Russian Psychology

To the memory of my parents,
Bertha and Joseph Joravsky

Russian Psychology
A Critical History

DAVID JORAVSKY

Basil Blackwell

Copyright © David Joravsky 1989

First published 1989

Basil Blackwell Ltd
108 Cowley Road, Oxford, OX4 1JF, UK

Basil Blackwell, Inc.
3 Cambridge Center
Cambridge, Massachusetts 02142, USA

British Library Cataloguing in Publication Data

Joravsky, David
    Russian psychology: a critical history
    1. Soviet Union. Psychology. Sociopolitical aspects
    I. Title
    302'.0947

    ISBN 0−631−16337−9

Library of Congress Cataloging in Publication Data

Joravsky, David.
    Russian psychology, a critical history.
    Bibliography: p.
    Includes index.
    1. Psychology − Soviet Union − History. 2. Communism
and psychology − Soviet Union − History. 3. National
characteristics, Russian − History. I. Title.
    BF108.S65J67   1988   150'.947   88−16833
    ISBN 0−631−16337−9

Typeset in 11 on 13 pt Bembo
by Setrite
Printed in Great Britain by
Dotesios Printers Ltd, Trowbridge, Wilts.

Contents

Preface

The Russian mind is my subject here, and so are modern claims to know what mind is or how it works. Skepticism shapes my history on both sides. A great nation's thoughts and feelings are no longer imaginable as a collective mentality progressing toward a goal, and likewise claims to know what mind is or how it works: they have tumbled about in too many separate heaps to fit within a conventional narrative of problems confronted and solved and knowledge systematically accumulating. But each project illuminates the other. Russians claiming to know the mind reveal their own distinctive minds in shifting patterns of clashing and confused beliefs, and we outside observers, reflecting on the process, increase our understanding of them and also of our own divided culture and fractious psychology.

We are not free as old-time scholars were with talk about the Russian soul or spirit, or even, with some hint of modern circumspection, the Russian mind. They saw the whole, or thought they did; we specialists permit ourselves mere glimpses of the parts. Preachers treat the soul, artists the spirit; mind falls between psychologists and philosophers, and such synthetic abstractions as a nation's mood or outlook are left to ideologues and politicians. I concede the triumph of the piecemeal age; indeed, I offer here in evidence the fissiparous growth of two disciplines in one country: neurophysiology and psychology in Russia from the 1860s to the 1960s. But my concession is grudging or even subversive; this is not one of those histories of science that respectfully follow specialists into their segregated disciplines to chronicle their accomplishments and problems as seen from within. I dwell on attempts at integration and on failure, on the persistent frustration of efforts to overcome the duality of brain studies and mind studies. I also dwell on fracture and frustration in the culture at large. Starting in the time of Marx and Comte, of Dostoevsky and Tolstoy, I ask how that old-time amplitude of spirit came down to Pavlov and his molecule of mind, the conditioned reflex. Or how the expectation of grand theorizing by revolutionary leaders declined to mindless bending of the knee before the printed works of Marx and Lenin, with Pavlov placed incongruously beside them, and laughing banned along with criticism.

Russian grandeur and Russian misery — I echo Stalin echoing Nekrasov — rule out a narrowly internal history of academic specialists poking at the problems of psychology. Even in such humdrum countries as our own psychology resists the pigeonhole approach of modern specialists. The word points both to claims of knowledge about mentality and to mentality itself, and within that double meaning of the word are four types, at least, of the twofold thing itself. Scientific psychology is the newest type, presenting claims that minds are functions of nervous systems, to be explained as nerves are, by experimental study of behavior, which slips away from nerves to subjectivity if verbal report is admitted in evidence, as it is by many of the schools at war within the would-be science. Some claim mind to be a function of social systems, and so lap over into sociology or more daringly into the realm of ideologists and political leaders, where it is taken for granted that minds express group interests and aspirations. This type of psychology I call ideological, since I understand ideology to be unacknowledged dogma that serves a social function, that is, clusters of unverified belief assumed to be proven truth because they serve the interests of the group that shares them. (That was the central theme in my study of the Lysenko affair.)

A third type of psychology seems quite at odds with the scientific or the ideological, for it resists the notion that minds are merely functions of nervous or of social systems, like digestion or waste disposal. This type takes for granted the obvious assumption of everyday life, that minds are expressions of persons, to be understood through their forms of self-expression, such as speech, singing, painting, or making all the other things that only human minds can make. This type I call aesthetic, and I look to it — especially as creative writers work it out for admiring readers — as evidence of the most widely recognized psychology, the type that sets agendas for would-be scientists or ideologists of mind, whether or not they are aware of their dependency. Finally, ancestral classics require acknowledgment of a fourth type, the philosophical, which tries to find the essence of authentic mentality — rationality, perhaps, or true community, or genuine creativity. The modern habit is to scorn all thought of essences; so thought of essences seeps into the other types of psychology not as deliberate philosophizing but as primitive assumption.

Awareness of those multiple and interacting psychologies has obliged my history of two disciplines in one country to look repeatedly outward, at political ideologists, literary artists, even an occasional philosopher. In such sorties I use exemplary instances of critically important views, and make no claim to offer thorough histories of ideological or aesthetic or philosophical psychologies. But even so, trying hard to be a proper specialist, I cannot keep away from two more historical problems that may seem quite alien to modern neuroscience and psychology: the relationship of Russia and the West, and along with that the relationship of Communist revolutions to the ancestral type in France or America, which proclaimed the overthrow of state intervention in the minds of free citizens. Is it Russian tradition or Communist revolution or the imperatives of power politics — or all together — that explain the efforts of Russian authorities to confine their subjects, scientists included, within the teachings of a state church, Orthodox Christian before the Soviet Revolution, Marxist-Leninist after it?

Russian culture is a provincial variant of European, and any study of it must confront the question: How different is it from the metropolitan types, and why? In particular, how and why did the Western revolutionary tradition take the Communist form in Russia — and in such other 'outposts of progress' as China, Yugoslavia, Vietnam, Cuba, and latterly even in the African 'heart of darkness'? I echo phrases of invidious comparison because European culture necessitates invidious comparison in its relentless diffusion from 'advanced' to 'backward' countries. The reader may prefer the gentler condescension of 'developed' and 'developing', but ahead-behind is not thereby avoided. 'Metropolis' and 'province' seem preferable to me because they point more plainly to mindsets than to supposedly inexorable realities of power and weakness, and so prepare the observer for startling inversions. Revolutionary minds can suddenly discover the true faith in Wittenberg rather than Rome, and colonial Philadelphia can proclaim 'the new order of the ages', still to be found on dollar bills. In Petrograd, 1917, the Bolsheviks and their lower-class militants vaulted Russia from the rear to the vanguard of nations, or so they believed, starting the process of 'overtaking and surpassing' that still preoccupies their heirs — and many other sharers of the dream further away from Europe's metropolitan centers, even in 'America's backyard'. Russia, the prime case of the Communist rupture in history, provokes the intensely ideological question, What kind of rupture is it proving to be, in ways of thought as well as politics and economic life? Expostulation comes far too easily. The factual question, What actually changed and what persisted?, still stands. I invite the reader to seek historical understanding through a study of changing psychologies among scientists, political ideologists, and imaginative writers during the last half-century before and the first half-century after the world's first Communist revolution.

THE ARGUMENT

The detailed table of contents and the index may invite readers to pick and choose according to their special interests, whether in neurophysiology or scientific psychology, in imaginative literature or political ideology. Such selective readers are likely to miss the connective themes or, worse yet, they are likely to be annoyed by what will seem to them an arbitrary emphasis on certain elements of their special interest and a high-handed disregard of others. I will therefore lay out here the major argument that connects the book's disparate materials. At the center is the problem of modern knowledge concerning ourselves, its multiplicity of forms and the role of ideology among them, that is, the role of group interests disguised as universal reasons.

Pluralism sets the problem: here are diverse groups of people claiming to achieve knowledge of human beings through incompatible modes of inquiry and self-expression. Philosophers of science tend to ignore such balkanization of knowledge; they usually assume that authentic knowledge must be grounded on some common rule of reason typified by physics. I assume that any common ground has to be discovered in the historical reality of the quest for knowledge, in confrontation not only with physics but also with claims to a knowledge of realities that physicists exclude from their inquiry, the jumbled claims offered by neuroscientists, by psychologists in their varied schools, by literary artists of even greater diversity, and by explicitly political ideologists who cluster in parties and bureaucracies that put their claims to harsh experimental tests, seeking rule over people or rebellion against rulers.

If you are aware of that jumble, you may not simply assume that physical scientists — in this case neurophysiologists — are the vanguard party of reason showing how to organize the data of experience. That assumption is a retreat to a new type of scholasticism, a fearful confinement of reason within one way of using it on one type of experience, and a willful refusal to examine the multifarious ways that other types of knowledge are created from other types of experience. Nor may you assume the contrary, that the scientists who study brain and mechanical behavior are the rearguard, which illuminates no more than the machinery of mind and the lowest levels of action, while the highest and most revealing levels are to be found in expressive thought. After all, neurophysiology and experimental psychology are also forms of human self-expression. They are typical of the forms that emerged in the nineteenth century, expressing a common sense that the conscious mind is a bizarre excrescence in otherwise mindless nature.

That is another part of the central argument: quarrelsome pluralism emerged out of metaphysical consensus. By tacit agreement educated people abandoned the soul, the immaterial substance that could formerly be invoked to explain mental processes and to justify the sacred quality of persons as distinct from other things. 'Naturalism', the more or less neutral term for the metaphysical vision that took possession of educated people, pressed the explanation of mental processes and the justification of persons to the margin of knowledge and beyond. 'Nihilism' seemed the unavoidable outcome: if mind is a neural function of ephemeral creatures in a universe without human meaning, explanation of mind seems to decline from philosophy or art to circuit maps, and justification of human values seems vain; they are functions of biological and social processes, no more justifiable than the mosquito's ways or the termite's. That prospect, clearly in view to thoughtful people of the mid-nineteenth century, provoked discordant patterns of response among imaginative writers, scientists, and political ideologists.

The term 'nihilism' first appeared among Russian writers of the 1850s and 1860s, in the special sense of disdain for any values but those to be found through scientific knowledge of progressive nature. But that was an ephemeral usage. None of the Russian writers who stood up for 'nihilism' in that optimistic sense, who argued that science shows us the progressive way of nature and its human offshoot, is read any more, except by historians tracing the ideological origins of the Bolshevik Revolution. The permanent meaning of nihilism emerged among writers who doubted or denied the scientistic faith, beginning with Turgenev and Dostoevsky. The metaphysical vision implicit in their classic works, still reverently studied not only in Russia but all over the literate world, finds no explanation of consciousness or justification of values in nature or historical process. The conscious mind is left to define and value itself, to assert the self in a world that nullifies self-assertion.

None of the classic Russian authors *liked* that vision. Each in his distinctive way tried to escape or overcome it, sometimes in explicitly ideological tracts, which proved to be ephemeral, and repeatedly in fictive representations, which proved to be enduring classics, of persons tragically or comically realizing themselves in a world that nullifies self-realization. I offer in evidence the best-known works by the most admired authors, to get at an outlook that great writers as a whole shared with the educated public at large. The diversity of the authors strengthens my argument. However different they were in explicitly declared ideologies — whether monarchist and Orthodox like Dostoevsky and Tiutchev, or revolutionary and atheist like Briusov and Babel, or somewhere in between like Tolstoy and Mandelstam — their fictive and poetic works expressed a common audacity, an implicit claim to know something more than naturalism seems to permit. They are aware that the conscious mind is an ensemble of biological and social functions, but their expression of awareness conveys knowledge of something more. Even when particular works ostensibly insist that there is nothing more, as, for example, Zola's *L'Assommoir* or Chekhov's 'A Dreary History' insist, the ostensible point is overborne by the pained consciousness in the work that makes it. Brooding over the absent soul, the literary imagination expresses something like a replacement of it, an insubordinate creative consciousness as the substantial quality of the person acting within its ensemble of roles. In contrast to that aesthetic vision scientific and political naturalists assume that the functional ensemble is all we know and all we need to know.

At first sight scientific efforts to explain the mind might appear as insubordinate as the aesthetic, and in the mid-nineteenth century there were some 'physiological materialists' who provoked traditionalist alarm and radical excitement at the prospect of the mind reduced to neural action, removed from moral judgment, freed perhaps to create new visions of itself. But the hubbub proved to be transient, in part because leading physiologists assured the public that their science was quite compatible with established values, but mainly because their science was not in fact trying to explain the mind, much less to dissolve moral judgment. Neuro-physiologists were turning their discipline into a rigorous natural science by conceiving nerves as purely physical systems, which entailed the exclusion of mental functions from their field of inquiry. The Russian experience was especially illuminating, for Sechenov, 'the father of Russian physiology', made an exceptional effort in the 1860s to bring the mind back into his science, and soon retreated from the effort in conscious failure. I offer a detailed analysis of the failure, not to belittle but to honor Sechenov, to retrieve his actual achievement from the Stalinist mythology that has cheapened it, and to disclose the duality of mind and brain that persistently re-emerges within serious scientific efforts to get rid of it.

Sechenov perceived the fundamental importance of the recent discovery that nerves not only excite muscles and glands to action but also turn them off or inhibit them. *Mental* processes, he surmised, must be elaborate forms of neural inhibition, something that happens in the brain between stimuli and long-delayed reactions. To test that inspiration he sought inhibitory effects in a frog's brain, and achieved them − but other researchers achieved the same effects throughout the nervous system. Sechenov quit the field in disappointment, but he encouraged his students to pursue the investigation of inhibition in all neural circuits and even in individual cells. Thus he founded the Russian branch of the major trend in neurophysiology which became best known in the West through Sherrington's classic work on the reciprocal functions of excitation and inhibition. In popular essays Sechenov acknowledged the mind-brain duality that his science could not eliminate, though he did not turn that into dual*ism* as conspicuously as Sherrington and other great British neurophysiologists have done.

At the turn of the century Pavlov and Bekhterev rebelled against that dominant trend in neuroscience. They differed in their immediate motives, and the band of disciples that each gathered about himself differed. Pavlov, who had won fame showing how the nervous system governs such macro-processes as digestion, was appalled by his discipline's descent from 'organ physiology' to the micro level. He feared that a chaos of disconnected facts would overwhelm the discipline unless he provided a framework of the general laws that govern the whole organism's normal interaction with its environment. Bekhterev, who was the chief organizer of backward Russia's medical neurologists and psychiatrists, felt a need to show the solidly scientific grounding of their embryonic effort to heal sick nerves and disturbed minds. So Pavlov was the more stubbornly devoted to laboratory research and 'the language of facts', while Bekhterev was the wider-ranging and more frankly speculative theorist, and each contested the other's priority in leading science to an explanation of mental function.

But for the long run their similarities were more significant. Both sought in neuroscience an escape from the 'subjectivity' of claims to know the mind; both thought that the 'conditioned' or the 'associative' reflex was the rock of 'objectivity' on which they would build authentic knowledge; and both were unable to solve the first two problems in that project. They could not find the neural mechanisms of the conditioned reflex, and they could not show how such reflexes might be combined to achieve the 'higher nervous activity' which is called mental in ordinary language. Thus, they failed to reduce mental processes to neural, but both — Pavlov especially — claimed that they *were* accomplishing that reduction, and they were believed, if not by the community of neurophysiologists as a whole, then by sufficient disciples to staff their laboratories, and by portions of the broader public who liked to imagine mind as a bundle of reflexes. They created a scientistic counterculture within the nihilistic trend of modern naturalism, nursing fantasies of mechanistic neuroscience winning mastery over mechanistic nature.

The most significant scientists among Pavlov's and Bekhterev's external admirers were the American psychologist Lashley and the Soviet physiologist Beritashvili, who began the serious effort to find the neural mechanisms of conditioning by recognizing that the search involved correlation of psychological laws with subcortical neural processes. Pavlov perceived that as a double defeat and strongly resisted it. That is, he refused to acknowledge that the laws of 'higher nervous activity' involved psychological concepts such as memory and representation, and he resisted the search for their neural substrate at the subcortical, much less the cellular, level. But his creative disciples moved away from his 'doctrine' in both directions, especially after the aged master died in 1936. Bekhterev and his disciples were far less resistant to the hybrid discipline that came to be called neuropsychology, for their 'reflexology' was in large measure a metaphor, which opened the door to psychological concepts from the start. Readers who fancy metaphorical flights from a base in neuroscience should not neglect Ukhtomskii, who rose from analysis of feline defecation to literary, philosophical, and even religious heights that entranced Bolshevik audiences.

In the problematic science of psychology the historian cannot sort out individual motives, group interests, and universal reasons without taking sides in an endless war of schools. I have taken the side of those psychologists — such as Brentano, James, and Vygotsky — who frankly confront the divided state of their discipline and thus acknowledge that the science of mind is not a science in the same sense as neurophysiology. 'Not *yet*', the psychologists insist, but I am an outside observer and do not share the group interest in repeating that 'yet'. The historical pattern impresses me. The psychologists' findings have persistently failed to cohere within a cumulatively developing body of knowledge, or worse: different heaps of data have been diligently accumulated by different schools, only to sink into pointlessness as the schools go out of fashion and new ones win favor.

So I am free to argue that the modern science of mind was predestined at conception to flounder between philosophy and neurophysiology and social science, as it has for more than a century now. I note that naturalistic philosophy irresistibly pointed psychology away from itself toward empirical science: mind is a process in nature, in the first place a function of nervous systems, and must be studied as such. At the same time the science of nervous systems pointed psychology away from *itself*: neurophysiology became a rigorous natural science by excluding anything like mind from the nerve action that was and is its object of study. All the while in everyday life, in such applied sciences as medical neurology and psychiatry, and in most of the emergent schools of psychological science, mental processes have been taken for granted as an autonomous reality, to be analyzed as such and correlated with neural processes and with the socio-cultural network that enmeshes the individual mind-brain. The behaviorist revolt against that hurly-burly did not end but added to it. So the modern discipline of psychological science is still what it was in its origin, neither philosophical fish nor physiological fowl nor sociological whale, but somehow all three at once, struggling to deal with a problem — What is mind? How does it work? — that each of the parent disciplines cast off from itself to be solved elsewhere.

Much of that academic struggle is cosmopolitan, but there are national peculiarities. The Russian branch of psychological science has persistently tended to theorize more than experiment, concerning itself with autonomous mental processes rather than with efforts to explain them away. (Pavlov's and Bekhterev's disciples, bear in mind, were perceived as physiologists in their native land, not as psychologists.) Both preferences — for theory over experiment and mind over behavior — reflect the culture of the intelligentsia, a self-conscious minority of modern thinkers within a backward country. A sense of provincial inferiority has also been a persistent part of that culture, an awareness of following after Western trendsetters and a compensating dream of leaping ahead, of showing the confused Western schools the way to unified truth. Stimulated by the Marxist excitement of the Bolshevik Revolution, those tendencies reached a creative peak in the 1920s, especially in the theorizing of Lev Vygotsky, but suffered crippling restraint in the harsh decades that followed.

That tragic arc is my central concern, not the catalogues of 'contributions' that pious psychologists compile when they construct their genealogies. I ask them to confront their actual history, which refuses to fit their dream of cumulative science. The founders of academic psychology in Russia are noteworthy for their institutional feat, and for the eclectic skill it required in rallying diverse tendencies − into schools of thought that proved ephemeral. That is no less true of Kornilov, eclectic organizer of the Marxist campaign in the 1920s, than of his pre-revolutionary mentor Chelpanov, who accommodated all schools by making eclecticism his chief principle. Vygotsky was unique in founding a school that has survived, but hardly in the way that he projected. Starting out as a literary critic, he tried to unify aesthetic understanding of the mind with scientific explanation of it, and so was drawn, in his most ambitious work, to analyze the divisions within scientific psychology, in hope of finding development toward coherence. His disciples admired the boldness of those projects but did not pursue them. His effort to sketch out an 'historico-cultural' psychology, that is, a phylogeny of mentalities that emerge at successive levels of development, got a modest start as a team research project, but was condemned by the ideological authorities in the early 1930s. So too were the other Soviet schools, though they all called themselves Marxist; they were all ordered to fuse into one, new, distinctively Soviet, truly Marxist psychology, which could be concretely described only in a negative way: it would *not* be like any of the existing schools, which were hopelessly 'bourgeois'.

Soviet psychologists shrank to fit within that framework, leaving grand theory to official ideologists and concentrating on empirical studies that might not be objectionable to the officials. Vygotsky's disciples retreated to the mental effects of brain damage and to child development studies rather like Piaget's, though constrained to deny the similarity. Their claim of a unique 'historico-cultural' approach was and remains an empty slogan. They could not give it substance without entering minefields of invidious comparison between group mentalities, such as 'primitive' *v.* 'civilized', or 'lesser' nationalities *v.* 'great' ones. S. L. Rubinshtein emerged as the chief theorist of Soviet psychology at an impasse, for he was especially skillful at decorating the impasse with abstract philosophizing − until the 'anti-cosmopolitan' drive of the late 1940s condemned the Jewish name that he signed to his works, and the works to boot.

That was when the ideological establishment formally enshrined 'Pavlov's doctrine' as the grand union of mind and brain in a single science. It was incontestably peculiar to Russia. Foreign scientists had absorbed his technique of conditioning but had set aside his neural explanation of the conditioned reflex and his conviction that it was the molecule of which all mental processes were compounded. Indeed, so had Pavlov's leading disciples at home. In 1950−2 neurophysiologists, psychiatrists, and psychologists were assembled in highly publicized meetings to confess their infidelity to 'Pavlov's doctrine', and to pledge correction of the sin. Yet at the same time Stalin was beginning to draw back from such scandalous and self-defeating methods of thought control. His death in 1953 accelerated the withdrawal, but it has been grudging and incomplete. Soviet psychologists have been allowed to reassert their affinities with Western schools, but not to disown the worship of 'Pavlov's doctrine' nor to criticize other worshipful approaches to basic theory. So Marxist and Pavlovian doctrines remained elevated above meaningful discussion, ritually avowed and practically ignored until Gorbachev called for *glasnost*.

Throughout these harsh decades psychological scientists showed a great capacity to keep their work within permitted limits, to avoid offense to men of power, to earn appreciation as scientists of the mind. None showed the pugnacious defense of the autonomous intellectual discipline that appeared among geneticists and physicists of the Stalin era. They did not need to; psychological science permits greater pliability to its adepts. Some neuroscientists — Beritashvili most notably — were as unbending as geneticists and physicists in defense of *their* discipline. It is 'harder' than psychology. But literary art was the hardest taskmaster, driving its votaries to revolt against Stalinist commands that writers must be 'engineers of human souls'. The soul-searching that drives a Mandelstam or a Siniavsky to such revolt is systematically excluded from scientific disciplines.

The mentality of the commanding officials, whether Tsarist or Soviet, is difficult to analyze, for they lack the scientists' and artists' compulsion to publish their thoughts. But their policies, and the stereotyped justifications offered for them, enable one to infer the animating mentality, especially during the last years of the Tsarist period, when officials retreated from efforts to suppress naturalistic explanations of the mind though still insisting upon the religious ideology that justified the established order. They were drifting toward the modern politician's separation from high culture, and also toward the collapse of their entire system. So too were the radical activists among the intelligentsia, a class that first appeared in nineteenth-century Russia, and is now commonplace in 'underdeveloped' countries. It combines intellectual, professional, and political functions that are separated in 'advanced' countries. 'Modernization' presses the intelligentsia toward the same separation, which many resist, seeing it as a decline in aspirations or even a desertion of duty. The emergent professional, such as Pavlov, expressed disdain for politics, but clung to the dream that his profession was the vanguard of Russia's necessary transformation. On the other hand radical activists among the intelligentsia disdained professional careers as a sellout to the Tsarist system, and came by the end of the century to the formation of parties struggling to overthrow the system. They showed far less interest than the radicals of the 1860s in such intellectual issues as the nature of the mind, yet they clung to the conviction that political leaders must be intellectual leaders as well.

It was such activists who came to power in 1917, and that conviction was one of the reasons for Russia's sharp reversion to thought control. But the major cause was the cultural isolation of the Bolshevik leaders. They were members of the intelligentsia who won power by leading a lower-class revolution, while perceiving their mass base as overwhelmingly 'un-civilized' (*nekul'turnyi*). They perceived the intelligentsia as the bearers of essential modern culture, who overwhelmingly refused to 'accept' (*priznat'*) the new regime. That precarious situation generated a protracted 'cultural revolution' at both levels. To transform the culture of their lower-class constituency the Bolsheviks turned to the intelligentsia, their political foes, with urgent demands for help; to achieve 'acceptance' of the new regime among the intelligentsia the Bolsheviks started campaigns for Marxism in all fields of high culture, and forcibly advanced workers and peasants into positions of authority. Unavoidably, issues of intellectual substance were entangled with lines of loyalty and opposition, within a political culture that tended more and more toward the equation of intellectual rectitude with place in the hierarchy of power: the higher up, the more 'correct' one's ideas were, until one reached unquestionable genius at the pinnacle.

Diktat seemed to have limitless potential within that system, yet it was always restrained and ultimately cut back by a variety of countervailing forces, including the Bolsheviks' faith in science. Even in problematic areas like psychology faith in science pushes believers toward the modern sep-aration of functions among intellectuals, professionals, and politicians. I am not endorsing the common notion that considerations of 'practicality' have been undermining 'ideology' in the CPSU as among Communists everywhere. 'Practicality' is itself an ideological artifact, another disguise of group interests within claims of universal reasons. Stalin insisted that 'the criterion of practice' guided the impositions of his ideological bureaucracy on high culture. By 1950 he was also beginning to invoke the same criterion to justify retreat toward recognition of free thought for specialists, and his successors have kept the same mixture going. Both tendencies have been at odds within the Bolshevik mentality all along; which one has prevailed in this or that field from one period to another has depended on contingent factors that can be discovered only through particular investiga-tion. Of course there has been an overall long-term pattern of change: from the self-conscious balancing of the opposed tendencies during the 1920s towards a self-destructive peak of know-it-all authoritarianism under Stalin, and then the slow climbdown toward recognition among men of power that they need to be limited if they are to be effective — indeed, if they are to avoid self-destruction.

Different groups of scientific specialists have played different roles in that long-term rise and fall of willfulness among Bolshevik leaders. In some fields the specialists' stubborn insistence on professional knowledge has obliged political bosses to see the need for retreat from intuitive notions of effective policies. The thirty-year war over Lysenkoism in agricultural policies was a case of that sort. The cases of applied psychology, which are analyzed in this book, were of a different sort. In industrial and educational psychology, however inconsistently the political bosses have fluctuated between opposed intuitions of effective policies, specialists have always been forthcoming with suitable theorizing and research to back up the bosses' intuitions. Yet both sides have felt the need for autonomous science, that is, the need to discover rational grounds for policies.

Psychiatry has a somewhat different, and even more illuminating history, for the political bosses have not been very assertive in this field. They have delegated authority over the insane to largely autonomous specialists. In Stalin's time there were a few gross political interventions, which I examine at length, for they show how a profession that prided itself on its liberalism was opened to the Stalinist mentality. But that opening does not suffice to explain the particular form that the Stalinist mentality took within the psychiatric profession, or the power of that mentality to go on dominating the profession long after Stalin was gone and external interventions had ended. Something within psychiatry, a persistent need to equate intuitive convictions with scientific knowledge, generated an enduring affinity between doctors of the mind and the authoritarian leaders of their country.

That affinity between psychiatrists and political leaders, the analogous obsequiousness of educational and industrial psychologists, and the pliability of pure psychologists contrast sharply with the refractory mentality of imaginative writers. Though many have produced the formulaic literature required by the ideological establishment, a persistent minority – the most gifted, the most capable of seizing public interest – have challenged and subverted the bosses' notions of 'engineering human souls'. Pondering the contrast, I return to the distinguishing feature of aesthetic psychology, its effort to find a self-expressive entity within the mind, not merely an ensemble of biological and social functions. That is basically at odds with the political *and* the scientific approaches, which agree that the mind is a function of something other than itself. Those who aspire to scientific explanation of the mind are therefore predisposed to collaboration with those who have the power of ideological mobilization, while those who aspire to aesthetic self-expression are driven to acts of defiance. That is why Soviet writers have done more to keep life in the spirit of revolution than the political leaders who have perceived themselves as servants of the revolution, while scientists of the mind have persistently tried to be servants of the servants.

No doubt such baldly stated judgments will strike some readers as infractions of scholarly objectivity. I ask them to consider the detailed evidence and the qualifications that I offer below, and to remember that objectivity requires self-consciousness in studies of psychology. That is generally acknowledged in the most inward appraisals of the individual self, but it tends to be forgotten in group psychology. Studying 'their' strange habits we tend to assume 'ours' as the standard of judgment. But a truly objective standard must be sought through endless questioning of our own psychology, all types of it, in constant comparison with others'. That is a major reason why Part I reviews the Western currents of thought that Russians took up and developed in their own distinctive ways. Beyond Part I the reader will find no more extended reviews of the Western developments that paralleled the Russian, but repeated brief ruminations on the similarities and the differences between 'their' psychology and 'ours'.

In short, I invite the reader to share with me, and with the contentious protagonists of the book that follows, a quarrelsome search for coherence. Those who harp upon the evidence of fretful discord, as I do, express that way the sense of something lacking, a true community of authentic minds. But something lacking is still something, if only in the mind's imaginary eye. A pattern of unresolved arguments may be a form of coherence; people arguing with each other may form a truer community than isolated groups ignoring each other's rival claims of knowledge.

Acknowledgments

I am deeply grateful to many institutions and individuals who have helped me with this study. It began long ago with the financial support of the National Science Foundation, which enabled me to read in Soviet libraries, and to request interviews with Soviet historians of psychology, none of whom would speak to me. The American Council of Learned Societies enabled me to try again, but the Soviet government refused to give me a visa. Part I was written during a stimulating year at the Kennan Institute within the Woodrow Wilson Center. (A portion of Part I was published in the Working Papers of the Institute.) The National Endowment for the Humanities and the International Research and Exchanges Board enabled me to set about completion of the book, though not in the Soviet Union as planned, since its government refused again to let me in. (I mention these details to explain why Soviet scholars are absent from my list of grateful acknowledgments, though their published works are overwhelmingly present in the notes.) Northwestern University has been generous in its support, both with grants of leave time and with funds for preparation of the manuscript.

Small portions of this book have previously appeared, in different forms, in the *New York Review of Books* (16 February 1974); in Sheila Fitzpatrick (ed.), *Cultural Revolution in Russia, 1928–1931* (Indiana University Press, 1984); in A. Gleason, P. Kenez, and R. Stites (eds), *Bolshevik Culture* (Indiana University Press, 1985); and in M. G. Ash and W. R. Woodward (eds), *Psychology in Twentieth-Century Thought and Society* (Cambridge University Press, 1987). I thank the publishers for permission to reprint. I also thank Faber and Faber and Harcourt Brace Jovanovich, Inc. for permission to reproduce excerpts from 'Burbank with a Baedeker Bleistein with a Cigar', in *Collected Poems 1909–1962* by T. S. Eliot, copyright © 1936 by Harcourt Brace Jovanovich, Inc., copyright © 1963, 1964 by T. S. Eliot, reprinted by permission of the publishers.

Josef Brozek and the psychologists that he assembled for a summer institute at Lehigh University were graciously helpful in showing me how psychologists approach the history of their problematic science. Similar assistance came from James Wertsch and Michael Cole. Fellow historians Mitchell Ash and Martin Miller were also helpful. I thank George Kline, Norman Birnbaum, Maurice Mandelbaum, Edward Geremek, and Philip Pauly for their thoughtful comments on Part I. Walter Reich opened up to me the central significance of psychiatry for my subject, and carefully criticized my chapter on the subject. Edward Shils also gave it a very careful critique, and I regret that I could not see my way to acceptance of his suggested improvements. I offer analogous apology to two anonymous reviewers of the entire manuscript, whose suggested improvements were counter to the book's main argument. Similar thanks with regrets to Loren Graham, Martin Malia, and David Bloor, who pointed me in radically different directions on important issues of interpretation.

No doubt Charles Rosenberg and Leo Haimson have long since forgotten the pointed questions that pushed me into deeper inquiries than I originally intended. My friend William Coleman did not realize how useful were the skeptical grunts and brief comments with which he punctuated my monologues on matters far from his major concerns. Too many living friends and colleagues have done me similar service to risk offense to some by listing others individually. David Hull and Josef Barton must be exceptions, for they wrote out their helpful comments. Many thanks to Roy Medvedev for giving me the complete works of Pavlov, to Marjorie Carpenter for skillful assistance in library matters, and to Ann Larson and Donna Oliver for preparation of the manuscript. To Doris Joravsky I owe whatever understanding of educational psychology may be found in the pages that follow.

Part I

Genteel Disintegration in the West

1

Psychological Science and Ideologies

NEUROPHYSIOLOGY

Mind and body are obviously connected but the connection defies understanding, especially in the century since experimental psychology became a
discipline apart from neurophysiology. Evasion is the contemporary style.
The body's machinery is a problem for the mechanics who service or junk
it, such as physicians and undertakers, but hardly for manipulators of the
mind, such as politicians and film-makers. Within universities philosophers
of mind ignore its neural machinery, while brain scientists, who pick at the
machinery, shun the concept of mind as specialists in acoustics shun the
concept of music.[1] Discharging fragmented services and having them performed upon ourselves, we are sufficiently unlike social insects to have
occasional feelings of incompleteness and incoherence, but we leave that
part of the divided self to other specialists, the various guilds of artists who
fill social space with symbols of expressive incoherence. They dull feelings
of disorder by making them chronic.

Sophisticated people have learned to evade questions that seemed urgent
a century ago. No one asks whether the science of physiology is subversive;
we know too well the answer to that question. Does the science of our
bodily functions rule out traditional concepts of spirit or soul? Obviously it
does, within the scientific discipline, and we are conditioned not to pursue
the question outside, lest traditional values, such as the reverence owed to
the person in the body, be overthrown along with its spirit or soul. That
evasion had to be learned. Conservatives once asked whether they should
not oppose the science of physiology, while radicals debated whether it was
an ideological weapon in the struggle against the old order or an instrument
of a worse new order. And poets − were they to confront 'the whole
goddam machinery' of nature,[2] as Lucretius did in that bygone age when
the machinery was only imagined, or were they to turn inward and
contemplate their imaginary souls?

It seems impossible to take such questions seriously any more. Informed that intelligent people once did so, prisoners of the current *Zeitgeist* shrug indifferently. Articulate prisoners draw a distinction between scientific and emotional levels of meaning, granting that controversies over scientific ventures in human understanding were emotionally significant to past mentalities in bygone cultural milieux, but denying that there was any scientific meaning in such controversies. Such sophisticates are trapped willy-nilly in a dominant ideology of our time, which blocks pure science from corrupting intercourse with other types of thought.

That antiseptic seal on natural science is a relatively new development. But it has acquired such a powerful hold on educated minds that it dominates even historians of science. Though their source material constantly reminds them of the confusing interaction between science and other types of thought in former times, they tend to brush the confusion aside or explain it away. It seems irrelevant, a primitive noise that the modern historian must filter out of his composition, so that the scientific themes can be perceived in their purely logical development. When ideological controversy *is* examined, it is not explained so much as explained away. We are told, to take the archetypal case, that the clash between Galileo and the Roman church was not the result of modern science subverting antique faith. Then, as now, soothing scholars assure us, everyone could and should have been nice. Genteel divorce was the obvious way to accommodate science and religion. But Galileo pressed for the divorce too swiftly, and the church authorities were too stupid or spiteful or, in the most generous of interpretations, too much the befuddled children of their Counter-Reformation times to appreciate the obvious logic of a neat separation between science and theology.[3]

Modernizing smugness — or modern fear of unmanageable problems — also organizes our vision of the ideological conflict that attended the rise of modern physiology in the seventeenth to nineteenth centuries. 'We' now have the pure science of physiology, which 'they' only glimpsed dimly through the acrimonious confusion of that science with alien compartments of thought, such as psychology, philosophy of mind, the literary imagination, ethics, political creeds, and religion. So we cut into pieces great thinkers who struggled for wholeness of thought and feeling. Here the archetypal case is Descartes, for he first clearly presented the basic metaphor of modern physiology *together with* the basic criticism of that metaphor by the self-conscious mind. He argued that the animal organism is a kind of machine, and he also argued that the machine metaphor will not explain the mind or spirit in the human animal. Tired of endless efforts to reconcile those arguments, we split Descartes into two or three non-communicating parts. His concept of a reflex mechanism operating the animal machine is assigned to neurophysiology. His treatment of the mind-body problem is relegated to academic philosophy. The possibility of a third Descartes, trying to keep a place for the soul in the neural machine that thinks and feels, is shuffled off to the literary imagination or to theology or to the museum of biographical contingency.[4] We may have an uneasy sense that we are murdering a great mind to dissect it so, if I may paraphrase Wordsworth. But that anxiety is mostly repressed, for Wordsworth and the other romantics have offered no alternative to dissection, and we all find security, however stultifying, in the specialized chambers of contemporary thought.

Diderot is another great thinker whom we cut into pieces to suit our mincing passion for clarity and efficiency in mental labor, and our fear of insoluble problems. He studied physiology intensively, pondered the central metaphor of the organism as a mechanism, and in different works expressed different reactions. In *D'Alembert's Dream* he developed the concept into an amused hedonism, relaxed, relativistic, ending with a comic forecast of genetic engineering and sexual liberation. In *Rameau's Nephew* he turned darkly comic: human beings become a loathsome sort of social insect, plagued by a self-contempt that foreshadows Dostoevsky's *Notes from Underground*. Those contrary reactions to a mechanistic view of human beings have become subject matter for cultural history and literary criticism, which avoid the question of whether the science of physiology does entail genial hedonism or manic *Angst*, or a fluctuation between the two, or no expressive values at all. Historians of science also avoid such terribly difficult questions. If they take note of Diderot's interest in physiology, it is to illustrate a bygone confusion in an embryonic science or a romantic spin-off from the science, not the implications of the science itself.[5]

With Lamettrie our compartmentalized minds have much less trouble than with Descartes or Diderot, for he was much closer to our age in his effort to avoid incoherence by stunting the intellect. He transformed Descartes' dualism (or trialism) into monism by 'downward comparison', as Robert Frost would say, erasing the line Descartes had drawn between humans and lesser animals. We are all machines and nothing more. The immortal soul is a fantasy of religious believers, and the celebrated mind that distinguishes us from lower brutes is to be explained physiologically, by reduction of mental states to bodily processes. Lamettrie had scant interest in the subtle problems that writers like Descartes and Diderot perceived in the reduction of mind to body. We may wonder if his alternating periods of cheer and gloom were a repressed analogue to the shift in Diderot's thought between *D'Alembert's Dream* and *Rameau's Nephew*. Perhaps the conception of one's self, of a person, as nothing more than a transient pattern of disturbances in an ephemeral tissue of nerve fibers induces such moody fluctuations in the part of the neural tissue that looks before and after and asks what for.[6]

Poetic anguish of that sort, the aspiration to be persons that is torn by the knowledge that we are things, is as old as *Ecclesiastes*, but modern science gave rise to a new form of it, the romantic complaint that science is to blame, since science reveals all of nature to be mere things. For the first wave of romantics, in the late eighteenth and early nineteenth century, the science of physics usually epitomized that 'mechanical philosophy' and its dehumanizing implications. The reduction of the rainbow to 'the dull catalogue of common things' was Keats's favorite example, referring to Newton's prismatic dissipation of the awe that the rainbow once inspired.[7] Schiller contrasted the ancient Greeks' naive personification of nature as a variety of gods with the modern knowledge that 'Nature, deprived of gods, like the dead beat of the pendulum clock, slavishly serves the law of gravity.'[8] Romantics of that sort did not doubt the truth of scientific knowledge. They were appalled by the separation of knowledge from feeling and yearned for a higher truth that would reunite the severed intellectual and aesthetic parts of the mind.

Physiology was conspicuous by its absence from such romantic complaints.[9] Indeed, it was possible for poets to find reassurance in physiology during the late eighteenth and early nineteenth centuries. Schiller did. He studied physiology in the course of his medical training, and wrote his first treatise, at the age of twenty, on *The Philosophy of Physiology*. Drawing on an ancient tradition that considered nerve action to be a force intermediate between mind and body, which Schiller called the *Nervengeist* or neural spirit,[10] he constructed a theory of human nature as a union of three impulses or drives. The material drive (*Stofftrieb*) was united with the ideal or formal drive (*Formtrieb*) by the playful drive (*Spieltrieb*), 'the aesthetic formative impulse' that expresses itself in creative activity which is both physical and mental at the same time.[11] Schiller deplored the breakdown of that natural unity not only in contemporary philosophy and science but also in social organization, which made human beings the specialized instruments of external constraint, thereby alienating the person from 'the full harmony of his essence'.[12]

Schiller was unusual among poets in the amount of attention he gave to physiology, but not, I would suggest, in his ability to find reassurance in it. Down to the 1840s most physiologists were still not committed to a thoroughly mechanistic interpretation of life. Some eclectic mixture of mechanistic and vitalistic principles was the rule. David Hartley, to take an influential example, argued that the neural mechanisms discovered by physiology proved the existence of a great design and reinforced Christian faith in the immortal soul.[13] Theology aside, his picture of the mind formed by sensations impinging on the nervous system appealed to Wordsworth and Coleridge. It seemed to be scientific support for their own notion of the human spirit vibrating in harmony with the rest of nature.[14]

Physiological psychology eventually turned into a thoroughly mechanistic discipline, which poets would find uninspiring if not repulsive, but the agents of the transformation were long unaware of the goal toward which they were evolving. Most physiologists of the eighteenth and early nine-teenth centuries were eclectics like Hartley rather than single-minded mechanists like Lamettrie. Yet something in their work was moving them toward the posthumous recognition of Lamettrie as a prophet of their science, not merely the zealot of a gray philosophy.[15] Robert Whytt, for example, who published his major works about the same time as Lamettrie, was temperately balanced on basic principles. He rejected extreme versions of vitalism, but assumed that something like a spirit — he called it a 'sentient principle' — must be the operative force in nervous systems.[16] Yet his experimental work tended to undermine any kind of vitalism, even the unthinking kind implicit in our everyday language.

If asked why an animal jumps when pricked, we commonly say it does so to escape pain. Thus we implicitly attribute to the beast feeling, purpose, perhaps even some primitive mind, in the sense of a capacity to plan ahead and to make decisions. (In certain circumstances we know that an animal can jump in anticipation of being pricked or can resist jumping when pricked.) Whytt's experiments made such purposeful language seem absurdly animistic. He took out a frog's brain, and found that the beast would still jump when pricked. Even when he repeatedly sectioned the creature — 'to section' became an antiseptic verb, cleansing the experimenter of inappro-priate feeling — the legs still made leaping motions when pricked. As long as the nerves serving the leg muscles were connected to a piece of spinal cord, the jumping response followed the pricking stimulus.[17]

It is hard to attribute feeling or purpose, much less mind or soul, to a frog's leg and a bit of spinal cord, or to other 'preparations' of isolated muscles and nerves.* Vitalistic physiologists argued for the existence of a 'spinal soul',[18] but their efforts turned into verbal shuffles and logic chop-ping in the mid-nineteenth century, as more and more neuromuscular automatisms were mapped out by such methods as Whytt had pioneered. The anal sphincter of a turtle, for example, can hardly be considered soulful or spirited when one sees it do its work for a decapitated and disembowelled turtle, opening when the colon is filled with water and shutting after relief, until it is disconnected from the spinal cord and falls open forever.[19]

Those who believed in a 'spinal soul' clung to the cord's capacity for switching signals in the 'wash reflex', to take the most famous example. A brainless frog will use its right hind leg to wipe at acid dropped on the right side of its body, but if the right foot is cut off, the stump will throb in

---

* 'Preparation' is another bit of antiseptic newspeak. It is only fair to note that few physiologists have been as thoroughly cleansed of inappropriate feeling as T. L. W. Bischoff. He was a German physiologist of the 1830s, who shouted 'Reprieve!' in the ear of a condemned man just after the preparation was sectioned — in non-scientific language, just after the man was beheaded.[20]

vain, and then the *left* leg will reach across the body to wipe at the acid.[21] It became increasingly difficult to construe such a simple switch as a proof of mind or soul, for more and more self-regulating devices of a purely mechanical nature were impressing themselves on the European imagination. The fantail keeps the windmill turned into the shifting wind; the float valve returns a fluctuating water level to the prescribed mark; the governor of a steam engine — the most popular of such images in the nineteenth century — adjusts speed and power to a changing load. Indeed, by the mid-nineteenth century mechanical self-regulation by systems that lack a genuine self had so impressed the European imagination that they were a common metaphor for entire human societies, not to speak of individual animals and their neural systems. Adam Smith's vision of society coordinated by 'an invisible hand' became, in Andrew Ure's hymn to the factory system, 'a vast automaton ..., all of [its parts] being subordinate to a self-regulated moving force. ... The benignant power of steam summons around him the myriads of willing menials.'[22]

The distinction between the sensory and the motor nerves, systematically carrying messages to the spinal cord and orders away from it, was the most famous reinforcement for the view of the nervous system as a self-regulating mechanical system. Mechanical analysis required the precise correlation of structures and functions, and the reflex arc furnished neurophysiology with a basic scheme for such correlations, capable of endless application: a sensory nerve carries information to the central nervous system, which sends out an appropriate order through a motor nerve to a muscle or gland. By the 1840s an angry quarrel over priority in the discovery of that scheme showed how firmly it had gripped the minds of physiologists.[23] The final blow to vitalism in neurophysiology was probably the mounting evidence that the motive force of the neural circuits is not some *Nervengeist* or 'sentient principle', or any other mysterious force inaccessible to experimental analysis, but a form of electricity, which moves at measurable speeds from a point of stimulus to a point of response.[24]

By the late 1840s and early 1850s the young German physiologists who were taking the lead in their discipline had pledged themselves to a principle of mechanistic reduction that takes the breath away with its astringent exclusion of anything like a spirit or mind from the science of living things: '... We have sworn to prove the basic truth that in the organism there are no forces at work except for the common physico-chemical ones.'[25] That famous oath said nothing explicitly about the human mind, but it too was scheduled for reduction, if not directly to the molecular level of physico-chemical laws, at least to reflex circuits in the brain. Such a thesis was independently and simultaneously published, also in the 1840s, by Thomas Laycock in England and Wilhelm Griesinger in Germany, founders of influential schools of neurophysiology and psychiatry.[26] What we call thought or feeling, they suggested, would prove to be interrupted reflexes, complex and time-consuming events in the cerebrum, which intervene between certain stimuli and certain long-delayed responses.

In the 1840s and for long afterward that notion of the mind as reflexes of the brain was hardly more than a metaphor. Much later it would prove to be more useful than the rival metaphor of mind as a secretion of the brain, on the model of the liver secreting bile or the kidney urine.[27] The reflex metaphor, as we shall see, lent itself to various kinds of experimentation and controlled observation, as the secretion metaphor did not. To be sure the reflex metaphor would also create great difficulties when it came to be pushed to the limit, that is, when it was used to push mind outside the bounds of physiology, or to deny its existence altogether. But the reflex metaphor was not pushed to that extreme in the mid-nineteenth century. Even popular evangelists of materialist philosophy talked of the mind as an autonomous entity, without concern for consistency.[28] As for Laycock, his practical purpose in proposing 'the doctrine of the reflex function of the brain' was to open the way toward understanding mentally disturbed people. His philosophical purpose in trying to correlate mental events with neural processes was reminiscent of Schiller and the ancient tradition of 'a scientific spiritualism'. He hoped to seize 'the link ... that connects the spiritual with the material world'.[29] Griesinger, the pioneer psychiatrist who published the reflex concept of the mind about the same time as Laycock, also moved back and forth, with little sense of inconsistency or difficulty, across barriers that have since risen between the neural and the mental world. He recognized great unsolved problems in the connection between them, but felt that they would be resolved as they were reduced from the metaphysical to the physiological level.[30]

Insouciance of that sort was characteristic of the mid-nineteenth century. Scientists who dismissed the notion of a 'spinal soul' operating the anal sphincter of a decapitated turtle felt free to invoke the mind or will to explain the operation of excretory sphincters in higher animals.[31] It is, after all, common knowledge that urination and defecation cease to be automatic reflexes when children or puppies are taught to hold back and let go 'at will'. Mentalistic terms of that kind occur freely in the writings of mid-nineteenth-century neurologists, though their twentieth-century descendants are uneasy at such violations of 'physiological orthodoxy'.[32]

The mechanistic tendency that drove the mind or psyche out of the spinal cord in Laycock's time has since then driven it out of the brain, or made its presence there seem a disconcerting inconsistency with the principles of physiological analysis. Mental functions constantly appear in higher neural circuits, not as 'a ghost in the machine'[33] — that joke is a philosopher's dismissal of a physiologist's problem — but as functions that cannot be explained yet cannot be ignored. As a result thoughtful neuro-physiologists have repeatedly indulged in mind-body dualism, on a specu-lative level, outside their work as physiologists.[34] Within the discipline mechanism won a complete, irreversible victory in the mid-nineteenth century. An historian of our day may warn that such talk ignores the diversity of views held by the defeated vitalists, some of them pointing toward issues that would not go away.[35] But a perceptive historian must also note the basic reason for the irreversible victory of mechanism: 'At the moment of closing with the organism in an experiment ... it is the only posture that will make biology go. ...'[36] No matter that the organism has to be carefully selected or willfully simplified to suit the experimental posture. The pioneers of thoroughly mechanist physiology knew that they were hacking out tiny clearings in endless forests, which might forever defy conquest by the ax. Far from daunting, that knowledge gave zest to their audacious venture. Passionate commitment is most intense and confident in its naive commencement.[37]

THE AESTHETIC REACTION

Modern industry was probably far more powerful than mechanistic physiology in winning converts to world views based entirely on positive science. Not modern industry in its fearful reality; that was just materializing in a few places, when the Crystal Palace Exhibition of 1851 lifted the eyes of admiring multitudes from the reality to the glittering dream. It was the vision embodied in the Crystal Palace, of easeful power magically flowing from applied science, which provided an eager audience for prophets exalting science as the only way to truth and perfection. Not only in England, but in provinces as distant as Russia and the United States, the 'synthetic philosophy' of Herbert Spencer became the most widely accepted version of the new creed. ('Synthetic' would become a sneer, a synonym for ersatz or phony, only in our own century, when applied chemistry would confer plastics on humanity.)[38] Spencer's synthesis was impressive less by virtue of its basic principles than by the sheer tonnage of contemporaneous knowledge and bourgeois homilies that he loaded upon them − without danger of the principles breaking, for they were vague enough to sustain any particulars.[39] The simple evolved into the complex, the homogeneous into the heterogeneous, 'militancy' (primitive, irrational, warlike society) into 'industrialism' (advanced, rational, peaceful society). It would be impolite to laugh; many people still believe that industrial societies are inherently more rational and peaceful than pre-industrial societies.

For those who preferred a streamlined, more radical version of the new faith in science, a famous trio of popular materialists, Büchner, Vogt, and Moleschott, preached that all the bewildering phenomena of nature, human nature included, were being reduced by science to one single substance or essence, matter in motion. The faithful simply took it for granted that scientific reduction would be complemented by scientific synthesis, that the world broken down into soluble problems within the particular disciplines would be put together again by aggregation of those same disciplines. For many believers, Spencer's voluminous works were a demonstration of the twin process; for others, the works of Comte and his disciples showed how to organize all knowledge and values into a harmonious system. The synthetic positivists even provided historical schemes to take the place of the ancient faith in God's successive revelations pointing humanity toward ultimate perfection. Spencer's two steps − 'militancy' evolving into 'industrialism' − captured the yearning imagination less effectively, or less durably, than Comte's three: religious thought progressing to metaphysical, and now the age of science or positive knowledge. From Comte's vocabulary (or St Simon's, to be meticulous in credit), came the most common term for the new faith, positivism.[40]

Hardly noticed in the mid-nineteenth century was the rival historico-philosophical scheme of Karl Marx, with its self-contradictory or dialectical acknowledgment of present incoherence joined to a dream of 'a single science' in the revolutionized future. More of that later, for it would become a mass faith in the twentieth century, when Comte and Spencer and the other rivals of Marx would be falling out of print, disintegrating into a sort of intellectual humus, the unnamed, unexamined creed of many scientists and their countless admirers, who simply take it for granted that science is the only way to truth and perfection. 'Scientism' is the derogatory label that twentieth-century infidels have put upon the relic of a faith once served by mighty, though mortal, thinkers. The neatest indication of the intellectual collapse that the faith has suffered is the transformed meaning of its most common name. In our century positivism has come to indicate a philosophy that strives to be purely analytical, that shuns efforts at a comprehensive synthesis of knowledge and values.

Great creeds often survive intellectual collapse. Belief is not as dependent on reasoned argument and verified knowledge as many of us like to imagine. Consider the older synthetic faith in science, characteristic of the seventeenth and eighteenth centuries, which interpreted mechanistic science as analysis of God's design in nature. It still has naive believers. They neither know nor care that serious intellectual efforts to interpret science as evidence of a transcendent design have long since withered away. Similarly, there are still many naive believers in the synthetic faith that flourished in the nineteenth century, who do not ask themselves why serious efforts at a positivist synthesis of all knowledge and values have also withered away.[41] When the failure of such efforts is noted, a pat formula is quickly invoked against the spectre of incoherence: the *amount* of positive knowledge has got out of hand, for the time being. An imperishable synthesis is, we are assured, still being spontaneously generated within the special disciplines, for example, by the reduction of psychology to neurophysiology, of biology to chemistry, of chemistry to physics, and of physics to the mechanics of elementary particles.

People who take that faith for granted are unwilling to confront a mass of contrary indications and the most obvious explanation of them: the breakdown of knowledge into isolated disciplines is the result of inconsistencies or even of irreconcilable differences in their fundamental assumptions and methods of inquiry, especially where the study of human beings is involved. Science, as a mode of critical inquiry, has spoiled the dream of science, as a unified understanding of the world and a guide to perfection. Success in analysis has entailed failure in synthesis. And the beginning of that self-defeat can be perceived already in the mid-nineteenth century, at the very time that the new synthetic faith in science was entering its great brief period of intense flourishing.

Consider the poets. No doubt it was even then a great exaggeration to call them unacknowledged legislators of the world. (For poets in our century it is a cruel joke.) It was also an exaggeration to call them engineers of the soul, a supposedly Stalinist metaphor that actually emerged in the late nineteenth century as a subtle insult to the poet and the soul.[42] But it is a fact that a large public in the nineteenth century looked to poetry for understanding as well as feeling, and it is also a fact that poets did not take to the new synthetic faith in science. Indeed, they showed an increasing tendency to lump science with scientism and to spurn both as inherently inhuman.

The modern split between the literary imagination and science is the result of a complex process, beginning with the romantic complaints against science in the late eighteenth century and culminating in the new romanticism of the late nineteenth and early twentieth centuries, with many variations by country, by school, and by individual.[43] But it can be epitomized very simply by reference to physiology, for there the poetic reaction was short, sharp, and universal. After the 1840s, when physiology turned thoroughly mechanistic, I can find no poet with a sympathetic interest in the science of physiology, such as Schiller, Wordsworth, and Coleridge had evinced back in the formative period when physiology was somewhat vitalistic.

Tennyson's *In Memoriam* (1850), to take for our example the great English case of a poetic mind struggling for a coherent vision in the age of mechanistic science, gave evolutionary theory the compliment of a long argument. Tennyson tried to reconcile the scientific picture of a mindlessly evolving universe with the aesthetic yearning for a grand design. Similar arguments with the theory of evolution were continued by other poets into the early twentieth century.[44] That theory was a grand, tragic challenge to poets still clinging to the universe as their subject, still resisting the 'journey to the interior', the concentration of the literary imagination on the inner, isolated self.[45] In contrast to evolutionary theory, mechanistic physiology seemed a trivial study of the plumbing and wiring that allow the mind to operate. If the science of physiology pretended to do more, to reveal the whole person, Tennyson dismissed it from poetic contemplation with curt, contemptuous finality:

> I think we are not wholly brain,
> Magnetic mockeries ...
> Not only cunning casts in clay.
> Let Science prove we are, and then
> What matters Science unto men,
> At least to me? I would not stay.[46]

There was a crucial ambiguity in those lines. Were they brushing aside the science of physiology or the nature of human beings, or both? If science actually proved that we are 'magnetic mockeries' − electrically powered models of persons − would the poet turn away from nature as well as the science that analyzed it? Baudelaire faced the issue and took the fateful step in the years 1846−52, earning a reputation as the originator of a new satanic type of romanticism, which would no longer yearn for harmony with nature but would rebel against it: 'The first business of an artist is to substitute man for nature and to make a protest against it.'[47] In time some poets and literary critics would take that line of thought to the extreme epitomized by this characterization of T. S. Eliot's outlook: 'The faith that science, rational knowledge of causes, will solve our problems, is a mean and pitiable delusion. ... Science has offered us a view of life that is unbelievable and intolerable.'[48]

At its height, from the 1850s to the 1880s, the new synthetic faith in science was no mean and pitiable delusion; it was a great creed which inspired intense feeling in its adherents as well as its opponents. There was even a major literary movement inspired by science, naturalism, whose most famous spokesman, Émile Zola, boasted in an early essay, 'On Science and Civilization in their Relations with Poetry' (1864), that he would do for modern knowledge what Lucretius had done for ancient learning.[49] He did not succeed − he did not even try − nor did the 'science poetry' movement, which produced mediocre verse and was soon forgotten.[50] On the other hand, Zola and some other naturalists were inspired by a scientific view of human beings to produce genuine masterpieces of the literary imagination − in prose, be it noted, not in poetry, and quite tragic.

Nowadays critics are inclined to brush aside the naturalists' claim of scientific inspiration as a faddish pretension, of little significance for their actual works of literary art.[51] I would suggest that older critics saw more deeply, when they noted a connection between the mood of mechanistic science and the tragic determinism that was so marked a feature of the naturalists' greatest creations.[52] To brush aside the naturalists' claim of scientific inspiration is not only a gratuitous insult to their intelligence. It is also an evasion of a basic question, whether the scientific study of human beings can generate aesthetic reactions, and if so, what kinds. As I read Zola's fiction, to take the most important case, I find repeated evidence of an aesthetic reaction to science — a sense of tragedy — at odds with the ideological reaction — a joy in progress — which he expressed in his tracts.

In his fiction Zola took scientific knowledge — or what passed for it in his day — and 'pushed things to nightmare'.[53] Consider, for example, how he transforms a clinical description of *delirium tremens* into a surrealist version of *l'homme-machine*, the basic metaphor of physiology, with some piece of a person left inside as a helpless observer and suffering victim of the machine:

> That day the legs were jumping in their turn; the trembling had gone down from his hands to his feet; a true puppet worked by wires, capering in the limbs but stock still in the trunk. The disease was steadily advancing. It was like some music under the skin, starting up every three or four seconds, pulsating a moment, then stopping and starting again, just like the little shudder that shakes stray dogs in the freezing winter in some doorway. The belly and shoulders were already quivering like water on the point of boiling. ... The puppet was actually doing a belly-laugh too. Giggles were running around the ribs, and the belly was gasping as if it were bursting with laughter. Everything was joining in the dance, and no mistake! The muscles paired off with each other, the skin vibrated like a drum, the hairs waltzed and bowed to each other. ... Coupeau might sleep, but his feet danced. O, their boss could snore, that wasn't their affair, they continued their routine, neither hurrying nor slowing down. Real mechanical feet, feet that took their fun where they found it. ... [His wife] Gervaise put her hand on his shoulder. ... The dance was going on right down to the bottom of his flesh, the very bones must be jumping. Tremors, waves were coming from afar, flowing like a river under the skin. When she pressed a little harder she sensed cries of pain from the very marrow. All you could see with the naked eye was wavelets hollowing out tiny dimples, as on a whirlpool, but inside there must be a frightful havoc. ... The bare feet sticking out at the end of the mattress were still dancing — they were none too clean, and had long nails. ... Suddenly they stiffened and stopped. Only death had stopped those feet.[54]

Here the physiologist's metaphor is no longer a mere guide for experimentation, but an aesthetic trope, a 'magnetic mockery' of a human being, as it seemed to Tennyson. Tennyson's ideology allowed him to dismiss the metaphor with swift contempt. Zola's scientistic ideology obliged him to return to it constantly, elaborating its implications for the person within the mechanism. It mattered little that Zola genuinely believed, on an ideological level, in the beneficence of the mechanistic vision. When he tried to embody that belief in a work of fiction that was supposed to sum up his life's work, he produced a tract instead of a novel, an embarrassing literary failure.[55] It mattered very much that Zola's powerful literary imagination accepted the physiological approach to human nature, and used it with extraordinary effectiveness to picture 'the puppet animal'.[56]

In short, ephemeral 'science poetry' and enduring naturalistic fiction were exceptions that tested the rule, and proved it true. Mechanistic science appalled the literary imagination even in the period when the synthetic faith in science was enjoying its greatest vitality. Tiutchev, the supreme Russian master of the meditative poem on man and nature, put the case with bleak simplicity in 'Our Age' (1851):

> Not flesh but spirit has rotted in our days,
> And man is desperately anguished.
> He strives toward light from night's darkness
> And, gaining light, grumbles and revolts.[57]

That poetic revolt foretold the intellectual collapse of the synthetic faith in science, which could hardly claim a genuine synthesis of knowledge while provoking belligerence between different ways of knowing, the scientific and the aesthetic.

It is worse than pointless to retort, as positivists commonly do, that the poet's reaction has been illogical, that the aesthetic sensibility may still regard the rainbow with awe after the intellect has ceased to do so, and the poet's fancy may put a person back in the neural circuitry after the physiologist's science has excluded it.[58] That retort is beside the point, for it simply ignores the artist's loss when knowledge of physical reality was cut away from the knowledge of mental realities that the literary imagination develops. The retort is worse than pointless in its implications for a theory of art. It is as if the positivist told someone mourning the death of a lover that she has in reality lost nothing but a pattern of pleasurable stimuli, which can conceivably be replaced, by synthetic sweets perhaps or maybe plastic dildos.

PSYCHOLOGY

Believers in scientism generally ignore the hostility of poets, or exhort them to accept their job of organizing the emotions apart from knowledge, since science alone provides knowledge. But that drastic surgery does not save the faith. Even if we assume that feeling can be so neatly separated from knowing — allowing the poet, let us say, to invite his soul or bid his spirit sing while knowing that he has no soul or spirit, and allowing the scientist to seek knowledge without spiritual purpose, merely with neural motives, as a dog seeks a bitch — even so, faith in science as the royal road to truth and perfection must still falter, if it contemplates the roads actually traversed by the human sciences. There are too many, running off in too many directions, too often petering out in barren isolation and mutual incomprehension.

That is of course a sore point for professionals in the human sciences, and they frequently reassure themselves by highly selective histories, like would-be aristocrats, who decorate their walls with a single family tree and ignore the enormous jungle within which their little families and big egos are momentary growths. Experimental psychologists, for example, like to call Wilhelm Wundt the father of their discipline, dismissing his philo- sophizing and his introspective method, and ignoring a host of disapproved relatives.[59] An outside observer lacks such uplifting selectivity of vision. He sees no single science of psychology emerging either from Wundt, or from Helmholtz, who trained Wundt in the physiological approach to psychology, or from E. H. Weber or Gustav Fechner, who were doing 'psychophysical' research before Wundt opened his famous lab in 1879.

The historian's problem is not the trivial one of establishing priority in psychophysics, nor the interesting but relatively minor question of differ- ences and similarities among those founding fathers of a physiological approach to the psyche. The major, intractable problem is the historian's awareness of many different, irreconcilable lines of descent. There is, for example, a line that runs directly from physiology to Pavlov and the *rejection* of psychophysics, indeed, of the psyche itself. There are lines running from Wundt and from Darwin to comparative studies of animal psychology (ethology, as it is generally called today) at odds with physio- logical reductionism. There are lines from Wundt and from E. B. Tylor to comparative studies of human societies (cultural anthropology, as it is generally called today) at odds with any kind of biological reductionism. There are complex lines from Franz Brentano and from psychiatry and from neurophysiology to Freud and 'depth' psychology. There are complex lines leading to Gestalt psychology, to cognitive psychology, to neuropsy- chology, to various schools of social psychology, and to the philosophical psychologies that reject or contemptuously ignore almost all of the above.

Constructing a history of the human sciences is quite different from recapturing the history of the natural sciences, for consensus on basics is lacking both in the past and in the present. Only a partisan can discern a grand line of development from past confusion to present knowledge — within the church that holds his faith. If the historian refuses to join a church, he is condemned to remain an analyst of confusion.[60]

Consider the strange origins of experimental psychology. One of the founding fathers was J. F. Herbart, Kant's successor at Königsberg, who rejected experiment as a way to understand the immaterial mind. Yet he was sufficiently enthralled by the exact sciences to work out mathematical correlations of mental phenomena, for example the 'thresholds' at which ideas emerge from subconscious formation to full consciousness. Herbart's textbook was still widely read in the mid-nineteenth century, but its mentalistic approach was being undercut by a growing tendency to consider mind a function of the central nervous system. Gustav Fechner, a physicist by profession and a spiritualist by conviction, sought to overcome that materialist *Nachtansicht* or 'night view' in favor of an idealist *Tagesansicht* or 'day view' − by experiment.[61]

At first sight that endeavor may seem as foolish as the seances of the Society for Psychical Research, where parapsychology had its nineteenth-century origins. But Fechner was no gullible dreamer seeking an ectoplasmic replacement for the spirit of traditional religion. He knew that the mind exists in everybody, or more precisely, in every body, interacting with the nervous system, controlling the most ordinary sensations of everyday life. As a physicist he also knew the methods of rigorous experiment, which he applied to 'the relations of dependency between body and mind.'[62] His 'psychophysical' experiments correlated precisely measured physical stimuli with verbal reports of sensations or perceptions. He correlated, for example, the changing weights that the subject lifts with the subject's reports, 'heavier', 'lighter', or 'the same'. Accumulations of slight, *unnoticeable* changes in such stimuli as changing weights or intensities of light become *noticeable* at certain thresholds, on the same mathematical pattern as Herbart's subconscious ideas emerging into the conscious mind. In short, Fechner established logarithmic equations between increments of physical stimuli and 'least noticeable differences' in sensation and perception. He presented the equations in *Elements of Psychophysics* (1860), arguing that they demonstrated the mind's autonomy in relations with the body.[63]

That argument was vigorously disputed from a variety of viewpoints, which intensified interest in experimental approaches to the science of mental life, and thus helped Wundt to found, in 1879, a laboratory for the training of experimental psychologists and a journal to publish their findings. Other labs and journals soon appeared for the new discipline. But disputes over the basic assumptions and methods of psychology were not washed away by the resulting flood of experimental data. On the contrary, the data were subject to charges of insignificance, if the critic did not share the experimenter's initial assumptions about the mind-body relationship that is involved in introspective reports of 'heavier', 'lighter', 'darker', 'brighter', 'the same'.[64] In short, experimental psychology and the philosophy of mind were caught in a vicious circle, from which estrangement seemed the only escape. Experimentalists would simply make the assumptions that suited them, without elaborate philosophical defense, while philosophers would theorize with less and less reference to experimental

findings. Moreover, experimentalists drifted toward internal splits of their
own, most notably the 'objectivist' or 'behaviorist' revolt against any
concept of mind in the science of mental life. That astonishing twist came
at the turn of the century in Germany, Russia, and the United States.
Tantum experimentum potuit saudere malorum, if I may modernize Lucretius'
thrust at religion. So much tormenting incoherence can experimental science
inspire, with or without the aid of philosophy.

The most influential agents of the drift toward behaviorism were not the
notorious physiological materialists (Vogt, Moleschott, Büchner), nor such
'shamefaced materialists' as Thomas Huxley, who likened the conscious
mind to the steam whistle of a locomotive to illustrate his oxymoronic
formula: 'We are conscious automata.'[65] Such popular authors used the
concept of mind quite freely, while arguing that the mind is nothing but a
secretion, or force, or property, or function of the brain. They took little
care to be precise or consistent. Büchner, for example, could sound very
much like the dualistic philosophers he was ostensibly rejecting:

> The origin of the nerves of voluntary motion must . . . be distributed
> in the brain in a certain topographic manner, in order that they may
> individually obey the will. This relation has very aptly been compared
> to the keys of a piano, upon which the person plays. The will, like the
> player, requires practice to learn this play, in order to produce particular
> movements by touching different keys.[66]

Not only consistency but also creative ideas for research were conspicuously
lacking in such popular tracts of physiological or 'vulgar materialism', as
Marx and Engels called them.[67] No doubt they had a considerable impact
on the general public, undermining religious faith and reinforcing the new
synthetic faith in science, but their influence on the actual work of psychologists and physiologists was indirect and remote.

The most influential agents of fragmentation and incoherence in psychological science were the leading physiologists of the mid-nineteenth century.
They did not intend to muddle the concept of mind or psyche; they only
wanted to get it out of their discipline. They were not materialists
in explicit philosophy. On the contrary, they prudently separated the
mechanistic methods of their science from the philosophy of materialism,
partly as a defense against the ideological furore over materialism — more
of that later — but even more, I would suggest, for purely professional or
scientific reasons. They made neurophysiology a rigorous experimental
discipline, a 'hard science', as we would say today, by deliberately limiting
it to neural impulses and muscular or glandular responses. Their characteristic way of justifying the exclusion of mind was to declare that an unbridge-
able gulf separated objective knowledge of neural processes from subjective
knowledge of the mind. Emil Du Bois-Reymond, most notably, in a
famous lecture of 1872, imagined 'astronomical knowledge of the brain', as

he chose to call complete knowledge of all the brain's atoms in all their interconnections. Even that 'highest knowledge of [the brain] that we can [hope to] achieve would show us nothing in it but matter in motion. Through no imaginable arrangement or movement of material particles, however, can a bridge be cast into the realm of consciousness.'[68] Or, as Hughlings Jackson, the great English neurophysiologist, put it: 'There is no physiology of the mind, any more than there is a psychology of the nervous system'.[69]

Whatever the practical justification for that view, it should be recognized as a partisan distortion of reality. Neurophysiologists cannot easily escape the psychic or mental aspects of neural functions when they are dealing with whole human beings, or indeed with dogs, as we will see in Pavlov's case. They sought such an escape by chopping apart the links in the chain that leads from physical stimuli to neural processes to sensations to perceptions to concepts to thought and sensibility. With carefully chosen 'preparations', such as a brainless frog, they could break off the first two links, physical stimuli and neural processes, and study them in isolation, by such simple acts as the muscular twitch or glandular flow that stops or goes on the stimulation of a nerve. It is quite practical for neurophysiologists to make such an arbitrary break. Their science became rigorous, at a truncated level. Even while their research was moving up the nervous system above the spinal level into the brain itself, they avoided confusion by refusing to rise above physical stimuli and neural processes in their system of concepts. Fritsch and Hitzig, who opened the field of electrical stimulation of the brain in 1870, were mavericks in their claim that they were demonstrating the action of the will on the nervous system.[70] The many neurophysiologists who seized upon their research technique ignored their psychological or philosophical interpretation, and concentrated on the purely mechanical mapping of relationships between the stimulated parts of the brain and the parts of the body that stop or go in response.[71]

Those who must deal with the whole human being were left to struggle as best they could with higher-level functions, such as thinking and feeling, which seem extraordinarily strange when the lower levels are separated from them. But the difficulties work both ways, troubling the most hard-nosed physiologist as well as the most freewheeling philosopher. Even such a low-level function as digestion is hard to disentangle from a psychic process, even in a subhuman animal. The reader will see how Pavlov, studying the flow of digestive juices in dogs, was troubled by psychic disruptions of his mechanical correlations between physical stimulus and glandular response. In fact he was so bothered that he finally decided to bring the purely objective method of physiology to bear on the psyche, as a sledgehammer is brought to bear on an obstructing boulder.

Much of this book will be concerned with areas where the modern specialization of intellectual labor goes awry, where the squirming facts exceed the squamous mind, if I may borrow Wallace Stevens's metaphor.[72]

The point here at the outset is the difficulty that began with nineteenth-century progress in neurophysiology, progress achieved by deliberate extirpation of the mind–body problem. That practical stroke left the mind more mysterious than ever by placing it beyond the reach of physiology. Experimental psychology emerged as a bizarre new discipline, applying the experimental methods of physiology to a problem that physiologists declared insoluble.

Wundt was 'the father' of the new discipline in this limited, sociological sense: he founded, in 1879, the first institution for the training of experimental psychologists as professional specialists, not simply as philosophers or physiologists who do psychological experimentation, which had been the situation previously. Sociologists may argue that Wundt thus unwittingly opened the way for a sharp separation of psychology from the other two disciplines, and indeed, for the sharp separation of experimental from other types of psychology. Communities of professionals tend to justify their existence by separating their enterprise from competition.[73] But one should stress that Wundt had this effect unwittingly. He intended no such separations. Quite the contrary, he insisted that psychologists must be interdisciplinary venturers, who would link physiology with philosophy in order to shed light on mental life. Indeed, Wundt ranged far beyond physiology and philosophy, to such fields as the study of animal behavior, anthropology, and comparative religion. His prodigious outpouring of books was one of the last great offerings to the dream of creating a comprehensive science of humanity by aggregation of many disciplines and doctrines, not by reduction to a single basic discipline founded on a parsimonious set of consistent principles. That explains in part the embarrassment of the behaviorists who call Wundt father, yet are skimpy and condescending in their treatment of him.[74] He started their professional enterprise, pointing it to an enormous task and a wide range of methods that they have shrunk away from or explicitly rejected.

The substantive reasons for this ironic process were probably more important than the sociological. How after all were experimental psychologists to analyze mind scientifically? Wundt's answer derived from neurophysiology and from the old notion of mind as a bundle of associations established by repeated experiences. The experimenter gets at those associations as Fechner did, by correlating physical stimuli with introspective reports of associated mental states — for example, by asking weightlifting subjects to report their perceptions of heaviness and lightness. Such a procedure is open to a number of objections, including the vicious circularity or question-begging that was mentioned above. Correlations of physical stimuli with verbal reports of sensation do not reveal the nature of intervening variables. One psychologist may put the word mind on such intervening variables; another may call them spirit or soul; a materialist may call them brain processes. The mere correlation of stimuli and responses will not settle their quarrel.

By the end of the nineteenth century a number of psychologists were sufficiently unhappy to draw the extreme conclusion, that the intervening variables should be left to neurophysiology, to the extent that they are brain processes, and to metaphysical speculation, to the extent that they are mind or soul. The experimental psychologist was left with the self-appraisal that concluded William James's famous textbook in 1892:

> ... 'Psychology as a natural science' ... means a psychology particularly fragile, and into which the waters of metaphysical criticism leak at every joint. ... A string of raw facts; a little gossip and wrangle about opinions; a little classification and generalization on the mere descriptive level; a strong prejudice that we *have* states of mind, and that our brain conditions them: but not a single law in the sense in which physics shows us laws, not a single proposition from which any consequence can be causally deduced. We don't even know the terms between which the elementary laws would obtain if we have them. ... This is no science, it is only the hope of a science. The matter of the science is with us. Something definite happens when to a certain brain-state a certain 'sciousness' corresponds. A genuine glimpse into what it is would be *the* scientific achievement, before which all past achievements would pale.[75]

James still hoped for 'the Galileo and the Lavoisier of psychology', who would make it an authentic science, though 'the necessities of the case will make them "metaphysical".'

The rebels against such a mixture of science and philosophy were not as thoroughly revolutionary as they imagined themselves. They carried forward not only Wundt's faith in experiment but also the 'elementism' or psychological atomism that seemed to be the founding assumption of psychological experimentation. Just as matter is compounded of elementary particles and living beings of cells, so mind or behavior in this view is compounded of elementary units of experience, repeated associations of certain stimuli with certain responses.

That atomistic picture of the mind was challenged by a number of thinkers — including Wundt in his philosophical works — who conceived the mind as an active entity or process, which shapes its own experiences in a purposeful way. The most important of these thinkers was Franz Brentano, another 'father of psychology', who strove as Wundt did to keep philosophy and psychology joined, and unwittingly contributed to their separation. In 1874, shortly before Wundt founded his laboratory, Brentano published *Psychology from the Empirical Point of View*, which opened with an unflinching recognition of disorder in the fledgling science:

> It is not so much abundant and many-sided theses that we need most in the psychic realm as it is unity of conviction [*Einheit in der Überzeugung*]. We must strive to achieve here what mathematics, physics,

chemistry and physiology have already accomplished, some earlier, others later: a nucleus of generally recognized truth to which, through the combined efforts of many forces, new crystals will adhere on all sides. In place of *psychologies* we must seek to create *a psychology.*[76]

Brentano hoped to start the unifying process, to create that nucleus of generally recognized truth, by rigorous philosophical analysis of the concepts and problems of psychology. Instead he precipitated splits even deeper than the behavioral revolt against father Wundt.

Brentano's central argument was that the mind is characterized by purposeful activity, or, if one must break the process into constituent units, by intentional acts, such as sensing, judging, feeling. Empirical study of the mind may take the form of experimentation, or observation of other creatures, or intuitive introspection, singly or in various combinations. Brentano saw no conflict among those methods, but his diverse intellectual progeny did.[77] They split into schools, using a variety of methods and assumptions, separately and antagonistically, not in 'unity of conviction'. The stress on mind as an active process rather than a bundle of associations − 'act psychology' *v.* 'content psychology' was the usual description of the cleavage − led some of Brentano's students (von Ehrenfels, Stumpf, and *their* students) to create Gestalt psychology. They contrived experiments to discover the organizing patterns or forms (*Gestalten*) of mental activity, in opposition to the Wundtian (and behaviorist) search for the rather passive elements or atoms of which the mind (or behavior) is compounded. It is also noteworthy that Sigmund Freud studied with Brentano, which may help to explain Freud's turn from a dream of neurophysiological reduction to his curious mixturē of biological reductionism with an introspective, mentalistic psychology.[78] From Brentano, through many intervening links and additions, one can also trace the school of L. S. Vygotsky, which has come to dominate Soviet psychology.[79] But the student most often linked to Brentano − or tied to him like the albatross to the sailor that shot him − is Edmund Husserl, the founder of the esoteric school of phenomenologists. They approach the mind as subjective experience, and turn it into an object of speculative analysis, which places them poles apart from any kind of experimental psychology. This approach can be called empirical − Brentano's term for his own viewpoint − only in a tortuous meaning of the word that fuses it with abstract speculation.[80] *Tantum philosophia potuit suadere malorum*, to modernize Lucretius once again: so much tormenting incoherence can philosophy inspire, with or without the aid of experimental science.

We find thus a double paradox in nineteenth-century German psychology. Its philosophical and physiological proclivities seemed to complement each other in the creation of experimental psychology as a hybrid discipline, but soon revealed inner antagonisms that split the unstable hybrid into segregated schools. Mental life, ostensibly banished from neurophysiology yet studied by methods that originated in physiology, became different mysteries for different schools. It is as if, trying to understand the singer apart from his song, one turned the song into a Platonic idea, or an abstraction from a pattern of physical sounds — or a jeering metaphor, such as a locomotive's steam whistle.

In the English-speaking world of the nineteenth century we find different sorts of paradox, with incoherence once again as the end result. Experimental psychology developed more slowly in empiricist Britain than in metaphysical Germany, which seems strange until we remind ourselves of the ambiguities in our terms. Metaphysics can mean 'an unusually obstinate effort to think clearly' — that is William James's definition[81] — which can drive the psychologist to distraction or to experiment, or to one after the other in either order. That is how it was in Germany. On the other hand, empiricism can be speculative, introspective, intuitive, as it was in the British tradition of associationist psychology. Locke and his disciples looked no farther than common-sense experience to infer that repeated association of sense-data creates the ideas that constitute the mind. In the nineteenth century John Stuart Mill continued that tradition of philosophizing about mind, and Alexander Bain, a self-taught scholar and admirer of Mill's, pushed it to the verge of experimental psychology.[82]

It seems strange that he stayed there on the brink, content with metaphors on the relationship of mind and body, holding back from the plunge into testable hypotheses. When we find analogous blockage in the other popular Victorian psychologists, William B. Carpenter and George Henry Lewes, each in his different way content with 'empirical metaphysics', as Lewes called his system,[83] we may wonder whether the common-sense tradition of British empiricism may not have blunted rather than sharpened the urge to test hypotheses about the mind. But there is no room here to indulge that wonder. By the end of the nineteenth century English-speaking graduate students were going to German universities — from America — and bringing back home the German obsession for experiment as the only way to get beyond common sense, to a scientific understanding of mental processes.[84] They were also nourishing the associated discontents that would make America the center of the behaviorist revolt.

With the advantage of hindsight we can see that Victorian England's most significant contribution to the human sciences was not the moribund tradition of speculative associationist psychology, but the new idea of evolution by natural selection. Hindsight is needed because associationism seemed to contemporaries to be *the* British school of psychology, and because the genuine significance of natural selection for the human sciences was long obscured by the factitious issues involved in social Darwinism. Darwin revealed the genuine significance when he reasoned that the intellectual and moral faculties must have emerged in evolution as a result of the enhanced survival value that they conferred.[85] That line of thought pointed toward an evolutionary version of biological reductionism, which would prove very different from physiological reductionism. Darwin's approach developed into comparative psychology − or animal psychology, or ethology, as it has variously been called − which sought, largely by field observations, to establish the different types of mental life or behavior that have emerged at different levels of evolution. Physiological reductionists sought, largely by laboratory experiments, to establish some basic element − tropism, taxis, or reflex − as the basic unit of which all behavior is compounded. Indeed, an admirer of Jacques Loeb reached below the animal level for the most sweeping vision of physiological reductionism: 'The movement of plants toward the light and the search for truth by mathematical analysis, are they not in essence phenomena of one and the same order?'[86]

In abstract logic the two viewpoints need not exclude each other. One may assume, as Loeb did, that the more complex types of mind or behavior, which emerge at later stages of evolution, are to be explained − in the famous last analysis − as compounds of the basic elements present at the earliest stage. But that assumption seemed to the comparative psychologists meaningless at best, if the last analysis was indefinitely postponed, and wrong at worst, if the last analysis was claimed in advance by speculative extrapolations from meager data of such physiologists as Loeb.[87] Accusations also ran the other way: the comparative psychologists appeared wildly speculative in their intuitive readings of animal minds. If Pavlov shocked psychologists by equating a mathematician searching for the truth with a plant turning toward the sun, George Romanes provoked the sarcasm of Jacques Loeb by supposing curiosity to be the force that moves the moth to the flame.[88] Whatever logical analysis may say about the ultimate compatibility of the two schools, the historical record shows that they regarded each other as opponents.[89]

More troublesome than that conflict between two kinds of biological reductionism was the division between biological and cultural approaches in the human sciences, and within the cultural approach the further division between evolutionary and non-evolutionary outlooks. Herbert Spencer and other Victorian polymaths, such as Lewes, blandly linked biological and sociocultural evolution in their speculative schemes. Marx and Engels assumed such a link in principle, but dismissed it as 'a mere phrase' when it was spelled out in speculative detail.[90] Very few specialists in the human sciences still argue, as the social Darwinists did, that natural selection explains the dominance of bosses over workers or whites over blacks. But the dwindling of such blatant ideology has revealed the deeper difficulties of reconciling the biological and cultural approaches to social evolution. The biological diversity of *Homo sapiens* is simply not great enough to account for the cultural diversity of the species. Natural selection is simply too slow to explain cultural change. A biological approach to understanding human beings has at best a peripheral interest to the cultural anthropologist, sociologist, or historian; like the study of physical geography, it indicates the broadest limits within which human societies can change. At worst a biological approach encourages the blatant error of supposing that the limits are the determinants of sociocultural variation. One might as well suppose that the physiology of hearing can explain the transformation of musical styles from Mozart to Stravinsky or the change in Russia's anthem from 'God Save the Tsar' to 'The Internationale'.

Within the cultural approach of nineteenth-century social scientists hind-sight reveals incipient fissures that have since become chasms. Victorian ethnographers such as Edward B. Tylor, collecting heaps of information about diverse human societies, were trying to organize their material according to schemes of cultural evolution, and, so doing, were unwittingly generating a revolt against the very concept of cultural evolution.[91] From a twentieth-century point of view the most obvious problem is ideology: it seems impossible to separate the concept of cultural evolution from European self-congratulation, for Europe was commonly assumed to represent the most advanced stage in the progressive emergence of an ideal culture. In the nineteenth century very few Europeans had begun to grow sick of such imperialist self-congratulation, but the technical or scientific problems of comparing a great variety of cultures were imperceptibly moving anthropologists away from the concept of cultural evolution.

Elements of a given culture, such as kin groups or religious beliefs or art styles, can be properly compared with elements of other cultures only if their functions within the given culture are first established. But concentration on functional analysis tends to undermine the ranking of cultures as higher and lower. If the strange kin groups of some primitive tribe serve to make it cohesive and self-perpetuating, the anthropologist finds it hard to declare those kin groups inferior to the family system of modern Europe. Unfortunately that line of thought threatens our confidence in science itself, the supreme measure of Europe's pre-eminence. If the magical beliefs of some primitive tribe serve to make it cohesive and self-perpetuating, the anthropologist finds it hard to declare magic inferior to the science of modern Europe. Ultimately, functionalism and anti-imperialism would come together in the twentieth-century revolt of cultural relativists against the assumption that the collective mentalities of human societies can be arranged on a scale of development from lower to higher, like the physical remains that rise from *Pithecanthropus* to *Homo sapiens*.

Whichever way that conflict is settled − if it ever is; recently there has been a revival of social evolutionism − cultural anthropologists seem destined, like plain old historians or imaginative writers, to be fundamentally different from physiologists. Analysis of conscious minds is excluded on principle from physiology; it is essential to the humanist disciplines, as it is to imaginative literature. Physiologists have limited their inquiry to non-mental processes, and with that have facilitated agreement on methods and results, and a swelling consensus on objective truth. The experience of psychologists has been very different, even for those who have aped the physiologists most slavishly, trying to exclude mental concepts from their field of inquiry. They have found themselves still embroiled with the taboo mind, if only by the mocking presence of rival, explicitly mentalist schools within the science they would purify.

Thus psychology comes to seem a dubious discipline. To those who would make it fit the standard of physiology, psychology seems too broadly questing and therefore amorphous. To those who would stretch the conscious mind's inquiry to encompass itself, including its abundant modes of self-expression, psychology seems neither a science nor a humanistic discipline, but a crippled bastard of the two. I favor a gentler metaphor for psychological science in its first century: disagreeable tribes claiming a single territory, shaping a history of dynamic tension within enduring wilderness.

2

Social Science and Ideologies

The wonder is that rulers were so nice to thinkers. Nineteenth-century materialism and positivism, in any of their forms, subverted the antique religions that rulers still invoked to justify their rule. In some forms they were directly linked with movements to overthrow the old order. But the urge to repress subversive ideas continued to recede, as it had in the eighteenth century — which is especially surprising when one notes the accelerating increase in audiences reached by subversive ideas. The rise of mass education and the mass press, of public lectures and free libraries, the coincident decline in working hours — all together gave more people more time and inclination to read and listen, with dangerous thoughts rather freely available. In most European countries the nineteenth century was also a time of revolutionary outbursts, and of great fear — or hope — that the outbursts might intensify to the point of a successful lower-class assault on their social and political masters.

Those processes would seem, on first thought, to have removed the social basis of intellectual toleration. In the eighteenth century toleration emerged on the basis of a sharp division between the unlettered masses, which could be presumed impenetrable by enlightened thought, and a tiny cultivated minority, which could be presumed too comfortable to use subversive ideas for anything but conversational toys. A split mentality allowed enlightened rulers to tolerate such thinkers as Diderot and Lamettrie, while using state churches to hold the masses in obedience 'for conscience' sake, not merely out of fear'.

It is not necessary to guess at subconscious attitudes; a double standard was quite consciously applied, at times with open cynicism. Catherine the Great maintained a state church so benighted that some of its censors still tried to ban the Copernican theory, that is, to arrest the movement of the earth about the sun.[1] Yet she had no fear of Diderot, who had been imprisoned in France for subverting belief in the immortal soul. Catherine invited him to St Petersburg, as an intellectual decoration of her court.[2] In Prussia Frederick the Great offered a refuge to Lamettrie, when he was hounded out of France and then even out of Holland, where a pioneering effort at religious toleration had not yet extended to godless materialism. Frederick not only rescued Lamettrie but delivered a eulogy over him when he died prematurely. In that speech Frederick the philosopher derided the Christian faith he maintained as a monarch.[3]

By the middle of the nineteenth century it is impossible to find a national ruler, whether king or president, courting atheistic thinkers and sneering at the traditional faith of his subjects. On the contrary; reverential posturing became an obligatory style in the political arena. But a split mentality of a different sort was becoming characteristic of modern political leaders. Hypocrisy would be an inaccurate term; it implies a mind that knows one thing while the mouth is saying another. More and more the political mouth was disconnected from the mind, and wired to a political calculator. Political authorities kept the appearance of a reverential outlook by stunting their intellects, simply ignoring conflicts between the religions or ideologies that they professed and the discordant visions implicit in science or pro-claimed in the name of science. Louis Napoleon, for example, still had enough old-fashioned pretensions to enlightenment to invite Claude Bernard to the palace for a lecture on new developments in physiology.[4] (In our century such pretensions to intellectuality have vanished from executive mansions, with the significant exception of Communist rulers fresh to power.) But Louis Napoleon showed no awareness of the conflict between science and the Catholic church, which he strongly supported for political reasons. Claude Bernard helped this mindless civility emerge by being a prudent professional, the thoroughly modern type of scientist. Though his work would have delighted Lamettrie by its mechanistic assumptions, methods, and findings, he carefully avoided inflammatory confrontations between the concept of *l'homme-machine* and the concept of *l'homme-esprit*, the physiologist's approach to the psyche and the churchman's or the humanist's. As for politics, he was an Orléanist, a moderate conservative, sufficiently candid to win a reputation of sturdy independence, sufficiently passive to cause the Bonapartists no anxiety.[5]

In Germany of the mid-nineteenth century the situation was different, on the surface at least, because of the tumult aroused by the popular material-ists, Büchner, Vogt, and Moleschott, who linked their radical philosophy to mechanistic physiology. They were forced out of their academic posi-tions, and even, in the case of Vogt, who was a revolutionary socialist as well as a materialist, into exile from the fatherland.[6] Other 'freethinkers' were tolerated in universities, on the tacit understanding that they would be less provocative than the 'vulgar materialists'.

That delicate balance set the tone of a major convention of scientists at

Göttingen in 1854. It was opened by a conservative old physiologist, Rudolph Wagner, who equated mechanism with materialism, and called upon his colleagues to earn the trust of state and society by repudiating the subversive doctrine in biology as well as philosophy. A debate was scheduled between him and Carl Ludwig, a young spokesman of the new mechanistic philosophy, but it failed to take place. Both sides seem to have backed off in fear, of political trouble in the case of Ludwig, of professional disgrace in the case of Wagner.[7] Subsequently, when Carl Ludwig heard that he had been refused a professorial chair at Bonn because of his reputation as an atheist, he wrote to the Prussian *Kultusminister* arguing that religious beliefs are quite separate from physiology, and citing in evidence an eminent physiologist who was a devout Christian and 'a good friend of the rest of us'.[8] Of course he did not directly acknowledge that 'the rest of us' were freethinkers, and he passed beyond diplomatic evasion to prevarication by citing a supposed proof of a personal God in a speech by Helmholtz.[9] But we must not be harsh. Compartmentalization of the mind was the central point in Ludwig's plea for modern civility. His letter was a little venture in politics, where evasion and prevarication are the norm. Among scientists Ludwig was renowned for his open, honest character.[10]

The notion that mechanistic physiology and evolutionary theory were intimately linked with atheism and radicalism became a sectarian belief during the latter part of the nineteenth century, more and more obviously at odds with reality in Germany as elsewhere. Leading biologists disowned the connection not only quietly, in the manner of Carl Ludwig, but also publicly, even noisily. Rudolf Virchow, who had fought for the revolution in 1848, when he was twenty-seven, caused a sensation at a scientific convention thirty years later by a political attack on the proposal to teach evolution in the schools. He linked evolutionary doctrine to socialism, and warned his fellow scientists that their academic freedom might not survive such challenges to the ideology that sustained the existing order.[11] Virchow was eccentric in his views on the problem of evolution, and he was exceptionally strident in his manner of expression, but he was probably close to the average German scientist in his conviction that scholars should protect academic freedom by confining it to the ivory tower, leaving ideology to the powers that be.

Emil Du Bois-Reymond, who had not fought on the barricades but had shocked German philistines with his extreme mechanism in the 1840s and 1850s, made amends in a more genteel fashion as he grew older. He gave philosophical lectures, which turned into popular pamphlets, arguing that science only seemed to be on the way to conquer the whole world of thought. On closer examination, science proved to be forever incapable of solving the most basic riddles that challenge the human mind, such as the question, What is mind itself? To those questions, he declared, scientists must respond *Ignorabimus* forever, We shall never know. Thus we leave humanity to its traditional faiths and metaphysical speculations.[12] Helmholtz, still closer than Du Bois-Reymond to the secluded academic type, published a quieter disapproval of the materialism that claimed support in biology.[13]

Thus, when Büchner founded the Freethinkers' League in 1881, he was clearly at odds with the leaders of mechanistic physiology, his own original discipline, which he pictured as the scientific foundation of materialist philosophy. He was also implicitly at odds with his own vision; like many an earlier preacher of a universal creed, he was establishing one more sect. He could not leave his philosophy to triumph spontaneously, along with the discipline of biology. His philosophy of biology had to be propagated by an organization of dedicated believers, who were increasingly ignored or brushed off by biologists. Thus the materialist philosophy implicit in modern biology was sinking from intellectual debate into the clutter of popular beliefs, this one shared with provincial fundamentalists, who loathe biological science for the same reason that Büchner exalted it, as a basis of godless radicalism. Whether the belief has intellectual value was coming to matter less than its value in the calculus of political forces.

For German politicians Bismarck's abandonment of the anti-Catholic struggle in 1879 was a major turning point toward the thoroughly modern separation of politics from theoretical ideology. The Freethinkers' League was not included in the *de facto* governmental coalition that emerged after Bismarck stopped fighting Catholicism, but intellectual incompatibility probably had little to do with the exclusion. Once Bismarck, a devoted Lutheran and an opponent of party politics on principle, made his political deal with the Catholic party, he had no need of the atheist party. In fact, his abandonment of the struggle against Catholicism may have precipitated the formation of the Freethinkers' League, by aggravating the atheists' sense of their own isolation. One might almost say that conservative politicians and conservative scientists conspired to drive radicals and materialists into sectarian impotence. It was not a conscious conspiracy. Things just happened that way, as politicians and scientists sacrificed their intellectual sensitivity in order to accommodate mechanistic biology and conservative ideology.

But then, of course, there is the exceptional radical, Karl Marx, whose admirers grew from sects to armies, first in Germany then the world. Did he not hand on from the nineteenth to the twentieth century the unbroken faith in materialist science and political radicalism one and indivisible, thought fused with action to comprehend and transform the world? That is not a rhetorical question. The devout ayes are too fervently pitted against the scornful noes for the issue to be dismissed with rhetorical gestures. We must ask quite seriously what there was in Marx's version of the nineteenth-century faith in science that saved it from the common wreck of all the others.

To ask the question is to enter an old quarrel. Many object that Marx's version of scientism was not saved but wrecked in its own special way: transformed from genuine thought into the crude ideologies of mass movements and regimes, which have not been 'really' committed to Marx's understanding of science and radicalism any more than the Christian churches have been 'really' committed to Jesus's teaching. Others find important continuities of belief linking Marx to his admirers, but only by dividing Marx in two: the scholar and the ideologist, the one inspiring an impressive array of thinkers to discuss his thought, the other inspiring movements and regimes to put his leonine head on their icons, of opportunism (Social Democratic version) or totalitarianism (Communist version). Still other commentators impatiently brush off Marx altogether, as a muddled violent thinker who earned his place on the wall-poster icons of left-wing totalitarianism. And then of course there are the millions of simple believers, who revere Marx as the one true founder of the science that will make us free: where all others failed he succeeded, as proved above all in the triumphant application of his teaching by Lenin and – Stalin? Mao? Castro? Berlinguer? After Lenin the militants cannot agree. Even for the least thoughtful the science in scientific socialism has become problematic, as it always has been for contemplative observers.

It is foolish to pretend an easy superiority to such conflicts of passionate opinion. There is no demilitarized zone for scholars. To claim impartiality is to be at war with all the other claimants on that sacred ground, and we can only hope to have something like reasoned discourse if we try strenuously to reduce differences of opinion to questions of fact, thrusting facts rather than weapons in each other's faces. In the factual record it is obvious that Marx *has* been singled out from the other nineteenth-century prophets of salvation through science, and he has been singled out by contemplative thinkers as well as political activists. His name, pinned to a variety of ideas, is constantly invoked in scholarly discourse as well as mass demonstrations, literally all over the world. If we ask what distinctive qualities may have earned Marx this uniquely broad and lasting appeal, and if we go back to Marx's own writings to find out, the first, most obvious distinction that strikes us is incompleteness. We find no grand synthesis of the universal process, as we do in Comte or Spencer, offered as the summation of all the sciences. Marx did not even produce a brief tract outlining his philosophical approach to the unified science of the future, such as Büchner and other prophets of that exalted century delivered to an avid public. At twenty-six Marx made a sketch for such a tract, and left it that way, an unfinished, unpublished sketch.[14] Approaching forty, he sketched a grand science of human history, and left that too unfinished and unpublished.[15]

For the twenty-five years remaining to him Marx concentrated his enormous energy on one piece of the grand science, the analysis of the capitalist stage in socio-economic development. At the same time, complaining of such interruptions to his serious scholarship, he kept returning to 'journalism', as he called his historical essays on contemporary affairs, ranging from the revolutions of 1848 to the American Civil War and British rule in India. Even in the 'journalism' one finds revelations of self-limitation beneath the appearance of unbounded self-assurance. Late in his life, for example, when Marx's first Russian admirers asked his opinion of Russia's path of development (Could the country skip over capitalism, directly to socialism?), he wrote several drafts of a pamphlet or article on the subject, and left them unpublished. He sent letters instead, saying he did not know enough to back up his tentative opinion (Yes, Russia might skip capitalism), and his Russian admirers kept the letters private, for Marx's Marxism was at odds with theirs (No, Russia could not skip capitalism).[16]

Obviously — if that word may vault us from fact to interpretation — two mentalities were at war within Marx. A revolutionary prophet, who strained to encompass the synthetic truth of the universal process, contended with an exacting, down-to-earth thinker, who kept breaking down the grand truth by trying to prove it. Marx's personality was notoriously assertive, imperious in presenting his own views, excoriating those who disagreed.[17] We hardly need the testimony of contemporaries; the harsh character is still urgently alive in the vehement, caustic style of his scholarly writing, no less than in his journalism. By comparison the treatises of Comte or Spencer are measured, judicious, almost academic. But their stylistic restraint conceals substantive pretensions far greater than Marx's. They not only dreamed of unifying all knowledge in the service of human perfection; they elaborated their dreams in detail and published them as systems. They were able to combine such grand pretensions with a sense of sober restraint, for they had a complacent view of science and society. From their viewpoint knowledge could be unified by summation of the existing disciplines, and the way to human perfection could be projected as a continuation of the dominant trends in existing society. Thus Comte and Spencer could enjoy very broad appeal, while confidence in steady progress was widespread. But their comforting message was also their undoing by the end of their century. As signs of upheaval in knowledge and society replaced confidence with a sense of crisis, the synthetic positivists were abandoned by an increasingly anxious public. They were proved not wrong but inane.

Marx had a far more audacious dream, expressive of angry disturbance even more than hope. He was profoundly revolted by the existing condition of knowledge and society, and therefore yearned for the unification of knowledge through the transformation rather than the aggregation of the existing disciplines — a revolutionary transformation of knowledge, to be accomplished in union with a thorough social revolution. That characterization is broad enough to cover the whole of Marx's intellectual development, from 1844, when he sketched his grand vision, to 1883, when he died, still laboring on *Capital*. It is also broad enough to explain why

enormous attention was paid to Marx after he died, as a sense of crisis —
and the reality of appalling crises — provoked a hunger for harsher analysis
and grimmer prophecy than the synthetic positivists offered.[18]

This characterization of Marx and his exceptional appeal, though true, is
evasive. It is too loftily detached to discern the painful choices that human
scientists must make, especially when they are revolted by the society they
are studying. If we approach closer, to see how Marx conceived the human
sciences, as they were and as he wished them to be, we do not find a single
consistent view, but an unresolved tension between opposed tendencies.

The romantic complaint, that modern society and science are intolerable
because they turn persons into things, was a central theme in Marx's
'Economic-Philosophical Manuscripts of 1844'.[19] But the complaint was
put in an historical context that made *Verdinglichung*, 'thingification' or
'reification', an inevitable stage in the dialectical process of *Vergegenständ-
lichung*, 'objectification', the self-contradictory way that human beings create
themselves by creating things, by transforming their essence into objects.
Following Schiller,[20] young Marx extended that line of argument even to
the physiology of the senses. He felt that society had stripped human
beings of the capacity to feel, even to see or hear, as whole human beings.
Humanity had disintegrated into a menagerie of one-sided creatures, but
the disintegration was leading to ultimate integration, to the emergence of
whole, genuinely human beings. In his own, quasi-Hegelian words:

> The formation [*Bildung*] of the five senses is the work of all of world
> history to the present. The sense that is subject to raw practical
> necessity has only a limited sense. For the starving man food does not
> exist in its human form but only in its abstract existence as food, ...
> and it cannot be said wherein his feeding activity differs from animal
> feeding activity. The worried, impoverished man has no sense of the
> most beautiful drama. The dealer in minerals sees only their commercial
> value, not the beauty and special nature of minerals; he has no minera-
> logical sense. Thus the objectification of the human essence [*die Ver-
> gegenständlichung des menschlichen Wesens*] is necessary in theory and in
> practice, both to make the human senses human and to create human
> senses corresponding to the entire wealth of human and natural being.[21]

That bewildering verbal play with the multiple meaning of 'sense' (*Sinn*)
can be translated into the pedestrian language that signals seriousness in the
academic world. The mechanical meaning of sense, the animal's capacity to
turn specific physical stimuli into specific nerve energies, is the only meaning explored in the science of physiology. Even sense as sensation, subjective feeling, is ruled out of objective science, not to speak of sense as
meaning and comprehension and aesthetic appreciation. Marx in 1844
disdained mere physiology as Tennyson did, about the same time and for a
similar reason: it did not grasp the whole human being, it did not get at the

human essence. Unlike Tennyson, Marx was not willing to supplement science with humanistic philosophy and poetry. He wanted to enlarge science to include humanism, to have science reveal the process by which creatures who have reified themselves will in the future transform themselves into authentic human beings.

To get at the human essence (*das menschliche Wesen*) Marx appropriated Feuerbach's concept of the *Gattungswesen*, 'generic essence', as it should be translated, instead of 'species being', as it usually is. The Latin root of 'generic', like the German *Gattung*, implies generation, not merely classification: the generation by human beings of themselves, literally, in the production of children and goods, and figuratively, in the creation of the human essence. Translation problems aside, the important point is that Marx was still clinging to the concept of human nature or essence. His German term, *das menschliche Wesen*, is much closer than the analogous English term, 'human being', to the metaphysical source, the urge to discover in our particular selves some universal quality that constitutes our humanity.

Such philosophical compulsions were being evaded by the separate disciplines that were emerging from philosophy. (Indeed, philosophy itself was on the way to its twentieth-century avoidance of metaphysics, including avoidance of speculation about essential human nature.) Political economy, sociology, anthropology, history were more and more shunning explicit assumptions about human *nature* in their analyses of human *activity*, and activity was not only separated from the problematic essence of the actors, but also chopped up into manageable parts – economic activity studied by economists, government by political scientists, primitive cultures by anthropologists, segments of advanced cultures by historians – with integration indefinitely postponed.[22] Physiology, as we have seen, was leading that disintegration of the human sciences in the mid-nineteenth century, and psychology was following along, on the way to becoming a discipline that deliberately avoids the question, What is the nature, the essence, of a human being?

In Marx's intellectual development we can see an especially tortured version of that transition from philosophical speculation about human nature to scientific investigation of human activity, broken down into manageable divisions. Already in 1844 he equated human nature, *das menschliche Wesen*, with *Gattungswesen*, the generic essence of humanity, which was not a permanent essence, present from first to last, but an historical process, ages of labor and struggle by which human beings have been paradoxically creating their essential nature and alienating themselves from it. Those who produce goods are alienated from the instruments and the produce of their labor, as ownership is vested in dominant classes of people who do not labor. Thus both producers and exploiters are alienated from a sense of creative participation in the work process, and therefore from a sense of community with other human beings. And thus they are alienated from consciousness of themselves as authentic human beings. That is, they do not comprehend the *Gattungswesen* that they and their ancestors have been generating.

Marx nowhere tries to end the incomprehension by attempting a full, substantive explanation of the human essence as it will emerge in the revolutionary future. He drops hints in his scattered references to free, conscious, integral activity — a dream of people who will hunt in the morning, fish in the afternoon, and do criticism at night, just as they please.[23] Those hints are fragmentary sentimental lapses from his grim main argument, which defines human nature by pointing to history, an endless, unfinished definition, 'the tradition of all the dead generations [that] weighs like a nightmare on the brain of the living'.[24] Scientific analysis of the nightmare process seemed to Marx the only escape from it. He thought to discover a human future by scientific analysis of an inhuman past, at the same time that he scorned the existing social sciences as apologies for existing society. He hoped that an authentically human science and an authentically human society would emerge together, each informing the other, in the course of a revolt against existing science and society.

Sneers will not solve the problem that had Marx in its grip. He was trying to define human nature by pointing to an endless process, which will have defined human nature when it ends, and he was trying to break out of that vicious circle by catching some anticipatory glimpse of a glorious end. He could not indulge such escapism at length without turning against science and reverting to metaphysics. That is, he could not attempt a thorough definition of authentic human nature without reverting to the 'drunken speculation'[25] that he began by rejecting in favor of science. He found himself trapped, along with other thoughtful people of his time and ours, in the disintegration of human nature by the alienating disciplines that are called, without conscious irony, the human sciences. Aspiring to a comprehensive understanding of authentic human nature, he made himself an economist. He forced himself to seek the human essence in the capitalist system, which he loathed for its negation of the human essence.[26]

To overlook that tragic self-defeat is to miss not only the central drama of Marx's intellectual development but also the continuing self-defeat of the human sciences, which have proceeded so far with the disintegration of their subject matter that even the dream of philosophical reintegration is widely regarded as an absurd relic. In such circumstances it is worse than a misreading of Marx to equate his frustrated aspiration with achievement, to say that he actually achieved a comprehensive philosophy, showing how all the human sciences are to be recast and integrated as a guide to the revolutionary transformation of humanity. It is also a cruel insult to misread Marx that way, for it turns him from a great living thinker into a fossil windbag, and burdens his admirers with the humiliating task of making themselves windbags or fossils. If we engage our minds with Marx's actual thought and its continuing impact, we find ourselves struggling with the central defects of the human sciences — incoherence and dehumanization — not a bogus correction of those defects.

ECONOMICS AND HISTORY

Even within political economy Marx's revolt exacerbated the defects he strove to correct. He pointed out the inadequacy of an economic science limited to the mechanisms of price formation and resource allocation within a capitalist system. Such a science is not only tainted with ideology, since it endows capitalism with an aura of inevitability; it is also scientifically crippled. It avoids the basic problem of change from one type of socio-economic system to another, a problem that has practical urgency as well as theoretical importance.[27] In the unpublished *Grundrisse* Marx tried to classify socio-economic systems in an evolutionary sequence. He could not make up his mind whether the pattern of commercialization and industrialization that he discerned in Western Europe applied to the whole world. In the published outcome of the *Grundrisse*, *The Critique of Political Economy* (1859), he dodged the problem, or rather, packed it unsolved into a very brief statement about stages of development, which included an undefined 'Asiatic mode of production', a system he thought might be indefinitely static. As his doctrine spread to Russia and to non-European countries, it provoked splits between universalists and nativists, as we may call those who have declared the West European pattern to be universal and those who have discerned distinctively non-Western types of socio-economic development — or stagnation. At issue is not only one more unsolved problem, but the nature of problem-solving in the human sciences. Economic science may be incapable of constructing a phylogeny of socio-economic systems that accords with historical evidence. The capricious particularity of human societies may be so great as to require that problem, like so many others, to be dumped in the unscientific discipline called history, the museum or junkyard of mere contingency.[28]

For the future as well as the past Marx raised problems of systemic transformation that may be beyond the capacity of science to resolve. He predicted a transition from a society shaped by commodity production to a socialist society, in which labor would cease to be a commodity and would become a free expression of creative human nature, like love or play. In that ideal society, freely given goods and services would be freely drawn from the public stock.[29] Marx was not a calm eclectic, who might be content to create a theoretically possible economics of socialism alongside the bourgeois economics that assumes the necessity of treating labor as a commodity. Theorizing of that sort leaves socialism a mere possibility, perhaps a utopian dream at odds with historical realities. Marx was intent on being realistic. He tried to prove that the inherent tendency of capitalist systems was to break down, thereby obliging people to make a revolutionary leap from bourgeois necessity to socialist freedom. Those who believe he succeeded stand hopelessly divided from economists who believe he did not, and the non-believers are divided among themselves. Some brush off Marx's concern with systemic breakdown as mere ideology, while others think he raised a genuine scientific problem, the problem of self-generated change within capitalist systems, including the possibility of the system transforming or destroying itself.[30] Economists who aspire to a universal science of choices in any possible system dump this problem too onto historians, politicians, and all the other impure types who must struggle with some particular version of the real world as best they can.

Sharper divisions occur among Marxists who must manage post-revolutionary systems. Marx was too fearful of utopianism to offer any more guidance than the general goal of abundant freedom, and the warning that the transition to that freedom would be subject to bourgeois necessities.[31] For some time after the revolution as before, the bourgeois calculus of price formation and resource allocation must still be used; human labor must still be bought and sold as a commodity rather than freely given and accepted as a spontaneous expression of the human essence. The rival claims of bourgeois calculation and socialist aspiration would be hard enough to reconcile in the calmest of scholarly seminars. In the actual turmoil of post-revolutionary regimes the rivalry usually turns into political warfare, and Marx's critique of bourgeois economics becomes a club to beat realistic calculators. Worse yet, the club is wielded by zealots of disciplined national power rather than abundant personal freedom, devotees of 'barrack socialism', as Marx called equalitarian deprivation under an authoritarian regime.[32] In the real post-revolutionary world the dream of socialism as emancipation from dehumanizing compulsion is driven back to its place of origin, the intellectual ghettos of capitalist countries.

I am suggesting that Marx and his disciples fell prisoner to the science he set out to humanize, when he tried to change economics into an historical sociology pointing toward the ultimate triumph of the human essence. It may be that economics cannot be humanistically transformed, that it can only be limited in its applications by a refusal on non-economic grounds to accept the complete determination of human life by mechanisms of commodity production and exchange. To raise that possibility is to go back to the original clash between the scientific socialist that Marx aspired to be and the utopian socialists that he derided as impotent dreamers. *Tantum economica potuit suadere malorum*, to resort to Lucretius one more time. Within so many vicious circles can economics entrap us.

Even if those problems of economics could be surmounted, it would still be unclear whether the other disciplines that study human beings could be fitted within the framework of an imaginable social science. Consider the discipline of history, to which Marx had frequent recourse in his efforts to explain social processes. On such occasions he did not feel constantly obliged to demonstrate the basic rule of his social science: that the historical process is determined by changing modes of production and by the class conflicts that derive from those modes. He felt free to attribute significance to accidents, personalities, ideologies, particular political and national traditions — even such as shape the modes of production and class conflicts. Occasionally he remembered to rescue the basic rule — or to set it aside — with some loose formula restricting the determining power of the mode of production to 'the long run', 'the last analysis', or 'the final account'. But for the most part, when he wrote historical essays, Marx kept his ultimate rule of explanation in the back of his mind, and explained as other fine historians do, according to proximate rules that resist explicit formulation, that strike the mind with explanatory force only when they are implicit in concrete examples and images. Such a discipline is a strange mixture of science and art, an art akin to the poet's or dramatist's. Its explanatory power derives as much from metaphor, the imaginative fusion of the particular with the general, as it does from the logical back-and-forth between clearly stated generalization and explicit inference, which is characteristic of science. The historian's ability to make us understand human beings also depends heavily on value judgments, which the natural scientist tries to avoid.

A couple of contrasting examples may help to clarify this intermingling of the scientific and the poetic. Sometimes the scientific mode of explanation can be isolated without much trouble, though with a significant moral and aesthetic loss. Toward the end of *Capital*, volume I, Marx argues at length that 'primitive accumulation' requires extra-economic compulsion. He supports that generalization with economic analysis and with historical examples, such as the eviction of British peasants by governmental edict, the abduction of Africans to slavery in the Americas, and British looting of the Spanish looting of American Indians. He sums up with a grotesque metaphor: 'Capitalism comes into the world smeared with filth from head to toe and oozing blood from every pore.'[33] A rigorous social scientist would interpret that metaphor as gratuitous decoration, an addition of moral judgment to an explanation that can and should be judged on its own, by reference to the economic analysis and the historical data, with the moral emotion set aside. In short, the scientific historian evaluates Marx's contribution to the human sciences by trying to sever his intellect from his feelings.

Usually the discipline of history resists such amputation. It would be impossible to separate explanation from judgment, intellect from feeling in Marx's essay, *The Eighteenth Brumaire of Louis Bonaparte*. The theme is set by a splendid metaphor in the opening lines: 'Hegel remarks somewhere that all great, world-historical facts and personages occur, as it were, twice. He forgot to add: the first time as grand tragedy, the second as shabby farce.'[34] I hope it is unnecessary to point out that that is not a literal generalization or 'covering law'.* It is a compound metaphor, and as such it is a master stroke of the satirist's art, introducing a comparison of the little Napoleon of 1851 with the great original of 1799. Each was raised to power by a revolutionary drama, tragic in the original, farcical in the later imitation. The metaphor is inseparable from Marx's explanation of Louis Bonaparte's triumph in the revolutionary events of 1848–51. 'I ... show how the class struggle in France created circumstances and relationships that made it possible for a grotesque mediocrity to play a hero's role.'[35] A bare précis such as that, which Marx offered in the preface to the second edition, drains his explanation of nearly all its persuasiveness, and even so the précis cannot dispense with the metaphorical equation of political conflict and tragicomic drama, in which human meaning is imparted to the action by the contrast between the protagonist's mediocrity and his heroic pretensions.

Implicit in that drama is an invitation to the audience to share the author's lofty view of the human essence, which the pretentious buffoon on stage illuminates by contrast, by his comic distance below it. The audience or readers see the contrast, even if they do not see it from the author's ideological viewpoint; they need only feel that the protagonist is at odds with *some* notion of a genuinely human essence. It is not necessary to accept Marx's explicit standard for judging Louis Bonaparte, which is offered as a supposedly scientific generalization: the age of bourgeois revolution, with its individual heroes, is giving way to the age of proletarian revolution, in which the masses emerge as a collective hero. The period 1848–51 is pictured as a moment in between; a pseudo-hero appeals to alienated masses of fearful peasants, petty bourgeois, and Lumpenproletarians, who will soon be transformed into collective revolutionaries as they are thoroughly proletarianized by the further development of capitalism. More than a century of hindsight tells us that Marx's supposedly scientific generalization was a pipedream, for France at least, but his essay nevertheless retains its power as an historical explanation. Indeed, the recurrent twentieth-century experience of fearful masses huddled in awe of dictatorial pseudo-heroes – some of them invoking Marx's name – heightens our readiness to be instructed by his essay. We may lack Marx's faith that proletarian revolution will emancipate humanity from history as absurd nightmare, but we share with him some battered sense of what a genuinely

---

* As condign punishment for their simplemindedness, believers in the 'covering law' model of historical explanation should be obliged to attempt a translation of such passages into literal statements. They would soon find their philosophy of lofty error repeated as low farce.

human history would be, and are therefore prepared to grimace appreciatively at his tragicomic caricature of it.

I am not suggesting that the modern discipline of history is identical with modern fiction or ancient mythmaking. Nowadays we expect the historian to be a reliable clerk, an accurate recorder of deeds. But we still expect him to infuse poetic meaning into the ephemera of our lives, to reveal a lasting human essence, as the ancient mythmakers did without great concern for facts. This strange modern art, which must verify poetic constructions by thrusting them upon facts, requires constant resort to metaphor. The particular fact must be imaginatively fused with the general rule, for explicit inference will not link them as we wish, whether 'we' signifies the wishful scientific intellect or the wishful poetic sensibility. If science begins with metaphors and ends with algebra, as a perceptive philosopher has remarked,[36] the discipline of history seems destined to remain betwixt and between. Even if such essays as Marx's *Eighteenth Brumaire* could be transformed into the equations of some future social science, the result would be as pointless as an algebraic translation of Flaubert's *Sentimental Education*, a reconstruction of the 1848 revolution as straightforward fiction. Our sensibility does not want what our intellect cannot in any case provide, what it can only dream of as science fantasy.[37]

After Marx as before, the discipline of history remains an anomaly to would-be social scientists. Herbert Spencer, who was far more singleminded than Marx in his dream of social science, neatly expressed the impatience with history that informs such a dream:

> My position, stated briefly, is that until you have got a true theory of humanity, you cannot interpret history; and when you have got a true theory of humanity *you do not want history*. You can draw no inference from the facts and alleged facts of history without your conceptions of human nature entering into that inference: and unless your conceptions of human nature are true your inference will be vicious. But if your conceptions of human nature be true you need none of the inferences drawn from history for your guidance. If you ask how is one to get a true theory of humanity, I reply — study it in the facts you see around you and in the general laws of life.[38]

Spencer offered a facile reconciliation: a science of human beings is possible, yet history will still be useful, as a teaching device, to make the laws of sociology vivid. History will be sociology teaching by example. A century later sociologists are far less confident than Spencer of their ability to frame laws for history to exemplify. On its side, the discipline of history, still a world apart from social science, is troubled now by infirmity of purpose. Some historians yearn for science, others for art, while most take fretful shelter in their clerkly role, as meticulous recorders of deeds.

And where, in the confusion between social science and history, should psychology come in? Nowhere, as far as the pre-revolutionary Marxists were concerned. Before the Soviet period they simply ignored the science of psychology. It is nowhere discussed in any of Marx's voluminous publications. One must go back to the manuscripts of 1844 to find the one place where he jotted down an opinion on the subject, and it is an opinion that makes the subsequent indifference understandable. Marx simply brushed off any science of psychology that would encompass less than the development of the 'generic essence', that is, the evolving human mind revealed in its socio-economic work through the ages:

> We see how the history of industry, and the existence of industry as something apart from us, are the book of humanity's essential human powers thrown open, human psychology presented to our senses. Up to now it has been comprehended not in its connection with the human essence, but only in an external, utilitarian relationship, because, moving within alienation, we could comprehend only man's general existence — religion, or history in its abstract general form of politics, art, literature, etc. — as the reality of humanity's essential powers and as the generic action of humanity. ... A psychology for which this book [the history of productive practice] ... is closed cannot become a real science with a genuine content. ...[39]

Young Marx made similar criticisms of philosophy and the natural sciences. In their past and present form they were theoretical expressions of human alienation, aspects of human experience turned into inhuman objects. In the future, as humanity overcame alienation, philosophy and the separate sciences would be fused into a single human science of man and nature together.

> The natural sciences have developed an enormous activity and have taken over an ever-growing mass of material. Philosophy, however, has remained just as alien to them as they remain to philosophy. ... But the more that natural science has in practice, by means of industry, laid hold of human life and transformed it and prepared for human emancipation, to that same extent its immediate result had to be the completion of dehumanization. Industry is the genuine historical relationship of nature, and therefore of natural science, to man. ... History itself is a genuine part of natural history, of nature developing into man. Natural science will later on incorporate into itself the science of man, just as the science of man will incorporate natural science into itself: there will be one science.[40]

If Marx had published that romantic effusion, and had gone on writing and publishing such dreams of a single humanized science overcoming the present clutter of alienated disciplines, he would have had very little influence either on his century or on ours. He would be remembered only by a few historians, as another of the philosophical critics of science who played a minor counterpoint to the dominant celebration of science during the nineteenth century.[41] As we have seen, Marx turned against such philosophical criticism; he scorned it as disguised surrender to an imperfect world on the pretext of changing it through criticism. He set to work on a joint revolution in social science and in society, and his greatest impact has been in the interaction of the two realms. Parties emerged invoking his teaching, claiming to be both scientific and revolutionary, insisting that philosophy and social science justify themselves in the arena of revolutionary *praxis*.

The mixture of such disparate elements can have many different results — sometimes exalting, sometimes catastrophic, sometimes absurd — but the first result was vapid. Outside of economics and historical sociology, where Marx did indeed begin an intellectual revolution, he and his disciples drifted with the tide of nineteenth-century thought, away from the metaphysical romanticism of his youth toward a sort of positivism in his old age.[42] In the political arena revolutionary *praxis* was constantly frustrated and postponed, while the desire to unify knowledge never got beyond the preliminary upheaval in economics and historical sociology. The result in thought as in political activity was that talkative expectation took the place of action to achieve the long-run goals. Dreams of great transformations in the future sanctified busy accommodation to present realities. The German Social Democratic Party and a Marxist version of synthetic positivism emerged together.

The first clear revelation of this trend came in the late 1870s, when Marx's growing appeal to German socialists was challenged by a rival thinker, Eugen Dühring, a blind zealot who taught at the University of Berlin until he was fired for his radicalism. He offered a complete system, a synthetic picture of the universal process and of human destiny within it — a 'scientific' system, of course, accompanied by denunciation of metaphysics.[43] Engels countered with a long polemic, *Mr. Eugen Dühring's Revolution in Science*, which not only attacked Dühring's system but offered a Marxist substitute, a vision of science and society developing together toward socialism. At least it was long accepted as a Marxist substitute, by Karl Marx to begin with. (As Engels wrote it, he read it to Marx, who contributed a chapter.[44]) In recent years philosophical admirers of the early Marx, scholars who would disembarrass him of scientific claims and responsibilities, have tried to construct a wall between his thought and Engels's popularization of it.[45] In creative philosophy or poetry such fictions are permissible, but not in the discipline of history. The voluminous correspondence of the two friends, which shows that they could and did disagree, does not offer the slightest evidence to suggest Marx's disapproval of *Anti-Dühring*.[46]

On the other hand, it is inaccurate to picture *Anti-Dühring* as synthetic positivism pure and simple, without any traces of the Hegelian philosophy that had been young Engels's point of departure as it had been Marx's.[47] To be sure, middle-aged Engels offered no talk of expanding the science of physiology to include sense as subjective feeling, as comprehension, and as aesthetic appreciation. Nor did he demand that the fledgling science of psychology turn to socio-economic history for an understanding of the human mind. He simply ignored psychology in his survey of the sciences, and portrayed physiology without criticism in the same rosy light as the other natural sciences. They were discovering the truth in their sectors as social science was in its, now that Marx had revolutionized it. Metaphysical speculation was no longer necessary:

> As soon as each separate science is required to get clarity as to its position in the great totality of things and of our knowledge of things, a special science dealing with this totality is superfluous. What still independently survives of all former philosophy is the science of thought and its laws — formal logic and dialectics. Everything else is merged in the positive science of nature and history.[48]

Within that main theme of synthetic positivism the reference to dialectics was a jarring echo of the Hegelian past. When Engels defined dialectics as 'the science of general laws of motion and development of nature [and] human society'[49] as well as of thought, he seemed to be resurrecting what he had just declared superfluous. Knowledge was to be unified not just by the aggregation of existing disciplines but also by a philosophical discipline of the whole, a discipline that would somehow transcend the others.

It would be a distortion of Engels's meaning to read a lot of metaphysical arrogance into his 'dialectical laws of motion' that govern natural and human history. In context they were a Marxist analogue to Spencer's laws of universal process: grand enough to inspire awe, vague enough to avoid refutation. They were a benediction on the work of scholars in their scattered fields, a prayer for future coherence, not a serious demand that all must come back together under the rule of philosophy. But implicit in that positivistic benediction were potential dangers far more serious than the vestigial metaphysics in the talk of dialectical laws. The positivist outlook pointed to some future time when the particular sciences would spontaneously cohere in a unified body of knowledge, which would bring great social benefit together with intellectual gratification. If that future should endlessly fail to arrive, would the faith in it wither, leaving scientists with a deadening sense of pointlessness? Worse yet, what if impatient believers should turn on the disappointing scientists and demand that the future arrive right away?

In the great ages of religious faith even the otherworldly dreams of the traditional creeds tended to provoke depression or rebellion by deferring

hope too long. The positivist faith in unified knowledge was more vulnerable to both of these dangers, for it scorned otherworldly dreams and
explicitly pledged fulfilment in this world. One way or the other *Anti-
Dühring* pointed unwittingly to the self-destructive nature of synthetic
positivism, its Marxist version included. Either the dream of the world
transformed by unified scientific knowledge breeds acknowledgment of
self-defeat, as it has in the case of twentieth-century positivists and some
communities of Marxists. Or the dream erupts in forceful revolt against the
actual, disappointing trends of intellectual and social development, as it has
among other communities of Marxists. Social and political conditions
within particular countries determine which temper will prevail. Human
scientists who are not Marxists have no right to feel smugly superior. They
avoid such dilemmas and embarrassments only to the extent that they
repress the yearning for intellectual coherence and social usefulness that
animated Comte and Spencer – and Mach and Durkheim – as well as
Marx.

Even with such stunted minds they cannot escape ideology, another self-
contradictory element in the human sciences. Marx's major contribution to
the subversion of faith in science was probably his concept of ideology as
false consciousness, the equivalent for social mentalities of rationalization in
individual psychology.[50] These kindred notions of Marx and Freud subverted naive self-assurance, and put self-conscious shame in its place: beliefs
about ourselves are subject to suspicion of self-serving, of being believed
not because they have been proved true but because they serve some
interest of the individual believer (rationalization) or the group of believers
(ideology). Non-Marxists who reject such an approach to their own beliefs
love to use it against Marxists, who are indeed an inviting target. If we ask,
for example, what features of *Anti-Dühring* won it primacy as *the* introduction to Marxism for two or three generations of Social Democrats and
Communists (from the 1880s to the 1930s), the most obvious answer is
that it gave them facile reassurance. It instilled confidence that Marxist
parties were guided by scientific truth toward the socialist transformation
of the world. It avoided disturbance of that confidence by avoiding the
perplexities that Marxism shares with other attempts at a scientific understanding of human beings. For example, Engels did not ask whether
Marxism might be another form of false consciousness.

Nevertheless *Anti-Dühring* is profound scholarship when compared with
the popularizations of Marxism that replaced it, such as Stalin's pamphlet
on dialectical materialism or Mao's 'little red book'. It is tempting to call
that sequence, from Marx and Engels to Stalin and Mao, a descent from
genuine thought to newspeak, to a mass ideology shaped more by the
psychological requirements of manipulating masses than by the logical
requirements of scholarly inquiry. But it is also possible to call that sequence
an ascent from the thought that only moves a scholar's pen to the thought

that moves masses. Either way one looks at the human sciences, with the philosophical interest in interpreting the human world or with the revolutionary interest in changing it — or the conservative interest in resisting change — one seems to be mocking at the effort to discover useful truth. Scientific truth and political utility seem to be mutually exclusive.

Consider the dilemma in general terms. If beliefs about ourselves are subject to the suspicion of self-serving, of being believed not because they have been proved true but because they serve some interest of the believers, the analyst of such beliefs is in a bind. He may seek some privileged vantage point, and there claim the unique power to explain without bias why the beliefs of others are biased. But that claim opens him to the charge of a self-serving double standard, and he is stuck again to the flypaper of ideology, which turns analysis into accusation, the scholar into the prosecutor. If he accepts that transformation, he moves the human sciences from a forum for reasoned discourse into an arena of warring interest groups, where ideas are valued for their effectiveness as instruments of social solidarity or conflict rather than for their demonstrable truth.[51] Either way the analyst of ideology subverts his own claim to impartial truth along with the claims he is analyzing.

Marx took the first course; he sought a privileged vantage point as the spokesman of the industrial proletariat, the class he pictured as having no interest in distorting the truth about society. Hence the passionate self-righteousness that inflames his arguments, and the unrestrained invective against 'hired prizefighters of the ruling class', as rival theorists often appeared to him. In that passion one may see Marx slipping unawares towards the second course, toward the arena where beliefs are weapons rather than proposals for reasoned discourse. If he had consciously chosen that course (and moved to a country with sufficiently flammable conditions), he might have arrived at Stalin's or Mao's elevation above uniformed masses chanting their devotion to his thought.

Scholars who recoil from that prospect may insist that reasoned discourse must obtain in the human sciences as in any field of inquiry. *Ad hominem* arguments must be ruled out of order here as elsewhere. Beliefs must be judged according to their logical and evidential merit, not according to the motives or interests we may impute to the believers. That way we escape the dilemma that the concept of ideology imposes, but we also lose the right to use the concept. We have forbidden ourselves to ask what interests or subconscious motives or latent social functions attach groups of people to various forms of false consciousness. Yet we can hardly forswear that inquiry while aspiring to an understanding of human beings, for the false consciousness of groups is an overwhelmingly obvious fact of social life. After Marx pointed it out, innocence of that fact became impossible, or self-serving pretense.

I confess that I have no solution to this problem. It is especially acute when it is least recognized, for example, among Western students of Communist societies, who tend to assume without question that 'we' hold the privileged ground of reason in analyzing 'their' false consciousness. When scholars recognize that 'our' privileged vantage point may well be another ideology, they may fall into cynical lassitude, or worse yet they may be tempted by the frankly irrational view that beliefs are mere instruments of social solidarity or conflict, to which the question of truth or falsehood is irrelevant. I reject that view. Better a struggle among contenders for the privileged vantage point of reason, even if it should prove unattainable, than descent into a chaos of prizefighters for warring interest groups. In such a situation it is tempting to grasp at William James's homespun advice, when he confronted the irremediable subjectivity of comparative psychology: 'The only thing then is to use as much sagacity as you possess, and to be as candid as you can.'[52]

But that is a milk-and-water antidote for the poisonous conclusions I have reached. The trouble with Marxism, as with other efforts in the human sciences, is not so much their demonstrable errors as it is their justifiable truths. They make sense separately, subvert each other when joined, and one way or another alienate non-scientific modes of understanding human beings, such as common sense, the literary imagination, and the ideological beliefs that bind people in communities. Physiology was one of the first undeniably successful applications of rigorous science to human beings, and it required mechanistic assumptions that excluded the mind from the body, or rather, excluded study of the mind from study of the body. The effort to create a separate science of mental life led back to the exclusion of mind, this time from the science of mental life, and also reinforced the chronic division of psychological science into irreconcilable schools. Poets and other humanists were alienated from any form of human science as a contradiction in terms: if scientific it cannot be human, if human not scientific, for science tries to avoid or even to explain away the conscious life that the humanities try to understand.

Some may think that a problem only for humanists, since scientists have shown little concern for it, while the robust men who do the world's business and run its governments have shown even less — with the significant exception of Communist rulers. There is indeed a standard repertory of incantations to fend off the incoherence of modern culture, whenever disaffected humanists call attention to it. The old-fashioned separation of faith from reason, refurbished in modern lingo as the independence of values and science, is constantly used to smother consideration of the moral and aesthetic implications of the human sciences. To those who murmur at the intellectual incoherence of the human sciences — never mind values and feelings — the stock reassurance is simply, 'Wait'. Division of labor, we are told, compels neurophysiologists, psychologists, sociologists, anthropologists, economists, and historians to study different aspects of human beings — and to split up further into rival schools — but this preliminary butchering of the subject will supposedly regenerate the whole creature later on. Sometimes that faith is expressed with the poignance of religious yearning for the circle that will be completed in the world to come. Wilder Penfield, for example, summed up a life of brilliant studies in the border-land between neurology and psychology with this confession:

> We have no basis on which to begin to understand the relation of mind to the brain. But the light of science will be brighter as the years pass, cast a wider circle, embrace things that lie beyond. I believe that understanding will come in time, with continued advance − not to us but to our successors.[53]

I intend no discredit to a great scientist and sensitive spirit when I note that the record of the human sciences in the past two centuries speaks against his faith. He might have lost the will to persevere in brain studies, if he had seen that incoherence and alienation in human studies are far greater now than they were in the time of Hughlings Jackson and Wundt, not to speak of David Hartley and Diderot. My purpose in calling attention to that bleak trend is not to cut the nerve of striving among human scientists or to start a crusade for some new approach to an understanding of human beings. My purpose is to shame the philistine narrowness and smug self-deceptions that are so widespread among twentieth-century specialists, and to overcome blind contempt for Marxist-Leninist ventures in the human sciences. Their self-defeating efforts to stamp out the fragmentation of culture derive in large part from the genuine crisis of fragmentation, which we share with them. Their reactions have been partly hallucinatory and partly stupid, but the crisis has been real. Traditional ideologies have been subverted by the human sciences, which cannot provide a viable substitute.

Marxists of the late nineteenth and early twentieth century shielded themselves from the intellectual collapse of the synthetic faith in science by declaring it a crisis of bourgeois ideology, not of Marxism or any other form of genuine science. Ignorance helped; they paid little attention to most of the human sciences. Edward Bernstein, and the minority who agreed with him on the need for a revision of Marxist thought, focused on particular socio-economic and political issues − such as the immiseration of the proletariat and the necessity of insurrection − not on the crisis of fundamentals that I have been stressing here.[54] The revisionists also in-itiated some debate on the philosophy appropriate to Marxism, for they were dimly aware that Marxism was an incomplete effort at a science of humanity.[55] Orthodox Marxists, as the anti-revisionist majority were not ashamed to call themselves, denied that Marxism lacked an adequate philo-sophy, and asserted that Marxism was the core around which a complete human science would naturally grow.[56] That confident equation of Marxism with social science pointed unwittingly in one of two very different direc-tions, either toward the dissolution of Marxism as a separate trend or toward a revolt against existing trends.

Which way particular groups of Marxists would turn depended in large part on the social and political conditions of their countries. In Germany, where the long awaited revolution finally arrived as a feeble victory of parliamentary government within an unchanged social order, Marxists tended toward intellectual fusion with other trends of social and philosophical thought. In Russia, where the revolution arrived as an irresistible lower-class upheaval and a complete collapse of the old social and political order, the Bolsheviks proved to be successful mobilizers of lower-class revolutionary energies, in part because of their zealous conviction that they were guided by the one true science of society. Thus they were in the frame of mind to get angry, when they discovered that the bulk of specialists in the human sciences not only opposed them in politics but stood apart from them on most issues in the human sciences. The incoherent clutter of those disciplines and their insolent indifference to Marxism were a greater provocation than the relatively few points where there was clear confrontation between Marxist and non-Marxist ideas. For the Bolsheviks to acquiesce in that situation was to shrink in self-perception as in reality into another one of the many discordant claimants to the non-existent science of human beings.

Thus the self-defeating and subversive force of the human sciences was brought home to the Bolsheviks, as an abomination within the faith that animated their revolution. If it had been a case, as so many commentators have imagined, of a clash between the human sciences and a comprehensive Marxist theory in point-for-point opposition to each other, a standoff might have been arranged rather easily, as it had been in states with traditional ideologies, which did not claim to be scientific. The Tsarist regime, as we will see, achieved such a standoff in the half-century before it collapsed. After the revolution there was a clash of the severest kind, within a single faith, which was already deeply divided against itself, exciting the Bolsheviks to political intervention in science, for the sake of science.

Part II

Genteel Disintegration in Russia

3

Neurophysiology and Obvious Ideologies

Russia has been the premier 'developing' power, the first to accuse itself of being 'underdeveloped', to set itself the task of 'catching up'. Not Russia as a whole; an educated minority of Russians fell into that form of national flagellation, when 'backward' was the accusation, before 'developing' was invented to console the victims of invidious comparison. Whichever words we use, we cannot escape the invidious element, flattering people in some nations, disparaging or insulting the others. So it is misleading to say 'we'. The inescapable comparison indulges Western observers in self-congratulation; from Russians comparison demands self-disparagement or even self-hatred as the first step to 'catching up'.

In a sense the educated minority of Russians have been outsiders within their own country. What the 'toiling masses' have thought of 'development' has been a mystery, except on those occasions when they have rebelled against the exploitation that it has aggravated. The articulate minority expressed divided opinions even in naming a modernizing new class, which emerged in the mid-nineteenth century. That was the time when the Latin word *intelligentia* shifted its Russian meaning from the special quality of educated minds to the special class that has such minds, the minority that brings in modern culture and envy of the advanced West, where the culture is supposedly taken for granted and no special class asks to be named 'intelligentsia'.[1]

Ideological imagination and social reality are all mixed up in matters of this kind. While the intelligentsia was emerging in Russia, in Western Europe 'intellectuals' became the new term for those who cultivate the mind intensively.[2] ('Philosopher' was shrinking into the name for an academic speciality.) In the Russian language individual *intelligenty* belong to the class *intelligentsia*, but Western intellectuals have no class to belong to, no collective term for themselves. At the turn of the century the word 'intelligentsia' was borrowed for the purpose, a metropolitan Latin root with a provincial Russian ending — and a sneer to boot. 'The Russian intelligentsia', quipped H. G. Wells, 'is an irresponsible middle class with ideas.'[3] In the West the term is still reserved for the exotic or the ridiculous. English or French speakers will readily refer to the intelligentsia of African or Asian countries, but they will not say 'I am a member of the intelligentsia' unless they are making fun of themselves. We deride intellectuals when we lump them in a class with a group mentality. The implicit metaphysics of our word-usage reveres the Nietzschean arrow straining in its self-created bow for flight to its own future truth, where other freely flying individualists will miraculously converge. Cultivated Russians in the late nineteenth century developed a different sense of the individual intellect and the collectivity. Many were proud to call themselves *intelligenty*, members of the intelligentsia, and many still are, though the Soviet state has tried very hard to change the meaning of the term and the nature of the class.

Since 1917 the state has been trying to make 'intelligentsia' nothing more than an occupational category, approximating to what we mean when we say 'the professional class'.* In unofficial usage 'intelligentsia' is still ambivalent, indicating both an occupational category and a spiritual fellowship, both special servants of the existing state and a communion of advanced minds contending with the authoritarian regime of a backward society. In short, the Russian intelligentsia was the first born of an inwardly divided type now found throughout the 'developing' world: advanced thinkers in backward milieux. The class came into existence arguing over its anomalous situation. Its ideal was 'critically thinking individuals' struggling for progress in a 'realm of darkness'.[4] Its growing reality was a professional class, making careers by selling special kinds of mental labor. The perennial issue was how to reconcile the ideal and the reality.

Modern science was central to that issue in the 1860s and 1870s. Was service of pure science appropriate for ideal *intelligenty* or only for self-seeking careerists? Would a life in science help to achieve truth and justice − *pravda*, 'rightness', combines both concepts − or would it be a retreat from struggle to the cloister (*zamknutost'*) of a new privileged class, a secular priesthood?[5] Such questions go beyond the issue of Russia's peculiar situation, and even beyond the broader question of advanced thinkers in backward countries. The hardest problems of combining knowledge with social responsibility are aggravated by the progress of modern science in advanced countries too. But let us begin with Russia, in the last half-century of the Tsarist system, and with the professionals of particular disciplines. Neurophysiology will be the first, for it seems nowadays to be

---

* Russian lacks a term as dignified as 'professional' to describe those who sell their special kinds of mental labor. *Spetsialisty* (specialists) is widely used, but it lacks the honorific sense of self-governing devotion to a calling. *Sluzhashchie*, 'those serving', is even less honorific, though it must not be confused with 'servants' (*slugi* or *sluzhanki*) − as in English, 'public servants' must not be confused with plain 'servants'. *Sluzhashchie* is rather like 'white collar', the English term that lumps professionals with all other mental workers.

a 'hard' and 'pure' science, distinct from its 'soft' and 'applied' relatives, psychology and psychiatry. But the distinctions were far from clear back then, and ideologies were entangled in the mixture. Perhaps the history of their entanglement will illuminate the meaning of ideology and science, and of hard and soft science. At the least we will discover the special qualities of genteel boundary mapping in a country undergoing 'development' — toward violent disintegration.

SECHENOV

Soviet authors love to tell the story this way.[6]

From the beginning Russian radicals and Russian scientists have been allies. In the 1860s N. G. Chernyshevsky, editor of *The Contemporary* and leading radical ideologist, found a comrade in I. M. Sechenov, the father of Russian physiology. So it came to pass that Sechenov's trail-blazing essay, 'Reflexes of the Brain', was written for *The Contemporary* and provoked the anger of the Tsar's censors. They altered it and banished it to a medical journal, hoping that the public at large would fail to take note. In vain. Everyone read it, and recognized not only a scientific breakthrough but also a revolutionary manifesto, marking the shift from romantic dreams of an ideal society to scientific struggle for its achievement. Chernyshevsky had been arrested before the essay appeared, but he managed, while in prison, to write *What Is To Be Done?*, 'the bible of the radical intelligentsia for a whole generation'. Its hero was a physiologist, modeled on Sechenov, who showed that humans no less than frogs are neuromuscular mechanisms. Directed by reflexes of the brain, the human mechanism seeks self-gratification, and reasons its way to the most gratifying form of self-gratification: loving service of humanity. At the turn of the century Chernyshevsky's radical ideology grew into Marxism-Leninism, while Sechenov's radical physiology engendered Pavlov's doctrine, the revolutionary psychology that is the natural ally of Marxist-Leninist social science and revolutionary politics.

That tale has been repeated so insistently that it has been commonly accepted, by Western as well as Soviet scholars. Yet it is mostly a mythic construct, expressing a dream of cultural coherence in defiance of fragmented reality. One can as easily construct a counter-myth of science separated from ideology within a Russian context of increasing pluralism. Indeed, most pre-revolutionary Russian scientists did that. They honored Sechenov not as a comrade of Chernyshevsky's but as a mild liberal in politics and an admirer of Herbert Spencer in philosophy and psychology. Since Spencer was perceived as a purely scientific philosopher, and science as a rigorous quest for objectivity, Sechenov and his admirers thought they were excluding ideology from knowledge. In the excited 1860s some people, non-scientists mostly, did talk about the inherent radicalism of physiology, but such talk soon died off. By the 1880s neurophysiology had become a purely academic discipline, as Pavlov earnestly believed. Ditto for the new discipline of psychology, which emerged in Russian universities as in the West, with much the same variety of schools, none of them looking to Sechenov or to Pavlov for inspiration. Marxists had no connection with such academic fields as psychology or physiology, whose adepts showed virtually no interest in Marxism. And the censors ceased all intervention in both disciplines. In short, cultural pluralism was coming to prevail in Tsarist Russia as in the West.[7]

This mythic vision has been kept alive by the émigré intelligentsia and by Western scholars who loathe all the Communist revolutions of our century but most of all the Russian original. They are provoked to anger rather than inquiry by the post-revolutionary campaigns for cultural unity; they sustain the pluralist vision by cursing the country's history, blaming it on the lunatic dreams and the power lust of tyrants who have torn Russia from its course. Before the Revolution many educated Russians nourished the beginning of that anger at their country's history. They directed their dismissive incantations at the Tsarist state, which was perversely obstructing the country's natural development into another England. They were stunned when the Tsarist state collapsed and England failed to emerge. In less than nine months the one-party Soviet state emerged, and the dreamers of Russian pluralism turned their angry disappointment, enormously intensified, against the madmen who sank poor Russia's ship in sight of port. (I borrow Winston Churchill's metaphor.)

The polar opposition of the Stalinist and pluralist myths is essential to an understanding of Russia, but it should not prompt outsiders to construct something in between. Pictures of angels and devils challenge us, not to paint creatures with angelic wings and satanic hooves, but to explain how Russians came to have such insistently opposed visions. In the 1860s there was fairly widespread belief in the natural alliance of radical ideology and physiological science, feared on the right, hailed on the left. That needs to be explained, and so does the fading of such beliefs in the following decades — and their furious revival in the post-revolutionary decades, as part of the mentality that came to be called Stalinist, or Maoist in its subsequent Chinese emergence. Even the mentality called Titoist clings to the vision of culture united for revolutionary progress. We are obviously dealing with an historical problem far broader than one country's aberration from the dream of pluralism. But let us start with that one.

The 1860s was an exciting moment in Russia's cultural history. A new Tsar started major reforms, in response to the humiliating lesson of the Crimean War. English and French forces had come into the Black Sea, easily destroyed the Russian fleet, landed armies in the Crimea, and right there on the Tsar's territory they had given violent instruction in Western values — as they did on Chinese territory in the Opium Wars (and as, for that matter, Russian forces were doing to the Chinese in the Far East; there are degrees of 'development' and of 'underdevelopment'). To catch up with the Western teachers of modern weaponry and civilized values, the Russian government turned not only to emancipation of the serfs and conscription of citizen soldiers, but also toward modern high culture. They put new emphasis on the development of science, retreating a bit from the late Tsar's efforts to shut out the ideologies linked with science, such as positivism and material- ism, which he and other conservatives associated with revolution.

At the same time the leftist intelligentsia turned toward their own ver- sions of toughminded realism, partly with similar feelings of national humiliation, and partly with special revulsion against the humiliation that their 'fathers' had suffered at the hands of the late Tsar. The 'sons' of the 1860s would not be feckless romantic dreamers, like the 'fathers' of the 1840s, easily repressed when the autocrat inclined that way. The 'new men' (and women) of the 1860s were determined to awake from idle dreams and see the world in its actual condition, however repellant. Hence a passion for science as the destroyer of illusory values, and hence the epithet 'nihi- lists', which was applied to the 'new men' (and women) by those who feared that all values might crumble before their radical assault.[8]

It would take us too far afield to attempt even the most cursory review of the diverse arguments about science and reality and values which erupted in the 1860s. Neurophysiology is our present focus, and one might expect that Russia's backwardness would not be an issue here. Yet it was, in part because Russian debates over physiological materialism in the 1860s were a belated importation of controversy that had been going on in Western Europe, especially in Germany, since the 1840s. Some of the Russian polemicists tended to harp on that fact. They saw the obsession with physiology as another case of the Russian intelligentsia making fools of themselves by provincial aping of passing fashions in the metropolitan West. Whatever the truth of the accusation in general, it misses the unique creativity of some Russian participants. Turgenev and Dostoevsky, who were quite sensitive to the foolishly imitative features of the intelligentsia, wrote extraordinary illuminations of the debate over physiological material- ism. *Fathers and Sons* (1862) and *Notes from Underground* (1864) reached through provincial absurdity to grasp the universal absurdity, and the pain, of seeing ourselves as natural objects burdened with conscious minds.

I will go to that level of the debate later on, when I will consider not only those two great novels of the 1860s but also later works on analogous themes by Tolstoy and Chekhov, and the poets Tiutchev and Solov'ev. In that realm of discourse, the literary reactions to scientific naturalism and its bearing on human self-consciousness, there was a continuous development of themes from the 1860s into the twentieth century. The novels of Turgenev and Dostoevsky are still meaningful to readers of our day, and not just in provincial Russia. But neurophysiology itself, which was a lively topic of general discussion in Russia of the 1860s, soon shrank into the exclusive concern of specialists. The popular tracts and polemics became dead artifacts of a bygone era.

To understand the general, but transient, interest in neurophysiology we must note the newly triumphant faith in scientific medicine. The mid-nineteenth-century public had very little evidence to support the faith, but few commentators challenged it. That is a persistent pattern. Widespread faith in the practical utility of a science wins social support before its works appear — if they ever do. Psychology and psychiatry, the 'soft' relatives of neurophysiology, have continually disappointed hopes of great practical utility, which has been one reason why they have continually been topics of debate among the general educated public. Neurology, the medical application of neurophysiology, has had a record of practical utility not only promised but delivered. Study of reflexes was already helping the diagnosis of neural diseases in the nineteenth century. But that news was hardly as exciting as the development of anaesthesia. Though it was largely empirical — clinical recipes for ether and chloroform, without scientific explanation — anaesthesia was perceived as a major scientific triumph. The public was therefore encouraged to surrender its neural mechanisms to professional specialists, asking only to see occasional popularizations, not to share the specialists' disagreements, however profound. Blind faith spared the mind from hard thought. In this respect the Russian intelligentsia were, and are, little different from Western intellectuals. However deep their ideological divisions over the mind and its works, virtually all of them have been willing to surrender the body, nerves included, to scientific specialists. Such 'hard' scientists demonstrate practical mastery of things, and therefore are elevated — or demoted — to the supposedly non-ideological level of technicians.

Russia in the 1860s was a momentary exception. Neurophysiology was a topic of general discussion because, in that place at that time, many perceived it as the royal road to a scientific understanding of the mind, and beyond that to a new morality, and so to a reconstruction of society. Even from a less grandiose, largely negative viewpoint neurophysiology seemed inherently radical, for it implied the reduction of the soul to functions of the nervous system, and thus subverted the ideology that sustained established church, autocratic state, and exploiting classes. Or so it seemed to excited readers of Büchner, Vogt, and Moleschott, who were widely translated and summarized, to the dismay of many conservatives, including government officials.[9]

Indeed, not all radicals were entirely pleased by physiological materialism, or agreed on its 'nihilistic' implications for morality. Even among the professed admirers, from the beginning of the discussion in the late 1850s there was a tendency to cling to the most admirable values of Christianity, to argue that they would not be lost but would receive a more secure foundation in a scientific understanding of the mind. Recall that physiological materialism pointed to selfless love of humanity in Chernyshevsky's *What Is To Be Done?* One can discern in such electicism a melding (some may say a mishmash) of Büchner's physiological materialism with Feuerbach's anthropological religion, and with J. S. Mill's magical extraction of altruism from the utilitarian calculus of pleasures and pains.

One can also discern, from the beginning of the discussion, leftist thinkers who leaned away from physiological materialism altogether, as inherently inappropriate for radical activists in search of a realistic understanding of human beings and their problems. P. L. Lavrov was especially influential in challenging the notion that scientific understanding of our neuromuscular machinery is equivalent to the understanding of ourselves. His *Historical Letters*, published in 1868–70, was a landmark event, a sign that radical obsession with physiology was ebbing away. He argued that the nervous system is but an instrument for a variety of cultures, that study of the historical evolution of culture should be central to those who want to understand the human world and to change it. That kind of argument moved radical thought from physiological toward historical materialism, away from worship of a life in science toward an impatient demand for social understanding fused with social action.[10]

M. A. Bakunin, a quintessential man of the 1840s, the notorious symbol of the impotent romanticism that the worshipers of science wished to reject, was hardly an unprejudiced observer of the process. But there was more than a sense of personal vindication in his summation on science worship and its end product: 'A new school of lonely, melancholy self-development in science and in life, independent of the people and set off from all political and social-revolutionary action.'[11] We may translate that into neutral language. Bakunin was observing a major rift between the increasingly sequestered world of academic scientists and the increasingly political world of the leftist intelligentsia. We can see the rift from the scientists' side as well as the leftists'. In Russia as in Western Europe, leading physiologists dissociated themselves from the physiological materialism that seemed in mid-century to be an ideological assault on the established order. In Russia, unlike Western Europe, they were also dissociating themselves from intensely serious revolutionary assault, which would go on mounting with or without physiological materialism.

The neatest expression of the rift was in two coincident funerals forty years after the excited 1860s. In November 1905, at the peak of Russia's first revolutionary convulsion, hundreds of thousands turned out for the funeral of a revolutionary beaten to death by reactionaries. Sechenov's funeral, a few days later, brought out only a few old friends.[12] Two little obituaries in liberal magazines recalled his radical reputation of long ago,

and emphasized the moderate views that he actually held.[13] At scientists'
commemorations fellow physiologists noted his academic seclusion as a
condition of achievement in science. N. E. Vvedenskii, Sechenov's most
distinguished student, found regal grandeur in his teacher's avoidance of
political involvement: 'Pursuing the true calling of the scientist, he carefully
separated himself from so-called social activity. ...' He was keenly interested in social problems, but the lonely search for truth imposed on the
scientist Pushkin's rule for kings: 'Thou art Tsar, live alone!'[14]

We have no cause to read political commitment in Sechenov's willingness to write an essay for *The Contemporary*.[15] He did not persist in
association with radicals or their journals. He went on writing popular
essays, mainly for *Vestnik Evropy* (*The Herald of Europe*), a major liberal
magazine.[16] Even in the 1860s his private correspondence shows no sympathy with the Russian radicals. It may show the opposite; Soviet editors
have excised part of a letter to his future wife where Sechenov begins to
comment on the 'nihilists'.[17] But his published letters do show a strong
urge to transcend narrow specialization. Through neurophysiology he
hoped to create a 'medical psychology', the foundation of a genuinely
scientific psychiatry. We shall see further on how Sechenov finally retreated,
baffled and discouraged, even from that fairly limited effort to unify
scientific disciplines in the service of humanity. The point here is that he
had the urge, and in the first essay, 'Reflexes of the Brain', he expressed it
with a brash confidence, which began to fade in later essays, until he quit
altogether.

That early brashness helps to explain his transient reputation as a radical.
In the 1863 essay he ignored qualifications that he would stress later on, so
that he seemed to be reducing psychology to physiology, and thus to be
endorsing physiological materialism. At one point he even seemed to imply
sympathy for political radicalism, if only in Italy:

> All the infinite variety of external manifestations of the brain's activity
> comes down finally to merely one phenomenon: muscular motion.
> Whether a child laughs at the sight of a toy, or Garibaldi smiles when
> he is persecuted for excessive love of his native land, whether a young
> woman trembles at the first thought of love, whether Newton creates
> universal laws and writes them on paper – everywhere the final fact is
> muscular motion. ... Thus, *all external manifestations of the brain's
> activity can really be reduced to muscular action.*[18]

But even in that first essay Sechenov tried to reassure non-radicals. Human
beings, he insisted, are neuromuscular mechanisms shaped by external influences, but that basic fact of life is compatible with traditional values. He
concluded the essay with affirmation of human dignity and Christian love:
'We value good and hate evil as we value a good machine and hate a poor
one. My doctrine has also this advantage: it is the basis for the highest of

human virtues — all-forgiving love, that is, complete forbearance toward one's neighbour'.[19]

The censors cut that grand finale. Still clinging to a vision of a unified culture which they knew to be outmoded, they thought he was mocking them. Most of his 1863 essay seemed to them a rehash of Büchner's *Force and Matter*, 'the catechism of the scientific faith professed by a majority of our young generation'.[20] And that mechanistic view of human nature seemed to the censors patently incompatible with Sechenov's closing affirmation of human dignity and traditional Christian love. Hence he could not be sincere; his declaration of faith was intended to strike the public as 'a supposedly forced, ridiculous concession to the requirements of the censorship'.[21] Later on we will see the censors perform analogous surgery on a profession of faith by Dostoevsky's underground man. They had just suffered a severe reduction of their powers; they knew that the educated public was looking forward to their complete disappearance; they were defensively hypersensitive.[22]

They were also rather dull concerning substantive issues. Sechenov had called his essay 'An Effort to Introduce Physiological Foundations in Psychic Processes', which implied some correlation of neural events with psychic processes, and might therefore be compatible with dualism. The censors, hoping to make the article seem narrowly scientific, without philosophical significance, suppressed the original title, which was replaced by the simplistic phrase, 'Reflexes of the Brain'.[23] Thus they unwittingly encouraged readers to put Sechenov on the side of those who simply identify the neural and the psychic. In later essays he complained about that, and took pains to make it clear that he did *not* deny the reality of psychic processes.[24] But during the 1860s he had the reputation of a radical materialist, thanks in part to the censors' dimwitted editing.

Their major contribution, however, was not in small changes of the 1863 essay, but in their effort to suppress it altogether when it reappeared as a pamphlet in 1866. Under the new law of the press their 'arrest' of the pamphlet was contested in open court, and Sechenov's lawyer — a Russified Pole gaining a reputation as a champion of civil liberties — won.[25] The 'arrest' of the pamphlet was revoked, whereupon the Minister of Internal Affairs wanted to know if Sechenov could be arrested, for subversion of faith and morals. The Minister of Justice explained that the new law required proof of intent, and he could not manage that, though he shared the other Minister's conviction that the pamphlet was 'harmful'.[26] So Sechenov was not arrested or tried, but news of these last-ditch efforts to keep science from undermining faith contributed to his reputation as a radical.

But most of all it was Chernyshevsky's ideological novel that gave Sechenov a radical reputation, and continued to maintain it, in some people's minds, for years after the censors and the Minister of Internal

Affairs lost interest in him. The reading public was convinced that the hero of *What Is To Be Done?* was modeled on Sechenov, and that the heroine was modeled on the young woman who married Sechenov's best friend and then abandoned him to live unmarried with Sechenov. The heroine in the novel did that, as a demonstration of the new freedom of radical men and women, and Maria Obrucheva, one of Russia's first women physicians, did it in real life. (I use her maiden name to call attention to her radical brother, who had been sent to Siberia for writing a revolutionary manifesto.)[27] To many minds here was dramatic proof that physiological materialism does indeed subvert morality. *Traditional* morality, said the radicals, and it deserves to be subverted. Morality as such, conservatives insisted, and it must be upheld against dirty books like *What Is To Be Done?* Either way, the coincident sexual scandal in Chernyshevsky's book and in Sechenov's life reinforced the physiologist's reputation as a radical, probably more than lofty issues in science and philosophy.

At the end of the 1870s, when public interest in physiology was largely spent, a reactionary colleague of Sechenov's tried to keep the controversy alive by publishing two abusive pamphlets that focused on sexuality and morals. He began by declaring that all the achievements of civilization rest on the repression of sexuality, and went on to find release in indignation at scientists like Sechenov:

> In the name of your latest scientific conclusions and the reflexes of the brain you have disfigured not only the moral physiognomy but even the outward appearance of the Russian woman. You ... have corrupted her mind and debauched her heart. In her mind was playfulness; you turned that into arousal. In her heart was enthusiasm; you turned it into lust. ... Admire her now: a man's cloak, a man's hat, filthy petticoats, torn dress, bronze or greenish color on her face, chin thrust forward, in her turbid eyes everything: weariness, anguish, malice ... [I omit a long outburst on bobbed hair.] In external appearance some kind of hermaphrodite; internally a true daughter of Cain.[28]

Darwin he found to be equally guilty of subverting morals, by his theory of sexual selection. 'One might think him not an English gentleman, but some old procurer.'

Sechenov and his Russian friends were the sole target of the second pamphlet, *What They Did in 'What Is To Be Done?'* What they did was to have a lewd *menage à trois*, until the complaisant first husband made it four, by bringing in another woman, who would be his second wife. The women would pose in the nude, and the men would kiss them all over, especially on 'the legs'. Sechenov, though unnamed, was obviously the lustful physiologist in the exposé, constantly seeking 'stimulation of the nerves'. There was even an insinuation of homosexual 'stimulation'.[29] Of course this pornographic reactionary was extreme, but there is evidence that Sechenov's love life was the topic of much gossip in the period when Chernyshevsky's novel was widely read. Prurience aside, the reading public gossiped about looks. How could Maria have left her very handsome husband for such an ugly man as Sechenov? His unusually broad face and very dark pockmarked skin reminded hostile gossips of a frog or toad. Friends admitted that he was 'rather ugly', but stressed his 'splendid eyes, intelligent, profound, piercing and kind at the same time. . . .'[30]

The similarity between Chernyshevsky's love story and Sechenov's love life is a puzzle. Chernyshevsky could not have known about Sechenov's liaison with Maria, because it began after he was put in solitary confinement, indeed, after he had written *What Is To Be Done?* Nor could he have sensed that Sechenov was about to fall in love with Maria, for he had only a nodding acquaintance with Sechenov, if any. Chernyshevsky may have had some sense of growing coolness between Maria and her first husband, Dr P. I. Bokov, for Bokov was a close friend. He helped to care for Chernyshevsky's son when Mrs Chernyshevsky, a cruelly selfish beauty, abandoned her child as well as her persecuted husband.[31] Since Chernyshevsky knew his own difficulties with his own wife when he took up his pen in solitary confinement, it seems most likely that the love story in the novel was a projection from his own experience, an embodiment of his own dream. He endowed the fictive version of the abandoned husband with the liberated calm that he aspired to. In his vision of women's liberation, the traditional double standard would have to be inverted for a time: a loving man must allow his woman a freedom to roam which he must deny to himself. Only thus would women learn the sense of freedom in love affairs which the traditional double standard had bred into men.[32]

There is not the slightest evidence that Sechenov held to that backbending view of love and liberation. He and Maria were unconventional in one sense; they lived together for many years before they went through the ceremony of marriage. But — or should we say therefore? — they were a model of faithful devotion in a protracted romantic union. The letters that Sechenov wrote during occasional separations show the tender affection that helped to keep them together, without giving any indication of a theory of modern love that they were trying to apply. We have only a slight hint of a theory in a memoir of Sechenov by a close friend. In his mid-forties Sechenov confessed a strong attraction to a young woman whom he was tutoring. He ascribed the attraction to 'a flow of blood toward the medulla', and repressed the emotion — a touching instance of physiological fantasy serving the discipline of monogamous romanticism.[33]

All this may seem mere gossip to readers who are interested only in lofty philosophical issues. I would remind them that women's liberation and the so-called sexual revolution of the twentieth century actually began in the nineteenth, and lofty philosophical issues were crucial to the pioneers.

Georges Sand, in her way, and John Stuart and Harriet Mill, in their different way, offered the public intensely reasoned attacks on conventional sexual attitudes, and high-minded defenses of their deliberate displays of extramarital love, their insistence that free self-realization is the essence of all human relations. Chernyshevsky's novel, which combined physiological materialism with a curiously self-denying theory of romantic love, reminds one again that nineteenth-century romanticism was constantly mixed with scientism — or positivism, to use the nineteenth-century term for the belief that there is no truth except the truth disclosed in science.

As the heart became a neuromuscular pump, and spirit was drained from an electrically operated nervous system, defiantly fictive affirmation of the immaterial 'heart' and 'spirit' intensified. Keeping in mind that continual mixture of bleak scientism and ardent romanticism, one need not imagine life imitating art in this particular case. That is, Sechenov and Maria did not need to learn a liberated view of romantic love from Chernyshevsky's novel, though that was chronologically possible. Nor vice versa; one need not imagine art imitating a particular life. Chernyshevský did not need to dream his love story on the model of Sechenov's experience, which was chronologically impossible. It is more sensible to regard them both as deriving their individual notions of modern love and freedom from an increasingly powerful tide of nineteenth-century thought and feeling, which did indeed separate love from the traditional sanctions of clerics, and did indeed seek a new and more honest understanding of love in some theorizing that would be firmly secular, if not scientific. A characteristic result was insistence on the liberation of love and intensification of romantic devotion, not a return to the aristocratic libertinism of the seventeenth and eighteenth centuries, nor a plunge toward the vulgar libertinism of our own age.

Count I. D. Delianov, who would become a notoriously reactionary Minister of Education in the aftermath of the Tsar's assassination, was upset by Sechenov's supposed combination of radical materialism and personal libertinism. He wrote to the supervisor of Odessa University, when Sechenov was seeking a position there, warning that the physiologist 'is an out-and-out materialist, ... not only in science but in life itself'. Might he not lead his students to corruption?[34] That was written in 1870, while Sechenov's supposed nihilism was widely accepted. Five years later the equally notorious reactionary, Count D. A. Tolstoy, who dominated higher learning for almost twenty-five years, approved Sechenov's return from the provincial university to a major appointment at the University of St Petersburg.[35] In short, despite Sechenov's love life, even reactionaries were coming to realize that he was not the dangerous radical he had seemed to be in the 1860s. As for censorship, after 1866 Sechenov never had any more difficulty, though he continued to publish speculative essays on a physiological approach to psychology, and supported such liberal causes as the shortening of the working day and the opening of higher education to women and to Jews.[36]

CLASS AND NATIONALITY

May we therefore conclude that higher learning in Tsarist Russia had arrived, after the turbulent 1860s, in the haven of toleration that supposedly sheltered academic intellectuals in the advanced countries of the West? Or, more modestly, may we conclude that mechanistic neurophysiology had been cut off from a transient association with radicalism, without lasting effect either on the traditional ideology by which the regime justified itself, or on the ideologies of the intelligentsia? And is the corollary also established, that the academic purification of neurophysiology had been completed, leaving no residue of ideological tension within the secluded discipline?

It would be rash to draw such conclusions, even though there is much in Sechenov's experience that can be generalized. After the 1860s the liberalized law of the press suffered reactionary amendments, but Tsarist censors made no more efforts to control anyone's publications in neurophysiology, or even in the much more sensitive field of psychology. (The only exceptions I am aware of were a brief ban on one of Ribot's many books and a lasting ban on Krafft-Ebing.)[37] By the turn of the century defenders of traditional ideology showed as little concern for physiology and psychology as did the varied critics of traditional ideology.[38] Their contention had moved to other fields of learning — such as evolution or theology — or directly to politics. And Russian neurophysiologists, like their Western colleagues, had learned to be rigorously 'pure' in their disagreements as specialists, allowing only hints of larger ideological disagreements in their scientific publications. But it would be misleading to leave the matter with these generalizations. If we examine the genteel world of higher learning more attentively, we discover considerable ideological turbulence, with a potential either for peaceful containment or for violent connection with the world outside academia, the world of Russia drifting toward total war and revolutionary upheaval.

Let us begin by noting certain kinds of turbulence that are usually ignored by high-minded historians of science, even when they try to go beyond purely internal analysis and to situate science in its social context. Let us consider class and ethnicity. I am using 'class' to include both the traditional *sosloviia* or *Stände* or *états* to which people were legally ascribed at birth (in modern English we have lost a generic word for such legally ascribed status groups), and class in the modern sense of extra-legal ranking, whether by relations of production or by supposed achievement, such as worker and boss, soldier and officer, clerk and professional. Academics like to say that the shift from traditional to modern society entails a shift from ascribed status, such as legally assigned *sosloviia*, to achieved status, such as extra-legal ranking of classes. That is true, but it tends to ignore forms of ascribed status that have been carried forward most powerfully from traditional into modern society. First of all there is sex, in its original meaning: the division of humanity into male and female with different status attached to each. Ascribed status also attaches to ethnicity, including not only such clear-cut national categories as Russian and Pole but also such ambiguous racial categories as Oriental and Caucasian, and such ambiguous ethnic types as Russified Pole or Jew. I will have little to tell in what follows concerning women in higher learning, for they were almost totally shut out except as students, and I am here concerned with faculties. I will have more to say about ethnicity and class, for academic faculties were not hermetically sealed in those directions as they were against women. Of course, they were not wide open to any males with records of scientific achievement. Clear rules of access and exclusion cannot be found. One finds patterns operating in largely inarticulate, partly subconscious ways.

Consider in this light some leading professors at Russia's major institution of medical training and research, the Military Medical Academy in St Petersburg, during the last half century of the Tsarist system. Sechenov is usually called the father of Russian physiology because he was the first thoroughly modern professor of physiology at that institution. He was born into the Russian landed gentry (*dvorianstvo*) in its time of rapid decline; in 1856 he sold his portion of the family estate to finance a few years of postgraduate training in Germany and France. He started teaching at the Medical Academy in 1860 and resigned in 1870, disgusted by his colleagues' refusal to appoint Mechnikov, a brilliant zoologist who was also from the Russian gentry, on his father's side, but had a taint of Jewishness on his mother's side.

Tsion, who took the professorship that Sechenov resigned, was 'from the lower middle class (*iz meshchan*),★ of the Jewish confession', to quote an official history of physiology at the Medical Academy.[39] The faculty voted against him, the administration nevertheless appointed him, and student demonstrations forced him to resign, all within the space of four years, 1871−5.

I. R. Tarkhanov (originally Tarkhnishvili), a student of Sechenov's and of Tsion's, who became the next professor of physiology, was a Russified Georgian prince with outspoken liberal views. He held the post longer than either of his predecessors, but was obliged to resign at the age of 48 by pressure from a reactionary administration.

★ That was the official designation of the traditional urban lower middle or lower class: *meshchanstvo* for the class, *meshchane* for its individual members. In the nineteenth century the term was already acquiring the extended, metaphorical meaning that it has to this day: people of limited, vulgar mentality. In this meaning it is often translated as 'Philistine'.

I. P. Pavlov, who succeeded Tarkhanov as professor of physiology at the Military Medical Academy, was the son of a Russian priest. He had been sent to a seminary in the traditional expectation that he too would be a priest, but he was won to the religion of science in the 1860s, and combined extreme mechanism in physiology with a determination to avoid political ideology of any sort. He held his professorship without interruption, even by the great revolutionary upheaval, until his death in 1936.

V. M. Bekhterev, who taught neurology at the Medical Academy, and challenged Pavlov's priority in the discovery of the conditioned reflex, came from another part of the social margin where the intelligentsia shaded into traditional orders of the lower sort. In Bekhterev's case it was not the priesthood but the *raznochintsy*, perhaps even the *meshchanstvo*, with a possible admixture of *inorodtsy*, though not of Jewishness.* In his autobiography he was careful to note that the widowed mother who raised him had been an educated woman, driven by need to run a boarding house.[40] Politically, he was an active liberal with radical inclinations, one of the few outstanding scientists who endorsed the Soviet regime soon after its establishment, and held his major post until his death in 1927.

Individualistic distaste for such labeling and stereotyping must not prevent us from pondering the effects of rapid change in the system of labels and stereotypes. Hereditary Russian gentry were giving way, in positions of distinction, to self-made men rising from some of the lower orders and some of the non-Russian ethnic groups — men such as Tsion, Tarkhanov, Pavlov, and Bekhterev. The reforms of the 1860s accelerated that shift, and thereby helped to provoke a counter-offensive by reactionaries, who prevailed over bureaucratic reformers within the government until the Revolution of 1905. Count Delianov tried to re-establish the traditional reliance on sons of the Russian gentry — repeat and stress: *sons* and *Russian* and *gentry* — as the most reliable source of leadership, in higher learning as in government. He issued the notorious circular of 1887, which ordered a halt to

> the entrance into *gimnazii* [academic secondary schools] of children of coachmen, servants, cooks, petty shopkeepers, and people of that sort, whose children, with the exception perhaps of those gifted with unusual abilities, should by no means rise out of the milieu in which they belong.[41]

And of course he restricted women and 'aliens' (*inorodtsy*), as 'primitive' subjects of the Tsar were officially labeled, and placed special restrictions on Jews, since more and more of them were shedding their traditional

---

* *Raznochintsy* were people 'of diverse ranks', who could not be assigned to the traditional *sosloviia*. *Inorodtsy* or 'aliens', signified non-Russians of oriental and primitive types. For *meshchanstvo*, see the note on p. 64.

clothes and separate language and striving to rise in Russian academic institutions.

Delianov was largely unsuccessful in his effort to check the replacement of gentry by Russian men rising from the *raznochintsy* and the *meshchanstvo*. There simply were not enough gentry, while men from those lower orders were increasingly pressing forward, and increasingly autonomous faculties were quite willing to receive them, recognizing their own kind of people: Russian men. On the other hand, Russian men of worker and peasant origin, and men perceived as not genuinely Russian, and women of all classes and ethnic origins, were largely blocked. Either they did not try to enter the world of higher learning, or the academics' consciousness of kind tended to exclude people of those categories, with or without directives from such Ministers as Delianov or Tolstoy — or such as A. N. Shvarts and L. A. Kasso, who vigorously revived restrictive efforts after the Revolution of 1905 had been suppressed.

Of course we should not expect to find some neatly predictable correlation between social status and frame of mind in each individual. While Count Delianov and Count Dmitrii Tolstoy were struggling to put back together the disintegrating old order, Count Leo Tolstoy was becoming a Christian anarchist. But we would be allowing the ideology of individualism to blind us, if we failed to note that far more of the gentry agreed with Dmitrii than with Leo Tolstoy, and that the leftist ranks of the intelligentsia were increasingly swelled by disaffected members of classes and ethnic groups below the Russian gentry. In short, we cannot avoid relating mentality to social status. But we can resist superficial stereotypes, if we cling to the old-fashioned intuition by which, in everyday life and in imaginative literature, we read the influence of social status in individual minds, groping even for those obscure depths where repressed anxieties and taboo dreams shape the quirky individuals who do not fit the average.

In Sechenov's mind and personality we find a model of graceful transition from gentry to intelligentsia. His family had only a small estate with few serfs, and therefore took it for granted, as most of the gentry did, that he would have to earn a living in some appropriately honorific occupation.[42] He was sent to a school of military engineering, where one of his classmates was F. M. Dostoevsky, son of an impecunious army doctor who had achieved gentry status as a function of his military rank. The future writer was therefore morbidly conscious of differences in social status, while Sechenov had the serene superiority to such matters that was the professed ideal of the intelligentsia. He had the authentic gentry status that he chose to scorn. That may have been an important cause of the sharp difference in their ideological development. Dostoevsky went to extremes — first left, then right — while Sechenov stayed with an even-tempered liberalism in the center.

Both of them strongly disliked the military career that had been chosen for them. Both dreamed of some other way to earn their living honorably. The traditional understanding of honor gained in government service, by climbing the table of ranks, was contemptuously brushed aside, in favor of the modern ideal of self-realization in the service of humanity, with its resultant plaudits, perhaps even glory. A twentieth-century reader may feel embarrassed by such highflown talk; nineteenth-century thinkers indulged in it freely. Sechenov's autobiography contains a sentimental reminiscence of the time in early manhood when he was infatuated with a beautiful young widow, a Russified Pole, who gently channeled his exalted yearnings to the cause of women's liberation and to medical service to humanity.[43] Since he shared the widespread disdain for the crude state of actual medicine, he fastened on the dream of its scientific future, and came thus to a life of research and teaching in physiology. When he finished his basic medical training at Moscow University in 1856, his widowed mother died, and his brothers offered him 6,000 rubles for his share of the family estate. He took the money, and used it for post-graduate training in the major centers of Germany and France.

Decades later Sechenov acknowledged his debt to the peasants he had exploited. Of course he did not use that harsh word. But an historian cannot ignore the harsh fact, packed as it was with violent consequences. Sechenov's brilliant career in science was financed by serfs at a time when the serf system was breaking down, with revolutionary upheaval as the long-term consequence. Nor should one ignore the responsive gesture of a repentant nobleman. In his will Sechenov set aside 6,000 rubles (out of modest savings that totaled 10,000) to be used for charity in the village he credited with financing his studies abroad.[44]

A leftist may sneer at the inadequacy of such a belated gesture, while a rightist may sneer at any sense of compensation owed to social inferiors. Sechenov was inclined to neither extreme. He was a quiet liberal, who did what he could for the peasants. He could hardly help them rise in science, for none of them sought that way out of exploitation and oppression. He left them charity in his will, and while he was alive he contributed an essay, during the famine of 1892, to a volume 'in aid of the starving'.[45] He also urged his students to work hard to earn the livelihood that the Russian *muzhik* was giving them.[46] Expressions of such sentiments − dilute populism, one might call them − were fairly common in Russian academic life during the last decades of the Tsarist regime.[47] They were gentle reminders that the sense of righteousness in the old order was draining away along with the gentry's land and status, while peasant expectations of full justice still to be done were growing. And they would be far from gentle when they came to find expression.

Perhaps Sechenov's sympathies for the downtrodden were stirred not only by the new sense of *noblesse oblige* that comes with the loss of land but also by the discovery that German scientists considered *him* a social inferior, because he was Russian. His autobiography recalls a lecture by Du Bois-Reymond on race, which credited 'longheaded' peoples with creative talents, while conceding to 'broadheaded' types powers of imitation at best. And that concession was a kindness to the Russians in the audience, for 'we were repeatedly made to feel that the Germans looked upon us as barbarians.'[48] Sechenov was calm in recalling such experiences: 'Could it have been otherwise? Neither in science nor in industry had Russians yet shown independence, while our broadheaded writers, Turgenev, Dostoevsky, and Tolstoy, were still unknown in Germany.'[49] His autobiography is wryly restrained in contrasting Du Bois-Reymond's utter refusal to speak to him, while he was a mere student, with the eminent German's amiability several years later, when Sechenov had himself become eminent. When he recalls the total silence he endured from Wilhelm Wundt during the year that both spent in the laboratory of Helmholtz, Wundt as an assistant to his great countryman, Sechenov as a Russian interloper, he adds, to be quite fair, that Wundt tended to be a recluse in general.[50]

In short, experience of Western disdain for Russians did not push Sechenov to extreme Russian nationalism, as it did Dostoevsky and Tsion, nor to the exaggeration of German strengths and of Russian weaknesses that we shall find at the bottom of Pavlov's nationalism. Privately, as Sechenov confessed in letters to friends, he was depressed by the contrast between the advanced countries where he had studied and his backward native land. Russia gave him the blues (*khandra*), and even prompted the thought of emigrating.[51] In print he struck a balance between recognition that 'we are novices in the work of civilization' and confidence that Russia's writers and scientists were bringing their 'race' (*rasa*) into 'the family of civilized nations (*kul'turnykh narodov*)'.[52]

Sechenov's calm dignity as a Russian may have rested on the double reassurance conferred by gentle birth and early achievement. (He was appointed to the faculty at the Medical Academy in 1860, when he was 33, and won a European reputation a few years later, when Claude Bernard sponsored publication of his pathbreaking article on the inhibition of spinal reflexes.) Even toward the end of a long life, increasingly burdened by a sense of early promise unfulfilled, Sechenov maintained a cheerful cosmopolitanism by dwelling on the warm friendship he had found as a young man in the laboratory of Carl Ludwig, who respected talent not only in the Russian gentleman, Sechenov, but also in the Russian Jew, Tsion, and the son of the Russian priest, Pavlov. (I am inserting the blatant stereotyping; Sechenov was always courteously vague.) All of them came to study with Ludwig at one time or another, published joint articles with him, and kept him fondly in their memories. To be sure, Sechenov noted that Ludwig was unusual among Germans in his cosmopolitan hospitality.[53]

Sechenov's broadmindedness was not unique, but he did repeatedly find himself in a minority, painfully frustrated by narrow-minded colleagues.

He tried to be aloof from the intrigue and backbiting that are generated by petty consciousness of kind, but he finally was caught, and the resulting conflict caused him to resign from the Military Medical Academy ten years after he was hired to modernize its teaching and research in physiology. His colleagues were divided on nationality or ethnicity. The looser term is more accurate, for labeling rested more on a sense of 'origin' than on clear-cut characteristics like language. A majority of the faculty was pushing for Russification, which is often pictured as an effort to replace Germans by Russians, since the Germans were mediocre — if they weren't, wouldn't they have professorships in Germany? — and arrogant, hardly bothering to learn the Russian language. No doubt the purge of such Germans was part of the process,[54] but it was far from the whole or even the major part of Russification. Sechenov was shocked into resigning when a majority of his colleagues rejected the appointment of Il'ia Il'ich Mechnikov, a scion of the Russian gentry who was winning an international reputation at an astonishingly young age.

Let us try to be precise, though we are entering a field of sensibilities that are maddeningly vague yet powerful. Mechnikov considered himself a member of the landed Russian gentry, for his father had been that. But his mother was, as the phrase went (and still goes), 'of Jewish origin'. Her father had been one of Russia's first assimilated and articulate Jews; he published the first Russian plea for fairness to Jews, and converted to Christianity. His son became an officer in the Imperial Guards and introduced his sister to a fellow officer of that elite corps, which resulted in a marriage and the little Mechnikov who grew up to be a brilliant scientist.[55] One might think such a man unquestionably Russian. Yet a majority of the professors at the Medical Academy in 1869 seem to have perceived him as a 'stranger' or 'outsider' (*chuzhoi*), not quite 'our own kind' (*svoi*).

The contemporary record may not contain those words, which are quoted by Sechenov in a reminiscence many years after the event.[56] The bitter letter that Sechenov wrote to Mechnikov just after the vote mocks the national sensibilities of 'the party' that rejected Mechnikov, but does not specify the Jewish question.[57] Perhaps the sense of ethnic difference was entangled with professional envy. Sechenov quotes the leader of the hostile 'party' declaring Mechnikov worthy of a rank higher than the Medical Academy could bestow, and wondering whether the Academy needed such an outstanding zoologist. By one smiling argument or another hostile motives were concealed in factitious explanations as Mechnikov was voted down. Sechenov felt 'such loathing and grief that I wept, but covered my face so as to give no satisfaction to the lackeys surrounding me.'[58] He determined to attend no more faculty meetings, and resigned in 1870, to join Mechnikov at the University of Odessa.

Odessa brought no escape from such conflicts. Not only Jews were centers of contention, but also Russified Poles — even a German, endorsed by Sechenov and Mechnikov for his talent, but stereotyped and rejected by the majority.[59] The two friends found themselves persistently outmaneuvered and outvoted, with the predictable result. After four years Sechenov wangled a return to St Petersburg, at the University this time; he refused to go back to the Medical Academy. In 1882 Mechnikov simply resigned, without a new appointment. With private funds he tried to start an experiment station for the control of infectious diseases. After a few discouraging years he decided to emigrate, and found a place in Pasteur's Institute. There he became famous, especially for his discovery of phagocytes, which won him the Nobel Prize in 1908. He rebuffed efforts to get him back to Russian institutions of higher learning, explaining — in the press — that they refused to hire the Russian Jews who came to study with him, whereas his French Institute did not discriminate.[60]

THE TROUBLES OF ZION

The appointment of Tsion — 'the first Jewish professor in Russian history' — as Sechenov's replacement at the Military Medical Academy did not mark an end to discord over ethnicity at that institution. Quite the contrary. His appointment was the occasion for a bitter quarrel that forced him to resign. In 1871 the majority of the faculty voted him down, in spite of strong recommendations by Sechenov, Claude Bernard, Carl Ludwig, and Helmholtz. The majority favored a non-Jewish Russian candidate who was not even minimally qualified — he was not a physiologist. They backed up their decision with an unsubstantiated attack on Tsion as a plagiarist and unscrupulous careerist, whose personal character made him unsuited to teach young people. A minority submitted a soberly factual endorsement of Tsion. Minister of War D. A. Miliutin, the leading bureaucratic reformer still in high office, who had authority over the Academy as a military institution, rebuked the majority and appointed Tsion. The majority prepared to publish their original report, Tsion prepared a public reply, and simultaneously expanded and intensified the acrimony by a public lecture defending traditional ideology against 'nihilist' misinterpretations of physiology, which he implicitly linked to his predecessor, Sechenov.[61]

Articles appeared in liberal and leftist journals, attacking Tsion. He replied with charges of a nihilist conspiracy. He was not only Jewish in ethnicity, he was aggressively reactionary in political ideology, determined to win recognition that the right, not the left, had reason to claim support from physiology. He was also abrasive in personality, failed an unusually large number of students, and offended others with his insistent ideology. When he handed out printed copies of his lecture against 'nihilism' in physiology, students whistled in derision and threw the pamphlets back at him. The administration refused his request for a policeman in the lecture hall. In 1874 student demonstrations disrupted his classes, forcing his withdrawal and, soon after, his resignation.[62] There would be no more Jewish professors at the Medical Academy until the Soviet period.

The case of Tsion is quite exceptional, and for that reason merits close attention. Exceptions do prove rules, in the original sense of putting them to the test, seeing whether they are actually rules, and if they are, seeing how they operate. Tsion's case involves three such rules, which we may try to separate in retrospect, though they were all entangled in reality: the virtual impossibility of Jews becoming professors, the ideal of academic seclusion against the politics of the outside world, and the ideal exclusion of ideology from a 'hard' science such as neurophysiology.

Tsion dressed and spoke like a Russian professor, to an extreme: he came to the Academy in a showy carriage, dressed as a dandy, was a vivisectionist showoff in his lectures. (That portrait from his detractors. His graduate student Pavlov admired and learned the quick sure manual skill that vivisection demanded of a physiologist in those days.) But Tsion had not yet converted to the Orthodox Church, so he was considered incontrovertibly Jewish, or even a 'yid' (*zhid*), the pejorative that a fellow ideologist of the right applied to him in private.[63] Could such a person hold an academic appointment without bringing into academia the outside world's rising conflict over anti–Semitism and Jewish emancipation? That question takes us to a test of the second rule, which Tsion intensified by his animus against 'nihilism'. He pictured himself as bringing to Russia the civilized separation of physiology and leftist ideology that Claude Bernard and Du Bois-Reymond were preaching in the West. But he put the stress on *leftist* ideology, and so appeared to be attempting not a separation but a reunion of science with ideology, rightist rather than leftist. Thus the third rule was being tested, in a peculiarly subtle way. Tsion explicitly endorsed the exclusion of ideology from science, and *on that ground* tried to prove that mechanistic physiology compels us to go beyond science to faith, for it shows that the heart is not only a pump but also the seat of the feelings, that is, the soul. That was the theme of his notorious public lecture.

Anything like a full consideration of the virtual ban on Jews in academic faculties would take us too far afield. Suffice to note the obvious fact. In 1912, as the Tsarist system approached its collapse, only seven Jews could be found on all the faculties in the Tsar's Empire, and none had the rank equivalent to full professor (*ordinarnyi*).[64] Only two features of the system that maintained this nearly complete exclusion are clearly revealed in Tsion's case. One is the role of increasingly autonomous faculties in keeping out the Jews. It was the liberal Minister of War, Miliutin, who appointed Tsion against the will of the majority, which caused academic autonomy to be an issue in the ensuing polemics. The other clear feature of the system is strangulated silence, the choked inability of almost everyone involved to confront the Jewish issue in public discourse. Tsion's case generated a considerable volume of polemics, but there is almost nothing in them concerning the man's Jewishness. There are only hints, gestures, and pregnant silences.[65]

N. K. Mikhailovskii, a major ideologist of the populists (*narodniki*), might be expected to have been boldly articulate. He was a leader of the left, an outspoken critic of the old order. And in fact he opened his long review of Tsion's case by noting that all those who had signed the majority report against Tsion's appointment had Russian names, while all who signed the minority report in his favor had names 'of foreign origin'.[66] 'Foreign' in this case meant German or Polish; 'of foreign *origin*' implicitly conceded that the men bearing the names were Russified. In effect, Mikhailovskii was waffling, gesturing toward a situation that defied rational analysis: the faculty was divided not so much by nationality as by consciousness of 'national origin' − by ethnicity, as we would say today. As soon as he gestured toward the bewildering division, Mikhailovskii set it aside with a piously cosmopolitan exclamation: 'Gentlemen, surely patriotism no longer grips the servants of truth and knowledge!'[67]

One is left wondering about Mikhailovskii as well as the academic servants of knowledge. Did 'patriotism' influence his decision to support the majority? He deplored their vehemence and their failure to provide convincing evidence for the charge that Tsion's character made him unsuitable to teach young people. Yet he endorsed the judgment, without adding supporting evidence of his own. If one is aware of the contemporary embarrassment on the left concerning the use of anti-Semitic propaganda among the lower classes, one may guess at a possible reason for Mikhailovskii's waffling. But he was also entangled in another mess. The parts of his case against Tsion that were long and detailed and comparatively plainspoken dealt with the familiar issues of physiology and ideology and ultimate implications for politics. Mikhailovskii conceded that Tsion must be a competent physiologist − how else explain the recommendations by eminent specialists? − but he could not approve the right-wing ideological implications that Tsion attached to his science.[68] Thus Mikhailovskii came close to declaring a scientist with Tsion's ideology unfit to be a scientist, but he refrained from so plain a challenge to the separation of science from ideology, so gross an intrusion of politics into academia.

Tsion's published comments are even more frustrating in their evasions and confusions. He was obsessed with his case, and told the story many times over not only while it was unfolding but for years afterward, while he was a permanent exile in France. He made farfetched charges of nihilism against his opponents at the Medical Academy, who were in fact quite conservative. He made the same charges against Sechenov, who had recommended him, and against Miliutin, who had appointed him.[69] Tsion ignored such inconvenient facts and focused on the supposed materialism of Sechenov and on the liberalism of Miliutin, both of which he linked with nihilism, and so by association came back to the source of his troubles.

Everywhere he saw the hand of the nihilists, and of the liberals who were soft on nihilism. Nowhere, as far as I can discover, did he openly consider the possibility that anti-Semitism might have been an issue in his case. He may have been hinting at it, in his first account, by deploring his inability, 'for reasons that are easily understood, to start analyzing all the motives that arouse my opponents to fly to the most reckless actions in order to close the doors of the Academy against me. ...'[70] But the reasons for that silence are *not* 'easily understood'. One assumes that he was hinting at some other motives than cryptic sympathy for nihilism, since he was quite free with that charge. He even made it against the government censors. In tedious, unconvincing detail he tried to prove that they had facilitated the publication of articles by his foes while trying to obstruct his replies.[71]

Tsion was reckless with such charges to the point of self-destruction. After he settled in Paris and started a new career as a French journalist and a Russian agent, he focused on Count Witte, the major bureaucratic reformer at the turn of the century, whom Tsion portrayed as the chief agent of Russia's ruin, collaborating with Jewish bankers to impose an unbearable national debt, which would cause bankruptcy and chaos and open the way to power for nihilists, socialists, and anarchists.[72] He finally got himself permanently exiled for slander. Yet he could not bring himself to make the accusation of anti-Semitism against those who drove him from the Medical Academy, nor even to take note of his Jewishness and to reflect on its possible effects.

Toward the end of the century the emergence of political anti-Semitism as a major movement prompted Tsion to publish a long essay on 'The Question of the Jews', which nowhere hinted at his personal 'origin' and blamed anti-Semitism on the nihilists, anarchists, and socialists. In that suitably distanced context Tsion unwittingly revealed the motives for his silence on the Jewish issue whenever he told of his troubles at the Medical Academy. The issue was irrelevant, for he was not Jewish, he was Russian. His either-or distinction forbade any possible confusion:

> One of the two: either the Jews are Russian subjects, having the same rights and the same duties as all the other subjects of this vast empire, ... Or the detractors of the Jews are right in representing them as a cosmopolitan people, incapable of being assimilated in the country that they inhabit — in which case, what right does one have to claim for them civil and political equality?[73]

From that opening declaration of his either-or principle Tsion proceeded to a logical conclusion, however extreme: the mass conversion of the Jews.

The Tsarist regime should not only remove all the restrictions it had been loading on the Jews — the forcible eviction from cities outside the 'pale of settlement', the 3 per cent or 5 per cent limit on enrollment in higher education, the widespread refusal of officials to consider Jewish converts (or even their children) as full-fledged Russians eligible for government employment. The government should stop such restrictions and go on to the logical opposite: full assimilation, including forcible conversion. He sketched a series of measures leading to the final decree: either convert or emigrate. One may call this the late medieval or Spanish solution to the Jewish question, bearing in mind that it was proposed, not in the late Middle Ages, when the nation states of Western Europe converted or expelled their Jewish subjects, but at the end of the nineteenth century, when *secular* nationalism was becoming the ideological cement that bound citizens in unitary states of the modern type. Secular nationalism entailed the shift from religious anti-Semitism to racist anti-Semitism, which Tsion opposed, as he opposed the separation of church and state and the shift to secular nationalism.

Of course Tsion was an exceptional reactionary, indeed an hysteric, shrieking at realities he could not think about. When he encountered secular nationalism in France, it was personified by Paul Bert, an eminent physiologist who got the Sorbonne chair that Tsion aspired to. Subsequently Bert became Minister of Education and excluded religion from the public schools. Tsion fired off another of his denunciatory pamphlets. 'Internal barbarians' were threatening France as well as Russia.

> Under the veneer of civilization man has remained the ferocious beast that he was in prehistoric times when he lived in caves. If religion and the gendarmerie disappear, the human beast will reappear in all his savagery. ... In the new flood that will submerge the civilized world two summits will remain standing, the Kremlin and the Vatican, if both of them remain true to their secular motto: *Keep authority intact!* Hierarchy alone is capable of vanquishing anarchy.[74]

His many political writings heave with stereotyped fulminations of that sort. They are all the more indicative of hysteria, when one notes the confession, *en passant*, that he was not 'a believer' himself; he insisted on the necessity of religious belief.[75] Evidently he converted to the Russian Orthodox church in 1886 as a willful assertion of ideological and political necessity in a world he found revolting and unmanageable. (He also hoped to become editor of a major Russian newspaper.)

The experiences that shaped this bizarre personality peep through his sloganeering only occasionally and accidentally, for he was too taut to indulge in self-examination. He could not stand the stinking German workers or their condescending socialist leaders; I gather that from a reminiscence of a brief attraction to Lassallean socialism while he was a student in Berlin.[76] He loathed most of the Russian intelligentsia, ostensibly for their liberalism or radicalism, but his expression of loathing for them is curiously abstract, lacking the smell of the German workers. It fills his ideological tracts without vivid examples drawn from personal experience.

One suspects, of course, the inexpressible anger of a man who insisted that he was Russian, while his supposed fellow Russians saw him as a Jew.

Concerning the Jews who constituted his unmentionable 'origin' he could be quite vivid, when he finally allowed himself to write on the Jewish question. He expressed sympathy with upper-class Russian revulsion against the handful of rich Jews who spoke poor Russian, had parvenu manners and might win power with their loans.[77] He shared the regime's anger at the leftist Jews who were increasingly prominent in radical movements, and the regime's worry about the disloyalty of Jewish organizations that facilitated emigration or disseminated separatist ideology among the Jews who stayed in Russia. Toward the great mass of poor Jews he expressed mixed feelings. They were sober, hardworking, commercially sharp, intensely competitive, all useful qualities for economic development. They also had a greater gift for abstract thought than the Russians, who were a 'younger' people, and therefore had healthier bodies than the sickly, undernourished Jews. Such faults could be remedied in time by mixture with the Russians and improvement in life style. The first step was for the Jews to shed their ridiculous clothes, their absurd hair styles, their separate language, and their subordination to fanatical rabbis. The power of the autocratic Tsar could get them to take those steps, at the same time encouraging them to spread out beyond the Pale and to dissolve in the Russian population. Autocratic power could also educate and, in the final analysis, could force the Russian population to accept the Jews as fellow nationals. 'The mob [*tolpa*, like *la foule* in French] is of the feminine gender; it respects only force.'[78]

Before we set Tsion aside as an unrepresentative hysteric, let us note two crucial respects in which he was not at all unrepresentative. In his career as a reactionary journalist he had the sympathy of the most important official ideologists in late Tsarist Russia: M. N. Katkov and K. P. Pobedonostsev. They — and Delianov — tried to get him appointed editor of a major newspaper, but could not overcome Alexander III's opposition. The documents reveal that the monarch's hostility to Jews was the insuperable difficulty.[79] In brief, Tsion's ethnicity was compatible only with irregular service of the ideological establishment. He could not be chief of propaganda in a system that held him in pariah status no matter how stridently he preached its values. Thus, Tsion's hysterical ideology reflected more than his alienation as a Russian Jew in a period of intensifying conflict over ethnicity. It also reflected the growing incapacity of Russian conservatives to think realistically about their country's transition to some version of a modern polity. They were drifting toward the chauvinistic mass mobilization that would be called fascist in the twentieth century, while clinging to the old-fashioned dream of empire over a politically passive population, quietly subordinate to royal and clerical authority. That incongruity inhibited effective mobilization of the population, and contributed to the collapse of the Tsarist system. It also inhibited explicitly racist anti-Semitism, which was emerging in the thoroughly modern, scientific context of German culture. Pobedonostsev's clerical anti-Semitism pointed toward conversion or emigration; Hitler's eugenic version pointed toward death camps. There are certain advantages in backwardness.

With respect to the academic profession that cast him out, Tsion seems at first to have been completely unrepresentative. Very few tried to connect rightist ideology to pure science.[80] An increasing fraction — perhaps a majority — were supporting varied forms of liberalism, with a growing sense of hostility to the autocratic regime. Even the minority of intellectuals who were attempting a religious revival were very far from Tsion in their political ideology, and poles apart from him in their commitment to religion as a free feeling, rather than a willfully imposed necessity.[81] Yet there was one crucial respect in which Tsion was representative of the profession that cast him out: they were as tongue-tied as he when confronting the ethnic issue in his case. Integration of the Tsar's diverse subjects into a single Russian nationality was a commonly expressed aspiration, but it was not realistically discussed, much less enacted. For example, the decrees that excluded Jews from state employment explicitly exempted those with advanced degrees, yet faculties overwhelmingly ignored that legal permission to integrate Jews into their sector of Russian society.

In this respect the little world of secluded professors reflected the enormous world outside. To be sure, the national problem may have been insoluble, as it proved to be in neighboring Austria-Hungary, where it was intensely debated, with complete disintegration as the ultimate result. It might have been impossible either to assimilate a highly diverse population into the dominant nationality or to devise some way of managing without the integrated nationality that is the typical basis of modern states. The academic profession shared the problem, and shared the failure even to discuss it in realistic terms. With rare exceptions professors were unthinkingly 'of our kind', indifferent if not hostile to the variegated consciousness of kind among 'them', the many different kinds of 'strangers' who lived within the Russian Empire but were not of it.

The irony is that many Russian academics, like many of the intelligentsia at large, thought of themselves as broadmindedly cosmopolitan. They simply ignored the obscure spokesmen of the lesser nationalities and ethnic groups within the Russian Empire. Their gaze was fixed, not downward in the hierarchy of status groups, but upward and outward, toward the supposedly superior nationalities of the West. They were perennially wondering when — or if — Russians might reach the level attained by German, French, or English savants. To such a mentality the accusation of Russian chauvinism did not signify supercilious indifference to non-Russians at home, but truculent denial of Western superiority, insistence that the Russian intelligentsia should stop kowtowing to Western culture. That kind of Russian nationalism was characteristic of conservative government officials and of the political right.

Diligent searching has turned up only one or two isolated scientists expressing such sentiments.[82] In 1894 V. F. Chizh, a neurologist and psychiatrist at Dorpat University, protested the tendency of his fellow specialists to ignore Russian achievements and 'to exaggerate the charm of everything abroad. We need ... self-respect. ... Contempt for everything of our own and kowtowing before what is foreign [*preklonenie pered chuzhim*], that is what holds our science down most of all.'[83] One must sympathize with poor Dr Chizh. He held the post vacated by Emil Kraepelin, who had gone back to Germany to win fame as the founder of the major trend in modern psychiatry. (Indeed, Russian psychiatrists would follow his lead and their Soviet successors still do, as we shall see below.) The editors of the major Russian journal of psychology would not even publish Dr Chizh's declaration of Russian pride until he nagged at them, and then they required him to rewrite it with specific evidence, which drained much of the force from his protest.[84]

Chizh's truculence was embarrassing evidence of a poorly controlled inferiority complex. Sensible pride required restraint, but some sense of inferiority was hard for a thoughtful Russian to avoid if he arranged nations on an evolutionary scale, as virtually everyone did in the nineteenth and early twentieth centuries – as we still do with our talk of 'developed' and 'underdeveloped' countries. Indeed, the dominant trend of evolutionary thought at that time made it hard to avoid worries that lower and higher in cultural evolution signified lower and higher in biological types. Even such a broadminded liberal as Mechnikov took measurements of bodies and heads among Central Asian nomads to confirm his notion that they represented a lower stage of evolution than Europeans.[85] I do not know whether he pushed that biological fantasy to the point of making distinctions among Europeans, with Russians showing more primitive traits than Germans or Frenchmen. Many nineteenth-century scientists did so.[86]

PAVLOV

Pavlov was one of those who indulged in biological fantasy about the relative standing of Russians and West Europeans, to the great embarrassment of reverential Soviet editors, who have surreptitiously excised most of the offensive passages from supposedly complete editions of his works. When Sechenov died, and Pavlov was asked to address a commemorative meeting, he called attention to the exceptional industry and self-discipline of the deceased – exceptional, Pavlov specified, among Russians:

> The type of the Russian man in general has not, up to the present time, achieved final development; it is, so to speak, a chaotic type,

only in the process of crystallization. Precisely the same thing must be said in particular concerning the type of the Russian scientist.

We are poor in firm characters. We are poor in steadfast scientists, who lay out for themselves a certain plan and follow it to the end, while it is absolutely clear that life is made only by such firm types. I. M. Sechenov was one of those scientists, who are extremely rare on Russian soil.[87]

It is unnecessary to imagine that Pavlov got that notion of a formless, chaotic Russian 'type' from his teacher, Tsion, though we can find it in Tsion's writings.[88] We can as easily find it in many other authors; it was something of a commonplace in the nineteenth and early twentieth centuries.

Pavlov took such notions seriously enough to incorporate one variant in a scientific paper. It was first presented in May 1917, just after the Tsar had fallen, and everyone was talking about freedom. But Pavlov's title, 'The Reflex of Freedom', was not consciously metaphorical. He thought he was solving a laboratory problem: Why is there a minority of dogs who will not quietly submit to experiments in conditioning? Answer: they must be the offspring of dogs that were not chained but ran free, and thus they have a strongly developed 'reflex of freedom'. Most dogs do submit quietly to conditioning, because they have the opposite, equally inbred, 'reflex of slavery'. And Pavlov made the extrapolation to humans, concluding with an invidious reflection on his country: 'How often and in what varied forms has the reflex of slavery appeared on Russian soil, and how useful it is to become conscious of it!'[89]

There were scientific reasons why Pavlov was unaware of slipping from physiology into political ideology in this instance. His concept of the reflex was willfully holistic, as some would say; sloppy, in the view of others. He was intensely annoyed by the growing tendency of neurophysiologists to pick apart the neuronal structure of reflexes until the concept becomes an 'artificial abstraction', as Charles Sherrington audaciously put it.[90] If we postpone that internal problem of Pavlov's discipline, and confine ourselves to his entanglements in obvious ideology, we are confronted with a paradox. Pavlov deliberately avoided ideology. Like the German teachers on whom he modeled his life, he expressed contempt for politics and ideologies, and prided himself on his steadfast separation from them. Yet it is impossible to overlook his continual, unwitting display of ideological beliefs, as in the cases just cited. That paradox was typical of a great many scientists at the turn of the century. Indeed, it is typical of a great many to the present day. Belief in the contrasting purity of science and dirtiness of politics, and consequent aloofness from politics, can serve as a haughty servant's self-deception, a way of concealing the subordination of scientists to political masters.[91]

Pavlov was the son of a priest and trained to be one himself, but he converted to a faith in science during the 1860s. Soviet scholars like to stress that, lumping him with the radical ideologists of the time, as a militant opponent of religion and of the state that justified itself with religious principles. In fact, while Pavlov became an extreme mechanist within physiology and an atheist in his private thoughts, he remained to the end of his life indulgently sympathetic to religion outside of the laboratory and the lecture hall. He remembered his priestly father with affection, and extended that sentiment even to the seminary where he got his basic education, clearly separating himself from the notorious reputation of ex-seminarians as especially vehement atheists and radicals.[92]

Pavlov married an old-fashioned woman with strong religious convictions, who kept hoping that she might win him back to the faith.[93] She failed, evidently because she found no spiritual torment or yearning to work upon. There is no sign in Pavlov's voluminous writing of the spiritual crisis that gripped so many sensitive nineteenth-century thinkers who found science incompatible with the religious faiths they were raised in. Pavlov held to a simple, unexamined faith that science would ultimately solve all human problems. He was equally thoughtless in his attitude to religion, and therefore was unaware when he slipped into ideological views concerning it. The neatest revelation of that common state of mind in polite society was a little incident in Montreal, late in Pavlov's life. He was visiting McGill University, accompanied by a grown-up son, who expressed indignation at the enormous iron-work cross on a hilltop overlooking the city. Pavlov told his son to hush up, out of respect for the feelings of believers.[94] He was indifferent to the feelings of non-believers, such as his son, and utterly insensitive to the victims of believers, who were plainly told on the cross why it stood there: 'To establish domination of the white man and his beliefs over the pagan Redskin of North America.'[95] To paraphrase Engels: Those who refuse to think about ideology are unwittingly entangled in the most vulgar species of it.

Pavlov's reluctance to soil his mind with conscious thought about politics and ideology was also evident in his response to the furore that erupted over Tsion while Pavlov was a graduate student at the Medical Academy. His actions showed intense feelings that his intellect would − or could − never discuss, not even in later years with his wife.[96] When Tsion was forced to resign in 1874, Pavlov withdrew from the Medical Academy, refusing to accept Tsion's successor, Tarkhanov, as his new graduate supervisor. Indeed, Pavlov made repeated demonstrations of his dislike for Tarkhanov for a long while afterward. To be sure, the bad feeling may have been prompted by Tarkhanov's status: he was a fellow graduate student, only three years older than Pavlov, when he was given Tsion's place.[97] We are left guessing at Pavlov's motives, for he simply would not discuss the Tsion affair.

Thirty years afterward, in 1904, when Pavlov won the Nobel Prize and received a congratulatory telegram from Tsion, then permanently exiled and disgraced, he responded with a warm tribute to the teacher who had made his triumph possible.[98] He called Tsion's attention to a public expression of his gratitude, in an autobiographical article that included a one-sentence account of Tsion's forced resignation, the only Pavlov ever allowed himself to make in print: 'A savage history; thanks to rotten influences (*skvernym vliianiiam*) a most talented physiologist was driven out of the Academy by the students.'[99] Soviet editors of Pavlov's 'complete' works have cut out the references to rotten influences and to students, evidently fearing that Pavlov can be read as agreeing with Tsion's attribution of his fall to 'nihilist' ideology among the students.[100]

Perhaps the archives contain decisive evidence on this issue, but my guess is that they do not, for Pavlov's reluctance to talk about politics and ideology was one of his most prominent characteristics. His other favorite domestic teacher was the clinician S. P. Botkin, personal physician to the Tsar, who had a similar reputation for 'indefinite' social and political views.[101] In fact Botkin was less 'indefinite' than Pavlov. He served in the Balkan War of 1877 and published his impressions, which were somewhat critical of the high command, and he got involved in practical politics concerning sanitation and hospital management.[102] After all, Botkin was a clinician, not so pure a scientist as Pavlov.

Pavlov was not a cool, phlegmatic type. A short thin choleric man with a pugnacious beard, he was proud to be passionately assertive, in science. When graduate students exasperated him, he might rap them on the head with a beaker. And that personality was consistent, I think, with an emotional tribute to his favorite German teachers – Carl Ludwig and Rudolf Heidenhain – for their 'childlike goodness of heart'. They managed to preserve it past childhood, Pavlov argued, because they were immured in their laboratories. That is where 'the only virtue, the only joy, the only attraction and passion, is the achievement of truth.' From such teachers he learned to 'invest one's whole life, all the joys and grief in it, in science and in nothing else.'[103] Later on, when the world outside his refuge was especially tormented by war and political upheaval, Pavlov would speak of scientific research as an anodyne.[104] At such times he seemed unwittingly to confirm Bakunin's characterization of a life in science as 'lonely, melancholy self-development, . . . independent of the people, and separate from all political and social-revolutionary action.'[105]

But in 1904, when he received the Nobel Prize, Pavlov expressed unqualified joy in the secluded scientific life. He was completely satisfied not only by his mistress science, but also by his helpmeet wife. She had been 'just as devoted to our family for her whole life as I have been to the laboratory'. She had freed him from all bother with the practical details of life. She even bought his shoes. Of course Pavlov did not refer to her as his good servant and bedfellow. He called her his 'comrade in life', a tiny vestige of the talk he had heard in the 1860s about the liberation of women. Mrs Pavlov made peace with her subordinate and self-effacing role, even when her husband cut her off from social intercourse. He would grow sullen and demonstratively leave a social gathering if she talked freely with other people. She suffered, she told her confidantes, in service of a worthy cause: her husband's career in science. Neither husband nor wife paid much attention to the movement for the equality and self-realization of women.[106]

Pavlov lived beyond the joyous moment in 1904, when he was thrilled to get a personal gift from the Tsar in recognition of his Nobel Prize — a desk set that he used for the rest of his life.[107] Like other loyal subjects he was soon dismayed to hear that Japan had defeated Russia in the Far East, and then he was dragged from the happy isolation of the laboratory by the Revolution of 1905. The students dragged whole faculties into conflicts with the political authorities, by holding revolutionary meetings on campuses that were supposed to be immune to police action, and ultimately by demonstrations and strikes that closed down many institutions of higher learning, including the Medical Academy. Digging in the records, one finds Pavlov on a few commissions or tribunals whose purpose was to keep out the police, quiet the students, and re-establish the academic routine.[108] He was almost always a silent member who quietly endorsed compromise proposals, the sort that student radicals condemned for their 'typical liberal phraseology: although on the one hand one cannot but acknowledge, on the other hand one cannot but admit ... [*sic*] By setting itself an illusory goal — to reconcile the irreconcilable — the tribunal rejected the sharp, direct posing of the question and concerned itself only in the moral evaluation of individual persons.'[109] It matters little that the question at issue was a picture of the German Marxist, Bebel, which had been taken off the wall of a student dining room, with disturbance following. The clash between reactionary and revolutionary personalities, who made an irreconcilable issue out of a picture on the wall, while scientists like Pavlov wanted above all to be isolated in the laboratory and the lecture hall, portended great trouble for all.

The trouble would be especially severe because the Tsarist regime was swiftly losing the loyalty even of people like Pavlov, and no centrist movement was getting a mass base. Pavlov confided to a former student that the destruction of the Russian fleet off the coast of Korea in 1905 was a turning point for him; he ceased to believe that the Tsarist regime could endure.[110] And when, in 1917 it suddenly collapsed, Pavlov was one of the overwhelming majority that showed not the slightest sign of regret, not to speak of efforts at restoration. Instead he was moved to give one of the very few political speeches of his life, welcoming the beginning of a new era, when free institutions would permit Russian scientists and engineers to catch up with the Germans, whose astonishing military power provoked envy in a Russian patriot's heart. (Soviet editors have used the scissors on this too.[111])

Of course Pavlov gave no thought to the workers and soldiers whose mass action brought down the old regime, nor to the revolutionary parties that emerged from underground and exile to organize the masses. He simply assumed that someone would organize a constitutional representative regime in Russia, as someone had in Western countries. Evidently he never saw that there was great political significance in his habit of disdainful abstention from political thought and action. (In all his life he is said to have signed a liberal petition only once, and to have rushed back soon afterward to remove the signature.[112]) Abstention from politics was a — perhaps the — most common form of submission to the powers that be. Scientists like Pavlov were — and still are — unwittingly confessing that they see no difference between the submission of subjects, which is enjoined by traditional forms of ideology, and the consent of the governed, which is demanded by modern forms. 'Unwittingly' must be stressed, for Pavlov consciously endorsed the abstract principle of representative government. It would be unfair to turn against him his own argument about Russians and 'the reflex of slavery', for it is not a meaningful concept either in physiology or in ideology. Moreover, Pavlov's temperament was fiercely independent — within the secluded territory where he chose to assert it, the laboratory and the lecture hall. We will see the curious results when the Bolsheviks invaded that sanctuary, with uncomprehending reverence for the great physiologist who had uncomprehending disdain for them.

I. R. Tarkhanov typified an attitude toward politics that was different both from Sechenov's mild liberalism and from Pavlov's disdainful quietism, not to speak of Tsion's reactionary hysteria. Tarkhanov was outspoken in the movement for a constitutional monarchy.[113] He considered political engagement more than a matter of personal preference; it was a citizenly duty to be involved. He was willing to make an exception for such a great scientist as Claude Bernard, who had gone on working in his laboratory during the Revolution of 1848. But even in that case, which was excusable because great discoveries came from Bernard's laboratory, Tarkhanov found aloofness from politics an indication of 'netsel'nost' lichnosti', a personality that lacked wholeness or integrity.[114] Tarkhanov carried into professional life the ideal of the intelligentsia as a sodality of critical spirits committed to the improvement of the country by something more than scientific research and teaching. Of course, he did not take the fateful step into political organization, which would have put him outside any permissible profession, for Russia was an autocracy, a system that forbids political organization to its subjects. Tarkhanov's opposed concept of citizenly commitment expressed itself in a sort of scholarly journalism.

Aside from politics, he published on a very wide range of subjects, including philosophy, literature, and history.[115] Whether he was involved in the movement for autonomy for his native Georgia is not clear. The stated reason for his dismissal from the Medical Academy in 1895, when he was only 48, was ridiculously trivial. (Presiding at a doctoral defense, he gave the floor to a scientist who had been dismissed for radical views, with 'disorder resulting' — that is, the disgraced scientist was cheered.[116]) Thereafter he taught at St Petersburg University as a *privat dotsent* — the lowest rank — and indulged his many different interests in a flood of publications. During the Revolution of 1905 Tarkhanov edited an ephemeral magazine, in which he urged the creation of non-governmental institutions of higher learning as the only assurance of academic freedom from political turmoil.[117] Evidently he gave little thought to the fact that such institutions had begun to appear in Russia, promoted, as often as not, by such non-political types as Pavlov. In 1889, when his only possibility of academic appointment was in provincial Tomsk, Pavlov persuaded Prince A. P. Ol'denburgskii to found the Institute of Experimental Medicine, which remained his chief base of operations even though he soon received an appointment at the Medical Academy — thanks to Tarkhanov, with whom Pavlov now ceased to quarrel.[118]

BEKHTEREV

If Tarkhanov's admiring gaze had not been fixed on the private institutions in the West, he might have pondered the achievement of V. M. Bekhterev, Pavlov's chief rival in the psychoneurological sciences, who was a medical and scientific entrepreneur on a grander scale than Pavlov, and was to the left of Tarkhanov in political thought and agitation — altogether an extraordinarily energetic and wide-ranging man. He studied not only neurophysiology (with Ludwig once again), but also experimental psychology (with Wundt), and psychiatry (with Charcot). While teaching in governmental institutions (first Kazan University and then the Medical Academy in St Petersburg), he did extensive research and publishing in neurology and psychiatry, and still managed to maintain a private practice. From wealthy patients and their relatives he gathered funds to start, in 1908, his own Psychoneurological Institute, which offered unrestricted admission to women and Jewish students, and appointed 'progressive' scholars to teach a broad array of subjects including even history and sociology. Bekhterev also managed, perhaps through connections with aristocratic patients, to get crown lands set aside for the support of the Institute.[119]

In his autobiography Bekhterev boasted both of the crown lands he won for his Institute and of the opposition he encountered from the Tsarist regime. Minister of Education Shvarts contested the appointment of 'progressive' faculty members, especially in such a suspect discipline as sociology, and his successor, Minister Kasso, notorious for his campaign against academic autonomy, refused in 1913 to approve Bekhterev as director of the Institute he had founded. (He continued to direct it in fact, though another person took over the title.[120]) When a police report informed the Tsar that the Psychoneurological Institute was the second most turbulent focus of student unrest in St Petersburg (the first was the University), the Tsar put a menacing question in the margin: 'Of what use is this Institute to Russia? I want a well-founded reply.'[121] Finally, student meetings became so 'stormy' that still another Minister of Education ordered the Institute to be closed. But that order came only days before far stormier demonstrations by workers and soldiers on the streets of the capital forced the Tsar to abdicate.

Much of this information comes from Bekhterev's autobiography, which was published in the Soviet period and may be suspected of exaggerating his pre-revolutionary radicalism. Yet there is independent evidence too. In the fall of 1906, for example, when the mass trial of the St Petersburg Soviet set the students at the Medical Academy back into action, adopting revolutionary resolutions at forbidden meetings, the Minister of War threatened to close the Academy. The faculty responded with an offer of compromise. If academic autonomy were respected, they would censure the students and would prohibit political meetings. In the discussion Pavlov made one of his extremely rare political speeches, offering tactical advice on the way to win acceptance of the compromise: Tell the authorities that they must either allow autonomy or militarize us and ruin the development of science. Bekhterev disagreed with any offer of alternatives or compromises, urging a simple vigorous demand for autonomy.[122]

Such boldness made Bekhterev a frequent spokesman, when academic types chose to express their discontent. What distinguished him from most of them was his radical theorizing and speaking on much broader issues than academic autonomy. Among increasingly narrow professionals he held to the tradition of the leftist intelligentsia. He even wrote a play, 'In the Dawn of the Revolution', preaching the need to rise above party politics on the left and thus to achieve the country's regeneration.[123] That remained unpublished, but a popular science magazine printed his argument for 'a religion of social heroism, in the sense of social self-sacrifice [*zhertvennost'*]'.[124] With this doctrine he claimed to have provided a scientific basis for the ancient belief in immortality. Speculative essays of that kind pointed toward the large treatise that he would publish soon after the Bolshevik Revolution: *Collective Reflexology*, broadening his physiological perspective into a social theory.

An unusual personality and the tradition of the intelligentsia pushed Bekhterev to the left of his colleagues at the Medical Academy, but the medical profession at large pushed him further. He was at his boldest when he mounted the tribune before assemblies of practicing physicians, who were distinctly more radical than academic scientists. In September 1905, when he addressed a congress of psychiatrists and neurologists, he sounded revolutionary. The Minister of Internal Affairs had permitted the congress on condition that the participants stay away from topics outside their speciality.[125] Bekhterev responded with a defiant keynote address on the impossibility of separating their professional problems from the broadest and most basic issues faced by the whole country. 'The Individual Personality [*lichnost'*]: The Conditions for Its Development and Health' — that was his 'professional' theme, the need to reverse, to overturn the country's traditional repressive system. 'We Russians disregard the needs of the individual personality to a greater degree than any other nations of Europe. A nation [*narod*] whose social life is utterly undeveloped, in which the individual personality is crushed, is doomed to decay and to the loss of its independence.' With the exception of the Japanese, who had defeated Russia because their society showed respect for individual initiative, 'the vegetative existence [*proziabanie*] of the nations of the East serves as the best evidence that the absence of social self-government and the despotism of those in power [*vlast'*] ruin the individual personality itself as the active unit of society.'[126] Thus, the decline of Russian power and the physical and mental degeneration of the population were two sides of the same process, which could not be arrested without a complete transformation of the social and political system. The congress of psychiatrists unanimously endorsed that belief.[127]

In part Bekhterev and his colleagues were declaring once again a belief that had been endlessly repeated among the intelligentsia. Back in 1859 Dobroliubov had argued that the crushing of the individual by pigheaded despots made Russia 'the realm of darkness'. (His actual words, *tëmnoe tsarstvo*, 'the dark tsardom', had a political daring that is lost in the usual translation.)[128] In 1905 psychiatrists were reaffirming that view in the context of mass demonstrations, large political strikes leading to the formation of workers' soviets or councils, and mutinies within the armed forces. At the climax in October 1905 the Tsar made an insincere pledge of constitutional representative government, which split the opposition, and permitted the government to beat down belated lower-class uprisings with gunfire, arrests, and exemplary hangings. Bekhterev and his medical colleagues were not among the diehards who took to arms, but they had been among the professional groups whose demands and protests helped to set the revolutionary process in motion.

A recent historian of the Russian medical profession argues that the need for professional autonomy pushed physicians into conflict with the autocratic regime.[129] That was indeed one of their arguments, and one can hardly doubt the sincerity of it. Yet one must note the extraordinarily broad meaning that they packed into the concept of professionalism. They were not just demanding internal control of the medical profession, which they already had in large measure. Bekhterev and his colleagues were stressing the professional mission to society at large — to protect the health of nervous systems and minds — and declaring that they could not fulfill that mission unless state and society were completely transformed. They proclaimed that vision when there were about 350 psychiatrists and neurologists in an Empire of approximately 160 million.[130]

A sense of professional futility was expressing itself in a utopian dream of the world transformed to make the profession useful. Of course there were more obvious, proximate reasons for the radicalism of the medical profession in Tsarist Russia. In the first place one notes the zemstvo movement. Many of Russia's physicians were closely connected with the local organs of representative government that had been set up in the 1860s and had managed to survive the reactionary counter-offensive of the late nineteenth century. The zemstvos had become organizing centers for a variety of professionals who wanted to combine practical help for the lower classes with political action for representative government. It was such professionals who helped to set off the Revolution of 1905 by organizing protests as the autocracy disgraced itself in the war with Japan. The congress of psychiatrists and neurologists in September 1905 was somewhat late in adding its voice to the outcry.

The zemstvo movement pitted a variety of professionals against the regime, after 1905 as well as before. Specifically medical or psychiatric issues were not very prominent. They appeared, surprisingly, in the scandalous Beilis trial of 1911–13. Beilis was accused of murdering a Christian youth to obtain blood for a Jewish ritual. The prosecution got Dr I. A. Sikorskii, an elder statesman of the psychiatric profession — he had been one of Bekhterev's teachers — to testify that such a murder was in accord with the Jewish mentality. The defense called Dr Bekhterev to argue the opposite, and a number of the country's leading neurophysiologists joined psychiatrists in a public statement deploring Sikorskii's misuse of professional expertise.[131] (One account lists Pavlov among the signatories, but I have been unable to confirm that.)

Sometimes medical issues created unusual alliances and conflicts. Alcoholism among the lower classes moved Bekhterev to request government support for a major research project into the causes and possible cures of excessive drinking. Pavlov vehemently opposed the project. He was a teetotaler not only as an individual but as a physiologist, convinced that distinctions between 'safe' and 'excessive' drinking were fraudulent. Simple abstention was the only cure for alcoholism. He went so far as to accuse Bekhterev's project of being a sly way of justifying the government's large income from spirits by fabricating pseudo-scientific arguments for a non-existent 'safe' way to consume alcohol. The government went ahead and funded the project, which seemed to Pavlov to reveal the hollowness of his rival's radical pretensions.[132] (In the same spirit, though on a much pettier level, Bekhterev was mocked for putting 'von' before his name when he published in German.)[133]

Such sneers and reproaches may not be brushed aside, however suspect in motivation or wrongheaded in reasoning. A Soviet author adds, as further evidence that Bekhterev was not a genuine revolutionary, the rank of general and the medals that were bestowed on him by the Tsarist regime.[134] Another Soviet author, expressing the prejudice in Pavlov's favor, pictures him mocking the regime by coming to lecture in the required officer's jacket — carelessly thrown over the laboratory coat that was his authentic emblem. Such authors do not tell whether or how Bekhterev wore his uniform and medals. In any case the clashing symbols of the Tsarist state and the biomedical profession matter far less than the reality they expressed: the internal tension, the inner conflict of a highly placed professional who worked for a state that he intermittently declared to be hopeless, incapable of using his services properly. Whether speaking for academic autonomy or testifying in the Beilis case or applying for funds to combat alcoholism or doing his daily routine of research and teaching and medical practice, Bekhterev was working within and for a system that he wished to see overthrown. His was something like the situation of avowedly revolutionary politicians, who had to decide whether participation in the newly established Duma would help or hurt their revolutionary goals. But we must bear in mind the enormous difference between such politicians, half-in and half-out of the conspiratorial underground, and professionals like Bekhterev, who were always part of the establishment.

When that basic fact of life is recognized — constant participation in the Tsarist establishment — the problem is to account for the revolutionary rhetoric that Bekhterev expressed, and his fellow psychiatrists and neuro-logists unanimously endorsed in 1905. Their declarations cannot be dis-missed as heady surrender to a turbulent moment. When the next congress of psychiatrists and neurologists met, in 1909, with Bekhterev presiding, reaction seemed triumphant. Yet he repeated, and his colleagues once again endorsed the same theme as in 1905: complete self-government was the only way to emancipate the individual personality and thus to save the population from degeneration. The practice of psychiatry required nothing less. At one point in his speech Bekhterev went even further: 'The capitalist system, that is the fundamental evil of our time. And we must do every-thing we can to achieve other, higher norms of our social life.'[135] He was not committed to any one of the revolutionary parties that preached the need to overthrow capitalism along with the Tsarist political system. But with all those parties, at some level of thought and feeling, he and his colleagues shared the conviction that complete overthrow was necessary, that it was chimerical to hope for the gradual improvement which they sought in their daily professional work. A Freudian would call them 'conflicted'. Whatever terms one prefers, it is crucial to note that these professionals were inwardly torn between faith and despair in the useful-ness of their calling within the context of the Tsarist system.

Let us return then to the disheartening numbers. In an empire of approximately 160 million, as it drifted into world war and revolutionary collapse, there were about 350 psychiatrists and neurologists. (A sharp distinction between the two specialities was not made until the 1930s.) Bekhterev's speeches expressed their dream of huge additions to their ranks, along with construction of many new mental hospitals, until the multitudes who needed hospitalization for neural and mental disorders could be taken in. In 1909 he estimated there to be about 330,000 such sufferers, languishing in need of care that the system could not provide.[136] The present-day reader may deplore that urge toward the 'institutionalization' or the 'medicalization of madness'. These heavy labels are favored by modern critics of modern societies, when they express their disappointment in psychiatry. We may share the disappointment, but must beware of anachronistic criticism. The handful of psychiatrists and neurologists whose dream was expressed by Bekhterev were not working within a 'developed' country, saturated with mental hospitals. He bitterly recalled turning away a patient with crippling neuritis, who had come to the overcrowded hospital for relief, and wept when he was refused admission.[137]

In theory, Bekhterev granted, the mentally disturbed would be better served in family settings than in large impersonal hospitals. In fact, he reported, most families were not only materially unable to support deranged relatives, but they had abominable attitudes toward the deranged, even beating and chaining them. It is not clear how accurate Bekhterev was in that perception of Russian mores, though I have found no other psychiatrist challenging his bleak picture of the treatment of the insane in Russian homes. The tradition of popular reverence for the 'holy fool' [*iurodivyi*] may have been an exceptional occurrence in everyday life; in the discourses of intellectuals it was important to the novelist Dostoevsky, not to Russian psychiatrists. And the population at large was eager to put its insane relatives in the hospitals.[138]

The chronic tension within the mentality of Russia's psychiatrists and neurologists toward the end of the Tsarist system was a version of the inner conflict that many other physicians acquired in daily intercourse with the population at large. Those professionals did not absorb the passions of the lower classes, which found revolutionary expression in 1905–6, and burst all restraints in 1917–18. Quite the contrary. Among the physicians who conflated revolutionary rhetoric with professional demands in 1905 and the years following, I sense apprehension concerning lower-class passions, a tendency to equate anarchic *buntarstvo* (violent, elemental outbursts) with the frightful memory of peasant assaults on physicians trying to control cholera epidemics. That apprehension was mixed with a condescending sympathy for the lower classes, and a nagging doubt of the physicians' ability to help, given their few numbers, given the unfair and inept Tsarist system, and given the lower classes' 'uncivilized condition' or *nekul'turnost'*. (That endlessly used term should not be translated as 'uncultured condition'. If one wants a sympathetic euphemism, 'cultural deprivation' will do.) In short, utopian dreams and revolutionary rhetoric were transmuted expressions of anxiety and despair among professionals whose daily experience kept alive the dream — or should we call it a nightmare? — of the intelligentsia as a tiny band of *Kulturträger* in a great 'realm of darkness'.

Chekhov, who was himself a physician and especially sympathetic to professional colleagues who made their rounds in provincial isolation, gave classic expression to that underlying mood in creating Dr Astrov, the rural doctor in *Uncle Vanya*. Within the play's opening scene Dr Astrov is reminded that he has aged prematurely and taken to drink. He responds with self-pity and brutal realism:

> Do you know why? I've worn myself out, Nanny. From morning to night always on my feet, I don't know rest. And at night you lie under the cover and worry that they'll come and drag you off to some sick person. ... Never a day off. How can you avoid aging? And anyhow, life itself is dreary, stupid, dirty. ... It envelops you, this life. All around you are nothing but eccentrics [*chudaki*], a solid mass of eccentrics everywhere. You live two or three years with them, and little by little, without even noticing it, you become an eccentric. ... I have become an eccentric, Nanny. Stupid I have not yet become, thank God. My brain is still in place, but my feelings have somehow been deadened. I don't want anything, I don't need anything, I don't love anyone. ...[139]

That deadening of feeling pointed toward the abdication of professional duty by other physicians of Chekhov's creation — the alcoholic doctor in *Three Sisters*, for example, whose refrain is '*Vsë ravno*' ('It's all the same; nothing matters'), or the sophistic do-nothing doctor in *Ward Six*.

Dr Astrov is still lashed to professional duty by feelings that he cannot justify intellectually:

> The third week of Lent I went to Malitskoe for an epidemic. Typhus. In the huts the people [*narod*] were laid out in rows. Dirt, stench, smoke, calves on the floor together with the sick people. Newborn pigs too. I was on the go the whole day, didn't sit down once, hadn't a bite to eat, and when I got home they didn't let me rest. They brought a switchman from the railroad. I put him on the table for an operation, and he went and died on me under the chloroform. And just then, when they weren't needed, feelings woke up in me, and tore at my conscience just as if I had intentionally killed him. ... I sat down, closed my eyes — like this — and I thought: Those who will live a hundred or two hundred years after us, for whom we

are now hacking out a road, will they remember us with a good word? They won't, Nanny![140]

Nanny is a peasant, and replies that people won't remember but God will. That bromide punctuates Dr Astrov's longing for rest and justification, and foreshadows the colloquy of tears and dreams that ends the play. A selfish professor, devoted to learning as a way to personal fame, has abandoned the backward countryside. Not Dr Astrov but two other members of the 'rural intelligentsia' — farm managers would be their sterile job description in a modern society — confront the disappearance of realistic hope from *their* lives. One weeps, and the other says not to weep, for some day death will bring rest from daily toil, and the spirit will ascend to rejoice with angels. The whole preceding play makes that consolation even more poignantly absurd than Dr Astrov's self-mocking thoughts of progress and the gratitude of posterity at the beginning of the play.

Of course those were fictive creations. But it is noteworthy that the medical profession quickly seized upon *Uncle Vanya* as an expression of its feelings, if not a tribute to itself — with the tacit approval of Chekhov. In 1902 the Moscow Art Theater put on a special performance of the play for a congress of physicians in Moscow. Chekhov, isolated with tuberculosis in Yalta, pressed his wife to describe their reactions. In the intermission, she reported, the congress of doctors presented the theater with a portrait of their 'colleague' Chekhov, a prearranged gesture she found difficult to interpret. But there was no mistaking the spontaneous reaction at the performance. 'Men were weeping; a woman was carried out in hysterics.' At the final curtain there was 'rapture, . . . an out-and-out ovation, they shouted thanks — in a word, an enormous success [*furor*].' By telegram the congress sent to Chekhov the special gratitude of 'zemstvo doctors from Russia's dumb little provincial corners [*glukhikh ugolkov*]'.[141]

Unfortunately for the historian who wants to sift out the peculiarities of pre-revolutionary Russia, audiences all over the world are still moved to tears by *Uncle Vanya*. Chekhov's play starts with the frustrations of the rural intelligentsia in the late Tsarist period, but reaches the sense of tragic absurdity that afflicts anyone who seeks consolation in dreams of earthly progress or visions of angelic afterlife. Great fictions achieve such universality; somehow they reach beyond the historical circumstances of their origin.[142] Listen then to non-fictional Dr Bekhterev, mortal witness of his place and time, speaking his own lines to the 1909 congress that endorsed his utopian dreams and revolutionary demands.

As he wound up the meetings, he took note of the transient pleasure they had all enjoyed, indulging in scientific discourse in luxurious rooms lit by electricity:

> But tomorrow you will be going back to the usual rut of the isolated workaday routine, where you will be all on your own, where you

will once again be face to face with the joyless reality of the people [*narod*], great in spirit but impoverished in the literal sense, with its sufferings and with the horrors that encompass its life.

For the majority of you, accustomed to work in the gloomy conditions of Russian reality, this contrast must be striking. It will for the hundredth time remind you of your duty to spread rays of spiritual life in our realm [*tsarstvo*] of darkness. Only by the harmonious cooperation of all the country's forces will light spread to the horizons of the gloom that presses in on us from all sides. And we will go on hoping that we will yet live to see better days for our unfortunate native land.[143]

Bekhterev's obvious intention was to play Gideon to the little band of psychiatrists and neurologists, praising them for self-sacrificing refusal of academic luxury as they returned to 'the heroism of little deeds' in medical practice. But this Gideon spoke like Dr Astrov, stoical rather than militant, sounding the cello rather than the trumpet. The basic tension was very much in evidence. Faith that day-to-day professional practice served a socially useful mission conflicted with a despairing perception of social reality, with the belief that only a complete transformation of state and society could make the mission feasible.

That physician's mentality helps us to understand why Bekhterev would be one of the few outstanding scientists to endorse the Bolshevik regime shortly after its establishment. Far from insisting on a wall of purity separating science from politics, he sought to join the two, to justify and purify both by a united effort to serve 'the people', or rather, to rescue them from their *nekul'turnost'*. He would offer the new regime not only his organizational and scientific skills but also his own universal science of human development. Far more than Pavlov, Dr Bekhterev would carry into the Soviet period the ideology of the professional as a member of the intelligentsia, a spiritual brotherhood of critically thinking individuals struggling to illuminate 'the realm of darkness'. The Bolsheviks, deriving from that same tradition, would warmly thank him, loudly praise him, and give generous support to his wide-ranging projects of research and education. Of course they would disagree with his universal science of human development, insisting instead on their own. The big question would be how long they would agree to disagree, to acquiesce in the genteel disintegration of the sciences that they and he wanted to mobilize in the service of revolutionary transformation.

4

Psychologies and Less Obvious Ideologies

In 1850 the Tsar abolished philosophy. To be precise, his government abolished the teaching of philosophy in Russian universities; the revolutions of 1848 had shown what modern reasoning could lead to. An exception was made for logic and 'empirical psychology', to be taught by professors of theology and church history.[1] That was one way to protect the faith that sustained the old order. We may call it the blindfold and earplug defense, and note once again that it was ineffective against the eager teachers of Western values who came all the way to the Crimea to drive their lesson home. They said they were protecting the Christian subjects of the Turkish Sultan from the imperialist protection of the Russian Orthodox Tsar. The active faith on all sides was in nationalism and power; Christianity of any variety had become a conventional piety, invoked when politically convenient, otherwise ignored. The bureaucratic liberals who reformed the Tsarist system in the 1860s hoped to keep the traditional faith unspoiled by modern reasoning, which had to be enlisted in the service of national power but kept separate from revolutionary ideology.

With such restrictions, in 1863, philosophy was restored in Russian universities. Theologians were entrusted with the delicate task of teaching it to vulnerable young minds, deeply affected just then by physiological materialism and by positivism.[2] P. D. Iurkevich, priest and professor, was the most notable agent of restoration. He moved from the Kiev Spiritual Academy to Moscow University, and extended his writing from religious magazines to a government journal of secular scholarship, and to the publications of Katkov, the journalist entrepreneur who promoted right-wing ideology among the educated public.[3] Iurkevich focused his offerings on the heart. It was still, he argued, the seat of the soul, as 'God's Teaching' insisted. It was not merely a muscular pump, as superficial interpreters of physiology would have us believe.[4] About the same time that Iurkevich was publishing that defense of a religious approach to psychology, the censors were trying to squash Sechenov's first effort to show how physiology pointed toward a new, scientific psychology. That conjuncture of events might seem to confirm the 'two-camp' stereotype of psychology: the simple choice then as now was between the radical, materialist 'camp' of Sechenov and the obscurantist, religious 'camp' of 'the so-called Russian school'. Soviet scholars dwell delightedly on that story.

In fact the Tsarist censors of the 1860s were more obscurantist than such scholars can bear to acknowledge. They tried to suppress not only Sechenov's first essay but also, and more determinedly, Wundt's first book in Russian translation. That clash is ignored by Stalinists, for they also assign Wundt to the enemy 'camp'. We outsiders are free to note that the censors belonged to an ancient tradition which lives on in Stalinist psychology, as it does in other embattled 'camps'. There are many more than two, but each one tends to divide the universe of discourse into two: us and all the rest, them. Each one knows a holy truth that must organize all thought, and therefore each one has a tendency to declare anathema on any inquiry that begins or ends outside its holy truth. The censors found poor Wundt even more offensive than Sechenov because he did not bypass their holy truth; he tried to include it in a modern synthesis. He tried to keep physiology and psychology and philosophy and religion all joined to each other, but not in the old-fashioned manner of Iurkevich. He did not start with 'God's Teaching' about the heart as the seat of the soul, and ask how physiology might fit within It. He started with physiology, and tried to link it with religions (plural, small r) through the new discipline of psychology. He asked, in effect, how the biologically created human mind creates its varied gods.

His book was offensive in its very title, *Vorlesungen über die Menschen und Tierseele*, which did not get the antiseptic translation that it would receive in English: *Lectures on Human and Animal Psychology*. The Russian translator went straight from *Seele* to *dusha* (soul), not hedging with the intermediate possibilities of *psikhika* (psyche) or *um* (mind, in the sense of capacity to solve problems). The book was called *Dusha cheloveka i zhivotnykh, The Soul of Man and Animals*. The censors considered it materialistic and sacrilegious to seek a physiological explanation of the soul, which comes from God; to blur the distinction between man, who has a soul, and the animals, which do not; and to attempt an anthropological explanation of religion, as Wundt did.[5]

The publisher's lawyer was once again, as in Sechenov's case, the Russified Pole Wlodzimierz Spasowicz, or Vladimir D. Spasovich. He offered modern counter-arguments, appealing to Wundt's declared intentions rather than the objective implications of his views, and to other distinctions that segregate the irreconcilable segments of modern culture, keeping them from war against each other. Wundt was not a materialist in philosophy; he said so explicitly in his book, and demonstrated the errors of materialism. He did not deny the religious doctrine of the soul's divine origin, nor did he equate the psyches of humans and lower animals. His book did not deal with theology but with the psychology of religious beliefs, and anyhow the publisher had excised the section on religion to mollify the censors.[6]

The Tsarist court in 1867 was not persuaded by those arguments. It upheld the censor's arrest of the book, fined the publisher, and ordered him to prison for a week. Spasovich appealed the decision, ultimately to the highest level − the Senate − and there won his case. The book was released, and even though the part on religion was still excised, a landmark victory had been won. (The trial record was printed as an appendix to Wundt's book.)[7] Henceforth it would be permissible to treat such sacred subjects as the soul from a secular point of view. Indeed, as Spasovich pointed out in the trial record, the permissive process had been under way for some time. The censors had previously allowed Russian translations of George Lewes and Herbert Spencer, who were far less sympathetic than Wundt in their treatment of religion. In short, the attempt to suppress Wundt was a capricious last-ditch effort to draw a line, to set some limit on secular inquiry. After it failed, the defense of the sacred would be less a job for censors than for philosophers like Iurkevich. Or rather, a job for philosophers who would be less and less similar to Iurkevich, by virtue of their increasing sophistication, the increasing diversity of their viewpoints, and their capacity, whether religious or not, to seem confusing or pointless to right-wing ideologists like Pobedonostsev and Katkov, or to left-wing ideologists like Plekhanov and Lenin − or to poetic psychologists like Leo Tolstoy and Anton Chekhov, who glanced at academic psychology and impatiently brushed it aside.[8] Modern professional psychology blossomed in Russia in its characteristic manner: fragmented, esoteric, seeking objectivity through separation of thought from feeling, or obscuring both in academic language. Whether such a discipline is therefore pure of ideology is a puzzle to the professionals themselves, and more so to laymen.

In 1867, the year that the court battle over Wundt won academic freedom for psychology, the profession passed another major landmark. M. M. Troitskii published the first Russian treatise on the new discipline.[9] Though a priest's son and a graduate of the Kiev Spiritual Academy, he had been converted to a secular viewpoint, indeed to positivism. His book was an attack on the German metaphysical tradition in psychology, which he considered 'a pathological state of mind'. He favored the British tradition of associationist psychology that derives from Locke. Indeed, he showed such enthusiasm for J. S. Mill and Alexander Bain that he was chastised for his 'slavish relation' to foreign scholarship by another young Russian who was then turning to psychology as a profession.[10] It is amusing to note that the critic − M. I. Vladislavlev − perceived nothing slavish in his own reverence for the German metaphysical tradition. It is important to note that Vladislavlev soon joined the faculty of St Petersburg University, while Troitskii became a professor at Moscow University after Iurkevich's untimely death in 1874. The 'problematic science' of psychology, divided into warring schools from its earliest beginnings, had begun its academic career in Russia. Iurkevich had failed in his crude effort to keep it a holy 'camp' walled about by sacred dogma.[11]

It is also important to note that Vladislavlev failed to win students to the declining tradition of explicitly metaphysical psychology. N. Ia. Grot, to take the most notable example of the lost opportunity, was a student at St Petersburg University in the early 1870s, but did not take his major inspiration from Vladislavlev. He was engrossed by the debate between Sechenov and K. D. Kavelin, who discussed the future of psychology in *Vestnik Evropy* (*The Herald of Europe*), the major journal of liberal thought. In one respect that debate in the early 1870s marked the end of an era: neither participant was a professional psychologist, and their forum was a journal for the general educated public. But in another respect their debate pointed ahead, revealing the framework within which professionals would henceforth conduct their increasingly esoteric arguments. Sechenov and Kavelin took the physiological approach for granted. They disagreed on the proper way to combine it with other approaches, but both agreed that physiology must play a major role in the new science of psychology, and each in his own manner turned against the traditional metaphysical approach. Young Grot enthusiastically set his mind within that new, positivistic framework.[12] When he became a professor at Moscow University, he joined Troitskii, the admirer of the British empirical school, in founding the Moscow Psychological Society, which launched Russia's major journal of the new discipline in 1889.[13]

Another ironic outcome of Vladislavlev's teaching was the turnabout of his student Alexander Ivanovich Vvedenskii, who succeeded Vladislavlev at St Petersburg University in the 1890s and became president of that city's Philosophical Society.[14] Vvedenskii continued the tradition of philosophical psychology — to the point of self-destruction. Drawing on the relentlessly critical element in Kantianism, he argued that there is no way of proving the existence of the psyche or mind or soul in another creature. We may find it useful to assume such a thing, but we might also find it useful to refuse such an assumption, and thus to develop a functional study of behavioral patterns, a 'psychology without any metaphysics'.[15] That was the goal sought by a variety of experimenters and theorists at the turn of the century, who are usually lumped together as 'objective psychologists', even if they professed disdain for psychology, as Pavlov did. Nevertheless, Pavlov's physiological study of salivation turned into the most famous of the 'objective psychologies', and A. I. Vvedenskii proudly claimed that he had predicted the Pavlovian revolution[16] (or pseudorevolution, as other philosophical psychologists considered it). Pavlov, as we will see, had no objection to Vvedenskii's blessing or the others' disapproval. Some of Pavlov's major disciples seized upon the blessing, for the philosophical dignity it conferred on their master and his school.[17] Either way, through disdainful indifference or smiling reassurance, experimental and philosophical psychologies learned to coexist.

Stalinist psychology has obscured that factual history within the myth of Sechenov and Pavlov at war with an official 'Russian school' that was metaphysical and religious, or simply 'idealist', an all-purpose pejorative for any and every thinker in the enemy 'camp'. The myth conceals plain truths that outside observers may plainly note. Grot and Troitskii − and the Stalinists too − could not escape some metaphysical commitment or some sense of the sacred in their efforts to create a science of the mind (or psyche or soul or behavior). Nor was Vvedenskii an exception. His 'psychology without any metaphysics' was one pole of an intellectual construct that had a metaphysical philosophy of mind at the other pole.[18] Nearly all the Russian psychologists − once again the Stalinists included − would spend more energy discussing approaches to psychology than doing experiments in it. That may be the most abiding distinction of the endlessly squabbling Russian schools taken as a whole, as an ongoing community in their discord.

The predominantly genteel pattern of the discord can readily be seen at the outset, in the debate between Sechenov and Kavelin. It was not, as Stalinist accounts picture it, a pitched battle between mutually exclusive 'camps'. The last battle of *that* sort, as far as psychology was concerned, occurred in 1870, when the defense of a dissertation at Moscow University turned into a public wrangle. Heinrich Struve submitted a Russian version of a metaphysical treatise he had previously used for a degree at Jena, and Iurkevich was willing to accept it. *The Independent Ground [nachalo] of the Soul's Manifestations* dismissed Sechenov's 'Reflexes of the Brain' as 'the catechism of materialism in the Russian literature', and spent most of its pages on lengthy quotes and paraphrases of German metaphysical speculation, to prove that mind or soul has its ground in a non-material substance, and therefore has nothing to learn from physiology. An overflow crowd attended the public defense, which lasted more than five hours, and was continued afterward in some articles and pamphlets. Struve's critics charged him with plagiarism, with misrepresenting Ludwig and Sechenov, and with insufferable condescension to Russians, treating them like ignorant provincials.[19] Nevertheless, with Iurkevich's support, he did get the degree, and went off to teach philosophy at Warsaw University. Sechenov never dignified Struve's criticism by any comment, and the episode faded from public memory.

Sechenov debated with Kavelin not as spokesmen of rival camps but as allies within modern thought. Indeed, their debate probably originated in friendly argument during soirées at the home of Dr Botkin,[20] who was

Russia's leading pioneer of scientific medicine, as Sechenov was the country's pioneer physiologist, while Kavelin was the major jurist and publicist of the liberal persuasion. When Kavelin moved the argument from Dr Botkin's salon to the pages of *Vestnik Evropy* (*The Herald of Europe*), Sechenov went along. He was a fellow liberal. Kavelin revealed the familiar obsession of Russian liberals: we must overcome repression of the individual personality and consequent lack of initiative, the innermost cause of the country's backwardness. He was concerned that Sechenov's insistence on scientific determinism in psychology, his argument against freedom of the will, might reinforce the ancient curse of passivity and helplessness.[21] Sechenov shared Kavelin's longing for vigorous individual initiative, but considered that issue irrelevant to his central concern as a psychologist, to move from the science of neural processes, physiology, to the science of psychic processes, psychology. Psychic phenomena, he assured Kavelin, are 'an incomparably greater riddle for naturalists than for humanists'.[22]

The riddle is inescapable, for the mind is a natural phenomenon. It originates and functions in accordance with laws that can be discovered scientifically, experimentally. That is the consideration that led Sechenov to deny freedom of the will, as a logical corollary of scientific determinism, without which it would be pointless to try to build a science of the mind. That is why he pictured the mind as reflexive, responding to the myriad external stimuli that provoke and shape it. Without those assumptions he could not conceive an experimental approach to psychology. Of course, in his psychological essays he was no longer using 'reflex' in its precise physiological meaning: a rapid, involuntary, invariant pattern of neuro-muscular or neuroglandular reaction to a physical stimulus. He was turning the reflex concept into a metaphor for any response to any external influence, however varied the response, however ancient the original influence, however complex and protracted the intervening psychic process.

Sechenov did not deny the obvious everyday distinction between voluntary and involuntary actions. In 'Reflexes of the Brain' he gave examples of voluntary inhibitions that can dominate involuntary reflexes, as in toilet-trained puppies and children, or, at an exalted level, in the hero's cultivated disregard for privation or death. He wanted the science of psychology to get to the bottom of that distinction. The psychologist could not hope to become a scientist unless he interpreted voluntary action as a delayed reflex or response to a stimulus experienced in the past – sometimes many stimuli in a distant past, such as play with toy swords or tales of heroism read in childhood.

For the same reason thought had to be regarded as a bundle of interrupted reflexes. The interruption could be quite prolonged; the brain processes intervening between stimuli and responses could be most complex. Those were fairly common notions in the mid-nineteenth century; Laycock in England and Griesinger in Germany had been the first to publicize them.[23]

Sechenov's innovation, as he saw it, was to focus on central inhibition as the neurophysiological mechanism that would explain the process. If thought is an interrupted reflex, then psychology will progress from a loose metaphor to precise experimental science as it discovers the brain's mechanisms for interrupting reflexes. More of that later, when we come to his intense experimental efforts to find centers of inhibition in the brain – and the frustration that he suffered, and his withdrawal from the field, in the period 1863–7. All but the first of his essays on psychology came after that frustration and withdrawal. They were not scientific presentations, as he himself notes.[24] They were popular defenses of the basic principles which, he was still convinced, were essential for the transformation of psychology into an exact science. That was the context within which Sechenov framed his broad question as the title of an essay – 'Who Is To Develop Psychology and How?' – and gave the pointed answer: the physiologist, using the methods and assumptions that have accumulated precise, reliable knowledge of neural processes.[25]

Kavelin declared himself in agreement with Sechenov's principles, as clarified in the essays following 'Reflexes of the Brain'. On basics, he was pleased to discover, he and the great physiologist were agreed. Sechenov was not a materialist. He said he was not, and he proved that he was not on concrete issues: he did not equate neural with mental processes; he did not preach the reduction of psychology to physiology; he allowed for the enormous importance of consciousness as well as voluntary actions.[26] Sechenov was not pleased by Kavelin's embrace. Even though he accepted those three principles, he disapproved of extensive philosophizing on such an abstract level, for that was regression to metaphysical speculation, the dead end from which some experimental strategy was the only escape.

It is worth quoting Sechenov at length in that vein, not so much to dispel the myth that he was an explicit materialist as to show how he fudged the choice between ontological assumptions such as materialism and spiritualism, turning away to practical assumptions and experimental strategies.

> We can understand therefore why no natural scientist tries to grasp 'matter' as a general ground concept [*obshchee nachalo*]. It represents an ideal point, toward which their exertions are directed; but for them it is a point in a dense fog, and they move toward it, guiding themselves not by it but by the closest points of the new horizons that are revealed to science in its slow, systematic forward movement.
>
> But philosophers of the antique temper, and Mr Kavelin following after them, instantly fly up in their subject area from the soil of concrete facts into the densest fog of a general ground concept (*obshchee nachalo*).[27]

In the very next line, without worrying about consistency, Sechenov conceded the necessity of using divergent 'ground concepts', involving soul or mind (*dusha*) as well as matter. He was confident that matter and soul would be shown in the long run to be 'variations of the same ground concept [*nachalo*]',[28] but he thought it pointless to make that issue the subject of discussion:

> Keep the soul in practical life, as the noblest part of man; accept it even in science [*nauka*] as a general ground concept [*obshchee nachalo*], in the same way that natural scientists regard matter. Let it even be the guiding star in psychological investigations. But how is it possible to explain anything by the inexplicable! That is taking up a thing not from the beginning [*nachalo*] but from the end. [The pun cannot be transferred into English. *Nachalo* means both a beginning and a ground concept.] The moral of all this reasoning is as follows: Mr Kavelin starts out in his philosophical system from shaky, unproven facts, and then takes the very step that has been the chief ruin of philosophy.[29]

In other places Sechenov conceded that Kavelin proposed not only metaphysical speculation but also concrete methods of psychological inquiry. In particular Kavelin stressed the inadequacy of the physiological approach, even if supplemented by experimentally controlled introspection. Laboratory psychology of any kind, he insisted, must be supplemented by cultural and historical studies, since the human mind is shaped by historically evolving cultures. Sechenov was not quite clear or consistent in his response to that argument. On the one hand, he backed off by pleading ignorance of historical and cultural studies.[30] He even granted that the physiological approach created mysteries by calling in question what cultural studies take for granted — the works of the mind. In the same vein he conceded that 'one of the most outstanding aspects of psychic phenomena — the conscious element — can be subjected to investigation only in ourselves, with the aid of self-observation.'[31]

On the other hand, more insistently and with more conviction, Sechenov warned against the anthropomorphic errors caused by absorption in the conscious self and by extrapolation from it to explain the external world, an attitude that he found typical of primitive rather than civilized minds.[32] He insisted most emphatically that invariance (*neprelozhnost'*) is essential to genuinely scientific laws. In addition to the experimental methods of the physiologist he could see only one other way of establishing invariant laws in psychology: the comparative study of animal behavior, what was coming to be called zoological or comparative or animal psychology and has since evolved — or split — into ethology and sociobiology. When arguing the supreme need for invariant laws, Sechenov implicitly withdrew the concession that historical and cultural studies might contribute to the science of

psychology. Invariant laws presupposed an invariant essence, to be discovered at the biological level: 'The basic features of man's thinking activity
and capacity to feel have remained unchanged in the various epochs of his
historical existence, independent of race, geographical condition, or level of
culture. . . .'[33]

That is one of many passages in Sechenov which prompt Soviet editors
to intervene with reassuring explanations. It is at first amusing to note such
an editor praising the quoted passage for its defiance of racism and respect
for the essential equality of man,[34] while ignoring the obvious clash with
Karl Marx's insistence that psychology must be an historical and cultural
discipline, since all aspects of the mind, even the senses, are a product of
historical experience. Amusement turns sour, however, when one notes
that this is not just a problem for Stalinist editors. It is their way of
fumbling with the endless clash between biological and cultural approaches
to the understanding of human beings.

If Sechenov was averse to extensive philosophizing, he was even more
unwilling to get involved in ideological combat. His critics insistently
raised the issue of moral responsibility, and not always on a dignified
philosophical level. Does not the scientist's rejection of free will subvert
moral responsibility? Has Sechenov not exculpated the criminal, whose
behavior is determined no less than the virtuous man's? Sechenov gave
only a brief reply. Whatever the cause of criminal behavior, society has the
right to protect itself. Such a statement had a punitive, right-wing resonance,
especially when Sechenov added the analogy with protection against wild
beasts. We do not blame them, but we keep them away from ourselves.[35]
In fact, he seems to have shared the liberal, reformatory attitude toward
criminals. It is often linked to determinism, with the argument that criminals
will be good people if the circumstances that shape them are changed from
bad to good.[36] Sechenov did not pursue such arguments in his psychological essays. On jury duty in Odessa he and Mechnikov found themselves
persistently more lenient than fellow jurors from the uneducated lower
classes,[37] but neither of the learned friends used that sociological observation to wonder whether philosophical ethics and psychological science have
much relevance to the notions of responsibility that we use in everyday life.
The peasants had their ideological beliefs, largely unexamined, and the
learned members of the jury had theirs, which Sechenov did not choose to
examine at length. He tried in his essays to avoid ideology, to constrict
thought within the purely scientific problem of transforming psychology
into an experimental science.

Those who fancy extensive philosophical or ideological theorizing can
seize on brief remarks by professionals like Sechenov — or peasants, for
that matter — and read extended implications into them. In the 1870s and
1880s a number of authors took the assumption of scientific determinism
and expanded it into lengthy discussions of ethical responsibility, crime,

social progress, individual freedom — the human condition, if one may use that worn-out phrase.[38] Consideration of that literature would take us back to obvious ideologies, which Sechenov and other professionals were trying to avoid. He could not help it if his specialized work obliged him to make certain assumptions that laymen expanded into extended argument over issues he chose to ignore. But one such process of expansion needs to be outlined, for it did not move away from physiology and psychology, as the debate over determinism and responsibility did within Russia and the Soviet Union. In epistemology, strange to say, Sechenov planted an assumption that would swell into a permanently inflamed area of Soviet psychology and philosophy.

Actually the process began with Helmholtz, from whom Sechenov took the distinction between physical and psychic processes.[39] The distinction is crucial to modern physiology, which excludes psychic phenomena, and to psychology, which brings them back in. The varying lightwaves that enter the eye are physical, subject to study by physical science. So are the corresponding patterns of neural excitation that the lightwaves stimulate within eye and brain. So are reflexes, such as the blinking eyelid or the contracting iris. So too, Sechenov argued, is the muscular movement of the vocal organs reporting what one sees. But he followed Helmholtz in arguing that *what* one sees, the psychic sensations and the perceptions constructed out of them, are not literally physical in the same sense that reflections in a mirror are physical. There is some correspondence between external physical objects and the sensations and perceptions of them in the brain-mind, but this correspondence is significantly different from the simple reflection of objects in mirrors. The brain-mind transforms physical stimuli into psychic sensations and perceptions, which the mind reads as representations (*Vorstellungen, predstavleniia*) of physical objects.

Helmholtz, and Sechenov after him, used the metaphor of symbols or hieroglyphs to suggest the way that psychic entities such as sensations, perceptions, and representations correspond to physical objects.[40] Their purpose was not to indulge in philosophy, certainly not in metaphysical theorizing, but to make neurophysiology a rigorously physical science by the systematic exclusion of psychic processes. Those excluded processes were handed over to the new science of psychology, and philosophers were left to worry about the ontological implications of the research strategy. Plekhanov was willing to regard those distinctions, that division of labor, even the metaphor of hieroglyphs, as consistent with the Marxist understanding of materialism.[41] Lenin was not, and attacked Helmholtz for 'physiological idealism'[42] — Helmholtz, not Sechenov. Either Lenin was unaware that Sechenov shared Helmholtz's view — in 1904 Lenin bought a book of Sechenov's, but no one knows whether or how much he read in it[43] — or else Lenin was aware, but chose to direct his criticism at the originator of the view, disregarding the Russian popularizer.

Lenin, as we will see, had a stronger tendency than Plekhanov to declare united what the learned world was breaking apart. His Stalinist successors had an even stronger tendency of that sort. They added Russian pride to the enforced reunion, and have transformed Sechenov into a, or even the, major founder of psychology, who pointed the new science toward a revolutionary materialist exit from the vicious circles of the idealist 'camp'.[44] Sechenov's contemporaries were quite unaware of that accomplishment. While he lived no Russian psychologist or philosopher even hinted at such a view of his essays on psychology. They were perceived as he himself pictured them: as popularizations, introducing into Russia crucial problems and concepts that had been developed in the West, of significance in the development of the Russian intelligentsia, not in the development of psychological science.[45] To be sure, Sechenov was a modest man; he may have built better than he knew. It may be discourteous of an outside observer to belittle an accomplishment that his Russian countrymen have acclaimed, however belatedly. But courtesy is no excuse for ignoring the factitious nature of the claim. Indeed, it is an ironic insult to Sechenov to inflate his significance by ignoring or distorting his central arguments, turning him from a serious thinker into a crude icon.

He called his psychological essays popularizations in two senses. They summarized for the Russian public ideas that Sechenov considered fundamental, without the claim of originality he attached to his scientific articles. He was especially fond of Herbert Spencer's psychological theories for their combination of physiology with evolution, and summarized them at considerable length with little criticism.[46] Sechenov's essays were also popularizations in the sense that they were limited to fairly elementary analysis, and deliberately passed by heavy involvement in philosophical discussion or technical problems. Sechenov was opposed on principle to the notion that psychology can be advanced by philosophizing about it, or even by scientific theorizing that does not lead to laboratory tests. His first psychological essay of 1863 helped to set him up for frustration; his experimentation took him into a dead end. The rest of his psychological essays were stoically calm popularizations of the basic reasons why he still held to his elementary assumptions.

If Sechenov was ever tempted to think that his psychological essays were framing concrete hypotheses for other experimenters to test — and there is not the slightest evidence that he was — he could not fail to note the accumulating evidence that no one was reading him that way. Russia's newly emergent profession of psychologists tended to do more theorizing than experimenting, and tended to show little or no interest in his central insistence on the correlation of neural and psychic processes, with special attention to the problem of inhibition.

Grot, who began his career in the 1870s as an enthusiast of the Sechenov-Spencer approach — he called it positivist, without an eponym — evolved into a highly speculative psychologist and philosopher. That evolution was especially ironic, for he began by dismissing philosophical speculation as mere indulgence in subjective feeling, and went on to analyze feeling as a psychological process. He came thus to realize that feeling is a component of cognition, and so wound up recognizing a cognitive element in speculative philosophy. Then he went deeply into such speculation. He claimed that a 'Copernican revolution' was accomplished by a psychology that regarded the psyche or spirit (*dukh*) as the unmoving center of the psychic universe, even though the psyche constructs the concepts which it then regards as independent of itself.[47] S. L. Rubinshtein, the exceptionally clever Soviet philosopher of psychology, has argued that Grot's 'Copernican revolution' revealed Sechenov's influence, by inversion of Sechenov's outlook.[48] That is plausible, if we think of Sechenov's fundamental outlook as philosophical materialism, the attribution of substantial reality to external objects and denial of such reality to the psyche. If, on the other hand, we note his express indifference to ontological choices, his stress on experimental strategies, then Grot's psychology is not so much an inversion of Sechenov's as a departure from it. In any case, Sechenov was probably untroubled by the evolution of Grot's thought, for there is no evidence that he bothered to read Grot or the other professional psychologists arguing about their subject on a philosophical level.[49] Much of the genteel calm in the disorderly world of academic studies flows from that aristocratic disregard of the disagreeable. One doesn't quarrel or seethe; one ignores.

There was one test of Sechenov's influence that he must have noted. It came in 1884, when an émigré Russian admirer published a French translation of his essays on psychology.[50] The book sank into instant oblivion, with a single brief review to mark its passage.[51] Another test came at home at the turn of the century, when Bekhterev and Pavlov published their first papers on the conditioned reflex, or the associative reflex as Bekhterev called it. Neither of them thought to mention Sechenov as their inspiration or even to put him in a footnote while he was alive, and he showed no sign of offense. Evidently he did not perceive their work as vindication of his experimental strategy, for they did not make rigorous correlation of conditioning with neural circuits.

Just after Sechenov died Pavlov was prompted by questioners to speculate that he must have experienced some 'unwitting' or 'hidden' (*podspudnyi*) influence from Sechenov, but he took pains to note differences as well as similarities between Sechenov's physiological approach and his own.[52] In later years Pavlov and his school — and Bekhterev's rival school of 'objective psychology' or 'reflexology' — would claim the inspiration of Sechenov without fussy qualifications. So too would the Soviet pioneers of neuropsychology. The Pavlovians would picture Sechenov starting complete reduction of psychic to neural processes; the neuropsychologists would claim him for the correlation of the two. Later still, Sechenov would be revered by such a heavily philosophical psychologist as S. L. Rubinshtein, by the cognitive school of Vygotsky, and by Soviet advocates of a cyberneticist approach. A familiar pattern in hagiography: the more distant the saint, the more diverse the appeals to his icon.

EDUCATORS, WRITERS, AND 'THE RUSSIAN SCHOOL'

Much of this may seem excessive labor to establish a rather modest point, that Sechenov dreamed of a particular kind of scientific psychology which he could not get going. But there is also a large, painful question that emerges when Sechenov is demythologized, as it does whenever one digs past the mythic constructs of the varied schools and unearths the actual history of psychological science. Why was his dream frustrated? Why were all the dreams of the nineteenth-century pioneers frustrated? Let there be no doubt about this fact, which contemporaries persistently noted and fretted over. Recall Franz Brentano in 1874 opening his major book with a lament on the unscientific clutter of psycholog*ies*, and starting more divisions with his project for a single united psycholog*y*. By the turn of the century Brentano seemed to be resigning himself to the indefinite continuation of two fundamentally different psychologies: '*Psychognosie*', or 'descriptive' psychology, which studied subjective experience, as opposed to 'genetic' psychology, which studied the objective conditions, mainly physiological, that attend or determine the coming and going of psychic events.[53] William James experienced a much more radical shattering of scientific dreams. The young man who went to Germany in 1867, eager to be in at the start of psychology as a natural science, came to the middle-aged conclusion that there was no science, only the hope of a science, accumulating data of dubious significance, and a great deal of inconclusive philosophical debate.[54] By self-mocking analysis he turned his disillusionment into a creative *tour de force*, a textbook of psychology that doubted the reality of the discipline, and so doing became a lasting work of art. His *Principles of Psychology* is a triumph of negative capability, as Keats called the fusion of contrary thoughts and feelings in artistic unity.[55]

Grot, doing a more conventional survey of the would-be discipline in 1898, took due note of its approach to anarchy: 'Never yet in the field of psychological problems has there been such a sharp struggle of trends, parties, and individual outlooks as there is at present.' Yet he also noted a countervailing

> striving for synthesis and reconciliation, a readiness on *particular* issues to reach agreement by mutual concessions. All psychologists, it seems, are looking for a general slogan of reconciliation, to found 'a single science' of consciousness and the mental activity of man and animals.

Since they are not finding it right away, they are developing psychology each in his own way, avoiding touchy problems (e.g., concerning the mind and its nature) or arguing about inessential details.[56]

The derisive irony of Grot's observation does not detract from its accuracy. Modern professionals in human studies do tend to avoid fundamental conflict by slogans, by evasions, and by limiting themselves to 'inessentials', keeping away from essences.

In such professional communities not everyone is ironic or derisive; there are cheerful souls who manage one way or another to see orderly progress. In 1893 N. N. Lange, one of Russia's pioneers in not only preaching but actually working at experimental psychology, argued for more laboratories by painting a rosy contrast between the anarchic dark age of speculative psychology and the harmony that dawned with the experimental approach.[57] He was soon reminded of the continuing anarchy, hardly concealed, merely eased by academic etiquette. At the defense of his doctoral dissertation in 1894 a senior professor of philosophy and psychology conceded only marginal value to Lange's work and to the experimental approach in general. He insisted on the more important understanding to be gained by 'the method of psychological introspection, which is so often and so unjustly condemned'.[58]

Twenty years later, when Lange published his textbook of psychology — it is often called the best Russian textbook of the pre-revolutionary period — he acknowledged the diversity of viewpoints, among experimentalists as well as other types.[59] At one point he even approached a Jamesian level of analysis by disclosing basic conflict within the head of an individual psychologist.[60] For the most part, however, he presented billiard-ball arrangements of the diverse psychologists, clustering them in rather simple-minded patterns within a Wundtian frame. The psychologist with inner contradictions had moved out of it. Freud had never given serious consideration to the Wundtian frame, and Lange repeated Wundt's payment in kind: Freud was not part of scientific psychology, he was trying to revive romantic notions from the age of *Naturphilosophie*.[61] No doubt there was a partial truth in that partisan label, but Wundt and Lange did not perceive themselves as partisans pasting labels on viewpoints they refused to consider. They avoided inner anarchy by resisting acknowledgment of everyone's unavoidable partiality, including their own willful way with a supposedly objective science.

Of course I am speaking in metaphors. Literal anarchy was erupting among Russia's social classes, ethnic groups, and political parties, not among academic psychologists. They were not literally partisan in the sense of forming parties of the parliamentary type, not to speak of the revolutionary type, which emerged in Russia at the turn of the century. The 'war of schools' among Russian psychologists, as among their Western

colleagues, was a metaphor for a highly mannered, courtly contest. Intermittent displays of rival views, as at Lange's doctoral defense, punctuated
stretches of studied indifference, and so did ceremonial gestures of respect
– bestowing the doctorate, for example, after belittling the dissertation.[62]
The discipline called psychology was a discipline less of thought than of
behavior, an etiquette that held mutually disdainful schools to a mannered
imitation of intellectual community.

Stalinist psychologists resist acknowledgment of that community of
manners, and of the diversity that it held in a semblance of order. They try
to picture Lange as a disciple of Sechenov, to see his doctoral examination
as an act of war, noting that the senior professor who attacked Lange was
himself attacked as a 'philosophical fascist'.[63] But in fact Lange was a
disciple of Wundt, not of Sechenov; he merely contributed a bit to the
posthumous veneration of 'the father of Russian physiology'.[64] And it was
not a fellow academic who flung the epithet 'philosophical fascist' at Lange's
critic: it was Lenin, in a completely unrelated context.[65] (The word I
translate as 'fascist' was *chernosotenets*, a member of the Black Hundreds,
Russian gangs that beat up leftists and Jews.) Nothing like Lenin's name-
calling, and certainly nothing remotely resembling the Black Hundreds'
physical assaults, are to be found in the pre-revolutionary arguments about
psychology.

The courtly jousting of academic psychologists involved occasional talk
of the violence that may be implicit in opposed theories of human nature,
but academics prided themselves on their ability to keep such talk confined
to talk. Words and deeds are completely separated in the higher studies of
human beings, even by those who deplore the separation. The pioneer of
animal psychology in Russia, V. A. Vagner, shared the social Darwinist
belief that protection of weak and defective individuals interferes with
natural selection and threatens to cause degeneration of the race.[66] Of
course he did not act on his theory. He did not kill deformed infants or
shut down hospitals or shoot intellectuals who preached humane mercy,
nor did his academic critics charge him with such proclivities.

Literary artists were much closer than academic psychologists to such
fusions of words and deeds – still in words, to be sure, but much closer to
deeds because they put words in dramatic action. Chekhov met Vagner at a
summer resort, argued with him about social Darwinism, and was moved
to write a tale, not a treatise. He imagined a virile advocate of social
Darwinism growing enraged at a feckless advocate of humanism, justifying
his approach to murder by scientific arguments that humanity must be
cleansed of such degenerates as the humanist. The result was one of
Chekhov's greatest tales, 'The Duel', with murder narrowly averted at the
end, and the chastened adversaries agreeing: 'No one knows what's really
right.' (Literally: 'No one knows real *pravda*', the famous word that
combines factual and moral rightness.)[67]

That tale expressed Chekhovian wisdom, as unprofessorial in its poignant skepticism as Leninist wisdom was in its organized fury. In the real world of academic rivalries — or are they the realists who call academia an artificial world? — in Russia as well as the West opposed psychologists tried to avoid forthright ideological confrontation, repressed murderous anger, and certainly refrained from mutual confession of ignorance. Chekhov would have produced an absurdist farce instead of a near tragedy, if he had imagined a professor of animal psychology literally shooting it out with a professor of the humanities. He transformed Vagner into a young field biologist, the feckless humanist into a self-pitying layabout.[68] Certainly the real Professor Vagner did not end his treatises with the *envoi*, 'No one knows what's really right.' He claimed to know scientific truth. Noting Pavlov's claim of a different truth, he challenged the physiologist with no weapon but the pen, and Pavlov, as we will see below, feared no dishonor in ignoring the challenge. That was his custom, a haughty indifference to those who questioned the adequacy of a physiological reduction of the psyche. It was not only a matter of personal temperament. When basic views are as deeply divided as they are in human studies, studied disregard of distant adversaries permits each school to get on with its self-centered line of work.

Bekhterev was exceptional in his broad conception of that strategy. He brought to the faculty of his Psychoneurological Institute and the editorial board of his journal not only neurologists and psychiatrists like himself but also the Darwinian zoopsychologist Vagner; also an educational psychologist specializing in personality studies, and a liberal sociologist, and an historian of culture, and even a religious philosopher who preached 'intuitionism'.[69] Bekhterev was exceptionally broadminded because he was exceptionally imperial in his reach. He thought to encompass all the diverse approaches to an understanding of human beings within his grand scheme of 'reflexology'. Perhaps we should not call it a scheme, but a phrase. Words that are loose enough to be slipped around every school may actually include none of them.

If psychology was to be something closer to a discipline than a blessing on everyone's venture, it needed academic entrepreneurs of a somewhat more focused or assertive type. G. I. Chelpanov was the Russian with the necessary qualifications. A student of Wundt's, he taught philosophy as well as psychology, first at Kiev then at Moscow University, where he replaced Grot. He insisted on keeping philosophy and psychology sharply distinguished, though constantly conversing with each other. The conversation might be pursued within the mind of a single individual, as it was in his. Indeed, he insisted that the future psychologists in his graduate program — a large number, rising above seventy in 1914 — must work their way through the history of philosophy, if only to become aware of various psychological theories during all the centuries when they were contained

within philosophies, before they emerged as a separate science.[70] That
seems to be the first level of meaning in the much quoted apothegm that
opened a well-known German textbook in 1908: 'Psychology has a long
past but a short history.'[71] At a deeper level admirers of the apothegm were
contrasting history in the progressive sense — a pattern of cumulative
development, as in the growth of a natural science — with philosophy in
the disparaging sense of mere speculation, wordspinning without progressive accumulation of knowledge.

Chelpanov not only insisted that his students review the clutter of
psychologies in past philosophies. He wanted them to be aware of the
divisive philosophical implications in the present-day choice of experimental
strategies and the interpretation of data. But philosophical disagreements
need not shatter scientific community, in Chelpanov's view. He believed
that scientific psychologists of all persuasions could accumulate a body of
experimental methods and data that all must acknowledge to be part of
their discipline. That may seem similar to the projects for 'objective psychology', or 'psychology without any metaphysics', which were emerging
at the turn of the century. Yet Chelpanov was critical of them. His stand —
for an argumentative separation but not a complete divorce between psychology and philosophy — may seem inconsistent, but we need not get
involved in his justifications of it.[72] For our purpose it is enough to note
that he kept philosophical criticism of rival schools in a realm of discourse
separate from experimental psychology. Therefore he could be eclectic in
psychology, eager to see a single discipline developed by a variety of
approaches, whether or not their advocates were fully aware of their
philosophical implications.

'Idealist' is the usual Stalinist label on Chelpanov. It is quite misleading,
for it implies an ontological commitment to mind or psyche as the immaterial substance investigated by psychology, and Chelpanov did not
require such a commitment of psychologists. S. L. Rubinshtein approached
the reality of Chelpanov's stand with this partisan summation: 'In general
Chelpanov had no psychological theory of his own.'[73] That is a mean way
of acknowledging Chelpanov's tolerant eclecticism. It is also a partisan
way, for it assumes that a distinctive psychological theory must have an
ontological commitment. Chelpanov was determined to encourage the
growth of scientific psychology by tolerating diverse ontologies, or none at
all.

That frame of mind at that time fitted Chelpanov to be an ideal organizer
of a large graduate program at Moscow University, which turned into
Russia's first full-fledged Institute of Psychology in 1912. Previously there
had been a number of small laboratories created at various institutions by
individual professors of psychology or psychiatry or pedagogy. From a
wealthy art dealer Chelpanov got a large donation that enabled him to put

up a new building, with the capacity, he boasted, to be the largest psychological institute in the world. He made a systematic tour of institutes in the West, including the United States, to plan his Institute in the most up-to-date fashion. At the opening ceremonies, in 1914, he looked forward to the time when psychologists around the world would speak of the Russian school with the same respect they felt then for German, English, or American psychology. Russian professionals, he declared, now had the material means to achieve that distinction, and they had the necessary professional consensus. 'The question, "Who is to develop psychology?" which only recently divided philosophers, psychologists, and physiological psychologists, has already, let us hope, become a thing of the past.' All would take part.[74]

In support of his cheery eclecticism Chelpanov could show messages of good will from a variety of schools, and not only of professional psychologists. A Russian Orthodox Bishop sent his benediction on those who were going to study 'the God-like nature of the soul'.[75] At the other extreme Pavlov, who insistently held up his pocket watch as the model of a man, sent Chelpanov his best wishes for a union of forces 'to solve the greatest task of human thought', ignoring for the moment his usual scorn for any psychological analysis of our clockwork selves.[76] Two Soviet editions of Pavlov's 'complete' works have omitted his congratulatory messages to Chelpanov,[77] for Pavlov's words upset the two-camp vision of psychology, unless one is ready to argue that Pavlov was not only a warrior for his camp but also a hypocritical diplomat. Perhaps, on some level of his mind, he was. He may have sympathized with another famous biologist, who did *not* send best wishes to Chelpanov's Institute, since he regarded it as 'a remnant of theology'.[78] On ceremonial occasions academics keep such hostility to themselves. But it is more likely that Pavlov actually felt a tolerant condescension toward Chelpanov's kind of psychology. It might soothe the impatient while neurophysiologists slowly reduced the mind to 'higher nervous activity'. Within that physiological approach, which Pavlov considered his realm, he was passionately intolerant, as we will see. Evidently Chelpanov's psychology seemed too distant to be worth a quarrel.

In educational psychology ideological issues were also strangely muted and obscured by genteel abstraction. A. I. Vvedenskii, for example, praised Chelpanov's 'rigorous methodological orientation' for restraining hasty applications of the new science in education.[79] With that decorously vague praise of rigor Vvedenskii was taking Chelpanov's side in a debate on educational psychology that began at the turn of the century and persisted through the Revolutions of 1905 and 1917 − until the 1930s, when the Stalinist regime would decree a final solution. In the post-revolutionary context the political campaign to 'push up' (*vydvigat'*) lower-class children would bring a rancorous quality to the controversy. Before the revolution psychologists could be nicely professional, for there was no organized pushing; the question was whether or how lower-class children might raise themselves individually.

Thus the educational problem for psychologists was raised to a lofty choice between pure and applied psychology. Could psychologists help teachers discover the talents and understand the problems of their individual pupils? Right away or later on? Chelpanov's response – 'later on' – protected the dignity and safety of the fledgling science. Like father Wundt he deplored the complete divorce of psychology from philosophy not only for intellectual reasons but also for defense of status. Cut off from philosophy, psychologists might become 'mere artisans', laboring in such manufactories or repair shops as schools or prisons.[80] Danger threatened along with indignity. If psychologists descended from philosophic heights to win public support by premature promises of practical benefit, public disillusion would follow, and support would collapse. Chelpanov repeated those cautions in a persistent debate with A. P. Nechaev, Russia's leading educational psychologist in the early twentieth century. Nechaev and his partisans insisted that their science was ready to help teachers, who should be organized into a nationwide system of psychological 'offices', collecting data and carrying out programs under the direction of his Institute and other centers of 'experimental pedagogics'.[81]

On a practical level tests were the focus of the debate. The Russians used an obvious neologism, *testy*, to underscore the distinction between traditional examinations, which are supposed to measure achievement, and new, scientifically designed instruments for measuring the different potentials, the inherent capabilities of individuals. Such tests responded to problems of efficiency and justice when placing individuals within increasingly large, impersonal, bureaucratic systems. Not only mass education but universal military training, modern prisons, hospitals, factories, and offices raised analogous problems of 'placement'. Sometimes psychologists indulged the utopian dream that tests, precisely measuring individual differences, would simultaneously improve efficiency and increase liberty by helping every individual find his ideal niche. Nechaev and Lange, for example, picked up American 'progressivist' talk of fitting the school to the individual child rather than the child to the school. In less utopian moods they pointed to humbler, more urgent tasks, such as discovering which children who failed had talents undiscovered by teachers' intuitive judgments, and which simply could not cope in ordinary schools but needed some special institution or program. Intelligence was not the only capacity to be measured. Two Russian psychologists pioneered in the construction of tests that were supposed to draw an accurate profile of the individual's personality, so that teachers would know the most sensible approach to each of their charges.[82]

Such issues were debated in pre-revolutionary Russia as in the West, but with less ideological heat in Russia. That may seem paradoxical in a country drifting into revolutionary upheaval, but the paradox is readily explained. The backward social context that made revolution a real possibility cast a futuristic aura about discussions of IQ tests and personality profiles. Mass education was still a dream more than a reality, which greatly reduced the urgency of 'placement'. In advanced societies supposedly democratic 'placement' had already become a widespread reality, constantly pitting belief in equality against perception of inequality, generating intense pride and envy, whose clash often centers on the schools, the social institution that is supposed to guarantee an equal start in the scramble for status. In pre-revolutionary Russia only the first steps toward universal compulsory education were being taken. Whether peasants and workers had earned their places at the bottom, whether the hereditary gentry deserved their dwindling share of places at the top, whether the intelligentsia merited positions of leadership – those were explosive questions, but they could hardly focus on the embryonic system of mass education. They pitted left against right in political conflict, with the angry parties appealing to historical grievances and justifications, not pedagogical. Psychologists tended to muffle such conflict in their professional discussions of education. They could all blame the government for the slow development of mass education. They could all be liberal believers in equality of opportunity, for they were debating it as a theme in *Zukunftsmusik*. To a large extent their 'practical' debate over testing concerned methods of placing future pupils in an imagined system of universal compulsory education when Russia would at last be modernized.

By and large they assumed without argument that the children of workers and peasants would reveal innate capacities to rise in such a system, supposing only that the people (*narod*) would be converted from its uncivilized condition (*nekul'turnost'*). They resembled Charlotte Brontë back in the 1840s imagining an ideal village schoolteacher for her developing country: undaunted by her meager salary and cultural isolation, she would check her revulsion against the boorish children of 'the British peasantry', she would tell herself that all were worthy of her efforts, some especially so, though she would naturally rise out of the classroom the moment she became 'independent', that is, found a more honorific source of income by inheriting money.[83] To that inconsistent dream the Russian psychologists of the early twentieth century added some scientific debate whether their contribution of IQ and personality tests might help the ideal teacher achieve an ideally efficient separation of the sheep and the goats.

When trial runs of Binet's intelligence test graded almost three-fourths of Russian schoolchildren significantly lower than corresponding age groups in Paris, Russian psychologists did not fall into arguments about genetic inequality. They took cultural explanations for granted. Chelpanov pointed to one Russian school where IQ scores exceeded Parisian levels, and noted that its pupils were largely children of the intelligentsia. That was offered as evidence that IQ scores were culturally determined, not as an argument for the genetic superiority of the intelligentsia over the peasants and workers. Indeed, Chelpanov accused all the intelligence and personality tests of failing to take into account the cultural milieux that shaped the minds whose individual capacities were supposedly being measured against each other. His other major criticism concerned 'mechanistic atomism'. The tests assumed that intelligence or personality is a mechanical sum of separable skills and proclivities rather than an organically functioning whole. In response to such criticisms Nechaev and the other advocates of testing acknowledged the imperfect nature of their instruments, but stressed the minimal accomplishments that could be proved, such as discovering which children could not cope with standard programs and would be turned against education for good if they were thrust into one that did not suit their individuality.[84]

Were there ideological elements in this division of professional opinion? No doubt, but it was impossible to distinguish them from the scientific elements. The opponents of tests preferred to rely on teachers' intuitive judgments in the grading of children. We could call that an ideological preference of political rightists, if we knew that tests favor the lower classes, that is, are more likely than teachers' judgments to discover hidden talents and soluble personal problems in lower-class children. If we knew the opposite, that standardized tests discriminate against the lower classes − are more likely to lock children in their parents' social status − then the *advocates* of tests could be labeled ideological rightists, perpetuators of the *status quo*. But we may not make such neat correlations, for ideology and knowledge are all mixed up in such issues.

In advanced societies bitter experience has inured us to explicit, vehement ideology in a debate that was originally supposed to be scientific. In pre-revolutionary Russia that form of ideological conflict was muted and obscured by the embryonic state of mass education. Not right *v.* left but pure *v.* applied was the dividing line between opponents and advocates of tests. Since pure *v.* applied may be linked with professionally cautious *v.* professionally bold, one might still argue that the advocates of tests were more 'progressive' than the opponents. The advocates were more willing to risk their professional dignity and safety for the supposed sake of social progress − to serve the people (*narod*), as Russians were likely to say. That is why they would be warmly supported by the Soviet regime, for a while. But it must be stressed that before 1917 both sides felt themselves committed 'to serve the people'. Even the purest of educational psychologists fancied themselves to be intelligentsia as well as professionals. To find the ideological tensions generated by that dual character, one must dig past their technical discussions of tests, down into their self-appraisals, their justifications of their careers in relation to 'the people' and its needs.

One quickly senses the presence of thoughts and feelings too painful to be confronted openly. The schoolteacher's lot in rural Russia — and that is where the bulk of 'the people' were waiting to be served — was very grim: near-starvation salaries and constant humiliation; a chronic sense of alienation both from the higher ranks of professionals and from the people they were supposed to be educating.[85] Were those teachers actually helped by educational psychologists doing research in urban institutes and universities? Or was that research an indulgence in privilege, an excuse for separation from the miseries of harrassed teachers in the freezing classrooms of rural Russia? Such painfully direct questions are missing in the lofty discussions of educational psychology. In most cases one finds occasional remarks that transmute such impermissible thoughts into reassuring pieties.

Consider in this light the career of K. N. Kornilov. He was a son of 'the rural intelligentsia', a fancy Russian way of saying that his father was a provincial bookkeeper. The son seemed locked into some equally humble status at the age of six by the father's untimely death and the consequent impossibility of a good education. He received only enough schooling to become at nineteen a village teacher or *'narodnyi uchitel"*, a 'teacher of the people'. That highflown title described the lowly job of thrusting very elementary education upon mostly unwilling peasant children in 'a dumb (*glukhoi*) Siberian village'. I am quoting an admiring Soviet biographer, who naively repeats the usual mixture of ritual respect and actual pity for 'teachers of the people', as he admires Kornilov for raising himself out of that servile dignity. Studying all on his own, Kornilov earned an *attestat zrelosti* ('certificate of maturity'). It happened to be 1905 when he passed the exam, and so qualified himself to enter Moscow University. Evidently he was singlemindedly devoted to his career, for he took no part in the revolutionary turmoil of the time. He studied hard and well, and on graduating in 1910 was invited to continue as a graduate student. In a short time he became a senior research assistant in Chelpanov's Institute, within sight of a university professorship. But he still believed in serving the people. As Kornilov piously explained in 1912: 'Cast up by a fortunate wave out of the mass of the people's teachers, I understood that I am obliged to devote all my energies to the service of those who have, in the past, been chastised by many but caressed by no one.'[86]

Neither Kornilov nor his admiring biographer perceived the incongruous mixture of narodism and careerism in such comments. I intend no caricature of Kornilov as an individual. Such unexamined pieties were typical of educational psychologists. In explanation I note two features of their professional context. Schoolteachers had very low status, but they could rise by leaving the classroom. They could rise by becoming either administrators, which is to say bosses over their former colleagues — as Lenin's father did — or academic specialists in 'pedagogics', which is to say teachers of

teachers and scholarly researchers in the mysteries of education and psychology.* In either capacity they had cause to wonder whether higher
status was earned merely by social elevation above 'the mass of the people's
teachers' or also by genuinely useful service to teachers and pupils. Once
again we have come to an area where knowledge that claimed to be
scientific was — and is — indistinguishable from ideology.

Consider what Kornilov did as a graduate student and research assistant
in Chelpanov's Institute. He accepted his mentor's prudent belief that the
science of psychology was not ready to deliver practically useful tests of
individual capabilities. So he attacked the underlying, purely scientific
issues. He studied individual differences in reaction times; they can be
measured with great precision and reliability. He established a scientific
correlation: the intervals between stimulus and response grow longer as the
experimenter increases the intellectual labor required by the response.[87]
Now I *am* indulging in caricature, partly because a solemnly detailed
picture of Kornilov's research would be unbearably dull. Besides, caricature
dramatizes the most striking characteristic of the subject: inanity, in Kornilov's case, as in so much research. Even if that harsh judgment of his
research is unfair, there is no room for argument about the incongruity of
his work as a scientist and his self-proclaimed obligation to serve the
people. His studies of reaction time had no visible connection with such
service.

But Kornilov, in common with all his elevated colleagues, hardly noticed
the lack of fit between his scientific work and his justification of it. He was
sensitive to the increasing separation between actual beliefs and ritual profession of traditional religion. He echoed the Western educational theorists
who considered that 'a grave disease of our age'.[88] As genuine belief ebbs
away, he argued, outward confession of faith becomes 'a yoke for testing
subordination' to political authority.[89] He refrained from such critical reflections on his own faith as a professional, his declared belief that a
successful career in psychological science served the people. In short, Kornilov was a sober solid citizen, a prudently wholehearted participant in the
world he found about him. That personality would carry him successfully
through the Revolution of 1917 as it had through 1905. If his mentor
Chelpanov, and their leading professional adversary, Nechaev, had a different type of personality, it was mainly in the greater assertiveness that
came with more years of professional advancement, the more solid sense of
self as they rose from giving deference to receiving it. After 1917 they

---

* Contrast the improvement of status by separation from pupils with the physician's pride
in maintaining some clinical practice as he rises. Before the nineteenth century, when
medicine began its fusion with natural science, 'doctors', the learned men of medicine, kept
an analogous distance from patients, whom they did not touch, and from the lower strata of
the medical profession, who did soil their hands on patients.

would find it very hard to change, while Kornilov would rise above them in the Soviet setting by transferring allegiance to new mentors.

There was in pre-revolutionary Russia at least one educational psychologist who was unusually critical of himself, his profession, and the world at large. That was P. P. Blonskii, avid seeker of truth in philosophy as well as psychology, ardent devotee of the people's liberation by revolutionary action, and — luckily for the historian — compulsive bearer of witness, whose autobiographical essays reveal more than he intended.[90] He was born to the impoverished gentry, sufficiently *déclassé* to hate the system that nurtured a sense of nobility and simultaneously mocked it, inwardly in his soul, as well as outwardly in his status. His father earned a meager living as a clerk, and deliberately elevated his mind to stoic dignity, flying out of temper only when his wife asked him to do some shopping or talk business with someone. An older brother cultivated important people in hope of juridical positions that conferred status with little or no pay until one was past thirty. His mother approved such dignified careerism, while despising those who fawn in hope of immediate reward. She grimly pinched pennies to keep the family in respectable clothes and genteel occupations, and passed on to Pavel Petrovich, as he genially confessed, a penny-wise-pound-foolish way with money. His obsession with small change was imposed by wretched circumstances; he rose above it with lordly disdain for big money.

As a university student Blonskii joined the Socialist Revolutionary Party, and suffered repeated spells in prison during the first revolutionary upheavals in 1904−6. But he also managed to become a professional in the emerging discipline of experimental psychology, with a special interest in educational applications. Thus he hoped, as the revolution seemed to fail, that he could serve the people as scientist and pedagogue, and earn a living in the process. He taught at secondary schools and pedagogical institutes, published scholarly pieces, and found himself drawn into Chelpanov's Institute at Moscow University half against his will, full of ambivalence and moral doubt as he rose toward a university professorship. He endowed his mundane career with the aura of a stoic *Kulturträger* by confessing the failed hope, the absurd striving to see a purpose in striving, the *fin-de-siècle* malaise that was especially acute among the Russian intelligentsia:

> It has long since become a hackneyed phrase to say that our time is one of intensified criticism, or rather, of skepticism. Our favorite writers, our journalism, our literature, the mood of people all about us — all are full of negation, exhaustion, an avid lust for some temple that is still uncreated. We have been moving along a road littered with the ruins of shrines, and our gait is sometimes indecisive and uncertain, sometimes nervously hurried and unnaturally bold, like the gait

of people who are tired of wandering and are rushing to rest somewhere, no matter where. And behind us our younger brothers are
coming; their negation is even stronger, their exhaustion even more
unbearable.[91]

Those were indeed hackneyed phrases when Blonskii published them, in
1908, age twenty-four. But he was not merely striking a fashionable pose.
He was indulging a wild romanticism, a self-critical revulsion against the
professional's life of small deeds and limited expectations. All that on the
level of grand ideology and philosophy, on which he published copiously
before the Revolution of 1917. On the practical level of pedagogy, where
he earned his living, he taught a lot and published comparatively little. Like
Chelpanov, he tended to doubt the practical usefulness of educational
psychology, until the Revolution of 1917 installed a regime whose wild
romantic yearning for a new order exceeded his own. Then, as we shall
see, he would be the very first psychologist to endorse the new regime, and
he would move his facile pen from speculative philosophy to educational
psychology, which became 'practical' in the post-revolutionary context.
Romantic personalities can be adaptable in their own ways.

I have been indulging in the advantages of hindsight more than many
historians would consider proper, using post-revolutionary eventualities to
illuminate pre-revolutionary characteristics of Russian psychology. Very
well. Let us play the 'pure' historian's game of make-believe. Let us
pretend we do not know what happened after 1917. Even so, restricting
our vision to the secluded world of professional psychologists in pre-
revolutionary Russia, we can sense the enormous trouble of the larger
society, which did not cease to disturb the professionals' dream of science
simultaneously serving the people and advancing one's career.

Consider the friendship of Grot with Leo Tolstoy, the turmoil that
resulted, and the disturbing questions that the turmoil raised – and that
Tolstoy persisted in raising – about the profession of the scientist. While a
young professor at Odessa University, Grot began to move away from
positivism, partly under the influence of Tolstoy's writings. He sent the
celebrated writer and prophet a copy of his first scholarly treatise, met him
on moving to Moscow University, and became a lasting friend. That
surprised Tolstoy, for he generally disliked academic intellectuals. But Grot
seemed to be an exception. He was genuinely interested in the tormenting
questions that had pushed Tolstoy to consider suicide, and

he was not interested in them, as most scholars are, only for the sake
of their academic chair. He studied them for his own sake, for himself.
It was difficult for him to emancipate himself from that superstition
of science in which he matured, in the service of which he achieved
outstanding worldly success. But I saw that his living, sincere and

moral nature persisted, involuntarily, incessantly, in striving for that emancipation.[92]

The 'superstition of science' that strained the friendship was the belief that reason can reveal the 'meaning of life', and thus discover what we should do with our lives. Tolstoy's celebrated conversion to a religion of his own intuition began with rejection of that 'superstition'.

When Grot started Russia's major journal of philosophy and psychology, he sent a copy to Tolstoy, who noted in his journal the reaction that he politely abridged in a letter to Grot. He was angry at an article that tried to explain human consciousness by an absurdly misplaced mathematical style of reasoning, and he found 'the journal as a whole a collection of articles without thought or clarity of expression'.[93] About the same time — 1889 — Grot dropped in with two other professors, interrupting Tolstoy's emotional response to George Kennan's book on the Siberian exile system, and intensely annoying him with their own preoccupations:

> cigarettes, *iubilei* [celebrations of leading academics on their anniver-
> saries], collections of articles, dinners with wine, and with all that, in
> the style of their profession, philosophical chatter. Zverev [a professor
> of philosophy and law, and a government official] is frightful in his
> madness. *Homo homini lupus.* There is no god, there are no moral
> principles — there is only process [*techen'e*]. Dreadful hypocrites,
> bookworms, and harmful.[94]

(The third professor, as it happened, was the one that Lenin would call a 'philosophical fascist'.) But somehow, in Tolstoy's judgment, Grot avoided complete defilement by his professional milieu. Tolstoy preferred him to V. S. Solov'ev, who was winning a reputation as the leading academic advocate of a religious revival, in opposition both to the dead formalism of the official Church, which excommunicated Tolstoy, and to the faith in science that prevailed among the intelligentsia.

> If you compare [Grot] with Solov'ev, both are equally superficial, but
> Grot is free and seeks truth everywhere, while Solov'ev is confused
> and can no longer seek truth anywhere except (excuse me) the fouled
> little refuge of the church. Solov'ev is more talented, that's true, but
> Grot is more broadly educated.[95]

The famine of 1891–2 occasioned a political test of the unusual friend-ship. Grot reacted to the famine with the characteristic gesture of the liberal academic intelligentsia: he prepared an issue of his journal, *Problems of Philosophy and Psychology*, 'to aid the starving', and asked Tolstoy for a contribution. Tolstoy's form of aid was a denunciation of the social system that brought the working classes to starvation while keeping a privileged minority, the intelligentsia included, physically comfortable and loftily cultured. 'The misery of the people is the condition of our well-being'. That brutal fact was too obvious to be concealed in Russia, unlike the advanced industrial countries, 'which feed themselves from their colonies'.[96] The censors arrested the issue of the journal carrying that inflammatory essay, but when it was published abroad a right-wing paper reproduced it in Russia, to stir up patriotic anger at Tolstoy and the left.

Revolutionaries like Lenin were overjoyed. It hardly mattered to the right or the left whether Tolstoy was denouncing the personal sin of those who ate while others starved or the social system which generated that sin, or both. Nor does it matter a great deal to the historian of high culture in pre-revolutionary Russia. The significant fact is Tolstoy's accusation against high culture: it was part of an exploitative and sinful order. The professionals who claimed to be serving the people were actually living off their misery. If they worked at the natural sciences and discovered practically useful truths, they were serving the system that exploited the people. If they worked at the humanities or at a hybrid discipline like psychology, they either asked pointless, factual questions, which science can answer, or they asked vital, moral questions, which science cannot answer. The most vital question, Tolstoy insisted, was what to do with our lives, how to live − *chto delat'*? What to do?[97]

I have followed Tolstoy's habit of running together questioning of one's purpose in existence with denunciation of the social order, and of both with his 'campaign against science', as it is usually called. The label is misleading if it implies a basic challenge to the factual claims of scientific knowledge. Tolstoy tended to concede those claims without examination, even in such an inchoate science as psychology, for he considered such factual knowledge largely irrelevant to the moral problems that obsessed him, which he pressed upon his fellow intellectuals with stunning simplicity:

> If the arrangement of society is bad, as ours is, and a small number of people have power over the majority and oppress it, every victory over nature will inevitably only serve to increase that power and that oppression. That is what is actually happening.[98]

To the human sciences, including the would-be science of psychology, Tolstoy presented a more severe indictment than to the natural sciences, reaching the level where moral accusation fuses with metaphysical horror. I shall examine that below; here I am making the elementary point that Tolstoy denied that natural science contributed to progress, and was doubly disrespectful of academic psychology. He broadcast that disrespect even in his posthumous tribute to Grot, who died of tuberculosis at an early age.[99] When some reading in Wundt or chance encounters reminded Tolstoy of other psychologists, he jotted disrespectful comments in his journal − mocking, for example, the intellectuals who tried to be fashionable by discussing Chelpanov.[100] Of course the reading public did not see Tolstoy's journal. What they did see, in the published fiction and essays that had an enormous resonance — and in the comedy *Fruits of Enlightenment* — was contempt for the human sciences, psychology included. That was an ominous portent for the field, since Chelpanov perceived that respect for higher learning was a more reliable support than hopes of practical utility, which might be disappointed. He might pride himself on the rich man's donation that founded his Institute, and on the modest success of his public lectures and popular booklets. But those were trifles compared with the influence of Tolstoy. It was to him and to other imaginative writers that the educated public looked for an understanding of the human mind, psyche, spirit, or soul — whatever it is that modern psychology claims to explain scientifically.

Of course, Tolstoy was unique or at least highly unusual in the new faith that he offered in place of science. Consider then Chekhov, who was also one of the most widely and intensely loved authors at the turn of the century, and was a great admirer of science. More discriminating than Tolstoy in his view of the sciences, he was more contemptuously dismissive of academic psychology. Tolstoy was willing to place Wundt's discipline on the same level as biology in its accumulation of factual knowledge. Chekhov was not. He took physiology and evolutionary studies very seriously, but brushed off 'bookish, academic [*uchenaia*] psychology' as 'a fabrication, not a science, something like alchemy, which it is time to put in the archives.'[101] If there were any imaginative writers at the turn of the century who took an active, respectful interest in academic psychology, I have not succeeded in finding them. It is also true that none of them made a public issue of their attitude toward academic psychology, as they did with respect to evolutionary biology or physics. One may therefore draw the obvious inference. Educated and thoughtful Russians shared with their imaginative writers a mode of inquiry into human psychology from which the academic discipline called psychology had estranged itself. The discipline was tolerated, perhaps respected to some degree, with other motives than the passion for self-awareness and social understanding that bound educated Russians and their imaginative authors in a highly contentious community of intense feeling.

For direct evidence of what those motives might have been, one might dig out rare scraps of 'popular psychology', as we now call reportage and commentary on the new science.[102] They are *rare* scraps, which may seem strange to Westerners, particularly to Americans, who are deluged with popular psychology. So much the better. The sense of strangeness may help us understand the distinctively Russian context within which the cosmopolitan science was trying to establish itself. In Russia one finds very few popularizations of psychology as a guide to health and success, a guide that requires us to regard ourselves and other humans as instruments, to be manipulated for practical ends.[103] That functional view of human beings, which seems to avoid the problem of a human essence, was developing within psychological science, and also within commercial life, but it was making little headway in the dominant fields of Russian high culture, that is, in imaginative literature and political ideologies. Liberal attitudes had progressed sufficiently to win toleration of psychological science, but little more. The characteristic attitude toward the human sciences, as one finds it expressed in the favorite journals of the educated Russian public, was epitomized by a 1914 article that noted 'the anarchy of thought', which Comte had feared might come with science. Straining to look beyond the anarchy, the author tried to justify hope for a positive answer to this grandiose question:

> Can we foresee in the near future the establishment of a broad, whole and viable world view, which would not only be an object or product of philosophical curiosity but could also serve as a thread of Ariadne in the labyrinth of life for all those who seek and strive, for all who ponder seriously the puzzling question of the 'meaning of life', of the goals toward which humanity is moving, of the earthly vale with its good and bad?[104]

Psychological science had little or nothing to offer such a mentality.

Russian journals of popular science were mostly indifferent to the new science, and so were religious journals, with this predictable difference: while the former took occasional notice of efforts to find physiological or chemical explanations of psychic processes, the latter made occasional efforts to see a spiritual essence re-emerging in a discipline that was actually moving toward some kind of functionalism. The functionalist trend is apparent in hindsight. At the time disorder seemed supreme, and neither physicalism nor spiritualism could derive satisfaction from 'the chaos of diverse trends that constitute at present the actual content of the science'.[105] I quote from an unusual, long review of Russian psychology that appeared toward the end of the century in a religious journal. The author hoped that Russian psychologists would overcome the chaos by reviving the Slavophile ideal of 'autonomous wisdom, corresponding to the basic principles of the old Russian educated mind [*obrazovannost*'], capable of subordinating the divided educated mind of the West to the whole conscious mind [*soznanie*] of believing reason.'[106]

That was a wistful dream, as the author virtually admitted, in tone if not explicit statement. Nothing so anemic as nostalgia for an imaginary wisdom of the Russian past could satisfy the yearning that educated Russians shared with imaginative writers and political ideologists. To the extent that there was a community of high culture in pre-revolutionary Russia, such writers and ideologists were its quarreling spokesmen. It was a typically modern community in its sense of anarchy, its constant reminders that modern knowledge is a clutter of fragments, wisdom a partisan claim, art at war with both. In Russia, unlike the West, that anarchic, extremely contentious quality of modern high culture corresponded to an explosively high level of contentiousness in relationships of class, of ethnic groups, and of politics.

Within such a context the tiny community of academic psychologists pursued the dream of quietly secluded scientists arriving at human under-standing through the patient summation of sensibly restricted investigations. The psychologists who sought public support through promise of practical help found few people interested in their kind of help, and anyhow they risked a backlash of disillusion, as Chelpanov warned. He and his sym-pathizers appealed to liberal intellectual curiosity concerning a possible science of the mind, which would be neither physiology nor philosophy, nor poetic vision nor political ideology. Such psychologists achieved a modest degree of public support, and seemed to risk only indifference – in the *pre*-revolutionary context. After 1917 they would face a regime inflamed with poetic vision and political ideology, convinced that revolution can create a new coherence in high culture which will then serve 'the people', free at last, raised to power over their learned servants.

5

Neurophysiology and the Poetry of the Problem

But Pavlov and Bekhterev, where did their scientific discoveries fit in? They did not fit, either in neurophysiology or in psychology. They were at the confused boundary between the two disciplines. Or maybe, if we accept Pavlov's scornful view of psychology, his discoveries marked the advancing boundary of physiology, with nothing beyond it but 'the poetry of the problem',[1] the subjective constructs of the mind contemplating itself. Yet Pavlov himself was twitted, by fellow physiologists, for leaving rigorous study of the nervous system to dabble in psychological fantasies.[2] Within the contentious discipline of psychology one strange new school, the American behaviorists, acclaimed Pavlov as their master: his studies of the conditioned reflex showed how to manage without the concept of mind *and without neural explanation*, though Pavlov insisted that he was achieving precisely that, reduction of mind to neural process. Was this clamor of tongues the cumulative progress of scientific knowledge or poetic creation of 'ruin upon ruin, rout on rout, confusion worse confounded?' I offer poetic creation as an optimistic alternative to the bleakest possibility: neither cumulative science nor poetic dialectic but incoherent babel, neither discourse nor music but noise.

When Pavlov shrugged off 'the poetry of the problem', he was using 'poetry' as many people do in an age of science, to point disparagingly at expression of feeling, mere subjectivity as opposed to objective knowledge. Pavlov was in his fifties when he joined the new movement to create an 'objective psychology', or simply to dissolve psychology in the laws of 'higher nervous activity'. Some turn-of-the-century polarization of mentalities drew him, late in his career, to declare that conditioned reflex experiments 'can exhaust the whole content of the so-called psychic function. The whole mind [*dusha*] can be compressed within certain rules of such objective research.'[3]

In the nineteenth century the most eminent physiologists had disclaimed such extremism; they had placed subjective knowledge in a privileged realm, beyond the reach of their science. The most famous disclaimer had been Du Bois-Reymond's '*Ignorabimus*': physiology could never reduce mental phenomena to functions of the nervous system, for physiology could not explain the least element of subjectivity, the most primitive sensation that a wriggling worm may experience. Objective science could explain the nervous mechanisms of wriggling; only poetic intuition could understand the feeling. That sort of distinction pointed toward a dualistic separation of body and soul, the one to be explained by physiologists, the other by poets, philosophers, churchmen. Psychologists tried to avoid such polarization. So did some physiologists, if not in their scientific work, at least in essays that sought some common ground for physiology and poetry − and thereby kept life in the tension between them.

Consider two representative examples, an 1865 lecture by Claude Bernard, and Tsion's adaptation of it for a Russian audience, the one groping for common ground, the other floundering toward polarization. To the diverse savants and literary artists assembled at the French Academy Claude Bernard set the following question: Does the physiologist's understanding of the heart as a pump subvert the significance that poets, and ordinary people in everyday life, have traditionally attached to the heart as the seat of the soul or at least of the feelings? On monistic philosophical grounds he ruled out the possibility: 'Truth cannot differ from itself; the truth of the scientist cannot contradict the truth of the artist.'[4] But he had no coherent argument to support his faith. He went off on a routine popularization of what was known about neural connections between the brain and the heart, 'the two most perfect gearboxes [*rouages*] of the living machine'.[5]

By emphasizing the interaction of the brain and heart *rouages* in the machine's functioning, Bernard was trying to imply a response to his opening question, but he was evidently aware of wandering from it, back into mere physiology. Toward the end of the lecture he began laboring to mix in poetry by conflating body and feeling, using 'heart' both as a name for the circulatory pump and as a symbol for emotional thinking. Thus he felt free to suggest 'physiological' justification for the belief that women have 'tenderer hearts' than men: 'cold reason' is less capable of restraining feelings in women than in men.

Finally, in a closing paragraph of honest inconsistency that does him credit, Bernard returned to the philosophical credo that he could not prove and could not abandon. He disagreed with those who said that 'scientific positivism is bound to kill [poetic] inspiration.' There might be epochs during which science is both too advanced and too imperfect, and therefore troubles the poet and the philosopher. That was, he conceded, the present case with physiology. But he declared it 'a transitory state, and I am convinced that when physiology will be sufficiently advanced, the poet, the

philosopher, and the physiologist will all understand each other.'[6] With
that gesture toward some positivist resolution of deeper troubles than he
cared to discuss, he stopped.

In Russia Il'ia Tsion took up these themes in an 1873 public lecture at the
Medical Academy, devoid of puzzlement or wavering. All basic issues
were already resolved: 'Science and art, physiology and poetry, as you see,
do not in any way contradict each other in their understanding of the heart
as the organ of the feelings.'[7] He based that conclusion on an anti–positivist,
dualistic credo. Science and art could not contradict each other, because
they worked in two different realms of being, the body and the spirit.
Between the two he perceived 'a whole abyss'. That was a favorite symbol
of romantic poets, but Tsion showed no sign of their anguish, their
yearning to leap the abyss. Maybe he was contemptuously indifferent,
maybe simply ignorant. Whatever the inner state of his spirit, his hand
wrote a cheerful sketch of mutually beneficial correspondence between
body and spirit, in a philistine's universe.

Physiologists, Tsion was happy to announce, could read the mind by
careful measurement of changing heartbeat and blood pressure. It was
possible to devise a lie detector, which could distinguish falsehearted suitors
from sincere lovers, to the inestimable benefit of rich men's tenderhearted
daughters. My paraphrase is mocking; Tsion was simply glad to tell the
practical advantages of science in a dualistic but complementary world. He
gave no thought to the possibility that different kinds of mental disturbance
might have the same effect on heartbeat and blood pressure, and he seemed
quite unaware of those tender hearts that are disturbed just by thinking of
human consciousness trapped within decaying flesh machines. Perhaps
Tsion was aware, but considered such emotional thinking unworthy of the
male heart. More assertively than Bernard he announced 'a complete
physiological foundation' for the traditional belief that women's hearts are
different from men's hearts: less rational, more emotional.

Of course Tsion did not pause to reflect on his switches in meaning, as
he used 'heart' sometimes to indicate the physical organ of circulation,
sometimes to point toward the emotional aspect of personality, and other
times to suggest one side of an ontological duality, spirit as distinct from
matter, separated by 'a whole abyss' yet miraculously cooperative. He was
reporting the conclusions of science, not the inconclusive arguments of
philosophy and ideology. Science, he told his audience, if it is properly
understood, would bring them back to the traditional pieties that had been
disturbed by certain physiologists.[8] He was hinting at Sechenov, his predecessor in the Medical Academy's chair of physiology, as he denounced
the materialist belief that physiology could explain the spirit along with the
body. His vision of maidens using lie detectors to choose husbands was
more vulgarly materialist than anything one can find in Sechenov, but
Tsion could not perceive that. Modern ideologies are most powerful when

they appear to their devotees as the obvious truth of science and practical experience.

Tsion was supremely confident of his opinions. Had he not won universal respect among physiologists by his discoveries? His major achievement — in association with Ludwig — was to establish the function of the depressor nerve, which helps to correlate heartbeat and blood pressure. Of course the experiments which established that function rigorously excluded any psychic element; they were done on rabbits, without concern for states of mind such as lying or truth-telling. Tsion was masterful in swift sure vivisection of warm-blooded animals, and brilliant in elegantly simple experimental design, two skills that he passed on to his admiring student Pavlov.

Tsion noted the contrast between the unforced consensus of physiologists in their restricted field and the world's violent discord on politics or ideology, but he denounced the positivist impulse to seek universal consensus by expanding the method of physiologists to encompass all spheres. Outside of science discord could not be reasoned away; it must be repressed by autocracy and established churches. His denunciation of positivism and materialism could hardly avoid vehement irrationalism. He did thoroughly materialistic physiology, while denying the power of physiology to understand psychic processes, urging the use of lie detectors to achieve such an understanding, and calling on arrogant scientists to learn the truths of the heart from authoritarian religions.[9]

SECHENOV'S VISION, AND RETREAT

Unlike Tsion — unlike Claude Bernard for that matter — Sechenov gave very serious thought to the confused boundary where physiology is entangled with psychology. His speculative essays on that subject were written for the general public, since he was consciously venturing beyond the bounds of the specialist's rigorous knowledge.[10] We must examine his work in physiology itself, if we would discover the process by which he was drawn to the boundary of his discipline, and then driven back by the intractable difficulties he found there.

At the outset Sechenov showed no interest in anything approaching psychology, not even in the study of neural systems. He began his work in physiology on the molecular level, which is prior to the cell, not to mention higher level biological systems. In his doctoral dissertation (1860) he analyzed alcoholic intoxication, in the biochemical sense of poisoning, not the psychophysiological sense of drunkenness. At one point he seemed to exclude the higher levels from his discipline by defining the physiologist as 'a physico-chemist who deals with phenomena of the animal organism'.[11] Shortly after he wrote that, post-doctoral work in Carl Ludwig's research group drew him out of such a severely limited view of physiology, to the analysis of nervous systems. He skipped over the nerve cell or neuron. It would not be clearly discerned until the 1890s, and Sechenov was not among the pioneering microscopists who were on the way to that discovery. He leaped from the molecule to the nervous system as the organizer of bodily motions. At the outset he shared the simple old belief that the function of nerves is simply to excite action in muscles. In his dissertation he flatly declared: 'Nerves holding back movement do not exist.'[12] That view was already obsolete, as he soon learned in the broad reading which would be his habit for the rest of his life. It is a habit that can interfere with creative leaps by loading too much information on the mind, but the early effect on the youthful Sechenov was to provoke a most insightful stroke of the scientific imagination.

German physiologists, he learned, had discovered that nerves can hold back or inhibit muscular action. When the vivisectionist stimulates the vagus nerve of a frog's beating heart, the heart stops, and starts again when the vagal stimulation stops. When he cuts out the frog's brain, the body's reflexes, working through the spinal cord alone, are intensified. Evidently some nervous structures turn off or diminish muscular action, while others turn it on or intensify it. Sechenov felt a surge of insight, joined to a great challenge:

> The problem ... I have always related to more passionately than all the others in physiology ... fixed itself in my head from the very first time I read [E. H.] Weber's thought that the intensification of reflexes after the [frog's] head is cut off may depend on the removal of mechanisms which tonically mitigate reflexes.[13]

In other words, the brain must contain centers governing inhibition as well as excitation.

If I may recast Sechenov's hypothesis in the favored jargon of our day: there must be a control panel with off- as well as on-switches. The central nervous system cannot turn the head simply by ordering one set of muscles to contract; it must simultaneously order antagonistic muscles to relax. That example comes from Sherrington in the generation after Sechenov's. We cannot help using hindsight, but we must be aware, as we do, that we are simplifying the difficulties confronting Sechenov. When we take Sherrington as our guide – I repeat: we cannot help doing so, the knowledge gained by neurophysiology is cumulative – we are excluding the psychophysical issue from the problem of inhibition. Sechenov tried very hard to include it. He had been attracted not only to Weber's hypothesis concerning inhibitory nerve action but also to Griesinger's notion that thought must be an "interrupted reflex'.[14] Centers of inhibition in the brain would be the mechanisms of interruption, hence of thought. The reflex concept of the brain-mind could be proven experimentally.

He was lucky to be working with Carl Ludwig when the bold idea came

to him. Part of Ludwig's greatness as a teacher was his genial encouragement of creative disagreement. He thought that physiologists tracing neural
circuits were not ready to reach into the brain. Experimental techniques
and the understanding of the brain's structure were still too crude. He told
Sechenov that one might as well try to analyze the timekeeping of a watch
by shooting bullets into it, hoping to correlate damage of particular parts
with particular alterations of functioning. But Ludwig offered such criticism
genially.[15] He did not obstruct, he challenged, and Sechenov made a major
discovery. By stimulating a frog's brain with salt or electricity, he inhibited
the animal's spinal reflexes. While he stimulated the brain, he could pinch a
foot without causing retraction. When the effect was strong, he could cut
off the foot with a shears, and the leg would not leap from the shears that
mutilated it. Sechenov reasoned that the spinal cord, which governs such
reflexes as the retraction of the foot, is itself governed by superior centers
of inhibition in the brain. He presented that argument in a landmark article
of 1863, under the sponsorship of Claude Bernard.[16] (The experiments he
had conceived in Ludwig's laboratory were carried out in Bernard's, but he
felt a disapproving coolness in the French scientist and regarded Ludwig as
his inspiring teacher.)[17]

The cosmopolitan community of neurophysiologists paid Sechenov the
compliment of vigorous reaction, disputing and testing his argument that
there must be centers of inhibition in the brain. Critics showed that it did
not matter precisely where the frog's brain was stimulated; inhibition of
spinal reflexes followed in any case. Indeed, a sufficiently powerful stimulus
to the peripheral nervous system had a similar effect.[18] Sechenov's response
to such criticism was to intensify his own experiments, testing a variety of
stimulants at varying strengths in diverse parts of the brain, trying to find
particular inhibitory effects on spinal reflexes. By the spring of 1867 nervous
exhaustion sent him to Karlsbad for a rest. Then he renewed his experiments at the University of Graz, where he felt a momentary climax of near
success, followed by a lasting sense of failure.

We can trace the curve, for he was sending constant reports to his wife.
In the fall of 1867 he wrote: 'My sweet little baby, these experiments will
not yield in importance one bit to what I did in Paris, and in elegance will
exceed all that I know of in the physiology of the nervous system up to the
present.'[19] She was wrong to reproach him for ignoring the writings of
psychologists. He saw no point in studying metaphysical psychology, but
since he expected to get heavily involved in 'physiological psychology', he
was reading such authors as Spencer and especially Bain. His great dream
was to put 'medical psychology' on a solidly experimental basis in neurophysiology. That would be his 'swan song'. He might 'perish, but leading
a great army'.[20]

Unfortunately, the Soviet editors who published those letters censored
them heavily. Sechenov may have diverged too flagrantly from their mythic

image of the all–conquering materialist hero, as he descended from the excited hopes he communicated to his wife in 1867. By the end of February 1868 he was stressing the great difficulties that were threatening his expected breakthrough: 'The deeper in the forest, the bigger the logs'. That proverb clung to hope, and so did his report of laughing at the explanations he sometimes imagined, of struggling desperately with 'the frightful complexity of the phenomena', of losing sleep. He sometimes felt that he would go out of his mind, but more and more he recognized the central, paralyzing difficulty: he could not find distinct neural structures to correlate with the distinct functions of excitation and inhibition.[21]

Correlation of structure and function, the classic method of biological science, had won major triumphs in neurophysiology when sensory and motor nerves were distinguished from each other, the ones carrying stimuli to the spinal cord, the others carrying reflexive signals out to the muscles. But the extrapolation of that scheme to the twin functions of excitation and inhibition brought great frustration, for those two functions could not be correlated with two distinct neural structures. Sechenov's critics emphasized that frustration, the capacity of any nerve to be either inhibitory or excitatory, depending on the intensity and duration of stimuli. They hypothesized that inhibition must be a product of intense or prolonged excitation. Since distinction of structure could not be made, they were trying to dissolve distinction of function.

In effect they were trying to return to the old notion that the sole function of nerves is to excite action in muscles. Inhibitory effects might be the result of an overload of excitatory charges, or of some wavelike interference pattern on the model of optics, or of fatigue in the neural matter with rest ensuing. Sechenov's hypothesis of distinct functions associated with distinct structures was not only difficult to square with known facts, it was horrendous in the future difficulties it conjured up: if centers of inhibition could not be found in the brain or in other gross parts of the nervous system, they might be located in particular nerve cells distributed throughout the system. How could the physiologist hope to explain the coordinated functioning of the whole system, if he faced the prospect of charting millions of microscopic rheostats and on–off switches?

In 1883, to take a notable example of the discussion, *Nature* published a long review of the conflicting hypotheses. The author began with 'the classic definition of inhibition', as it is now conceived: 'the arrest of the function of one neural structure by the activity of another neural structure'.[22] He went over the evidence that pointed away from Sechenov's hypothesis of inhibitory centers in the brain, but recoiled from the inference that inhibitory structures − distinct 'fibers', as he imagined them − must exist in every nerve cell. He preferred to imagine interference effects produced by nerve fibers that could be either excitatory or inhibitive, depending on the waves of impulses going through them.

Back in the 1860s Sechenov caught glimpses of that fearful complexity when, for example, he thought there must be 'centers of inhibition' in the spinal cord as well as the brain.[23] By 1869 he was ready to quit. He abandoned research on neural networks, and went back to the molecular level where he had started out. For the rest of a long life — he lived to 1905 — he would pump gas into liquids, trying to establish the physico–chemical mechanisms of gas absorption in the blood, returning only rarely to bits of research in neurophysiology. Not only foreign critics but also his best students rejected the hypothesis of inhibitory centers in the brain. Indeed, Sechenov himself tacitly abandoned the largest vision of it.[24]

It would be misleading to brush aside Sechenov's hypothesis as a wrong guess, significant only for the impulse it gave to other lines of inquiry. His most distinguished student, N. E. Vvedenskii, made that mistake in an otherwise perceptive and admiring biography.[25] Vvedenskii had persevered with the neural mapping that his mentor had abandoned along with the hypothesis of centers of inhibition. He had watched Sechenov's retreat to largely unproductive studies of gas absorption, and had noted the virtual disappearance of public interest in Sechenov's essays on psychology. Perhaps Vvedenskii had been infected by Sechenov's sense of failure as the years obscured his youthful triumph. Sechenov not only refused all rituals of tribute, the periodic 'jubilees' or anniversary celebrations much favored by Russian savants. He took flight as he approached his sixtieth birthday in 1889; simply resigned his professorship at St Petersburg University, with nothing to take its place but fruitless wandering in Western Europe and a beginner's position (*privat dotsent*) subsequently arranged at Moscow University. The unspoken motive for flight was embarrassment by the decline from youthful triumph.[26]

The profession maintained filial respect for Sechenov as 'the father of Russian physiology', the first to win a European reputation and to start a Russian center of research and teaching in thoroughly modern physiology. Moreover, he was an erudite father who knew what the sons were doing. In 1890, when he offered a series of public lectures on the current state of neurophysiology, Moscow's physicians crowded the hall. He was still a great lecturer, though he could offer no great unifying ideas. He told, for example, of recent experiments showing that electrical stimulation at certain points in a dog's cerebral cortex excited muscular movements in the legs, but he noted that those much-discussed experiments failed to resolve the old debate over localization of functions in various parts of the brain.[27] In short, the elderly Sechenov had retreated from bold theorizing to reasonable balancing of inconclusive possibilities — on the one hand localization, on the other equipotentiality, and so on.

At a distance from the Russian scene, unaware of such biographical particulars, Charles Sherrington perceived the major significance of Sechenov's hypothesis concerning centers of inhibition. In a masterful

review of neural inhibition, published in 1900, Sherrington acknowledged
the antiquity of the notion that action in one part of the nervous system can
be inhibited by action in another part. He even had an appropriate quotation
from Hippocrates. But up to Sechenov, he noted, the idea had been merely
'psychological', an intuitive inference from subjective observations, such as
the subsiding of pain in one part of the body when a greater pain visits
another part. Sechenov had transformed that vague psychological idea into
'a working physiological thesis'.[28] His mode of experimental reasoning had
fostered rigorous tracing of inhibitory and excitatory effects of particular
segments of the nervous system acting on other segments, with muscular
motion or rest as the chief indicator of excitation or inhibition.

The search had moved down to very precise, extremely laborious testing
of networks mediated by the spinal cord. When the testing reached up to
the brain, it was to some artificially simplified version of a warm-blooded
animal's complex brain. The experimenter tested particular functions before
and after he extirpated particular neural structures, moving from higher
levels down to lower, like a mechanic figuring out the operation of an
unfamiliar engine by piecemeal disassembly and reassembly, with repeated
efforts to run the component parts in combinations that exhaust the possibilities. To be sure, a living animal is not as mechanical as an engine; the
component parts of a mutilated dog or monkey could not be put back
together, but another whole specimen was always available for the next
disassembly required by the logic of 'successive degenerations', to use
Sherrington's term for the method. He and likeminded experimenters –
including N. E. Vvedenskii, who claimed priority in the discovery of
reciprocal innervation[29] – were not seeking the neural mechanisms of
learning or emotion. They were mapping the circuits that governed physical
reflexes, such as the scratching movement of a dog's hind leg when its back
is rubbed.

With staggering patience Sherrington confronted the ubiquity of inhibitory 'centers' throughout the nervous system, and brought them within an
experimentally proven rule: 'The augmentor [excitatory] innervation of
one muscle group seems regularly to be accompanied by inhibition of
another muscle group; this mode of innervation I have termed "reciprocal".'[30]
That rule was central to Sherrington's comprehensive picture of 'the integrative action of the nervous system'. It is customary to acclaim his picture
as the foundation of twentieth-century neurophysiology, and it deserves
such acclaim.[31] But we must not forget that it was comprehensive within a
deliberately limited framework. Sherrington mapped neural circuits in 'the
puppet animal', as he called his mutilated 'preparations'. He was a dualist,
many people say, implying some willfully metaphysical choice to believe in
Descartes. He was a dualist, I say, meaning that dualism was the necessary
presupposition of his experimental reasoning, reinforced by its success.

Descartes died long ago. It is the physiologist's mode of experimental reasoning that has constantly regenerated some version of mind-body dualism. Sherrington was keenly aware that he systematically excluded the psyche or mind from the analysis of such neural processes as inhibition. When he credited Sechenov with starting systematic physiological research on inhibition, he was evidently unaware that Sechenov had done so with the hope of *including* the mind. The centers of inhibition that he sought were to be the neural mechanisms governing not only leg retraction in frogs but also thought in human beings, conceived as brainy interruptions of reflexes. Sechenov's Russian colleagues were very much aware of his goal, and were therefore inclined to perceive him as starting up a blind alley, backing away with speculation about the mind-body problem, and then going off to pump gas. He pumped it by hand, and came to value the daily exercise for the mind-numbing fatigue it induced.[32]

I am combining apparently contradictory views. Sechenov abandoned his work in neurophysiology because − not although − he started a crucially important line of research on inhibition. It did not lead where he wanted to go. Whether pursued by N. E. Vvedenskii in Russia or by Sherrington in England or by Hering in Germany, that line of research pointed away from explanation of the mind, toward an implicitly dualistic separation of neurophysiology from psychology.[33] Sechenov started with dreams of founding 'medical psychology' in rigorous physiology of the brain, and saw his research carrying physiology away from the higher levels of the brain, at least for a long time, and away from the mind, perhaps forever.

No doubt other attractions and revulsions were at work. He had begun his work at the physico-chemical level, and he returned to it when balked in the analysis of neural networks. But we cannot attribute flighty impatience to Sechenov, for he demonstrated enormous perseverance in his largely unrewarding studies of gas absorption in the blood. He did lack the degree of callousness that seemed increasingly demanded for mapping neural networks. He was willing to cut up living frogs in order to see how their neural machinery works, but he was not willing to do the same to dogs or monkeys, the victims of choice to physiologists like Sherrington or Pavlov.

It is worth inquiring whether vivisection of warm-blooded animals was essential to the next stage of neurophysiology. This is partly a technical issue. Cold-blooded animals lack, for example, the depressor nerve whose function Tsion discovered by cutting up live rabbits. But this is also a question of outlook or mentality among scientists. The human depressor nerve is structurally different from the rabbit's, yet physiologists cannot check the functional significance of the difference by doing vivisection of humans. The ethical obstacle is not 'merely' emotional or social; it rests on knowledge, intuitive knowledge that a kindred soul or mind or psyche would be killed in vivisection of a human. We might wonder whether Sechenov's refusal to do vivisection on any warm-blooded animals rested on a broader empathy, which may be essential to the dream of keeping psychology joined with physiology. The vivisectionist of a dog or monkey must overcome his intuitive knowledge that he is killing a psyche akin to his own, getting it out of the way in order to tease out the functioning of a nervous system akin to his own. Wordsworth would have said that he murders to dissect. Some prisoners of the mentality that Wordsworth denounced overcome the problem by denying the reality of the psyche in dogs or monkeys, or even in humans.[34] Others — Sherrington, for example — acknowledge that they murder a kindred psyche to dissect a living nervous system. They deplore the cruelty that is necessary to the advancement of knowledge. That has been a common outlook among neurophysiologists. Sechenov's inability to go along with it, while encouraging students to do so, suggests that deep inside his mind he was hung up on some holistic outlook like Wordsworth's while the tide moved to some mutilating dualism like Sherrington's.

But speculation about the subconscious is not essential to an understanding of Sechenov's isolation at the boundary between physiology and psychology. What is essential is the sequence of biographical events as perceived by professional colleagues, by ideologists, and by historians who claim to have no *parti pris*. After an intuitive vision of 'centers of inhibition', Sechenov wrote 'Reflexes of the Brain', projecting a strategy for neural analysis of the human mind, extending even to Garibaldi's heroic disregard of suffering and Newton's abstract thought. The course of neurophysiology quickly rebuked that strategy, and he dropped research in the field, but he persisted for a good many years in writing popular essays on psychology, reaffirming the faith in a neurophysiological approach to an understanding of the mind. In short, he kept pointing at the boundary problem as he left off working on it. His professional colleagues in Russia perceived him as a leader who was making himself increasingly marginal.[35] In the early twentieth century, when Pavlov and Bekhterev began their efforts to move physiology over the boundary and into psychology, colleagues asked whether they were reviving Sechenov's dream. Their replies, as we shall see, were both a retrospective evaluation of Sechenov and an expression of their own views on the major issue at the boundary, the mind-body problem.

In this area historical reality is a shifting tension of opposed judgments. To the extent that the mind-body problem seems inappropriate for physiological science, Sechenov's venture shrinks toward inanity, a homily for those lost in alien wilderness, the psychologists. His most illustrious student, N. E. Vvedenskii, straining to tell a 1906 congress of psychologists what made Sechenov "one of the country's mightiest prophets and heralds of psychology as an experimental science', could specify nothing more than aversion to metaphysical speculation and 'close connection with other sciences, above all with physiology'. That was the entire 'methodology' that Vvedenskii found in 'Reflexes of the Brain', his trivial reason for this condescending accolade: 'one of the most remarkable and brilliant models of scientific popularization'.[36] He gently brushed aside Sechenov's later essays on psychology; they seemed intractably obscure to Vvedenskii, virtually private explorations of the great man's puzzlement.

At the other extreme is the Stalinist magnification of Sechenov, which became official doctrine in the 1930s, and is still adhered to in the major biography, by M. G. Iaroshevskii, whose main interest is not physiology but psychology. He cannot avoid the Stalinist insistence that the mind-body problem is solved, in the first place by the Russian vanguard of revolutionary materialists. Thus Sechenov is the towering genius who foresaw the true science of psychology. And that, in Iaroshevskii's account, is why Sechenov quit experimental work in neurophysiology. He saw so far into its future fusion with psychology that he outran the experimental possibilities of his time.[37]

The eager reader who wants to know the scientific solution of the mind-body problem, and how Sechenov anticipated it, is repeatedly frustrated by Iaroshevskii. At times he endorses the official doctrine that Pavlov turned Sechenov's vision into experimental science, and ignores the obvious objections: Pavlov's experimental method and reasoning were quite simple, entirely within the range of possibilities available to Sechenov, who showed no interest. Indeed, he lived long enough to read the first papers on conditioned reflexes, and ignored them, evidently seeing little in common with Pavlov. Sometimes Iaroshevskii ignores Pavlovian doctrines, and ascribes to Sechenov 'cybernetic' modeling of a brain that is simultaneously a mind, but he is hopelessly vague both about the model and about Sechenov's anticipation of it. He picks on words, 'signal' and 'self-activation' (*samopodvizhnost'*), which Sechenov used much too loosely to be considered cybernetic concepts.[38] What is worse, Iaroshevskii is obliged to note and to explain away Sechenov's persistent concessions to a dualistic position on the mind–body problem. If he anticipated any trend in neuroscience, it was neither the Pavlovian reduction of mind to nervous activity nor the cybernetic fusion of the two but what is now called neuropsychology, which correlates psychic and neural processes. But that is too broad to capture Sechenov's unique genius; many neuroscientists have long worked that way, which may be called Cartesian or Leibnizian, if one wants to read into scientists' labors the abstract philosophy they mostly try to escape.

It is a partisan distortion to assign Sechenov the role of prophet for some twentieth-century school. Any retrospective modernization of his views gives the history of physiology-cum-psychology a coherent continuity that the disorderly facts reveal only to true believers in one or another of the rival schools. In his own time the most outstanding feature of Sechenov's speculation on the boundary between physiology and psychology was his effort to make the reflex concept work in both fields, as the elemental unit of which neural and psychic processes are compounded. If he could analyze the role of central inhibition in reflex action, he believed he would be on the way to analyzing the mechanism of thought. That basic proposition involved him in two separate disputes. The neurophysiological argument over inhibition focused on experimental data concerning the fine structure of nerves, and pointed away from the higher levels of the nervous system. The psychological argument was persistently speculative, which is why Sechenov dropped out of it after a while. After all, he had begun by insisting that psychology could become a genuine science only if it became solidly experimental. But while he did participate in speculative arguments about basic concepts, he rejected the simple view that the psyche is a compound of neural reflex arcs; the *interruptions* of reflexes revealed the psyche. And that is how fellow Russian physiologists categorized his position on the mind–body problem. Sechenov, they were in the habit of saying, considered the psyche a middle element in some reflex arcs, a sort of inhibition intervening between stimulus and reaction. Some physiologists remembered that as a point in his favor, others as a mark against him. But mostly they stayed away from the messy boundary with psychology where bold young Sechenov had suffered defeat.

PAVLOV'S CONVERSION

Thus we are in a position to understand Pavlov's response, when he was first confronted with a comparison between his 'conditioned reflex' and Sechenov's 'reflexes of the brain'. It was just after Sechenov's death, when Russian physiologists were remembering 'the father' of their enterprise. At a conference in May 1906, a batch of papers by Pavlov's students was presented, and two former students of Sechenov's rose in the discussion period to note the differences between their mentor's approach and Pavlov's. Sechenov had thought of the 'psychic element' as 'an intermediate something' (*nechto srednee*) in cortical reflexes, and he had searched rigorously for the neural mechanisms. Pavlov's experiments failed to show which part of the brain mediated conditioned reflexes, and did not 'get at the psychic process itself. What you are getting is the result of a process, the result of a series of associations, but you are not investigating the process itself.'[39]

Pavlov replied defensively on the issue of brain localization – more of that later – but aggressively on the psychic process. The 'psychic method' must give way to 'the objective, physiological method' in the analysis of higher nervous activity. With the latter 'we are studying all the organism's reactions to events of the external world. What more do you need? If you find it nice to study, so to speak, the poetry of the problem, then that is already your business.' It was not the business of 'naturalistic inquiry'.[40]

As for Sechenov, Pavlov promised to speak his piece at a forthcoming commemorative session, but he offered this judgment extemporaneously:

> For the honor of the Russian intellect one must say that Sechenov was the first to begin scientific study of psychic phenomena, and if Sechenov himself was not a genius but only very talented, still in this attempt I see a flight of positive genius in Sechenov's thought. ... But, once he presented the thought, he could not carry it through, he began to admit a psychic element, from a physiologist he began to make himself a philosopher. That is why I trace the starting point of our research to the end of 1863, to the appearance of the well-known essays [sic] by Sechenov, 'Reflexes of the Brain'.[41]

Subsequently Pavlov declared that he had worked under Sechenov's influence unwittingly. He surmised that the 1863 essay had been 'the main impulse to my decision [for physiological study of the psyche], even though it was not a conscious decision then', when he read the essay in his youth.[42] He was not invoking the Freudian unconscious. He was simply evading uncomfortable questions about his relationship with Sechenov.

It is invention to declare, as many authors have, that Pavlov was Sechenov's student.[43] He was not, either in a literal or a figurative sense. The two men, twenty years apart in age, were acquainted for something like thirty years until Sechenov's death in 1905. They were persistently distant and cool, taking note of each other only rarely, without much respect, not to mention enthusiasm. In Pavlov's dissertation Sechenov is fleetingly listed among those professors to whom the candidate had demonstrated experimental findings.[44] While scrabbling for a decent academic appointment, Pavlov once offered Sechenov's name as a reference.[45] If a letter resulted, it has not been published. In 1889, when Pavlov was competing to be Sechenov's successor at St Petersburg University, Sechenov recommended a different man. By a single vote Pavlov lost the appointment to a third candidate, Sechenov's former student N.E. Vvedenskii.[46]

A few years later one finds Sechenov suggesting that a veterinary should go and study with Pavlov, Russia's best vivisectionist of warm-blooded animals.[47] Did that bit of praise, the only one on record, suggest that Pavlov was merely the master of a bloody technique, without creative ideas? Pavlov revealed analogous ambiguity when he broke his habitual silence. The second and last time, during their thirty years of acquaintance, that he cited Sechenov in print was in an article on vivisection, written for a medical encyclopedia. 'The father of Russian physiology', as Pavlov dutifully called him, was too sensitive to cut warm-blooded animals.[48] That observation was part of Pavlov's response to criticism of vivisection by the lay public. We are left wondering whether he pointed to Sechenov's tender heart with respect or condescension, or a little of both. In 1904, when Pavlov won the Nobel Prize, Sechenov sent brief congratulations, but did not contribute to the Festschrift that honored Russia's first laureate.[49]

Soon after Sechenov's death, as the reader has seen, his questioning students provoked mixed praise and criticism from Pavlov. In later commemorations the criticism dropped away, and Pavlov lent his voice to the replacement of the real Sechenov by an icon. Even the initial, comparatively realistic remarks began the mythic habit of evading inconvenient realities. More than thirty years elapsed between young Pavlov's reading of 'Reflexes of the Brain' and his conversion to the belief that physiologists should carry the reflex concept into the analysis of psychic processes. He used the word 'conversion' (*obrashchenie*) in the opening of his first article on conditioning, for he had held a contrary view during those thirty years. He had persistently said that physiologists must acknowledge 'the psychic element' in animal functioning and must take steps to exclude it from their work as physiologists.[50]

That long-held view may have been instilled in him by his actual teacher at the Medical Academy, Il'ia Tsion, but it was so common among physiologists of the mid-nineteenth century that any assignment of copyright would be foolish. At the beginning of the twentieth century Pavlov announced that he was changing his mind; physiology could and should include — or rather, dissolve — 'the psychic element'. The first paper announcing that change was published in 1903, which happened to be the fortieth anniversary of 'Reflexes of the Brain', but Pavlov made no mention of the once famous essay.[51] Either he remembered and judged it irrelevant, or he had simply forgotten. It had slipped from many people's memory; it came back as Pavlov's (and Bekhterev's) new doctrines called it back to mind.

If not Sechenov, then who did move Pavlov away from the traditional exclusion of the psyche from the physiologist's competence? We have Pavlov's answer in his 1903 'history of a physiologist's conversion from purely physiological questions to the field of phenomena that are usually called psychic'.[52] He gave credit to Jacques Loeb, but he laid much heavier stress on laboratory experience as the source of his conversion. So we should ask *what* rather than *who*. What accumulating experience in physiological research brought him to the boundary with the troubled science of the mind and pushed him into it, philosophizing with a hammer?

The characteristic reply by Pavlov and his student assistants pictured themselves drawn along by force of factual research, almost without theorizing, certainly without philosophizing. Analysis of digestion entangled them in analysis of the psyche. 'The problem arose', as one disciple put it, 'not as a question that Pavlov set for himself, but as a corollary experimental inference from his work on digestion.'[53] The flow of publications from Pavlov's laboratory at the turn of the century confirms that retrospective assessment, as long as we refrain from probing below the surface.

In the late 1890s Pavlov was still insisting on 'the reality of the psychic element as a stimulus' to the flow of digestive juices, which had been the focus of his research since 1883. 'A psychic event, a passionate desire to eat, is undoubtedly a stimulus to the [neural] centers of the salivary glands.'[54] To acknowledge that fact of everyday observation, while attempting to exclude it from physiological research, was to be entangled in especially difficult problems. Consider this example: food in the dog's mouth stimulated a simultaneous flow of saliva in the mouth and gastric juice in the stomach, but acid placed in the dog's mouth stimulated salivation alone, no gastric juice. Should the physiologist go looking for the neural circuits that govern the discrimination between pleasant and unpleasant stimuli? Or should he be content to draw the veil, as Pavlov did in November 1899, saying that the influence of the psyche is weaker deeper down: strong in the mouth, less so in the stomach, hardly apparent in the pancreas?[55]

Neural analysis of the psyche might be put aside, but that would not remove persistent troubles at the most elementary level of factual observation. In dogs habituated to feeding experiments salivation was highly erratic. It depended not only on the length of time since the previous feeding but also on the experimenter's movements as he prepared to feed the dog, and even on individual differences among experimenters. Indeed, one unfortunate young man felt obliged to leave the team because he provoked constant salivation in the expectant dogs, regardless of their hunger or satiety, in spite of all his efforts to move about inconspicuously. (He went off to Switzerland and became a psychiatrist.)[56] What was worse, even a single experimenter found it hard to achieve consistency in his own observations with a single dog over a period of time.

As late as 1901–2 Pavlov was arguing with his student assistants whether to go on speaking of the 'psychic element' in the dog's salivation, for example, at the sight of the acid bottle in the experimenter's hand. An alternative had emerged: to dissolve the unmanageable psyche in a new concept, the 'conditional reflex'.* They were making statistical correlations of salivation to 'indifferent stimuli' – for example, to the bottle flashed on the eye rather than the acid placed on the tongue – and they were imagining the neural linkages in the cortex that connected sight and salivation, unsure whether they were still involved with the 'psychic element' or were establishing a new kind of reflex. It was a student assistant, not Pavlov, who first published the term, 'conditional reflex', in 1902. (Later on, when he left the laboratory, he and the master had a tangled little dispute concerning priority and the meaning of the term.)[57]

L. A. Orbeli, who would succeed Pavlov as the chief Pavlovian, recalled that the term 'conditional' emerged in their discussions not only to indicate

---

* *Uslovnyi* should be translated as 'conditional', but endless repetition of 'conditioned' has made that mistranslation stick.

that a certain kind of salivation was conditional on past experience — if associated with acid on the tongue, the sight of the bottle caused salivation; if not, not — but also that the hypothesis was conditional: the scientists were not sure that the correlation of experience and salivation was reducing psychic secretion to a newly discovered type of reflex.[58] By 1903 Pavlov had made up his mind. The conditional reflex was not a new word for a psychic process; it was a newly discovered reflex, of revolutionary significance. It was the elemental unit of which all 'higher nervous activity' is compounded. From indisputable physiology of the digestive process he had moved to supposedly physiological analysis of supposedly psychic phenomena. He insisted on the second 'supposedly'; his critics insisted on the first.

That account of Pavlov's conversion by force of laboratory experience is obviously true, but just as obviously inadequate. Even the surface evidence in the flow of published papers suggests depths and difficulties that were being willfully passed over. Pavlov constantly insisted that he was replacing 'philosophy' with 'the language of facts', but that was usually a rhetorical device, permitting him to indulge his basic assumptions without arguing them. Certainly he never ceased appealing to such undefined concepts as 'objectivity' and 'determinism' to justify his revolutionary move — into physiological fantasy, according to such eminent neurophysiologists as Sherrington; into behaviorist psychology, according to his American admirers. Soon Orbeli and other disciples were offering explicitly philosophical and historical arguments to justify their overthrow of convention, implicitly acknowledging that Pavlov's 'language of facts' was not enough to win neurophysiologists' approval of his doctrine.[59]

The retrospective observer of this scientific revolution cannot fail to note the contrast with Einstein's theory of relativity, which was published about the same time and won rapid acceptance among physicists. The philosophical and historical debates that relativity has engendered have been a tribute to its large significance, not a struggle over its acceptability as physical science. Evidently the phrase, 'scientific revolution', means different things in the two areas of investigation. In the study of the psyche it entails a war of schools and a confusion of disciplines, which cannot be evaded by an easy distinction between the science that is agreed upon and the philosophical interpretation that is disputed. I am deliberately disagreeing with Pavlov on that point. Even the historical observer is pulled away from milksop neutrality, into the belligerent neutrality of those who see claims of objective truth as temporary constructs, the ephemeral products of transient historical circumstances. When every claim to overcome the war of schools becomes the start of a new one, what else can the historian do? Nor should one be apologetic. It is the historian's ancient habit to seek understanding of human beings in the changing and inconsistent ways they understand themselves.

Pavlov, let us recall, was born in 1849. He went through his scientific training in the 1860s and 1870s, when physiological materialism, linked with political radicalism, was very much in vogue. That fact has been used for extravagant attributions of influence to Russia's 'revolutionary democrats', as Stalinist ideologists like to call their predecessors of the 1860s and 1870s. They can quote from Pavlov's reminiscences the customary tribute to Pisarev's influence in his choice of science as a way of life.[60] Youths of the 1860s who became scientists regularly invoked the memory of Pisarev, which is evidence that he infused moral virtue in their choice of a career, as opposed to Lavrov or Mikhailovskii, who cast moral doubt on the scientist's flight to the ivory tower. We have already examined that general problem of ideology, which concerned all the sciences and diverse trends within them. The problem here is Pavlov's decision to become a physiologist, and his belated conversion to a physiological assault on psychology.

We have his own attribution of decisive influence to G. H. Lewes's *Physiology of Common Life*, which he read in Russian translation while he was still a schoolboy.[61] Lewes was a popular Victorian positivist, who offered the public a vigorous argument that materialism and dualism were equally pointless to physiology, a science which showed that mind and body are two aspects of the same thing, the functioning system of a whole human being. It would be foolish to seize on that, or some other major themes in Lewes's book, as distinctive shaping influences on Pavlov. They were undoubtedly shaping but they were hardly distinctive, either to Lewes or to Pavlov. To be sure Lewes made great show of originality, of standing bravely against 'the established doctrine' respecting mind and body.[62] But it was a set of philosophers' doctrines that he was not so much standing against as brushing aside, in favor of a fairly commonplace belief, that empirical science would resolve any worthwhile problems in otherwise pointless metaphysical disputes. The reader has seen Sechenov produce his spontaneous version of that common positivism, when pressed by Kavelin on the mind-body problem.

Pavlov never allowed himself to be drawn into extended arguments of that sort, even in the late period of his life, when he had philosophers and psychologists buzzing about his claim to compress 'the whole mind within certain rules' of physiological research. We will see him respond with an agnostic shrug when a meeting of philosophers tried to pin him to a choice between materialist and dualist ontologies. No doubt implicit metaphysical choices can be discerned in the two stages of his thought, first the conventional acknowledgment of 'the psychic element' that must be excluded from physiology, then the radical decision to include and dissolve it. But the ontologies in those choices were inarticulate moods, Pavlov's determinedly unexamined responses first to a mid-nineteenth-century climate of opinion, then to a turn-of-century transformation.

It is easy to brush past the influence of the obscure professor who taught

Pavlov physiology while he was an undergraduate.[63] To be sure, that teacher's modest publications reveal hypothetical constructions of brain processes that Pavlov would cling to with obsessive persistence, in spite of mounting evidence against them. I note in particular the notion that sensory signals spread through a mosaic of 'centers' in the cerebral cortex — from, say, the visual centers, which receive the sight of the acid bottle, to the feeding center, which activates the salivary glands. What will require explanation is not where Pavlov picked up those once common notions of brain processes, but why he clung to them in growing isolation during his old age. An opposite problem is raised by his other teachers of physiology, Il'ia Tsion and two famous Germans, Carl Ludwig and Rudolf Heidenhain. He warmly thanked them for their shaping influence, but they cannot be said to have prefigured the experimental technique or the theory of conditioned reflexes. Except, I shall argue, in a negative fashion, by starting Pavlov down a heavily traveled road, which grew increasingly irksome to him, until he took a sharp turn into the wilderness.

From Tsion Pavlov absorbed not only his first area of research (the innervation of the heart) but also the skills of a master vivisectionist, indeed, a virtuoso's pride in the art. Surgical techniques were fairly primitive, and warm-blooded animals were far more vulnerable than frogs to simple destruction when the physiologist started taking them apart to see how they worked. The physiologist had to conceive experiments within the limits set by the animal's fragility and his personal speed and sureness of touch. Tsion's personal best was a legendary performance on the way to the theater, in formal dress with a large expanse of starched white shirt that he disdained to cover. Not a drop of dog's blood was on that shirt when he put on his top hat and left. What Pavlov thought of such theatricality is not in the public record. He measured his personal best within a scientific frame, pointing proudly to the isolation of a portion of a dog's stomach with all its nerves intact and functioning, ready for experimentation. He was also proud to have implanted a fistula or drainpipe in a dog's pancreas, once again without cutting the nerves that govern the secretion. On the way to such successful 'preparations', to use the antiseptic euphemism of the trade, he killed a lot of dogs unintentionally, but physiologists counted the number of unintended 'sacrifices' (another favorite metaphor) as a measure of spectacular achievements. We may consider that a scientific variation of an ancient role played by hunters' dogs: the more formidable the beast at bay, the more dogs sacrificed in bringing it down, the greater the hunter's renown.

Pavlov was left-handed by nature, ambidextrous by training, and thoroughly mechanist in the management of affection. He trained dogs to be cooperative friends in the experiments he did on them, in contrast to E. L. Thorndike who thrust cats howling and clawing into experiment boxes, and discovered thus the 'law of effect': learning how to open the boxes had a calming effect and vice versa: calm facilitated learning. (Of course that is my mocking formulation of the law; Thorndike avoided terms that claimed knowledge of the cats' mental process. Evidently he was repressing something in himself as well as in the cats.) Pavlov had the serenity of one who sees only a machine in the dog that he pets in preparation for cutting — indeed, who sees only a machine in the hand that pets or cuts and the higher nervous activity that generates one kind of joy while caressing, another kind while cutting.[64] I am drawing not only on his own account, but also on the reminiscence of a former student assistant, who watched a dog with an esophagotomy and a stomach fistula run up to be petted before its accustomed false feeding.* And Pavlov, caressing, asked: "'Where are people's heads if they can think that there is a qualitative difference between us and animals?'"[65] The former student also accompanied Pavlov on a visit to a relative who had suffered a stroke, which had caused a peculiar disruption of speech: the subjects of sentences halted in his mouth, but the predicates flowed smoothly. When the visitors left, Pavlov said to his student: "'A machine, a machine, and nothing more. An apparatus. . . . Where are people's heads if they can see in this anything but an apparatus?'"[66]

With that outstanding complex of manual skills and mental aptitudes, Pavlov systematically extended knowledge of the digestive glands, paying special attention to the nerves that govern them. He published his results in the customary research papers, and then in a brief, clearly written course of lectures, *The Work of the Digestive Glands* (1897).[67] Soon translated into German and English, it brought him specialized fame in place of comparative obscurity. (He had sometimes been confused with two other Pavlovs at the Medical Academy.) In 1904 he was awarded a Nobel Prize. The explanations of the digestive process, which won him the prize, were quietly absorbed into the accumulating body of physiological science, quite apart from psychology, unmarked by the label 'Pavlovian'.

Pavlov was founding the 'Pavlovian' doctrine of 'the so-called psyche' as the Nobel committee was honoring his previous work. Vivisection and study of digestion led up to the change, but fell into an ancillary role as a result of it. In 1895 he and an aide devised a simple fistula to the salivary gland, with a little pouch at the opening of the tube to collect saliva for careful measurement, still with neural regulation of the digestive process as the focus of experiment. That effort led to an assault on 'the psychic secretion', as Pavlov and other physiologists called the anticipatory flow of

---

* In plain terms: the dog's esophagus had been cut and brought to an opening in the skin, so that food taken through the mouth would drop out of the artificial opening rather than into the stomach. The fistula to the stomach enabled the experimenter to insert or extract substances, testing, for example, whether gastric juice flows in the empty stomach of the 'feeding' dog (it does), and whether the juice flows if food is slipped into the stomach while the mouth is not 'feeding' (it does not).

saliva when the habituated dog was taken to the laboratory for feeding experiments, or when it saw the acid bottle in the experimenter's hand — or when the unhabituated dog was first put in harness on the experiment table, trembling and slavering in fear. A conventional experimenter excluded such disturbances by waiting for the 'psychic secretion' to stop, or by concealing such signals as the acid bottle — and in the first place by training the dog to stand quietly on the table.

Implicit in that experimental common sense of the physiological profession was the attribution of psychic processes to the dog — learning, anticipating, liking, fearing — and the assumption that the neural mechanisms of those psychic processes were beyond the reach of the physiologist. In the first years of the twentieth century Pavlov challenged that conventional wisdom. He devoted the rest of a long life to the challenge. Until he died in 1936, at the age of 87, he focused on it not only his own phenomenal energy but also the factory-style research of teams that grew to 29 salaried scientists and 162 trainees (*praktikanty*) by the eve of the First World War.[68] The start and stop of the salivary response to 'indifferent stimuli', such as a bell or a light or an electric shock, were to serve as indicators of processes in the cerebral cortex, the same ones, he assumed, that governed all 'higher nervous activity', whether canine or human.

THE SOURCES OF PAVLOV'S CONVERSION

There must have been some accumulating urgency, gathering force over many years, which transformed a solid analyst of digestion into a rash conquistador of the psyche at the age of fifty-four. (I am echoing Freud's defiant characterization of himself, though Pavlov did not like comparison with that other even bolder adventurer, who also moved from neurophysiology into psychology at the turn of the century.)[69] Pavlov's study with Carl Ludwig may recall Sechenov's turn to brain studies back in the 1860s. But there is no evidence that Pavlov felt challenged, as Sechenov did, by Ludwig's skeptical analogy between physiological probing of the brain and shooting bullets into watches to see how their timekeeping is altered. On the contrary, Pavlov came to share Ludwig's abiding conviction that drastic intervention in the living brain is an unlikely way to discover its laws of normal operation.

Rudolf Heidenhain, the teacher Pavlov most respected, favored such intervention. He cut pieces out of the living brain and poked at it with electrical stimulation to discover effects on the animal's behavior. He also argued that 'every conscious process' must be translated into 'objective terms', such as bodily motions, or be ruled out of consideration by the physiologist. That formulation comes from Karl Lashley, the American pioneer of neuropsychology, who thought he saw in Heidenhain's translate-or-exclude a major source of Pavlov's conditioned reflex.[70] But a rule that excludes some mental processes is a restriction of the physiologist's competence, and Pavlov was rebelling against such restrictions when he declared in 1906: 'The whole mind [*dusha*] can be compressed within certain rules of objective research', meaning the rules of conditioning.[71] His claim of universality was especially audacious since his experimental animals were trained to passive reaction, not to conscious action. The dog's salivation at the sight of the acid bottle, like our own at the sight of a lemon being cut, is closer to an involuntary eyeblink than to a deliberate wink. But Pavlov leaped to the inclusion of conscious and voluntary processes in the laws of involuntary slavering and blinking. It is also noteworthy that he turned to such problems long after 1881, when Heidenhain, in association with a different Russian student, published the article on brain studies which seemed to Lashley a foreshadowing of Pavlov's doctrine.

Lashley, as we shall see below, persistently tried to fit Pavlov's conditioned reflexes within the dominant trend in brain science, a trend that annoyed Pavlov until he turned to set it right, and annoyed him even more in the aftermath, when men like Lashley tried to set *him* right. He often masked his annoyance. In 1897, when Heidenhain died, Pavlov eulogized him as 'a physiologist of the cell, a representative of that physiology which is due to replace our contemporary physiology of organs, and which may be said to foreshadow the final stage in the science of life — the physiology of the living molecule.'[72] In that farewell to a man he revered as a model scientist, for his devotion to physiology 'and to nothing else', Pavlov refrained from disclosing a critical reservation. He believed that the cellular and molecular physiology of the future would be wretched chaos, unless old-fashioned systemic physiology, 'our contemporary physiology of organs', provided grand laws of coherence. In physiological science Pavlov was a sort of tory radical, convinced that bold adherence to old principles was the only assurance of orderly progress.

In the twentieth century his disciples would look back and discover the first intimation of the master's radicalism at the very end of his doctoral dissertation (1883), which offered a systemic account of the innervation of the heart. He had been working in the laboratory of Dr S. P. Botkin, the famous clinician whose salon, as the reader may recall, started Sechenov and Kavelin debating the relationship between physiology and psychology. Pavlov wound up his dissertation with a special tribute to Botkin's 'deep and broad nervism, which often runs ahead of the experimental data'.[73] To some extent that curious tribute was a courteous way of saying what Pavlov would put in plain Russian after Botkin died: The wise old doctor 'did not like to enter into physiological criticism' of Pavlov's findings; he preferred to draw on the intuitive understanding of physiology that comes with clinical practice.[74] To some extent the tribute may also have reflected Botkin's challenge to a very careful young scientist who aspired to be daring and original. Pavlov was replying to Botkin: the dissertation herewith presented *is* daring and original. (At the defense Tarkhanov criticized Pavlov for pretending more originality than the dissertation actually showed.)[75] Those are minor points, except as they may reveal young Pavlov's intensely ambitious scientific personality. The important question attaches to 'nervism', the cryptic concept that enables one to 'run ahead of the experimental data'. What did he mean by that?

In the twentieth century, when he became famous for the doctrine of conditioned reflexes, Pavlov's students began putting the question to their master, asking him to explain the concept that might allow *them* to run farsightedly ahead of their data. Pavlov's printed explanation was little help. Nervism, he wrote, is 'the attempt to extend the influence of the nervous system to the greatest possible number of the organism's activities.'[76] Such a platitudinous rule of strategy hardly seemed to warrant a special new term. In conversation Pavlov was less laconic. A former student recalled that he used 'nervism' as an opposite of 'chemism'.[77] Of course he was not against chemical analysis in physiology. He opposed 'nervism' to 'chemism' in the sense that he opposed 'organ physiology' to cellular or molecular physiology. In the jargon of our own time Pavlov yearned for a biology of the system, while the tide was running strongly toward molecular particularism. His parsimony in written explanations of 'nervism' showed the repressed nature of that feeling. His dissatisfaction with 'chemism' was not a denial of its legitimacy, but a conviction that something must transcend it. Increasingly, in the last years of the nineteenth century, that yearning for some larger vision became a commitment, shaping his research strategy and his students', while they belonged to his highly disciplined collective.

In print Pavlov explained himself with diplomatic courtesy, as in this passage from *The Work of the Digestive Glands* (1897), justifying his type of physiology:

> This is not a question of the essence of life, or the mechanism or chemism of cellular activity, a question whose final solution will remain the task of a countless series of scientific generations, as a desire that constantly beckons but can never be completely satisfied. At our, so to speak, level of life, in organ physiology (as opposed to cellular), in many of its sectors one has the right to be soberly confident of the possibility of a complete explanation of the normal connection of all the apparatus' separate parts (in our instance the apparatus is the digestive canal) among themselves and with the objects of external nature that stand in a special relationship to them (in the given instance the objects are food). At the stage of organ physiology

we as it were abstract ourselves from such questions as these: What is the peripheral ending of the reflex nerve? By what means does it receive this or that stimulus? What is the nerve process? How, by force of what reactions and what molecular structure, do these or those enzymes arise in the secretory cell, is this or that digestive reagent produced? We accept these properties and these elementary activities as accomplished, as given, and, by grasping the rules, the laws of their action in the whole apparatus, we can within certain limits govern the apparatus, have power over it [*vlastvovat' nad nim*].[78]

Was Pavlov claiming superiority for his 'organ physiology', a right to 'govern' or even 'have power over' cellular and molecular biology? If so, the claim was only an implicit possibility, waiting to emerge in future controversies.[79] The point here is Pavlov's growing discontent in the 1890s, his anxious sense that the whole animal in its normal functioning might be slipping out of the physiologist's control. Passing fifty, seeing his kind of physiology losing its claim of mastery, the conventional analyst of digestion turned into the radical conquistador of 'higher nervous activity'.

The most vivid picture of Pavlov's prodromal disturbance comes from A. F. Samoilov, who worked in Pavlov's team from 1893 to 1896, and then moved to Sechenov's laboratory for a seven-year apprenticeship, which turned him into a leading electrophysiologist. Pavlov obstructed what Sechenov encouraged: study of tiny bioelectrical discharges across microscopic synapses between neurons, which achieve summation as the gross impulses that excite or inhibit muscles and glands in reflexive feedback loops, which are integrated by the spinal cord and the lower brain in the functioning of 'the puppet animal' as a whole, which is in turn transformed into a lively self-activating animal or even a person by higher brain processes, which operate at such levels of complexity that the scientific imagination may not simply be staggered, as the usual cliché describes it, but quite overwhelmed. Samoilov was sufficiently broadminded to sympathize with Pavlov's revulsion against that prospect, even though it was the one he chose for himself. He recalled Pavlov angrily throwing down a journal full of articles on the fine structure and microscopic functioning of nerve tissue, exclaiming: 'Yes, if you work on such questions and such objects, you won't go far! ... Would that my eyes had not looked upon all that!'[80]

Samoilov's reflections, honoring Pavlov while sticking to his own viewpoint, are worth quoting at length:

From my earliest acquaintance with Ivan Petrovich I was struck by his imperious temperament, by the force and power of his scientific personality. In the tasks that he set himself and in his moves carrying them out, one sensed a kind of bravery; if I did not fear that I might be misunderstood, I would say recklessness.[81]

Samoilov gave homely examples from everyday life in the laboratory. Pavlov harried his little army of researchers, demanding not only laborious execution of his orders but invigorating argument from supposedly independent minds; yet he flung aside, with a wish he had not seen it, a journal full of fine-scale studies that threatened to subvert his approach.

> At the time all that [fine-scale studies] seemed to me in the highest degree interesting and valuable. I confess that now too, thirty years later [he was writing in honor of Pavlov's seventy-fifth birthday] I have the same view of this matter as I did then. The general physiology of excitable tissues has justified its existence and needs no special defence. But it seems to me that I understand what was guiding Ivan Petrovich when he reacted with such disapproval, even hostility, to the trend of physiological research I am talking about. All those investigations that concerned separated points of the body seemed to him excessively isolated from the animal mechanism as a whole, from the whole organism; they seemed to him excessively abstract, distracting, untimely; in his vision they were out of order.[82]

From a distance Samoilov could admire the commander's willful plunge toward mastery of the whole organism. He saw in Pavlov 'a gift of intuition, ... of direct, as it were, poetic discovery' — a questionable compliment, considering Pavlov's contempt for 'the poetry of the problem'. Samoilov defended 'poetic discovery' by noting that predictability is not unique to science. Consider, he wrote, the excitement one feels watching a tragedy on stage and sensing how things are bound to end. He dignified his analogy between the scientific and literary imagination by the predictable reference to Goethe, and also by calling to witness the great Helmholtz, who typed Faraday as a scientist with the poet's intuitive grasp of major truths.[83]

Of course Pavlov was an intensely mechanistic poet, as Samoilov demonstrated. The union of thorough mechanism with reckless intuition was the source of the fundamental 'breakthrough' (*lomka*) that Pavlov achieved in the study of higher nervous activity. It was an epochal breakthrough, Samoilov declared, comparable to Einstein's in physics. Yet he recalled Du Bois-Reymond's '*Ignorabimus*', and agreed: 'As we cannot square the circle or build a perpetual motion machine, exactly so we cannot connect the objective world with the subjective world by the use of one and the same terms.'[84] He credited Pavlov with showing how to extricate the study of higher nervous activity from that bind, yet he wondered whether Pavlov's 'hostility to general neurophysiology' could be overcome, perhaps by some other methods than conditioning, some methods that would achieve a truly physiological explanation of the higher functions.

That seesaw appraisal, rising and falling between awe and skepticism, was characteristic of physiologists' reactions to Pavlov as he carried into the study of higher nervous activity what he insisted was not hostility to neurophysiology but 'organ physiology' or 'nervism', an older, grander strategy than the new focus on the cell and the ion. His first paper on conditioned reflexes, presented to a physiologists' congress in 1903, criticized the predominant form of research in brain processes as 'psychopathological experiments', since the principal method was extirpation, removing parts of the brain to see what disruptions resulted in the animal's behavior. Such experiments were not developing 'steadily and according to a definite plan', for 'the researchers have lacked up to now a more or less significant and detailed system of the animal's normal relationships to its surrounding world, so that one might make an objective and precise comparison of the animal's condition before and after operation' on the brain.[85] The method of conditioned reflexes would provide such a system, a supposedly neurophysiological account of the whole animal's normal reactions to its environment.

Nowadays the catchword 'systemic' or 'holistic' would be used to label Pavlov's distress, while 'reductionist' would also be applied, however paradoxically, to describe his reactive flight toward a comprehensive doctrine of 'higher nervous activity'. In emphasizing that internal paradox — his aversive reaction, as a mechanist, against the profession's descent from systemic to cellular and molecular physiology — I am not doubting the positive reinforcement he got from other scientists. He was not alone in dreaming of mechanistic unity in life studies. The most notable visionary of that sort was Jacques Loeb, the Jewish physiologist who had left his native Germany for the more congenial atmosphere of the United States. Loeb experimented with lowly orders, such as caterpillars and worms, to prove that all movements of living beings could be reduced to invariant physico-chemical reactions. The variable behavior of higher animals was the result of 'associative memory', which was not to be understood in psychic terms. The nervous system associated — in the sense that wires connect — one series of automatic reactions with some other series, as changing circumstances required such temporary connections, which gave rise to the appearance of willful decisions based upon learning. Loeb's vision lumped the ingeniously variable behavior of higher animals with 'tropisms', the caterpillar's invariable crawl toward light, the ladybug's mechanical reversal of direction when pointed toward the earth, even the plant's clocklike pursuit of the moving sun. Pavlov relished such mechanistic extravagance. He liked to hold up his pocket watch as a model of a human being. In his first paper on conditioning he paraphrased Loeb's argument in a single rhetorical question: 'The movement of plants toward the light and the search for truth by means of mathematical analysis, are they not in essence phenomena of one and the same order?'[86]

Later on, without such flamboyance, Pavlov also noted his debt to an 1899 article by a trio of German biologists, who proposed the invention of a thoroughly objective terminology to cleanse their science of all subjectively tainted words, such as memory, learning, or voluntary action.[87] He also gave credit to H. S. Jennings, a zoologist who had done experimental studies of learned behavior in lower animals, and to E. L. Thorndike, the pioneer of American behaviorist psychology: they had started experiments similar to his own, independently and a few years earlier.[88] Pavlov's students compiled longer lists of predecessors and analogous contemporaries, partly to show how deep and broad was the sense of need for 'objective psychology', and also to prove the unique value of their physiological doctrine in satisfying the need.

Such lists of predecessors have also been used by detractors, to dissolve Pavlov's doctrine into banality.[89] But it is irrelevant to note that Claude Bernard put a fistula in the salivary gland of a horse, and got a profuse flow of saliva when oats were shown to the beast.[90] Bernard was content, as Pavlov was before the twentieth century, to consider such salivation a psychic reaction and to exclude it from physiology. That standard approach was very different from the assertively monistic doctrines which emerged more or less simultaneously at the turn of the century — Loeb's theory of 'tropisms', American 'behaviorism', Pavlov's 'conditioned reflex' theory, Bekhterev's 'objective psychology'. Their origins are not to be found in the innumerable preceding observations of bodily reactions to mental stimuli, but in a revulsion against such observations, a suddenly intense desire to prove that talk of mental stimuli belongs to primitive animism, to the rain dances and the blessing of fields by which primitive people 'cause' rain to fall and crops to grow. Erasmus Darwin, to take an example that antedates Pavlov's conditioned reflex by a century, needed no experiments to prove that the mind influences the body. He merely noted the obvious: dogs salivate at the sight of food; a mother's nipples rise when she takes up a baby for nursing; even sleeping flesh stands to salute imaginary women in the minds of dreaming men.[91] Pavlov's breakthrough (*lomka*), and analogous breakthroughs by other scientists at the turn of the century, were efforts not to prove but to stop such common observations of the mind moving the body. To escape subjectivity they went to the laboratory, not to correlate mind and body, but to eliminate mind.

DISCORD AMONG OBJECTIVISTS

To situate Pavlov in the revolt against subjectivity is to confront an essential paradox of the movement. Those who sought to reduce mental processes to a coherent, thoroughly objective natural science were not only intensely subjective in their appraisals of each other's achievement; they were discordant on matters of substance, thereby subverting each other's claims of coherent, objective science. Outsiders — for example, the old-fashioned majority of medical neurologists, who went on correlating mental and neural processes — were more sympathetic to the would-be monists, Pavlov included, than the rival sects of that crusading minority were to each other.

American behaviorists and Russian Pavlovians seemed at first to prove the opposite; from their widely separated provinces of modern European culture they made gestures of deep respect for each other. In 1909 R. M. Yerkes, a biologically oriented behaviorist — and racist and class snob in his vision of objective psychology — celebrated Pavlov's studies of the conditioned reflex.[92] In 1915 J. B. Watson, delivering his presidential address to the American Psychological Association, hailed Pavlov as 'the master'.[93] Watson was the major propagandist of black-box behaviorism as a makeshift for physiology; he was deficient in experimental rigor, and, on the practical level, he preached manipulative values to justify society's winners, and corrective labor institutions and 'etherization' to certify the criminal and hopelessly insane losers[94] — but none of that disrupted expressions of mutual respect between American and Russian objectivists. Experimental science spoiled the mood. Karl Lashley tested Pavlov's neural explanation of conditioning, by running rats through mazes and excising parts of their brains to see what the precise correlations of brain and learned behavior might be. The result, when he gave his presidential address to the American Psychological Association in 1929, was an angry protest from the Russian master, for Lashley's results ruined his neural schemes. As it happened, the original Russian influence on Lashley was less Pavlov than Bekhterev, who seemed to Americans to be doing the same work as Pavlov, yet was continually quarreling with him at conferences in St Petersburg. Disputes over priority were not the main issue in their strangely discordant claims of objectivity. The competitors were as jealous of first prize as any other scientists, but they found it hard to quarrel about who came in first when they could not agree on the course to be run.

It may be tempting to call this another eruption of materialist philosophizing, this time in the guise of experimental science. But the guise cannot be brushed aside. The proponents of objective psychology hardly mentioned Lamettrie or Cabanis, Büchner or Moleschott, and certainly not those drastically different materialists, Feuerbach and Marx. They were determined to be experimental scientists, not speculative philosophers. And certainly not radicals in a political sense; the one-time link between philosophical materialism and political radicalism was conspicuously absent from the twentieth-century revolt against the concept of mind. Most proponents of objective psychology were men of the academic establishment, far from the political left. Inarticulate ideology may be dug out of their insistence on emancipation from philosophy and political ideology, but the digging cannot bypass the layers of articulate denial. The rational arguments of the objectivists may have been shaped by glandular secretions and fields of social force, but their labors did not show the way to such depths. The only way down there is still intuitive analysis of their expressive minds, as they disputed rival strategies for the reduction of expressive thought to neural process.

Cultural geography is another type of determinism that must be postponed. The anti-mentalist crusaders of the early twentieth century were concentrated in the United States and Russia, two peculiar provinces of European culture, each with its own form of the provincial tendency to seize a metropolitan fashion — in this case the mechanization of man — and to exaggerate it, sometimes to a grotesque extreme. But speculation of this sort once again points toward excavation of inarticulate thought and feeling, which I am postponing. Suffice here to caution against hasty generalization. Anti-mentalist schools of scientists remained minorities within their provincial American and Russian cultures even at the peak of their meteoric fame in the early twentieth century, and subsequently declined into sectarian groups, wasting their missionary fervor in internecine strife, until they finally came to grudging reconciliations with the still dominant believers in the concept of psyche or mind.

Consider Bekhterev's version of the objectivist vision, which pointed toward eclectic compromise and thus embroiled his school in conflict with Pavlov's, a conflict that persists to this day in the Soviet Union. Eight years younger than Pavlov, Bekhterev started out with similar training in medicine, but on the postgraduate level turned himself into a different kind of scientist. He was as broad and wide-ranging as Pavlov was narrow and sharply focused. After studying psychiatry, experimental psychology, general physiology, and physiology of the brain, he combined medical practice in neurology and psychiatry with research in both fields and writing on an astonishing variety of topics.[95]

He came to brain studies, not circuitously and belatedly, as Pavlov did, but directly and young, as a specialist in neurology. In the 1880s he cut away parts of the brain in dogs, cats, and birds, trying, by disruption, to discover which parts governed which particular forms of behavior. He imagined that there are areas of the brain where repeated stimuli are associated or linked with the habitual actions that they provoke — for example, a dog's anticipatory retraction of the foot in response to a signal repeatedly associated with an electric shock. That was Bekhterev's experimental analogue to Pavlov's anticipatory salivation. The question of priority is hard to resolve, for the crucial issue is not salivation or leg retraction but anticipation, neural analysis thereof, which remained an unsolved problem. From Flechsig, or from the old tradition of 'associative psychology', Bekhterev took the name that he applied to habit-formed anticipatory automatisms: associative reflexes. He also made the customary assumption about brain localization: the neural mechanism of associative reflexes must be in the cerebral cortex.

That assumption was shaken when he discovered that the experimental animal might lose the reflex for a time after removal of the cortex, but subsequently would learn once again to withdraw the foot in anticipation of a shock. Bekhterev reasoned that subcortical ganglia can be trained to 'compensate' for the normal functions of the missing cortex, just as human victims of a stroke or other brain damage can sometimes train the healthy remainder of their brains to assume functions formerly mediated by the damaged parts. On the other hand, clinical experience also showed that some functions are lost beyond possibility of compensation, and Bekhterev found confirmation of that too in his experiments.

His earliest extirpations showed that animals deprived of the cerebrum could still bark, miaow or chirp, but only in response to external stimuli. Self-activated barking, miaowing or chirping disappeared along with the cerebrum, thereby reinforcing the traditional association of higher functions with the higher levels of the brain.[96] That deepened the neurophysiological puzzle of the decorticate animal's ability to learn some associative reflexes. It also increased the physiologist's need for some classification of functions above the level of the innate reflex, some hierarchical scheme in which the associative or conditional reflex would be an intermediate level, higher than the kneejerk but lower than the deliberate kick. To attempt such a classification was to leave the solid ground of physiological science and enter the slippery arena where schools of psychology engaged in dubious battle.

Little of the experimentation or reasoning that Bekhterev did along these lines at the turn of the century was considered startlingly new, certainly not epochal, either by the profession at large or by Bekhterev himself. Rather, his work was part of the dominant tendency of brain studies to generate more problems than solutions, to create an inconclusive opposition of various hypotheses playing upon incoherent data. Bekhterev's response resembled Pavlov's in one broad sense: he looked with growing intensity for some principle or strategy of research that would be simultaneously 'objective' and unifying. But his style in the search was drastically different. He did not present the associative reflex as the building block — or the philosopher's stone — that would bit by bit put up an entirely new, unitary structure to replace the makeshift clutter of the human sciences. That was Pavlov's style. Bekhterev's project of unification was ecumenical rather than sectarian, a banner for coalition of existing congregations rather than creation of yet another. He even included speculative philosophy, instead of dismissing it with a sneer. He favored a sort of Spinozist ontology: mind and body, he declared, are two aspects of one substance, energy, which manifests itself sometimes as matter, sometimes as mind.[97] On that basis he was willing to include in the grand coalition even parapsychology, as we would call it. If energy manifests itself as matter or as mind, and matter has fields of force that act at a distance, then 'the influence of [disembodied] thought across space' becomes a possibility to be tested in the laboratory, where he proved it to be an indisputable fact. An experimenter would think of a number, and a dog would give just that many barks.[98]

That bit of science is offered to indicate Bekhterev's uninhibited eclecticism, not his eccentricity. He was quite the opposite of a crank in the perception of the scientific community. He was a superb organizer of diverse disciplines and schools, on an institutional if not an intellectual level. The Psychoneurological Institute, which he founded in 1908 with private and governmental funds, was too modest in its title. Within five years Russia's chief medical journal was describing it as a veritable university or academy, for Bekhterev had groups of specialists working on:

> general and experimental psychology, psychiatry, the doctrine of the nervous system in normal and in sick conditions, the doctrine of hypnosis and suggestion, pedagogical and social psychology, general sociology, criminal anthropology and the psychology of the criminal, and also the philosophical sciences that have a clear connection with the psychology of man.[99]

On the intellectual level Bekhterev tried to fit such diverse studies within a vision of 'objective psychology', which he first presented in an essay of 1904 and then developed into a three-volume treatise that began to appear in 1907 and grew steadily through succeeding years in various editions and translations.[100]

In 1912 he began using the term 'psychoreflexology' or simply 'reflexology' as a synonym for 'objective psychology'. The new term suggested an extreme form of physiological reductionism, but it was only in a loose manner of speaking that Bekhterev asserted the reduction of all animal behavior to reflexes. Indeed, he explicitly broke the reflex concept into three different categories or levels: 'ordinary reflexes', 'associative reflexes', and 'general reactions'.[101] The first was the physiological reflex in the strict sense — what neurologists are looking for when they scratch the sole of the foot or tap the knee, to see if certain discrete, automatic, involuntary functions of the nervous system are operating normally. 'Associative reflexes' were similar to those that Pavlov callēd 'conditional': habit-formed automatic reactions to repeated stimuli, which fade away when the stimuli cease. (I am postponing a bundle of difficulties with that simplified definition.)

By adding 'general reactions' as a separate category of 'reflex' action, Bekhterev broke quite free of the strictly physiological concept, turning it into a loose metaphor that he could drape over any type of behavior, or indeed of interior thought and feeling. In that eclectic vein he drew an explicit distinction between reflexology as a kind of physiology and reflexology as a kind of psychology. Thus he felt free to include within reflexology any school or trend in human studies — even Marxism, after the Soviet Revolution made it significant for academic psychologists. Bekhterev, we may say, had a rubber-sheet sense of consistency; he could stretch the reflex concept to cover a variety of views that less flexible thinkers found incompatible.

Even so, in addition to such conscious and explicit eclecticism, there are unwitting incongruities in his voluminous publications. For example, he sometimes indulged in the imaginary cortical explanation of conditioned or associated reflexes which, at other times, he amended to allow for subcortical hypotheses. Bearing in mind his freewheeling, easygoing habit of thought, we should not try to press too firm an interpretation upon his ultimate definition of reflexology: 'the objective biological investigation of the personality of man as a biosocial being'.[102] He was simply raising the reflex concept out of its physiological rut, turning it into a benediction on − or a claim of sovereignty over − any form of human studies that somehow or other acknowledges our biological nature. Such usage was slovenly, but − or therefore − Bekhterev was free to be quite rigorous in neurophysiology. Pavlov, on the other hand, who was trying to stretch the physiological concept of the reflex to be, literally, the element of which all behavior is compounded, had a powerful incentive to ignore or explain away much of the disorderly data in brain studies.

So it is hardly surprising that the two advocates of objective psychology clashed in their unavoidable encounters at St Petersburg conferences − once Pavlov had converted to the study of conditioned reflexes. As late as 1899 they were still amiable, while discussing a paper by one of Bekhterev's students. He had done electrical stimulation of a dog's brain to obtain a flow of gastric juice, and he opened his report with a tribute to Pavlov's school for its pioneering investigation of psychic secretions, whose neural mechanism he was trying to illuminate. In the discussion Pavlov and Bekhterev both accepted the dualism of psychic *v.* reflexive secretion.[103] But only three years later, when Pavlov had made his plunge for the dissolution of the psychic element in a general theory of conditioned reflexes, he was quite sarcastic to Bekhterev: 'You poison, you operate, you keep the animal in an unnatural situation, and thus you create extremely shaky ground' for experimental results.[104]

Bekhterev could strike back with more telling force, since he was a hardnosed neurologist as well as an eclectic theorist. He was free to recall neurological facts that were quite inconvenient to the more single-minded Pavlov. In the course of an extended exchange at a 1908 session of the St Petersburg Medical Society, Pavlov was pressed back to his rhetoric about 'facts alone' deciding, verbal disputes settling nothing, while he was actually evading the specific facts that Bekhterev kept thrusting upon him: instances of 'compensation', as Bekhterev called the conditioning of animals after removal of the cortex.[105]

Pavlov also fell back on historical argumentation. He deplored the trend of brain physiology since the 1870s, when the vogue of electrical stimulation had begun. 'Nothing new', he declared, 'has been accomplished. Petty elaboration of details has of course gone on, but fundamental guiding ideas, fundamental methods have been exhausted ...'[106] Yet he denied the charge that he was rejecting electrical stimulation and extirpation in brain studies. He insisted, as usual, that he would show what those methods could yield later on, after his school had established 'the normal operation of the cerebral hemispheres' by working out the laws of conditioned reflexes.

In the meantime Pavlov could even the score in private. In opposition to a three-man committee, which recommended a prize for Bekhterev's *Foundations of the Science of Brain Functions*, Pavlov wrote a confidential review that blocked the prize with a variety of criticisms. Some of them applied as much to his own school as to Bekhterev's: he had a tendency to treat hypotheses as if they were proven theories, to make an inchoate field of inquiry seem clearly laid out, to present the work of his own laboratories and to ignore others'. On one point Bekhterev may indeed have been more vulnerable: he 'constantly mixed up psychological and physiological points of view'.[107] An outside observer would amend that a bit: Bekhterev came closer than Pavlov to an *explicit* mixture of the two viewpoints.

Since the participants in those debates were Russian physiologists, not American behaviorists, none of them put off the problems of neural mechanisms in favor of the black-box approach to objective psychology. That is, no one described the laws of associative or conditioned reflexes as statistical correlations of stimuli and responses, which could be a new, supposedly autonomous science of behavioral studies, formerly obscured within psychology, the would-be science of the so-called mind. Russian physiologists were too much imbued with the conviction that mind and body are essential realities, even when they were discussing the possibility of reducing one to the other. The reader may recall how a student of Sechenov's reproached Pavlov for failing to 'get at the psychic process itself. What you are getting is the result of a process, the result of a series of associations, but you are not investigating the process itself.'[108] Pavlov did not reply, 'So much the worse for the thing in itself.' He shared the general assumption that psychologists investigated 'the psychic process itself', which he derided as 'the poetry of the problem', to be set aside by scientific study of the neural process. The black-box behaviorist notion that one might set aside *both* things in themselves − the neural as well as the mental process − was hardly considered, except in the context of philosophers' debates.

Russian physiologists in their professional disputes occasionally edged toward such issues, but only inadvertently, when, for example, they debated the question: Is salivation a good choice as a representative bit of behavior? Bekhterev thought it was not. He thought salivation too erratic and variable, by contrast with an either-or bit of behavior such as leg retraction, and he thought it too simple to be representative of higher complex functions.[109] The first objection — too variable — was the criticism of a modern physiologist; he wants a 'preparation' as artificially simplified as possible, approaching in its schematic structure a single neuron turning a single muscle fiber on or off. The second objection — too simple — was a psychologist's criticism; he wants, not a 'preparation' but a 'subject', as close as possible to the whole natural animal behaving in its normal manner, though still 'subject' to controlled study. (Note the critical ambivalence of 'subject', which means an active agent *and* an object of study.) Thus the stress of American behaviorists was, from the start, on cats in problem-solving boxes or rats in mazes, that is, animals which must take some action to achieve some result. The Americans were mainly psychologists, on the way to 'operant conditioning', as they would call the reversal of Pavlov's and Bekhterev's sequence. Putting the response before the stimulus — the rat must go through the maze to receive some food — the American experimenters were coming perilously close to reading intention, which is to say mind, into the behavior of the experimental animal.

Both Pavlov and Bekhterev were physiologists in their experimental approach to objective psychology. They trained the subject (or object, or subject conceived as object) to act like a 'preparation', that is, to stand quietly in a harness, passively waiting for a signal of forthcoming pleasure or pain. Russian experimenters would come to the American viewpoint in the 1920s and 1930s, when some would argue that Pavlovian or 'classical' conditioning revealed only a limited part of the animal's repertory, that 'natural experiments' with free running animals were necessary to study more varied roles. In the pre-revolutionary debates Bekhterev pointed in that direction, but only inadvertently. He was still a physiologist, though he had a loose habit of thought that permitted him to perceive the reflex concept not only literally, in the physiologist's sense, but also metaphorically, in the psychologist's, while still believing that both were part of 'objective psychology' or 'reflexology'. Pavlov was more vehemently opposed to the subjectivity of psychological science, and therefore he was less objective in his physiology. Insisting that the same concept of the reflex applied in both disciplines, he was boxing himself into increasing isolation from both.

He was also boxing himself into conflict with evolutionary biology, though he chose to ignore the fact. V. A. Vagner, a zoologist on the staff of Bekhterev's Institute, who inspired Chekhov to make an ironic fiction out of the challenge that a Darwinist presents to a humanist, in reality challenged objective psychologists to confront Darwinism, without success in Pavlov's case, while Bekhterev stretched reflexology to include Vagner's evolutionary approach to psychology. It may seem quite objective to note that natural selection has established increasingly complex levels of behavior on ascending levels of animal species, but subjectivity creeps in when one tries to explain the intentional behavior of the higher species. Jacques Loeb triumphed over mind-reading psychologists when he demonstrated that caterpillars are drawn toward certain patterns of light in rigidly mechanical fashion, but when he declared that every level of animal behavior could be explained by such 'tropisms', he was indulging in fantasy no less subjective than reading curiosity into the moth that seeks the flame.

Trouble inheres in very simple factual observations, such as: a cat can solve more problems than a caterpillar, and a human far more than a cat. Pavlov tried to prove that all levels of animal behavior are chains of conditioned reflexes.[110] For example, if his team could establish salivation to a light that precedes a bell that precedes a feeding, they would prove that a man going out to shop is responding to a chain of conditioned stimuli which end in feeding.[111] They had a testable hypothesis, and the tests brought disappointment. Pavlov and his team could not establish even short chains of conditioned reflexes. One link seemed to be the limit in conditioning. The dogs salivated to immediate signals of feeding, not to anterior signals of signals that preceded feeding – regularly to the bell that comes before the feeding, rarely to the light that comes before the bell, never to the shock that comes before the light that comes before the bell that comes before the feeding.[112]

My talk of signals rather than stimuli may violate the objectivist rule against mind-reading, for signals have intentional meaning, if not to a telephone apparatus, to the human beings talking at each end of it. To ask which parts of the human nervous system are analogous to the telephone apparatus, as opposed to the parts that understand meaningful signals, is to be entangled in the difficulties which drove Sechenov from neurophysiology. Bekhterev pointed to the cerebral cortex as the area where future research would resolve such difficulties, while rallying various schools and specialties to the slogan: 'Break the yoke of subjectivism.'[113] Pavlov thought to escape neurophysiological difficulties right away by showing that the cortex was the area of conditioned reflexes, and that chains of conditioned reflexes were equivalent to meaningful signals. Both efforts quickly led to criticism and frustration, which occasionally caused Pavlov to waver a bit in his basic commitment, as we will see. But mostly his reaction was to dig in more and more stubbornly, insisting that the cortex *is* the site of conditioning and that the conditioned reflex *is* the elemental unit of which all so-called mental processes are compounded.

But let us postpone for a while the divergent roles of Pavlov's and Bekhterev's schools in the development of neurophysiology and neuropsychology. We must first account for the revulsion against subjectivity that they shared with each other, and with other thinkers at the turn of the century. For that we must consider the poetry, not just of the neurophysiologist's problem, but of the human thing, aware of the incongruity between thingness, existence as a natural object, and subjective consciousness. I will argue that the scientific urge to extreme objectivity, like the artistic urge to extreme subjectivity, and the ideological call for grand union in progressive action, all took their rival shapes from the acutely discordant self-consciousness of the age, acting out, as it were, the mocking boast of Emerson's Brahma: 'When me they fly, I am the wings.'

6
The Poetry of the Thing, and the Politics

In November 1916 the Petrograd Philosophical Society drew Pavlov into an unprecedented discussion. It was unprecedented for them, who normally disregarded physiology, and for him, who routinely disregarded philosophy and psychology. He opened the session with a characteristic exposition of his 'doctrine' (*uchenie*) of conditioned reflexes, presenting it as a set of unavoidable inferences from the experimental data of physiology.[1] But as soon as the assembled philosophers and psychologists started arguing, they pushed him away from his chosen ground, the supposedly unanswerable 'language of facts'. (Bekhterev was the only one to challenge him there; he gave a long critique of Pavlov's hypothetical brain processes, which the philosophical editor omitted from the printed record as a technicality.)[2] Pavlov, driven to philosophize about his technicalities, surpassed his usual metaphor of man as a clock to show that the psyche is a function of a mechanical system, as timekeeping is of a watch. Paving stones in the street, he said, constitute a functioning system. If a concept like the psyche is unnecessary to analyze a street made of paving stones, why bring it in to analyze an animal made of cells?[3]

The philosopher who pressed him that far accepted the analogy, as an introduction to his own metaphysics of systems analysis, a way to overcome both the materialism that he perceived in Pavlov's doctrine and the psychophysical parallelism that he perceived in other neurophysiologists. That was evidently too much for Pavlov, who tried to get back to his usual rhetoric of pure science:

> I have not gone into that, the philosophical part. For me my subject and my principles have only methodological significance. I cannot agree that my methods constitute pure materialism. I pursue only the methods of useful research. The point at issue is only by what procedure it is most fruitful to work. I say that thus and so is necessary,

that thus and so proves itself in reality. You have brought up something else and have got involved with Weltanschauung. I have little acquaintance with that; I have always limited myself only to practice, to methods.[4]

The assembled philosophers and psychologists refused to be satisfied by such talk.* In particular, A. I. Vvedenskii gave Pavlov a lecture on the inevitability of philosophical decisions, if only to justify the choice between his objective psychology, which dispensed with the concept of mind, and the usual subjective approach, which assumed the reality of mind in order to analyse it.[5] Pavlov, replying, repeated his satisfaction with science alone, his indifference to philosophy and psychology. Even his courteous acknowledgment of the other disciplines' right to exist implied an inferior existence for them: 'I do not absolutely reject psychology; I only say that with this object, an animal, there is no scientific benefit in connecting one's research with the internal state of the dog, when I proceed more surely without that, and a serious scientific result is achieved.'[6]

A. I. Vvedenskii, as the reader may recall, liked to boast that he had virtually predicted objective psychology, on philosophical grounds, before Pavlov and Bekhterev and the American behaviorists created it in scientific fact. If Pavlov had proved to be the Darwin of the new century, as he liked to fancy himself, A. I. Vvedenskii might have been its Herbert Spencer. But historical reality has been unkind to both. Psychology has stubbornly resisted reduction to physiology, which has casually ignored Pavlov's schemes of brain function, and twentieth-century culture at large has mocked expectations of unified knowledge even in eclectic forms. Neither Pavlov's nor any other version of objective psychology has become the central doctrine of the age, organizing thought about the human mind and its place in nature. As for A. I. Vvedenskii's eclectic philosophy of science, justifying both objective and subjective psychologies, it has fallen so short of an influence comparable to Spencer's that forgetting him may seem an act of sensible charity. But it is unfair to single him out for invidious oblivion. Disregard for all philosophers of science was evident in Pavlov's aloof response to Vvedenskii; he shrugged off any offer of philosophical justification. On the other hand he did not object when a few of his disciples approved Vvedenskii's grounding of their science in neo-Kantian philosophy. That was a little seal of academic respectability — until the Bolshevik Revolution made Marxism the seal, and a few of Pavlov's disciples put *that* upon their master's doctrine.[7]

That range of attitudes — from the master's express disdain to fickle displays of concern by a few scientists, with a stolidly silent majority in

* And Soviet scholars have refused to take note of it or even to publish it, in two editions of Pavlov's 'complete' works or in supplementary volumes of Pavloviana.

between — shows the humble place of philosophers of science in twentieth-century culture. Their cogitation is hardly the place to seek the basic assumptions that scientists bring to their work. Philosophers' arguments have been symptoms rather than causes, after-the-fact commentary in another of the sequestered disciplines that clutter the landscape of high culture. I do not doubt that philosophical assumptions were working in Pavlov and other creators of objective psychology. On the contrary, I am calling attention to the inarticulate assumptions that they kept stubbornly concealed within the 'language of facts', protected by deaf ears against the arguments of academic philosophers. Nor am I doubting that a few twentieth-century philosophers have had very broad cultural influence, which must have had some effect on scientists like Pavlov — unacknowledged, indirect, perhaps negative. I insist upon such influences. We can hope to identify them if we begin by noting an obvious feature of this century's otherwise fragmented culture: the few philosophers who have had exceptionally broad influence have offered wisdom to the educated public, not knowledge alone; they have favored the literary imagination over scientific modes of inquiry as the way to wisdom.

Positivist philosophers sequestered in English-speaking universities may snort in derision, but the educated public pays little heed to them. Certainly this has been the case in continental Europe. Among educated Russians, V. S. Solov'ev epitomized the exceptionally influential philosopher during the last few decades of the Tsarist system, in large part because he reached most vividly beyond the limited vision of the positive sciences.[8] That was the theme of his doctoral dissertation, *The Crisis of Western Philosophy: Against Positivism* (1874), which broke out of academic obscurity, provoking discussion in the 'thick journals' of the educated public. For the rest of his short life — he died in 1900, aged forty-seven — Solov'ev wrote as much for that larger audience as for his professorial colleagues. He linked speculative philosophy with dissident religion and mildly radical political ideology; he even used verse to join thought and feeling in unashamed subjectivity. In such verse, widely read and quoted, we may hope to find the philosophical beliefs actually at work in the minds of educated Russians.

The communion of minds mediated by imaginative writers and political ideologists — that is where one must seek the most widely shared, most basic philosophical assumptions which Pavlov and the other objective psychologists were reacting to, when they strove to wall themselves off in pure science, protected by objectivity — from what? That question is as hard to answer as it is important to ask. It makes little or no sense to focus the search for an answer on a particular philosophical system, not even one as famous as Solov'ev's. Pavlov probably did not read him, or any other philosopher after Spencer; Bekhterev may have glanced, at most. Since we are dealing with scientists who were determined to escape introspective psychology and speculative philosophy, our first clues are the stereotyped phrases that they used on exceptional occasions, when they felt obliged to contrast their claims of objective science with the non-scientific modes of thought they were trying to surmount. Gestures of negation were their manner of tacit discourse with the dominant literary and political mentalities of educated Russians.

In this respect Bekhterev's record is a much more difficult source than Pavlov's, precisely because he was much more voluble on many more exceptional occasions. He was less narrowly compulsive in his striving for scientific objectivity, much freer with the language of the literary and ideological imagination. Perhaps the most illuminating example is his criticism of Freud, the supreme master of the eclectic style that invokes objective science to put the reader in awe of the literary imagination.[9] Bekhterev began his critique of Freud with approval of the basic assumption: 'sexual arousal is reducible to a chemism', which will ultimately be explained by endocrinology and neurophysiology. So far, both scientists conceded, little was known of the sexual 'chemism', yet both were courageously free with hypotheses, which quickly rose from tentative introductory notes to the boldest tones of objective knowledge. Bekhterev noted that dubious pattern — surmise palmed off as certainty — in Freud's writings, which he therefore accused of 'extreme subjectivity'. He preferred the 'chemism' of a Russian colleague, who built a model of sexual arousal on an analogy with itching and scratching in eczema.

But the mechanism of coupling was only a minor point of initial disagreement. Bekhterev rose with Freud to analysis of love, which required intuition of feelings, even in a nursing infant. He rehearsed Freud's vivid picture of the infant's eager motions and lustful sounds while seeking the nipple and sucking, noted the flushed sleep of repletion — and sharply disapproved Freud's analogy with adults in copulation. That was a degradation of the special love between mother and child, which must have a different neural and endocrine mechanism since it was obviously different from sexual love, not to mention lust. It would be extremely difficult to isolate the objectivist urge in such a free mixture of imaginative chemism with imaginative reading of an infant's mind and imaginative taxonomy of love. I intend no disrespect to the imagination; I merely wish to note that three different types of imaginative thought were mixed together as objective science by Bekhterev, and by the master of such mixtures whom he was criticizing.

Pavlov furnished fewer and simpler tangles, which lend themselves more readily to unraveling. Consider again his initial lecture on conditioned reflexes, the 1903 'history of a physiologist's conversion from purely physiological questions to the field of phenomena that are usually called psychic'.[10] Mostly he insisted upon the unavoidable logic of laboratory experience, which obliged him and his colleagues to seek escape from the disagreement that occurred 'in our psychic — let us use that word for a while —

experiments on the salivary glands'. When they tried to interpret a dog's state of mind, they had no constantly reliable way to settle arguments. How could they decide, for example, whether a dog's 'psychic salivation' was prompted by anticipatory pleasure or fear or mental association that turned into mindless habit? They had to rule such debates out of order — literally: fines were exacted from members of the team who lapsed into mentalist language.[11]

But Pavlov did not limit his defense of objectivity to the logic of experimentation. He reached outside the laboratory for a broader justification of the objectivist flight from inherently disagreeable mind-reading:

> Furthermore, does not the persistent misery of life consist in the fact that people for the most part do not understand each other, cannot enter into one another's condition! Where then is knowledge, where is the power of knowledge in the possibility that we might, perhaps even truly, reproduce the condition of another?[12]

At the end of the lecture he resumed that pathetic appeal to put objective science in place of intuitive efforts at mutual mind-reading. The method of natural science, he insisted, was the way 'to illuminate our innermost nature, to clarify the mechanism and the meaning of life in that which concerns man most of all — his consciousness, the torments of his consciousness.'[13]

If I call those phrases stereotyped — and I do — I may be condescending to the style of expression, but I am not doubting the genuineness of Pavlov's feeling. On the contrary: like bits of imitative verse in a dismissal of poetry, such phrases evinced genuine feeling, of distaste. Pavlov was momentarily indulging an alien mode of expression to show why he was determined to avoid it. I do doubt, I expressly deny, that Pavlov, in the 'innermost nature' of his own personality, was genuinely concerned with 'the meaning of life in . . . [man's] consciousness, the torments of his consciousness.' He was genuinely concerned to brush aside those preoccupations of educated Russians, so that all might share his faith in 'clarify[ing] the mechanism' as the only way to subject our unruly selves to 'knowledge, . . . the power of knowledge'.

His personal letters, the stenographic records of his extemporizing (usually at sessions of physiologists but also in psychiatric wards), the reminiscences of him by students and friends — none of that abundant evidence shows anything more than occasional observation, from without, of his contemporaries' endless talk about the torments of consciousness, the failures of mutual understanding, the tragic condition of humanity everywhere but especially so in Russia. For one brief period, his courtship in 1880–1, Pavlov read Dostoevsky to please his fiancée. His letters to her indulged in some awestruck oh-ing and ah-ing over the great writer's insights, but ended by telling Serafima of the true mind that would subdue hers in marriage: literary insights were unsatisfactory because they yielded no power. Only natural science could disclose our real nature by giving us predictable mastery of it.[14]

Pavlov was an assertive little one-sided man, quite untroubled by doubts concerning natural science, especially physiological science, as a way of life for himself and, in its future perfection, a guide to life for all. Perhaps the neatest revelations of his mentality came in psychiatric discussions, when he was such a celebrity that stenographers attended his visits to bedlam. The case of a 27-year-old 'mild hysteric' is especially illuminating — 'a nice hysteric', as her psychiatrist put it, to distinguish her from the usual 'difficult' type.[15] A cluster of specialists discussed the case with Pavlov at length, mingling physiological fantasies of 'signal systems' and neurological 'types' with snap judgments about the young woman's particularities. She had an undeveloped uterus, very irregular periods, and a record of 'sexual perversions': masturbated in childhood, dressed as a boy in ballet school, broke off with a young man after reading Freud, vomited when asked about sexual relations. She had come to the mental hospital because of convulsive seizures in facial muscles, headaches, extreme insomnia, and — what troubled her most — fear that she was losing her capacity for work. She dreamed of becoming an artist; she had read philosophy. When she was brought from the ward to the learned conclave, Pavlov opened with that:

Pavlov   Well, are you studying philosophy now, are you paying attention to it or not?

Patient   No, I used to be interested in it.

Pavlov   And what did you read?

Patient   Many different books. The last I was interested in was Hegel.

Pavlov   What? Did you like him?

Patient   Very much.

Pavlov   What did you like? Didn't it strike you that Hegel has little connection with reality?

Patient   Since I came to Hegel from Marx, that did not strike me. I accepted it as natural.

Pavlov   Did you read his various conclusions and representations about human and universal relationships? Did all that seem real to you, and not a purely verbal construction?

Patient   From his point of view it is real. For me it was of course an abstraction.

Pavlov   Didn't the fantastic quality hit you in the eye?

Patient   But that seemed natural to me.

Pavlov   What? Did you read him as a fairytale or as something serious?

Patient   As something serious.

Pavlov   But what is serious consists in reality, in drawing conclusions
         as they originate. Then it is interesting. Or is this interesting
         as a fairytale? How does this seem to you? How does this
         please you, as a verbal picture taking in a mass of phenomena,
         or ... [*sic*]
Patient Hegel also has his ground.
Pavlov   Purely verbal. Is it like reality, does it relate to reality?
Patient Of course it does.[16]

Pavlov would not stop badgering, and she would not give in. Did she
not prefer Spencer to Hegel? Her reflexive 'Hegel, of course', provoked his
reflexive 'language of facts': 'But Spencer is related every minute to reality.'
To which the young intellectual sneeringly countered: 'Yes, creeping reality;
he is too empirical.' Finally a learned doctor broke in: 'It's clear that she
likes philosophy which concerns reality, is not cut off from reality, but
which includes a philosophical system, and is not a crudely mechanical
arrangement of facts. Did I understand you?' 'Indeed. Thanks for the help',
the patient replied. Pavlov retreated to a brief query about her interest in
art, a brief interrogation about her convulsions, and the conclave of scientists
let her go back to ordinary bedlam.[17]

Temperaments differ, among mechanistic scientists as among other
believers. Reading of Schopenhauer brought Jacques Loeb through melancholy to a calming vision. If will is reducible to the biological forces that
hold a person in thrall, escape is impossible. Freedom is an illusion, but we
can ease our servitude through understanding of the forces that knock us
about in our transient lives. That is a modern version of an ancient tradition,
which perceives genuine freedom in recognition of necessity, in disdain for
the illusion of free will. A sense of tragic dignity has often accompanied
that philosophy, in its Stoic or its Spinozist forms, and Promethean defiance
inspires some of the Marxist versions. But the scientistic varieties that
flourish in our century aspire to the dream of technical power rather than
the dignity of submissive understanding or the defiant pride of the rebel. It
is such a dream, of science as technical power, that one finds in Pavlov.
There were times when he saw the laboratory as a refuge from a mad
world of war and revolution, but the soothing effect depended on the belief
that his sequestered labor was preparing objective knowledge to master the
madness outside.[18]

He did little reading and less writing apart from physiology, not even in
evolutionary theory, which might have made his faith less serene, certainly
less simple. Perhaps the arguments of his Darwinian critic, V. A. Vagner,
warned Pavlov to stay away from deep thought about evolution and
psychology. Vagner shared Pavlov's disapproval of subjectivity in the
dominant schools of psychology, and also sought countervailing objectivity
in a biological approach to the psyche. But that frame of mind did not

shelter him from such themes as 'Renan and Nietzsche; On the Beast in Man' or 'The Old Naturalism and the Philosophy of World Pain' (he rendered *Weltschmerz* into Russian).[19] Vagner connected biological science with such issues through his basic concept of emergent levels in evolution. At successively later and more complex levels — Vagner said 'higher' levels without worrying about the taint of subjective judgment — new patterns of instinct and capability emerge. They are reducible to biological processes in an historical sense, by the mind engaged in retrospection. They are not presently reducible in the physiologist's laboratory by the mind proving its technical mastery. Unrepeatable series of past biological events extending over many millions of years have established in humans such unique mental qualities as consciousness, which are not presently reducible to the reflexes that govern canine salivation. That is how Vagner set evolutionary 'biopsychology' against Pavlov's simpler version of the mechanistic faith; emphasis on process and emergence opened his biologist's mind to consideration of Nietzsche, naturalism, and *Weltschmerz*.[20]

If Pavlov worried about the compatibility of his doctrine with evolutionary theory, he could find reassurance in the writings of K. A. Timiriazev, the most well-known Russian Darwinist, who also ignored Vagner's insistence on emergent levels of mentality and uncritically admired Pavlov's insistence that behavior at any level can be explained by reflexes. Timiriazev celebrated Pavlov's doctrine as a victory of objective science over subjective psychology, which he scorned.[21] Whether that simple dichotomy was spoiled by Vagner's 'biopsychology' Timiriazev did not pause to consider. Since he was the most eminent popularizer of natural science in late Tsarist Russia, a master of old-fashioned ornate rhetoric, his writings reveal more abundantly than Pavlov's the dike of scientism that both were raising against 'the reactionary wave of "the decadent epoch", . . . when the cult of the inane word, sound, color has replaced the cult of clear, definite thought coming from observable reality. . . .'[22]

Another distinguished biologist and admirer of Pavlov's quoted Timiriazev to sum up the age:

Among our ravished ideals and shattered hopes it may be only science, positive science, unified by positive philosophy, that is crossing the threshold of the century without wavering and doubt, in calm consciousness of its obligation fulfilled and of unexampled success in the past and with bold confidence that nothing has the power to stay its triumphant march into the future.[23]

That stereotyped talk of 'ravished ideals and shattered hopes' at 'the threshold of the century' acknowledged the *fin-de-siècle* mood from which believers in scientism claimed exemption, even if they had to achieve it by ignoring problems that nineteenth-century biology had created.

I substitute 'scientism' for Timiriazev's talk of 'positive philosophy', because Comte and Spencer were losing the unifying and uplifting power they had had among educated people in the bygone days of Timiriazev's and Pavlov's youth. Positivism was becoming a narrowly analytic philosophy, struggling to specify exactly what distinguishes genuine knowledge from spurious imitations, losing its confident visions of unified knowledge and progress, chastened by cultural trends that Timiriazev and Pavlov could not reason away. They could only point, with phrases of revulsion, at the chaos that their scientific objectivity was supposed to master. In effect, they were becoming internal exiles. Their scientism — the belief that natural science is the only form of genuine knowledge — was a fortress mentality. It sheltered them from the literary and ideological culture that had been carrying educated Russians — and Europeans at large — away from the grand positivism of the 1860s.

We must see ourselves as natural objects, the advocates of objective psychology insisted, filling their journals and books with theoretical schemes and supporting detail, and stubbornly ignoring the very different visions of ourselves as natural objects which filled the poetry, the novels and plays, and the ideological tracts of the time. Such a self-isolating culture cannot be understood without some sense of the larger world that is being excluded. The profane culture of the gentiles inspires the shuttered faith of the ghetto more than either side can bear to acknowledge. The literary and ideological culture of educated Russians at large will reveal, if we factor it properly, some common denominator of belief to which Pavlov and his comrades were reacting. Themes and works that were generally known, if not at first hand at least by constant allusions and derivative variations, will disclose the mentality that was coming to dominate the age, the naturalism that objectivists hid from in laboratories with loyal comrades sworn to use no mentalist language.

NATURALISTIC VISIONS: POETRY

My map will show ironic circularity: objective psychologists unwittingly confined themselves within the mentality they thought to exclude. Claiming to reduce the mind to functions of the nervous system, they were actually surrendering to the belief that the human mind is incongruous with the rest of nature.

The sense of incongruity between ourselves as natural objects and ourselves as conscious subjects came to dominate educated Russians as the nineteenth century turned into the twentieth. Some of the visions that I will offer in evidence bridged naturalist metaphysics and political ideology, and to that extent softened the underlying conviction that the human being is a natural object afflicted with consciousness, born to die like any other animal, yet requiring knowledge of purpose or meaning that reach beyond its brief existence. Political ideologies offered such transcendent knowledge, but the literary imagination relentlessly undermined it, working down to the bleak bedrock of naturalism, the vision of human beings as natural objects and nothing more.

Nihilism is the usual term for that 'nothing more' naturalism, and modern science is inseparable from it. The view of nature that is essential to science seems to make nothing of the long-term values and purposes that are essential to the human mind, to consciousness. Writers might declare themselves opposed to such a nihilistic vision, but their literary imagination persistently recreated it in poetry and fiction. And that occurred within a Russian context of great upheaval, amidst cries for fervent belief in the public thing, whether leftist *res publica* or rightist leviathan, the aggregation that is supposed to realize the values and purposes inherent in each of its units, or maybe the other way round: the units acquiring values and purposes by aggregation into the public thing. Or maybe both. Or neither, on the argument that the sum of pointless lives is a pointless collective life.

Maybe history can disclose patterns in chaos. The vision of ourselves as natural objects has provoked a variety of reactions in many countries over a long period of time. The limited question here is whether we can discern a modern Russian type, emerging in the 1860s and becoming a more and more distinct species as cultural crisis merged with political convulsion in the twentieth century. I think we can, if we construct a montage — turn-of-century snapshots set within flashbacks and forward glances — to get the sense of a mentality developing in conflict with itself from the 1860s to the Bolshevik Revolution, and beyond.

Note as preview the paradoxical fate of the three most famous treatments of 'nihilism' that appeared in the 1860s and long outlasted that moment of peaceful reform: Turgenev's *Fathers and Sons*, Chernyshevsky's *What Is To Be Done?*, and Dostoevsky's *Notes From Underground*. While Turgenev's and Dostoevsky's troubled brooding grew in creative influence throughout the world, Chernyshevsky's celebration of 'nihilism' was elevated above creative thought, within Russia alone. In other countries his book was largely ignored; in Russia it turned into an icon for radicals, bowed to rather than read or thought about. By creative political action, increasingly separated from creative thought, radicals carried forward Chernyshevsky's optimistic faith that natural objects can create meaningful lives, indeed paradise on earth, if they apply scientific analysis to themselves. At the turn of the century movements inspired by that faith were organizing parties for the overthrow of the Tsarist system, though they were no longer reading the revered statement of the creed by Chernyshevsky, their martyr hero.

Those are complex cases, which require extensive analysis of collective mentalities. Let us approach them from within an individual mind which reached maturity at the turn of the century, revealing its own creative thought at odds with its ideological faith in science. A startling case in point is *The Republic of the Southern Cross*, a fantasy published in 1905 by V. I. Briusov.[24] He imagined a society so overwhelmingly scientific in its organization that the alienated citizens explode in self-destructive anarchy to prove their freedom, as if they were acting out the predictions of Dostoevsky's Underground Man when he reflected on the Crystal Palace, the first world fair, prime symbol of industrial society. Certainly Briusov's fantasy was not the dream of Chernyshevsky's Faith (*Vera*), the heroine of *What Is To Be Done?* She saw herself emancipated from a dark basement (*podpol'e*, 'underground', Chernyshevsky's symbol of egotistical isolation before it was Dostoevsky's), and guided by gentle young physiologists to the sunny fields where 'love of humanity' reveals herself to be the guiding spirit of science. Briusov's fantasy took Dostoevsky's side of the argument, though Briusov declared himself a disciple of Chernyshevsky and wound up supporting the Soviet regime, even joining the Communist Party.

Concerning his lifelong ideological commitment Briusov's autobiographical notes seem unequivocal:

> Over my father's desk there always hung portraits of Chernyshevsky and Pisarev. From the cradle, so to speak, I was raised in the principles of materialism and atheism. ... It hardly needs to be said that in our house there wasn't even a memory of religion: faith in God seemed to me the same kind of prejudice as faith in household spirits and fairies. ... That is what created my world view, my psychology. And I think that what it was in childhood, such it has remained, and will be to the end of my life.[25]

Against that background it seems quite appropriate to find Briusov in 1909 declaring the need for 'scientific poetry', which would

> endow our knowledge with the unity that the scattered fields of science are not capable of giving. ... Poetry must give meaning to reality, establish its relations to the constant laws of history and sociology. Using its methods of intuitive synthesis, poetry can become the foreteller of the future, and the poet can regain his ancient name – *vates*, prophet. ... To the scientist, accustomed to observe the world in a single section, it will give broad generalizations. ... It will help the political activist make sense of the given historical moment. ... To every thoughtful person it will give a harmonious, rigorously thought-out world view.[26]

That was hardly the world view of Chernyshevsky and Pisarev, who had exalted positive knowledge. Briusov found science inadequate, until transformed by poetic vision.

Back in the eighteenth century expectation of a modern Lucretius had been fairly common; the sciences and the arts seemed then to be progressing in harmonious ensemble, which a great poet would soon express. The nineteenth century spoiled the pretty dream, though Comte and Spencer churned out many prosaic tomes on its behalf. The sciences that explain nature made undeniable progress — further and further away from the arts and the ideologies that express human values, and turn-of-century intellectuals were acutely conscious of the rift. In that context Briusov's declaration of the poet's mission to unify science and art and social process was another instance of his notorious audacity in defying common sense. He was not the only modern poet who shocked. Only a few endorsed his dream of 'science poetry',[27] but some assault on common sense was characteristic of the movements that would be retrospectively labeled 'modernist'. Briusov's was an especially bizarre case of defiant modernism, for he revered Chernyshevsky, who had presented the positivist dream as the obvious common sense of modern times.

The discord appeared within Briusov's poetic works as well as his manifestoes. His 'science poetry' was mediocre, in fact and in public evaluation, while his 'decadent' or 'symbolist' poems made him scandalously famous, and keep his reputation alive to the present time, among émigrés and in the Soviet Union. As an example of the lesser verse, consider 'Life', a Darwinian transformation of the romantic reproach to indifferent nature. The opening sounds grimly naturalistic — 'Faceless [life], it has forgot the count of faces' — but heaps of transient creatures tumbling through the poem turn at last into a modernist version of Schiller's worm joined by joy to the man in the shroud glimpsing angels *in excelsis*:

> O brothers: man! bacillus! tiger! pink!
> And dwellers in unknown other planets!
> And hidden spirits, non-appearing faces!
> We are all mere fleeting sparkle on the endless sea of years![28]

No doubt the author hoped for aesthetic rescue of a human essence by artistic expression of its dissolution, and no doubt the Russian original is closer to such an aesthetic triumph than my prosaic translation, but it still falls short. The deepest trouble is not in the particular poem. Suppose the music of its verse forever enchanting, even when there will be no ears to hear it. Worship of such an essence — the eternally singing sparkle of a momentary wave — is quite at odds with worship of the evolutionary progress that culminates in human social and scientific progress, joining past-present-future in hymnable unity of emergent essence. It was *that* vision — grand positivism — which Chernyshevsky and the other 'nihilists' proclaimed in the 1860s. At the turn of the century leftist ideologists still clung to it as the metaphysical justification of their project. Briusov could join them as an ideologist, but his poetry could not serve the cause.

The conflict was not an external opposition; it was at work within the poet's mind when explicit political ideology was absent. His diary records a trip to the Crimea in 1898, when he 'played the tourist' and tried to make himself 'fall in love with nature' like an old-fashioned poet. His inwardly focused soul or mind (*dusha*) refused; it was still 'above everything', his essential reality. The universe without, analysed by scientists and apostrophized by old-fashioned poets, was mere dust compared to the world within:

> Clearcut lines of mountains;
> A palely-untrue sea . . . [*sic*]
> The enraptured gaze fades,
> Drowns in impotent space.
> I've created in secret dreams
> A world of ideal nature.
> In face of it what is this dust:
> Steppe and cliffs and seas![29]

Some such rebellious inversion of the old romanticism, constructing beauty out of alienation from inhuman nature, has been a characteristic trend in modernism, in the visual arts as well as literature. 'Through art', Picasso said, 'we express our conception of what nature is not.'[30]

On occasion Briusov would push that inversion to revolt even against the sense of the self as a continuous thing within the human object, a thing in time: 'Not man, but the moment is the measure of things. That is true which I recognize as true, and recognize now, today, at this moment.'[31] At one extreme, that may be literal solipsism of the present moment; it may approach actual madness. At another extreme it may become a toy model of madness in reassuring salons, where intellectuals come and go talking of daring overthrow. In between are various combinations of madness and metaphysics, authentic belief and make-believe, all with political significance, sometimes trifling, sometimes momentous, the significance always dependent on the social context, never to be inferred from philosophic content alone.

In 1905 Briusov greeted Russia's first revolutionary convulsion with a poem predicting more and still more, a hymn to 'coming Huns'. 'In the dark depths of his soul', a critic has commented, 'lay the primordial Russian *nihilism*. He loved order, peace, and system, but he was instinctively driven toward chaos. Within Briusov the European sat an ancient Hun.'[32] That was written after 1917, by an émigré critic trying to explain the Bolshevik victory and Briusov's endorsement of it. Soviet critics put their explanations of Briusov and Bolshevism within a very different framework of political and philosophical assumptions.[33] They share the émigrés' tendency to read political significance into philosophical beliefs quite freely, but that freewheeling Russian habit is restrained a bit by the Soviet insistence on an essential distinction: the 'nihilism' of the 1860s and the nihilism of the turn of the century were different. Bolsheviks are proud to claim descent from the former while denying any connection with the latter. The problem is that Briusov revered Chernyshevsky but lived at the turn of the century. It was the latter, genuine nihilism without quotation marks, which he audaciously acclaimed and Lenin abjured and the émigré critic found inherent both in the Russian national character and in the scientific vision of ourselves as natural objects – and in Lenin's Bolshevism, which is supposed to combine the worst features of both: the rage for chaos in the Russian soul and the scientific collapse of values into transient functions of a social process.

What a tumult of ideology and metaphysics! We will have to follow Briusov and his critics into such turbulent mixtures, but we need first to see the metaphysical vision calm and pure, as expressed by an earlier and more famous poet. F. I. Tiutchev, who died in 1873, is still the meditative poet most admired by Russians regardless of ideology. Dobroliubov, radical positivist critic of the 1860s, admired him.[34] Tolstoy, Christian anarchist, was moved to tears by Tiutchev's longing to escape from consciousness of self into 'the abyss', which the poet's godless vision perceived in the natural universe and in its human by-product.[35] Solov'ev, who was much closer to Orthodox Christianity than Tolstoy, demurred from Tiutchev's obsession with 'the dark root of being', but admired – indeed, imitated – the poetry that expressed that obsession.[36] Briusov, admirer of Chernyshevsky, of atheism, and of political radicalism even in its Bolshevik form, was proud to be considered the major heir of Tiutchev in Russian meditative poetry. And Nabokov, aesthetic dandy, satirist of Chernyshevsky's legacy, ostensibly disdainful of any ideology but especially revolted by Bolshevism, was so enamored of Tiutchev that he did translations of him into English verse, though Nabokov believed that the marriage of sense and sound in great poems is essentially untranslatable.[37] Aside from such idiosyncratic eminences, there is commonplace evidence of Tiutchev's universal appeal to educated Russians, regardless of their ideological warfare: he has been persistently republished and commented upon both within the Soviet Union and among Russian émigrés. At the peak of Stalinist fervor in the 1930s and 1940s, there were new editions of his works and a laudatory article in the *Big Soviet Encyclopedia*.[38]

It is Tiutchev's philosophical poetry that has had this hold on Russian minds. His political verse has usually been brushed aside in embarrassment, along with his career as a Tsarist diplomat *and as a censor*. It may seem small-minded to stress his service as a Tsarist censor, but my purpose is not to belittle the poet. It is to credit his astonishing achievement. Though a servant of the Tsarist system in one of its most despised activities, when he indulged his poetic vision of the universe and the human situation in it, he mesmerized the whole reading public. There can hardly be stronger evidence of the attractive power that metaphysical nihilism has had on educated Russians.

Religion did not shelter Tiutchev's imagination, for he lost his faith at an early age. His anguish at the loss, at the consequent bleakness of naturalistic vision, provided the theme of some of his best poems. On a mundane level he did not hesitate to draw shockingly anti-intellectual inferences from the incompatibility of faith and reason. He believed Christianity to be indefensible but indispensable, so he disdained efforts to work out some reasonable version of the faith. 'The only philosophy compatible with Christianity is entirely contained within the catechism.'[39] As a censor he did not follow that belief to its logical extreme; he did not urge the suppression of all philosophical works. Such inconsistencies reflect more credit on his heart than on his intellect, if I may adapt the distinction offered by an astute critic, who deals with Tiutchev's embarrassing ideology by questioning his 'intellectual honesty', while insisting on his 'deep emotional sincerity'.[40] The important point for present purposes is the great poet's refusal of reason when he turned to political ideology. He summed up that refusal in a jingle that delighted nationalists — the last line passed into the language as a common saying — and embarrassed thoughtful Russians:

> You won't grasp Russia with the mind,
> Or take her measure with a footrule:
> Her character's a special kind —
> Believe in her is all you can do.[41]
> (*V Rossiiu mozhno tol'ko verit'*.)

Liberals and radicals condemned such irrational nationalism as evidence of the old order's intellectual bankruptcy. Some may have felt that Tiutchev's philosophical nihilism was a fitting basis for a bankrupt political ideology, but no one published such criticism of him, as far as I know. He scorned modern science for enslaving the mind by trying to impose order on inherently chaotic nature, while the radical Briusov praised science for disclosing the chaos. That difference mattered little to the metaphysical vision they shared, for theirs was not a reasoned, discursive metaphysics, such as an academic philosopher would expound. It was a felt philosophy — 'métaphysique émue' — inseparable from the poetry that expressed it.[42] Of course, many critics have recast Tiutchev's central ideas in discursive prose. Briusov, for example, offered this paraphrase of a well-known poem that begins 'Nature does not know knowing of the past', and ends with a characteristic plunge into 'the all-engulfing and world-creating abyss':

> Genuine being is possessed only by nature in its entirety. Man is merely 'a daydream of nature'. His life, his activity, are merely 'a pointless heroic feat'. That is Tiutchev's philosophy, his innermost world view. Virtually all his poetry is explained by this broad pantheism.[43]

Pantheism is the wrong name for a world view that vividly denies any divine presence and seeks fusion with a universal essence — or anti-essence — symbolized by night and silent space. Here is Nabokov's version of one of the best-known poems, '*Sviataia noch' na nebosklon vzoshla*', which Nabokov entitled 'The Abyss':

> When sacred Night sweeps heavenward, she takes
> the glad, the winsome day, and folding it,
> rolls up its golden carpet that had been
> spread over an abysmal pit.
> Gone vision-like is the external world,
> and man, a homeless orphan, has to face
> in utter helplessness, naked, alone,
> the blackness of immeasurable space.
> Upon himself he has to lean; with mind
> abolished, thought unfathered, in the dim
> depths of his soul he sinks, for nothing comes
> from outside to support or limit him.
> All life and brightness seem an ancient dream –
> while in the substance of the night,
> unravelled, alien, he now perceives
> a fateful something that is his by right.[44]

Nabokov's English lacks the musical enchantment of the original – and restrains the mystery of the parting lines by inserting orderly concepts of 'substance' and 'right' – but it comes closer than other translations to conveying the feeling that we are essentially nothing, but a nothing that thinks and feels.

One paradoxical corollary, repeatedly expressed, is the vanity of self-expression by the human nothing. 'Shut up', Tiutchev exclaims,

> conceal yourself and hide
> Your thoughts, your visions!
> Just learn to live within yourself.[45]

In the self-contradictory writing of such lines there may be some dialectical triumph, looking within the isolated mind and without at mindless nature, seeing 'nothing that is not there and the nothing that is'. (I borrow another expression of that persistent modernistic theme from an American poet, Wallace Stevens.)[46] When Tiutchev published the rhetorical questions:

> How is the heart to express itself?
> How is another person to understand you?
> Will he understand wherewith you live?[47]

he was inviting both the obvious negative – 'No, we cannot understand each other' – and the less obvious positive response: 'Yes, we can understand our common inability to understand.' 'The thought expressed is a lie', Tiutchev concluded, contradicting the meaning of the words by the saying of them.[48]

From such contradictions, when they are artfully wrought, a painful

beauty is born. When a poet watered 'the dark root of being' with a little
Platonism of true hearts, 'symbolist' verse sprouted into sentimental kitsch:

> Dearest friend, don't you sense
> That the one thing in the world as a whole
> Is only that which heart to heart
> Speaks in dumb hello?[49]

That is not Tiutchev but Solov'ev, in a poem once much admired, now
mercifully ignored. I exhume it here as further evidence of a widespread
state of mind among educated Russians at the turn of the century. Even
Pavlov, who probably read no poetry, invoked that theme — 'people for
the most part do not understand each other, cannot enter into one another's
condition' — as a reason to drop the effort to understand and to study
conditioned reflexes instead.

My invidious classification — great poetry in Tiutchev's case, less great
in Briusov's, sentimental kitsch in Solov'ev's, a stereotyped phrase in
Pavlov's turn to conditioned reflexes — is intended to convey something
more than individual taste. Some kind of classification is necessary, for all
those thinkers were reacting in their different ways to a commonly shared
vision of human beings as 'an accidental product of nature, not to be
distinguished from beings that lack endowment of consciousness'.[50] Once
again I use Briusov's prose version of the metaphysical vision that he
absorbed from Tiutchev — and from Chernyshevsky and Pisarev — and
turned into modernistic self-assertion, crafting poetic evidence that individual consciousness was his supreme reality, however accidental or inessential
in the cosmic order that lacks consciousness.

NATURALISTIC VISIONS: PROSE

Some readers will no doubt wonder whether poets expressed a widespread
state of mind. They should recall that poets were once regarded as oracles,
before modernistic retreat into expression of an inexpressible self withered
the public's veneration, and even their interest. That withering was only
beginning in Tsarist Russia. In any case the prose fiction of the Russian
masters, whose hold on the educated public cannot be doubted, reveals an
analogous vision of incoherence between consciousness and natural being.
In prose fiction the vision is less starkly revealed. It is embodied in everyday
happenings, but it is present. That is so even in the tender novel that was
the classic beginning and a persistent source, keeping the problem of
nihilism alive for successive generations of Russian readers: Turgenev's
Fathers and Sons, published in 1862.

A bold young physiologist stands at the center of the novel, angry at the
phony pretenses that hide reality from most people. He seeks the human

essence in physiology, lumping humans with frogs in the search. Trouble attends this angry young man. He cannot express love or accept it; he radiates no sweetness and light, as Chernyshevsky's loving young physiologists do, in *What Is To Be Done?*, a 'nihilist' book that is actually more fairy tale than novel. Its scientist heroes overcome their difficulties with astonishing ease and are living happily ever after as the story ends. *Fathers and Sons* follows its hero into self-imposed isolation and death by his own young hand, victim of disdainful — or suicidal? — neglect of sensible precautions against infection while doing autopsies.

On his deathbed he achieves some self-mocking dignity by noting his similarity to 'the wriggling of a worm broken under a wheel', a worm that might imagine itself a frustrated giant with great deeds left undone. But Turgenev cannot bear to leave the tale so naturalistic. The inconsolable grief and the graveyard rituals of the hero's old-fashioned parents hardly subdue the nihilistic outlook of their dead son. So Turgenev enters the tale in his own person, mounting the son's grave at the very end to make tearful declaration of his agreement with old-fashioned people, his faith in something more than the dead man's nihilism. The author speaking in his own voice asks the flowers on the grave to speak, not only of indifferent nature and the troubled heart buried below, but 'also of eternal reconciliation and life everlasting'.[51]

The censor withheld the blue pencil from that parting declaration of traditional faith, though the context invites a disbelieving smile from the reader. I intend no disrespect for Turgenev. The smile of disbelief is tearstained and admiring, deliberately crafted by the author. Coming after starkly naturalistic deathbed scenes, the parting speech in his own voice is romantic counterpoint, yearning for traditional faith rather than offering the faith itself.

Dostoevsky's *Notes from Underground* (1864) drew harsher treatment from its censor; he cut out the anti-hero's confession that only religious faith could rescue him from the torments of nihilistic consciousness.[52] That censor may have been excessively fearful of the reading public's skepticism, or he may have been appropriately skeptical of the text. The Underground Man is unrelievedly ridiculous and repulsive. He may earn the reader's pity, which he does not want — like Camus's Stranger he prefers to be loathed — but the novel that presents him is unrelentingly cruel, in its comic elements no less than its tragic. It contains no softening elements, such as the Byronic defiance in Turgenev's nihilistic hero, or Turgenev's repeated digressions from that hero to picture good-natured people and the beauty of external nature. In *Notes from Underground* the one good-natured person is pitiable rather than delightful, and nature is 'not pretty scenery but the whole goddam machinery,' to borrow from another American poet, Robert Frost.[53]

Dostoevsky wrote the book in reaction to *What Is To Be Done?* He imagined the Underground Man taking Chernyshevsky's naturalistic vision to a mad extreme: If a human being is nothing but a self-serving machine, calculating the egotistical costs and benefits of social intercourse, he will not arrive at genuine love of others and the creation of a beautiful social order, as Chernyshevsky's heroes fondly imagined. He will stay in the basement or underground of egotistical isolation. To come out is to risk humiliating dependence on other people, or to amend the supreme rule of self-realization, which is indistinguishable from self-assertion. The anti-hero will assert himself all by himself. He tells his notebook that the naturalistic vision inherent in science, and the complementary anthill organization of modern society, mock the pretense that self-realization is the supreme value for human beings, while pushing people away from any other supreme value, such as subordination of the self to love for others. In the original text Dostoevsky had the Underground Man cry for religious faith as the only way out of that cruel trap. The religious passages may have been a jarring intrusion of the author's ideology into his character's self-portrait. Perhaps, after raging at the censor's deletion, Dostoevsky came to feel that the cut improved the novel, for he did not try in subsequent editions to restore the Underground Man's cry for faith.[54]

In any event the text remains thoroughly nihilistic, one of the major scriptures of modernism, inspiring an unending procession of wretchedly free anti-heroes, forever destroying themselves to prove that the conscious self is something more than it seems to be. It seems to be merely a bundle of biological and social functions, held on course by the organizing function called self-consciousness. Yet an underground type can transcend that mechanistic appearance by willful disorganization. By spurning the functions that nature and human society have prescribed for him, he can prove that the inner person, the self, is a genuinely independent reality. At the start of the novel the Underground Man is boasting that he will not submit, he will not even go to the doctor, though his liver is ailing and he has been indoctrinated to believe in scientific medicine. At the end he is insulting and chasing away the pitiable whore whom he has beguiled into loving him − out of spite, first annoyed by her cold indifference when he used her body for pay, then annoyed by her entangling affection when she loves him for nothing.

Self-assertion not only leads to isolation from other selves; it merges into self-destruction. Suicide, in this mad philosophy, becomes the ultimate assertion of authentic dignity, an individual person's declaration of freedom from enslaving nature and society. In subsequent novels Dostoevsky elaborated that feverish vision, inserting repeated cries for religious faith and insisting that there would be political hell to pay if faith did not overcome nihilism.[55] Thus he made his great novels a special problem for ideologists, especially those of the left. It is not necessary here to review their struggles to separate the commendable from the despicable aspects of Dostoevsky's universally acknowledged classics. For my present point it is enough to note that such ideologists have been unable to ignore Dostoevsky; his vivid power in exploring the mental landscape of nihilism has had too great a resonance in the reading public, first in Russia, then in the modern world at large.

Dostoevsky was obsessed with extreme characters, marginal to respectable society. Calmer writers could use solid citizens to reveal the horror that assails self-consciousness when the naturalistic outlook lays hold of it. Tolstoy pictured a middling juridical official, Ivan Il'ich, proving his individual worth by accumulating symbols of social standing, mindlessly satisfied with the process until he is confronted with death by cancer. The certainty of extinction cancels all ephemeral satisfactions and puts metaphysical anguish in their place: a dying body imposes lack of choice and inability to act on a mind whose essence is to choose and to act. Toward the end Ivan Il'ich glimpses a reassuring possibility of choice and action even in the process of dying. He tells himself: 'One can do "this", one can' – and instantly asks the subversive question: 'but what is "this"?'[56] If 'this' is dying of cancer, it is self-deception to imagine that he, Ivan Il'ich, can consciously choose to do 'this'. Aylmer Maude, the Quaker author of the best-known English translation, eased the bite in Tolstoy's naturalism by changing the self-contradictory 'this' – what the conscious self 'does' as the body dies – into a moral choice. In Maude's version Ivan Il'ich tells himself that 'one can do *the right thing*', and then pauses to consider 'what is *the right thing*?'[57]

Softening the text by inserting new words is of course much less common than ignoring what is in it. In present-day America 'The Death of Ivan Il'ich' is favored by authors of how-to-die manuals and by other sentimentalists who fancy that Tolstoy drew the sting from dying by showing how naturally it proceeds.[58] Changes of animal consciousness from resistance to resignation are indeed described in 'The Death of Ivan Il'ich', but the description does not equate natural with humanly acceptable. (In another tale Tolstoy attempted the equation, and achieved a preachy parable, largely ignored by critics and readers.)[59] On the contrary, the gruesome natural details of Ivan Il'ich's dying evoke uniquely human awareness of his 'helplessness, his terrible loneliness, the cruelty of man, the cruelty of God, and the absence of God'.[60] The story is full of 'a terrible truth', which Tolstoy had perceived long before he wrote 'Ivan Il'ich'. In an 1860 letter to a well-known poet he expressed it directly, without the mask of fiction, describing the death of a favorite brother:

A few minutes before he died he dozed off, then suddenly woke up and whispered with horror: 'But what is this?' He had seen it – this swallowing up of the self into nothing. And if he found nothing to grab hold of what should I find? Even less. ... As soon as a man reaches a higher stage of development and ceases to be stupid, it becomes clear to him that everything is rubbish, deception, and that the truth which he nevertheless loves more than anything else is a horrible truth. That as soon as you see it well, clearly, you wake up and say, as one should: 'But what is this?' Well, it goes without saying, while there is the desire to eat, you eat, to shit, you shit; while there is the unconscious stupid desire to know and speak the truth, you try to know and speak it. That is the one thing left to me from the moral world, higher than it I cannot rise. It's the one thing that I'll go on doing, only not in the form of your art. Art is a lie, and I can no longer love a beautiful lie.[61]

Once again, as in Dostoevsky's case, the moral and religious doctrine that Tolstoy preached is largely beside the present point. The issue here is the nihilistic vision that he was struggling to subdue, and his failure in the effort both within his mind and among the educated public. Only a minority became Tolstoyans in ethics and political ideology, but the reading public as a whole venerated such naturalistic fiction as 'The Death of Ivan Il'ich'. There were, and still are, readers and critics who would like to split Tolstoy as they do Tiutchev, to shrug off his ideological writings as eccentricities easily separated from his universally admired fiction. But that splitting evades the naturalistic antinomies that gave force to his fiction precisely because they were never quite subdued, and in analogous fashion gave force to his ideological writings.

At the center of Tolstoy's trouble was the 'terrible truth' of life's point-lessness versus the meaningful patterns read into human lives by fictive art. He anticipated Nietzsche's famous aphorism, 'Art exists to save us from truth' — and went on creating works of art as embodiments of truth. He thought he saw an analogous trouble in science.[62] It claimed to show the world as it is without human values, but actually concealed painful reality by separating the natural from the human world, pretending that the mind can be coolly indifferent in its picture of nature. Both forms of deception, artistic and scientific, catered to the comfortable classes, which derive corrupting profit from things as they are and do not want to know the terrible truth of how they really are. His argument was clearest concerning the social order, but was not limited to it. In his extravagant manner Tolstoy was struggling with a problem that bothered a number of thinkers at the turn of the century, the claim that knowledge is achieved by separation of fact from value, the realm of is from the realm of wish-it-were. Tolstoy passionately denounced such separations as impossible and intolerable deceptions, while his own mind continued to make them.

Since his time the social sciences have been continually pounded by accusations of presenting wish-it-were as is or must-be. That is a major reason why the social sciences are often called 'soft'. The natural sciences are called 'hard' in large part because they have won far more acquiescence to their claim of identifying things as they really are, apart from the ways we wish them to be. Tolstoy therefore seems most extravagant when he attacks that claim, charging that natural scientists, by distancing themselves from humanly important problems, have moved from truthseeking to play with unreal abstractions and trivia. He even denounces the experimental method:

> Our science, in order to become science and to be really useful and not harmful to humanity, must first of all renounce its experimental method, which causes it to consider as its duty the study merely of what exists, and must return to the only reasonable and fruitful conception of science, which is that the object of science is to show people how to live. ... The study of things as they exist can only be a subject for science in so far as that study helps towards the knowledge of how one should live.

Inconsistencies are not hard to pick out. Time and again Tolstoy implicitly assumes what he is trying to deny: that natural science achieves genuine knowledge by distinguishing between objective nature and subjective consciousness and by portraying only nature. The inconsistency is evident in the stunning indictment that sums up his major essay on 'Modern Science':

> If the arrangement of society is bad (as ours is), and a small number of people have power over the majority and oppress it, every victory over nature will inevitably serve only to increase that power and that oppression. That is what is actually happening.[63]

The assumption that science achieves victories over nature is hard to reconcile with other parts of the essay, which deny that science achieves genuine knowledge — unless one is prepared to argue that genuine knowledge is different from powerful techniques, that modern science is increasingly abandoning knowledge in favor of techniques, leaving the search for wisdom in thrall to the lust for power.[64] To press Tolstoy's inconsistency to that level is, I think, to approach a basic antinomy of the naturalistic outlook, which began as a comprehensive vision of truth and wisdom, and has been turning into an instrument of power, physically enormous and morally incompetent. Sometimes 'nihilism' is used in that special accusatory sense, to designate that monstrously lopsided conception of knowledge as amoral power becoming an end in itself.

That is a problem that will not be eliminated by ridicule of Tolstoy's self-contradiction in analyzing it. Likewise with the problem embedded in his political extremism: society is either good or bad, its science included. Moderate men of the judicious middle, in Russia as in the West, saw the obvious rebuttal. Outside of the extremist's head good and bad are often mixtures of more or less rather than extremes of either-or. The lower-class

victims of an oppressive social order, to take Tolstoy's favored point of
ethical reference, can and do benefit from such victories over nature as the
control of epidemics. They even benefit from modern military technology,
which requires a literate and healthy nation to kill and be killed in the most
obedient and effective manner. Evidently there are vicious realities that
cannot be brushed aside by noting Tolstoy's extremism in railing at them.

Before we get deeper into the politics of the thing, let us take a final look
at mundane realities, expressed by a prose artist who shied away from
political brawls. Anton Chekhov limited his explicit ideological argumentation to private talk and correspondence, and even there tended to be
skeptical of grand schemes. Against Tolstoyan criticism of science he
offered some of the points that come easily to moderate men of the
judicious middle. He noted, for example, the obvious benefit of scientific
medicine in the improvement of health, and thought that science was
making progress though literature was stagnant.[65] But his stories and plays
did not express even such limited faith in singleminded fashion.

The reader will recall Dr Astrov's depressing account of his unavailing
efforts to improve the health of peasants, his self-mockery for dreaming of
progress through applied science, and the tears of self-recognition in the
congress of Russian physicians that watched a special performance of *Uncle
Vanya*. Russian critics, who expected grand prophecy of their great writers,
were upset by the persistent subversion of prophecy in Chekhov's stories
and plays. *Uncle Vanya* achieves its poignancy not only by Dr Astrov
mocking his own faith in scientific progress but also by the exquisite
counterpoint of unavailing religious faith in the famous curtain speech of
another character trying to overcome the sense of pointlessness that attends
her forecast of day-in day-out labor until death.

Chekhov's 'lack of a general idea' has provoked much controversy,
which can be skipped over here except for one crucial point. He was
skeptical of grand solutions, not indifferent to major problems. He offered
keen analysis of the problems, even metaphysical ones, leading to no
solutions. In 'A Dreary History' he did his version of 'Ivan Il'ich'. As
Chekhov explained the story to his publisher, a narrator reflecting on his
life would come to realize 'what was already known long ago, that a life
thought through [*osmyslennaia*] without a definite world view is not a life
but a burden, a horror'.[66] That is very like Tolstoy's agonized impulse to
religious conversion and prophecy, but Chekhov stopped at the beginning.
He limited himself to creating a bleakly naturalistic story of a man facing
what Tolstoy called 'the swallowing up of the self into nothing'.

Chekhov came to that ultimate problem unexpectedly. Annoyed by his
own celebrity, he began by thinking about the self or person not as a
bundle of social functions – in this case the famous writer – but as an
interior essence, the actor who knows he is something apart from the roles
that he plays. He planned to make a comic story of that distinction, 'My

Name and I', but while he was writing, his brother died and the weather turned very hot. He fell into 'the rottenest mood', and his story pressed beyond the relationship of *persona* and person to the insoluble problem of the inner person as a thing in itself, a conscious thing wondering what it might be in itself as it faces extinction.[67]

To point up the irrelevance of social role and achievement, Chekhov imagined a man of distinction: a physiologist who has achieved eminence and is facing death after the conventional three-score years. His scientific knowledge of the body permits no illusory hopes of escape from its diseased process, nor does his outlook permit the slightest thought of any divinity or of 'life everlasting'. Nor does his human creator, Anton Chekhov, intervene in the story with Turgenev's romantic yearning for transcendence, or with Tolstoy's awesome pointing toward 'the cruelty of God, the absence of God', certainly not with Dostoevskian prescription of the balm in Gilead to heal the sin-sick soul. As Tolstoy once observed, Chekhov was 'absolutely godless, but a good man'. He felt for the person confronting engulfment by nothing, but had no words that could save or comfort him.

The dying physiologist still believes that science is fascinating and worthwhile, but he finds the belief quite irrelevant to the problem he has suddenly confronted: discovering the essence of the inner self, the person who is to die. The distinguished scientist, the *persona*, has become a hateful burden to the inner man. The scientific enterprise will continue, but he will not be part of it for he will not be. Perhaps the inner self is to be found in communion with other sufferers? Chekhov's physiologist seeks and does not find. He finds only persons like himself, utterly absorbed in their separate ephemeral selves. Examination of his life comes then to 'evasive twisting in confrontation with himself' (*vil'ian'e pered samim soboi*), as Chekhov explained to a friend.[68] ('I play tricks in confrontation with myself' − *khitriu pered samim soboi* − the physiologist says in the story itself.)[69]

'A Dreary History' leaves the man still alive physically, isolated forever from any other person, quite blocked in his effort to understand the meaning or purpose of such existence. The relief of seeing the sufferer extinguished at last, which Tolstoy granted to the readers of 'Ivan Il'ich', is withheld by Chekhov. The romantic softening that Turgenev offered, by discovery of Byronic defiance in the 'broken worm', is absent. There is not the slightest hint of a Dostoevskian solution, whether suicidal defiance or saintly conversion to transcendent love of others, or the intermediate madness of Ivan Karamazov. It was characteristic of Chekhov to pretend no metaphysical solutions, to leave his audience overwhelmed by knowledge that they have shared an insoluble problem with the author and his fictive creatures. If there is a hint of sufferers' communion in that knowledge, it is modernist and bare, much more severe than Tolstoy's deliberate wringing of compassion from his readers.

No doubt some readers are inclined to share Pavlov's revulsion against that kind of knowledge, even deny that it is knowledge. Is understanding of ourselves to be found in fictive subjects confessing essential ignorance of their inner selves and ultimate isolation from each other? The historian's reply is that nearly all educated Russians assumed that self-knowledge was to be found in such fiction and poetry. The simplest proof of that sweeping generalization is to be found in the 'thick journals', the favorite reading matter of the educated public. Those magazines showed virtually no interest in Pavlov's objective way to human understanding, very little in the academic study of subjective psychology, and an unabating passion for imaginative literature and the ideological arguments that buzzed about it. Hence the major significance of the persistent nihilism in famous works by venerated writers. To educated people seeking self-knowledge literary illuminations revealed an essential darkness. Modern naturalism at work in the imagination spurred the likes of Pavlov to scientistic flight from the literary imagination, others to the inverse, impatience with science as technical manipulation of inhuman nature devoid of human significance. But all that in contemplation; in practical action a revolutionary minority strove to create the authentic humanity that science and the literary imagination found lacking. The activists would create what no one could describe.

ACTIVIST RESISTANCE: THE BOLSHEVIK MENTALITY

In the 1860s Russian leftists turned from romantic philosophizing to positivist visions of science overthrowing the old order and traditional values. When critics expressed alarm at such 'nihilism', some radicals defiantly accepted the epithet. They did not mind shocking. Their talk had some of the make-believe qualities of the intellectual salon, and anyhow they were confident that faith in science was compatible with faith in emergent values loftier than those of the traditional order. Natural science, their model of knowledge, disclosed the order of nature, which seemed progressive, inherently moral, to the 'nihilists' of the 1860s (hence my use of ironic quotation marks).[70]

By the end of the century, when nihilism without quotation marks was endemic in Russian literary culture, and scientists were dropping talk of progress inherent in the natural order, radicals were branching out from salons and student circles, forming underground parties to agitate among the masses for actual overthrow. Much more audacious in political action than the radicals of the 1860s, they were less so in philosophical talk. They refused to call themselves nihilists with or without quotation marks, and most rejected anarchism, the supposedly natural order of humanity, in favor of some revolutionary state. They loved the imagery of popular wrath exploding the old order, and to that extent gloried in disorder. But only some wild fellow travelers like Briusov glorified chaos as a meta-physical principle. A practical leader like Lenin took a very different view. He insisted on order and discipline not only in the dream of a revolutionary state, but right away within the revolutionary movement. Like the conservatives and the right-center liberals, he strongly condemned what he perceived as a Russian tendency to 'elementalism', as he called it: *stikhiinost'*, from the Greek *stoicheion*, the elements of nature. *Stikhiinost'* became a major Leninist curseword, and we should stop translating it as spontaneity, which is *spontannost'* or *samoproizvol'nost'* in the narrow sense of willful action from within, or *samodeiatel'nost'* in the extended social sense — 'manifestation of personal initiative' — which Lenin very much approved. *Stikhiinost'*, which he strongly disapproved, is the random quality of elemental nature, unregulated by mind.

A responsible historian of Russian Marxism will not glibly ascribe to its leaders the combination of anarchic nihilism and worship of despotic authority with which critics have repeatedly charged them. Nevertheless one cannot brush aside such ascriptions simply because the ideologists in question have persistently done so. The frequency of the charges, and the analogy in Lenin's exaltation both of revolution and of discipline, oblige the historian to pause and reflect on the issue. It is obviously related to the allegations that disorder, chaos, nihilism, elementalism, or formlessness are inherent in the Russian character, along with surrender to absolute rule. They have been pictured as mutually reinforcing extremes, each fastening the other in Russian souls. The long-term frequency of such observations must be evidence of some important feature in Russian culture, but what might it be? Is it a fact that Russians have been exceptionally inclined to disorder unless repressed by tyrants? That they readily accede to tyranny because they fear the self-destructive rage for chaos in their hearts?

That may be an attractive construct for homilies, but it seems small use to concrete historical inquiry, until we note an obvious social pattern in such comments. It has been educated Russians — and foreigners echoing those educated Russians — who have persistently offered such analyses of Russian character. Conservatives offered them in justification of autocracy, established religion, and traditional social hierarchy. Revolutionaries used their versions to justify faith in the real possibility of popular upheaval, and sometimes, as in the case of Lenin, to justify insistence on discipline within the revolutionary movement. Cautious liberals have used other versions to justify some go-slow approach to 'European' liberties, that is, to chartered rights for self-restrained souls when they have learned to repress the supposed rage for limitless freedom. In all that diversity there has been one obvious common element — anxiety among the educated concerning the 'uncultured' mentality of the masses — and one less obvious but no less important element: anxiety among the educated concerning their own incongruous mentality. An acute sense of social isolation intensified both nihilist soul-searching within the individual mind and fierce drives to break out of tormenting isolation, to join forces with 'the people' in creation of authentic humanity.

Practical action could hardly be limited to naked acts. Explanation was required, if only to recruit more activists and to keep a common course. In short, the will to change the world required some pause to interpret it, but not so much as to suspend action indefinitely, which was the paralyzing habit of radical intellectuals in the West. In a backward country drifting toward collapse of the old order, the radicals' will to change the world was not only fiercer than their Western comrades'; it entailed more audacious claims of knowledge and more impatient refusals of thought.

Here is another paradox like that of the scientists walling themselves within scientism, refusing serious thought about the naturalistic mentality that they shared with educated Russians at large. The activists' connection with the common mentality also found expression in gestures of negation and phrases of revulsion. When they flinched from thought and fell to sloganeering, or flew into a rage over symbolic trifles, they were expressing features of the common mentality, the parts of it that they did not want to share but could not reason away. Psychological science provoked such symptoms in telltale fashion: sparse, evasive, self-deluding, ultimately angry, for the activists claimed scientific understanding of humanity yet − or therefore − resisted entanglement in the science of the mind.

The very small first generation of Russian Marxists came to intellectual maturity in the late 1860s and the 1870s, and therefore picked up some of the contemporary enthusiasm for physiology as the way to understand human beings. P. B. Aksel'rod (born in 1850, a year after Pavlov) talked for a while of going to study with Sechenov (as Pavlov did not).[71] Aksel'rod had heard that Sechenov was a comrade of Chernyshevsky who could teach one how to be both scientific and revolutionary. He soon turned to Marxism as the embodiment of that dream, and to party organization as the way to realize it − he became in time a leading Menshevik − and he never gave careful thought to the question how the viewpoints might be combined. He simply assumed that physiology provided the science of the psyche, while Marx's analysis of socio-economic formations provided the science of society.[72]

G. V. Plekhanov, also born at mid-century (1856), 'the father of Russian Marxism' as he came to be known, shared the assumption that physiology and Marxism were complementary sciences, also without giving much thought to the matter. His prolific writings on historical materialism contain a sprinkling of references to physiology as the scientific basis for under-standing the psyche. He had occasional words of respect for Wundt, 'the father of experimental psychology', who was supposedly building it out of physiology.[73] But those were gestures without substance. Plekhanov was unaware of the gap between Wundtian psychology and neurophysiology;

his mind was not seriously involved with either discipline. The historical development of society was his obsessive concern – to explain it so as to change it.

When he repeated the Marxist formula about the 'material being' that determines 'consciousness', the 'being' at issue was not individual nervous systems but socio-economic formations, and the 'consciousness' at issue was not the individual stream of it in each person's head, but the collective oceans of it, the mentalities or ideologies of social classes. The dependence of the individual consciousness on the central nervous system was a simple philosophical assumption to Plekhanov, who was uninterested in the technicalities. In each head were the coils of wire and the little electromagnetic field that connected the individual with collective mentalities and social systems, which were Plekhanov's field of study. I have made up these mechanical metaphors, rigidly segregating individual and collective, body and mind; Plekhanov only implied such sharp compartmentalization, for he was passionately committed to materialist monism. He would not cool the passion by thinking too much about the staggering problems it raises for the human sciences.

The Marxist use of 'materialism' and 'monism' was becoming increasingly Pickwickian, or should we say positivistic? Turn-of-century Marxists, like other *au courant* thinkers, assigned separate problems to separate disciplines, and recited inane formulas of reassurance over the moribund problem of the whole. It seemed congenial for a materialist to observe that experimental psychology was emerging from physiology, but too disturbing to look closely at the process. Plekhanov knew that the celebrated Wundt was decidedly opposed to materialism in philosophy, but he brushed that off with a formula which regularly separated science from the philosophizing of scientists: the natural sciences are inherently materialistic even though natural scientists are usually inhibited from acknowledging the fact. After all, they are bourgeois in ideology. Plekhanov, and Marxists generally, were not so easygoing with social scientists and philosophers. They felt obliged to get inside such disciplines as economics, history, or philosophy, and there, on those specialized fields, to battle the 'hired prizefighters of capitalism', the 'diplomaed lackeys of clericalism'.[74] But Marxists avoided any such challenge in experimental psychology, so long as they could lump it with physiology and consign the unexamined lump to natural science, an ideologically privileged realm of pure hard knowledge. Thus Plekhanov criticized Wundt's explicit philosophy, while indifferently approving his psychological science.

And thus Marxists at large did not know or care about the objectivist revolt at the turn of the century. Mentalist philosophers challenged Pavlov on the issue of materialism, and he declared his indifference, but Marxists did not rise to defend their philosophy in the science of the mind or brain. No one has been able to find a single reference to Pavlov or to Bekhterev in any pre-revolutionary Marxist publication. (Many Soviet scholars have searched, since *ex post facto* they joined Pavlov to Marx to Lenin in holy trinity.) Such a uniform anomaly could not have been an accident, to borrow a favorite phrase of Marxists. The explanation – of the original indifference and the *ex post facto* myth of affinity – must be sought in some aspect of false consciousness, to borrow another catchphrase – or in repressed consciousness, to borrow a third.

Lenin's generation of Russian Marxists did not live through the enthusiasm for physiology as a revolutionary way to scientific understanding of human beings. That petered out in the 1870s, when Lenin was a child. The new men picked up recollections and ran them together with the emergent disdain for any philosophizing about human nature. Both the recollections and the disdain appeared in Lenin's first publication, in 1894, when the future Bolshevik was only twenty-four. He was polemicizing against a populist critic of Marxism who had complained that Marx's writings contain no systematic exposition of historical materialism, which should begin with a definition of basic terms, such as human being, and should culminate in a scheme of universal history, a map of where we have come from and where we are headed. Lenin scorned that as metaphysics, a digression from the Marxist task of 'scientifically explaining the functioning and development of a particular social formation'.[75] Marx had never pretended to explain the whole of history. He had merely analysed the development of one socio-economic formation, capitalism. Implicit in Marx's analysis was a method that could be extended to other formations, but Lenin strongly opposed such an extension. Indeed he opposed philosophical generalization altogether. 'From the viewpoint of Marx and Engels', as he declared in another early publication, 'philosophy does not have any right to a separate, autonomous existence, and its material has been divided among the various branches of positive science.'[76]

Lenin could name what he could not philosophize about, the method that uses concepts which may not be defined for fear of metaphysics. The method is 'practice'; the concepts are scientific as they emerge in practical applications, not in philosophical treatises. He explained by offering illustrations. Chemists and biologists analyze material processes without stopping to define matter as such, or even to define chemical affinity or life as such. In psychology young Lenin thought he saw another illuminating example of metaphysics overborne by scientific practice:

The metaphysical psychologists debated the question, What is mind? The method itself is absurd. ... Progress here must consist precisely in casting aside general theories and philosophical constructions about what mind is, and in finding a way to put on a scientific basis the study of facts that characterize these or those psychic processes. ... The scientific psychologist has cast aside philosophical theories about the mind, and has turned directly to the study of the material substrate of psychic phenomena – neural processes – and he has produced, let us say, analysis and explanation of this, that, and the other psychic process.[77]

The vagueness of Lenin's gesture toward 'this, that, and the other psychic process' was as revealing as Pavlov's gestures of dismissal. So was his indifference to the possibility that dualism is implicit in a psychology which distinguishes between psychic processes and their neural substrate, or more generally between subjectivity and objectivity. An effort to deal with that problem would have involved him in the very kind of reasoning that he was dismissing as useless metaphysics.

Even an effort to give a specific example of 'this, that, and the other psychic process' would have drawn him into a conflict between the materialism he espoused and the positivism he had unwittingly absorbed. It is extremely difficult – perhaps impossible – to explain, say, visual perception by reduction of psychic phenomena to neural processes in the eye and brain. It was tempting to avoid the difficulty by assignment of psychic and neural processes to separate disciplines, and to smooth over the resulting philosophical problem by appeal to a composite category, 'experience', which was supposed to encompass both psychic and neural processes. Ernst Mach and Richard Avenarius were doing that smoothing job at the turn of the century, and Lenin's comrade, A. A. Bogdanov, was spreading the good news among Russian Marxists. Initially Lenin liked what he read in Bogdanov.[78]

Straining for action to change the world, rather than philosophical interpretation of it, in 1902 Lenin published *What Is To Be Done?*, the insistence on party discipline which polarized Russian Marxists into hard and soft factions, Bolsheviks and Mensheviks. Beneath a title that evoked the sacred memory of Chernyshevsky he utterly ignored the martyr's theory of human nature. He focused instead on the way to build a party sufficiently militant and disciplined to lead the masses in successful revolution. The immediate result was the famous split within the band of would-be leaders, and that paradoxical syndrome – a fury for unity with splits resulting – continued to plague Communist parties.

The splits of Russian Marxists have been retold and argued over in exhaustive detail, but almost always with this anomaly left out: in the formative first years of Bolshevism Lenin's distinctive insistence on action and discipline was associated with the philosophy that Bogdanov took from Mach and Avenarius and turned to revolutionary purposes. Historians have been so hypnotized by Lenin's break with Bogdanov, and by his vehement denunciation of Machism in 1908, that they have tended to overlook an obvious reason for his extraordinary vehemence. In 1908 he was denouncing philosophical views that he had shared, and which had come to be generally associated with the Bolshevik version of Marxism, while the Mensheviks had been associated with materialist orthodoxy.[79]

There was a certain plausibility in those associations. The Mensheviks forecast a protracted revolutionary process in two separate stages, bourgeois and socialist, each determined by objective social processes. The Bolsheviks forecast an accelerated revolutionary process, in which organized consciousness would speed the tendency of a backward country to compress the bourgeois and socialist stages into one 'uninterrupted' process – 'permanent revolution', as Trotsky called his version of the compression. It seemed logical to associate the Menshevik outlook with old-fashioned insistence that material being determines consciousness, and to associate Bolshevism with the new philosophy that fused object and subject in a single category of experience and stressed the active role of the conscious mind in shaping reality. In theory Machism seemed to go with Bolshevik insistence that discipline is needed to heighten and focus decisively important consciousness, while materialism seemed to go with Menshevik revulsion against such willfulness – 'Jacobinism' or 'Bonapartism', as Lenin's critics first described his views. Menshevik declarations of respect for the autonomous development of lower-class consciousness seemed logically connected with historical materialism, while Bogdanov's 'empiriomonism' seemed a logical justification of Lenin's insistence on a disciplined vanguard party bringing advanced consciousness to the lower classes.

The historical process disrupted that logical scheme. Lenin turned savagely against Bogdanov's philosophy, Bogdanov turned ruefully away from Lenin's politics, and the Mensheviks found themselves in 1917 fatally at odds with lower-class consciousness, which erupted with revolutionary demands that the Bolsheviks knew how to mobilize. Some historians respond to such contretemps with sneering dismissals of theorizing among leftist intellectuals: see how wrong those leftists were, by contrast with us who have hindsight and no need to act. Less complacent academics cannot doubt that theorizing minds intent on action shaped the revolutionary process, even as they were tumbled about and shaped by it. So we who would use hindsight and academic distance for some better purpose than self-congratulation must inquire into the insistent theorizing that was central to the developing Bolshevik mentality. Bogdanov's is a crucial test, for he seemed at first to epitomize Bolshevism on the philosophical level. Not only Lenin thought so but also Bukharin, eighteen years younger than Lenin and his successor as chief Party ideologist in the 1920s.[80] The main problem here is to discover commonality rather than differences, in hope of glimpsing a broader commonality, the culture that the Bolsheviks were reacting to.

Trained as a physician, committed to revolutionary action, Bogdanov was mostly a writer, on the grandest theoretical level. He was building toward a system of all systems: philosophical, natural scientific, sociological, cultural. No one knew at the time that such grand theorists were an endangered species, among Marxist activists as well as academics. No one suspected that Marxist chiefs would someday lead in lordly silence, with bands of specialists to work out justifications of their peremptory politics. In the first decades of our century Marxist leaders still felt obliged to do their own grand theorizing, showing enough science to chart the way to the future while dismissing metaphysical claims to know it all. Bogdanov was so skillful at the art that Bolsheviks saw him as their leading philosopher. That respect persisted after 1908, when Lenin had him expelled from the party. Subsequently Lenin tried to bring him back in, most crucially in 1917, but Bogdanov declined.[81] He perceived the Bolshevik Revolution as a willful adventure, which had the support of soldiers and urban workers who had been radicalized by the war but otherwise lacked the cultural level required for a genuine democracy of workers' and soldiers' soviets.

He emphasized culture, consciousness, psychology — he tended to use the terms interchangeably — as the critical element in organizing ever higher levels of social existence. That emphasis joined him with Lenin on the far left in the original split between Bolsheviks and Mensheviks and in the revolutionary disintegration that reached a climax in 1905. The semiconstitutional interlude that followed, and the profoundly revolutionary disintegration of 1917, separated Bogdanov from Lenin's politics, though he remained sympathetic enough to stay in Russia and support the Soviet regime in his own way. (He pressed for an autonomous development of 'proletarian culture', and when Lenin insisted on party discipline in that area too, he retreated to science, studying blood transfusion as well as social transformation, until 1928, when he killed himself with a rash effort at total transfusion.)[82] There is always some slippage of thought as theoretical principles mesh with practical applications. The slippage increases rapidly in an age of cultural disintegration, when ideologies become rallying cries more than systems of thought, which hinder the rallying function if they are considered too deeply.

Even the creative essays of young Bogdanov reveal the rising disinclination to examine the faith too closely. He called an early collection *From the Psychology of Society*, though he showed little more interest than other Marxists in the actual discipline of psychology. He was content with the usual vague declaration that physiology was generating an authentically scientific psychology. If he was aware of the discipline's dominant commitment to subjective methods, its continuous war of schools, and the objectivist revolt as the newest episode in the war, he chose to appear ignorant. It is far more likely that he knew nothing of such specialists' problems, and did not care to know. He had a purely epistemological motive for the vague declaration that psychology was becoming an exact science as it was increasingly 'based upon the introduction into it of the physiological viewpoint and of physiological methods'.[83] He was arguing for reductionism as a general principle. Bogdanov noted that 'almost all' the other Marxists who thought about the subject were eager to set limits on reduction, to warn in advance that the laws of social development could not be reduced to biological laws. He called that 'eclecticism' rather than monism, for he perceived in such a view different epistemologies for different levels of knowledge. Mysticism threatened in that direction, but Mach and Avenarius had saved modern thinkers from the threat, by showing that all levels of knowledge were ways of analyzing and organizing a single category, experience. Hence the name Bogdanov put on his system: empiriomonism.[84]

It may well have been this monistic feature of Bogdanov's argument that Lenin found initially attractive. He thought that Plekhanov might be the author, using a new pen name, for Plekhanov had been stressing the need for a monistic world view to counter the paralyzing belief that social reality is too complex to be mastered. But Plekhanov in his own name began publishing criticisms of Bogdanov's empiriomonism.[85] He found 'experience' an evasive category to put in place of matter, an attempt to fudge the problem of subjective minds interacting with objective processes, to evade the consequent necessity of deciding which category has priority, subjectivity or objectivity, mind or matter. He accused the Machists of shirking the unavoidable choice: either materialism, the philosophy of those who submit to the tests of objectivity because the historical process is on their side, or idealism, the philosophy of those who need to conceal material reality with self-serving subjective beliefs, that is, with false consciousness or ideology.

Lenin picked up that argument from Plekhanov, and turned it into the central theme of *Materialism and Empiriocriticism* (1908). But his version was distinguished by its extreme crudity, which provoked condescending amusement from Plekhanov and shock from other reviewers, and is still a puzzle to readers who respect Lenin's intellect. Why was his first fling at philosophical analysis so willfully simple-minded, or 'wooden-headed', to borrow Plekhanov's expression?[86] And why was his tone so shrill, his language so abusive?

If the reader thinks that I am being shrill and abusive, let him consider an example of Lenin's reasoning, his charge of 'physiological idealism' against anyone, Plekhanov included, who demurred from the belief that visual perceptions 'reflect' external objects. Helmholtz had noted that analysis of the processes which turn light rays into visual perceptions requires the analyst to make basic distinctions between neural and mental processes, between signals as bioelectrical impulses and signals as meaningful symbols. He used the metaphor of hieroglyphs to suggest the nature of the signals that the eye delivers to the brain-mind, which has the job of interpreting, of deciding what external objects the hieroglyphs correspond to. Sechenov liked the metaphor, and Plekhanov passed it on to the Marxist community. It illuminated the materialistic or realistic argument that visual perceptions correspond to patterns of neural stimuli which correspond to patterns of light reflected from external objects. But Lenin denounced any theory of correspondence as an idealist mystification, a subversion of materialist realism. Without bothering to distinguish light rays from neural stimuli from sensations from perceptions from concepts, he simply shouted that what we see in our heads are 'copies, pictures, mirror images, reflections' of external objects.[87]

Lenin felt free to indulge such extreme simple-mindedness, because he disengaged himself from the internal problems of physiological and psychological science, even from the elementary distinctions between light rays and neural stimuli and sensations and perceptions. He left all that to the specialists, declaring that he was dealing only with philosophy, not with science. Did he realize that such a dismissive maneuver moved the Marxist philosopher away from rational discourse with science, toward a protective fortress of blind faith? At some level of his thinking he did realize that. His notebooks enable us to say so with confidence. After publishing his furiously simple-minded book he did not stop studying philosophy. Especially during the enforced leisure of the war years in Swiss exile he took many reading notes on philosophy, and sketched out some ideas of his own, including some that the author of *Materialism and Empirio-criticism* had denounced as utter idealism. For example: 'The consciousness of man not only reflects the objective world but also creates it.'[88] Within the fortress mentality a critical mind was still at work.

Why then had he put his mind within a fortress? That question applies to many more individuals than Lenin. Why did the majority of pre-revolutionary Marxists, Mensheviks as well as Bolsheviks, keep repeating simple-minded formulas, ignoring or angrily rebuffing the small minority of comrades who wanted to open up discussions of issues that the orthodox declared closed? Note the telltale pride in 'orthodox' scientific socialism, defying the connotation of religious orthodoxy.[89] Even Bogdanov, who criticized orthodoxy and became the arch 'revisionist' of Bolshevik Marxism, preferred empty formulas of unified scientific understanding to serious thought about the actual discord in the human sciences.

One instance has been noted: his inane declaration that psychology was being reduced to physiology, without attention to the disputes and the frustration that attended claims of reduction. There is another, more revealing instance. Bogdanov allowed himself to be drawn — briefly, to be sure — into the problem of the individual self, 'the I', as the Russians and Germans say.[90] (It is confusing to translate '*das Ich*' as 'the ego', which connotes pride or selfishness, or an English-speaking corner in the Freudian triangulation of the personality.) The Russian educated public was obsessed with the problem of the self, as the reader has seen, but Marxist activists brushed it aside as a disease of bourgeois intellectuals. Commitment to revolutionary action was the obvious cure. Once the advancement of authentic humanity becomes one's 'cause', the organizing force in a person's existence, the problem of the self dissolves. That was the standard formula, which Bogdanov recast in his own style. Yet he was sufficiently pensive to confront the counter-argument that one cannot be sure what constitutes the advancement of authentic humanity or how to achieve it in one's particular situation unless one knows in advance what an authentically human self will be and do in a genuinely human society.

Trying to show that progress toward authentic self-realization can be defined, Bogdanov ventured an analysis of personality. He offered a tri-angular diagram of his own, very different from Freud's, very Marxist: perception-and-feeling, lumped together at one corner, cognition at another, and action at a third. The wholeness of each part he declared necessary for the harmony of the ensemble:

> The greatest fullness and harmony of life are only possible for man when, at the moment of feeling he gives himself up entirely to feeling, at the moment of knowing to knowing, at the moment of action to action. ... In the absence of such wholeness we have, not mighty harmonious unfolding life, but wretched, stunted [*polovinchatoe*] existence.[91]

To talk of such wholeness, he acknowledged, was to dream of an ideal. In most cases 'up to now man has emerged precisely as a stunted, dishar-monious being.'[92]

That indulgence in philosophizing about the essential nature of a whole person was quite brief and most unusual. Most often Russian Marxists refrained from efforts to specify the ideal human nature they were striving to create, or to release from the crippling social systems of past and present. Philosophizing of that sort led away from action toward meta-physics, or toward literary mooning over the insoluble problem of self-realization in existing society. Bogdanov's little venture recalls young Marx's fleeting dream of the whole person in the socialist society of the future, who will hunt in the morning, fish in the afternoon, and do criticism at night, 'just as I please'. Keeping such dreams, but keeping them tensely repressed by fear of utopianism, by the urge to be practical, has been a persistent source of strength to Marxist movements. The dream that can only be hinted at must be striven for, created by political action. In modern literary culture, the dream of self-realization is shamelessly exposed, des-cribed, picked at. Marxists may become sensitively involved in that culture − at the risk of disillusion with the ideal self to be created through political action.

Bogdanov's brief indulgence was not very risky, for he showed little sensitivity to the problem of self-realization in literary culture, and did not note the implicit conflict with his usual scientism. At one point, and I use his own emphasis, he declared: '*All mysticism and all metaphysics have precisely this significance*: they are undifferentiated forms, in which knowing has not yet been liberated from will and emotion, and still bears their coloration.'[93] That aspiration to liberate knowing from feeling was a scientistic fission of the personality. He was extrapolating the supposed ideal of natural science to the mind at large, ignoring the fusion of knowing and feeling that is essential to imaginative literature. He was also ignoring the disputes in social science over the separation of cognition from evaluation, whether it is possible or desirable. And of course he ignored Tolstoy's argument that, even within natural science, it is a fraud and a sin to claim separation of factual and evaluative knowledge, science and wisdom.

Lenin's *Materialism and Empiriocriticism* was also willfully indifferent to that issue within natural science, but passionately assertive of *partiinost'*, partyness or partisanship, in all other realms of thought. *Partiinost'* was Lenin's strange new word for the influence of collective interests on cognition. When the class interest of thinkers is threatened by the objective trend of social reality, Lenin argued, their knowledge will conceal or deny the threatening reality. And conversely: when thinkers take the side of progressive classes, whose interests will triumph with time, partyness has the opposite effect; it generates realistic discovery of objective truth. But that sociology of knowledge did not extend to natural science. Within physics and physiology as such, in natural science as distinct from philosophical interpretation of science, Lenin brushed aside the principle of partyness. He took it for granted that truth concerning nature is constantly discovered by scientists who share the class interests and the ideologies of the exploiters, and therefore cannot be trusted the moment they move from science to philosophical interpretation, from nature to mind and society. In short, a dualistic epistemology is implicit throughout Lenin's famous book on the philosophy of science. Of course the dualism is not explicitly confronted. Lenin was a furious believer in monism, all the more furious for the need to repress problems that might turn active faith into academic discourse.

In 1908 – and afterward, to his death in 1924 – Lenin made no effort to assert the party principle in physics or physiology, and he never mentioned psychology after the early work noted above.[94] Even when he insisted on 'partyness' in philosophy he used the term in a metaphorical sense, to signify the age-old contest between the 'party' of reactionary exploiters and the 'party' of progressive humanity. His main political motive in writing *Materialism and Empiriocriticism* was to dissociate philosophical doctrines from parties in the literal sense, to prove that orthodox materialism was not exclusively Menshevik, nor Machism the distinctive philosophy of Bolshevism.[95] It is certainly reasonable to ask whether the Stalinist interpretation of partyness was not implicit in Lenin's argument, given the principle of the vanguard party bringing consciousness to the lower classes, and given the need for discipline within the vanguard. The obvious answer is that the Stalinist interpretation was *implicit*, along with other possible interpretations. Which would actually be chosen by the Bolshevik Party would depend on its changing mentality, shaped by changing circumstances in successive periods of its history.

Zealots, whether Communist or anti-Communist, refuse to acknowledge the multiple possibilities of the Bolshevik mentality; they insist on a mono-lithic quality present from the start. Such zealous faith in essences must ignore inconvenient facts. Some proved to be of small long-run significance: Lenin's original sympathy with Bogdanov's philosophy, his conversion to orthodox materialism by the Menshevik Plekhanov, his insistence that the rival Marxist parties were not rivals in philosophy. (He held to that view even in the Soviet period.) The most important feature of the Bolshevik mentality that threatens zealous faith in a monolith is its inward division between subjectivity and objectivity, between the willful urge to create social reality and the thoughtful urge to discover it.

Concerning physical reality, as discovered in everyday experience and in natural science, Lenin and his comrades were naive realists, who wanted to hear no sophisticated arguments about unavoidable subjectivity. He rejected not only Bogdanov's empiriomonism but even Plekhanov's realistic doctrine of correspondence between the perceiving mind and the reality perceived. Lenin insisted on a doctrine of 'reflection', as if the mind were a mirror or a camera. But in the realm of social reality he vehemently insisted on the mind as agent or subject, grasping reality or disguising it, as class interests require. In the social realm the wish is father to the thought, which proves realistic if it helps to create the emergent reality that it wishes to perceive. That may be called a dialectical contradiction, a vicious circle, or an inconsistent muddle. The name matters less than recognizing the tension inherent in such an outlook, its potential for creativity, for destructiveness, or for deadlock.

Lenin did not assert that social reality is created by the future ruling class and its party, by those with a sufficient will to power. Such a view – may we call it Nietzschean? – expresses disdain for any social reality but the will of the strong, a disdain that can become self-destructive madness – of the Nazi variety, to take an extreme example. Nor did he simply sub-ordinate the party will to disinterested comprehension of objective social realities. That way lies surrender of the social process to the powers that be – or the utter ineptitude of the Mensheviks and the liberals in a time such as 1917, when the powers that be suddenly ceased to be, when social reality became, for the lower classes and their parties, an extremely flammable mixture of is and wish-it-were rising to irresistible shouts for must-be.

In his crude, passionate manner Lenin tried to have things both ways: as an orthodox materialist to separate what empiriomonism claimed to unite – knowers and things known – yet simultaneously to reunite them in practical action, the method by which knowers create the things they know. He was trying to hold opposites together, the subjective will toward revolutionary creation of a new reality and the objective knowledge of a solid old reality, external to and ultimately determinate of the Party will. The startling Bolshevik triumph in 1917, the astonishing victory in the consequent civil war, the social retreat (to the New Economic Policy) at the moment of military victory, and the subsequent renewal of civil war (collectivization) in a time of social peace — that staggering course of Soviet history expressed the tension within the Bolshevik mentality, sometimes tending toward respect for objective facts, sometimes toward insistence that social reality is what the vanguard wills it to be, and sometimes toward deadlock.

From the start there were critics who perceived no multiple potentialities in Leninism. They saw a closed mind, fanaticism, despotic tendencies. But they were likely to point an accusing finger at Russian Marxism as a whole — if not the entire Russian left — not exclusively at Leninism. In 1908 Karl Kautsky, the chief of orthodox German Marxists, deplored the ideological extremism of the Russian comrades. He perceived the Mensheviks as materialists, the Bolsheviks as Machists, and lamented their common tendency to make a party issue of philosophy. He thought it should be a matter of private judgment, especially since 'Marx proclaimed no particular philosophy, but the end of all philosophy.'[96] Rosa Luxemburg, a native of the Tsar's realm who migrated to Germany as the most advanced center of the revolutionary movement — so she thought, so many comrades thought — was more biting in her assessment of the Russians' philosophical disputation. 'Tartar-Mongol savagery [*dich'*]', she called it; their 'Tartar Marxism grates on the nerves.'[97] That taint of racism in the sociology of knowledge was moved further east by a Russian comrade who broke with the Marxism of Lenin and Plekhanov. In 1910 he accused both of 'Marxist Chineseism [*kitaizm*], a complex and weird mixture of dogmatism, the closed mind in ideas [*ideinaia zamknutost'*], arrogance, and underestimation of the opponent's forces.' He declared Lenin and Plekhanov prisoners of the tradition that Marxists must be ferocious know-it-alls, with a papal attitude that masks the poverty of their thought.[98]

Those pre-revolutionary critics were anticipating notorious features of the mentality that came to be called Stalinist as it emerged in the 1930s, and some readers will leap upon such evidence that the Stalinist potential was evident in the Leninist mentality from the start. The eager accusers should pause to reflect. Do they agree with the first critics' accusation of Russian Marxists or leftists as a whole? Do they agree that 'backwardness' was the social determinant of that mentality, and will they add the racist twist to their sociology of knowledge by repeating the clichés 'Chinese', or 'Tartar-Mongol'? Lenin, I must note, also had the habit of using 'oriental' as a label for backward traits. We may sensibly discard such racist tendencies, but we are still left with the question of how much truth there is in the derivation of the Stalinist mentality — or the Leninist anticipations of the Stalinist mentality — from socio-economic and cultural underdevelopment, as polite people nowadays call the condition of a peasant country with a modern intelligentsia.

The problem I am pointing at is much too large to be treated adequately within a special study of Russian psychology. But a few observations are necessary, if only to avoid superstitious exaltation of Lenin and his comrades as the gods or devils who created history for millions of lesser folk — not only in Russia, but in all the countries that have had Communist revolutions and may still have them. Visibility creates tricky problems. Revolutionary intellectuals stand out too prominently in the drift to 1917, and anti-intellectual party bosses come too powerfully in view after 1917. We must remind ourselves that Russian intellectuals who wished to be revolutionary leaders were actually very marginal figures until the moments, in 1905 and again in 1917, when mass upheavals suddenly raised them to the tribunals that govern revolutionary politics. Previously they were very often marginal even in a physical sense: in exile, trying to persuade themselves that appearance and reality were inside out, that some among their splinter groups spoke for the oppressed multitudes back home while others would forever be the chattering isolates that they appeared to be. One obvious consequence of that persistent pattern in Russian political culture was the tendency of exiled radicals to substitute their particular party for the lower classes and their own mind for the party.[99] They had constant reason to turn anxiety into exaggerated assurance, to hear one's own voice as the future thunder of oppressed multitudes, while dismissing other marginal voices as isolated chatter. And one or another was to be proved right in the course of sudden upheaval back home, to the astonished dismay of rivals and the protracted puzzlement of historians.

The moments of mass upheaval were crucial tests of social knowledge, not only for exiled intellectuals trying to imagine the interests and the passions of the oppressed masses back home. For the last twenty years before the complete collapse of the Tsarist system, there were significant numbers of political activists back home. The leaders in exile had contacts inside Russia, mostly underground but partly in the open, especially during the final ten years, after the revolution of 1905 had won some rights of political action. Revolutionary theorists were interacting with the lower classes, directed by such leaders as J. V. Stalin, who went abroad rarely and briefly. They stayed at home to organize the party cadres (note the military usage), to spread the word and make propaganda (note the religious usage), to agitate (note the pride in stirring lower-class emotions). Sometimes dodging police and escaping jailers, sometimes caught, such activists wrote comparatively little, and that in a strikingly simplified style, much closer to sloganeering than to theorizing. We must assume that this new breed of revolutionary leaders were absorbing consciousness from within, not just bringing consciousness into, the urban lower classes of the Russian Empire. But it is extremely difficult to discover what they were absorbing until, in the aftermath of 1917, cadres recruited from below came to dominate the Party and quite subordinated the intellectuals. Even then we may not automatically assume that we are seeing the triumph of lower-class passions and thoughts, for the freshly promoted cadres had sudden power, which transforms anyone's mentality.

Only the articulate have left self-portraits. Even the bosses of lordly silence who triumphed in the Soviet period have pictured themselves as they signed decrees for changing policies and ordered changing justifications from learned underlings. I will examine such Stalinist self-portraits in due course. Here I am concerned with pre-revolutionary origins. Some traits of Stalin's mentality have been charged against – or credited to – the lower classes that he moved among, including its criminal elements. The inarticulate cannot defend themselves – or claim credit. They have left only murky evidence of their beliefs on such issues as an authentically human life. Some deeply felt sense of equalitarian justice shaped lower-class visions at that basic level. I take that for granted because their spokesmen talked that way in 1905 and again in 1917, when the old order collapsed and the lower classes seemed suddenly free to build the human world anew, on foundations of their own design. Of course the articulate architects they chose were mainly from the radical intelligentsia, and the Bolshevik vanguard quickly became an irreversible tyranny which choked off autonomous expression of lower-class visions. The historian is left wondering how much long-term concordance there was between leaders and led, not only in visions of justice but also in tendencies to violence and tyranny. That is an enormous problem for historians of lower-class culture in developing countries.

I am concerned here with radical intellectuals rather than their lower-class constituency, especially with the Bolsheviks who became the chief tribunes of the people in 1917. If we ask of Lenin what vision of an authentically human existence fitted him for supremacy among the people's commissars, his writings offer thousands of pages in reply, all concentrated on social analysis and politics, none devoted to the justification of an authentic human being as such, much less the claim that he was it. Even in private letters the innermost vision of his own person, what he wanted his self to be, was rigidly encased within the social mission ostensibly imposed by history. Service to the cause was the only justification of a person, the only way out of an otherwise pointless or immoral existence. The same modest – or supremely arrogant – equation of self and cause marks the man in reminiscences by those who knew him most intimately.

Let us turn then to Trotsky, second in command during the Bolshevik Revolution and notorious for extravagant self-display. That notoriety emerged in contrast with Lenin's extreme reserve. In Trotsky's writing the display of self is actually modest, if we measure it by contrast with explicitly subjective revolutionaries, who identify their personal intuition with the people's will. Trotsky was a Marxist, and presented himself as a social scientist. Or should we say that he constrained the self within that role? In any case he had absorbed much of Russian literary culture, and its characteristic anxiety over personal justification resonated in his scientific analysis of impersonal process. Consider the dialogue of the scientist and the activist, the objective process and the human creator, which emerged in an essay on the twentieth century, written in 1901 when Trotsky was twenty-one.

> If I lived the life of celestial bodies, I would be absolutely indifferent in my relation to the contemptible ball of dirt lost in the infinite universe, I would shine all the same on the evil and the good. ... [*sic*] But I am a *man*! And 'universal history', which seems to you, dispassionate priest of science, bookkeeper of eternity, a negligible second in the budget of time, to me is everything! And while I breathe I will struggle for the sake of the future, that resplendent and bright future, when man, strong and beautiful, will master the elemental [*stikhiinym*] flow of his history and will direct it to limitless horizons of beauty, joy, happiness!
>
> And against the contemptible philistine, with his denial of changes in the sublunar world, the optimist of the future opposes the bookkeeping calculations of science that were directed against him. 'Look!' he cries: 'out of five seconds of universal history less than half a second was allotted to your petty bourgeois [*meshchanskoe*] being, and maybe less than a tenth of a second is left till the end of your historical existence. Here's to the future!'
>
> The indifferent centuries have passed in a file, like the movement of the earth about the sun, and only dramatic episodes of the ceaseless struggle for the future have added bright coloration to these bare arithmetical conventions, to these giants of calendrical origin.[100]

The new century seemed to be bringing intensified racism and war. Instead of nineteenth-century radicals' dreams coming to life, Trotsky saw:

> hatred and killings, famine and blood. ... 'Death to utopias! Death to faith! Death to love!' thunders the twentieth century in volleys of gunfire and thudding of cannon. 'Submit, contemptible dreamer! Here I am, your long awaited twentieth century, your "*future*"!'
>
> 'No!' answers the refractory optimist; 'you are only the *present*!'[101]

Is there not a glint of nihilism within that florid cascade? The scientific self, knowing past and present to be inhuman, provokes revolt by the activist self. Trotsky strains toward a future that may prove to be no better than the past; he finds in the dream of something better and the strain to accomplish it the only justification of his otherwise negligible moment. Yet Trotsky also, and more characteristically, mobilized troops for battle with claims of scientific knowledge: the historical laws discovered by Marx ensured the victory of socialism. Hung up for years between Menshevism and Bolshevism, criticizing the one for *attentisme*, the other for tyranny, he came down on Lenin's side in 1917, and was soon the supreme military commissar, the legendary organizer of revolutionary victory.

To grasp that startling overthrow of traditional Russian values, an American might try to imagine a black abolitionist such as Frederick Douglass commanding a revolutionary army, guaranteeing the seizure of estates by former slaves, of factories by former operatives, all determined to ignore the question of race. Of course Trotsky did not call attention to his Jewishness; he was culturally assimilated to the educated Russian type, like the multitude of Jews who quickly rose to prominence in the course of the Revolution. Enemies of the Revolution called attention to the sudden upsurge of assimilated Jews as a terrible sign, along with peasant seizure of the gentry's land, workers taking over factories, and soldiers ordering officers about — all shocking signs that Russia was being destroyed. The retrospective outsider notes that Trotsky and his lower-class soldiers defeated the anti-Semitic class enemy in civil war, but still the distant observer finds cause to wonder how long Russia could have been held together by workers and peasants seeking justice, led by Bolshevik intellectuals who brushed aside the Jewishness of Trotsky as an irrelevant trifle. Very soon after 1917 the lower-class seekers were being harshly disciplined, by Trotsky among others, who would in turn be ground down by a harsher tyrant.

Joseph Conrad, Polish exile from the Russian Empire and outsider everywhere, saw Bolshevik intellectuals as continuing the Russian tradition.[102] They were trying, by violent action, to fill the moral void, with no other knowledge of what they sought than that it must be different from the hated society they were born into. Conrad simply ignored the Marxist argument that the improved future can be scientifically predicted. Perhaps, had he known the writing of young Marx, he would have liked the argument that alienated human beings struggle to create authentic humanity without knowledge of what it will be, compelled in that direction by instinctive rejection of obvious inauthenticity, and trapped by their rebellion in some new form of inauthenticity. Conrad's fictional heroes reveal that pattern. At the heart of Europe's civilizing mission in Africa Marlow discovers futile rapacity and place-seeking; recoiling against that, he finds himself entangled with mere violent self-assertion, and with a lying pretense of chivalric service when he returns to the European metropolis.[103] Similarly in tyrannous South America or Russia: heroes struggling for some dream of justice find themselves imprisoned in vicious circles of unending violence and reinforced tyranny.[104] At the heart of metropolitan civility in England, which Conrad admired above all other patterns of culture, he discerned either mindless commitment to rules of order or the stodgy pragmatism of the policeman endlessly circling the ultimate terrorist in *The Secret Agent*: to shoot him from ambush would affirm his scorn for law and order; to attempt arrest would be counter-productive, for an infernal machine is on the terrorist's body, set to blow up a city block if the policeman touches him.

The machine that blew up Europe was not an absurdly simple combination of nitroglycerin and malevolence. It was an intricate arrangement of nationalist ideologies, arms races, and imperial contests, all wired together by alliance systems that were supposed to cow any adversary by threatening instant transformation of any local conflict into total world war. So a pistol shot at one man could detonate the massed machine guns and mountains of shells that killed ten million, and in the sequelae killed tens of millions more, and have still not stopped the mechanized killing but only slowed it down somewhat while the enormous machine – the ideologies, the arms races, the imperial contests, all wired together by the alliance systems – is intricately rearranged to destroy many hundreds of millions more, if not the entire race.

Back at the very beginning of this century the outsider's imagination of Joseph Conrad enabled him to perceive the mental hollowness, the intellectual nihilism that gave the lie to the outward thrust of the politicians' jaws, whether upward in some version of the 'idealist' posture or resolutely downward in the stance called 'realist'. Conrad's fiction presaged the revulsion and the horror of the writing provoked by the First World War, and the persistent distrust if not loathing of power structures that has dominated serious writing ever since. Yet he himself, during the First World War, vehemently endorsed the Anglo-Franco-Russian cause; he was one of those old men who send off children, ardent for some desperate glory, preaching 'Dulce et decorum est pro patria mori'. I call attention to that incongruity of thinker and citizen, the inconsistency between the piercing vision of his fiction and the deadly banality of his everyday politics, because it too presaged a characteristic pattern of our century. Serious thought may guide the writer's hand, but not the public mouth. Organized violence drags everyone up its ever rising waves, with ideological shrieking that the best minds often join. Lenin and his Party were determined to stop that. By violent action they were determined to create a truly human community, to replace the exploitation, the oppression, and the periodic mass slaughter that they knew to be inhuman.

Part III

Genteel Integration in Revolutionary Russia

7

A Great Unifying Idea

Did the Congress of Soviets proclaim a republic of workers and peasants, or did the Bolshevik Party seize power? The answer of course is both, but the overwhelming majority of the intelligentsia was in no mood to acknowledge a new kind of revolution emerging in twentieth-century backward countries. Nearly all longed for the British or the French system, refined products of bygone revolutions, not mad dreams of direct democracy by uncivilized (*nekul'turnye*) workers and peasants under the actual dictatorship of a single party. No matter that the political parties dreaming of the British or French system in Russia could not draw workers and peasants away from *their* dreams, which the Bolsheviks knew how to organize into the Soviet regime (power or regime, *vlast'* means both). No matter that four years of civil war and foreign intervention against the one-party *vlast'* of workers and peasants gave deadly proof that it was indeed the supreme power in the land, superior even to economic collapse and famine. Such brute facts could force the intelligentsia to submit (or emigrate), but 'inward acceptance of the Soviet *vlast''* — the constant Bolshevik demand — could still be refused in the privileged realm of high culture.

The history of Soviet Russia seems to writhe forever in that vicious circle: inward refusal aggravated by the persistent victory of external compulsion, and not only among the intelligentsia. In 1917-18 the toiling masses could seize farms and factories spontaneously, but they could not spontaneously run them as a modern system. They lacked the resources, the knowhow, the rational self-discipline; centralized compulsion was a poor substitute, a remedy for underdevelopment that intensified the trouble. The masses' liberating anger at the old *vlast'* of landlords and capitalists turned easily into non-cooperation with the new *vlast'* of Bolsheviks, or worse. Peasants tried a few hopeless insurrections — there was no Bolshevik Party to organize a revolution within the revolution — and then easily slipped back into the cunning servility that masks evasion of power.

The Bolsheviks themselves were changed by the triumph of their power, more than any other group. Their numbers increased enormously, and so did the percentage of lower-class members, with minds turned from hated subjection to — what? The end of all subjection forever? So they said, with a passion that belies disbelief, while forcefully mobilizing peasants and workers to win a ferocious civil war and build a new state system of extreme authoritarian severity. An outsider may pooh-pooh the animating idea of an end to state systems, and note that this newly swollen Party of lower-class people fought their way from beneath one power system to the top of a new one built for themselves. But the outsider's indifference to the frustrated idea misses an essential feature of Bolshevik minds. They moved from the 1917 dream of the world renewed by lower-class democracy through civil war into the chronic anger of devout rulers, the bitter insistence that a stubbornly sinful world must be governed by righteous violence. As the dream of stateless freedom shrank into a glimmer on the furthest horizon, like the Christian second coming or the Wilsonian world made safe for democracy, the romanticism of righteous violence swelled to fill the intervening space, for Bolsheviks as for Wilsonian Americans. While the world would persist in wicked refusal of the virtuous way, the virtuous would prove their devotion in warfare.

There were other homelier elements in the romanticism of the newly swollen Party in power. *Shturmovshchina*, taking the goal by storm, grew from a military tactic into a general way of thought. The odds against Bolshevik victory were so great as to cast doubt on realistic calculation of odds, to make it seem an un-Bolshevik or 'bourgeois' procedure, while uncalculating leaps toward maximal goals came to seem the triumphantly Bolshevik kind of practicality. Lenin warned repeatedly against *komchvanstvo*, 'Commconceit', a coinage to describe Bolshevik delusions of superhuman knowledge and power.[1] But he was far from undercutting his comrades' belief that 'We Bolsheviks are people of a special make. ... With a passionate will we can accomplish everything, we can overcome everything.'[2]

That quotation is from Stalin, not Lenin; speaking in the early 1930s, not the 1920s. Putting it in here is an unhistorical leap forward to 1929, when Stalin revived the spirit of the Civil War to press upon the population a new 'revolution from above', as he called the sudden collectivization of farms, the forced industrialization, and the all-out assault on the 'bourgeois' intelligentsia. If we are true to the ethos of 'bourgeois' historians, we must hold back for a while and consider the possibilities of the intervening period. We may not simply assume without argument that Stalin's second revolution was predetermined by Lenin's first, even though every Communist revolution in our century has followed something like that two-step pattern. Perhaps the Russian original could have been different.

So let us give thought to the strange interlude following the 1917 revolution from below, the civil war it set off, the Bolshevik victory in a devastated land, the concession of autonomy to the peasants and the intelligentsia — and the consequent tension of opposed tendencies within a system aspiring to prophetic unity. After all, no one then knew what hindsight tells us now. Many then believed that unity of opposites was the prophet's way, and Stalin was the leader of the center in the mid-1920s, seeking unity in balancing. Bukharin, the chief ideologist of the period, identified dialectics with equilibrium, and Stalin did not object before 1929. We should not endow him with godlike prescience; Stalin had to learn the way we call Stalinist, the plunge for unity through deliberate revival of civil war.

We do not need to guess at the opposed tendencies within the new system. The most obvious, such as the standoff between *vlast'* and intelligentsia, were abundantly discussed by the Bolsheviks themselves. Two days after Soviet power was decreed Lunacharsky, the first Commissar of Education, warned that 'functionaries without ideas [*bezideinye chinovniki*] are rather likely to come to our side, while all the officials with ideas [*ideinye rabotniki*] stubbornly defend their opinion that our power is a usurpation.'[3] Lenin sometimes warned that the new regime might be trapped in the old 'realm of darkness' that Dobroliubov had mapped: the vicious circle of *samodurstvo* and *obezlichka*, self-assertive pigheadedness above and self-effacing irresponsibility below, the mutual stultification of the foot-stamping master and the grovelling slave. At other times Lenin swung about and claimed that revolting workers and peasants were turning themselves into civilized (*kul'turnye*) agents of socialist modernization. At a terrible low-point in the Civil War he angrily denied any need for the hostile intelligentsia. They were 'lackeys of capital who fancy themselves the nation's brain. In fact they are not the brain but the shit.'[4]

That outburst was a momentary extreme, but it vividly revealed the potentially violent ambivalence that attended Bolshevik efforts to enlist the intelligentsia in the cultural revolution. At the point of a gun the intelligentsia were asked to teach the masses not only essential knowledge and skills but a complete change of spirit. Under duress the intelligentsia were to draw the masses away from the heritage of duress, from *samotek*, planless drift, and from *stikhiinost'*, the ancient 'elementalism' that knows only inertial torpor or anarchic chaos. The Greek root is still alive in Russian as *stikhiia*, the elements or chaos. Trotsky told a conference of Russian educators: 'Man is himself *stikhiia*', inviting them to help the Communists change human nature, to create 'a new, "improved edition" of man'.[5] But in the next breath he acknowledged such talk to be

> of course, music of the future. We, along with you, must lay the first stones of the foundation of socialist society. And the cornerstone is raising the productivity of labor. We will be able to speak of the real, complete, and irreversible victory of socialism only when a unit of human energy will give us more products than under the rule of private property.[6]

By excitedly running that plodding task – raising Russia to the capitalist level – together with a futuristic mission for all humanity – creating a new man – the Bolsheviks generated some enthusiasm among the intelligentsia. A minority became 'fellow travellers' (*poputchiki*), but the fundamental antipathy persisted. It emerged as a basic theme in Trotsky's exhortations to imaginative writers; even the fellow-traveling minority annoyed him. They declared their sympathy with Bolshevik goals, but their writing was less inspirational than naturalist; the Bolshevik ideal was less in evidence than the unruly elements of actual human beings. The revolutionary commissar was especially annoyed at writers who thought to picture the Revolution sympathetically by dwelling so vividly on lower-class upheaval that vanguard vision was lost:

> ... It is bad, it is criminal that they cannot make their approach to the present Revolution otherwise than by dissolving it into blind revolts, into elemental uprisings. ... As Pilnyak says, 'peasant life is known – it is to eat in order to work, to work in order to eat, and besides that, to be born, to bear, and to die.' Of course that is a vulgarization of peasant life. However, artistically it is a legitimate vulgarization. For what is our Revolution, if it is not a mad rebellion in the name of the conscious, rational, purposeful and dynamic principle of life, against the elemental, senseless, biologic automatism of life, that is, against the peasant roots of our old Russian history, against its aimlessness, its non-teleological character ...?[7]

He wanted writers 'to understand the Revolution from within, ... to look at it with the eyes of its greatest dynamic force, of the working class, of its conscious vanguard.'[8]

Trotsky's famous book, *Literature and Revolution*, was an extended effort to mobilize the miscreant imagination of creative writers, scolding most of them, holding up as a model an oldfashioned versifier who wrote to order for *Pravda*.[9] He endorsed 'complete freedom of self-determination in the field of art, *after* putting before [artists] the categorical standard of being for or against the Revolution'.[10] He explained the categorical imperative, 'being for the Revolution', with a formula that plainly anticipated what Stalinist officials would call 'socialist realism': 'a new art ... incompatible with pessimism, with skepticism, and with all the other forms of spiritual collapse. It is realistic, active, vitally collectivist, and filled with a limitless creative faith in the Future.'[11] The revolutionary boss was beginning a protracted conflict. It could hardly be avoided, for both sides, writers and revolutionaries, took very seriously the notion that 'man is himself *stikhiia*.' The writer's craft was to order the elements in aesthetic forms, the revolutionary boss's to transcend or at least to order them in other than aesthetic forms, in hierarchies of power.

The Bolshevik leaders could not simply turn away from high culture and the intellectuals, as twentieth-century leaders have done in advanced countries. Russia did not have the kind of modern mass culture that cements leaders and led while excluding the intelligentsia. Which is another way of saying that Leninists shared the misgivings of educated Russians concerning lower-class culture, or 'non-culture' (*nekul'turnost'*), as they preferred to say. The leaders used such disparaging language constantly, in startling discord with their faith in the sacred masses. President Kalinin taunted an academic audience at the Agricultural Academy by conceding that the dictatorship of the proletariat might entail the barbarization of culture, as many intellectuals feared. He professed no alarm at the prospect. Did not the fall of Rome show that the barbarization of culture could serve progress in the long run? But that gibe at the self-importance of the intelligentsia was only a small part of a speech which ended by exhorting agronomists to carry the light of science to the dark peasant masses.[12]

In a speech to the Academy of Sciences Commissar of Education Lunacharsky was less provocative, and unusually frank. He assured the scholarly audience that the political triumph of the lower classes was not a threat to high culture, for the masses did not rule directly. They had created a dictatorial regime which was a friend of high culture. Genuine self-government, he promised, would not come until the masses were enlightened. In the meantime he called upon the old 'bourgeois' intelligentsia to help raise a new, red, Soviet intelligentsia out of the lower classes.[13] In other words, he asked the existing intelligentsia to transmit their knowledge, their culture, without the non-Marxist ideologies that saturated it.

That tangle of ambivalent hopes and anxieties dragged the Bolsheviks into offensives on two ever-widening sectors of the cultural front: against the uncivilized tendencies of the masses, and against the subversive tendencies of the intelligentsia. Shouting hollow claims of victory, the Bolsheviks were actually staking fortified outposts in alien territories. They called themselves comrades of the natives on both fronts, while they knew that they were a tiny army of occupation, struggling to avoid assimilation by the uncivilized masses on the one hand, by the subversive intelligentsia on the other. My military metaphors are drawn from the Bolshevik vocabulary, but I am obviously twisting their words to expose an underlying hysteria, a self-deceiving refusal to see intolerable realities, which expressed itself in overcompensating boasts of a new culture being created by campaigns against the old.

PAVLOV AND THE BOLSHEVIKS

On their side of the confrontation the intelligentsia were by no means of a single mind, but a characteristic type stands out in the record. Pavlov was representative, probably of a large majority in higher learning, who had learned under the old regime to sneer quietly at power, to combine a distant dream of constitutional representative government with disdain for current politics. The combination gives intellectuals a sense of purity, while masking submission to whoever commands the dirty world of politics. (I use the present tense, for such purified submission is by no means unique to Russian intellectuals or to a bygone era.) Such people did not respond to the Bolshevik Revolution by emigrating or by joining the Whiteguard armies, or even by parading in the streets or signing public protests. They simply disapproved, while getting on with their lives as best they could. Pavlov did not conceal his revulsion against the new regime, but he remained as ever aloof from 'politics', which is to say from organized agitation or action. He stayed where he was in Petrograd and continued his work, until the economic collapse that attended the Civil War made such normality impossible. Then he turned to the new authorities with a threat to emigrate unless he received special help.

The public record does not reveal which lesser officials said what in the palaver, but we get decisive insight in the letter from the very top which gave Pavlov what he demanded. Lenin wrote to Zinoviev in June 1920, saying that Pavlov was threatening to emigrate, since it was virtually impossible for him to continue his work in Petrograd. Lenin thought it would

> hardly be rational to permit Pavlov to go abroad, for he has previously spoken out openly in this sense, that, being a truthful person, he will be unable, in case appropriate discussions are started, to refrain from speaking out against the Soviet regime and Communism in Russia.
>
> At the same time this scientist constitutes such a big cultural value [*bol'shuiu kul'turnuiu tsennost'*] that it is impossible to think of keeping him in Russia by force, in conditions of material deprivation.[14]

Therefore, Lenin reasoned, Pavlov should get an extraordinarily large food ration, and an especially comfortable place to live.

In a government decree spelling out the details some months later, exceptional provision was also ordered for publication of his scientific work. (There was a terrible paper shortage at the time.) The cryptic characterization of Pavlov in Lenin's letter − 'such a big cultural value' − was slightly expanded but hardly clarified in the decree: 'Academician Pavlov's absolutely exceptional scientific achievements . . . have significance for the toilers of the entire world.'[15] Evidently Lenin and his comrades did not know enough to be less vague. Nor is there anywhere else a word of Lenin's to support the legend that he saw in Pavlov's doctrine the way to a Marxist reconstruction of psychology. A few years after 1920, when a campaign was launched for such a reconstruction, its point of departure would be the explicit recognition that no one had ever before thought of Marxist psychology, and that no one knew exactly how to create it.[16]

In 1920 Lenin and his colleagues may have been moved to favor Pavlov by the simple fact that he was the only Nobel laureate in Russia. What he did to win the Prize, his studies of digestion, may have been 'the big cultural value' that was decreed to be of exceptional significance for the toilers of the entire world — in short, an object of blind worship. If the leaders were aware of his post-Nobel writings, which claimed to reduce the psyche to neural processes, they could hardly have considered them a pure boost for Bolshevik ideology. His 1918 paper, 'The Reflex of Freedom', was extravagantly reductionist and implicitly anti-revolutionary. Pavlov began with a laboratory puzzle — some dogs could never be trained to stand quietly in the experimental harness — and proceeded to indulge his imagination. The untrainable dogs had the 'reflex of freedom', because their ancestors had not been chained, while trainable dogs had the 'reflex of slavery' because they came of chained animals. He finished by lamenting how often Russians exhibited the reflex of slavery.[17] When that was published the Bolsheviks were entering the Civil War; it is quite unlikely that they were paying attention to academic fantasies of freedom and slavery as neural reflexes. Nor is there any evidence that they thought of Pavlov as a psychologist. Even in 1921 Bukharin's textbook of Marxist sociology cited Wundt and Lévy-Bruhl as its authorities on psychology, without a single reference to Pavlov or conditioned reflexes.[18] To be sure, his citation of big names in psychological science does not prove that he preferred their mentalism to Pavlov's physiological reductionism. He was probably unaware of such distinctions; he was concerned only to evoke respect for his science of man by associating respectable names with it.

In 1921, as the Civil War drew to an end, Bolshevik leaders turned seriously to problems of higher learning. They moved to undercut the hostility of its adepts by restricting academic autonomy and by starting rival institutions to train 'red professors' for a future takeover. The immediate result was a clash with the existing professors — strikes broke out at some universities — which ended in an uneasy compromise. Statutory autonomy was restricted as the Bolsheviks insisted, and 161 scholars in philosophy and the social sciences were demonstratively banished from the Soviet Republic because of their inimical doctrines. (Lenin himself took a direct hand, singling out the sociologist P. A. Sorokin as an obnoxious example of the higher learning that the Republic did not need.)[19] But then the highest leaders turned about and made conciliatory gestures to the much larger number of scientists and scholars still in place. (A very approximate estimate would be ten thousand 'scientific workers' inherited from the old regime.)[20] As long as they refrained from organized political opposition, they were free in the 1920s to think and teach as they wished, even to express courteous disagreement with some aspects of Communist ideology. That compromise, and the Bolshevik effort to unify culture within a Marxist frame, occasioned peculiarly Soviet debates in a variety of scholarly disciplines. Seeking cultural unity without throttling dissidence, the Bolsheviks achieved something like genteel discourse among diverse interpreters of Marxism and experts in various fields of higher learning.

Even Pavlov, who normally held himself silently superior to ideological disputation, opened the academic year in the fall of 1923 with a lecture at the Medical Academy explaining why Marxism was not authentically scientific. The lecture has never been published, but its central argument is apparent in the rebuttals that three of the highest leaders published. Lenin was silent — he was paralyzed and close to death — and Stalin was just edging toward his first venture into the theoretical foundations of Leninism, a series of lectures designed to prove that he was more than the chief administrator of the Party. The Party chiefs who were already recognized theorists — Zinoviev, Trotsky, Bukharin — were stung to rebuttal not only by Pavlov's unpublished lecture, but also by an ideological thrust that he had got into print. In a preface to his collected papers, which the state publishing house had been ordered on Lenin's instructions to bring out, Pavlov celebrated the triumphant progress of the human mind in natural science, and lamented what the mind produces in other fields:

> The same human being, with the same mind, governed by some dark forces acting within himself, causes incalculable material losses and inexpressible suffering by wars and by *revolutions with their horrors, which take man back to bestial relationships.* Only the ultimate science, the exact science of man himself — and the most reliable approach to it from the field of all-powerful natural science — will lead man out of the present darkness and cleanse him of the present shame of inter-personal relations.[21]

I have italicized the obvious insult to the Revolution, but the reader should also note the implicit rebuke to the Marxist claim of social science. Pavlov spelled that out at length in his unpublished lecture: his doctrine of conditioned reflexes was the only genuinely scientific approach to an understanding of mental phenomena. Marxism was pseudoscience, as one could easily see by noting its failure to make verifiable predictions. 'The leaders of our ruling party believe that there will be a world revolution. But I want to ask: how long will they go on believing? You see, it is necessary to set a limit.'[22] The students laughed, and the Party chiefs used such media as *Pravda* to rebut the amusing professor. That seems an exciting sign of intellectuality in high places, until one reflects that the chiefs were replying to the stenographic report of an unpublished lecture, plus a few lines of published disdain for their revolution and the claim of social science that justified it.

The most interesting reply was Trotsky's, for he showed some under-standing of Pavlov's field. He thought that psychological science was divided into two rival schools, Pavlov's and Freud's. Whether he had known of Pavlov's school before the Revolution Trotsky did not say. He had known of Freud's. While in Viennese exile he had even attended some meetings of Freudians, and noticed that they 'combined physiological realism with almost belletristic analysis of mental phenomena'. Trotsky compared them

> to people looking into a deep and rather turbid well. They have ceased to believe that this well is an abyss (the abyss of 'the soul'). They see, or they divine, the bottom (physiology), and they even make a series of guesses about the characteristics of the bottom, which determine the character of the water in the well — guesses that are clever and interesting but scientifically arbitrary.[23]

Pavlov's approach seemed to Trotsky the opposite: it 'goes down to the bottom and rises experimentally to the top'. Before he published that judgment of psychological science, Trotsky wrote to Pavlov asking whether he agreed with the metaphor of the well, or with this version: 'the doctrine of conditioned reflexes includes Freud's theory as a particular instance.'[24] Pavlov disdained to reply, or wrote a letter that Soviet editors have considered improper to publish. (He did, however, remember the metaphor of the well, and used it in conversation to express his scorn for Freud's method and confidence in his own.)[25]

Trotsky's little flight of imagination, repeated and expanded a bit in publications of the mid-1920s,[26] was closer than any other Bolshevik leader came to a consideration of issues in psychology. It is impressive by contrast with the ignorance one expects in twentieth-century leaders, but that is scant praise. To Trotsky, as to the literate public at large, Freud and Pavlov were the founders of psychological science, period. He did not know that they were both outside critics of psychological science. He had no inkling of the actual schools that were struggling within the discipline to make a unified science of it. He gave no thought to the contradiction between his most fundamental conviction, that Marxism explains the mind in historical evolution, and his casual assumption that psychological science reduces the mind to physiology. In short, his sense of psychological science was that of the average educated person, Marxist variety. But he was Trotsky, major Bolshevik leader. When he put such banalities and blank spots into print, they were elevated in significance, foreshadowing official positions of a later time.

The major blank spot — no thought to reconciling Marx and Pavlov — was the most significant foreshadowing, but the evaluation of Freud as against Pavlov was the most striking. Trotsky was very close to the view that would become official wisdom, when he noted that Freud as well as Pavlov laid claim to the reductionist way in psychology, and declared that Pavlov's was the authentically scientific claim. Of course, Trotsky was far from peremptory in offering such judgments. Like the rest of the educated public, he did not take psychology and physiology nearly as seriously as he did imaginative literature, where he expressed his judgments frequently and forcefully. He offered only a few passing thoughts on psychological science, calmly noting the 'belletristic' attraction of Freud's ideas, smiling at their lack of scientific rigor, grimacing in proper revulsion at their exaggeration of sexuality — and coming down on the side of Pavlov as the authentic scientist of the brain-mind.

None of the Party leaders who responded to Pavlov thought it necessary to get deeply involved, for a simple division of labor seemed the obvious way to unify his knowledge and theirs. Zinoviev, Bukharin, Trotsky, all chided the great physiologist for straying into social science, their field of expertise, and for revealing ignorance and class prejudice while trespassing. All three eagerly declared their ignorance of his field, and unwittingly proved it by the unquestioning equation of his doctrine with psychological science. They were simply carrying into the post-revolutionary era the unexamined assumption that reduction to physiology was the only way for psychology to become a science, and they were adding the unexamined assumption that Pavlov's school was leading the way. They were unaware of the multiple divisions among academic psychologists, and of course they knew nothing about Pavlov's growing separation from the world community of neurophysiologists, as he imagined cortical processes of conditioning in disregard of the evidence mounting against him. Nor did the leaders show any wish to know about such issues. The scientistic faith endures by ignoring the major problems of science, by blithely brushing them off to the specialists who deal with technicalities. 'Technical' is the magic word that absolves the twentieth-century mind from the necessity of thought. Calculation suffices, each mind within its own speciality.

BUKHARIN'S VERSION

Bukharin, the Party's chief ideologist through most of the 1920s, touched on psychology and neurophysiology repeatedly, always with evasive vagueness. His *Theory of Historical Materialism* was the most important occasion, for it was an official textbook until his break with Stalin. It was reductionist but unaware of Pavlov and conditioned reflexes. Then there was the long reply to Pavlov's attack on Marxism, which Bukharin published in a 'thick journal' and republished as a pamphlet and yet again in *Attack*, an anthology of his essays that enjoyed many readers and no significant criticism before his fall.[27] He also wrote a scornful polemic against Emmanuel Enchmen, a former Socialist Revolutionary who saw in Pavlov's doctrine the forecast of a purely proletarian culture based directly on conditioned reflexes, without necessity of conventional language or thought.[28] In those polemics as in his textbook, whenever Bukharin touched on psychology and neurophysiology he deliberately limited himself to touching, careful to avoid entangling particulars. He wanted to show respect for physiological explanation of the mind, while proving that Marxism is the self-sufficient sociological explanation. His method of combining the two projects was to be extremely brief and philosophically abstract concerning the physiological.

That had been Bogdanov's way of combining Marxism with physiological reductionism, and Bukharin still admired Bogdanov, though he briefly apologized for his youthful infatuation with empiriomonism.[29] He no longer sought monism in the universal category of experience, but in the universal principle of equilibrium, and he was pleased to note that Pavlov adhered to the same principle.[30] Freud also assumed that the nature of animals is to be at rest or to seek re-establishment of rest when disturbed, but Bukharin was not aware of that kinship, or refrained from telling his readers that he was. In any case we can pass by his principle of equilibrium, for it had little influence on other Soviet Marxists, who favored more dynamic visions of the human animal, and anyhow the principle was anathematized in 1929 as the philosophical root of Bukharin's 'right deviation', that is, his resistance to Stalin's sudden revolution from above. But two of Bukharin's remarks on psychology had considerable resonance in the Soviet Marxist community, thereby revealing some of its characteristic mental habits. Indeed, one of them has been a central feature of Pavlov-worship in the Soviet Union, though separated of course from the taboo name of its originator.

The two remarks were not full-fledged thoughts. They were figures of speech, helping Bukharin to say something while avoiding entangling particulars. There was the simile of the sausage, and there was the metaphor of the weapon. While chiding Pavlov's notion that physiology alone yields scientific understanding of human beings, demonstrating the paramount importance of social experience in shaping the mind, Bukharin quoted Kuzma Prutkov, the fictive humorist much loved by Russians of that time: 'Many people are like sausages: whatever is stuffed into them, that they carry in themselves.'[31] The whiff of mockery in that trope was wiped away by Bukharin's martial metaphor: whether Pavlov realized it or not, his doctrine was 'a weapon from the iron arsenal of materialism'.[32] The sausage simile was ambiguous, but the weapon metaphor was clearly intended as clangorous praise, and was repeated in that spirit, even by those who disapproved of Pavlov's doctrine in psychology.[33] That bears repeating, for the incongruity marks Soviet thought to this day. Even scholars who disapproved of Pavlov's doctrine in psychology felt obliged to repeat Bukharin's ideological blessing on it, as 'a weapon from the iron arsenal of materialism'. He did not analyze the doctrine or use it; he simply made it a sacred weapon.

A profane observer may note the ambiguities that Bukharin and the other Soviet Marxists ignored when they equated Pavlov's doctrine with materialism. Subjective consciousness is not explained by studies of conditioned reflexes; it is ingeniously excluded from the experimental inquiry. The experimenters know that the dog expects, fears, likes, puzzles; they construct clever procedures to cut all that out of their communication with the dog and with each other. Bukharin did not ask whether the amputation of consciousness limits inquiry to automatic behavior and thereby cripples Pavlov's claim of a method to explain the whole mind. Nor did he note that Pavlov's doctrine had been linked to agnostic or neo-Kantian philosophy, in the first place by a pre-revolutionary philosopher, and then by some of Pavlov's disciples, including one whose book was graced with an admiring endorsement by Pavlov himself in 1923.[34] (That endorsement has been omitted from both editions of Pavlov's 'complete' works.) Bukharin simply disregarded the agnostic argument that one may assume either conscious persons or neuromuscular systems as the realities to be studied by psychological science, that different psychologies will be the result, without either type having the right to claim knowledge of mind or of matter as the metaphysical essence of the creature. Bukharin's materialism may be called Spinozist, for he felt that mental and neural processes are two aspects of one substance.[35] But it would be misleading to give his declaration such fancy names. He laid down the bare conviction, and left it unexamined. Which was just as well, since he could not have maintained his scorn for metaphysics if he had tried to explain and justify the two-aspects-of-one-substance, much less to show the connection with Pavlov's doctrine, which lops off one aspect.

Sacred beliefs may require clouds of unexamined questions. By its reverential intent the weapon metaphor stifled analytical philosophizing about conditioned reflex experiments as the way to explain mind. The sausage simile was less stifling than slippery, and frustrated analysis in a different manner. Bukharin first used the sausage in *The Theory of Historical Materialism* (1921), before he was entangled with Pavlov, but was already mocking the notion that the individual is the elemental unit of which society is constructed: 'If we consider the individual person [*lichnost'*] in its development, we see that it is in essence like a sausage skin stuffed with the influences of the environment.'[36] His obvious purpose was to ridicule the individualist approach in social thought, but the metaphor can also be read as mocking the individuals cranked out by socialization, perhaps even the socialization process itself. In 1924 Bukharin turned the figure of speech against Pavlov, who was repeating phrases that had been stuffed into him concerning the unscientific dogmatism of Marxism.[37]

Was the sausage simile also intended to ridicule mechanistic psychologies, which deny the existence of autonomous minds that shape the world in creative ways? That was an unintended implication, at odds with Bukharin's mechanistic main theme. To sustain his social theory he wanted seriously to believe that 'the individual person is precisely a clot of compressed social influences, bound in a little knot.'[38] This metaphor was part of his solemn textbook argument, widely repeated by respectful Soviet Marxists while Bukharin was still respectable. A leading psychologist of the 1920s even combined the two metaphors, the sausage and the clot − adding, on his own, a spongy suggestion of some slight self-activation: the individual person soaks up ever new experiences as a sponge soaks up water.[39] Other Soviet Marxists took advantage of Bukharin's slippery trope to favor some less mechanistic psychology. They quoted the sausage simile in deliberate derision of Pavlov's doctrine, and of American behaviorism and any other school that would reduce a conscious person to a system inherently inert, moved to action only by upset of its natural tendency toward equilibrium.[40]

Bukharin deserves his reputation as an exceptionally erudite and brilliant chief ideologist. He deserves it by comparison with Stalin, who took over the job in 1929, and certainly by contrast with the golems who have followed after Stalin in the ideological bureaucracy. Only ghoulish humor can attach intellectual adjectives to the monotonous muttering of Stalin's successors. Such forward comparisons are quite flattering to Bukharin, and backward comparisons − with Plekhanov or Marx − may be simply unfair, like measurements of twentieth-century American politicians against Madison or Jefferson. The historical process since the Enlightenment has irresistibly severed political leadership from intellectual thought. So I intend no disrespect for such passionately thoughtful leaders as Lenin, Trotsky and Bukharin when I call attention to their place in the descent from Marx to Suslov. They did what they could to resist the descent. Considering its irresistible power, we may say that Bukharin's brilliance expressed itself in the brevity and ambiguity of his remarks on issues like the mind-body problem.

He came close to explicit defense of philosophical brevity and ambiguity, when he told a Comintern Congress of 1924 why it was necessary, not dangerous, for Communist parties to require belief in Marxist materialism. It was necessary in order to combat the disruptive effects of bourgeois philosophies. It was not dangerous since Marxist materialism is not very restrictive, it is 'a rather elastic formula'.[41] An outsider might say that he was reaching for the kind of distinction that Galileo offered to traditional churches: between religious knowledge, which is sacred and changeless, and scientific knowledge, which is profane and transient. But Bukharin was caught in a tradition that rejects such distinctions. Marxist knowledge was not sacred and changeless, it was scientific and − transient? He was obliged to be brief and evasive in epistemology as well as psychology.

As examples of disruptive bourgeois ideologies, which must be suppressed by Marxist materialism, Bukharin cited 'voluntaristic' interpretations of Marxism, evidently with George Lukács and Karl Korsch in mind. To sustain scientific socialism their interpretations of it would be prohibited.

Within Russia he saw a greater danger in 'agnostic positivism'. He offered the example of 'comrades [who] take their stand on the doctrine, incorrectly understood, of the Russian physiological school, so-called reflexology'.[42] They considered Marxist materialism obsolete and were trying overtly or covertly to replace it. He may have had in mind the admirers of Bekhterev, who was worrying Party ideologists by his effort to annex Marxism, to make it seem a part of reflexology. But if that specific case was on Bukharin's mind, he refrained from saying so, and Soviet Marxist critics of Pavlov, not only of Bekhterev, liked to quote the anti-reflexological passage from Bukharin's Comintern speech.

To some extent Bukharin was undoubtedly deliberate in his ambiguities and silences. Stalin, as the reader will see, was far more reticent and enigmatic, if only because he was far closer to possessing godlike power over the poor scribes whose job it was to interpret his oracular pronouncements. By comparison, Bukharin could be considered loquacious and straight-forward, though he too leaves us guessing — for example, whether his understanding of issues in psychology was as crude as M. N. Pokrovsky's.

Pokrovsky was the chief Bolshevik historian of the 1920s, and an administrator of higher learning in general. In 1926, during an extemporaneous exchange at the Communist Academy, he declared that 'the study of the brain by the Pavlovian method is the latest word of materialism, spoken quite unintentionally by the old idealist Pavlov. It sometimes happens that way; a man will say a new word at odds with his personal world view.' Pokrovsky grew still cruder as he tried to explain wherein Pavlov's doctrine was materialist: 'It abolishes the spirit, in the most obvious manner it abolishes the very concept of the soul.' And he offered an example that he could not forget: an ape, which had previous experience of morphine, staggered drunkenly merely on seeing the needle, before actual injection.[43] None of the Marxists in the audience, including the famous historian who had been objecting to Pavlovian research at the Academy, called attention to the superficiality of Pokrovsky's argument and the irrelevance of his example.[44] (The *mechanism* of suggestion is the issue in appraisals of Pavlov's doctrine, not the age-old observation of the occurrence.) The handful of Marxists with a genuine understanding of issues in psychology and physiology were at other institutions — chiefly the Institute of Psychology — and there were few of them in any case. Pokrovsky and his audience at the Communist Academy were representative of the Party's ideologists and scholars; they cared little about psychology and neurophysiology, and knew less.

One likes to imagine that Bukharin's understanding was not so superficial or crude, but there is no good evidence one way or another. He was careful to be philosophically abstract in his publications, and he was too exalted a boss to engage in extemporaneous discussion at the Communist Academy.[45] In any case, issues of personal biography are not nearly as important as the problem of the collective mentality, the Party's framing assumptions, of which Bukharin was the chief interpreter. The central question is why he and the other Bolshevik leaders were entangling their minds in issues that they had a sensible inclination to evade, if only because they were conscious of their limited knowledge and the urgency of other tasks. An unpublished lecture of Pavlov's could have been ignored by busy statesmen; the republic would probably have endured without its chief ideologist chiding Pavlov's sneer at Marxism but blessing his doctrine of conditioned reflexes. Why did busy practical leaders bother?

The first step in explanation is to note that Pavlov's sneering lecture went unpublished, though a stenographer recorded it (the leaders quoted from that record), and hectograph copies seem to have been made for Pavlov's students. (Seventy years later it is still unpublished and deliberately ignored by Soviet scholars.) Censorship had collapsed with the Tsarist regime in the spring of 1917, but the Bolsheviks re-established it in the fall for an obvious political reason – to suppress opposition to their rule. There is no obvious reason why they subsequently extended censorship to a range of cultural matters far more extensive than Russian censors had touched since the 1860s. Nothing of Pavlov's had ever been suppressed before the Bolshevik Revolution. Nor had the work of any other Russian psychologist or physiologist, once the landmark cases of Sechenov and Wundt had been won in the 1860s by the proponents of free expression.[46] By 1917 the Tsarist censorship was largely restricted to politics. Why did the Bolsheviks in their cultural revolution reverse that fifty-year withering away of thought control?

One must grope for motives through a study of cases. Already in the comparatively liberal 1920s there was a growing index of prohibited works. Freud was not on it at first. The Bolsheviks did not come to power with minds closed against his ideas, unless one imagines that their silence means dissent. A series of Russian translations of Freud was not only continued but expanded in the early 1920s, stimulating animated discussion of the compatibility between Freudianism and Marxism.[47] But in the late 1920s the translations dwindled to a dead halt, and genuine discussion of Freudianism was swamped by one-sided denunciations.[48] Less famous Western psychologists – the behaviorist Watson, the Gestaltists Köhler and Koffka, the cognitivist Piaget – continued to be translated into the early 1930s, but with special introductions warning Soviet readers against ideological contamination. By the mid-1930s even that filtered flow was stopped.[49]

Bukharin's ideological essays offer revealing insights into the mentality that was putting up such a wall against 'the old world', as he characterized the diverse thinkers labeled 'bourgeois', who were increasingly denied to Soviet readers except as interpreted and denounced by trustworthy Marxists. That 'old world', he explained, 'has no future, and therefore it has no great unifying idea that could draw people together, that would cement their relationships.'[50] The Bolsheviks had such a great unifying idea, and they had to protect it. With it their society would flourish while the presently developed countries would be sinking into decline. If revolutions failed to arrest their decline, mass migration would set in to the USSR, the socialist America of the future. Then everyone would recognize the truth and the unifying power of Marxist ideas, which was presently apparent only to the vanguard. So Bukharin called on Bolsheviks to be on 'guard — let them laugh at this as much as they like, the philistines of all sorts and ranks — we must guard our Marxist purity.'[51]

Bukharin was obviously uncomfortable in that fortress mentality. He was boasting that his Party was guided and unified by a scientific doctrine, and he was defending his science with the age-old methods of state churches: exiling infidels and heretics, prohibiting subversive texts, polemicizing against thinkers forbidden to be read. When G. I. Chelpanov, dean of experimental psychology, complained of 'the dictatorship of Marxism in ideas [*ideinaia diktatura marksizma*]', Bukharin defiantly accepted the phrase and boasted of the conversion (*pererozhdenie*) that the dictatorship was achieving among intellectuals. He felt sure that some converts were honest, but he worried about those who were trying 'to smuggle in hostile ideologies under oaths of devotion to Marxism'.[52] In short, Bukharin sensed his entanglement in the law of enforced belief, as we may call the rule that hypocrisy springs up where free thought is cut down. But he felt cause to hope that those were temporary difficulties, which would recede as the intellectual bankruptcy of 'the old world' and the contrasting vitality of Marxist thought became increasingly evident. Meantime he and Stalin and the other Party leaders of the 1920s allowed some latitude for free thought, enough to permit the absorption by Soviet Marxists of what was still worthwhile in the culture of 'the old world' — not only its absorption, but its creative development, *and* its fusion in a Marxist synthesis, 'a great unifying idea'.

It is too easy to brush off Bukharin's project as a hopelessly self-contradictory fantasy. Its absurd unreality is so easily demonstrated that one too easily overlooks the evidence of its realistic feasibility. There *was* creative thought and genuine discussion within the circumscribed community of Soviet Marxists in the 1920s, and also between it and the much larger universe of non-Marxist thinkers, many of whom lived and expressed themselves within the Soviet Union. To examine such creative thought and discussion we must descend from the exalted level where Bukharin and other Party chiefs were trying to combine grand politics with simplified slogans about a unifying idea in the cultural revolution. Down below, in academies and universities and the 'thick journals' that were still the favored reading of the educated public — now with titles like *Red Virgin Soil* — we find Bolsheviks and their sympathizers arguing with each other about ways to overcome the cultural disintegration of the 'bourgeois' world. The reader who wants to know right away 'Yes or No? Were they achieving genuine Marxist integration or not?' is willy-nilly pressing toward the Stalinist mentality that suddenly emerged in 1929–30. Whoever is willing, like Bukharin, to avoid that question with evasive posturing, with ambiguities and procrastinations is capturing the spirit of the Soviet 1920s.

Of course one of the questions being evaded was, and for historians still is, 'How long could the game go on?' That is very similar to the question that anxious people have been asking about cultural fragmentation in the West, for so long that some combination of political unity and cultural disunity begins to seem indefinitely possible. The political and social circumstances of Soviet Russia in the 1920s were radically different, and they seemed to the new bosses to require a major effort at cultural integration. But if we look closely, we see that the integration was largely make-believe, masking a continuation of the creative disorder that is distinctive to modern culture.

8

Psychology and Philosophy

In psychology the first preacher of Marxist unity was not a boss, nor even a member of the ruling Party. He was P. P. Blonskii, soul-searching son of the *déclassé* gentry, would-be servant of the people's liberation, Socialist Revolutionary, philosopher, psychologist, educationist by profession, who was thirty-three when the Bolsheviks proclaimed the republic of workers and peasants.[1] He may have been the very first of the intelligentsia to 'accept Soviet power'. The day that it was proclaimed the teachers' union responded with a strike, and Blonskii wrote a letter to *Izvestiia* deploring the action, calling on his fellow teachers to join him in continuing service to the people.[2] The union instantly expelled him, and Blonskii felt compelled to choose one side or the other. In political ideology his 'acceptance' was brief, brusque, crude. He did not reason his way out of Socialist Revolutionary ideology. He simply turned away, as a convert takes the decisive step from darkness to light, saving reason for the other side, in the world lit up by the new faith. 'October clearly showed me the two sides of the barricade; I perceived keenly that there can be no middle ground, and since November of 1917 I have known the joy of being on the side of the people.'[3]

That slam-bang manner of the convert, the abrupt choice that protects the mind against unbridled reason, extended into Blonskii's new writing on philosophy and psychology. During the darkest days of civil war and famine he published two little treatises very like the political pamphlets of the time, in appearance – gray pulp paper, smudged print – and in content: too ardent to care about consistency or profundity.[4] Revolutionary war was subjecting the intelligentsia of a backward country to the vanguard party of the masses, and Blonskii shouted that his class had earned its humiliation. He did not talk of the nation's shit pretending to be its brain – nor did Lenin in public – but the insulting accusation was plain enough: 'The intelligentsia knows how to snicker over Marxism, but it absolutely does not know how to master politics. In an epoch of great social events the intelligentsia has discredited itself most cruelly, blundering about under everybody's feet and earning only contempt from everybody.'[5] The intelligentsia must choose between class suicide and service to the people, which requires that all learning be revolutionized. And the way to that goal is to 'take our stand on the Marxist viewpoint as the only scientific one, ... not only in economics but also in social science generally, ... and in psychology, and also in philosophy, and in all of science'.[6] That was the first time — at least I have found no pre-revolutionary case — that every branch of knowledge was summoned for transformation by 'the Marxist viewpoint as the only scientific one'.

Blonskii was abandoning professional prudence in an effort to be thoroughly sincere. He was trying to amalgamate the new ruling ideology and his professional knowledge as complementary approaches to an understanding of human beings. If there was heroism as well as self-abasement in that project — and I think there was — it was the absurd heroism that typifies synthetic theorizing about human beings in our century. Out of the flood carrying the intelligentsia from critical thought to specialized service of the powers that be, Blonskii threw little cries of exhortation, urging all to rise above constraint in revolutionary scientific vision, to see the hydraulic system in which conscious individuals would be freely flowing drops of operative fluid. That is not Blonskii's metaphor. It is my adaptation of Robert Musil's vision of the modern self as a drop of urban fluid slightly conscious of the sewer walls that channel its flow.[7] Perhaps Musil adapted that from Whitman's leaves-of-grass metaphor for individual persons *en masse*. Our century is less outdoors and upright than Whitman's.

Blonskii's revolutionary treatises were synthetic in the mocking sense — ersatz, inauthentic — that twentieth-century chemistry has forced upon a once dignified term. He skimmed over the hard problems that had caused psychology to split away from philosophy, and to split further into incompatible schools. He grabbed randomly at theories of the mind proposed by a variety of thinkers — Hume, Kant, Titchener, Freud; even Jacques Loeb's and Ivan Pavlov's reduction of mind to tropisms or to reflexes — and threw them together with Marxist declarations that modes of production determine and express the evolving mind. Striving for synthesis, he achieved eclectic clutter. And intermittently he subverted the whole project by denouncing psychological science as an obfuscation, an escape from action that would change the world into academic exercises at interpreting it.[8]

It is not clear whether anyone paid attention to Blonskii's tracts as they appeared in 1920–1. Lenin had one in his personal library,[9] but there is no evidence that he read it. Krupskaia, Lenin's wife and a leader in the creation of a new educational system, was associated with Blonskii, as he became a major theorist of the Soviet educational effort. When the crusade for a Marxist psychology was proclaimed in 1923, he was surprisingly absent, though he was probably influential, for the headquarters of educational reform seem to have been the crusade's point of origin. Perhaps Blonskii inspired others in conversation, while his premature treatises showed what to avoid, a self-defeating extreme in super-revolutionary rhetoric.[10]

The two who proclaimed the crusade were much closer to calculating professionalism, though they differed markedly in backgrounds, interests, and personalities. A. B. Zalkind, who was twenty-nine in 1917, was a physician, especially involved in the mental health movement and Freudian theory as well as education; Jewish in nationality, of unknown class origin and unknown date of Party affiliation. (Not known because he fell victim to the terror in the 1930s — he seems to have cheated it by suicide — and did not collect the ceremonial biographies that are periodically pinned to Soviet scholars who march through 'jubilees' to respectable graves.[11])

In any case Zalkind was not the intellectual chief of the campaign for Marxist psychology in the 1920s. K. N. Kornilov was — that provincial bookkeeper's orphaned son who became a village schoolteacher, and then worked his way up to a post at Moscow University, rising finally, on the eve of the Revolution, to the rank of senior assistant in Chelpanov's newly established Institute of Psychology.[12] He was thirty-eight in 1917, the same age as Stalin and Trotsky, if the life cycle of academics and political leaders is measured by a single calendar. In 1922 he claimed that he had been a Social Democrat — of the 'internationalist' variety — as early as 1905, but he must have been referring to the passive sympathy of a *Kathedersozialist*, for there was no evidence of political activity in his career until he issued the call for Marxist psychology in January 1923. Nor was there any previous sign of professional disagreement with his mentor Chelpanov, who was still director of the Psychological Institute where they both worked after 1917 as before. In 1922 they probably began to quarrel, as Kornilov headed toward his new mission, and sometime in 1923 they broke. In November, 'Chelpanov was ordered to hand over the Psychological Institute to Kornilov'.[13] 'When you chop wood, chips fly', as the Russians say, a proverb that would be much quoted by Stalinists in the 1930s, when multitudes of people would be chopped away from more precious things than directorships.[14]

For the first four years after the Bolshevik Revolution Kornilov had seemed still absorbed in his specialized profession. In 1919 he took a small stand on a related political issue, by publishing *The School and the Law of God, against* the teaching of atheism in the public schools.[15] After a variety of non-Marxist arguments, at the end of the pamphlet he drew on the deterministic side of Marxism: Religion could not be eliminated by fiat; it would wither away with the social conditions that engendered it. That little venture into public affairs was uncharacteristic; most of his energies still went into research. In mid-1921 he finished a large treatise that summed up the experimental study of 'reactions' which he had started ten years earlier under Chelpanov's direction.[16] I put quizzical quotation marks around reactions, for I am not sure whether Kornilov was studying physical reflexes or psychic activity or a muddled mixture of the two. He caused delays in the reaction times of his experimental subjects by inserting intellectual tasks and emotional complications between sensory stimuli and motor responses. He hoped to gain understanding of psychic variables intervening between stimulus and response, by physical measurement of the variable timing and force of muscular responses. He did not claim to eliminate the psyche from psychology, as Pavlov and Bekhterev did. Quite the opposite. He measured the simplest physical effects that his intuition imputed to the psyche.

Kornilov offered no philosophical analysis of his basic concepts and methods. At the beginning of the treatise he endorsed the principle of 'a complete and decisive separation of psychology from philosophy', but did not credit Chelpanov with teaching him that principle.[17] He declared himself a follower of Titchener, the chief Anglo-American disciple of Wundt, and of Wundt himself, ignoring the fact that the 'father of experimental psychology' had opposed the divorce of psychology from philosophy. Kornilov paid special tribute to a Danish psychophysiologist for showing how to measure the relationship of emotional and physiological changes. To Chelpanov, who was his original teacher and still his director at the Institute of Psychology, he offered a gesture of conventional gratitude deep within the text.[18] About Marxism he said nothing, but he did express sympathy with 'energeticism', which he may have considered an approach to Marxism.[19] A few years later, when Kornilov had become the leader of the campaign for Marxist psychology, he claimed that the 1921 treatise showed his break with the past.[20] I find no evidence of such a break in the text, unless personal disengagement from Chelpanov was a first step. I assume that Chelpanov in 1921 was already winning notoriety for resisting 'the dictatorship of Marxism in ideas'.

Sometime in 1922 Kornilov stopped teetering. He was converted, by what combination of external persuasion and internal reflection, he and his respectful biographers have never tried to say. Indeed, they have tried to cloud the fact of conversion by claiming that he was a Social Democrat as early as 1905, by ignoring the 1919 pamphlet, and by trying to explain away his 1921 endorsement of psychology's independence from philosophy.[21] (Kornilov quietly removed that endorsement from subsequent editions of the book.)[22] In January 1923 he revealed his new outlook, by preaching Marxist reconstruction to an astonished congress of specialists in the psychoneurological sciences. He acknowledged at the outset that the project was utterly new, that it might seem an absurd effort to restore the subordination of psychology to philosophy. But Marxism, he declared, was not any old speculative philosophy; it was 'intrascientific', an outlook and a methodology that inhered in the practice of experimental science.[23] He did not confront the obvious question – 'Why then put the name of

Marx on such a philosophy?' – nor offer the obvious answer – 'To demonstrate ideological solidarity with Russia's new rulers.' Marriages are made for love in our time, not for calculation of advantage, and we have no reason to doubt the sincerity of his newfound love.

Kornilov made his appeal for Marxist psychology near the end of the 1923 congress of psychoneurologists, their first since before the Revolution. Until he spoke the congress had seemed a humdrum resumption of the old ways.[24] Not only were most presentations the usual specialist reports, but the leading personnel were unchanged: Bekhterev was elected honorary chairman, Chelpanov and his school were a – perhaps the – major presence, and Nechaev, the leading pre-revolutionary specialist in educational psychology, was head of the organizing committee and author of the staid report that appeared in *Pravda*.[25] He showed the willingness of his profession to serve the new regime by stressing practical applications in education, medicine, job placement, criminology, and 'racial improvement'.

His article in *Pravda* simply ignored Kornilov's sensational demand for a Marxist reconstruction of the discipline, and the politically charged debate that had ensued. In the debate Nechaev and Chelpanov joined in defense of professional autonomy, which was more important to both than their pre-revolutionary disagreement over the use of experimental psychology in education. Now they both objected, Chelpanov bluntly, Nechaev diplomatically, to Kornilov's demand that experimental psychology be subordinated to philosophy, indeed, to a single school of philosophy.[26] Chelpanov may have repeated his complaint about 'the dictatorship of Marxism in ideas', which Bukharin picked up and transformed from a scholar's protest into a politician's warning.[27]

After that first confrontation, polemical articles and books began to pile up, but they debated *how*, not *whether*, psychology should be reconstructed on a Marxist basis.[28] The limitation was enforced by the administrative action that followed the congress: Chelpanov was dismissed and Kornilov installed as director of the country's single Institute of Experimental Psychology.[29] The new limits of discussion were then dramatized at a second congress of the psychoneurological sciences, in January 1924, which was staged as a public triumph for Marxism and rebuff to its enemies. There were also twice as many participants as the year before – over 900, as against 500 or so – and teachers outnumbered medical people among them, for Party activists found teachers more tractable than physicians on the average. At the plenary sessions the gallery was packed with students, who cheered appeals to Marxism and showed special enthusiasm for Zalkind's rousing oratory. He wrote the report in *Pravda*, concluding that 'the revolution has conquered [*zavoevala*] not only scientists but science itself.'[30] A long account in *Red Virgin Soil* showed critical respect for venerable scientists like Bekhterev, who were pictured as trying sincerely to accommodate their theories with Marxism, and for young scientists on the way to dialectical materialism, even if they were hesitating to make the decisive commitment. L. S. Vygotsky was offered as the prime example of that young, interested but hesitant type, the promise of future triumphs for Marxist psychology. Chelpanov was pictured as the chief 'idealist' opponent of Marxism in psychology, the miscreant role that he still plays in Soviet accounts.[31]

In fact, Chelpanov was sufficiently realistic to recast his arguments within the obligatory new frame, arguing no longer that psychology should be kept apart from Marxism but that it should be well and truly linked. He got his polemics into print through private and cooperative publishing houses — that was still possible in Soviet Russia in the 1920s — so we need not guess his argument from the attacks on it in the state press. We can read at first hand the instruction he offered to Marxists on the proper way to apply their doctrine in psychology.[32] He did not claim to be a Marxist. The polemicists who jeered at him for changing his creed under pressure were misrepresenting. He explicitly declared that he held to his former philosophy. He simply claimed to understand Marxism, as he did other philosophies, by reading its principal authors, including Bukharin and Lenin as well as Marx. The implicit assumption — that Marxism is merely one more philosophy, without privileged status — effectively continued Chelpanov's long-standing insistence that the discipline of experimental psychology did not rest on one special philosophical system, that it was a philosophically neutral meeting ground for any and all who sought knowledge of psychic phenomena.

Chelpanov admitted, not a change of heart, but a correction of error. He had been wrong, he confessed, to think that materialists were necessarily mechanistic, in the style of Büchner. He had discovered that genuine Marxists held to a Spinozist version of materialism, which justifies psychophysical parallelism, not the reduction of mental to neural processes. He was too diplomatic to note that Lenin and Bukharin were vague and inconsistent on that point. He accused lesser Marxists, such as Kornilov and Blonskii, of mixing up Marxism with the 'vulgar materialism' that would reduce the mind to neural functions. Properly understood, Chelpanov argued, the philosophy of Marx and Lenin and Bukharin justified a discipline of experimental psychology that would rely both on neural analysis and on subjective report, and would investigate inward consciousness as well as outer behavior. Turning from philosophical justification to the science itself, Chelpanov found 'extreme confusion and disagreement' among 'the psychologists of the left front'.[33] Some required psychology to become social psychology, but they had no idea how to accomplish that worthy task. Others tried for impossible combinations of physiological reduction with introspective experimental psychology or with introspective speculative systems such as Freud's or even Bergson's. In short, Chelpanov found Kornilov's new school an eclectic mishmash of non-Marxist psychologies draped with quasi-Marxist slogans.

Such charges — misinterpreted Marxism, eclecticism, lack of scientific innovation or accomplishment — were occasionally conceded, in softened self-critical forms, by Kornilov and other leaders of Soviet Marxist psychology in the 1920s.[34] In the 1930s such criticisms were recast as violent denunciations by new leaders, and they have since been repeated with less severity by the psychologists who rose to leadership in the period after Stalin's death. The pioneer Marxists of the 1920s are conceded little more than the merit of starting, of *trying* to recast their scientific fields. Misunderstanding of Marxism, eclecticism, lack of scientific achievement are still routinely charged against them. Yet none of the critics have credited Chelpanov with making any telling points in the opening debates that marked the emergence of Soviet Marxist psychology. He was labeled then, and he still remains, the alien with nothing useful to offer, the chief 'idealist' who opposed Marxism in psychology.[35] That persistent unreasoning antagonism reveals the confessional nature of the Soviet Marxist mentality as it took shape in the 1920s and continues to this day. Not everyone had an equal claim to discuss Marxism, as one does monadism or meteorology, with no other commitment than to rational discourse and respect for facts. One had to *be* a Marxist, to join the congregation, if one wished to understand its doctrine, to see its application in particular disciplines.

That is the logic implicit in the stony refusal to give Chelpanov a fair hearing. Yet once again historical reality is not neatly congruent with logic. The treatment of Chelpanov was not a rule for all. Pavlov was much more alien; he openly mocked at Marxism as a pseudoscience, yet his doctrine of conditioned reflexes was blessed by the chief of Bolshevik ideology as 'a weapon from the iron arsenal of materialism.'[36] And there were other, less extreme cases of Soviet Marxists showing respect for outsiders who expressed skepticism about Marxism in science. In 1928 Kornilov ruefully agreed with Iu. V. Portugalov, a child psychiatrist in Samara, who had exclaimed in mock dismay at the Marxist campaign in psychology: 'Why, at present there are so many schools and tendencies fiercely struggling with each other that one easily becomes completely confused.'[37] Portugalov gave his taunt a deferential stoop by asking how a provincial clinician or pedagogue was to satisfy the giants at war in the metropolitan centers:

> It is no easy task to choose: abolish psychology altogether — Kornilov won't approve; recognize it — Pavlov won't approve; recognize materialism — Bekhterev won't approve; recognize energeticism — Kornilov won't approve; assume the spatiality of the psyche [*psikhizm*] — Pavlov won't approve; assume the non-spatiality of the psyche — Kornilov and Bekhterev won't approve.[38]

The poor provincial heaped up more instances of such disarray within the metropolitan avant-garde, cleverly framing them with quotes from Lenin and Krupskaia that deplored avant-garde extremes in the cultural revolution. Thus he justified sticking to his pre-revolutionary stance in psychology, a skeptical questioning of scientific claims for one or another philosophical system such as Marxism. Kornilov of course brushed aside that skepticism, but he conceded that Portugalov's 'caricature' of the discord in psychology was realistic.[39]

At one point a presumptuous outsider was given a respectful hearing though he struck at the heart of all the campaigns for Marxist transformation in the sciences. In 1926 *Under the Banner of Marxism*, the chief journal of philosophy, published an article by A. F. Samoilov, a student of Sechenov's and a major neurophysiologist, who criticized dialectical materialism as a philosophy of science.[40] From the operational viewpoint of a practicing scientist, he argued, mechanism was still the philosophy that worked. His discipline, for example, was making great progress by analyzing the fine structure of neurons and their bioelectrical functioning. He challenged dialectical materialists to suggest better methods of research that would lead to important discoveries in neurophysiology, and he promised that he and his colleagues would rush to become dialectical materialists. Otherwise they would remain indifferent or bemused by talk of Marxism in science. The dominant school of Soviet philosophers replied that such a mechanistic view of science, and such a positivist view of philosophy's role, were wrong-headed.[41] Kornilov responded quite differently. As a fellow scientist he accepted Samoilov's challenge.[42] In psychology, he agreed, Marxists must prove their doctrine by achieving experimental results which would command the respect of the entire profession, and they had yet to pass that test.

Of course Kornilov went beyond that admission and tried to show the triumph that was on the way. He offered as an example his own research in 'reactions', claiming that his results were 'dialectical', since a certain pattern of reactions reversed itself when a threshold intensity of stimuli was passed. He declared that Marxist philosophy could predict or foresee (*predvidet'*) such dialectical regularities (*zakonomernosti, Gesetzmässigkeiten*):

> And it is precisely in this *foresight* [*predvidenie*] that all the colossal significance of this method lies, for from the Marxist point of view only that method has vast significance which makes it possible to *foresee* the appearance of some new regularity [*zakonomernost'*], because *foreseeing* signifies also *mastering* and thereby also *regulating* a pheno-menon, which constitutes in the final analysis the meaning of *all scientific knowledge*.[43]

Such bombast hardly altered acceptance of Samoilov's instrumental or positivist philosophy of science. Kornilov's was a decorative Marxism, a cloud of generalities in which foresight and hindsight and verbal shuffles were indistinguishable. He had joined a congregation of Marxists, but he would not let the sectarian act cut him off from the cosmopolitan profession of experimental psychologists. In ideology they were overwhelmingly 'bourgeois' − the standard Soviet equivalent of gentile or heathen − but as a profession they still decided claims of knowledge in psychological science. The Marxist faith, Kornilov was saying, would win over professional psychologists as Marxists met their heathen tests of experimental prowess.

It is very difficult to follow that rule, to submit one's beliefs about mind and personality to the test of acceptance by professional experts in experimental psychology. If one could imagine such a naively worshipful positivist, one could not find a profession sufficiently coherent or sufficiently informed to answer his questions. He would be confounded by a war of schools the moment he asked about matters that have been investigated, and he would be dumbfounded by the persistent 'Not yet' that would set aside his most important questions about mind and personality. In marked contrast, our naive positivist would have little difficulty with neurophysiologists. Concerning nerves as physical systems scientific consensus has accumulated on many important matters. Psychologists are different; mind and personality have mostly eluded their persistently contentious scientific quest. And all the while extra-scientific understanding of mind and personality is endlessly demonstrated in everyday experience, in the arts and humanistic studies, in ideologies and religions. Such extra-scientific knowledge is even cumulative, in sprawling, disputatious ways − such as legal traditions or the literary canon − which present a hugely diverse fund of knowledge about ourselves, far richer than experimental psychology and essentially at odds with its notion of proof.

It is a rare psychologist who openly confronts that awkward situation, and asks where his would-be science fits in the age-old ways we have of knowing our minds and personalities. James was such a rare thinker; Vygotsky was another, as we shall see. Kornilov lacked the heroic boldness and breadth of those two. He shut his eyes to the difference between knowledge of nervous systems, which develops in the pattern of the natural sciences, and knowledge of minds, which does not. He dreamed of psychology as a natural science, liberated from the endless clash of basically different beliefs, a science that would compel the assent of all sound minds regardless of philosophic creed, political ideology, artistic sensibility, or cultural context.[44] He called the dream Marxist rather than positivist, but the change of names did not change reality. The discipline that he presided over was still a tension of competing schools, and he was a fair administrator over them, though he was intellectually unfair to the man who taught him that style. He misrepresented Chelpanov's outlook, exaggerating the differences between them. In plain fact Kornilov continued much of Chelpanov's tolerant eclecticism, after he inscribed 'Marxist unity' on the wall and sat down at the director's desk.

Within the Institute of Experimental Psychology Kornilov encouraged advocates of various psychologies, so long as they were willing to consider how their favored schools might fit within 'the future system of Marxist psychology'. He forecast *'a synthesis of the so-called empirical or subjective trend with the psychology of behavior, reflexology, or, as it is still called, objective psychology.'*[45] That was the dream goal of his own research in 'reactions'. Vygotsky, who rapidly became the major theorist in the Institute, added 'historico-cultural' psychology: study of socially determined mentalities would synthesize the subjective and objective trends. But Vygotsky honestly observed that all such projects of unification were dreams of logic at odds with messy history. [46]

As a sensible administrator Kornilov by no means limited colleagues to his 'reactology', which sought physical measurement of psychic processes. On the assumption that Marxists would find a way to make everything fit, he approved schools that excluded the concept of psychic processes: both Russian variants of conditioning (Pavlovian and Bekhterevian) and the behaviorist new wave in America. Kornilov's colleagues did not do experiments in conditioning, whether Russian 'classical' or American 'operational'. They expressed approval of such presumed allies, while working at their own favored schools: reactology, comparative or animal psychology, Freudian theorizing, Gestalt, and an emergent cognitive school rather like Piaget's plus talk of the 'historico-cultural' sweep that would bring together all of the above.

The immediate result was a hodgepodge, unified by the yearning for unification within a Marxist framework. Vygotsky pictured the situation honestly in a 1928 review: 'What has the new [Soviet] psychology succeeded in yielding? Not much so far. ... some methodological premises, the outline of a science, its plan; ... but what is most important: Marxist psychology has an objectively and historically justified will toward the future.'[47] Marxism was the ideology that 'objectively and historically justified' that 'will toward the future'. The contentious schools of 'bourgeois' psychologists provided the scientific starting point, or rather, the multiplicity of possible starting points.

Anything like a detailed review of the arguments over basic principles, much less the actual theories and findings in psychology and neurophysiology, would take us away from the central question here: did this genteel mode of Marxist unification generate the Stalinist mode that soon replaced it? The diversity tolerated by Kornilov certainly was not part of the generative process, except in a negative way. Repeat and stress the 'not', and Kornilov's school turns Stalinist. It was precisely the toleration of virtually every 'bourgeois' school which Stalinists furiously attacked as they leaped to control of the discipline in the early 1930s.

Their fury has subsided, and Kornilov is once again credited with leading Soviet psychologists toward Marxism, but the Stalinist mentality is still evident in the embarrassment of Soviet psychologists whenever they recall the diverse psychologies that were given serious consideration by Marxists in the 1920s.[48] Kornilov's demand for a single system of Marxist psychology pointed toward Stalinism, but his readiness to pause in response to the demand, to consider nearly all existing 'bourgeois' schools as potential contributors, pointed away, toward a continuation of intellectual pluralism within a Soviet Marxist setting. In the Soviet Union of the 1920s psychology was still a discipline that defines itself by consensus less on matters of substance than on patterns of dispute, by an unending tension among opposed schools.

PHILOSOPHERS AND FREUDIANS

But what was Marxist in that case, other than the will toward future unity within psychological science and external concordance with the state ideology? The question is implicitly Stalinist, for it assumes that a diversity of Marxisms is not authentically Marxist. Yet intellectual diversity among Marxists has been their persistent condition. Even limiting our observation to Soviet Marxism, we must recognize that it has never been a monolithic system of thought except in aspiration. The aspiration has always been mocked by the reality of disagreement, which tempts thinkers and bosses in opposite directions, either to intensified argument or to a campaign against argument, to thought or to 'rectification of thought', as the Chinese admirers of Stalin would call the Bolshevik style of mobilizing thinkers.

In Soviet culture of the 1920s the opposed tendencies balanced each other. In philosophy, for example, Marxist thinkers sought unity through vigorous disputes, which ideological authorities organized into a two-bloc scheme as a basis for their choice of one. On one side were the 'mechanists', officially out of favor. On the other side were the 'dialecticians', called Deborinites by their critics, for A. M. Deborin was the officially favored leader of philosophy — until 1930–1, when Stalin renamed him and his comrades 'Menshevizing idealists' and dumped them on the rubbish heap of counterfeit Marxists along with the mechanists.[49] We heathens can pick through the discarded artifacts of the 1920s without the activists' need to choose the 'correct' line, or the Stalinists' subsequent need to denounce all available choices, to insist that authentic monolithic Marxism-Leninism was always a real presence though beset by alien deviations. We can be plainly matter-of-fact archeologists of knowledge. In the 1920s the ideological establishment turned against positivist versions of Marxism, in favor of a neo-Hegelian version, and then turned against it too. Yet all the while, and afterward too, particular Soviet thinkers did not cease to follow their individual ways with Marxism, though increasingly obliged to put on masks of conformity or to fall silent.

If the two-camp arrangement of philosophers had a strong element of make-believe for administrative convenience, attaching Marxist psychologists to one or the other philosophical camp was even more arbitrary. Yet such attachments were announced and have been widely credited. The so-called mechanists in philosophy have been linked with reductive psychologies – Pavlov's or Bekhterev's or American behaviorism – while dialectical philosophy is tied to voluntarist talk of creating a 'new man', the Soviet improvement of *Homo sapiens*.[50] Such correlations appeal to the desire for governable order, whether bureaucratic or ideological, but they hardly fit the historical facts.

Consider, for example, Liubov Aksel'rod, or 'Aksel'rod the Orthodox', as she signed her publications in the pre-revolutionary days of exile, when she was a disciple of Plekhanov's, a Menshevik in politics, Jewish in nationality, and a Swiss Ph.D. in philosophy. Deborin had the same background, minus the Ph.D. – and of course both cut off their Menshevik politics after 1917.[51] In the philosophical disputes of the 1920s they found themselves sharply opposed to each other. Aksel'rod was intensely annoyed to be stigmatized as a mechanist, while Deborin won official approval as the leader of authentic Marxists. Aksel'rod did not consider herself a mechanist, and any fair observer must agree. She opposed Deborin's neo-Hegelianism on other grounds. At the Institute of Red Professorship she focused her seminar on the history of philosophy, and the publications that issued from their studies pointed distinctly away from reduction of the mind to biological or even to social functions.[52] That is to be expected. To study the history of philosophy is to assume the conscious mind as something to be understood in its changing expressions, to be explained, not to be explained away.

Aksel'rod summed up her anti-reductive attitude in a thought experiment. Imagine, she wrote, that the fondest dreams of neurophysiologists have been realized, that the expert could get inside the active brain of a conscious person and discern every neural process. Such a triumph of biochemistry would be irrelevant to psychology, for the neural processes alone would tell the observer nothing about the feelings and thoughts of the person whose brain was under observation.[53] In effect she was modernizing Leibniz's image of the brain as a factory, within which an observer walking about, studying the machinery in motion, would be unable to discover what is being manufactured. One could turn the experiment around and imagine an omniscient neurophysiologist of the future taking up a product of a thinking brain, say Tolstoy's *War and Peace*, and working backward to reconstruct Tolstoy's neural processes as he wrote every sentence. The result would be a book of formulas, far bulkier than the novel and utterly pointless to anyone interested in the novel as a novel, or in Tolstoy's mind as a novelist's mind.[54]

Such arguments could have turned into a critique of Pavlov or Bekhterev.

But Aksel'rod never descended that far from abstract philosophy of mind into psychological science, into its actual schools. She avoided their contention. Brief allusions show that she shared the common assumption of Soviet Marxist philosophers concerning Pavlov's doctrine: it dealt with the neural substrate of the mind, not the mind itself, the mechanisms of the speaking mouth, not the words and thoughts that the brain-mind is directing the mouth to speak.[55] Thus one could hold a materialist position, broadly defined – no mind without a living brain – or even repeat Bukharin's materialist blessing on Pavlov's doctrine, and still insist that one was not casting doubt on the reality of the conscious mind or the knowledge of it that is achieved by ordinary people, storytellers, philosophers, or experimental psychologists who use subjective report.[56]

As the example of Aksel'rod suggests, in the relations between philosophical and psychological trends it is easier to show what was *not* the case than it is to discover what was. She was labeled a mechanist in philosophy, but she was certainly justified in her angry denial. She opposed reductive theories of the mind. On the other hand she did not criticize psychologists who assumed such theories as the basis of their research. But then the Deborinites were even less inclined to tangle with Pavlov or Bekhterev, though the Deborinites boasted of their opposition, in philosophy, to the reduction of mind to neural processes. They gave their blessing to Kornilov's leadership of psychology – after it was established – on a level of abstraction that avoided difficult issues within psychology itself. Kornilov was also superficially accommodating and fundamentally evasive. He was willing to accept the philosophical blessing of the Deborinites, and to use it against psychologists who criticized him in the name of Marxism, but he stayed away from the special quarrel with Aksel'rod and in general avoided philosophy of the mind.

On both sides the alliance was more show than substance. Deborinite philosophers ignored the positivist elements in Kornilov's writings. Perhaps they were being diplomatic with him; perhaps they were genuinely indifferent to the whole field. They also ignored Vygotsky's theorizing, which drew on the history of philosophical psychologies for an extended dialectical critique of the warring schools in twentieth-century psychological science. The Deborinites had nothing substantial to say about any school of psychology, however alien or allied it may seem to their school of philosophy. Mannered gestures prevailed over significant discussion in the intercourse of philosophers and psychologists. They were engaged in academic gamesmanship rather than serious efforts to combine philosophical analysis and psychological science. At stake was leadership (*rukovodstvo*) of the separate disciplines, and leadership was decided in the final instance by unsophisticated officials such as the historian Pokrovsky or the economist Miliutin, or the ideologist Bukharin, who supervised appointments, the disbursement of funds, and the organization of decisive conferences.

Leadership, *rukovodstvo*, was – and still is – a crucial concept in Soviet discussions of higher learning no less than political and economic affairs. Its prime meaning is plain: they are leaders in scholarly disciplines who sit in directors' chairs at research institutes and learned journals. The ultimate source of such leadership is supposed to be intellectual deference flowing from the profession at large, looking to those in the directors' chairs as authentic spokesmen of truth in particular disciplines. There is an obvious similarity between Soviet talk of 'leaders' and the constant references to 'eminent authorities' in Western psychology and philosophy. Of course there is a major difference in Western efforts to keep such scholarly authorities separate from political authorities. In the Soviet Union the dominance of political and ideological leadership was undisguisedly asserted at the end of the Civil War. But during the 1920s that dominance was not so blatant as to mock the very notion of autonomous scholarship. The profession could see that ideological chiefs raised Kornilov to leadership over psychology in 1923, and the reason why was quite obvious – he endorsed the project of Marxist reconstruction – but the profession found its own reasons to respect Kornilov and his lieutenants, especially Vygotsky, who became the abiding genius of Soviet psychology.

In spite of their ideological stance as revolutionaries, the leading Soviet psychologists behaved very much like authorities in the 'bourgeois' West. Indeed they called attention to the similarity in the habitual manner of cosmopolitan scholars, who love to reinforce their local authority by showing that other authorities in distant lands agree. As late as 1930, to take a notable example, when Vygotsky and Luria offered an initial outline of the 'historico-cultural' approach to psychology, their little book borrowed heavily and quite respectfully from such Western authorities as Piaget and Freud, showing that the Westerners' discoveries blended nicely with a much smaller amount of findings by Soviet psychologists, and with a very light dusting of references to Marx and Engels.[57] Once again, if we focus our retrospective gaze on what Soviet psychology of the 1920s was *not*, we can see how it turned into Stalinist psychology. It was not at war with 'bourgeois' psychologists, and such non-belligerence was furiously denounced within the year that Vygotsky's and Luria's book appeared. They still had an irenic attitude toward 'bourgeois' psychologists; they were not only preaching Marxism as domestic ideological and political leaders wished them to, they were also continuing the advancement of psychological science in harmony with Western colleagues. To the furious Stalinists of the 1930s that evidence of professional legitimacy was evidence of pseudo-Marxism.

But that is to anticipate. In the 1920s Stalin and Bukharin, Pokrovsky and Miliutin, conferred leadership on psychologists who acquired authority by decorous participation in cosmopolitan learning. Analogous synergy was present even in philosophy; a combination of ideological and professional appeal was a distinctive feature of the Deborinites. Their rivals sought the same combination without success. They were lumped under the derogatory label of mechanists because some of them, trying for a comprehensive vision of the universe and the human place in it, sounded embarrassingly out of date, rather like Büchner or Spencer. Other opponents of the Deborinites were professionally in tune with the times, but they undermined the possibility of a comprehensive world view by favoring contemporary positivism, looking to particular disciplines for grainy understanding, putting off the problem of the whole. Against the One-in-all philosophizing of the Deborinites they flung demands for precision, which of course they did not get. In neo-Hegelian discourse the specialized knowledge of particular disciplines was 'sublated' (*aufgehoben, sniat*), raised to the level of generality where knowledge merges into inanity and the One-in-all becomes incontrovertible. Spears of positivist logic were pointless in such neo-Hegelian clouds, which were blessed by the ideological establishment under Bukharin.

In short, prudent professionals kept to their separate trades, while leaders preached the end of such isolation. Philosophy and psychology were drifting apart in the Soviet Union much as they were in the West, but the leaders would not acknowledge the void. Deborin's function in philosophy and Kornilov's in psychology, like Bukharin's in social theory and grand ideology, was to fill the cultural void with talk of plenary knowledge and wisdom. One might compare their function to Henri Bergson's in the 'bourgeois' West, except that the designated leaders of Soviet thought did not exude such complacent reassurance as that oracle to the comfortable classes of advanced countries. They were struggling to organize an integrated world view for a politically dominant but culturally besieged minority in a confessedly backward country.

That context could foster an urge to repulse non-Marxist thought, to reject at once all 'bourgeois' learning. Soviet scholars showed very little of that repulsive urge in the 1920s, but the political leaders and their ideological establishment showed a lot, swelling toward fulmination in the 1930s. The increasingly belligerent process was most apparent in political ideology, but revealed itself also in the mounting anger at Freudianism, the one type of psychology that was becoming popular as well as academic. Official hostility to Freudian ideas was well in evidence by the mid-1920s, while Stalin was still comparatively moderate and Bukharin was in charge of ideology. A detailed history of Soviet Freudianism and the official backlash would take us far afield, but we must note the chief features of that history, for they point strongly toward the psychology of Stalinism.

Many people, even educated ones, identify Freud with the science of psychology; they know little and care less about the actual schools that have claimed the allegiance of academic psychologists. Soviet leaders shared this common misperception of the discipline, to which they added a dim notion of Pavlov as the brain scientist who was creating a rigorous psychology, and a dimmer sense of the Institute of Psychology having something to do with education. Freud's exceptional hold on the educated public rested on much more vivid stuff: scientific dramatization of the agent within the human animal, the person or self which presumes to be the manager but may actually be the servant of the biological creature and its social relations.

Freud's popular success quite overshadowed other would-be human scientists who also tried to show that the presumptuous manager is in fact the servant, that the person or self is a central regulatory function, co-ordinating all other biological and social functions within each skinful of flesh and nerves, much as the governor of a steam engine adjusts that machine's functioning to changing circumstances. Bukharin's textbook of historical materialism favored such a reductive vision, without much lasting appeal. On the other hand, artists and judges and ordinary people get at the self in a radically different way: by questioning it, implicitly assuming a conscious essence, an 'I', that can account for itself as everyone does in everyday life — as Bukharin did in his autobiography.[58] Among Soviet Marxists of the 1920s, as in other intellectual communities, there were thinkers who longed to unite the different approaches. That was one of the main reasons for Freud's rapidly growing popularity, in the Soviet Union as in the West. He seemed to unite 'the' scientific and 'the' literary visions of ourselves as natural objects and as conscious subjects. And that was a major reason why the Bolshevik ideological bureaucracy came down early and hard against Freud. His claim of a unified vision was too obviously in competition with their own.

A fair number of Soviet Marxist thinkers — Vygotsky, Luria, Zalkind were most notable among the psychologists — tried to turn the competition into complementarity, to show that Marx and Freud could be united.[59] They were struggling against the letter and the spirit of Freud's writings. He sneered at Marxism, and, worse yet, his vision was expressly tragic if not pessimistic. He brushed aside any project of socialism as a sentimental dream, incompatible with his conviction that human beings are essentially envious, that growing up within any social system is necessarily a repres-sive process, and becomes more so as the advancement of civilization lays an increasing burden of anxiety on the individual's sense of a guilty self.

No matter that left-wing Freudians rejected this feature of the master's doctrine, appealing to Marx for proof that revolution will eliminate repres-sion; they were told that Marx's theory was Promethean fire to Freud's submissive ice. Theoretical argument among intellectuals hardly mattered; it crashed on the Communist conviction that self-realization can be con-ceived only within the movement, the organized cause. Bolshevik activists were convinced — to the point of self-destruction, as many would prove in the 1930s — that each person realizes himself only within the Party, con-tributing to a better society. It was simply unhealthy to probe more deeply than that into the needs of the individual self.

Within that restrictive framework Soviet Freudians were able to save the medical part of Freud's doctrine: it showed how to analyze and treat unhealthy persons. In the officially approved view of Freud that emerged in the mid-1920s the psychiatrist was separated from the ideologist. Freudianism was sanctioned as a therapeutic method and a concomitant explanation of abnormal personalities, while Freudianism was condemned as a theory of the normal personality, and certainly as a social theory and ideology.[60] That division was superficially similar to the way that Bukharin saved Pavlov's doctrine, by separating the scientific theory from the scientist's 'bourgeois' ideology. Indeed, I would expect the archives to show that Bukharin was personally involved in establishing the line on Freudianism. The crucial difference was in the materialist blessing he bestowed on the doctrine of conditioned reflexes, which carried forward the traditional association of Russian radicalism with physiological reductionism. If Freudianism was grudgingly allowed to be materialist in part, it was in the sick part, in knowledge of how to treat the neurotic person before the triumph of socialism would make every person healthy.

That sickly aura was one reason why, though the official line continued formal toleration of psychoanalysis as therapy until the 1940s, even psychiatrists were abandoning Freudian talk in public discourse by the late 1920s.[61] Bolshevism aside, there were other, professional forces pushing in that direction. Russian psychiatrists were strongly influenced by German models, who were largely followers of Kraepelin and skeptical of psychoanalysis. Russian social conditions intensified that intellectual influence. In a poor country with very few psychiatrists and mental hospitals, extreme pathological cases were the main concern of the profession and psychoanalysis was little or no help with such patients.

In a 1929 presentation to the Communist Academy Wilhelm Reich, the well-known 'Freudo-Marxist' from Austria, implicitly acknowledged the practical irrelevance of psychoanalysis in a backward country. If the Five Year Plan succeeded, he argued, then Soviet psychiatrists would have plenty of neurotic patients and therefore much need for psychoanalysis. In the meantime he urged the Russian comrades not to turn against Freud's psychological theory just because his social theory was reactionary.[62] If Reich had known the Soviet situation in detail, he could have cited Dr Zalkind as a fellow 'Freudo-Marxist'. Zalkind was one of the few psychiatrists with a favorable interest in Freudian theory, in keeping with his unusual clientele: he was trying to organize a mental health movement among Party activists. He preached the need for hard-pressed leaders and mental workers to guard against neuroses, and to seek psychotherapy in case preventive measures proved inadequate.[63] Most Soviet psychiatrists were overwhelmed by much more seriously disturbed patients than neurotics, and Party activists were annoyed by public talk of their mental health. By 1929 Zalkind felt obliged to retreat so far from his original Freudianism that he said nothing of it in his hostile comments on Reich's presentation.[64] Reich thought him a complete opponent of Freudianism.

Here again the drift toward full-fledged Stalinist psychology was mainly revulsive, in this case against neurotic self-absorption. In the Soviet Union as in the West masterful men knew that getting out of oneself, proving one's worth in progressive social activity, is the practical answer to the sickly self-absorption of quitters and losers. That conviction would reach a fevered climax in the 1930s, but in the 1920s it was already strong enough to press Soviet Freudians toward hostile interpretations of their own doctrine, or toward a dignified silence. We can see the turnabout most clearly in Zalkind's efforts to separate himself from his reputation as a Freudian. The most striking example of dignified silence is to be found in a history of psychiatry published by the Communist Academy in 1928, with passages on Freudianism that were extremely brief although – or because – the author was known to be a sympathizer.[65] His laconic statements on Freudianism conveyed sympathy without supporting arguments, and Zalkind's review accordingly deplored the absence of 'methodological analysis', especially the absence of the mandatory attack on Freudian social theory.[66] In fact, Zalkind's experience argued for silence; within a thickening fog of unreasoning hostility his 'methodological analysis' sounded like alien apologetics to Stalinists, denunciations to Freudians. By 1936 he would be driven to suicide.[67] The Stalinist atmosphere was not generated within academic psychology, but academics could not avoid breathing it.

9

Literature and Psychology

THE LITERARY IMAGINATION

Modern literary artists have been obsessed with the search for an authentic self or inward person, in the Soviet Union as in pre-revolutionary Russia and the West. The problem, after the Bolsheviks took over, was to find some room for that quest within the conviction that self-absorption is a sickness, within enthusiasm for the cause that takes people out of themselves. One solution was to agree with the revolutionary bosses, to turn their crude conviction into sophisticated analysis of self-absorption as a kind of alienation which Marxists cannot ignore. On that basis in 1927 Mikhail Bakhtin, a young linguistic philosopher and literary critic, published *Freudianism: A Critical Essay*, which disclosed 'the spirit of contemporary Europe, the psychology of *déclassé* people trying to create a world on the far side of the social and the historical.'[1] Along with the doctrines of Rudolph Steiner and Henri Bergson, 'the psychobiologism and the sexualism of Freud define the physiognomy of the contemporary *Kulturmensch*, his three altars of worship: *magic, instinct, sexuality*. Where the creative paths of history are closed, there remain only the blind alleys of individual adaptation to a meaningless life.'[2]

Working toward that conclusion, the critic managed to convey substantial understanding of Freudian theory, and to justify Marxist interest in the problem of the self — among intellectuals, at the risk of offending practical types, who are antagonistic to any self-analysis subtler than chest-thumping. In the world of practical men that healthy hollow sound is sufficient notice of the person within, who proves his essence by what he achieves, not by agonizing over what he may really and truly be. The little treatise of 1927 was the last substantial examination of Freudianism that appeared in the Soviet Union — until 1978, when free-spirited psychologists in the Georgian Republic organized a symposium on the unconscious as a problem in science, without talk of alienation from the authentic human essence.[3] It took half a century to move the Soviet discussion of Freudianism beyond frank ideology, through simple denunciation, to pretense of pure science.

A similar difficulty inhered in the suddenly swollen explicit sexuality of the new age. Earnest Bolsheviks were offended no less than 'bourgeois' believers in the strenuous life. The Bolsheviks called themselves materialists, but certainly not in the everyday sense of hedonistic self-seeking. Though their chief ideologists wobbled a bit, as the reader has seen, between historical and physiological materialism, it was physiology of the traditional sort that they had in mind, in which the sexual appetite is hardly as powerful as the need to breathe, drink, feed, excrete, and most of all to work, to satisfy the drive that satisfies all the others. Sexual gratification was a safety valve in the hardworking man-machine, not the main boiler. Lenin made such a point in his famous interviews with Clara Zetkin, as *Pravda* recalled in a 1925 swipe at Freudianism as a doctrine of sensuous license, ignoring the fact that Freud had his own version of the safety-valve doctrine for hard-pressed *Kulturmenschen*.[4]

Lenin's central figures of speech were not of valves and boilers, but even so his argument was functionalist rather than soulful. He disapproved of free red love, whose advocates had been comparing sexual gratification to drinking a glass of water. Lenin countered: 'Of course thirst must be satisfied. But will the normal person in normal circumstances lie down in the gutter and drink from a puddle? Or out of a glass whose rim is greasy from many lips?'[5] The Bolshevik ideal repudiated three types that make too much of the sexual function, whether as vice or virtue or sentimental mixture of the two: 'Neither monk nor Don Juan, nor the intermediate attitude of the German philistines.'[6] What survived the triple taboo was a Bolshevik version of Benjamin Franklin's advice to 'use venery rarely', only 'for health or offspring, never to dullness, weakness, or the injury of your own or another's peace or reputation'.[7] Of course Lenin focused on the social cause rather than the individual career, but the resulting prescription was a similarly hygienic regime: 'Joy of life and power of life ... Healthy body, healthy mind! ... The revolution requires concentration, increase of powers, ... no weakening, no squandering, no waste of powers. Self-control, self-discipline is not slavery, not even in love.'[8]

On that basis there was room in the 1920s for a mental health movement and some sex education. The rage to acknowledge no need for safety valves, no limit on the strenuous life, would not erupt until the 1930s, as a by-product of the all-out drive for industrial socialism within an impossibly short time. The heroes of Five-Year-Plan novels would hardly pause to eat or sleep, not to speak of languorous coupling, and denunciation would fall upon the mental health movement in the early 1930s, as we shall see. That rage would exhaust itself in a fairly short period, and a more permissive functional view of sexual gratification would reassert itself. (To be sure, some monkish resistance has persisted; it appears, for example, in Soviet republications of Zetkin's reminiscences which omit Lenin's comments on sexual matters.)[9]

Soviet Communists can hardly avoid a functional view, for theirs is a mentality of the modern sort; they are devoted to practical achievement above all, anxious to feel emancipated from fear of sexuality as a snare for the soul that might otherwise be free for divine pursuits. The proscribed monk is still present, in the ranking of natural functions below the soul's grand purpose, but he cannot be acknowledged. 'Positive heroes' of routine Soviet fiction couple in the same excessively incidental way that they eat or excrete, to keep the fleshy engine working at the practical achievement that is their loudly trumpeted supreme purpose in life.[10] Like American worshipers of personal success, they identify the person with the functions it performs, and repress the question why some are worthier than others, the anxious wonder whether there is at bottom any essential person of inherent value. The creative writer's imagination seizes on that underlying anxiety no matter how much − maybe because − the bosses say to cut it out. From the 1920s to the present day political leaders and ideologists have demanded that writers glorify 'positive heroes', but a persistent succession of willful writers have balked. They have dwelt perversely on the question, Who or what is the real person within the deed, the authentic inner agent of the creature's external action?

That conflict has far too complex a history to be recounted here even in summary outline. Nevertheless, a few cases must be examined, if only to illuminate the refractory type of inquiry that has been common among writers of fiction, yet rare among scientific psychologists and psychiatrists. Psychological science tends to identify the person with the cluster of roles that it plays, which gives a scientific basis to the cult of practicality and deadens the nerve of resistance to masterful men, who go a step further: the person is identified by its place in the social hierarchy of roles, with the political chief at the apex. Psychological science can fit in that political ordering of human beings, but imaginative literature causes trouble even where the artist tries to fit in.

Consider *Red Cavalry*, Isaac Babel's classic of modernistic self-examination, which has sent a shock of recognition through a worldwide audience, including readers who thought they had nothing in common with Bolsheviks and fellow travelers. The book seems a disjointed group of short stories and anecdotal fragments until one perceives a jagged unity in the types that are being portrayed, especially in the emergent self-portrait of the first-person narrator. Not a portrait in the usual sense, but a jumble of incompatible persons: writer Bolshevik intellectual Russian Jew joined with Cossacks (the red minority of them) in time of civil war and national conflict (Russians *v*. Poles with traditional Jews in between). The identities conflict, which makes tragicomic self-contradiction of the narrator's effort to discover his authentic self by telling precisely what he felt as he saw, heard, acted for Lenin's cause.

Since Babel's narrator is always looking intently without no less than within, other people are knotted into his self-contradictory appraisals.

Actual commanders of the red cavalry appear with their real names, but not as they wanted to see themselves or their troops.[11] Even the sacred name of Lenin is drawn into the dialectical soul-searching. In 'Gedali', for example, the narrator has an old Polish Jew telling him – fellow Jew but young Bolshevik Russian – about

> 'the International – we know what the International is. And I want an International of good people. I would like them to put every soul on the list and give it a first-priority ration. There, soul, please eat, have your own satisfaction in life. The International, Pan Comrade, you don't know it, what it is eaten with. ....'
>
> 'It is eaten with gunpowder', I answered the old man, 'and flavoured with the best blood.'

And instantly bloodthirsty young Bolshevik dissolves into pacifist old Jew. The narrator sees Friday evening arriving – 'the young Sabbath rose to her seat out of the blue shadow' – and he asks Gedali: '"Where are Jewish biscuits to be got, and a Jewish glass of tea, and a little of that pensioned-off God in a glass of tea." "Not to be had,"' the old man replies; '"they are weeping in the inn where good people used to eat."' He does an absurd little ritual of warding off evil, and goes off to a synagogue in a top hat with a big prayer book under his arm, grotesque 'founder of an impossible International.'[12]

That comic dialectic of old faith and new faith occurs early in the series of sketches; at the end there is a keening reprise. Typhus-ridden peasant refugees, 'a monstrous and inconceivable Russia, tramped in bast shoes on either side [of the red cavalry train], like a swarm of body lice'.[13] A rabbi's son who has turned into a revolutionary soldier lies sick with typhus on the floor within the train, his clothes so tattered that 'his sexual parts, this puny tender curlyhaired manhood of the wasted Semite', are exposed to the stolid gaze of Russian women. (Posthumous editors excise the peasants as body lice, but leave the ethno-sexual imagery.) Among the scruffy belongings of the rabbi's son the narrator finds 'portraits of Lenin and Maimonides side by side, the knotted iron of Lenin's skull beside the tarnished silk of Maimonides' portraits'. Entangled in a further jumble of mementos – Communist, Jewish, poetic, erotic – is the dying man's confession: he has failed the revolutionary cause as well as his parents' religion. The author's voice breaks from narration to its own confession, closing the story and the book: 'He died before we reached Rovno. He died, the last prince, among poems, phylacteries, and foot-wrappings. And I – hardly containing in an ancient body the storms of my imagination – I took in the last breath of my brother.'[14] That was the very end through the book's first six editions, until 1933, when Babel yielded to his ideological critics and added a softening (or hardening) touch: a new final tale suggesting that the intellectual narrator achieved fusion with the revolutionary Cossacks.[15]

Ideological critics were understandably disturbed by Babel's confusion of

identities, and have never ceased to be — except for a fifteen-year silence
after 1939, when he was arrested as an 'enemy of the people' and became
unmentionable. After his posthumous 'rehabilitation' in the 1950s, a Soviet
critic found a Leninist essence in *Red Cavalry* by reading it as the author's
ironic portrait of the mixed-up narrator. The *narrator* is torn between the
Bolshevik model of authentic humanity and a variety of miscreants, but the
ironic art of the *author* distances him (and the reader) from the absurd self-
contradictions of the narrator. A sensitive American critic countered that
Soviet reading by noting the inseparability of narrator and author in *Red
Cavalry*, but she could not endure the usual conclusion that other critics
have drawn: this author-narrator's divided self mirrors the grotesque
incongruities of his society, if not humanity at large. The American critic
added her own transcendent essence, different from the Bolshevik transcendence which the Soviet critic read into the book: 'The grotesque is
accepted . . . as the revealing sign of the individually human quality, the
divinely human.'[16]

I single out these opposed ideological readings, in respectful disagreement with both, to show how particular social contexts and personal faiths
can deflect modern literary sensibility from its nihilistic tendency. I think
that the customary reading is truer to Babel's text and the modernistic
outlook that it expresses. Its tragic power derives from grotesque incongruities that the author-narrator cannot transcend, not in society at large
nor even within his divided soul — if I may follow his example and still use
that antique term. Dreams of righteous order, whether Gedali's or Lenin's,
antique religion or progressive ideology, point up the horror they are
supposed to point beyond; they express the mind's need to justify a history
that mocks justification. That compulsive circularity drags the shrinking
reader through Babel's civil war as relentlessly as it does through Kafka's
penal colony or through Conrad's civilizing assault on Africa. Babel's
classic has the special bite of a revolutionary dream that was supposed to
justify history by transforming it yet disclosed all over again the ancient
nightmare of killing as the supreme justification.*

Along with that timeless significance for any reader, *Red Cavalry* is
particularly illuminating about the Soviet intelligentsia of the 1920s: it
shows one of them, a fellow-traveling *intelligent*, picking at the divided self
that sets him apart from single-minded masterful men, and ensures subordination to them. Submission is implicit in such self-examination, but it
is submission with a paradoxical sting of resistance: the fatally divided self

---

* Stalinist commentary is complacent — 'Babel's whole book is a justification of obligatory
mercilessness, of violence in the name of its future abolition'[17] — but the common reader
finds no complacency in the book itself.

can neither assert itself nor surrender itself wholeheartedly, without qualifications that disgust and enrage single-minded masters of society.

Some would call this a self-destructive form of fellow-traveling, and would guess that the administrators of terror punished Babel for the divided mind evinced in *Red Cavalry*. I doubt they were so intellectually sensitive in their choice of victims.[18] But the relentless anti-Communist insists upon a broader question: Was not the triumph of administered terror in the 1930s facilitated by the fellow-travelers' submissive aid to Communism in the 1920s? It is cruel and unhistorical to answer yes with swift smug self-assurance. In the 1920s Communism contained milder prospects than it had revealed during the Civil War. Babel and his sort thought to aid *those* prospects, not the shooting of a woman for a black-market bag of salt or the cutting of an old Jew's throat on suspicion of espionage or getting even with a landlord by kicking him to death. They were fellow-travelers, not single-minded fanatics or servile hacks; they could see multiple possibilities. Their visions, embodied in works of art, became a part of Communist history that the administrators of terror could not stamp out.

Consider another masterpiece of the 1920s, the novella *Envy*, by Iurii Olesha, a son of the *déclassé* gentry, further disoriented by a mixture of nationalities and religions: Russified Polish, with a Catholic upbringing and a lost faith early on.[19] His father, proud to be called 'Squire' (*barin*) though he had lost his estate, took a salary for killing time as an 'inspector' at a distillery. He urged his son to recover status by becoming an engineer and an owner of real estate. All this Olesha confessed after the Revolution had separated him from such values, and from his parents, who emigrated during the Civil War, while the son joined the Red Army. His experience of the Civil War, though not as violent as Babel's, was ultimately as disturbing to the sense of self. Work as a signalman drew him into propaganda and then to writing satirical verse for the newspaper of the railway workers' union. He took 'Chisel' for his pen name, as he chipped out and pieced together material from readers' letters to create humorous exposés. He liked the feel of that, ceasing to be a self-seeking careerist, becoming instead an anonymous instrument for the expression of mass sentiments in the construction of a new society. Some of his fond reminiscences of that newspaper work remind an American of Carl Sandburg's dream of himself as a steel spike holding up a skyscraper. Olesha's populist imagination was excited less by rising steel frames than by expanding communications networks, created by and creating a cheerful community of collectively self-improving individuals.

After he left the paper and began to write fiction in his own name, other visions disturbed Olesha. *Envy* (1927) was the major result. His characters were rival ideal types: feckless intellectual dreamer at one extreme, super-efficient constructor of heavy industry at another, in between an earthy emperor of sensuous delights (sausages in this case, not ice cream as in the famous poem of Wallace Stevens), and an intellectual madman at war with machine society. The super-efficient constructor of heavy industry is a perfectly single-minded super-athletic 'new man', his sweetheart is an ideal young woman love machine; an enemy of machine society creates a female robot to destroy it from within. The book was — and is — fun to read, obviously satirical, and ultimately disturbing in its double-edged thrusts. Which of the ideal types was the butt? At first reading official ideologists applauded the book for satirizing relics of the old order, but soon they swung about and chastized Olesha for making the super-efficient constructor of heavy industry seem a mechanical monster rather than an authentic human, and for seducing readers into sympathy with the feckless intellectual dreamer. He is a likeable underground man, apologizing to modern society for the sensibility that is an obstruction to progress.[20]

In the course of the ensuing controversy Olesha wrote a confession for *Izvestiia*, which deepened the mystery of authorial ambivalence in the very act of denouncing it. He telescoped a picture of himself as a self-seeking child of the *déclassé* gentry and himself grown up to be a 'lonely writer', who sees everyone aspiring to be engineers though no longer owners of real estate. The Revolution made the difference, opening his eyes to something more attractive than high social status or even engineering: to *justice*, the emancipation of the oppressed, an ideal that his parents had never taught him.

> And what did they drum into that head of mine? A desire to become rich, a desire to force society to bow down before me.
>
> I grab in myself my very self, I grab by the throat that me that suddenly wants to turn back and stretches out its arms to the past.
>
> That me that thinks that the space between us and Europe is only a geographical space.
>
> That me that thinks that everything that happens is only its own life, the unique and irrepeatable, all-embracing life of me, which will terminate by its end everything that exists outside of me.
>
> I want to crush in myself a second 'me', a third and every 'me', which are crawling out of the past.
>
> I want to annihilate petty feelings in myself.
>
> If I cannot be an engineer of the elements [*stikhii*], I can be an engineer of human material.
>
> That sounds grandiose? Let it. Grandiosely I shout: 'Long live the reconstruction of human material, the all-embracing engineering of a new world!'[21]

Note how Olesha has internalized Lenin's famous '*Kto kogo?*' — 'Who will do in whom?' — and is unsure who will.

His desire to become 'an engineer of human material' anticipated the 'social command' that Stalin and Zhdanov would lay upon writers in the

1930s, the order to be 'engineers of human souls'. Yet Olesha was also echoing previous uses of the metaphor; neither he nor Stalin can justify copyright. In *À rebours* (1884) Huysmans used it — 'un ingenieur savant de l'âme' — in praise of writers who debunked the pretentions of soulful thinkers.[22] Bertold Brecht used it in 1926, explaining the theme of a satirical play: 'It's about a man being taken to pieces and rebuilt as someone else for a particular purpose. ... [by] three engineers of the feelings.'[23] No doubt a thorough search would turn up other instances. The equation of the literary artist with the engineer was there in the iron arsenal of modern culture, to adapt Bukharin's phrase, ready to express the functional ideal of modern human beings and simultaneously to mock at it.

The political bosses who read Olesha's confession in 1929 probably did not grasp the needling ambivalence in the particular metaphor; Stalin and Zhdanov used it quite simplistically in the 1930s, as they crushed the soulful expressiveness of writers. But they could hardly overlook Olesha's explicit theme of the inward division that one must suppress to become an engineer of souls. As he pledged to crush the old self, the one that defines itself by 'a desire to force society to bow down before me', Communist bosses must have stirred uneasily, reading such stuff in *Izvestiia*. And when he denounced the self that sees a void at the end of its individual life, one imagines them going back to Lenin's tomb for a reassuring sight of the rouged mummy and a yearning inspection of the wall nearby where a select few of the faithful win individualized eternity in little bronze plaques. For all other less distinguished souls the rock of ages is there grandly visible as redbrick fortress, ancient Kremlin standing against modern doubt with a new red star on the tower and a tomb of polished granite at the base, holding the corpse that does not rot.[24]

Olesha was trying to convert himself to the psychology of Stalinism, to be a self-assured engineer of souls, but the effort was frustrated by the modern writer's deepest urge to strip away mechanical models and find the authentic self. For the twenty-odd years of high Stalinism he could not do any serious writing. In the mid-1950s he started again, when a friend asked if it was true that he was writing an autobiography. He forced himself to try by putting something on paper every day, hoping that a life would emerge in the excretion of fragmentary memories. He agonized over the question: 'But who am I? Who? This question must be resolved, must be answered. What is my world view?' — and characteristically darted away from telling what he was to telling what he was not, recalling a quarrel with a priest over funeral arrangements for his sister.[25] The autobiography never became a complete life.

I have gone ahead of the 1920s to disclose the lost potential of that decade. The subsequent void in the creative lives of Olesha and Babel sets off their masterpieces as a peculiarly Soviet type, 1920s variety. Political authorities were demanding that writers serve the construction of an ideal new human being, and imaginative writers of the fellow-traveling sort were responding with soul-searching, trying to discover the contrasting essences of engineer and 'human material', constructor and clay, in that grandiose project. They were mostly talking past each other, the political leaders and writers of the 1920s, but each side was trying to persuade. In the 1930s the bosses would violently disrupt that genteel dialectic, and the ostensible revival in the 1950s would be angry accusation on both sides, quickly deadlocked.[26] In the 1920s, while all that was still future, unknown, a tense civility prevailed between politicians and writers; from it emerged a uniquely Soviet, politicized version of the modern writer's search for the authentic person, the genuine human being.

PSYCHOLOGISTS

The person seeking its authentic self belongs to imaginative writers. Personality, in its twentieth-century usage, has been appropriated in the West by psychotherapists, a trade that identifies the person with its bundle of traits in their functional relations and calls the bundle personality. That vacuous circularity sounds scientific — like equating value with price in economic science — and it suits the practical purpose of 'adjustment'. The goal is neither to philosophize about the quality that constitutes a person, which was the old meaning of personality, nor to make a new society for authentic persons, which was the dream of revolutionaries, but to remake the individual specimen, to fit it more efficiently into existing society.

In pre-revolutionary Russia such functionalism was already in evidence among psychologists. They were trying to get metaphysics out of their speciality and were no more interested in revolutionary creation of authentic persons than revolutionaries were interested in psychological science. To be sure, the orientation of personality studies was not toward psychotherapy — there was no such industry — but toward education and psychiatry, which fostered a similar approach. Children and the insane, everyone agrees, cannot be left as they are; they require 'adjustment' to existing society, and psychological science was supposed to show how to accomplish that.[27] After 1917 a revolutionary patina was laid upon such studies, with talk of going beyond traditional adjustment in schools and mental hospitals. A Marxist psychological science would show educators and psychiatrists how to create a new man for a new social order. But that was never more than talk. Something in the science of psychology, reinforced by the cultural politics of the revolutionary era, restricted even the best minds to humble tasks of adjustment. The lifework of A. R. Luria provides the most revealing case in point. He began as a broadly ranging student of personality, and wound up in 'defectology', correlating particular types of brain damage with particular disturbances in behavioral functions.

Luria's name was as obviously Jewish as Tsion's, but his way was not obstructed by the stigma as Tsion's had been. The Soviet government campaigned against anti-Semitism during the 1920s, opening the way for Jews in many careers. Yet Luria's autobiography, written in the 1970s, is as tensely silent about his Jewishness as Tsion's published accounts of *his* academic deeds and troubles back in the 1870s. Luria is proud to tell of his father's status — a physician who won a teaching post at the Kazan medical school before the Revolution — but he represses the phrase that the Soviet reader would supply: even though father was a Jew. Ethnicity is a troublesome ghost, banished with this curt description of the family background: 'We considered ourselves progressive and had no religious tradition.'[28] That tense dismissive gesture is typical. Principled disregard of 'Jewish origin' was a common characteristic of the numerous Jews who were encouraged to rise by the revolutionary campaign against 'Great Russian chauvinism'. Upwardly striving Jews were being assimilated to a genteel Russianness that disdained invidious distinctions between Jew and gentile. 'Soviet' was the supra-ethnic identity, which failed to dissolve the ethnic obsessions of less exalted souls.[29]

Luria came to higher education at Kazan University in 1918, as the Civil War was beginning, and he stayed. If the great upheaval inspired any desire to go off and fight, or to escape into emigration, his autobiography passes over such vagrant feelings in silence. He repeats the standard phrases about the Revolution breaking down old limits, opening up grand vistas, sweeping 'us' into a great historical movement,[30] but only one of 'us' emerges from such generalities, a vividly remembered 'I' against a gray background of anonymous others.

He gives only the faintest hint of the first clash between academics like himself and the waves of lower-class students sent into higher education by the Bolshevik authorities. In 1918 they tried 'open admissions', as we call it in America nowadays, and then turned to 'workers' faculties', where largely unwilling professors were made to provide compensatory education for inadequately prepared lower-class students. Luria brushes past that turmoil with a few evasive phrases.[31] He concentrates on a list of formative authors and books, the customary start of any academic autobiography in pre-revolutionary Russia or the non-revolutionary West. The only distinctively Soviet feature of his autobiography is its reticence on distinctively Soviet issues. He avoids touchy matters in pure thought no less than politics or ethnicity. In his catalog of formative authors he tells how Höffding set him against associationist psychology (and refrains from saying what that did to his view of Pavlov); how Dilthey and Rickert showed him the qualitative difference between *Geistes-* and *Naturwissenschaften* (and refrains again from criticism of Pavlov, and from comment on Marx's view of the difference between the natural and the human sciences); how William James and Carl Jung excited him with their analyses of religion (and ignores again the comparison that begs to be made with Marx); how Freud's writings suggested a way to analyze the personality (and inserts a ritual warning against Freud's unconvincing speculations).

No doubt the exciting first years of the Soviet Republic stirred young Luria to boldness, of an academic sort. He sent letters to Freud and to Bekhterev, seeking their blessing — and getting it — for starting the 'Kazan Psychoanalytic Association' and for founding a journal on 'the psychophysiology of labor'. Such youthful enterprise won him the attention of Kornilov and a call to Moscow at the age of 21. That was, no doubt about it, a remarkable outburst of energy, but it was hardly revolutionary in the sense of Babel's or Olesha's quest as they joined the Red Army and began their soul-searching writing about the Soviet experience. Luria's autobiography is unquestionably accurate in noting that his research interests were shaped for fifty years by 'the central themes that guided my initial efforts' during the Civil War.[32] He merely neglects to specify one of the most obvious of those 'central themes': political caution, a scientist's effort to avoid ideological conflict, and a consequent retreat from field after field of research interests as ideological authorities extended *their* interest to and in them.

Luria was never as bold as Blonskii or Zalkind in ideology, or as bold as Vygotsky in the breadth and critical bite of his theorizing about psychology, but in the 1920s his intellect was far from timid:

> *Together with* [Kornilov's] *doctrine of reactions and* [Pavlov's and Bekhterev's doctrines] *of human reflexes, psychoanalysis provides a solid foundation for the psychology of materialist monism, the psychology that gets at the psyche of the whole personality in a positive way* [*pozitivno*, i.e., factually, not speculatively].[33]

Thus in 1925 he laid out his theoretical framework as he began experimental studies of conflicts within the personality. His boldness lay in the breadth of his reach — 'the psyche of the whole personality' — not in his choice of authorities. At the time Kornilov was the established leader of the doctrine of reactions, and of psychological science in general. Reflex doctrine had been blessed by Bukharin. Even the appeal to psychoanalysis was not yet, in 1925, a daring act for a Soviet Marxist.

Luria was somewhat defensive in plumping for Freudian concepts, but his defensive argument was addressed to experimental psychologists rather than Marxists. He acknowledged Freud's 'imprecision', but he praised that quality as 'scientific pragmatism', being loose enough to get on with the major job. Excessive precision, he argued, leads to abstract philosophizing or to trivial experimentation in psychology. He praised Marxism for being as creatively imprecise in social science as Freudianism was in psychology. With those related types of 'scientific pragmatism' providing his basic concepts, Luria hoped to replace mystified rationalizations of behavior with 'sociobiological explanations', experimentally verified.[34]

However freewheeling and creative that program sounds, it had a hollow
quality that prefigured collapse. Luria's Marxism avoided concrete issues.
The avoidance was quite obvious in his study of conflicts within the
personality: he never asked to what extent they may be functions of class
conflict. And he certainly did not ask the reverse question, which might
have been quite subversive: to what extent may class conflict be a function
of a disturbed personality? He simply ignored such politically charged
issues both in the design of his experiments and in the interpretation of the
results.[35]

Somewhat like Kornilov, he used 'the combined motor method' to study
emotional reactions. He measured the pressure of a hand on a rubber bulb
as the subject was taken through word associations charged with affect, or
was asked about hypothetical situations that set off internal conflicts of
feeling. Luria used three types of subject: students in the anterooms of
'purge commissions' (that is, commissions purging higher education of
students with the wrong combination of class origin, political outlook, and
academic achievement); criminal suspects in police stations before and after
the catharsis of confession or − rarely − exculpation; and volunteers for
induced neurosis under 'experimental psychoanalysis'. The volunteers would
be hypnotized, told that they would be unable to say certain words when
awake, then waked and tested, with precise observation of their aphasia
and trembling when asked to repeat forbidden words. All those types
would have been very suitable for class analysis − note especially the
students confronting 'purge commissions' − but Luria made no effort in
that direction. His preliminary reports in journals, and the large book, *The
Nature of Human Conflicts*, which summed up this protracted work of the
1920s, simply ignored Marxism. The book has a fragmentary quote from a
Marx who may be Karl − it is too tiny to be identified − and quotations
aside, it has no ideas or concepts distinctive of Marx, not to speak of Lenin
or Stalin or Bukharin, or even Pokrovsky and all the other social theorists
who wrote at considerable length on class conflict as the determinant of
beliefs and attitudes. Their ideas and concepts belonged to historical
materialism or sociology. They were quietly excluded from Luria's discipline, his 'compartment', as the Germans say.

The avoidance of social analysis by a scientist pledged to create a Marxist
psychology was not at all peculiar to Luria. Toward the end of a 1928
review of Soviet psychology in its first decade, Kornilov remarked: 'How
strange it is for the position of Marxist psychology in the Soviet Union
that one must speak of *social* or rather *collective psychology* at the very end,
while it would seem that one ought to speak of it at the very beginning.'[36]
But he could not avoid the fact: he and his colleagues had done almost
nothing in that field. He found some excuse by noting the predominance of
'bourgeois' traditions in psychological analysis of 'the crowd', took some
comfort in the beginnings of Soviet Marxist theorizing about 'the collective', and boasted of the graduate students he had recently assigned to

concrete research. 'The task of the next decade', he pledged, 'is to direct young people to research in problems of collective psychology, to make it possible for the field to lead psychology instead of trailing at the rear, as we see at present.'[37]

An outside observer is free to note the obvious explanation for the neglect of social psychology by Marxist psychologists. Prudent professionals stayed away from the politicians' domain. Even in personality studies, where political issues could be avoided as they were by Luria, the ideological need to combine adjustment and revolutionary transformation put the scientist in a deadlock. How could he focus both on the imperfect present and on the glorious future, on existing disorders of personality and society and on the splendid harmony that was to come? Listen to Zalkind, early in 1929, telling psychologists how to construct a new personality along with a new society:

> In the USSR as nowhere else enormous attention is drawn to the study of *human personality*. The personality of man, in the conditions of constructing socialism, is subjected to influences without historical precedent, and is developing a number of qualities and possibilities unknown to pre-socialist epochs. The new social system presents man's personality with original requirements, which are giving rise to a special type of thought and feeling. The toiling masses, the *mass* human personality, growing swiftly and creatively, expanding the boundaries of their aspirations, have come to power, to culture, to construction. These masses, ignored by bourgeois science, must be studied anew both in the sense of identifying their genuine characteristics and in the sense of identifying methods of educational influence on them.[38]

If such grandiose talk had any concrete meaning, it pointed away from the academic laboratory, toward 'the great social experiment' of the political bosses. It was less a program of research than a gesture of deference.

As the leading Communist on the psychoneurological front, to use the lingo that came into vogue in 1929, Zalkind could hardly offer down-to-earth marching orders. Psychologists were to help the managers of the Soviet system by showing how to combine 'maximum benefit for socialism with minimum cost to the personality'. He conceded that 'this colossal command of the revolution will not be an easy job.' The first step for the profession was '*to define itself anew ideologically*, ... to achieve an *integral, single system*' of scientific knowledge concerning man.'[39] His own professional efforts hardly fit that grand vision. As a psychiatrist and advocate of the mental health movement, he had been urging Party cadres and students to ease the strains on themselves by sensible ordering of work and relaxation, and by recourse to psychotherapy when stress became unbearable.

During the 1920s, while the plunge for the ideal personality lay somewhere in an indefinite future, alongside grandiose talk of humanity transformed there was autonomous space for Zalkind's humdrum preaching of personal adjustment to existing society, and for Luria's non-political study of present people and their inner conflicts. When present and future would run together in Stalin's great leap forward, that autonomous professional space would be squashed into politics. Poor Luria wrote up his book of personality studies a year too late; he finished in 1931 just as angry Stalinists were demanding right away the combination of utopian and practical studies that had previously been a distant dream. Essentially a work of the 1920s, *The Nature of Human Conflicts* was not published at home in Russian. It appeared abroad in English, with an admiring introduction by a leading American psychiatrist, who did not notice the absence of class analysis or of practical advice on the leap to a society without conflicts.[40]

In the early 1930s Luria tried to meet the Stalinist demand for work of practical relevance in Soviet society by offering field studies of peasant mentalities – only to provoke intensified anger and further blockage of publication.[41] The poor psychologist was damned if he did and damned if he didn't; whether he prudently avoided politically sensitive issues, as the culture of the 1920s permitted, or engaged in them, as the early 1930s seemed to require. In the mid-1930s Luria went to medical school and began his correlations of particular behavioral disturbances with damage to particular areas of the brain. The 'strategy' he adopted 'was to study the dissolution of higher psychological functions as the result of some kind of insult to the organism.'[42]

The pity of it is that Marx can be read as a philosopher of human nature with a distinctive argument on the creation of an authentically human person in a genuinely human society. Yet even in the comparatively liberal 1920s I have been able to find only two Soviet scholars who read Marx with that problem in mind and perceived the relevance to psychological science. One was an historian of ideas digging out evidence of alienation in modern culture. The other was a literary scholar who became entangled with the psychology of art and thus with the clash between expressive understanding of the mind and scientific explanation of it.

T. I. Rainov was the philosophical historian of ideas, a bookkeeper's son who completed his higher education just before the First World War. His doctoral dissertation, *A Theory of Creativity*, revealed no sign of Marxist influence, though Kant and Hegel were very much in evidence. Rainov argued that subjective minds create knowledge by acts of fusion with objective realities that transcend particular individuals and indeed particular generations of living individuals. Those objective realities are not only the material universe but also the human realities of 'culture as such', 'values in the flow of historical being'.[43] The creation of knowledge merges the individual mind with that process. Preoccupation with that theme of classical

German philosophy may explain why Rainov was one of the very few pre-revolutionary philosophers who made a successful transition to Soviet Marxism. He was following young Marx's route to Marxism. Perhaps that is also a major reason why he never became a leader among Soviet Marxists, who have mostly shunned the daring of young Marx, the idea of philosophers rising to a grand 'historico-cultural' understanding of *praxis*, above political leaders' day-by-day understanding of current practice. The merest hint of such an elevated vision among philosophers would be condemned by Stalin in 1931 as 'Menshevizing idealism'.[44]

Whatever the reason, Rainov was always a peripheral figure. He taught philosophy at a provincial teachers' college until 1923, when he moved to the Communist Academy in Moscow, but only in the modest post of bibliographer. In the metropolis but still on the intellectual margin, he wrote with great erudition on a wide range of subjects, turning constantly about the process of creating knowledge by creative fusion of individual subjective minds with the objective reality of historically developing culture. Psychological science intrigued him by its growing determination to ignore such an obvious process. Psychologists not only turned away from explicit metaphysics, but also tried to separate the mind from the cultural process that is its inseparable producer and product, within which individual minds are both creators and created. In 1926 he published 'The Alienation of Action', a long critique of American behaviorism, of Bekhterev's reflexology, and of Pavlov's doctrine. (At the time no one doubted the basic similarity of those three trends.)[45] They turned human action into 'behavior', or into 'reflexes', in order to equate it with physical action, to separate action from any concept of a person who acts. Rainov compared that compulsive separation with signs of analogous alienation in modern society at large, ranging from objectivist trends in art to the use of working people as appendages to machines. 'Evidently somewhere in the depths of social being in our time it has become necessary to treat actions as processes, and those who act as machines.'[46]

Perhaps the most significant feature of his analysis was its isolation. His long article came out as three installments in a major journal, *The Herald of the Communist Academy*, but it was ignored, though a similar line of analysis was beginning to appear among Western Marxists.[47] It would turn into the focus on alienation that has mesmerized Western Marxism since the Second World War. Soviet philosophers have deliberately looked away, and they were doing so already in the 1920s, as we can see in their willingness to publish but not to discuss Rainov. Soviet psychologists were even less responsive to his argument that 'objectivist' trends in their discipline express the alienation of modern industrial society. To debate the notion that we have an essential nature from which we can be alienated was to go back to an issue that psychologists had simply put behind them when they turned away from philosophy — and also from common sense. Rainov tried to recall them not only to the esoteric ideas of Kant and Hegel but also to the commonsense knowledge that a human being acts in accordance with his intentions, choices, decisions, dreams. The search for unintentional determinants of intentional actions, whether in the nervous system or the social system or both together, implies the absence of a real inner actor or agent; the person using the complex machinery of his nervous processes, hormones, and bodily urges becomes a mechanical function or a helpless observer of the machinery. Rainov challenged Soviet psychologists to debate that implication within a Marxist frame of reference, but they proved as deeply reluctant to do so as their 'bourgeois' colleagues at home and abroad.

In this respect professional psychologists were in fundamental sympathy with Bolshevik political and ideological leaders, who despised philosophizing about the nature of an authentically human person. They preferred to get on with the practical business of constructing him, or (to be precise) building the new society in which 'the new man' will be both constructor and constructed. Never mind speculating in advance what he will be like when the project is complete. Functionalist social scientists and practical Communist chiefs have shared, then and still, a deep-seated refusal to spell out their underlying assumptions concerning human nature. They feel no need to justify their escape from a metaphysical quagmire to the firm ground of practical activity and experimental science. The evasive act is to be its own justification; doing is to be proof of knowing.

Rainov may have perceived that ubiquitous similarity of modern minds, that implicit ideology linking practical Communist leaders and Soviet Marxist psychologists with practical 'bourgeois' leaders and 'bourgeois' experimental psychologists, but he had more political sense than to point it out. On the contrary, he claimed Communist leaders for his cause; he listed Bukharin among the Marxist critics of Pavlov's doctrine and the alienation that it expresses. He simply ignored Bukharin's exaltation of Pavlov's doctrine as 'a weapon from the iron arsenal of materialism'.[48] Such bits of opportunism in an otherwise honest scholar are properly ignored.

THE EMERGENCE OF VYGOTSKY

The other thinker of the 1920s who called Marxist colleagues back to the neglected depths of psychology was L. S. Vygotsky. He acquired much greater influence than Rainov; indeed, he founded the most important school of Soviet psychology. He could have such effect because he did not stay on the periphery of psychological science, criticizing it from without. He came up to it from humanistic studies, but then entered fully in, and criticized from within, repressing the metaphysical issue of a human essence and alienation from it. Accepting the ethos of the profession, he revealed its basic problems with the persuasive power of a comrade. We aspire to a science of psychology, he reminded his colleagues, and we have created several of them, just as Franz Brentano, one of our founding fathers, noted back in 1874.[49] He challenged his colleagues to scorn the easy escape, which is to immure oneself in a single school and pooh-pooh the others. He laid out a most ambitious program of unification with an 'historico-cultural' approach as the central feature. Though tuberculosis cut him off at a very early age, Vygotsky left prolific disciples, most notably Luria and A. N. Leont'ev, who founded the Vygotsky school of cognitive psychology, focused on brain damage and on child development.

There is a great irony in that history: preaching a comprehensive science, Vygotsky started one more school. Much of his work was actually concealed by his avowed disciples or by the censorship, or by some combination of timid disciples and fearsome censors. His major books were withheld from publication, for forty years in one case, fifty-five in another.[50] When they finally appeared, his admirers had become thoroughly specialized adepts in one or two parts of his comprehensive project, conditioned to ignore the rest. There are peculiarly Soviet features in this ironic history, but there are also striking analogies to the fate of Wundt or James among Western psychologists, who also profess reverence for founding fathers and ignore their central ideas.

Like Luria, who was among his earliest and most intense admirers, Vygotsky was obviously Jewish and defiantly superior to ethnic labeling. Or maybe he was more stoical than defiant, as he carried through Russian academia the telltale combination of Russified Polish name and Mediterranean face. The rare photograph shows large dark eyes lit with gentle intensity rather than arrogance, reinforcing the disciples' talk of an 'enchanting personality'. We must make do with guesswork from bits of evidence, for extensive material is not provided. If he left an autobiography, it is still among his unpublished papers along with self-revealing letters, which must have been written, for he had a warm outgoing nature. The disciples tell us that, but they themselves are utterly ungiving of documents, and close-fisted even with elementary details of his life. They refuse to tell Soviet readers anything about family background beyond the bare statement that his father was a *sluzhashchii* (literally: a person in service). That means a white-collar or salaried person, in contrast to a blue-collar or wage-earning person, and includes levels of status far above poor clerks or bookkeepers. Foreign readers are permitted to learn a little more; a recent biographical sketch, published only in English, acknowledges that Vygotsky's father was a bank officer, and gives a little reminiscence of the family's secular Jewishness.[51] The son was an outstanding student, who worked jointly at Moscow University and at Shaniavskii University in law and 'philological studies' (read: imaginative literature and cultural history), and was making a name for himself as a literary critic by the time of the 1917 Revolution, when he was only twenty-one.

- Jean Piaget's Stage Theory
- Lev Vygotsky's Social Contextualism.

That is another part of the legendary aura that radiates from Vygotsky: the incredibly young genius who had to do his enormous work at great speed, while tuberculosis was pushing him to periodic bedrest and early death (in 1934, aged thirty-seven). The admirers who stress the doomed youth's intense engagement with his calling are strangely vague about his path through the revolutionary storm.[52] He may have consorted with non-Bolsheviks in 1917, for he published in a Jewish periodical and in one edited by Gorky which was critical of the new dictatorship and was soon shut down by it.[53] Studied silences suggest unpleasant news. The disciples say nothing about his politics in 1917–18; for the ensuing years of Civil War they tell us only that he taught at a pedagogical institute and advised a theatrical company in a small Belorussian town. They refrain from republishing or even from adequately describing the earliest articles he is known to have published in 1915–23, though literary art was their topic. If he wrote anything on politics, it has been kept in the dark.

When we contemplate the skimpy accounts of Vygotsky's major intellectual transformation, from literary critic to psychologist, one large fact quickly emerges. The accounts are skimpy because his distinctive ideas about literary art are not to the taste of his disciples in psychological science. They admire the psychologist that emerged from the literary critic in the period from 1915 to 1923, but they have been unwilling or unable to confront the critic, or the influence of the critic on the scientist. *The Psychology of Art*, the dissertation that summed up the emergence of one from the other, and earned Vygotsky a doctorate in 1925, waited forty years to be published (heavily abridged in 1965, 'corrected and enlarged' in 1968 and enlarged yet again in 1986 and 1987).[54] Editor A. N. Leont'ev asserts, without offering evidence, that Vygotsky himself withheld the book from publication since he was acutely aware that he had not solved the problems he was struggling with.[55] That may be true, but it is much more obviously true that Vygotsky died in 1934, and his disciples – Leont'ev included – waited thirty years before they could bring themselves (and the ideological establishment) to set aside the master's perfectionist scruples and put the book before the public. Archival information would help, but one can discover the major reason why without access to the archives. One need only consider Vygotsky's argument concerning art, and compare the disciples' one-sided summaries, when they have felt obliged, briefly and perfunctorily, to report it. He discovered antinomies in modern views of the expressive imagination; they prefer to brush the antinomies aside, mumbling about the imperfect stage of psychological science in his day and hurrying back from the expressive imagination to the problem-solving intelligence.[56]

This was the basic antinomy: the belief that imaginative literature (or art in general) is merely a manner of signalling, like birdsong or ratsqueak, to be explained by its biological and social functions, versus the belief that it is also a major thing in itself, to be not only explained but also understood as beautiful truths accumulating in a cultural process, which creates the human mind even as it is created by it. Vygotsky began with the second belief, was drawn against his aesthetic inclination toward the first, tried to fuse them, but did not succeed.

He started in particular with an intensive study of *Hamlet* and the critical controversies that have accumulated about it. He wanted to understand the appeal of art works called classic, a persistent appeal that must be evidence of some persistent structure of thought and feeling inherent in the human mind. If the fictive tragedy of *Hamlet* is a perennial stimulus of pleasurable feelings, and it is, whoever would explain that paradoxical fact — tragedy stimulating pleasure — cannot ignore either literary analysis of the drama or psychological analysis of author, actors, audience, critics. Until 1924 Vygotsky concentrated on the author's text and the critics' debate, with splendid results. His literary essays remain the most original and exciting part of his writing on the psychology of art, though ostensibly they only lead up to it, passing on to psychological science a problem that literary criticism cannot solve.

Literary analysis revealed to Vygotsky that *Hamlet*'s dramatic tension derives from the opposition between the plot formula and the actual plot; what the audience expects to happen (criminal outrage corrected by vengeful justice) is opposed to what the audience actually sees (random violence, insanity, and vengeful justice dissolving into absurdity). Adult audiences know that there are such distressing incongruities between the expected and the actual pattern of life. Why their enactment in fiction pleases the distressed mind is a question that carries the critic from literary to social and psychological analysis. Vygotsky's response was a version of 'catharsis', interpreted in Freudian fashion as the patterned discharge through dramatic fiction of suffering that would otherwise be destructive. That seems to be a functional, scientific explanation of tragic fiction. But Vygotsky also argued, with a rare combination of erudition and clarity, that the two types of analysis have been increasingly at odds with each other. As psychologists have separated their discipline from philosophy and modeled it on the natural sciences, they have moved toward a psychology of art 'from below', functional analysis of stimulus and reaction that is primitively crude, incompatible with literary analysis of such texts as *Hamlet*. And vice versa. As critics have separated their discipline from metaphysical doctrines of 'the soul' or 'the mind', they have kept alive a psychology of art 'from above', but it has been increasingly deprived of a psychological theory that might justify it.[57]

Vygotsky turned to Marxism, not for a ready-made theory of art or psychology or unification of the two, but for a methodology that might help him to overcome the antinomy he was struggling with. He emphasized that Marxism was not opposed to aesthetic theory 'from above'. Young Marx, he noted, asked the same question about the persistent appeal of

Greek classics that he was asking about *Hamlet*.[58] How could it be that the beautiful works of a slave-owning society are still beautiful in a capitalist society and will be under socialism? The persistence of the appeal challenges the Marxist theory that social superstructures, mentalities included, change with transformations of the social base. Vygotsky had to emphasize that Marx recognized the problem, for Marxists tended to regard their doctrine as an approach 'from below', a sociological analysis of the class feelings communicated and shaped by art.

The reductive inclination was reinforced after the Revolution by official disapproval of 'formalism' in literary studies, a label of disapproval for emphasis on qualities that inhere in works of art regardless of changing social relations and psychological mutability.[59] In the post-revolutionary context a 'formalist' approach seemed to imply the superior isolation of the artist, elevating the 'engineer of human souls' above the leaders who tell engineers what needs to be constructed.[60] Vygotsky's brilliant internal or structural analyses of literary art came dangerously close to such 'formalism', and his respectful attention to the chief bugbears of 'formalist' theory (Potebnia and Shklovskii) must have inclined the ideological establishment against publication of *The Psychology of Art*.

But there were also professional reasons for his disciples' reluctance to confront his essential argument. Literary analyses of *Hamlet* seem as alien to psychologists who have no fear of Party ideologists as to those who do. The Western psychologists who came to admire Vygotsky in the post-Stalin era have shown no more interest in his psychology of art than have his Soviet disciples.[61] A complementary indifference to Vygotsky's psychology is observable among literary critics, East or West, who are unresponsive to suggestions that 'the biological basis of art' may be found in 'the possibility of releasing into art powerful passions which cannot find expression in normal, everyday life'.[62] In support of that idea Vygotsky cited both Nietzsche and Sherrington, trying to combine intuitive understanding of bardic frenzy with physiological analysis of the nervous system, the poetic striving for harmonic order in our emotive thinking with the mechanistic image of art as a safety valve that relieves an overburdened steam boiler. (Yes, he too used that reductive metaphor.)[63] Vygotsky has had no more success in the West than at home in his efforts to bridge the 'two cultures', or rather to show that works of art may be used as such a bridge, since they are created by the mind in a dense context of social and biological functions, demanding both humanistic and scientific approaches in order to be fully understood and explained.

Vygotsky is known at home and abroad primarily as a cognitive psychologist, rather than a writer on literary art. His disciples have been persistently eager to tell at length about his investigation of problem-solving development in children, and to give lip service to his 'historico-cultural' project for psychology, but they are not at all clear or convincing

in their accounts of how he came to that work, or even how he came to the
Institute of Experimental Psychology where he pursued it. They note his
emergence from provincial seclusion in 1924, but do not say who invited
him or why. We simply learn that he was a major speaker at the Second
Psychoneurological Congress in January of that year, the meeting that
proclaimed the campaign for a Marxist reconstruction of psychology.[64]
Vygotsky must have been known as a Marxist sympathizer in the psychology of art and of education, but the disciples do not say whether he
chose or the organizers of the Congress chose for him a more elemental
and sharply controversial topic: consciousness (*soznanie*, the thinking and
feeling mind), as a problem for physiology and psychology.

Whether intended by the organizers or not, that is what he spoke about,
with such eloquence and clarity that witnesses felt the excitement of attend-
ance at an historical event.[65] Yet they have been persistently vague and
inaccurate in recounting what he said and explaining why it constituted an
historical event. The reporter who wrote a long account of the Congress
for the major intellectual journal, *Red Virgin Soil*, thought that Vygotsky
epitomized a brilliant young psychologist on the way to Marxism but
hesitating en route.[66] Yet the reporter gave no evidence for that judgment,
nor have subsequent admirers, who picture Vygotsky as a full-fledged
Marxist. They imply that he was *the* Marxist hero of psychological science,
who turned his errant colleagues away from an infatuation with reflexology,
to a proper interest in the conscious mind.[67] But they offer no evidence to
support that legend, nor can they, for Vygotsky did not criticize fellow
psychologists, who did not have an infatuation with reflexology. He criticized some physiologists, most notably Pavlov and Bekhterev, and refrained
from naming Marxists who shared the assumption that consciousness is to
be explained by physiological reduction.

Both the contemporaneous reporter and the subsequent admirers have
been gesturing toward a kind of disagreement which they may not speak of
frankly: between academic professionals and Party leaders. It was not
professional psychologists who were infatuated with reflexology, it was the
Party's chief ideologists. After 1917 as before Kornilov deliberately included subjective elements in his 'reactology', and the central Institute of
Psychology, which he directed, sponsored no research of the purely objectivist kind, whether Pavlovian, Bekhterevian, or rat-running American
behaviorist.[68] Bukharin and the other ideological leaders of the Party were
either unaware of the psychologists' outlook or unsympathetic to it; either
thoughtlessly or threateningly they equated scientific psychology with
Pavlov's and Bekhterev's reduction of mind to reflexes.[69] From the tribune
of the January 1924 Congress Vygotsky was arguing explicitly with Pavlov
and Bekhterev, the non-Marxist leaders of physiology, but implicitly with
the Party leaders who took it for granted that those physiologists had
founded psychological science. His fellow psychologists were an enthusi-

astic audience, for they shared his conviction that subjectivity and consciousness are central to the science of the mind, but they had not known how to reconcile that conviction with Bukharin's Marxism.

In the Soviet, as in the pre-revolutionary period, nearly all of Russia's professional psychologists took it for granted that their discipline must analyze consciousness, though they disagreed on the proper way to do that. With one or two exceptions, they did not polemicize against Pavlov or Bekhterev. They praised studies of conditioning as a physiological foundation for psychology, not a replacement of it, and they had cause to wonder whether the distinction was clear to laymen, especially the new rulers, who simply assumed that the study of conditioning was psychology *tout court*. The psychologists had been encouraged in 1923 by an article of Bukharin's ridiculing an extreme left version of Pavlov's doctrine — Enchmen's 'theory of new biology', which predicted that conditioned grunts and gestures of the proletariat would replace the verbal culture of 'bourgeois' society.[70] But soon after that encouraging article was published the Party leaders gave psychologists new reason to be anxious, by their gentle response to Pavlov's ridicule of Marxism. In November 1923 *Pravda* published replies by Zinoviev and Trotsky, who limited their criticism of Pavlov to social theory and politics, while reverently accepting his reduction of psychology to conditioned reflexes.[71] In January 1924, while the Psychoneurological Congress was meeting, the first part of Bukharin's lengthy reply to Pavlov was either at the news-stands or on the way.[72] And Bukharin, the Party chief of ideology, pronounced Pavlov's doctrine of conditioned reflexes 'a weapon from the iron arsenal of materialism'. He also repeated one of the reductive figures of speech that he had put in his textbook of historical materialism: 'If we consider the individual personality [*lichnost'*] in its development, we see that it is in essence like a little sausage skin stuffed with the influences of the environment.'[73]

That was the context that challenged Vygotsky when he rose to defend psychology as the science of the conscious mind. He opened with Marx's well-known contrast — it occurs in *Capital* — between the clumsiest human architect or weaver and the most unerring bee or spider. The human sees his intended construction in the mind's eye before physical eye and hand put a sketch on paper or a physical structure on the ground or the loom.[74] The bee and the spider are much simpler machines: they excrete their hives or webs in unchanging stereotypes without intentional preliminaries. So a passage from Marx himself disproved the widespread notion that radicals favor physiological reduction of the mind, while psychologies of the conscious mind are musty relics of old-regime metaphysics, if not the church. Vygotsky made the ideological point all the more effective by abstaining from stereotyped use of such labels as mentalist or materialist; he showed, quite artfully, how the physiological materialism of Pavlov and Bekhterev forced them into dualist inconsistency. Nor did he indulge in flag-waving talk of 'bourgeois' versus Marxist in psychological science. After citing Marx on the unsolved problem of consciousness, he set his analysis within the framework of classless science.

He noted, for example, that Pavlov's hypothetical brain processes were at odds with the findings of major neurophysiologists such as Sherrington.[75] He did not drag the audience into obscure technical issues, but brought the clash of basic concepts to vivid life by contrasting Pavlov's switchboard model of the working brain — random temporary associations as called for by external stimuli — with Sherrington's metaphors of highly structured organization: funnels collecting and concentrating neural energies, or better yet a big busy house with small doors controlling the flow of business in and out. Vygotsky also called Sechenov to witness against Pavlov, reminding the audience that the father of Russian physiology had defined thinking as an *interruption* of reflexive activity, which opens the way to a non-reflexive psychology of thinking.[76] By such appeals to physiological authority and by matter-of-fact argument he demonstrated the need to supplement neurophysiology with a psychology that analyzes 'the structure of our [conscious] behaviour, ... its composition and forms'.[77] Obviously the Gestalt school was a major influence on this omnivorous consumer of all psychologies. He also had the literary flair to make everyone see the necessity of assuming inherent mental structure, the absurdity of Pavlov's opposite, associationist assumption: 'A human being★ is not at all a skin sack filled with reflexes, and the brain is not a hotel for a series of conditioned reflexes accidentally stopping in.'[78]

That witty negation of Bukharin's sausage simile, to ridicule simple-minded faith in Pavlov's doctrine, was probably the reason why the reporter for *Red Virgin Soil* typed Vygotsky as a hesitant, incomplete Marxist; how else explain a scholar who quotes Marx and mocks Bukharin? But the reporter refrained from naming the butt of Vygotsky's witty thrust, as Vygotsky refrained in the printed record. Whether in extemporaneous speech he named the leaders who were too exalted to be engaged in public dispute with mere academics, archival records may some day reveal. His admirers did a little prevaricating shuffle to respect the leaders' exaltation above criticism. They pictured Vygotsky as challenging the vogue of reflexology among 'Marxists'. They carefully ignored the difference between Marxist Party ideologists like Zinoviev, Trotsky, and Bukharin, who shared in that vogue, and Marxist professional psychologists, who did not.

In a short time the prevaricating shuffle became a standard formula, which is repeated to this day in Western as well as Soviet histories: reflexology dominated Soviet psychology until the mid-1920s, when Vygotsky and his disciples called psychologists to the social or 'historico-cultural'

★ *Chelovek*, 'man' in the generic sense, not the male 'man', which is *muzhchina*. Russian separates the two meanings that English lumps in a single word.

study of the conscious mind that is appropriate to Marxists.[79] In fact Kornilov, Luria, and the other Marxist psychologists were using subjective methods and studying consciousness before Vygotsky appeared at the Congress of January 1924 to defend such studies. He showed them how to justify their disagreement with reflexology and with the Party ideologists who favored it.

There was something much more important than a tactical evasion of scandal in Vygotsky's argument. He showed psychologists a sophisticated kind of Marxism, which went far deeper into their problems than the simplistic formulas of Bukharin or Trotsky or Lenin; he took Marxism into serious analysis of the war of schools. Of course his tactical smoothness was essential to that deep discussion. He had a style of argument that fitted the mores of the 1920s, combining criticism with respect for such non-Marxist eminences as Pavlov and Bekhterev, on whom the government was lavishing favor, and artfully honoring the taboo on explicit criticism of Party leaders, while actually disagreeing with them. One must give credit to the administrator — Kornilov, in all likelihood — who recognized the value of such a thinker, and invited Vygotsky to join the Moscow Institute of Psychology soon after the Congress of January 1924.[80] One must also give credit to Bukharin, for keeping quiet. Indeed, he even hinted, in a 1924 speech to the Comintern, possible disapproval of reflexology.[81] Given his power as Stalin's right-hand man, and given the fact that on this issue he expressed the superficial opinion common to Bolshevik ideologists, any further public statement of his views on psychology would have had a stifling effect on professionals in the field. His forbearance enabled them to engage in fairly free discussion, though they constantly bore in mind the latent discord between themselves and the ideological establishment.

Within that cagey community Vygotsky had an exhilarating way of speaking clearly on basic issues while avoiding scandalous conflict. He named Bukharin and Trotsky only when ostensibly agreeing with them.[82] Toward lesser mortals he was courteous in a more forthright manner. He could, for example, write penetrating criticism of Luria's effort to mix Freudianism with Marxism, and still keep Luria's adoring friendship.[83] He could criticize his immediate chief, Kornilov, and still hold his favor.[84] He had by all accounts an unusually attractive personality, but he had a far more important intellectual advantage, which is obvious to the outside observer reading through the publications of those psychologists who called themselves Marxist. Vygotsky was the only one who had thoroughly absorbed Marxism. He had studied Marx, Engels, and Plekhanov — probably before the Revolution as his disciples claim. (I am inclined to believe them even though they offer no evidence; it would probably show some heretical form of Marxism.) He had studied 'the classics of Marxism' for deeper reasons than political convenience or ideological fashion, as he studied Spinoza, his favorite philosopher. He was seeking unified understanding of human beings as natural objects with conscious minds.[85]

VYGOTSKY'S 'CRISIS'

Vygotsky showed his exceptional intellectual breadth and seriousness of purpose most notably in his major book, written in 1926–7, while he was committed to bedrest by an acute attack of tuberculosis. His title was ambivalent. 'The Historical Meaning [*smysl*] of the Psychological Crisis' suggested not only significance in some functional sense – as in 'the evolutionary significance [*znachenie*] of the grasp reflex' – but also meaning in the humanly goal-seeking sense – as in 'the meaning [*smysl*] of life'. Moreover the curious phrasing at the end – 'psychological crisis' rather than 'crisis of psychology' – invited thought about psychology as mindset along with psychology as science, about a crisis in self-knowledge as reflected in a crisis of science. To be sure, that ambivalence was implicit rather than elaborated, in the body of the book as well as the title. (I am assuming that the editors have not silently omitted substantial chunks of the text.)[86]

Vygotsky focused his explicit argument on psychological science, which had been in a chronic crisis since its emergence as a separate discipline, for each of its warring schools had hold of an indubitable truth, but all the partial truths together had formed a wrangle instead of a consistent science. He noted also, as an obvious truth, that literary art still provides far more important understanding of our minds than scientific psychology does. Such truths seem to call for retreat from faith in a single psychological science to acceptance of 'two psychologies' in permanence: 'understanding' or humanist as opposed to 'explanatory' or natural scientific.[87] But Vygotsky would not accept the permanence of that division. It implies a pluralist universe, in which human consciousness is an anomalous presence, to be *explained* by natural science but *understood* by artistic self-expression and by everyday forms of intuitive self-analysis.

Implicitly Vygotsky accepted that vision, as an accurate characterization of human understanding at odds with nature in past and present; explicitly he rejected such pluralism for the future. There would be no *permanent* division between the conscious mind and unconscious nature, he insisted. The tension between reality and aspiration resonated in the quotation from Spinoza which he had used as epigraph to his previous book, *The Psychology of Art*. He had quoted Spinoza defending monistic naturalism against the objection 'that solely from the laws of nature considered as extended substance' one cannot 'deduce the causes of buildings, pictures, and things of that kind which are produced only by human art; nor would the human body, unless it were determined and led by the mind, be capable of building a single temple.'[88] That objection to the monistic vision is very like Marx contrasting the mindful architect or weaver to the mindless bee or spider, and indeed like countless others observing the obvious difference between a mind with intentions and a physical body without them. Spinoza's reply to the objection is that 'the objectors cannot fix the limits of the body's power, or say what can be concluded from a consideration of its sole nature.'[89] Evidently Vygotsky liked Spinoza's philosophizing to prove that in principle mind and body *can* be explained by a single science of 'extended substance', but his twentieth-century mind turned deliberately away from philosophizing about such a science to the concrete problems of building it.

A unified psychology was not in sight, even in the mind's eye; he showed that quite vividly by reviewing the war of schools. The psychologies rooted in natural science were persistently opposed to the psychologies rooted in literary and philosophical reflection on ourselves. He avoided going back to philosophy by affirming Marxist faith in the future. Evolving together in emergent unity, a new society and a new human being would create a new, unified science of psychology. That affirmation concludes 'The Historical Meaning of the Psychological Crisis'. It seems almost certain that he used — and the editors have deleted — his favorite quotation from Trotsky: 'Man is himself *stikhiia*', *stoicheion* or elemental chaos, which is yet to be shaped into an authentic human being or superhuman, as Kautsky predicted, in another quotation that has probably been deleted.[90] The editors have let stand the book's final paragraph, which drew again on Spinoza:

> In the future society psychology will be in actuality the science of the new man [*chelovek*]. Without that perspective Marxism and the history of science would not be complete. But that science of the new man will still be psychology; we now hold in our hands the thread leading to it. Never mind that that psychology will resemble present-day psychology as little as — in Spinoza's words — the constellation Canis resembles the dog, a barking animal.[91]

With that the book ended. And somehow that futuristic yearning, pitting Spinozist faith against the incoherent pluralism of contemporary culture, had the acrid flavor of modernist absurdity. Psychologists aspiring to a unified science, a dog barking beneath the constellation named for him — that summed up 'The Historical Meaning of the Psychological Crisis'.[92]

Perhaps the effect was not consciously intended, for the bulk of the text preceding the final paragraph was a respectful analysis of the contending schools in modern psychological science. Vygotsky classified them according to three basically different approaches. Psychologists proceeded either from analysis of the normal adult mind (for example, in Gestalt), or from the pathological mind (for example, in psychoanalysis), or from subhuman animal behavior (for example, in Pavlov's doctrine of conditioned reflexes). At times those categories tended to blur and to fission, but it would take us too far afield to offer an adequate sampling of Vygotsky's subtle analyses. One must however note the resemblance between his views on the crisis of psychology and those offered by Karl Bühler and by William James. He drew on them, and on many other Western scholars, in an open, generous spirit that seems unSoviet to those who know only the Soviet publications of the 1930s and after. They have insisted on a heavy-handed distinction between Soviet and 'bourgeois' scientists, who may not be trusted in ideologically sensitive matters. Vygotsky's 'Historical Meaning of the Psychological Crisis' seems at first to be utterly different, showing what Soviet psychology was *not* until Stalin's 'revolution from above' transformed it.

The most obvious contrast is between Vygotsky's sensitive cosmopolitan attitude and the crude secessionist rage of high Stalinism. He included Soviet Marxist psychologists within the worldwide discipline and thus within its crisis, for the obvious reason that he and his colleagues followed much the same lines of thought as the schools contending with each other in the West. He paid no attention to Lenin's talk of a crisis in science at large, the supposed result of its adepts' 'bourgeois' ideology, their ignorance of dialectical materialism.[93] Stalinists in the 1930s would seize upon that Leninist argument to hammer the point that Soviet scientists must separate themselves from 'bourgeois' science by applying dialectical materialism to their disciplines.

The outside observer with the advantage of hindsight can see the secessionist spirit of Stalinist psychology emerging in the 1920s within talk of 'Marxist psychology', or *Psychology Presented from the Viewpoint of Dialectical Materialism*, as Kornilov entitled his textbook in 1926.[94] Vygotsky opposed that kind of talk. He argued that it confused three different levels of knowledge: psychology as a specific science, which must be distinguished from the particular methodology appropriate to it, which in turn must be distinguished from the most general methodology of knowledge as a whole. Dialectical materialism, in his view, was the Marxist version of the most general methodology. It could be translated into specific methodological principles for psychology only in the context of protracted, concrete labor within the science, overcoming thus the war of schools: 'Our science will become Marxist to the degree that it will become true, scientific; and we will work precisely on that, its transformation into a true science, not on its agreement with Marx's theory.'[95]

Monism was one of the central assumptions of the truly scientific and therefore Marxist methodology: mind and body constitute a single reality in the functioning human being, and therefore a single science must ultimately describe and explain the unity. That assumption was shared not only by Marxists but by most specialists in the human sciences, in the West as well as the Soviet Union. That was a major reason why Soviet Marxists in the 1920s so confidently described their philosophy as 'intrascientific'. They were making explicit a methodology that was already implicit in the practical assumptions of scientists who did not yet think of themselves as

Marxists.[96] Vygotsky took that familiar theme of reassurance to scientists and made it fearsome, by showing its dreamlike, futuristic contrast with reality. No existing school of psychology nor all of them lumped together achieved the monistic ideal of a single science of the mind-brain. What they were contradicted what they hoped to be. He nevertheless clung to reassurance by preaching patience: 'That psychology of which we speak does not exist yet; it is still to be created, and not by a single school. Many generations of psychologists will labor on it, as [William] James said. . . .'[97] Such millenial calm is disturbing to specialists hoping for perceptible gains in their own lifetime. To the frantically impatient mentality that erupted in Stalin's revolution from above, such calm would be simply unthinkable. For those Stalinists the protracted tension of opposed schools would be plain evidence that they were in a 'bourgeois' dead end, from which Marxists must effect a great leap forward, to a completely new, genuinely monistic science of psychology.

Am I therefore placing Vygotsky completely outside the drift to the psychology of Stalinism? I am not. He did, after all, collaborate in the furtive semi-concealment of his views, the public show of unity and progress that camouflaged the back-and-forth of opposed tendencies among Soviet Marxist psychologists as among their 'bourgeois' colleagues at home and abroad. By withholding his most serious writing from publication he was implicitly accepting for psychology the rule of secrecy that Stalin established for political discourse early in the 1920s: the most sensitive issues should be thrashed out within a small circle of wise initiates, and a unified front must always face the simple-minded public.[98] Vygotsky went further than mere withholding of troublesome debate. He prevaricated on occasion. It is startling to compare his semi-private writing on 'the psychological crisis' with the rah-rah review of Soviet psychology that he published in a 1928 volume celebrating the social sciences during the first decade of Soviet power.

He opened the review with his favorite theme: the problem of psycholog*ies* aspiring to be psycholog*y*. And he ended with quotations from Trotsky and Kautsky on the new society and the new man that will emerge from past and present human *stikhiia*, elemental chaos, along with a new, unified, practically useful science of psychology. In that respect the essay was a condensed version of his unpublished book. But his tone was quite different; there was no breath of Jamesian resignation to many generations of labor toward an ideal that might possibly prove to be unrealistic. At some points he must have consciously doubted what he put on paper. For example:

If in the doctrine of conditioned reflexes our psychology has found its *biological foundation*, and in materialist dialectics *its philosophical formalization* [*oformlenie*], in psychotechnics − in the broadest sense of the word — it has found *its practice*, i.e. the mastery of human behavior in deed, the subordination of it to the control of reason.[99]

All three parts of that claim were at odds with Vygotsky's beliefs, as he had presented them elsewhere and at length. He had shown that Pavlov's explanation of conditioned reflexes clashed with neurophysiology. He had also observed that the would-be 'foundation' did not match 'the roof', that is, that conditioned reflexes could not explain higher nervous functions such as thinking and speaking.[100] He had argued that dialectical materialism is not a ready-made philosophy for psychology, yet here he described it as the 'philosophical *oformlenie*', which means formalization in the bureaucratic sense of registering a marriage or drawing up a treaty, quite different from the open-ended emphasis of Vygotsky's passages on Marxism in 'The Historical Meaning of the Psychological Crisis'. And the enormous claim made for psychotechnics, that it had already found practical mastery of human behavior, was another incongruity. Like other Soviet writers on psychotechnics, Vygotsky normally stressed its embryonic or inchoate condition.[101]

Evidently the telescoping of aspiration and actuality, which comes so naturally at jubilees, took hold of Vygotsky on that occasion. It would hardly be worth mentioning, if it did not anticipate so clearly the Stalinist habit of requiring such a telescoping, of forcing present reality to collapse into future dream. To be sure, Vygotsky concluded his celebratory essay with a clear statement that 'Marxist psychology' expressed a will to the future rather than a present achievement.[102] His was a comparatively small step toward the collapse of present reality into future dream. But small as it was by comparison with the tub-thumping extremes that were to come, it was still there in his published work, disturbingly at odds with the dominant theme of the major work that he had just finished, which was circulating in manuscript, and would remain unpublished until 1982, fifty-five years after he wrote it.

My account of Vygotsky has deliberately paid scant attention to the features of his work that have been habitually emphasized by his admirers, both Soviet and Western: his cognitive studies of children, his interest in cognitive disorders of mentally ill and brain-damaged people, and his project for an 'historico-cultural' approach to general psychology. That habitual emphasis distorts historical reality. Whether we judge quantitatively or qualitatively, Vygotsky's emphasis in the 1920s was on the issues that I have stressed: the psychology of art and the discord among rival schools of psychology. When he came to cognitive psychology, he did preliminary theorizing far more than experimental research. And when he came to preach 'historico-cultural' psychology, his theorizing was quite thin and derivative. He ostentatiously put the 'historico-cultural' slogan at the center of his program for psychology, yet he worked at the subject only belatedly and briefly. His first published venture was a little survey that he and Luria brought out in 1930, mostly reviewing theories of Western psychologists: *Studies in the History of Behavior; Ape, Primitive, Child.*[103] Stalinists immediately attacked the scheme of behavioral evolution that it presented as essentially 'bourgeois'.[104] Vygotsky's defensive and aggressive responses — restricting his freewheeling thought, attacking 'bourgeois' elements in Piaget — belong to the Stalinist 1930s.[105] The point here, respecting the 1920s, is that even then, in a relatively liberal atmosphere, Vygotsky resembled most other Soviet psychologists in his paradoxical combination of insistence that social psychology be the center of the discipline and his evasion of serious work at that center. Even this extraordinarily venturesome thinker tended to stand clear of an area charged with ideological and political passion, while solemnly calling on Soviet psychologists to make it their focus.

Vygotsky dreamed of a psychological analogue to the 'biogenetic law', that ontogeny recapitulates phylogeny.[106] He supposed that the individual mental development of the child recapitulates the mental development of humanity, with primitive and peasant adults somewhere on the evolutionary ladder between completely childlike and completely civilized. In their actual work as psychologists he and his school got stuck in parts of ontogeny. The cognitive development of children and cognitive disruption in brain-damaged people became, in the 1930s, the major area of their research and their main claim to world renown in the decades following the master's untimely death in 1934.[107] That prudently lopsided development of the school can already be discerned in the 1920s, if only in embryo. Vygotsky first became involved with problems of child development as early as the Civil War, while he was teaching at a pedagogical institute in a small Belorussian town. The practical emphasis of his earliest writing on the subject was never lost, even when it was nominally subordinated to the grand theorizing that preoccupied him after moving to Moscow. The link to teacher training would keep his school alive during the years of high Stalinist insistence on practicality, when the whole discipline of psychology was threatened with destruction. On the other hand, the link of child development studies to a general 'historico-cultural' psychology never got very far beyond general pronouncements, not even in the 1920s.

At Kornilov's Institute there were colleagues working on comparative or animal or zoopsychology (it was called all three names, and not yet ethology). They were supposed to work out the levels of development below 'historico-cultural' psychology, and they had a tendency to stay down there, avoiding upward comparisons with human behavior. In the 1930s Stalinists would denounce them for reducing human psychology to bestial patterns, but the denunciation was quite unmerited. If anything, they deserved praise for cautioning Pavlov and Bekhterev against simplistic reduction of human psychology to supposedly universal patterns of conditioned reflexes. They argued for emergent levels of increasingly complex behavior, with full-fledged consciousness emerging at the human level, and they tended to restrict their investigations to worms, fish, and apes, stopping short of serious inquiry into continuities and discontinuities with the human level.[108] The little book that Vygotsky and Luria offered in 1930, as their first effort at such inquiry, ran into a stone wall of ideological disapproval.

One major feature of Vygotskian studies in child development has been entirely overlooked by admirers and commentators, whether Soviet or Western, since it is so common to the whole field: within the race of Cyclops the single eye goes unnoticed. That feature is the concentration on problem-solving, the virtual neglect of expressive understanding. Consider, for example, the report by Vygotsky and Luria of a conversation between a five-year-old boy and his mother. She called his attention to the planet Jupiter. He wanted to know 'For what [*zachem*] is Jupiter?' and refused to be turned away to naturalistic disregard of the question. His mother finally turned his question back upon him − 'And you and I, for what are we?' − to which the child instantly replied: 'For ourselves.' When the mother surrendered − 'Well, then, Jupiter also is for itself' − the boy was pleased and started a list: 'And ants, and bedbugs, and mosquitoes, and nettles − are they also for themselves?' As his mother wearily agreed, he laughed with joy. William Blake might have turned that into a poem, but Vygotsky and Luria repressed any joy with their Gradgrind analysis: 'In this conversation the child's primitive teleologism is quite characteristic. Jupiter must obligatorily exist for something. Precisely this "for what" [*zachem*] most often replaces, for the child, the more complex "by what rule" [*pochemu*].'*[109] And the two scientists pointed a warning finger at adults who continue such childlike thinking when they should have the scientific and practical turn of mind.

It is hard to believe that was written by the same scholar who began his investigation of the mind with sensitive analyses of imaginative literature, and had some familiarity with the philosophical tradition that pondered the difference between the thing in itself and the thing for itself. The further away from aesthetic studies, the deeper into psychology − even the part of the science that studies 'consciousness' − the more Vygotsky tended to repress his original concern with expressive thought, to ignore the effort to understand humanly as well as explain scientifically.[110]

I am tempted to picture Vygotsky, like the best literary artists, as a person in search of the essential self, but one turned increasingly away from the search by his determination to find the self in psychological science. Some future biographer, with full access to his papers, will perhaps discover how close to the man's inward life this guess may be. For present purposes the important issue is the collective mentality that he was assimilating, the functionalist ethos of professional psychologists in the twentieth century.

* *Pochemu* parallels *zachem* in linguistic construction: literally 'in accordance with what', contrasted to 'for what'. Both are usually translated into English as 'why'.

In their congregation the component elements of personality are explained by the functions they serve, the whole is the sum of those functions, efficiency is the measure of the integrating function, and any questions about an essential person are turned aside as relics of a bygone metaphysical inquiry into the spirit or soul.

All the subjects of this history were self-assertive individuals. Whether scientific psychologists or imaginative writers, neurophysiologists or political leaders, all sought to put themselves forward, to call attention to themselves, if only by publishing their individual names at the head of impersonal scientific studies. The anonymous labor of the toiling masses was not sufficient to express their sense of self. Yet each of these assertive types had a sharply different manner of self-expression.

The scientists put their names over works that claimed to exclude the subjective individual. Their proud assertion of authorship laid claim to impersonal knowledge of human beings as a natural species, not as subjective persons. Godlike arrogance inheres in such a claim. You may fancy yourself to be a person, the conscious center of your intentional life, but scientists know you to be an ephemeral specimen of replicating nervous systems and a replaceable part of an impersonal social system. There is an unwitting affinity here with the political leaders' claim to know the interests and the passions of the toiling masses better than subjective individuals within those masses know what they need and feel.

Both the scientific and the political claims seem to contrast sharply with the apparent humility of imaginative writers, who express the tormented or comic search for a self worth telling about. But the writers' overweening humility may contain an implicit challenge to godlike claims. Everyone can see that imaginative writers touch nerves of feeling and understanding of which political leaders claim mastery, and of which scientific psychologists claim impersonal knowledge. Writers and readers communing thus with each other implicitly push pretentious statesmen and scientists aside, toward irrelevance, maybe absurdity. Even if the whole business of that literary communion is imaginary, Soviet political leaders have taken far more interest, often alarmed or worried interest, in the apparently humble works of imaginative writers than in the apparently arrogant claims of psychological scientists.

I am groping for the reason why the boldest psychologists in the most liberal periods of Russian history — pre- as well as post-revolutionary — have been quite tame politically, have provoked only a little ideological controversy compared to the most creative imaginative writers. If one may indulge in antique language, the writers challenge politicians to struggle for our souls, while scientific psychologists turn away, striving to extricate themselves from any entanglement with the soul, the essence of a human being. The determined phenomenalism of modern science helps to win it acceptance — or toleration, or indifference — while the essentialism of imaginative writers keeps many people intensely interested, sometimes in awe, sometimes in anger.

Perhaps the oddest feature of these modern ways to knowledge of ourselves is the reverential credence widely given to neurophysiologists with sweeping claims. Pavlov and Bekhterev and Ukhtomskii were not content to work out neural circuitry but made vaulting extrapolations to mental and social functioning. Yet Bolshevik ideologists were largely deferential, quite gingerly in criticism. Indeed Pavlov was canonized, elevated above criticism along with Marx, whose claim to scientific knowledge Pavlov ridiculed. But that absurdist chapter in modern intellectual history belongs elsewhere, perhaps with the assimilation of behaviorism in the culture of God-fearing America.

10

The Truth in Neurophysiology

Neurophysiologists had a privileged stronghold in the human sciences, sheltered from the doubts cast upon psychologists. If you consider that only natural, since neurophysiology is a natural science — or perhaps you say 'hard', to distinguish it from a 'soft' science such as psychology — you are worshiping at the same shrine as the Bolsheviks. They revered the truth in natural science, and that reverence went beyond factual knowledge concerning nerves as physical systems; it gave license to theorizing that connected the nerves to the psyche and even to the social nature of human beings, where the Bolsheviks usually claimed a Marxist monopoly of truth. Pavlov was a champion of the game; he managed to hold the reverential favor of the new rulers while he wrote about 'the reflex of freedom' and 'the reflex of slavery', and openly scorned their Marxist claim of social science. His case is especially astonishing when we note that his hard science was soft in critical spots: his neural explanation of conditioned reflexes was increasingly at odds with factual knowledge concerning nerves as physical systems.

But his paradoxical triumph with a flawed physiology can be explained only in context, compared with less exceptional cases. We must pay special attention to neurophysiologists who were bolder than Pavlov in speculative leaps from neural facts to psychic and social hypotheses, but were more cautious with respect to neural facts. Or should I say more rigorous? They were more careful in distinguishing between proven neural processes and hypothetical ones, while they were bolder in grand extrapolations to mental and social processes. In the 1920s that style of finding the truth in neurophysiology enjoyed more Bolshevik favor than Pavlov's, but it would prove more vulnerable in the 1930s, when Stalinists revolted against rigorous distinctions between the little truths that are proven and the big truth that we hope to prove.

In the first place there was V. M. Bekhterev, who kept first place among

Russia's neurologists and psychiatrists under the new regime as under the old. Of course he had to repress his habit of openly criticizing the regime, as all his colleagues in the medical profession did. The only alternative was civil war, which the Bolsheviks won, or emigration, which did not alter their victory. It is not clear by what moves Bekhterev changed from outspoken critic of the old regime to quiet collaborator with the new. He seems to have resigned himself to the inevitable, by attributing the Bolshevik Revolution to the absence of self-governing habits among the masses, their lapse from 'patriotism' during the First World War, and their consequent susceptibility to 'demagogic internationalism'.[1] We can only speculate on the man's internal balance between political revulsion and professional concern for his large scientific enterprise. His Institute's private endowment vanished with the abolition of private capital; continuation of its government funds now depended on the abolitionists. The negotiating steps are not in the public record, only the result. By the spring of 1918 Bekhterev had budgetary support for his Psychoneurological Institute and a pledge for future expansion, to create an Institute of the Brain.[2]

Unlike Pavlov, who openly and long disapproved the regime from which he took support, Bekhterev soon began to find elements of shared ideology. He did not join the Communist Party or renounce the left liberal dreams he had eloquently expressed as a leader of the medical profession before 1917, when physicians were politically assertive. He continued to believe in Russia's need for a social order that fosters autonomous individuality — the essential source of modern civilization, in his view — but the belief turned from an immediate goal to a distant dream, while present disasters allied him to the Bolsheviks. In January 1920 he published an appeal to the countries of the Entente, asking them to lift the blockade of their former ally:

> Do you want the destruction in body and soul of your partners [*sobrat'ev*] who have absorbed a great deal from you, out of the inexhaustible source of your spiritual culture, and have contributed from their side a certain portion of creative activity to the rich treasurehouse of all-human knowledge? Obviously you do not! For we live on one planet, whatever the dissension of political tendencies, and our situation as neighbors cannot be set aside by any ultimatums, nor can cultural connections be broken. ... I appeal in particular to my own colleagues, the doctors of all countries, to whom human suffering is closer than to anyone else. Raise your voices on behalf of a nation that is biologically perishing. ...[3]

An émigré read careerist motives into Bekhterev's new politics, but we have no reason to do so. Famine, pestilence and war were in fact decimating Russia; even some émigré liberals began urging an armistice with the

Soviet regime, since it was the only possible Russian government, the only means to save the homeland from extinction.[4]

As if to compensate for the restriction of political expression, Bekhterev enlarged his scientific theorizing. From 1917 to his death in 1927 at the age of seventy, he brought out his grand summation, *The General Principles of Human Reflexology*, in four ever larger editions.[5] The book's physical volume more than tripled, as it came to encompass the universe, nothing less. He joined physiology and its psychological offshoot not only with biology at large but also with physics and astronomy, by interpreting their 'laws' as special cases of a universal pattern. Indeed he perceived the ontological ground of all in all. Matter had been shown to be a fiction; energy was the universal substance, whether expressed in solar fire, animal metabolism, or human thought. If he had read Lenin's polemic against such 'energeticism', he chose to ignore it.[6]

In 1921 Bekhterev even ventured bulkily into social science, with a large treatise on *Collective Reflexology*. That was where he incidentally explained the Russian Revolution. The masses, suddenly liberated but without previous experience of autonomous politics, readily succumbed to 'demagogic internationalism', and indifferently watched the country fall apart, leaving the Bolsheviks to put it back together. *Collective Reflexology* provoked a little flurry of polemics from the ideological establishment, most notably from V. I. Nevskii, who ranked below Bukharin or Trotsky in political standing but was closer to Leninist purity in creed.[7] (Lenin commissioned him to do a post-revolutionary update of *Materialism and Empiriocriticism*.) He did not battle with Bekhterev in neurophysiology; he called him back to the boundary imposed by specialization.

Nevskii mocked the notion of universal laws that rule the heavens, the earth, and the human mind. If they were not meaningless, they were absurd: sunspots correlated with human upheavals, thought transmitted by extrasensory waves. (When Bekhterev and his colleagues thought of a number, a gifted dog would bark that number of times.)[8] Nevskii ridiculed the reduction of social science to imaginary natural science, but he stopped respectfully short of any attack on the central idea of reflexology, the reduction of psychology to 'associative reflexes'. After all, there was a long tradition of left-wing reverence for physiology as the destroyer of religion in explanations of the mind. Bukharin was just discovering Pavlov within that revered tradition, and outsiders could hardly distinguish between the conditioned and the associative reflex. (The former was Pavlov's, the latter Bekhterev's.)

Nevskii did not even distinguish between Bekhterev's reflexology and Kornilov's reactology, which Bekhterev criticized for its subjectivism.[9] Journalists and philosophers were increasingly aware of that disagreement, and they were taking Kornilov's side in the mid-1920s. That is, they were

becoming aware of the difference between psychological science and reflexology, and were showing a preference for psychology, especially after
Vygotsky came on the scene. But no one urged the suppression of one in
favor of the other. Each discipline was supposed to be working in its own
way toward the comprehensive science of man — until the 1930s, when
both would suddenly be condemned as 'bourgeois', hopelessly alien to
authentic Soviet science.

Neurophysiologists were not of a single mind on reflexology, but they
wasted no time arguing about it in public. Those who were skeptical of
Bekhterev's extravagant union of their discipline with all other sciences and
even with the energetic all-in-one probably expressed themselves in the
closed meetings where funds were distributed among competing scientists
and institutes. Backstage charges of superficiality and speculation are alluded
to by present-day admirers of Bekhterev, who have bitter memories and
access to the archives.[10] They are happy to note that the master's grand
project prevailed over small minds and petty jealousies in the 1920s, but
they may not openly disapprove the sharp cutback that came in the 1930s,
for that is still official policy. Bekhterev's disciples must even now confine
themselves to neurology and psychiatry, narrowly construed.

An outside observer cannot miss the drastic change or fail to wonder
why. In the 1920s Soviet authorities supported Bekhterev's work not only
in basic neurophysiology, medical neurology, and psychiatry, but also in
the reflexological school of psychology, the psychophysiology of labor
(associated with a new field called 'the scientific organization of labor'), and
even in such fields as criminology and pedagogy. He and his disciples liked
to think of their Institute in Leningrad as 'a university of the human
sciences', and the dream won official sanction. In the mid-1920s the Institute
became the Academy of Psychoneurological Sciences, with seven constituent institutes and a very large staff.[11] When Bekhterev died in December
1927, *Izvestiia* featured President Kalinin's eulogy, stressing the great man's
scientific genius, his solidarity with the Soviet cause, and brushing aside his
problematic relationship with Marxist ideology.[12] But that was a brief
peak. By 1929 reflexologists were under ideological attack; in the 1930s the
doctrine would be condemned, the Academy dismantled, and Bekhterev's
reputation posthumously deflated. The persistent weight of self-limiting
specialists must have been present all along, overridden in the 1920s by
Bolshevik fondness for freewheeling theorists, revealing its crushing power
in the 1930s, when the Bolsheviks changed their mind.

We will have to ask later on what there was in the Stalinist mentality
that loudly insisted on the boldest breadth in theorizing and simultaneously
gave the triumph to narrow specialists. Here the problem is the fragile art
of the 1920s, the concealment of intellectual pluralism within world-
sweeping pictures of monistic unity. Bekhterev had been engaged in that
art since pre-revolutionary days. Not the mode of production but the reflex

concept was supposed to unify the human sciences. He deliberately stretched the concept to include all possible types of animal activity: not only the innate nerve action intended by 'reflex' in physiology (such as automatic retraction of a shocked paw — his model experiment — or automatic salivation when food or acid touch the mouth — Pavlov's model), but also the acquired habit intended by 'associative' or 'conditioned reflex' (such as retraction or salivation to a signal of forthcoming shock or food or acid), plus 'reflex' as any reaction of the whole animal to any signal (such as 'the orientation reflex', the turn of ears–head–body toward some sound or sight), and finally 'reflexology' as the study of conscious human behavior, including even such 'behavior' as silent thought.

Bekhterev and his disciples were obviously cousins of the American behaviorists, who were flourishing at the same time. They shared the dream of escape from subjectivity to a thoroughly 'hard' science. The most important difference would prove to be the ideological and political context, which encouraged behaviorism in the USA for a long time, while sustaining Bekhterev's reflexology in the USSR for a single decade. At the time the most important difference seemed to be the attachment of American behaviorism to the science of psychology, while Soviet reflexology had its base in physiology and seemed to demand the reduction of psychological science into physiology.

Kornilov and the other psychologists sought to avoid conflict by drawing lines of specialization: reflexology studies 'higher nervous activity', psychology studies psychic behavior. Bekhterev's school objected to that division as a continuation of mind–body dualism, the body to be studied objectively, the mind subjectively. They did not propose the suppression of psychology as an autonomous discipline; they argued that its goal should be reduction to reflexology in some long–run or metaphysical sense, not right away or literally. None of the parties to this academic dispute preached active intolerance. All endorsed, in theory, the principle of monistic unity, while respecting, in practice, the plurality of incongruent disciplines and schools in the human sciences. Fully in the spirit of the time, Kornilov's school tended to brush over its differences with reflexology. Bekhterev was less in tune with the time, more eager to advance the pretense of unity, with his theory as the synthetic organizer.

For a while that seemed a virtue rather than a self-destructive mania, especially when Bekhterev reached out to include Marxism within his synthesis. The move began as a comradely gesture in the preface to the 1923 edition of his *General Principles of Human Reflexology*. Without any taint of fawning, not even dropping Marx's name, much less Lenin's, Bekhterev simply recalled the famous maxim that 'being determines consciousness', not the other way round. Thus he sought to reinforce the argument that psychology must find ultimate explanations in reflexology.[13] In the next edition, sent to press in 1925, he inserted two little passages paying homage to Marx's explanations of social processes, trying to show that they were similar to reflexology.[14] In the same year he wrote a pamphlet defending reflexology against a Marxist critique, and so became entangled with the question, What constituted authentic Marxism?[15] Willy-nilly he was emerging from the privileged stronghold of pure 'hard' science, entering fields where explicit ideologies clashed.

His abiding purpose was 'to break the yoke of subjectivity in the scientific appraisal of those complex activities of the human organism which establish man's correlation with the environment'.[16] In 1926 he took his crusade to the philosophers, who were showing increasing approval of Kornilov's school, though not yet disapproving Bekhterev's. For *Under the Banner of Marxism*, the central journal of philosophy, Bekhterev wrote 'Dialectical Materialism and Reflexology', a dreary assemblage of long quotations and paraphrases from his previous works, laced with brief characterizations of Marxist views formulated so as to resemble his own.[17] The editors expressed satisfaction that 'some of the greatest natural scientists are turning to dialectical materialism', though 'stipulating their own disagreement with some of the authors' positions', left unspecified.[18] Death cut short Bekhterev's effort at accommodation with Marxism, but some of his disciples persevered, until they were told that theirs was an imperial expansion of reflex studies, incompatible with Marxism-Leninism.

Bekhterev's original base of support was not neurophysiology so much as the medical profession; he imagined that he carried it with him in his crusade for reflexology. Early in 1923 he could boast that three conferences of medical specialists had endorsed his proposal to make reflexology an obligatory course in all medical and pedagogical institutes.[19] But beyond that little gesture physicians were unwilling to go. Even his fellow neurologists and psychiatrists were largely cool to reflexology. Of little or no help in their practical work, it threatened to drag them into otiose ideological disputes. As for educationists (or pedagogical scientists, as they are called in the Soviet Union), Bekhterev could boast of their support, but he was bothered by its mushiness. He proudly quoted the praise that reflexology received from Dr Zalkind, a Party leader in education as well as psychiatry and psychology, but he could not explain why Zalkind had included some of the praise in a foreword to a philosopher's critique of reflexology.[20] Zalkind endorsed the philosopher's effort to restrict reflexology to the physiology of 'higher nervous activity'.

A similarly restrictive pattern came to prevail in 'pedology', the interdisciplinary study of children that was heavily promoted by the educational establishment. The chief journal of the field showed respect both for psychology and for reflexology, each in its proper place, complementary disciplines rather than rivals. That was itself an endorsement of Kornilov's attitude and a rebuke to ardent reflexologists, such as Dr A. G. Ivanov-Smolenskii, one of the very few psychiatrists devoted to the grand project of unifying the human sciences within reflexology. He attended the major Congress of Pedology in January 1928, and was upset to see a victory for Kornilov's school. Its leaders dominated the sessions on educational psychology and used the occasion to justify their 'subjectivist' viewpoint. Ivanov-Smolenskii went home and wrote a polemic, which unwittingly revealed a true believer's bitter sense of growing isolation, and preached the usual remedy: return to the true and original doctrine. He lamented Bekhterev's dilution of the basic truth by interpreting the reflex concept so loosely as to allow 'subjectivist' studies within his school. Pavlov seemed a truer prophet to Ivanov-Smolenskii – he had studied with both masters – because Pavlov stuck to the basic proposition that the physiological reflex is quite literally the elemental unit of which all animal behavior is compounded.[21]

Ivanov-Smolenskii could not calmly analyze the paradox that he was struggling to deny. Bekhterev was a nuts-and-bolts investigator of neural pathways, and for that reason could not be a reflexologist in a literal sense. In nuts-and-bolts neurophysiology the reflex explained only a small part of behavior, and anyhow the neuron was undermining the reflex arc as the elemental unit of explanation. The grand doctrine of reflexology could accommodate that situation only by resort to futuristic dreams: all psychic processes would someday be translated into behavioral processes, which would someday be explained by reflex arcs, which are compounded of neurons. That vision yearned toward a very remote future, contrasting sharply with the limited array of muscular twitches and glandular drips that could be linked with neural reflex arcs in existing laboratories.

To claim the all-inclusive power of reflexology in his own time Bekhterev simply denied the obligation to map the neural circuits of all behavior: 'Reflexology does not study the functions of the brain in a direct fashion, but studies the associative reflex activity of man, however it may be understood, and independently of this or that basis in the brain which this associative reflex activity may have.'[22] Thus he cut the physiological ground from beneath present-day reflexology, leaving himself only a philosophical or ideological pulpit to preach for a future physiology of the mind, against 'subjectivists' who would obstruct its realization. And he was ultimately self-defeating in such preaching, if only because the 'objectivist' faith that he expounded pointed away from the pulpit to the laboratory as the sacred place where truth is proved, not preached. In unadorned reality the particular truths to be found in the laboratory were insufficient for a mind that aspired to a great unifying truth. Yet he insisted on the laboratory as the temple of truth.

That was the cause of a persistent sponginess in the blows that Bekhterev struck for his cause. He might, for example, start with a jibe at Kornilov for claiming that his school of psychology was materialist since it acknowledged the psyche to be a function of the central nervous system. 'To say that the psyche is one of the manifestations of organized matter is quite similar to Molière's hero explaining the sleep-producing action of opium by its soporific quality.'[23] Bekhterev could not press that argument home, for he was in the same position. He had no more evidence than Kornilov to prove that particular mental processes are functions of particular brain processes. He denied that reflexology is obliged to prove such direct linkages, and seemed unaware that he had placed himself alongside Kornilov in the position of Molière's hero.

Similarly, when Bekhterev deplored the 'subjectivism' of Kornilov's school, he did so abstractly. He never demonstrated concrete instances of errors or arbitrary elements in the psychologists' work, which they might have avoided if they had followed the model of the associative reflex. Nor did he have enough sympathy with Bolshevism to pinpoint spots of ideological vulnerability in the work of psychologists. For example, he approved Kornilov's classification of personality types and the resulting rule of job placement: 'The transition from mental to physical work is easier than the reverse process.' He failed to see that the rule clashed with Bolshevik determination to 'push up' (*vydvigat'*) workers and peasants into managerial and intellectual occupations. Bekhterev merely complained vaguely that Kornilov's study of 'reactions', from which his personality types emerged, was 'not devoid of subjective coloring'.[24]

Against Pavlov Bekhterev did make one specific, telling criticism. He showed that Pavlov's essay on the 'reflex of freedom' and the 'reflex of slavery' was an expression of disgust with Russians for submitting to authoritarian rule.[25] Certainly it was not hard science. Bekhterev noted how arbitrary Pavlov was in his move from 'observations of one lively dog' to sweeping conclusions about inherited tendencies to freedom or slavery. But such effective thrusts were comparatively rare. More often Bekhterev's criticism of Pavlov seemed limited to proof of his own priority in the investigation of associative reflexes, as he chose to call them, and to the superiority of the motor reflexes that he used rather than the salivary reflex that Pavlov favored. Bekhterev did not develop his pre-revolutionary criticisms of Pavlov's imaginary neurology of the conditioned reflex, which seems surprising until one recalls that he expressly separated reflexology from obligatory demonstration of underlying neural processes. Other scientists, who accepted that obligation, were much keener critics of Pavlov's imaginary neurology.[26]

In short, Bekhterev organized a scientific school around a dream of unification in the human sciences. As he spelled out the dream, he contributed to the school's downfall, for he was pushing it too obviously out of the specialized safety of physiology, into the arena where ideologists and philosophers decided what Marxism required for the unification of the sciences. The trend that Ivanov-Smolenskii sensed in 1928 was brought home to other reflexologists in April 1929, when the Deborinite philosophers celebrated their supremacy over the 'mechanists'. At a large conference of Marxist-Leninist institutions philosophy was the central concern; psychology and physiology were distinctly subordinate issues, but even so the pattern could not be missed. The three speakers who considered psychology and physiology dissociated themselves from Bekhterev's synthetic project.[27] The speaker who must have been particularly galling was himself a reflexologist, associated with the Communist Academy's tiny Institute of Higher Nervous Activity. He reported that his group originally admired Bekhterev's theory, but recently decided that it goes against Marxism – and so too, he pugnaciously insisted, does Kornilov's psychology. Pavlov's doctrine, his group had decided, comes closest to the correct Marxist approach.[28]

He proved to be a prophet without honor, that pugnacious Pavlovian at the 1929 conference. He was Dr A. N. Zalmanzon (b. 1892), a psychiatrist and neurologist distinguished within the profession by his unusual involvement in Marxism and the Communist Academy. Brushed off in 1929 as a 'mechanist', he did not reappear at later conferences to claim credit for anticipating the Party line on Pavlov. That would have been a criminally presumptuous claim anyhow, but Zalmanzon was never tempted to make it; he vanished in the mid-1930s, a probable victim of the mass terror.[29]

Those who assume a rational explanation of his destiny will be disappointed. There is no one-to-one correlation between positions taken in disputes of the 1920s and victimization by terror in the 1930s. The other two who spoke on physiology and psychology at the April 1929 conference did not dispute Kornilov's approved ascendancy or anticipate the future line on Pavlov, yet they also would fall victim in the 1930s. Those unfortunates were Dr A. B. Zalkind (b. 1888), who would be publicly cursed in 1936 for killing himself as denunciations grew against him,[30] and Dr I. D. Sapir (b. 1897), who ranked just below Zalkind in the 1920s as a Party leader among physicians and physiologists. He was exiled from Moscow to Mogilev in the early 1930s, sank into uncharacteristic silence, and resurfaced after the War in far-off Krasnoiarsk, which suggests some years in the Siberian camps.[31] The Jewish taint in all three was probably less fateful than their political eccentricity: they stepped out from the crowd by joining the Party and preaching Marxism in the 1920s, when scientific specialists were free to be their usual unpolitical non-Marxist selves. In the 1930s, when the administrators of terror raked over everyone's past, such eccentricity must have seemed suspicious.

Those who stayed low as water and still as grass were the large majority of scientific specialists in post- as in pre-revolutionary Russia, or in any other twentieth-century country. Narrowly focused on limited projects, they paid scant attention to philosophical or ideological debates at the outer bounds of their safe disciplines. Only a small minority of neurophysiologists participated in discussions of their relationship to psychology, and to the mind-body problem that 'you won't see if you don't look at it'. The Revolution did not change that basic division between the fraction that speaks to large issues and the majority that is obscurely absorbed in mundane research and teaching. Before 1917 the articulate minority probably spoke for the rest when they advocated 'psychology without any metaphysics', but probably not when they backed up the slogan with neo-Kantian arguments on the essential unknowability of things in themselves, whether mind *or* body. After 1917 very few persisted with such talk;[32] accommodation with Marxist materialism became the new slogan of the articulate minority. Since their supporting arguments had less to do with Marxism than with the grand theories of famous scientists, the silent majority of specialists might conceivably have become involved, if the grand theories had been rich with implications for mundane research and teaching. But they were not.

Bekhterev did have disciples, who proved their commitment by continuing to stand up for reflexology after the ideological establishment turned against it. Twice in 1929 the Bekhterev Institute of the Brain held conferences to discuss the growing official disapproval of their creed. In the spring they defined the issue as a choice: 'Reflexology or Psychology'.[33] Later in the year, giving way but not giving in, they redefined the issue as a conjunction: 'Reflexology and Neighboring Tendencies'.[34] The either-or choice that they discussed in the spring moved them to some self-criticism, but mostly to reaffirmation of the faith, which was put into a formal resolution:

> One cannot fail to recognize as firmly proven that reflexology is not reducible to the morphology and physiology of the nervous system (as it seems to its opponents); it is an autonomous science, which studies all of man's coordinating activity as a developing system of his active relationship to the surrounding world.[35]

The both-and formula that they discussed later in the year provoked more self-criticism and a formal resolution that looks at first glance like an act of self-destruction by the school. They resolved that the war of schools was deplorable, and offered reconciliation with 'the reactological trend of Kornilov, behaviorism, the theory of conditioned reflexes [that is, Pavlov's doctrine], and the materialist part of research in structural psychology', by which they obviously meant the Vygotskian trend.[36] That plea for peace implicitly cut back reflexology from the grand all-in-one discipline to one among others, and crippling self-criticism did not stop there. The disciples of Bekhterev pledged to give up the social study of human beings to Marxist sociology (or historical materialism), and to concede that the mind requires independent studies of consciousness. Such divestitures would logically shrink reflexology into neurophysiology. But Bekhterev's disciples managed, however inconsistently, to affirm once again the all-embracing nature of reflexology. Their speeches showed continuing faith in their imperial dream, not in the self-restriction that they put into the formal resolution at the end of the conference. But it would prove to be a dream without substance, as the faithful lost the right of universal sloganeering to Marxism-Leninism and its official ideologists. There was no concrete research program to link neurophysiology with the all-in-one.

If one searches, one can find a happier case than Bekhterev's, that is, a scientist who captivated Marxist-Leninists in the 1920s, when it was not compulsory to court their approval, yet escaped repudiation in the decades following. A. A. Ukhtomskii was such an exceptional case – unique, I would say. He enthralled Soviet Marxists, though he should have been a scandalous offense. He was worse than a 'bourgeois specialist', he was highborn, an actual prince, and his face avowed religious faith even when his mouth was shut: his beard tumbled untrimmed toward his waist in the style of an Orthodox monk. (The Bible says we are made in God's image; it does not say that God cut a single hair of the Almighty Beard.) Ukhtomskii combined the narrowest investigation of neural circuitry with the broadest traffic between scientific and philosophical concepts. And it is there, in his vivid facility with such metaphorical intercourse, that one finds his appeal to Soviet Marxists. He satisfied their yearning to find expressive meaning in physiological explanations of ourselves, and vice versa, scientific justification of expressive meaning.

Until 1917, when he turned forty-two, Prince Ukhtomskii showed the world a neatly trimmed stylish beard (like Freud's), and limited his publications to neurophysiology narrowly construed. Inwardly he was making a circuitous journey from the banal outlook of his father, who cultivated court circles on behalf of his sons' careers, through religion and philosophy to experimental science, searching for 'the path to absolute truth'.[37] First an older brother and then Aleksei upset the father by going from an elite military school to St Sergius Trinity Monastery, a walled-in medieval complex near Moscow where priests are still trained and services are chanted before the Saint's black mummy in an open gold coffin. (It may be brass but it shines like gold.) The older brother stayed with his religious calling, as a missionary to Siberian pagans, ultimately as a bishop. Aleksei, who loved to read Spinoza and Hegel, decided to 'steel himself' by studying physiology. Exactly what he intended by that phrase is no doubt spelled out in the diary from which a Soviet biographer has taken only timid fragments.[38] The frustrated reader is left guessing at the faith that Ukhtomskii was putting to the test, and at the world view that was developing from the interaction of religion, philosophy, and experimental biology. He did not publish his deepest thoughts until middle age, after the Revolution provoked him to bear witness, perhaps by its sharp attack on religious faith.

In the patriotic canon of Soviet historians Sechenov trained N. E.

Vvedenskii to take his place as chief physiologist at St Petersburg University, and both trained Ukhtomskii to step in when Vvedenskii died in 1922. Thus a distinctively Sechenovian line was preserved in neurophysiology. That is historically accurate, but it is also true that the line was basically similar to the one called Sherringtonian in the West. We need not guess at the likeness. Ukhtomskii was so taken by Sherrington's classic, *The Integrative Action of the Nervous System* (1906), that he published a Russian summary of it in 1910.[39] No envy was mixed in his admiration, no claim that Vvedenskii and he had anticipated Sherrington's central discoveries: reciprocal innervation and the final common path. Soviet writers who have been making such claims since the 1940s either ignore their hero's deference to Sherrington or disapprove of it. Both the big man's deference and the little men's claim of Russian priority on his behalf are evidence of an international community, a shared outlook that has persistently spanned the national separation of Russian from Western countries.

To be precise, a shared *physiological* viewpoint has united English- and Russian-speaking specialists, while pushing them toward divided opinions on the psyche, which is carefully excluded from their common approach to the nervous system. Their physical methods of correlating structure and function in nervous systems restricted consensus for the most part to the puppet animal — Sherrington's term for 'preparations' with the cortex peeled from the brain or the whole cerebrum removed — and to microscopic analysis of bioelectric discharge across synapses. The excluded higher levels of nerve function have constantly beckoned thoughtful neurophysiologists to speculations about the psyche, which resist translation into precise hypotheses for physiological testing. Sherrington's intuition was plainly dualist: the psyche, he was sure, is accessible only to expressive understanding, as in everyday conversation and imaginative literature, which cannot be reduced to neural analysis.[40] Such dualism has been a persistent tradition among leading neurophysiologists in the English-speaking world. In Russia the dominant tradition among articulate physiologists has been speculative groping for some monistic principle.

Bekhterev's prominence was partly due to his taking the lead in such speculation, which he tended to present as established science, centered in neurology, thereby flattering the self-importance of physiologists and the medical profession at large. Ukhtomskii offered a different type of monistic speculation: far less scientistic than Bekhterev's, far more inclined to draw on literary and philosophical modes of thought, even at the risk of dissolving physiological concepts while ostensibly fusing them with psychological concepts and expressive values. We may call this the Freud phenomenon, to honor the supreme master of the hybrid art, which reached its apogee in the first half of our century, when some great minds were still struggling to keep the culture whole. Ukhtomskii's contribution was 'the dominant', supposedly a physiological concept, actually a product of his

unusual journey through religion and philosophy to physiology, which
was brought to grand theorizing by the Soviet cultural revolution in its
initial stage of genteel integration.

At first the Bolshevik Revolution provoked 'dismay and wavering' in
Ukhtomskii.[41] He went away from Petrograd, as he had in 1905, but some
experience of the Civil War, only vaguely suggested by his timid biographer, sent him back, prepared to 'accept' the Soviet regime, and even to
cooperate with it. Late in 1919 he won Bolshevik gratitude by willing
participation in the 'workers' faculty' at Petrograd University, and again in
1920 by standing for election to the city soviet. Those symbolic acts of
'acceptance' helped to reassure the Bolsheviks that this outspokenly religious scientist was not an enemy. Positive friendship began in 1923, when
Ukhtomskii started to publish his thoughts on 'the dominant' (*dominanta*,
the same as the musical term). He plainly declared that he was taking the
word and the idea from Avenarius, the German physiologist and positivist
philosopher whom Lenin had castigated for 'idealism', if not 'fideism'.[42]
Soviet Marxists seemed not to know or care what Lenin would have
thought. They listened with awed respect when Ukhtomskii spoke on the
dominant at the Psychoneurological Congress of January 1924; they
published him on the subject in the *Herald of the Communist Academy*, and
they continued to treat 'the dominant' with uncritical respect even in the
worst periods of hostility to 'bourgeois' science.

On the level of experimental physiology the term signified the capacity
of one nerve center to dominate the activity of others. Ukhtomskii's
favorite introductory example was the inhibition of leg movements in a
defecating cat.[43] He and Vvedenskii had observed it within the laboratory,
while administering small electric charges to the parts of the brain that
excite movements in the legs. The onset of bowel movement suspended leg
movement, suggesting a temporary subordination of one neural network
to another, 'the dominant'. Ukhtomskii extrapolated from that to the
everyday observation that a free cat becomes 'rooted to the spot' when
defecating. He leaped from there to the universal observation that the
human mind, when intensely concentrated either in deep thought or great
emotion, shuts off many sensory inputs. His intuition made many such
extrapolations, downward from the defecating cat to experimental testing
of neural impulses and motions in the jellyfish, and also upward to a host
of mental examples in human beings. He felt free to invoke, in illustration
of the dominant, the description of Natasha's feelings in *War and Peace* or
the analysis of insomnia in a poem by Pushkin. The overall effect of
Ukhtomskii's theorizing was a sense of vibrant oneness in the living universe, somewhat disturbing but thereby also thrilling to the belief that a
distinctively human meaning inheres in nature, to be realized by the two-
legged animal that reasons.

Style is essential to such thinking, which may easily provoke mocking laughter among twentieth-century minds, fearful of transgressing the limits that confine them. Perhaps Ukhtomskii's religion overcame his share of that fear. Whatever the personal source of his calm grandeur, the public result was most effective. He did not put his audience on guard by defensive display of abstract philosophy or other elaborate shields against ridicule. With infectious ease he went straight through vivid instances of the dominant, taken from laboratory experience, everyday observation, and literary art, to illuminate the human place in nature and its implications for human values. He laid out his grand vision without a trace of Pavlov's belligerent self-certainty or Bekhterev's imperial condescension. He even knew how to disagree pleasantly. He did not, for example, name Pavlov or Bekhterev when he argued against the reductive views for which they were famous. He named them only when approving other features of their work, and managed to sound approving even when contrasting Pavlov's hypothetical neurology with his own guess about the neural basis of conditioned reflexes. His was, he stressed, no less a guess than Pavlov's, and both must remain so, for neurophysiology was unable as yet to test either.[44] Christian charity – or diplomacy? – kept him from noting that Pavlov presented his guess as if it were proven.

The most impressive display of Ukhtomskii's unique appeal was a lecture to students at Leningrad University, which was published by the Communist Academy in 1927 and republished both at the rigid climax of Stalinist hysteria (1950) and during the post-Stalin relaxation.[45] He opened with apparent acceptance of the belief that the reflex is the elementary unit of all behavior, only to subordinate both concepts, reflex and behavior, to 'the dominant'. Sherrington had declared the reflex to be an 'artificial abstraction',[46] but Ukhtomskii avoided such a provocation to the common sense of things. Not only specialists but all sharers in modern culture know that the pupil contracts when light shines in, the leg jerks when a tendon is struck, the sphincter opens to a dose of salts. Ukhtomskii relaxed such rigidly stereotyped thought by offering experimental evidence of deviations from the fixed pattern, such as 'reflex reversal': the emetic that can cause defecation, the purgative that can cause vomiting, the response depending on the manner of administering the stimulus and on the state of the whole organism. Thus he worked up to his central physiological principle: each neural subsystem operates in labile fashion, depending on the purposeful operation of the whole system.

'Whole system', properly speaking, is the organism up and doing within its natural environment, rather than the drowsy dog trained to stand quietly in a laboratory harness while its separate subsystems are tested with arbitrary buzzers, flashes of light, and electric shocks. Such artificial conditions sustain the belief that living systems operate according to the principle of least action, the inertial aimless way of non-living systems. That belief, Ukhtomskii argued, is the ground of faith in the invariant reflex arc as the element of all behavior, and of the conviction that the whole organism is 'an aggregate of reflex arcs more or less accidentally tied in a bundle'.[47] He did not say 'Pavlov' or 'Bekhterev' when he disagreed with that conviction. Vygotsky had named them both, when he denied that the brain is 'a hotel for a series of conditioned reflexes accidentally stopping in.'[48] Ukhtomskii may have liked that wisecrack, but he was irenic rather than contentious, for his vision dwelt, not on the unresolved tensions of opposed schools, but on the harmony that could be achieved by subordinating them to 'the dominant'.

He did not make heavy use of opposed abstractions such as holistic and reductive, systemic and atomistic, dynamic and static, though his thought lends itself to such philosophizing. By favoring homelier abstractions and abundant concrete examples, Ukhtomskii made his case for dynamic holism far more effectively. He also avoided the abstract opposition of vitalism and mechanism, while he shielded his theorizing from suspicion of vitalism, which is forbidden to twentieth-century minds. He proved that his thought was mechanistic, without using the word, by contrasting the law of least action with the persistent disequilibrium in the living organism's absorption of energy from its environment — its lifelong reversal of entropy, as Schrödinger would say.[49] Ukhtomskii also stressed the high level of randomness and inefficiency in vital processes such as reproduction, which he summed up in a neat apothegm: 'Life is obviously wasteful, expansive.'[50] That artful admission of persistent loss — 'wasteful' — as the other side of persistent gain — 'expansive' — was his typical way of running together evaluative judgment and scientific report. Starting so unobtrusively, he rose to numinous metaphors as if they were self-evident generalizations of factual science. He noted the persistent appearance in aging creatures of 'the scholastic dominant', as he called the uncritical subordination of present experience to the stereotyped past. Against that 'scholastic dominant' he set 'the dominant of youth, in which nothing has as yet been subordinated to sclerosis and necrosis, but life is broad and entirely open to what is ahead.'[51]

Ukhtomskii did not dispense easy optimism. He stressed the open-ended, uncertain nature of human experience, and came thus to talk of 'man's tragedy'. He found it in the lack of 'a portable, convenient, handy "criterion of truth", *except for the real test of man's expectations in direct collision with concrete actuality.*' Great men, he declared, take humanity into especially great collisions. There was not only an echo of Nietzsche in that passage but also a disturbing reminder of Soviet talk about 'the great experiment' that Bolshevik leaders had started. If the audience sensed that suggestion, they must have been thrilled by the daring of this man with the wild religious beard, and also by his reassurance that tragic waste was the natural price of progress. Bolsheviks and fellow-travelers, earnestly striving to transform backward Russia, must have been especially thrilled to hear him insist that 'the whole task of human culture' is to improve ourselves, to create new reflexes and instincts: 'We are not observers of being but participants in it. Our behavior is labor.'[52]

At that grand level of disagreement with behaviorism and reflexology, defending a central concept of Hegel's and Marx's (*praxis*) against the central concept of Pavlov and Bekhterev (reflexive behavior) and enhancing his expressive utterance by keeping those distracting names out of it, Ukhtomskii had an irresistible appeal to Soviet Marxists. When he talked openly of God and the soul, they might grumble,[53] but they could hardly object when he transformed love-thy-neighbor into a scientific concept: 'the dominant on the person of the other [*dominanta na litso drugogo*]'. By that he meant the capacity to put oneself in another's life, to understand the other person as 'an independent essence [*sushchestvo*]'. He conceded that this ultimate dominant was only a dream so far, but insisted that the dream must be a pledge of future reality. It was essential to overcome 'the curse of a selfish [*individualisticheskoe*] relation to life, a selfish world view, a selfish science. . . . From the moment that the person of the other is revealed, man himself for the first time deserves to be spoken of as a person.'[54] It may have been obvious to many Soviet Marxists that this peroration was a thinly disguised appeal to acknowledge the soul or personhood as the essence of a human being, but they could hardly call Ukhtomskii back to the science that has no place for soul or essence. Marxism was itself too vulnerable to such disheartening separation of hope from experience; Marxists were eager to be reassured that heroic dreams are scientifically justified.

Specialists in physiology also listened benevolently, making no objection to Ukhtomskii's elevation of their discipline into prophetic vision. The dignity conferred on the narrow discipline could not be harmful, for Ukhtomskii kept each thing in its proper place. He did not try to force the metaphorical meanings of 'the dominant' back into the experimental science from which he derived it. Within neurophysiology he was content to emphasize the labile, systemic nature of functions that are usually considered invariant operations of subsystems. (See again the emetic that can act as a purgative, and vice versa.) When particular cases of that sort were at issue, Ukhtomskii and the rest of the profession discussed them in the customary terms, without reference to the dominant. The concept hovered somewhere between science and philosophy, too modest to enter and become a permanent presence, or a nuisance, in either.

PAVLOV AND HIS CRITICS

Ukhtomskii was not unique in his gentle way of disagreeing with Pavlov on the neural explanation of conditioning. Indeed, he was somewhat less indulgent than most of the physiologists who commented publicly on

Pavlov's doctrine, for he called attention to the unsubstantiated guesswork in it. The usual pattern was to heap praise on Pavlov's experimental investigation of learned behavior, and to pass over his hypothetical neural explanations without criticism. In short, the professional community gave Pavlov courteously imprecise praise. They liked, or they quietly tolerated, his combination of rigorous laboratory technique and freewheeling speculation, which was laying claim to the 'higher nervous activity' that mediates learned behavior, hitherto a closed world to neurophysiologists. He was compared to Galileo, Newton, Darwin, and Einstein — by fellow specialists who knew that his hypotheses were at odds with their knowledge. When Pavlov turned seventy-five, in 1924, he received a gratifying heap of such tributes.[55]

In private Pavlov and his disciples remembered other reactions, such as Sherrington's amused condescension during a visit to St Petersburg in 1912. Dogs conditioned to salivate at a painful electric shock — because food was presented after the shock — reminded him of saints who welcomed martyrdom as a signal of salvation.[56] Pavlov defiantly interpreted that as a tribute, though he was angrily aware that Sherrington did not accept his neural explanations, and considered his doctrine no more a part of physiological science than the metaphorical equation of tortured dogs and martyred saints. Pavlov also kept in mind the advice of an eminent Swedish physiologist who was a close enough friend to speak plainly: 'Drop that fad and get back to real physiology.'[57] From his first paper on conditioning (1903) until the mid-1920s such offhand criticism was the only sort he received from fellow neurophysiologists.

He should have known that the Galileo or Darwin of 'higher nervous activity' would have had a more vigorous response. He boasted 'a hundred collaborators',[58] but they were actually subordinates, disciples perhaps, working in his laboratories under his stern direction. When they gave papers to physiological conferences — charts of precisely measured stimuli and responses arranged within the master's constructs of neural analyzers and temporary connections, cortical irradiation and concentration, inhibition and disinhibition — one or two outsiders, Bekhterev most notably, might rise in the discussion period to point out discrepancies with commonly known facts and generally accepted beliefs.[59] But outsiders were not sufficiently provoked or intrigued to try Pavlovian experiments for themselves and see if they could improve the hypothetical explanations, until the mid-1920s. Even then very few took the trouble, and Pavlov was not overjoyed to see his celebrity tarnished by serious interest. For it was critical. A first step of the first scientists who took him seriously was to correct the obvious flaws in his 'neurologizing'.[60]

'Cortical dogmatism' is the usual shorthand for the most obvious flaw, Pavlov's stubborn assignment of all learned behavior to 'temporary connections' in the cerebral cortex. The other side of that central dogma was his near indifference to subcortical structures and processes. It was quite paradoxical, that combination of cortical localization with a sweeping reduction of all learned behavior to the conditioned reflex. In the highest level of the most advanced nervous systems he located the mechanism of a very primitive mode of learned behavior, the conditioned reflex, and he refused to think of other modes. He assumed two levels of animal reaction to stimuli: the unlearned, inborn or unconditioned reflex, which is mediated by the subcortical brain and spinal cord, and the learned or conditioned reflex, which is mediated by the cerebral cortex. In Pavlov's doctrine those two types of reflex were the elemental units of which all behavior is compounded, as matter is compounded of atoms and molecules.

That simple assumption provoked both neurological and evolutionary objections. A dog whose cortex has been peeled off, after recovering from the surgery, learns once again to salivate on hearing a buzzer or to retract a threatened paw when a light signals imminent electric shock. Many animals in the natural state reinforce the objection. Far down the evolutionary scale, where animals get through life without a cerebral cortex or even without a brain or spinal cord, individual behavior is constantly adapted to changing circumstances as signaled by patterns of changing stimuli. Earthworms learn. Their nervous system is vastly simpler than the dog's, and so too is their repertoire of learned behavior, but conditioning is within their brainless ken. A worm in a T-shaped tube filled with earth will learn to avoid the arm of the T that is soaked with salt, to move routinely to the arm that contains food. In 1906 an American zoologist published a host of such findings even in protozoans, which have no nerves, only a primitive forecast of them.[61]

Of course, one might argue that the cerebral cortex of higher animals plays a critical part in integrating the most primitive types of acquired reaction, such as the conditioned reflex, with the most advanced, such as thought and willful action. The dog without a cortex will learn to salivate at a ringing bell but will not respond to his name; he can be conditioned to retract a paw when a light flashes, but he stumbles about without visual comprehension of his surroundings. He hears and sees without understanding, if one may retreat from 'objective psychology' to the common-sense language of Hermann Munk, a slightly older physiologist than Pavlov, who did pioneer studies of the decorticate dog.[62]

Pavlov stubbornly refused to make such a retreat, or to confront the evolutionary problem. To admit qualitatively different levels of behavior seemed to him an abandonment of mechanistic determinism at the higher levels, a surrender to subjectivity, the enemy of science. There were two levels and no more. The most complex patterns of human behavior would ultimately be shown to be great chains of conditioned reflexes, reinforced by unconditioned stimuli. To be sure, there were moments when he seemed to falter, to acknowledge that the neural mechanisms of conditioning were unknown, that speech and conscious thought might be qualitatively different from conditioned reflexes, that subjective psychology might still be of some value in understanding human beings. But those lapses are properly appreciated only as dark moments, accenting not altering the interpretive scheme that he brought to bear. Most often he simply ignored the reasons to doubt that his binary scheme could contain the overflowing diversity of animal behavior, or that his imaginary circuits could map the nervous systems which accomplish even the simplest conditioned reflex.

Some of the contrary evidence appeared within his own laboratories, in spite of experiments rigorously designed to exclude the unmanageable complexities of natural behavior. Milk-fed puppies were a revealing case in point. One of Pavlov's disciples kept newborn puppies on a milk diet for several months and then checked to see if they salivated at the first sight and smell of meat.[63] They did not, and Pavlov was delighted to report that fact repeatedly, as evidence that instinct, inborn proclivities, need not be inserted in his binary classification between unconditioned and conditioned reflexes. In his summation of the mid-1920s, *Lectures on the Work of the Cerebral Hemispheres*, he told of the clean-slate puppy mind this way: '... All by itself the sight of food is not a stimulus of the salivary reaction, is not an agent connected with it before birth. Only when these puppies had eaten bread and meat several times, only then did the sight alone of bread and meat start the flow of saliva.'[64]

A hard judge might convict Pavlov of misrepresentation, for his subordinate had clearly reported something else. When first shown meat, the milk-fed puppies strained to get at it, and a single taste was enough to establish subsequent salivation at the sight and smell. Nor would that reaction fade away in the absence of reinforcement, as salivation to a buzzer or a light – 'indifferent stimuli', in Pavlov's vocabulary – fades away when food repeatedly fails to follow. The disciple felt that one must distinguish 'natural conditioned reflexes', which are easily and permanently established, from 'artificial conditioned reflexes', the occasional, transient reactions to truly indifferent stimuli. Pavlov not only rejected this blurring of the distinction between unconditioned and conditioned reflexes, which raised the specter of instinct; he mis-stated the facts, when he declared that 'several' experiences of meat-eating were necessary to establish salivation at the sight. He avoided plain falsehood by lumping bread with meat, and by omitting reference to the smell.

A crucial difficulty, which Pavlov did not glide past with slippery phrasing, was the failure of his laboratories to establish extended chains of conditioned reflexes. They were essential to his insistence that the most complex forms of behavior are actually compounds of many conditioned reflexes, ultimately reinforced by some unconditioned stimulus. To prove that hypothesis it was necessary to show that a dog would salivate not only when a buzzer signalled the approach of food, but also when a black square in the dog's field of vision signalled the imminent buzzer, and when a metronome signalled the square which signalled the buzzer which signalled the food — and so on indefinitely. Otherwise, how explain the multitude of animal activities that have no proximate reinforcement of the unconditioned sort? No food or drink or sexual congress rewards the busy dog making his inquisitive rounds with reflexive pissing on posts and stiff-legged scratching of the earth, or the human in sedentary thought seeking the solution to a mathematical problem or perfection in some lines of poetry. In Pavlovian experiments it was extremely difficult to achieve a chained reflex of only two links; three were an exceptional triumph of experimental cunning, and therefore readily disputable as evidence of the nervous system's normal functioning. Beyond three links Pavlov himself acknowledged failure, so far.[65] One could always hope for the concealed obstacle discovered, the breakthrough to proof that endless chains of conditioned reflexes do bind all learned behavior to some primal unconditioned stimuli.

Such were the difficulties encountered within Pavlov's laboratories, where most of the Russian work on conditioning was done. From outside his realm of direct control criticism came in four converging streams — mere trickles at first. First there was V. A. Vagner, the zoologist who founded comparative or animal psychology in Russia. He was arguing even before the 1920s that patterns of behavior must be classified on a scale of evolutionary emergence, rising from tropisms to authentically learned behavior, with human speech and conscious thought at the most advanced level, remotely linked to the foot's jerk from the fire or the mouth's watering at the fictive representation of a cut lemon.[66] In the 1920s other comparative psychologists picked up this sort of criticism, most notably V. M. Borovskii, a leader of the struggle for a Marxist psychology who was in charge of comparative or 'zoopsychology' at Kornilov's Institute.[67] Psychologists who had little interest in subhuman animals or in neural explanations of conditioning intermittently objected to Pavlov's simplistic, reductive view of the conscious mind — sometimes with dramatic effect, as in Vygotsky's speech to the Psychoneurological Congress of January 1924.[68] Signs of discomfort also appeared among psychiatrists and neurologists who specialized in the study of brain-damaged people. Their habitual respect for 'pure' research extended to Pavlov, but it was occasionally clouded by realization that their empirical correlation of mental disorders with physiological disruptions was at odds with his rigid insistence on physiology alone, his effort to banish mental concepts from brain studies.[69] Finally, and most important, neurophysiologists and neuropsychologists outside Pavlov's laboratories began in the 1920s to offer their specialist criticism, directly bearing on Pavlov's central arguments, for some of them began to imitate his experimental correlation of brain processes and learned behavior, and immediately diverged from his picture of the brain processes.

It is not mean, it is magnanimous to approach Pavlov this way, through the slowly gathering judgments of serious critics. Their objections to his doctrine disclosed its significance. He was too vain or too zealous to appreciate that dialectical process, but it rescued a major place for him in the history of brain studies. If the community of neurophysiologists had gone on smiling with inane courtesy, as they did during the first twenty years of his effort to be the Galileo of 'higher nervous activity', we would have to classify Pavlov as another Bekhterev: a physiologist who drained significance from his narrow discipline by extending it so broadly, flattering it with speculative universality.

Certainly Pavlov had a tendency in that direction. Witness his essays on such 'reflexes' as purpose, freedom, and slavery, or his talk of the 'investigative or what-is-this? reflex' to explain a dog's general alert at an unexpected sound or sight. Physiologists had to ponder the latter — the orientation reflex, as they came to call it — for it preceded the conditioned reflex in Pavlov's experiments, and he offered hypothetical processes in the cortex to explain how a general alert shrinks into mere salivation. But they could ignore his 'reflexes' of purpose, freedom, or slavery, for Pavlov indulged only occasionally in such rhetoric and never offered neural mechanisms in explanation of them. His imagination was mostly confined within the laboratory. He was sufficiently narrow-minded to believe that his salivation experiments would prove the universal explanatory power of the reflex concept, literally, while Bekhterev had enough breadth and flexibility to split the concept, to separate its literal laboratory meaning from an extended set of metaphorical meanings, suitable for universal application in speculative books. Pavlov was so insistent in presenting his speculation as 'the language of facts', so intent on entangling his hypothetical explanations in heaps of experimental data, that a few physiologists outside his corps of subordinates were finally challenged to take up the project, to try to improve his audacious venture into the neurophysiology of learned behavior.

I. S. Beritov was the first, and probably the most significant, of those outsiders. He emerged in the line of neurophysiological thought that ran from Sechenov through N. E. Vvedenskii to Ukhtomskii, who did graduate work alongside Beritov in Vvedenskii's laboratory at St Petersburg University from 1908 to 1912. Then Beritov went off to Kazan University, to study electrophysiology with Samoilov, another student of Sechenov's. On the eve of the First World War he finished off his graduate training in the West, working with an eminent Dutch physiologist who did precise mapping of the complex neural mechanisms that accomplish subconscious feats, such as walking, or simply holding the body erect.[70] The realm of the psyche was excluded from Beritov's studies until 1915, when he joined the faculty of Odessa University and became a fully independent scientist. There, aged thirty, he started his lifelong effort to extend physiological science into 'the neuropsychic activity of the brain's cortex',[71] beginning with critical reflection on Bekhterev's and Pavlov's doctrines. The associative or conditioned or individually acquired reflex attracted Beritov as a problem at the boundary, where the neurophysiologist may glimpse connections between brain and mind.

It is tempting to think that Beritov was returning Sechenov's school to the large problem that the founder had vainly struggled with and abandoned back in the 1860s. To be sure, Beritov's earliest articles on the subject contained no references to Sechenov. It was Bekhterev and Pavlov who had inspired him to do conditioning experiments, and he gave them explicit, generous credit. He even declared that 'Pavlov and his followers ... have explained the fundamental laws' of individually acquired activity of the central nervous system.[72] Yet those first articles also revealed disagreement with Pavlov on two fundamental issues that had long separated Sechenov's students from him: Pavlov was impatient to leap over fine-scale neural processes in the effort to explain higher nervous activity, while Sechenov's students had an obsessive interest in them; and Pavlov was obsessively bent on the exclusion of psychic concepts from the effort, while the Sechenovian school was sufficiently relaxed to use them. Beritov's initial choice of conceptual terms, 'the *neuropsychic* activity of the cerebral cortex', pointed away from Pavlov's strict insistence on physiology alone, toward the hybrid discipline, 'neuropsychology'. Within a few years he would be writing plainly of memory, a term that Pavlov avoided, and even of the 'representation' (*predstavlenie, Vorstellung*) that guides a dog to the place where it remembers finding food. If not consciously aware that Sechenov had inserted a psychic element in 'reflexes of the brain',[73] Beritov was unwittingly retracing the founder's way.

Toward the end of his long life Beritov recalled his initial teaching experience in Odessa as the time he 'first sensed the profound difference between Pavlov's theoretical representations [*predstavleniia*] of this activity [conditioned reflexes] and the laws of central [nervous] activity which I was teaching to my classes.'[74] But at other times he recalled that he had been Pavlovian in his first articles on conditioning, and pictured himself breaking away in the late 1920s and early 1930s. His actual publications in the mid-1920s can sustain either recollection: they were full of praise for Pavlov's doctrine, but they firmly corrected its hypothetical neurology. The corrections were more important than the praise, for Beritov published in prestigious English and German journals, so his work struck the worldwide communities of physiologists and psychologists as the first extended critique of Pavlov's neural doctrine. That is how Beritov won an international reputation.[75] Evidently the young scientist had an instinct for the vulnerable points of a famous reputation, and a habit of bowing with respect as he put the knife in. He also revealed, in the decades that followed, an enormous capacity for work and a stubbornness that matched Pavlov's.

He stuck to criticism of Pavlov's doctrine while Stalin's ideological establishment demanded worship, and to neuropsychology while the Stalinist machine demanded rejection of it. Beritov fully earned a tribute for 'heroism' from a disciple of Pavlov's who was struggling during those same years to reform the master's doctrine from within.[76]

Perhaps Beritov proved to be such a prickly independent because he was a Georgian in nationality and a rebel against a religious upbringing. The son of a priest, marked for the same vocation, he 'came to hate religion' while in a seminary. The cryptic biography that quotes that snippet of self-analysis does not even specify the church he was being trained to serve.[77] It was probably the same as Joseph Stalin's, who was also turned into an anti-religious militant, perhaps in the same seminary. After the Revolution, when Soviet Georgia declared its independence, Beritov went home from Odessa, to found a department of physiology at the newly established University of Tiflis, or Tbilisi, as Soviet Georgians persuaded Soviet Russians to call the capital city. In 1919, when Beritov came home, Mensheviks were in charge of Soviet Georgia, but the public record does not show how he felt about that anomaly, or about its forceful correction in 1921, when the Red Army came in from Soviet Russia and put Bolsheviks in charge. In time his national pride would be sufficiently developed for him to restore his authentic un-Russified name, *Beritashvili*, which I will call him from now on. His resistance to the sanctification of Pavlov's doctrine in the period of high Stalinism may have been in part a Georgian's resistance to Russian domination, but the sanitized public record contains no evidence on such issues.

At the outset Beritashvili's criticism of Pavlov's doctrine was combined with matter-of-fact acceptance of the central Pavlovian concepts, 'analyzers' and 'temporary connections'. 'Analyzer' lumped in one category the entire network of nerves that receives a specific physical stimulus (the airborne vibrations of a buzzer, for example), and transforms it into a nerve impulse and a sensation and a perception. 'Temporary connection' then explained how an 'indifferent' sense perception (buzzing sound) is transformed into a meaningful signal (buzzing sound signifies food forthcoming) and into anticipatory action (salivation). By lumping many things in one the analyzer concept evaded 'the so-called physiology of the sense organs', as Pavlov dismissively referred to the tradition of Helmholtz.[78] He disliked its distinctions in the analysis of perception − the external physical, the neural, the sensational, and finally the perceptual − for they obliged the science of physiology to confront the fact of subjectivity and to confess defeat, to acknowledge that subjectivity is a natural fact which lies outside the realm of natural science. Pavlov overleaped all that with his 'analyzer' concept. It jumped directly from a point of reception at a sensory nerve ending to a corresponding point of arrival in the cerebral cortex, the site where some perceptual function was pronounced done, *basta*. Then, to link perception to signal to appropriate action, his doctrine shifted from lumping to splitting, by constructing a 'temporary connection' in considerable detail, mostly imaginary.

From the analyzer of hearing he pictured excitation spreading quickly through a mosaic of other analyzer terminals in the cerebral cortex, as an incoming alarm might be connected with all the possible terminals in a telephone switchboard.[79] Among them would be the taste locus, where such stimuli as meat touching the tongue are analyzed and impulses are sent to 'the feeding center', which activates the glands and the muscles used in eating. Pavlov was deliberately vague on the structure of such 'centers' of vital functions and their connections with the cortical 'points' where 'analyzers' terminate. He felt sure that there must be such structures, and he was quite sure that his experiments were establishing their functional relationships with cortical analyzers. Like Newton or Darwin, he was providing the masterful framework of functional laws; the morphological and bioelectric details would be filled in by future researchers grateful to him for guidance.[80]

Here then, in the Pavlovian language of facts (and hypothesized facts), is the mechanism of a conditioned reflex. When a buzzing sound to the ear repeatedly precedes the touch of meat to the tongue, the initial excitation of all points on the cerebral cortex shrinks into an association or temporary connection between two, the analyzers for hearing and for taste. Thus the feeding center comes to be activated by an 'indifferent' stimulus, a buzzing sound. The connection is temporary, for it depends on reinforcement (food on the tongue following buzzing in the ear); repeated failure of reinforcement 'extinguishes' the temporary connection. If reinforcement is renewed, the connection is restored.

In short, Pavlov translated associationist psychology into physiology. He took the old scheme that explained mind as a product of repeatedly associated sense impressions, and translated it into a scheme of repeated neural associations, constructed on the model of an old-fashioned telephone switchboard, with a mosaic of receptor points constantly connected and disconnected according to demands coming in from the animal's environment. The translation thrilled him as the ultimate triumph of natural science. It was no longer necessary to say that association of mental representations corresponds to association of physical events yet is somehow radically different, for example, in the mind's capacity to run ahead of the temporal sequence that it has absorbed, to anticipate future events and act accordingly. In Pavlov's doctrine the process of learned behavior became temporal association of physical events in the nervous system, with before and after in the proper sequence of cause and effect even though the dog seems to be salivating in anticipation of a future event. Future feeding is not causing present salivation; precise analysis of neural processes shows that the salivation is a reflexive response to past events.

Beritashvili in his first articles seemed to like that Pavlovian project. But he did make changes in neural details, which would quickly subvert the whole scheme and restore talk of mental representations and of acts directed toward future events. He attempted an outline sketch of the route that a nerve impulse follows from a receptor surface to the cortex, and then out to a muscle or gland. Using the best available knowledge of the nervous system, he showed how peripheral nerves are connected with the spinal cord and with the brain, and he inset sketches of synaptic connections between neurons, showing excitation and inhibition as reciprocal functions performed at that microscopic level.[81] Thus he felt obliged at the outset to reject Pavlov's understanding of inhibition, which showed no concern for tiny bioelectric discharges across synapses or for the precise amounts of time that are appropriate to that elemental process. This problem is worth considering in some detail, for Sechenov had tried to make inhibition serve as the bridging mechanism between neural and psychic processes, and he had been frustrated by his respect for the inconvenient details of neural structure and function. Here was Pavlov much too handily turning inhibition into a universal explanatory label. Which is another way of saying that disregard of neuron processes is often cited, along with cortical dogmatism, as the basic flaw in Pavlov's doctrine.

A dog's first reaction to the buzzer is general alert, which Pavlov called 'the investigative or what-is-this? reflex': the dog turns toward the sound, its ears pricked, its whole body expressing heads-up, taut-muscled attention, as one would say in plain language, which was too subjective for Pavlov (and for Bekhterev, who called the initial alert of the experimental animal its 'orientation reflex'). In prosaic neurology, then as well as now, the term 'reflex' was not used for such general reactions of the whole animal, but only for particular neuro-muscular or neuro-glandular automatisms, such as the famous knee jerk when the tendon is struck or the scratching motion of a dog's hind leg when its back is rubbed or the flow of particular digestive juices when stimulants touch particular nerve endings in the alimentary canal. The metaphorical equation of all behavior with that automatic model raised more than verbal problems for Pavlov as he analyzed events following initial alert. If buzzing is repeatedly followed by feeding, reflexive salivation comes to be provoked by the buzzer, while the generalized alert drains away. The conditioned salivation may properly be called a reflex, and its neural mechanism explored on that assumption, but how is one to connect that specific reflex with extinction of the 'what-is-this? reflex'? Plain language says that the dog grows used to repeated buzzing and bored with it, even to the point of falling asleep in the middle of the experiments. Pavlov forbade such mentalistic language — literally: fines were exacted from assistants who lapsed into plain talk. Pavlov insisted on saying that generalized excitation of the cortex is being differentiated, by inhibition of all cortical loci except the two — hearing and feeding — that are getting a temporary connection.

Similarly in the case of 'extinction', as Pavlov called the suspension of salivation to the buzzer when reinforcement is suspended a sufficient number of times. Once again Pavlov's explanation was inhibition, in the taste analyzer and in the feeding center that activates the salivary glands. If at some later time reinforcement starts again, reflexive salivation to the buzzer also starts again, much more quickly than was required for the initial establishment of the conditioned reflex. 'Disinhibition' was Pavlov's explanation of this quick revival. One must not say that the dog has remembered what it once learned even while it has not been using the memory. That would have opened the forbidden lexicon of mentalistic terms. In particular it would have raised the head-cracking problem of memory: how does a neural system store information and draw on it at appropriate times? Pavlov pushed such issues out of sight, under the universal explanatory label: inhibition and disinhibition.[82]

Beritashvili began with a firm rejection of that Pavlovian catch-all. It clashed with 'contemporary views. The inhibition associated with inborn reflexes is an active process like the excitation; it is provoked by stimulation, it develops and passes off as it [does], and, like the excitation, it irradiates rapidly from its primary focus into other parts of the cerebrum.'[83] So Pavlov could not invoke inhibition to explain long-term processes. Certainly inhibition 'cannot last for hours, still less for days or weeks, after the stimulus has ceased'. Yet that is what Pavlov assumed when he attributed to inhibition the 'extinction' of a conditioned reflex that is not reinforced, and to disinhibition its swift resumption when reinforcement begins again. It was clear to Beritashvili that 'some other process' was at work in the coming and going of learned behavior according to the presence or absence of appropriate circumstances. One could seek that 'other process' in some improved understanding of neural processes or in some type of psychological science, or in some combination of biology and psychology. But one could not solve the problem by brandishing the word 'inhibition' in disregard of its precise physiological meaning.

Just before the First World War a Lamarckian zoologist in Germany had suggested that experience 'engraphs' or writes its traces, 'engrams', on living matter.[84] Occasionally Pavlov spoke in analogous terms, of 'traces' left or imprinted in the nervous system.[85] Evidently he sensed that inhibition and disinhibition are not an adequate substitute for the concept of memory and recall. For a while he gave credence to demonstrations that traces of acquired behavior may be hereditarily fixed in animals. Mice trained to respond to a dinner bell engendered mice which learned the habit more quickly than their parents. But it turned out that the experimenter was not improving the inherited dinner bell responsiveness of mice; he was unwittingly improving his human skill in teaching them.[86] Pavlov issued a brief disavowal of his belief in the Lamarckian results, and showed signs of sympathy with the rapidly growing science of genetics.[87] (A Division of

Evolutionary Physiology was created within one of his institutes, and a bust of Mendel was erected in front of another.)[88] Heredity aside, Pavlov mostly evaded the concept of memory and so avoided the problem of its neural mechanisms.

Nor did Pavlov and his Soviet followers ever get seriously involved in the American or rat-race style of conditioning, which came to be called operant or instrumental, as distinguished from Pavlovian or classical conditioning. The Americans put the response (maze-running) ahead of the stimulus (food at the end of the maze), which took them dangerously close to mentalistic concepts. In Germany Gestalt psychologists went all the way. They tested the ability of chimpanzees to get an out-of-reach banana by piling scattered boxes into a pyramid for climbing, or by jointing a long stick for reaching, and they used mentalistic terms to explain the animals' thoughtful behavior. Pavlov and his disciples preferred dogs trained to stand passively in a harness, waiting for stimuli to impinge upon their nervous systems. Thus stimulus and response were kept in satisfying before-and-after sequence, as long as the experimenters ignored the precise timing of excitation and inhibition in neuron networks, while invoking those processes in explanation of their animals' reflexive behavior.

When Beritashvili broke out of the Pavlovian frame in the late 1920s, he set the dog free to run an obstacle course, somewhat as the Americans did with their rats. He preferred the term 'natural' to describe his experiments, rather than operant or instrumental, and that preference caught on in the Soviet Union. In natural experiments the dog is trained to move about within a specially designed problem chamber. (See plate 00.) Its bed is in a fixed spot, where it has been trained to stay without physical restraint until the experimenter signals permission to go to a concealed feeding place that had previously been shown to the dog. The concealed experimenter can introduce complicating factors, such as 'indifferent stimuli' (buzzers, flashing lights), and also 'biologically significant stimuli' (the appearance of food in some other place than the usual one). The 'indifference' of conditioned stimuli was Pavlov's concept; Beritashvili was subversive in his serious acceptance of it, for he saw that it is implicitly opposed to 'biologically significant'.[89]

Pavlov liked to emphasize that even such a stimulus as an electric shock, presumably unpleasant in itself, can evoke pleasurable salivation if feeding regularly follows. The stimulus is thus inherently 'indifferent' as a signal. Sometimes the dog greedily licked the apparatus that shocked it. Pavlov liked to emphasize such grotesqueries, to support his contention that all conditioned stimuli are essentially 'indifferent': their specific significance to the animal depends on what comes after them. Invariant signalling power inheres only in unconditioned or inborn stimuli, such as meat actually touching the dog's tongue. Pavlov did not like to hear that some conditioned stimuli must be 'biologically significant', as opposed to 'indifferent', for such distinctions pointed once again toward a breakdown of his binary classification of all reactions.

In America extreme behaviorists shared his either-or tendency. J. B. Watson's analogue to the dog licking the shocking apparatus was a baby crying at the sight of a stuffed toy. Every time the baby had reached for any soft furry object, the experimenter banged metal bars, until the child learned to shrink and cry at the sight of a teddy bear.[90] Underlying such demonstrations was the determination to avoid mentalist concepts at any cost, to prove that learned behavior must always be the mechanical product of stimulus and response. The experimenters were not only training their animals, they were simultaneously training themselves to observe taboos and syndromes of avoidance. Pavlov, by restricting himself to 'classical' conditioning of dogs trained to be passive, had a comparatively mild case of compulsive avoidance in his verbal behavior. Behaviorist psychologists in America, venturing more freely in their rat-running experiments, were forced into more restrictive contortions when explaining. They needed baroque circumlocutions to avoid joining the subject 'rat' — or 'child' — to the predicate 'expects'.[91]

In the Soviet Union psychologists were largely free of such behaviorist taboos and elaborate syndromes of verbal avoidance. Indeed the dominant psychologist in Soviet Georgia was D. N. Uznadze, who had written a pre-War German Ph.D. dissertation on Solov'ev, Russia's best-known metaphysical philosopher.[92] After the Revolution he turned to psychology and founded a school whose central concept was mental set (*ustanovka*), analogous to the German concept of *Einstellung*.[93] His school would withstand Pavlovian pressures in psychological science as stubbornly as Beritashvili's group did in physiology. Indeed, each reinforced the other, as both resisted the Russian nativism that fastened on Pavlov.

Whatever the varied influences at work on Beritashvili, the significant result was his turn to mentalistic concepts in neuropsychology. He said plainly that the dog in his experiment chamber was guided along its shifting path not only by indifferent conditioned stimuli, such as buzzers and flashing lights, but also by biologically significant stimuli, such as the appearance of food in an unusual place, and by internal 'representations' (*predstavleniia*, *Vorstellungen*) of feeding places. If a dog once discovered food in an unusual place, or once experienced pain at an unexpected spot, its subsequent perambulations would regularly deviate toward the one and away from the other. That recalled the milk-fed puppies, who were taught by a single taste to salivate at the smell of meat, but the difficulty for the Pavlovian scheme was greater. The milk-fed puppies raised the problem of instinctual behavior, which Pavlov grudgingly noted, if only to set it aside by equating instinct and reflex. Beritashvili's freely moving dog raised the problem of mental representation, which Pavlov simply refused to consider, certainly below the human level, and often even there. Beritashvili did not succeed in finding the neurological basis of mental representation, but he effectively highlighted the inadequacy of Pavlovian efforts to avoid the problem. An American observer of Pavlov cannot help recalling Mark Twain's cat, which once sat on a hot stove-lid and thereafter avoided all stove-lids of any temperature. Beritashvili insisted on studying such behavior, rather than emulating it.

In the 1920s he was just beginning the hybridization of neurophysiology and psychology, which he would subsequently learn to call neuropsychology, that is, the systematic correlation of neural and psychic processes. At Kornilov's Institute of Experimental Psychology V. M. Borovskii was moving toward a similar hybrid, starting from comparative or animal psychology. In part his move was defensive, for Pavlov scorned 'naive zoopsychology', which 'merely indulges in fantasy and cannot answer one serious question'.[94] Indeed, in 1923 Pavlov went beyond scorn and explicitly denied that zoopsychology has a right to exist.[95] Borovskii was not so aggressive, but he did turn the accusation back on Pavlov, whose experimental data, he respectfully declared, merited better explanation than the neural fantasies which Pavlov offered. Inhibition was of course a major item in his bill of particulars, and he drew an interesting new charge from embryology or 'developmental mechanics', as the field was sometimes called.

Far below the level of behavior where mental concepts are at issue, careful study of embryonic processes cast doubt on Pavlov's doctrine. The reflexive swimming motions of certain fish had been shown to originate as generalized thrashing about just after the tiny fish hatches, a thrashing about that gradually becomes differentiated and thus turns into the co-ordinated reflexes which accomplish effective swimming. Thus Pavlov's rigid distinction between inborn and acquired reflexes was called in doubt, and so too was his assignment of the operative mechanisms to different neural networks. Borovskii drew that embryological argument from the work of American scientists, as he did several other substantial objections to Pavlov's explanations of conditioning. That was especially ominous, for American experimenters were showing much more active interest in Pavlov's doctrine than scientists in his native land. That is how he was drawn into a confrontation at a 1929 conference in the United States, which finally provoked the old man to dignify his critics by an extended public reply.

Before 1929 Pavlov cultivated an air of aloof self-sufficiency, in science as well as politics. He demonstrated his disdain for the new regime, which honored his work, by systematic absence from Soviet congresses of physiologists, who also did him honor. They signalled it with telegrams announcing his election *in absentia* to their honorary executive committees, but meaningful recognition in the form of papers on conditioned reflexes was mostly lacking, except in distant America. To a disciple who had emigrated to America Pavlov sent a warm expression of respect for that assertion of independence. He was appalled at the lack of dignity among those who stayed in the Soviet Union: 'All around me I am astounded to observe an absence of the feeling of human dignity. People who have been thrown two or three times into prison without any grounds for it, like a dog attached to a chain, forget that so quickly, without any acknowledgment of spiritual defeat.'[96] In 1924, when a young disciple wrote an article on 'Dialectical Materialism and the Problem of the Psyche', Pavlov angrily insisted upon the excision of any comment on conditioned reflexes.[97] But he limited himself to that bit of censorship. Outside his laboratories and his doctrine, where his authority was unquestioned, he admired individual freedom and liberal ideology.

The 'Bolshevization' of the Academy of Sciences in 1929 provoked Pavlov to some unusual action on behalf of that ideology, behind the scenes and for a short time.[98] Before and afterward he was aloof to any cause but his doctrine. The help he gave to A. K. Lents fits the pattern, for Lents was a psychiatrist who admired the doctrine of conditioned reflexes. He had written a wildly speculative book whose publication was blocked for several years in the mid-1920s, perhaps because of its extravagant equations between human and canine behavior, perhaps also because of its off-hand chauvinism.[99] Lents offered a reflexive explanation for any and every human experience, including low levels of morality 'among the less civilized nations and individuals': their physiological 'type' was simpler, closer to the salivating dog's, than the physiological types found in superior people.[100] Pavlov helped get the book published by writing an introduction of unqualified approval, a blurb in short, which has been omitted from both editions of his *Complete Works*, perhaps because Lents became a 'repressed' or non-person in the 1930s.[101] His scheme of evolutionary physiology did not vanish with him. Pavlov mostly avoided that huge problem, but when he chanced to touch on it we find him ascribing a simple 'type' of neurophysiology to 'animals and primitive people, until the latter have developed into real people and have approximated our condition'.[102]

No doubt Pavlov was a vain self-centered little man, but he was also a great physiologist, and one must wonder how he resisted the evidence that the cerebral mechanisms in his epochal doctrine were largely imaginary. Perhaps unpublished correspondence will some day shed some light. The voluminous public record intensifies the puzzle. In the early years of the century, when he first presented his cortical explanation of conditioning and immediately heard the obvious criticism — decorticate animals can be conditioned — Pavlov offered a brief, extemporaneous defense: his explanation was tentative, subject to improvement as experimentation would proceed. Removal of the cortex was a crude interference with normal function, and its full significance must depend on further refinement of techniques and on the general laws of the normal animal's behavior, which his group was establishing. Within such initial, defensive parrying he had one precise counter-blow. The pupillary reflex was known to be subcortical, and his team had proved that it could not be conditioned. The iris would not contract when a buzzing sound signaled a forthcoming flash of light, but only when the light actually struck the eye. Hence, the temporary connections that establish conditioned reflexes cannot be in the subcortical region where the pupillary reflex is mediated.[103]

Was there a vicious circle in that reasoning? It is tempting to say so, especially when one notes Pavlov's resistance to inconvenient experimental evidence. Some Americans reported limited success in conditioning the pupillary reflex. It was achieved with electric shocks or loud sounds that provoked fearful alarm in human subjects, and thus pointed once again toward complex relations between lower and higher levels of neuropsychology.[104] Pavlovian resistance to such issues was predictable, maybe even rational, but it also appeared on a more basic level of neurophysiology. To take a critically important example: he and his team omitted electrical stimulation of the brain to see which glands might secrete or muscles twitch in response to impulses from hypothesized 'points' and 'centers'. Since 1870 many researchers had been accumulating data by such experiments; Pavlov occasionally signalled brief respect for them – and brushed aside the results as incoherent and irrelevant to his project. A few of his disciples were drawn toward such studies, most notably P. K. Anokhin (b. 1898), the same young man who annoyed the master by writing on dialectical materialism and the problem of the psyche. In the mid-1930s, just after Pavlov's death, he would plainly declare the need to end our 'separation from world neurological thought'.[105] While Pavlov lived, he curbed such impulses among the disciples. He showed intermittent awareness of his school's separation from world neurological thought, majestically ascribing it to his vanguard role.[106] The electrical stimulators of the brain had the task of catching up, not of showing the way.

Toward another crucially important method, surgical alteration of the nervous system, Pavlov's resistance was not simple but complex. The surgical researcher correlates structure and function by removing particular neural structures to see which behavioral functions will then be impaired. Though Pavlov decried such disturbances of normal function, and insisted that the 'pathological' results must be placed within the framework of normal laws established by his studies of unimpaired animals, he nevertheless set some of his people to work on extirpations, and he reviewed their findings in a fairly long section of his *Lectures* in the mid-1920s.[107] Bewilderment and frustration attend the reading of those sections, partly because Pavlov himself felt those emotions, but even more because the reader watches Pavlov turning constantly in a vicious circle.

He recognizes that the decorticate animal can be conditioned, but he does not even consider the obvious inference: neural mechanisms of conditioning must be sought in subcortical structures. Instead, he emphasizes the differences between the conditioned behavior of the decorticate animal and that of the unimpaired dog. Munk, the German pioneer of such studies, had characterized such differences with free use of psychological terms — for example, the decorticate animal hears or sees without understanding. Pavlov disapproves of such a subjective concept as understanding, and labors to show that it can be avoided, if one takes out limited portions of the cortex, and then makes precise reports of consequent alterations in the animal's response to conditioning. He offers such detailed descriptions, explaining them with his original scheme of cortical points, irradiation, and inhibition — the very scheme that was thrown in question by the brute fact of conditioned reflexes in the completely decorticate animal.

Pavlov did not repair that illogic by his intermittent recognition that brain localization is an unsolved problem, or by conceding that the cortical 'points' involved in 'temporary connections' were probably not points in a literal sense but 'kernels' or 'nuclei' of indeterminate areas of brain activity. A sympathetic reader might say that Pavlov was verging on a dynamic theory of brain localization, moving away from assignment of particular functions to sharply delimited structures, toward a picture of labile interaction among structures that perform a variety of functions. The important fact is that he only verged, he did not go over the edge.

He did not, to take a glaring omission, give serious consideration to the evidence that surviving parts of a damaged nervous system can take on functions normally performed by the lost parts. In a cruelly simple demonstration, the motor nerves of an animal's rib muscles and diaphragm are cut, but breathing does not stop; the muscles of the pharynx take on the job of moving air in and out the lungs. In another experiment the leg muscles are paralyzed, and the crippled rat somersaults through the maze to get food at the end. The functioning of the whole organism is not only determined by its constituent reflex arcs; as a whole system it also determines which arcs perform what functions; it improvises to achieve its ends. Neurologists who treat brain-damaged people are constantly involved in extremely complex efforts to achieve such substitutions or compensations. Pavlov could not confront their significance without once again putting in doubt his reduction of all behavior to the automatic compounding of automatic reflex arcs, which are either innate and fixed or acquired and temporary.

For a retrospective outside observer it becomes hard to understand the neurophysiologists who acclaimed Pavlov as the Newton or Darwin of higher nervous activity — until one notes their accompanying stress on the obscurity and confusion in that part of the discipline where Pavlov was making his bold entry. Indeed, one recalls, in Pavlov's defense, that Darwin's theory of natural selection endured a long period of apparent incongruity with important bodies of fact and significant lines of biological thought. Virtually complete consensus of thought in favor of Darwin's theory was won by the synthesis of natural selection and genetics which began in the 1920s, at the very time that Pavlov's doctrine was becoming the target of increasing criticism. Natural sciences can develop in that bumpy discordant fashion. Believers in a grand explanatory hypothesis may be jostled by disbelievers for a considerable time, until new discoveries and deeper insights make one or another side give in. Indeed, all sides may give in, to a general sense of failure.

Pavlov was not the philosophical type to use such analogies – certainly not the pessimistic sort – but he evidently expected vindication of the Darwinian sort. He was sure that he and his team were laying out the framing laws of higher nervous activity. They must not be deterred by incongruous details, whose fit would be discovered in the future. That stubborn self-confidence was reinforced by the lavish compliments of many specialists outside his team. One may doubt that he was entirely pleased to see himself compared to Columbus, who believed himself in Asia when he had stumbled on America.[108] But even that dubious compliment helped him resist the bleak suggestion that he had found no continent at all, no neural substrate of all individually acquired behavior, merely a precise technique for distinguishing one type of such behavior.

He would have been edging toward such a modest assessment of his accomplishment, if he had conceded merit in criticisms of his imaginary brain mechanisms and his binary classification of behavior. Instead, he resisted consideration of such criticisms, and so, unwittingly, he began to immure his school in its own little world of sectarian discourse. The doctrine that claimed to be a universal framework was becoming a garrison mentality for Pavlov's school. Active appreciation of their growing isolation would come in the 1930s, but the advantage of hindsight enables us to see the pattern emerging in the 1920s, in Pavlov's refusal to give serious consideration to urgent challenges in neurophysiology and evolutionary biology. Yet he seemed at one point to offer a major concession to the psychologists studying the human mind: his laws of conditioned reflexes might not be sufficient to deal with speech and thought.

That startling departure from his usual self-assurance came toward the end of the *Lectures on the Work of the Cerebral Hemispheres*:

Of course, for man speech [*slovo*] is just as real a conditioned stimulus as all the others that he has in common with the animals, but at the same time it is also so all-inclusive [as to be] like no other stimuli, and in this respect speech does not permit any quantitative or qualitative comparison with the conditioned stimuli of animals. Speech, thanks to the whole preceding life of a grown person, is connected with all the external and internal stimuli that have reached the cerebral hemi-spheres, it signals all of them, takes the place of all of them, and therefore can arouse all those actions, the reactions of the organism, that have been conditioned by those stimuli.[109]

In the 1930s, when Pavlov was to get heavily involved in psychiatry, he would develop this line of thought into the postulation of a 'second signal system', which may have implied a special neural network that mediates speech and thought. Whether he intended that implication, and whether it was a serious breach in his doctrine, I will consider later on. In the 1920s few people noticed the exceptional nature of the passage just quoted. His doctrine was not sacred; its every word did not require close scrutiny. He was not a god but an eminent scientist, praised or criticized for his usual insistence that 'our upbringing, education, discipline of any kind, all our possible habits obviously consist of conditioned reflexes.'[110] That character-istic declaration opened the lecture which included the concession that speech is qualitatively different from conditioned reflexes. Everyone thought of Pavlov in his characteristic stance, the scientist who equated all thinking and acting with a dog's salivation to a bell. Momentary concessions to common sense were not nearly as interesting or important as that sensational claim.

Pavlov was happily aware that behaviorist psychologists in the United States were much more actively sympathetic than psychologists in Soviet Russia. The behaviorists praised him for undermining all mentalist concepts, for showing how to analyze the mind without them, and he in turn credited the Americans (Thorndike in particular) with an independent start in conditioning experiments.[111] He did not approve their indifference, as he supposed, to the neurophysiological mechanisms of conditioning. He obviously had in mind J. B. Watson, the major propagandist of behaviorism, who had hailed Pavlov as the master in his 1915 presidential address to the American Psychological Association.[112] Perhaps in expectation of more such encomiums Pavlov decided to attend a major congress of psychologists in New Haven in September 1929. He was invited to be one of the two main speakers at the plenary session. A Gestalt psychologist was the other, which implied a deliberate balancing of opposed schools in a deeply divided discipline.[113] But the newly elected president of the American Psychological Association was Karl Lashley, a well-known behaviorist who had a strong interest in neural mechanisms. He had been giving Pavlov's doctrine the sincerest form of tribute, by testing it in his laboratory, and he devoted his presidential address to a review of 'Basic Neural Mechanisms in Behavior'.

This detailed tribute turned quickly into repudiation. Lashley flew past the basic principle: 'we all agree that the final explanation of behavior or of mental processes is to be sought in the physiological activity of the body and, in particular, in the properties of the nervous system'.[114] That was

Pavlov's faith, but his translation of it into the reflex creed had not survived Lashley's tests:

> In the youth of a science there is virtue in simplifying the problems
> ..., but there is a danger that oversimplification will later blind us to
> important problems. In the study of cerebral functions we seem to
> have reached a point where the reflex theory is no longer profitable
> either for the formulation of problems or for an understanding of the
> phenomena of integration.[115]

Lashley did not specify Pavlov as the chief author of that 'over-simplification', once useful, now unprofitable. He hardly needed to, considering Pavlov's fame for the reflex theory of learning, among the public at large as well as the specialists. Moreover, Lashley concentrated on the central principles that Pavlov brought to his experimental data: that conditioned reflexes are the elemental units of individually acquired behavior, and that they can be precisely correlated with neural processes in the cerebral cortex. Lashley did not claim to know what were the functional units or the neural substrate, but he did know that Pavlov's doctrine was wrong. He was precise in negating, confessedly vague in affirming:

> ... The units of cerebral function are not simple reactions, or con-
> ditioned reflexes as we have used the term in America, but are modes
> of organization. The cortex seems to provide a sort of generalized
> framework to which simple reactions conform spontaneously, as the
> words [of a speaker] fall into the grammatical form of a language. [He
> had been reading Gestalt as well as Pavlov and Bekhterev.] ... The
> nervous unit of organization in behavior is not the reflex arc, but the
> mechanism, whatever be its nature, by which a reaction to a ratio of
> excitation is brought about. ... Such notions are speculative and
> vague, but we seem to have no choice but to be vague or to be
> wrong, and I believe that a confession of ignorance is more hopeful
> for progress than a false assumption of knowledge.[116]

His precise negations were supported by vivid experimental results. The rat that somersaults through the maze when its legs have been paralyzed was proof that learned behavior is not literally reflexive in the same sense as the knee-jerk or the infant's grasp. That is, maze-running was not the automatic performance of particular functions by specialized neural arcs. Lashley showed that he was aware of the Sherringtonian tendency to dissolve even such literal reflexes into extremely complex reactions among neurons, but he turned aside from that descent toward elemental chaos. He shared Pavlov's urge to find the neural mechanisms of the whole animal's systemic behavior, and therefore shared the conviction that the literal reflex of traditional neurology is a meaningful unit of analysis. To state the conviction more broadly: 'the essential feature of the reflex theory is the assumption that individual neurons are specialized for particular functions. The explanatory value of the theory rests upon this point alone, and no amount of hypothetical elaboration of connections alters the basic assumption.'[117] If the paralyzed rat threads through the maze by somersaulting instead of running, its behavior cannot be reduced to the particular reflex arcs that were part of the initial learning experience.

Lashley pursued this line of criticism into the examination of cortical processes. He removed this, that, and the other part of the cortex, and at each stage compared time in learning the maze with the time of unimpaired rats. He found that the particular regions of removal had no effect; only a large amount of cortical tissue taken from any region could slow down the rate of learning. Hence his law of mass action: 'The rate of learning is not dependent upon the properties of individual cells, but is somehow a function of the total mass of tissue.'[118]

That was a version of equipotentiality, the principle that had been at war with cerebral localization all through the nineteenth-century disputes of brain scientists, who cannot avoid such protracted contention because their data are so baffling. Of course Lashley did not deny any and all specialization of brain cells for particular functions, but his emphasis in 1929 was on the contrary evidence that he had been getting in trying to locate cortical areas which were responsible for learning the maze. The contrary evidence was enough to reject Pavlov's image of learned behavior as the establishment of temporary connections between cortical points that specialize in analyzing particular types of sensory inputs. On the positive side hindsight might credit Lashley with groping for some hypothesis of dynamic localization, heavily dependent on metaphors as he groped: 'The same cells [of the cortex] may not be twice called upon to perform the same function. They may be in a fixed anatomical relation to the retina, but the functional organization plays over them as the pattern of letters plays over the bank of lights in an electric sign.'[119] (Beritashvili liked that figure of speech.)

Pavlovian legend pictures the master rising immediately with a scathing reply from the floor, there among the American infidels in New Haven. In fact, spoken English did not penetrate his mind quickly enough, and Lashley had not waved a red flag by explicit citation of Pavlov. It may be that Pavlov was told right away what Lashley had said and argued with him *viva voce* after the public session,[120] but the important reaction came a couple of years later, when he had read the published speech in the *Psychological Review*, and a similar critique by another eminent American behaviorist with an interest in the neural mechanisms of learning.[121] In the country where Pavlov had his greatest following his doctrine was being brushed aside – by the followers. For once in his life Pavlov broke from his lofty disregard of criticism, and wrote 'The Reply of a Physiologist to Psychologists', which appeared in an American journal in 1932.[122]

It came too late, this solitary venture into polemics. Before and during the 1920s he had acquired an American following among behaviorist psychologists, inspiring some of them to seek the neural mechanisms of learned behavior. Their first discovery was the inadequacy of the master's doctrine. 'Temporary connections' between 'analyzers' in the cerebral cortex are not the neural mechanisms of conditioned reflexes, which are not the functional units of which all individually acquired behavior is compounded. Conditioned reflexes are only one type of such behavior. Now they were moving on, as Beritashvili and Anokhin and some other physiologists were in the Soviet Union, into the hybrid discipline of neuropsychology. The arguments that Pavlov flung at their dwindling backs will be examined below, as part of the evidence, mounting rapidly in the 1930s, that Pavlov and his school (the uncritical members of it) were more and more talking to themselves.

But the general public continued to think of Pavlov's doctrine as the hard truth in psychological science. After all, that laurel wreath had been laid on Pavlov by fellow specialists, who did not take it away as they began to use his technique to subvert his doctrine. In reverence for founding fathers scientists resemble religious congregations; by highly selective memory they maintain myths of continuous revelation, the holy spirit of truth descending from father to son to living communicants in the progressive present. Bolshevik ideological authorities were part of the larger congregation, the general public that knows the scientific truth as they hear it from scientists. That is how the Bolsheviks knew that Pavlov's doctrine was the basis for a genuine science of the mind. Physiologists and psychologists had repeatedly said so; their technical quibbles hardly mattered.

Part IV

Plastic Unity

11

Comrade Stalin and his Party

Stalin's entrance was a dramatic astonishment. He was the supreme boss, the chief (*vozhd'*), the practical leader so completely in charge that mere theorists never approached disagreement with him. Yet he walked on un-announced, at the end of a convention of 'agrarian Marxists' in December 1929, irritably objecting to the insolence of their theorizing.[1] It was, he insisted, disrespectful to *praktiki*, the practical activists whose chief he was. By action, by organizing peasants into collective farms, the *praktiki* were proving vitally useful new truths, while the agrarian theorists talked with each other about possibly useful knowledge. Theory and practice must be united, with practice serving as the criterion of truth. The job of theorists was to end their separation from practice, to declare the truths that practical activists were proving. In effect Stalin was recasting Marx's thesis on interpreting the world and changing it. He was turning a thesis into a state edict, with an anti-intellectual sting: philosophers must not think to improve the world, they must teach the world to revere what practical improvers think.

The assembled Marxists were too stunned to defend their intellectual autonomy. Maybe they gave the mandatory 'stormy and extended applause', maybe not; the sources are not consistent.[2] What mattered was the over-whelming presence of Stalin himself on the cultural front. The nationwide audience of Party activists and intellectuals divided. All hailed the chief, of course, but none were quite sure whether or how much his criticism of 'theorists' applied to their particular fields. In philosophy, most notably, a quarrel broke out between the established Marxist leadership and a group of their students, who charged the teachers with 'separation from practice' and 'formalism'. The angry dispute dragged on till December 1930, when Stalin made another of his rare, dramatic interventions in high culture. He had the young rebels in for an interview, to tell them that their attack was

justified but too cautious. The former philosophical leadership was guilty
of a sin much worse than 'a formalist deviation leading to idealism', the
strongest accusation that the young Stalinists had made up to that point.
Stalin sharpened that down to 'Menshevizing idealism'. Philosophical
separation from practice not only led away from materialism toward idealism; it reached that reactionary philosophy and pointed insolent theorists
on toward treason, the Menshevik politics of the class enemy.[3]

Early in 1931 the Party's Central Committee put that judgment in a
decree ordering appropriate changes in *Under the Banner of Marxism*. The
old philosophical leadership was removed and reviled for false pretense of
Marxism, and similarly in all other areas. On all sectors of the cultural
front — note the revived Civil War style of speech — militant Stalinists
pressed campaigns against analogous deceivers. Whatever the particular
issues in various fields, the Marxist leaders of the 1920s were unmasked as
pseudo-Marxists. The universal call to authentic Marxism-Leninism stressed
'practice', active participation in 'socialist construction', and that meant not
only the building of tractor plants, steel mills and collective farms, but also
a militant new psyche battering at any suspicion of an ivory tower.
(*Zamknutost'*, the fortress quality of higher learning, and *kastovost'*, the caste
quality of its adepts, were the Russian pejoratives; not scornful and dismissive, as 'ivory tower' is, but angry and demanding.) In high culture
practical aid to socialist construction meant above all *partiinost'*, the party
quality, infusion of Party spirit in the arts and sciences.[4]

Lenin had used the word *partiinost'* a few times, in a loose broad sense
analogous to French leftist talk of intellectual *engagement*. He and his comrades had urged such an orientation on thinkers without explicit demand
for subordination of their thought to Party control, indeed, with repeated
assurances that no subordination was intended.[5] Throughout the 1920s, the
Party's call in higher learning had been for Marxism broadly construed, to
be developed by autonomous scholars. Now suddenly, in 1930, talk of
'partyness' became an insistent drumbeat for an essentially new concept,
brutally explicit in its denial of autonomy on principle, as in this declaration by a young Party boss of mathematics and natural science (Ernest
Kol'man):

> Now it is clear to everyone that the basic lesson of the philosophical
> discussion is this: philosophy, and every other science as well, cannot
> exist in the conditions of the proletarian dictatorship separate from
> Party leadership. Now it is clear to everyone that all efforts to think of
> any theory, of any scholarly discipline, as autonomous, as an in-
> dependent discipline, objectively signify opposition to the Party's
> general line, opposition to the dictatorship of the proletariat.[6]

That was high Stalinism in full cry, as it would be heard almost continu-
ously for the next twenty-three years, with occasional brief rests. When

burst blood vessels removed Stalin in 1953, the volume dropped and portions of the theme were blurred, as we will see, but the central insistence on obedient service to the Party, the denial of intellectual autonomy on principle, continued to frame the Soviet Communist mentality, until Gorbachev's call for 'new thinking' in 1987.

We are obviously confronting a collective mentality far more extensive and persistent than the dark little mind of the Russified Georgian who suddenly, in December 1929, proclaimed the new 'criterion of practice'. Long after and far away, in Chinese streets professors would be paraded in dunce caps, even beaten, for cultivating learning apart from the Party cause, and in comparatively courteous meeting halls of France intellectuals eager to serve the working class would be told to go away, back to the bourgeoisie if they must have cultural autonomy. Evidently the new manner of subjecting theory to practice, which Stalin announced at the end of 1929, signalled the emergence of a mass conviction, a faith that won so many militant minds, in properly receptive milieux, that it ruined the sacredness of the original apostle and his Party. Their criterion of practice can deify any Comrade N who wins supremacy in one's own best-loved Party O. That separatist capacity revealed itself very early. While Stalin lived the Chinese and the Yugoslav comrades showed that the faith they shared with him mobilized their practical minds about their own revolutionary chiefs. And right after Stalin's death in 1953 his own lieutenants' attack on the cult of his person dispelled any lingering notion that the mentality called Stalinist was merely a self-serving contrivance of Stalin's personal rule, a system of strings to make his puppets dance, as anti-Communists used to say.

It was and is a self-replicating structure of minds in communion, so extensive and persistent as to recall the state church offshoots of the Protestant Reformation. To understand such collective mentalities it is much more important to see them as social constructs than it is to explore the individual minds of the founders, even such as Luther and Calvin, who were far more expressive of their deepest beliefs than Stalin, and thus more individually causative. Stalin was notoriously close-mouthed — 'secretive and concealed to an extreme', as Roy Medvedev observes[7] — a quality that grew especially intense after he became the practical-theoretical man-god of the party–state. As his sacred authority came to be invoked in all fields of thought and action, the public heard less and less from a distinguishable individual named Stalin. It became harder and harder to tell which was more formative of the other, the individual mind of Stalin or the collective mentality organized as a Party, within which the General Secretary personified the criterion of practice. The man and the principle jointly justified everyone's position in both senses of position: bureaucratic place and mental stance.

Yet Stalin was a real administrator before and while he was a symbolic man-god. The first wave of full-fledged Stalinists rose in response to his call for revolution from above, united by faith that the individual who uttered such a startling phrase was the creator of their mentality, not just its namesake. We can hardly avoid asking to what extent he did shape the collective mentality that made him god — and vice versa, to what extent it shaped him. But the important point is their joint achievement, the construction of their hysterical resistance to mental individuality, their fervid insistence that group action must construct group thought, with a practical leader as clearly designated commander-in-chief of the revolutionary but highly disciplined process.

Stalin's personal biography is of little help. He has had many biographers, some admiring, mostly hostile, the best of them scholarly equilibrists. None has saved individuality. None has been able to prove that native disposition and early experience molded the individual mind which then stamped its essence upon the collective mentality. What passes for evidence of the individual's essential mind is almost entirely retrospective hearsay, entered in the public record after he had become the focal point of a collective mentality. He is pictured, for example, as inherently suspicious and vindictive to a pathological extreme, but we cannot tell how much of that picture is retrospective, a projection from the monstrous suspicion and vindictiveness that gripped him and his Party in the 1930s and 1940s. We may feel inclined to believe Trotsky's recollection — in Mexican exile, in 1940 — that hatred gleamed in Stalin's yellow eyes at their first meeting, in Vienna in 1913.[8] (That was one of the very few times that young Stalin made a brief trip abroad to meet the intellectuals who were the leaders in exile of the Party which he served underground, within Russia.) But how can we test our inclination to believe Trotsky? How can we prove that the mind of pre-revolutionary Stalin really was organized by resentment of intellectual émigrés, or of rivals for revolutionary leadership, or of Jews, or of the world at large? We lack specific, confirming evidence from the period in question.[9]

We may be inclined to believe the hearsay report that Bekhterev, after a conversation with Stalin in 1927, confided to a fellow psychiatrist his professional judgment: their country's supreme leader was paranoid. But how far can our credulity stretch? The alleged diagnosis followed a single conversation, and the fourth-hand report abuses our trust by pressing too much upon us: Stalin was jealous of Bekhterev's reputation, somehow knew his diagnosis, and instantly had him poisoned.[10] Once started in the collection of such memories and reports, and reports of other people's reports and memories, we must consider the allegation that Stalin raped a thirteen-year-old girl, that he boasted of the sweetest sleep after arranging the destruction of an unsuspecting adversary (or supposed adversary), that he found amusement in cutting the throats of sheep. (Trotsky, whom we wish to believe about the hateful yellow eyes in pre-revolutionary Vienna, is our source for the cutting of sheep throats in post-revolutionary Moscow.)[11]

The 'rude' (*grub*) quality that Lenin noted in his 'testament' is an exceptionally important clue, for it was entered in the record in January 1923, when Stalin was just emerging from his reputation as a 'gray blur' among the revolutionary leaders, a backstage administrator rather than a tribune of the people or ideological prophet. (In fact, the 'gray blur' appraisal was entered in the public record about the same time, in the most famous memoirs of the revolution.)[12] Lenin, contemplating death and his successors, saw no backstage blur but a formidable potentate. He perceived Stalin along with Trotsky as 'the two outstanding chiefs [*vozhdi*]', and worried that Stalin was 'too rude' to continue as General Secretary, supreme boss of personnel. His memorandum therefore advised the comrades to replace Stalin in that post with someone 'more tolerant, more courteous, and more considerate of comrades, less capricious'.[13]

Like the German *grob*, *grub* means not only discourteous but coarse, gross, vulgar; Lenin's word choice suggests the division between the revolutionary intelligentsia who had cultivated their minds in Western exile and sons of the lower classes who had their minds shaped by years of illegal, sometimes criminal struggle in the Russian underground. If testimony of that sort were more abundant, and more explicit, and pre-revolutionary as well as retrospective, one might weigh it against contrary evidence, such as the unqualified enthusiasm that Lenin expressed in a 1913 letter to Gorky. Stalin was staying with the Lenins in Krakow, doing his own bit of émigré intellectual work, and Lenin was delighted: 'A wonderful Georgian has settled in with us',[14] to write the article on Marxism and the national question that would be Stalin's only claim to distinction as a theorist until 1924, when Lenin died. Then, midst the grieving exaltation of Lenin, chief administrator Stalin tried on the prophetic mantle of the leader who 'lived, lives, will live!'[15] Which is to say that Stalin went to a Communist University in April 1924 and gave a series of lectures on 'The Foundations of Leninism'.[16] The resulting pamphlet was reviewed by one of the philosophical leadership with complete deference to Stalin's explanation of Leninist politics, but condescending correction of his inept mumbling about Leninist philosophy.[17]

With a lot more of such *sic et non* a biographer might hope to draw a particularized profile of Stalin's authentic mind as revealed in its interactions with other individual minds, before his became the public embodiment of the ruling Party's collective mentality. But such bits of good evidence are too rare and too disparate, as in the sampling offered here, to cohere in a reliable, particularized profile of an authentic, individual mind. Invariably Stalin's vulgar biographers fall back on legend, while serious biographers defeat their own purpose and unwittingly start a different project. Lacking sufficient information about the individual mind in its development, they start describing the group psychology that can reasonably be projected into or out of Stalin; they analyze the Party's changing habits of thought and action as the chief expressed them or was pictured as expressing them. Either way, legendary or scholarly, the biographies portray 'a new world seen through one man', as a French Communist subtitled the icon he painted in 1935,[18] neglecting to specify: the new world of a Party vanguard pressing a revolution from above upon a rearguard population.

Consider a major element of the vanguard's mentality, animosity against the intelligentsia. That has often been declared a major element of Stalin's mind, mostly concealed until he had achieved full control of the Party, then imposed upon an enormous country. Evidence from the period of concealment is of the yellow-eye-gleam sort, or it is inference of what Stalin must have felt when he compared his meager writings with the showy output of such rivals as Trotsky and Bukharin — look what he did to them when he got the power to show how he had felt all along.

Such arguments about one man's fiendishly concealed feelings are hardly convincing. Unmistakable evidence of systematic animosity against the intelligentsia first appeared during the Civil War, when Lenin was in charge, and the Party was still led by people like him, the tiny fraction of the intelligentsia that chose to be Bolshevik. Recall the systematic bias of the Cheka against educated people, Gorky's protest to Lenin, and Lenin's outburst to Gorky about the shit that imagines itself to be the nation's brains.[19] Systematic animosity subsided in 1922, only to reappear at the end of the 1920s in show trials of learned 'wreckers', which were obviously approved, if not initiated, by Stalin. In the early 1930s such terror erupted on a mass scale, with tersely reported 'shootings and arrests' of 'wreckers'[20] in all sorts of cerebral hiding places, from historiography to soil science, theatrical direction, and educational theory, not to mention applied fields such as engineering, agronomy, and economic planning, where the press could give concrete examples of expert knowledge willfully misused to obstruct the great leap forward.

In short, mass terror was turned upon the intelligentsia as it was on the peasantry during the revolution from above. The purpose was 'to encourage the others', the Spartan method of inspiring martial ardor in unreliable troops by orders to shoot every tenth soldier. The Soviet press of the 1930s explicitly declared the intention of forcing reliable service from suspect professionals, whose esoteric knowledge presumed to set limits on the Bolsheviks' blue-sky plans. Another obvious purpose was to relieve the Party's collective anxieties by discharging blame on slide-rule scapegoats: *they* were responsible for the jarring contrasts between projection and achievement in the great leap forward. Systematic mistrust of autonomous professionals also justified mass advancement of new Party bosses, the 'pushing up' (*vydvizhenie*) of reliable rude young men, abruptly placing them in charge of engineers and economists, public health specialists and educators, scientists and artists. Stalin's endlessly publicized insistence that practice has priority over theory was the keystone of faith in the *vydvizhentsy*: individuals 'pushed up' with scant regard for educational qualification, who had learned from practice how to manage suspect professionals.[21] One *vydvizhenets* boasted that he used 'snout-pounding' (*mordobitie*) to extract from experts the information they otherwise held secret.[22] He hit them in the face till they said what he wanted to hear.

Within that mentality in that period of its development Stalin became the man-god. In May 1935, addressing the graduating class of the Red Army Academy, he won 'Stormy applause, shouts of "Hurrah,"' when he boasted of his part in snout-pounding, or rather 'denting the sides' (*pomiat' boka*) of cautious skeptics, those who had doubted the realism of the Party's fort-storming assault on backwardness.[23] In the fall of 1935 he permitted himself some more intensely publicized praise for 'the boldness to smash the conservatism of some of our engineers and technicians', the daring kind of science that 'does not fear to raise its hand against the obsolescent, the old, and keenly listens to the voice of experience, of practice'.[24] He called on Bolsheviks to end their dependence on alien specialists not only by raising the hand to pound and dent and smash, but also by mastering science and technology with their own heads. That should not be hard for men of the special stuff that had won the Civil War and pushed through collectivization.

But that was only one side of a complex mentality. The emphasis in the 1930s was on aggressive disdain for elaborate calculation of costs and benefits, yet Stalin constantly republished his 1924 insistence that Leninist 'style' combined 'Russian revolutionary sweep' with an 'American business-like quality' (*amerikanskaia delovitost'*).[25] At critical moments in the 1930s his establishment frowned upon anti-intellectual hysteria and scapegoat sacrifice of learned specialists. Stalinist lieutenants in charge of ideology and higher learning spasmodically warned against attempts to revolutionize the sciences without genuine understanding of them.[26] And Stalin in his own person deplored *makhaevshchina* (the doctrine of Machajski, 'demagogic assignment of the intelligentsia to the exploiting classes') and *spetseedstvo* (literally cannibalism of specialists, 'a hostile attitude toward non-Party specialists, . . . toward the intelligentsia').[27]

Without access to private communications and confidential meetings we are bound to be puzzled, as the Soviet public was, by such fluctuating signals, which continually excited hostility to the intelligentsia but intermittently inhibited it. In 1938–9 Stalin tried to explain the fluctuation as an historical progression, from mistrust of the old 'bourgeois' intelligentsia to full faith in the new Soviet intelligentsia, which had been 'pushed up' out of the lower classes. But he confounded his own supposed history as he laid it out. He located the greatest hostility to Bolshevism in the most knowledgeable stratum of the intelligentsia, and vice versa: he assumed that the less knowledgeable strata had been the most likely to serve the Bolshevik cause.[28] Of course Stalin did not draw the disturbing conclusions, that Bolshevism and expert knowledge were inherently at odds, that ignorance was the surest ally of his Party. He slid over the problematic relationship between knowledge and power by simply equating the new, authentically Soviet intelligentsia with the *apparat* of Party and state, indeed with the 'commanding cadres', yet he was annoyed to observe that many Bolshevik officials regarded the new intelligentsia with much the same suspicion as they did the old. In November 1938 a decree of the Central Committee ordered such officials to get such absurd suspicion out of their minds.[29]

We are left guessing whether this back-and-forth on the intelligentsia expressed a dominant idea at war with persistent realities, or a jumble of inconsistent ideas and moods in a confused mind and a complex Party lurching between war and peace with masters of expert knowledge. Either way, we must also wonder how far Stalin was the creator, how far the creature, of such a dominant idea, or of such jumbled ideas and mood swings among Party militants, himself included. We may be sure that he liked to have his public wondering, to have them fuse in collective straining to understand their half-hidden divinity. Without their unifying fear and awe, we distant observers are condemned to share their wonderment. We are as unable as they were to know how much Stalin understood, how clearly he foresaw where he might be leading his Party and state. Chances are there were only a few blinding visions in a dark little mind, as he and his Party plunged toward catching up with the advanced powers.

SMASHING THOUGHTS

That was the central compulsive vision, the loathing of Russia's impotent backwardness, the wild urge to leap out of it all at once. In 1931 the most emotional speech that Stalin ever gave seized ten out of the blue, ten years to escape otherwise disastrous reality: 'We have fallen behind the advanced powers by 50–100 years. We must run through that distance in ten years. Either we will do that, or they will smash us.'[30] His 'ten' was accidentally accurate: Nazi Germany attacked in 1941, on the largest front, with the greatest armed force in the history of warfare, furiously committed to the destruction of Communism and the enslavement or even the extermination of 'inferior races'.

The inconsistencies in the defensive preparations of Stalin and his Party, their denunciation of the advanced nations that smash backward ones combined with a fury to make Soviet Russia one of those that smash, the nearly fatal wounds they inflicted on their own nation in the mad rush to compress its industrialization within a single decade – all that is too easily apparent to outside observers looking back. A taint of smug absurdity inheres in the outsider's question, Why did Stalin and his Party fail to see what is so obvious to us, the wastefully destructive — the nearly *self-destructive* — irrationality of the policies they called *practical*? Better to acknowledge the disability in the outsider's tranquility, his intrinsic incomprehension of berserkers, especially as he sees them submit to incarceration, torture, and execution at the hands of their own comrades in arms. Better to start with less stupefying problems than the Party's acceptance of the terror turned against itself, to consider situations where Comrade Stalin and his Party showed self-confident understanding of the obvious distinction between 'us', who deserve mutual confidence and protection of law, and 'them', the alien elements who do not.

Perhaps the chief significance of Lenin's 1923 judgment that Stalin was too rude to remain General Secretary is to be found in the 1924 decision by Stalin's comrades to hide that 'testament' of Lenin's, in Trotsky's self-defeating vacillation on the issue of hiding or publishing, and in the applause that Stalin won from the comrades in 1927, as he delivered the final oratorical blows to the completely defeated 'Trotskyite opposition':[31] 'Yes, I am rude, comrades, in relation to those who rudely and treacherously wreck and split the Party. I have not hidden that, and I do not hide it. It may be that a certain softness is demanded here in relation to splitters. But they won't get it from me.'* A rude soldier of the revolutionary army, proud to obey until called to command, his mind focused on disciplined, revolutionary service, whether giving it to the great Lenin or commanding it in Lenin's name — that was the mentality projected by Stalin and admired by his Party as they raised him to supremacy over themselves. It remained the Party's ego ideal until the current challenge of 'new thinking' and 'reconstruction'. To the extent that this ideal controlled printed thought and public action, it systematically frustrates the outsider's effort to discern individual minds. They were proud to present themselves in self-effacing uniform; they were fearful of deviance, even the slightest appearance of it.

The revolutionary context that shaped such a mentality is crucial to an understanding of its repressed discordance. Revolution is the breaking of rules, discipline obedience to them. Efforts to combine such opposites are more or less forced, the more or the less depending on the extent of unforced consensus in society at large. In pre-revolutionary Russia there was little consensus, even (or especially) among those who called themselves Marxist. They were continually 'split' by rival theories, leaders, and factional fighting. Such splits were briefly overwhelmed by mass revolution from below in 1917–18, an irresistible tide of consensus among workers,

* The Russian for political 'splitters' is *raskol'niki*, the same as the term for schismatics in Russian church history. That suggests another hypothesis, which is intriguing, but untestable: the influence on the Stalinist mentality of Christian hatred for deviance, a corollary of faith in almighty truth.

peasants, and soldiers, which carried Lenin and his party to power. But the approach to catastrophe during the Civil War, 1918–21, broke up the consensus, or alienated the Bolsheviks' mass base.

Either choice of concepts, liberal talk of consensus or Leninist talk of mass base, points to the same reality. Most of the peasantry and much of the urban working class manifestly turned against the policies of 'war communism', while the intelligentsia persisted in its visceral disapproval of the Bolshevik 'usurpers', who had spoiled the dream of a constitutional representative system. And economic activity declined past crisis, to collapse and famine. In such a context the natural tendency of revolutionaries, to argue vehemently and to split, could easily have cost them their power to rule. In fear and anger, disillusion and willful hope, the Bolshevik Party came to the paradoxical decision of 1921: they abandoned 'war communism' and offered a liberal compromise to the peasantry and the intelligentsia, while clamping a tyrannical ban on 'opposition' within their own Party. In society at large opposition was to be placated, if only for a time, while the Party in power was immediately to intensify its urge to unity through discipline. Loyal opposition quickly became an intolerable contradiction in terms; any disagreement within the Party was perceived as an opening wedge for the multitudinous 'class enemy', who had to be tolerated and placated outside the Party. The vanguard Party was besieged within its nation, within its own mentality.

Stalin emerged as the chief administrator of that discordance. His rivals for leadership saw him as a dull Party boss in a time of retrenchment, whose greatest distinction was his capacity to run the Party though lacking in distinction. 'The most outstanding mediocrity in our Party', Trotsky sneered.[32] He felt obliged to add a sociological explanation for the mediocrity's irresistible power: Stalin was 'the personification of the bureaucracy that is the substance of his political personality', whose 'rudeness and disloyalty are no longer mere personal characteristics [but] the character of the ruling faction'.[33] Trotsky flung that scornful sociology at a Party conclave of 1927, in the last speech they allowed him to give before expulsion. He was drowned out by the derisive racket of the 'bureaucrats' he was attempting to deride.[34] They saw themselves as practical leaders, and their chief, Stalin, as the quietly effective replacement of super-revolutionary speechifiers like Trotsky, who had attained a flashy eminence in the momentary storm of revolution from below. Those opposed views of Stalin in the 1920s were really one, charged with radically opposed feelings. If an outsider such as Max Weber had lived to see the process, he might have said that Stalin administered the routinization of insurrectionary charisma, to the satisfaction of most Party cadres, the disgust of a minority.

And then Stalin suddenly turned about, became super-revolutionary in administrative commands. In 1928–9 he turned the Party machine back to its Civil War job of seizing grain from resistant peasants, and then ordered the machine into 'a socialist offensive along the whole front'. The most extravagant part of the offensive was 'the liquidation of the kulaks as a class', which meant the transport of millions to distant waste places, while the luckier peasants at home were pushed into collective farms, where they could no longer set limits on the state's extraction of surplus product (except by sullen slowdown and deliberate ineptitude). After Stalin's fiat had committed the Party-state machine to that monstrous war, he got around to requesting approval from the representative bodies that were supposed to decide such matters, and to mobilizing public opinion with a huge propaganda drive. His role was dramatized by occasional emergence from headquarters, dressed in a severe military tunic, brusquely encouraging militants and threatening laggards. That was the context that put stunning force in the news of Comrade Stalin's personal appearance at the conference of agrarian Marxists to scold theorists for their separation from practice. A similar shock to intellectuals was the angry public letter that he sent in 1931 to a journal of revolutionary history. Until he barked at them to fall in line, the editors had been permitting 'archive rats' to make Party history a matter of discussion. Henceforth no one was to imagine that Marxist-Leninist comrades had ever disagreed among themselves; revolting oppositionists disagreed with truth, and they were miscreants, not comrades, in the past as in the present.[35]

His sudden change was a puzzle, and still is. From the calm chief of the center, brushing off demands of the left as irresponsible adventurism, he suddenly moved to a left extreme that made Trotsky seem quite timid. The larger puzzle was, and is, the spirited turnabout in the organization that he commanded. They threw themselves so ardently into the revolution he proclaimed from above, that they transformed it, as Stalin boasted, into one supported and pushed through down below. 'They' were, in the first place, administrators of the existing Party-state, yet they followed Stalin back to revolutionary upheavals, more extreme than those of 1917–21, quite dangerous to the rule they had so narrowly won.[36]

Many outsiders have argued that the centrist persona of the 1920s was a mask, concealing the inner essence of Stalin and his organization. Limitless power lust, in this view, was the essence. It approached a self-destructive extreme during the period of 'war communism', backed off for a few years of rest, and then madly revolted against the humiliating restraints of those few quiet years – against bargaining with the peasantry, against conceding high culture to the 'bourgeois' intelligentsia, against the power of any autonomous social groups to obstruct instant achievement of industrial, socialist power for the state. But talk of power lust trivializes a mentality distinguished by the grandeur of its claims. If we wish to be pejorative, we may say megalomania rather than grandeur, but with either term the puzzle is still the hugeness of aspiration, not the banality of power lust. Activists in any political system reveal a lust for power by being activists, especially as they rise to the top. It is a common passion; the historian's problem is to understand its different modes and varying intensity of expression in one or another country, from one period to another.

The grandeur or megalomania of Communists in power has been repeatedly checked by contrary tendencies, including realistic self-appraisal. Lenin, for example, coined the term *komchvanstvo*, 'comconceit', to caution against the delusions of grandeur that threatened Soviet Communists in power, the readiness to believe that there were literally no fortresses they could not storm, that any goal could be reached simply by nerving themselves to lunge for it. Those extravagant figures of speech were not Lenin's confection in mockery of *komchvanstvo*. It was Stalin who quite earnestly declared the Bolshevik power to storm any fortress, to achieve any goal by willing to achieve it.[37] With such slogans he led Soviet Communists into their revolution from above — after he had established his identity as the chief of a realistic bureaucracy committed to centrist policies.

Such swings have been apparent far beyond the person of Stalin, not only in the organization that made him chief boss and followed his lead first one way and then the other, but also in other Communist parties, which have developed on their own, without Stalin's personal control. Nearly every Communist party that has come to power has lurched spasmodically between rampage and restraint. Initial wildness has helped to win power, and consequent responsibilities of rule have generated some restraint, which has nearly always given way — rather soon — to convulsive impatience with restraint, to flailing at every obstacle, until, checked short of instant industrial socialism, the collective monopolists of power have subsided into a long period of diminishing swings between restraint and outburst, sullen realism alternating with bull-headed *shturmovshchina* (the fort-storming style of leadership) or *kampaneishchina* (the campaign style).*

Stalin's biography and his Party's history jointly reveal a mentality of that spasmodic, zigzag type. To credit him with creating the type is to go beyond the evidence — beyond rationality, to a vision of Stalin as the demiurge of contemporary history not only for the Soviet population but also for the entire third of humanity that has come under Communist rule, and even now for the unexpected corners of the underdeveloped world where his type of vanguard intermittently recurs. They are trapped in mythic thinking who exalt Stalin so. And so are they who recoil from such a 'cult of the individual' and exalt abstract ideology, that is, revere (or execrate) Marxism-Leninism as the demiurge. Many scholars perform that

---

* These terms are pejorative in the Soviet lexicon, though Stalin was anything but disapproving in chanting of no fortresses that Bolsheviks could not storm. Indeed, spring still brings earnestly proclaimed campaigns to make peasants plant crops in time, though the professed goal is peasant self-activation (*samodeiatel'nost'*), and *kampaneishchina*, the campaign way, is theoretically disapproved.

mythic turn. They picture Marxist-Leninist doctrine as the force that has brought to life vanguard parties in backward countries, and has generated in them protracted spasms of assault and accommodation at the approaches to a heaven they cannot storm.

Such exaltation of Marxism-Leninism or of Stalin (or Mao, or ... Comrade N) is a mobilizing myth for political activists. The scholar surrenders his own mind to their myth when he explains Communist activists by pointing as they do to their holy books, and to the Comrade who is the current chief interpreter of the texts because he is the current chief of the activists. They must keep their minds in operational focus by such a surrender, that is, by mythic exclusion of distracting perceptions. It might cut the nerve of action to consider, for example, that Marxism inspired Social Democrats as well as Communists, and to consider further that Leninism inspired Bukharin and Gramsci and Berlinguer, who bent back toward Social Democracy, as well as Stalin and Mao and Pol Pot, who bent forward toward total war of the revolutionary party-state against its recalcitrant population.

We outsiders — if we are authentic outsiders, and deliberately take our stand outside the mythic frame of mind that constrains Communists and anti-Communists within their compulsive contests — we are free to note such complexities. We can perceive the mentality called Stalinist as an historical *Gestalt*, a joint product of many willfully disciplined personalities, whose grandly simplistic ideological visions justify breakneck assaults on social and cultural 'backwardness', and provide a political sociology to guide the assaults. 'Backwardness' is the common shorthand for the invidious situation that generates the personalities, inflames the visions, and enables the assaults. All together that circle of mutually inflammatory factors can produce a revolutionary vanguard with sufficient zeal and know-how to gain control of a rearguard population. Thereafter the vanguard is locked into spasmodic lurching between combat and accommodation with the rearguard — including the rearguard qualities of its own mentality as well as those of the population at large. In the process what began as grand theorizing tends to become the cadence counting of a disciplined mass, now fast, now slow, rhythmically shouted on command. Yet Communists may not mock the intellect explicitly, as fascists did and religious fundamentalists still do. On the contrary, the Stalinist army wears a badge of fealty to rational discourse — to science, if you please — not to the irrational will of a leader or the literal truth of holy writ, and certainly not to the strangulated tensions that have actually governed its spastic cadences.

The pattern was starkly revealed in the history of high culture, which seemed largely exempt until the 1930s, when it was suddenly declared totally included. Before 1930 only the political arena exhibited repression of mental discord by shouted boasts of monolithic unity. In high culture during the 1920s unity was a dream of the future, a premise of Marxist theorizing, which was creatively discordant in its quest for unity. The division between politics and high culture was clearly expressed in a separation of powers. Stalin was chief of political practice, Bukharin of Marxist-Leninist theory; autonomous Marxist scholars were leaders of campaigns for Marxism in particular fields of higher learning, and within those fields avowedly non-Marxist specialists were respected masters of knowledge. That multiple division of labor, the genteel disintegration of modern culture in a Soviet form, broke down as Stalin mobilized the Party for forced industrialization, including assaults on the peasantry and the intelligentsia. In 1928 he and Bukharin disagreed backstage over the swing from a politics of compromise to a politics of assault. As the swing accelerated in the spring of 1929, Bukharin was publicly denounced. He was called the leader of 'the right opposition', though he and his sympathizers were far too timid or too well-disciplined to have earned such a showy label. He was reviled anyhow, as a warning to any who might secretly question the breakneck policies that he had questioned backstage. The position he lost as chief of theory was amalgamated to Stalin's as chief of practice, and the ethos of high culture was amalgamated to that of politics by abrupt decree, in disregard of actualities.

Gross incongruities between phrase-making and fact were immediately apparent. The approach of Stalin's fiftieth birthday in December 1929 was the occasion for a campaign to make him the single incarnation of the triune prophet, Marx-Engels-Lenin, though he had almost no prophetic writings to set beside theirs. At the Communist Academy one man jūstified the boss as prophet by saying that Stalin had discovered the error of Bukharin's social theory because Stalin was a *praktik* (practical person) and therefore a better *dialektik* (dialectician) than abstract philosophers. To which another man objected that such a formulation belittled Stalin and practical leaders in general:

> Stalin is a practical dialectician because he is a good theoretical dialectician. Stalin's correct practical standpoint results from a correct theoretical standpoint. . . . It is impossible to be a practical dialectician without being a theoretical dialectician. . . . I categorically deny that the chiefs [*vozhdi*] of our Party are only practical leaders. If they were not theorists they could not determine the Party's general line.[38]

With any formula of justification this new view might seem to have ruled out any form of theory but obsequious commentary on the intuitive convictions of practical leaders. Yet the supreme chief of practice was carefully close-mouthed, and simultaneously insistent upon scholarly theories to justify the intuitive convictions that practical leaders revealed in action. He declared his 'reverence before science', while boasting of readiness for 'very rude interference' when practicality required it.[39]

Scholars in the human sciences found themselves in precarious tenure of their special fields, commanded to theorize boldly in hope of pleasing the half-hidden man-god and in fear of offending him. To be precise, hope and fear were administered by an ideological bureaucracy, which had even more precarious tenure of its special field, Marxism-Leninism, under the direct supervision of an administrator who sat at Stalin's feet in the Polit-buro. At all levels, administrators of ideology were randomly snatched by administrators of terror, who were themselves subject to sudden snatching – until 1939, when the witch-hunting paranoia of Stalin and his militants declined from unendurable frenzy to hysterical stasis. That did not relax the cult of Stalin. With or without mass terror to stimulate fervor, the ideo-logical bureaucracy and the scholarly and artistic communities declared themselves worshippers of the 'coryphaeus', the choirmaster of all knowl-edge and art, as Stalin was often called without intentional mockery. His actual appearances on the choirmaster's podium were dramatic rarities, intensely enigmatic for all the apparent simplicity and directness of his style. Bureaucratic politics of a highly fearful and secretive type roiled about his demonstrative gestures – for this trend (apparently), against that (implicitly), and dreadfully Delphic or Sphinx-like concerning all.

In 1938 he made what seemed to be a public declaration of guiding principles for administrators of the intellect. At a Kremlin reception for officials of higher education, he proposed a toast:

> ... To science [*nauka*, i.e., learning in general], to its flourishing, to the health of the people in science.
>
> To the flourishing of science, of that science which does not fence itself off from the people, does not keep its distance from the people, but is prepared to serve the people, prepared to hand over to the people all the conquests of science, which serves the people not by compulsion but voluntarily with desire.
>
> To the flourishing of science, of that science which does not let its old and recognized leaders shut themselves up complacently in the shell of priests of science, in the shell of monopolists of science, which ... recognizes that the future belongs to the youth of science.[40]

The toast lasted ten or fifteen minutes – a short speech, actually, with ominously vague praise for scientists who respect traditions but are not slaves of them, who have 'the boldness to smash old traditions, norms, outlooks'. Galileo, Darwin, and Lenin were his only examples of smashers in the past; the speed-up miner Stakhanov and the polar explorer Papanin were his only current examples of 'the model man of science, who boldly leads the struggle against obsolescent science and lays down the road for new science'.

Along with the 1929 insistence on the priority of practice, that was the closest Stalin came to a program, a statement of guiding principles for the administrators of ideology and higher learning. His celebrated essay on dialectical and historical materialism (1938) was too inane for any use but tub-thumping celebration of the great author. In 1950 he put such choruses to shame by decrying authoritarianism in science, declaring 'the clash of opinions, the freedom of criticism' to be essential to the development of knowledge.[41] But even before Stalin published that blessing on liberalism, opinionated clashes repeatedly disrupted the rhythmic chants of Marxist-Leninist unity in Soviet culture. Kotowing to sacred texts and to 'the lessons of practice' did not lessen, it intensified, the fury of Stalinist 'discussions', either by bringing into scholarly disagreements the war of the sacred and the sinful, or by political manipulation of that war, or both. Such 'discussions' continually mocked the claim that Soviet culture had transcended the chaos of 'bourgeois' culture, which still tormented the decadent West.*

The absurd inconsistency could not be escaped by application of Stalin's guidelines. They demanded unification of higher learning through concentration on serving the people and smashing obsolete views, but the demand was either too precise or too vague. Too precise, if it set up Soviet or 'proletarian science' as the automatic opposite of Western or 'bourgeois science', and thereby outlawed any views shared with Western scholars. Too vague, if it allowed for the distinction between ideology, which is partisan, and science, which is all-human. Stalinist ideologists wavered on that crucial distinction, ended by endorsing it, but never have resolved the difficulties that attend it.[42] Nor could veneration of practicality put an end to the war of schools, least of all in such predominantly academic subjects as psychology. On many academic issues the cult of practice was irrelevant — for example, on the neural mechanics of the mind-body problem. Where the intuitions of practical leaders had some bearing — for example, on intelligence tests — scholars were more and more conditioned by the Stalinist system to look away from issues to leaders, and especially to look for signals from the chief (*vozhd'*), the supreme reader of practical experience. But he was mostly a silent reader in the realm of high culture, or maybe an icon, staring down from every wall though still alive in the Kremlin, capable of rare speech and 'very rude interference'.

---

* Stalinist 'discussions' differ from authentic discussions, which may go on without closure or may proceed to unforced consensus, because the community strives for standards of judgment that will be impersonal or equalitarian or conventional. In a Stalinist 'discussion' the boss's will is the implicit standard for an exasperated push to establish unity, a quick-as-possible herding of the community to a foregone conclusion, which may erupt in new 'discussion' when the boss changes his mind or leaves the scene.

PRETENTIOUS THOUGHTS

May we infer that the erratic policies of Stalin's ideological bureaucracy from 1930 to 1953 expressed the discordant pattern of his individual mind? Obviously not, for he could not have kept himself informed, if he had wanted to, of all the positions that the bureaucracy took in a wide variety of esoteric subjects. But obviously so, for the equally self-evident reason that the major positions taken were publicized in the central press, and must have had the chief's approval if only tacit or provisional or after the fact. The public was left guessing at the extent of his involvement, all the more because occasional spotlights of publicity would give brief glimpses of Comrade Stalin intervening in person on the ideological front: giving encouragement to the rebels against 'Menshevizing idealism' in philosophy, denouncing 'archive rats' in historical scholarship, shouting 'Bravo, Comrade Lysenko!' to a bold smasher of obsolete biology, rebuking economists for denying the reality of land rent in a socialist system. In the last few years of his life he even published two essays on intellectual topics, laying down the laws of socialist economics and of linguistics.[43]

Yet, in the very act of decreeing truth to those sciences he denounced such acts on principle: he decried the dictatorship of a crankish school of linguistics, which his ideological establishment had maintained for almost twenty years, and declared 'the clash of opinions, the freedom of criticism' to be essential for the flourishing of science.[44] Was he unaware of his self-contradiction, or proud of it as a sign of dialectical profundity − or contemptuously indifferent to such logical difficulties for intellectual types? Perhaps all of the above. His inner thoughts were concealed, but we must assume that he approved the cat-and-mouse consequences of the yes-no-maybe that he uttered on academic autonomy: learned specialists were batted about by his subordinate ideologists as mice are by cats, whose sport requires some autonomy in mice. Maybe the image should be dogs barking at skunks, since it was unusual for harassed scholars to get killed, and ideologists with excessive zeal could raise such a stink as to be excluded from decent society.[45]

No spotlight of publicity ever revealed Stalin directing neurophysiology, psychology or even literary art. In those fields his directing hand was flicked upon the public screen twice, so briefly as to suggest subliminal messages from a realm too deep for discussion. Certainly subordinates were not supposed to debate in public what the chief might intend by enigmatic gestures. They could only praise in general terms, and hope their praise would be found acceptable. But we outsiders cannot avoid puzzling over the brevity and the vagueness, as well as the signals themselves, wondering what they revealed of Comrade Stalin's psychology, and his Party's.

Maxim Gorky, newly returned from emigration and transformed from a critic of Lenin's dictatorship into a major propagandist of Stalin's,[46] had a special interest in Pavlov's Institute of Experimental Medicine. In Gorky's apartment, on 7 October 1932, Stalin, Molotov, and Voroshilov met with 'a group of scientists' from that Institute, including L. N. Fedorov, the Communist director, but not Pavlov himself.[47] A week later the press announced that the Council of People's Commissars was raising Pavlov's Institute to All-Union status, designating it the center for the 'all-round study of man', the Magnitostroi or Dneprostroi of the medical sciences.[48] (They were gigantic industrial and hydroelectric creations of the Five Year Plan.) Did the authorities intend to imply that the 'all-round study of man' would henceforth be based on Pavlov's doctrine? There is no telling.

Intense debates among rival schools of psychology had just reached an impasse. All the schools had been labeled bourgeois, all journals in the field were ceasing publication. May we infer that Stalin was breaking the deadlock, giving the nod to one of the schools? The question is still beyond the bounds of permissible discussion by Soviet scholars, who may only praise the favor shown to Pavlov's school, without comment on the possible relevance to the contemporaneous impasse in psychology. When Pavlov was hailed as a truly Soviet scientist, in 1935, Molotov would be the highest official at the ceremony.[49] Stalin's 1932 nod to Pavlov's school retained its elliptic quality. He did not plant his irresistible authority on a spot that might prove inconvenient, and he most certainly did not encumber his busy mind with the complexities of physiology or of psychological science.

Nevertheless, there was the mighty finger on a public screen pointing in a certain direction. We need not be surprised that it was the same direction as that in which Bukharin had pointed ten years earlier, when he praised Pavlov's psychology while rebuking the old scientist's politics.[50] Nor should we be surprised that it was the same direction — as far as laymen knew or cared — which Chernyshevsky had applauded in the 1860s, when Sechenov offered a speculative reduction of the mind to reflexes of the brain. Radical interest in such matters had ebbed away, but the feeling persisted that there must be some affinity between physiological materialism and the left, in spite of Marx's discouraging sarcasm. Stalin's distinctive contribution to the problem was to put a disciplined army of ideologists to work, by a Delphic gesture of approval for Pavlov, and thus to lay upon serious psychologists the labor of dissembling, pretending to belong to a tradition that ideologists proceeded to construct.

We will note their archaizing labor below, their mythic marriage of Sechenov to Chernyshevsky, of both to Pavlov, all to Marx, and so to Lenin and Stalin and the luminous Soviet point in the forefront of advancing world science — still at the forefront in the 1930s and 1940s, under Stalin's leadership, as in the 1860s, when Sechenov was miraculously inspired by the 'Russian revolutionary democrats'. Suffice here to note that Stalin and his Party hardly cared to know about the complexities and frustrations that attended efforts to reduce mind to brain. Radical interest in the subject had declined to a crude generality: radicals believe, and reactionaries deny, that the mind is a function of the brain. The generality was now to be justified by specialists at the chief's apparent say-so, though he would not, maybe could not, offer a philosophical justification, not even a few vague metaphors such as Bukharin's. That too was characteristic of the Stalinist mentality, that peremptory commitment of specialists to stereo-typed memories of nineteenth-century visions. Stalin and his Party left cities overwhelmed by such commitments in ornate buildings and pompous statuary, blotting out the few spare modernist structures that had gone up in the 1920s, when high culture enjoyed its brief autonomy.

On 26 October 1932 Stalin returned to Gorky's apartment, to 'converse with a group of writers'. This time three of his actual words were engraved in the public record: 'engineers of human souls' (*inzhenery chelovecheskikh dush*). That is what Comrade Stalin said, that was the job category, the administrative slot that he found for imaginative writers.[51] The momentous placement was announced when all previous organizations of schools and trends of literary art had been dissolved, and writers were mobilized in a single Union. At the founding Congress of the Writers' Union in August 1934 Andrei Zhdanov, Party chief of ideology, took the supreme chief's three-word assignment for the theme of his keynote address. He spelled out the job specification by reference to 'socialist realism', another combination of opposites that may be profoundly dialectical or logically inconsistent, or simply the Soviet variety of kitschy goo:

> Comrade Stalin has called our writers engineers of human souls. What does this mean? What duties does this title confer upon you? ... The truthfulness and historical concreteness of the artistic portrayal should be combined with the ideological remolding and education of the toiling people in the spirit of socialism. This method ... is what we call socialist realism. ... To be an engineer of human souls means revolutionary romanticism, ... a combination of the most stern and sober practical work with a supreme spirit of heroic deeds and magnificent future prospects. Our Party has always been strong by virtue of the fact that it has united and continues to unite a thoroughly businesslike and practical spirit with broad vision, with a constant urge forward. ...[52]

Stalin does not deserve the worldwide copyright that is now his for 'engineers of human souls.' My ruling is not simply based on chronology, the metaphor's appearance in previous comment on the writer's trade. In 1928 Stalin had probably read Olesha's use of it in *Izvestiia*, but he had probably not read Brecht's in the German press, and he almost certainly did not know that Huysmans had used it in a pre-revolutionary sneer at the notion of writers discovering exalted principles in human minds.[53] The metaphor was in the common culture of the age, but Stalin's meaning was new. Previously the notion of writers as engineers of souls suggested some absurdity in modern society, which produces human souls that can be engineered and writers that can do the engineering. Stalin and his ideologists caught up the phrase in apparent ignorance of its nettlesome ambiguity, and their naive approving usage might conceivably have won out. (Note how the public relations industry in the West has removed mockery from talk of 'image making'.) But Soviet writers would not forget that nettlesome quality of the metaphor, and the naively approving Stalinist usage faded away.

Even at the Congress of Writers in 1934 there was a hint of the pejorative in Isaac Babel's ostensibly reverent speech hailing Comrade Stalin for transforming writers into engineers of human souls, but worrying that the engineers might not write under the weight of such responsibility, without the ancient privilege of writing badly.[54] Explicit mockery made the phrase unmistakably pejorative after 1953, when Stalin was laid beside Lenin in eternal glory, only to be taken out within a decade and turned to routine ashes in the Kremlin wall. The successors who used his corpse so inconsistently are embarrassed by his phrase, 'engineers of human souls', and do not use it. They still want imaginative writers to produce the Soviet equivalent of supermarket literature, which engineers poor souls in the West, and they continue the crude Stalinist method of seeking to overtake and surpass the production of supermarket literature: a centralized publishing industry controlled by a disciplined army of editors and censors. But − or therefore − 'engineers of human souls' has become the exclusive property of dissidents and antagonists, who use the phrase not so much to ridicule the writers' trade as to scorn the Stalinist way of bossing it.[55] Such is the cunning of history; the coryphaeus' gift to literary theory turned back against his system.

I am assuming that Stalin was unaware of such nuances. Of course I may be wrong. He may have decided, quite deliberately, to show contempt for the intelligentsia by putting imaginative writers in a job category that mocked their independent creativity and the autonomy of their audience's souls. One recalls Lenin's 1905 essay, 'Party Organization and Party Literature', which called writers 'screws and cogwheels' in the social mechanism, imagined the intelligentsia's screams of outrage, and shushed them with an assurance of respect for individual creativity, and with the observation that writers who disliked his Party's line could peddle their stuff elsewhere.[56] My guess is that Stalin was incapable of such ironic swordplay, because he was too crude or too superficial in his view of writers. But I cannot be sure of that, for his style as man-god was the minimal act, with subsequent explanations ground out by the ideological bureaucracy.

1 (above, left) I. M. Sechenov, the father of Russian physiology, as a young man

2 (below, left) I. F. Tsion, the first Jewish professor, teacher of Pavlov, or Élie de Cyon, as he presented himself in the West

3 (above, right) Sechenov's major students, N. E. Vvedenskii (seated, second from left) and A. A. Ukhtomskii (seated, third from left), with their students, about 1912

4 (below, right) V. M. Bekhterev in 1903, Russia's major neurologist, psychiatrist, and 'objective psychologist' or 'reflexologist'

5 (above, left) I. P. Pavlov, Nobel Laureate, 1904

6 (above, right) Pavlov at the Military Medical Academy, 1911

7 (below) Pavlov in the laboratory, 1928. L. A. Orbeli, crown prince of the Pavlovian realm, is seated at his right hand

8a,b Pavlov endorses the Soviet cause. Front page of *Izvestiia*, 18 August 1935. Stalin and Voroshilov review their forces at the top of the page. Molotov and Pavlov celebrate the International Congress of Physiologists at the bottom of the page. Between them is I. A. Akulov, the Party official in charge of the Congress, and second from right is G. N. Kaminskii, Commissar of Health, both of whom were subsequently 'repressed'. The other men are foreign scientists

9 Molotov and Pavlov as they appear in Pavlov's *Collected Works*

10 Orbeli in 1957, restored to eminence

11 I. S. Beritashvili, independent continuer of Pavlov's and Bekhterev's research

12 P. P. Blonskii, the first psychologist to announce his acceptance of the Soviet regime, and the first to call for a Marxist psychology

13 K. N. Kornilov, eclectic leader of the campaign for a Marxist psychology in the 1920s

14 S. L. Rubinshtein, chief theorist of Marxist-Leninist psychology from the 1930s to the 1960s

15 L. S. Vygotsky, the muffled deity of Soviet psychology, in the photograph that accompanied his obituary, 1933

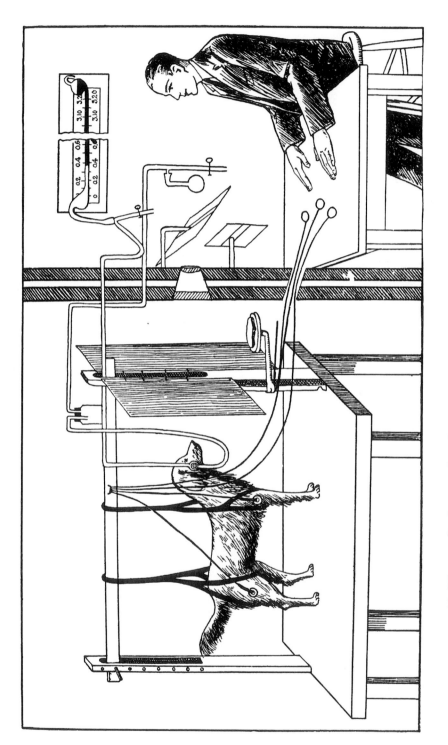

16 Diagram of Pavlovian or classical conditioning. The dog is held in place by a harness, food is presented or withheld by the rotating dish, stimuli (sound, light, electric shock) are delivered by the experimenter pressing buttons, and saliva is automatically drained off and measured

17a,b Photograph and diagram of Beritashvili's "natural" experiments in conditioning. The chicken, released from its cage (center rear) two minutes after food has been placed behind the screen to its left, runs directly there, not to the screen on its right. In the diagram of experiments with dogs, L is the dog's station, K is its regular feeding place, which may be open or shut, S' and S" are screens concealing containers A–H from the dog. He is led to one that has food in it, allowed to eat, and then returned to his station. The dotted line shows the path of the dog when subsequently released from his station. He shows a highly reliable memory of the place where he has found food, even if the containers have been removed, as in the diagram on the right. Explanation, Beritashvili argued, requires such mentalist concepts as representation, which are taboo in Pavlov's theory

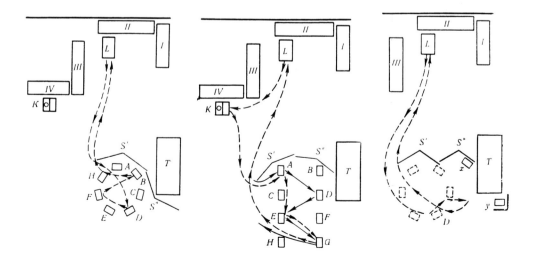

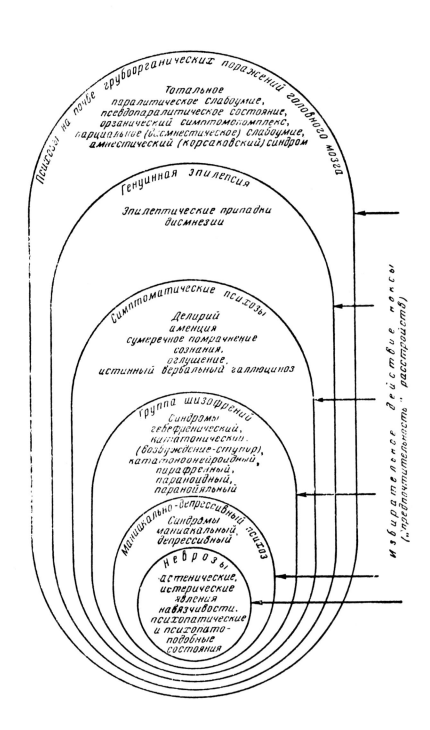

18 Snezhnevskii's 1960 diagram of his classification of mental illnesses, showing
"the nosological specificity of psychopathological syndromes". The progression
is from neuroses in the smallest circle through "the group of schizophrenias"
and "genuine epilepsy" to "psychoses on the basis of grossly organic brain
traumas" in the outermost circle

That was how he continued to perform the large intellectual role expected of the Marxist-Leninist chief. As such he could hardly avoid the ideological contest in imaginative literature, for that traditional passion of the Russian intelligentsia was still intense. It had not been shriveling into unexamined catchwords, as the interest in physiological psychology had. Even in the exile culture the young Vladimir Nabokov was annoyed by worship of Chernyshevsky and 'civic spirit' (*grazhdanstvennost'*), the ancestral version of 'party spirit' (*partiinost'*). He wrote a novel satirizing that Russian tradition, which precipitated experimental proof of his point: the émigré publisher cut out the satirical portrait of Chernyshevsky. When Nabokov became a famous American writer, he published an uncut English translation, with a preface wondering when his native land might have a regime that would tolerate satire of the civic-spirited tradition.[57]

In Soviet Russia even in the comparatively liberal 1920s Party chiefs felt compelled to give writers guidance on the shaping of their readers' souls. Trotsky's *Literature and Revolution* was the best-known work of that sort, an extended mixture of exhortation and complaint to fellow-traveling writers.[58] Stalin did not produce a comparable book or even an essay; he did not give a speech or interview on the subject. He continued the tradition in his own godlike manner, by uttering a three-word job description for writers, leaving Zhdanov and his establishment to figure out what the chief had in mind. Then to thousands of editors and censors fell the endless job of applying the chief's grand, though inarticulate, scheme, with thousands of vehemently obsequious critics to measure literary works against it.

Glorifiers of Stalin's intellect took for granted that vast industrial display of the mentality that he shared with his Party. They glorified his mind for utterances that bore his personal seal, especially those that went beyond three words. There was most notably the 1938 *Short Course* of Party history, written by a committee of persons unnamed, except for the chief himself, who claimed individual authorship of the chapter on dialectical and historical materialism.[59] Praised without limit while the chief was there to hear, it fell into oblivion once he turned to dust in the Kremlin wall. The 1913 essay on Marxism and the national question, and perhaps the 1950 essay on Marxism and linguistics, enjoy a little life beyond the author's life, along with speculation about the ghosts who may have helped to write them (Lenin or Bukharin in the first case, an eminent Soviet scholar in the second). Analogous speculation (of plagiarism in this case) attaches to two essays of Mao Tse-tung's that laid claim to philosophizing,[60] which occasioned choruses of boundless gratitude while the presumed author could appear on the tribune to wave back at the cheering masses. Thus leader and led attested the continuing tradition of the prophetic mind: Marx-Engels-Lenin had a worthy successor.

The hysteria of those efforts evinced the repressed knowledge that the

age of enlightened prophets was actually gone. Now none can doubt that
Stalin and Mao were the shrunken ends of a disappearing genus, the post-
Enlightenment hybrid of political leader and universal intellectual, species
Marxist. They were twentieth-century politicians, with little heart or mind
for the intellectual part of the inherited role that they could not or would
not abandon. They delegated the actual work to a bureaucratic machine,
which extolled the chief as the living heir to Marx-Engels-Lenin while itself
manufacturing the product of his mind.

That is the source of a great paradox in Soviet cultural history: Marxist-
Leninist intellectual commitments were enormously expanded in the 1930s
to the 1950s, just when the intellects at work grew shrunken and shallow.
A big bureaucracy of little minds claiming scientific knowledge of the
world could make far more intellectual commitments than any individual
thinker striving to understand the world, even such an audacious polymath
and would-be activist as Karl Marx. What drove the little minds to huge
expansion and what they did in various fields of learning cannot be derived
from their simple invocation of the chief's immeasurable genius or their
insistence on the universal reach of their ideological heritage. Neither Stalin
nor the sacred texts of Marx-Engels-Lenin were ever involved with such
matters as brain localization or mental illness or experimental psychology.
What moved Stalinist ideologists into such fields and what they did there
are questions to be answered by particular historical inquiry. Believers in
the determinist power of sacred or diabolical creeds may wince at such
crippling of their unhistorical faith; the historically minded student of ideas
may smile in weary satisfaction. Coherence is lost, but a kind of freedom
appears, even for true believers in great creeds.

But one large pattern was obvious everywhere: anti-intellectualism in an
intellectual guise. The vast bureaucratic expansion of Marxist-Leninist
ideology camouflaged a retreat from live thought. Comrade Stalin and his
Party almost completed the transition to the mental world of typical
twentieth-century politicians, who are sheltered from serious intellectual
labor by staffs of ghostwriters and other obsequious experts, and beyond
that rampart are protected from serious thought by intensifying specialization and the withering of grand ideology in the intellectual world at large.
For typical twentieth-century political leaders slogans and clichés suffice,
fragments and vestiges of once grand ideologies, while newspaper writers,
magazine pundits, and academic pontificators rework the fragments and
vestiges in their progressively heavier styles. In some respects Stalin and his
Party belonged to the dominant political species of our century. In range of
genuine intellectual interests they were almost as narrow, in depth almost
as shallow, as their typical 'bourgeois' counterparts in the West, almost as
exclusively obsessed with arranging people in hierarchies of domestic power
to enhance national power abroad, 'ours' in competition with 'theirs'. Yet
the burden of their revolution dragged Stalin and his Party into extravagant

denial of their own nature, into wild pretensions of intellectuality, insisting with guns in hand that the intelligentsia hear and obey.

At the time outside observers sensed a rage for some metaphysical order, which could be appeased only by continuous total war on the actual world. That became a favorite theme in Western explanations of Stalinism at mid-century.[61] They ignored a strange complacency within the Stalinist mentality. Surrender to things as they are was often contained within insistence on total revolutionary change. That was especially common in higher learning. Much academic autonomy persisted through vehement insistence on the party principle. Incongruities of label and content became a common feature of learned publication. Decorative passages of Marxist-Leninist denunciation prefaced sober expositions of the 'bourgeois' learning that was ostensibly denounced. The intellectual world rose on new foundations more in pretense than in fact.

The mental mechanism of that pretentious process can be seen in Stalin's habitual talk of grasping the main link or seeing the big picture. Those metaphors were his way of dismissing what did not fit his schematic thought, of rising above the chaos that threatens to overwhelm a lesser person. Were not his intuitive judgments proved right by his successful mastery of affairs at the top? So too for every lesser boss; the petty truths seen by those down below could be brushed aside. The rule that practice has priority in the determination of truth justified subordination, not only of academic theorists to practical leaders, but also of practical people to those who stood higher in the pyramid of power, and thus had claim to see the bigger picture. Soviet pragmatists could see little or no middle ground between such hierarchical ordering of claims to knowledge and hopeless conflict of each person's practical intuition with all others'. If I may offer a simple translation of this central Stalinist conviction: human beings learn truth through many forms of practice, but most of all through bossing.

Where a critic sees grotesque pretense that things are as officials suppose them to be, the Stalinist feels obliged to declare the future reality already present to the mind's eye of a sufficiently farsighted leader. Or the Stalinist may be simply uninformed of particular discrepancies between official schemes and grubby realities. The higher up the pyramid of power, the more effective are the baffles against information at odds with the bosses' schemes. Either method of reassurance, the imperious look to the future or the screening out of inconvenient information, can serve to justify war with mundane reality or acceptance of it, or some combination. The only way to know which pattern prevailed is to study the Stalinists at work in particular fields of endeavor, for they were pragmatists in action as well as ideology, continually adjusting their claims of knowledge to the lessons of experience. They even knew how to correct themselves when experience, even at the pyramid's peak, kept proving their beliefs to be dangerously at odds with reality. Within a system that concentrated power at the top and responsibility below, the top could always blame its errors on the bottom. Stalin was a master of that rude art.

All this has emphasized perhaps too much the enduring Stalinist system, the features that outlasted the decade in which the system was violently created. The exceptional wildness of those years — most notably the collectivizing assault on the peasants, the terrorist assault on the intelligentsia, and finally on the Party itself — have been perhaps too casually noted in this analysis of the mentality at work in Stalin and his Party. So too have the murderous assault of Nazi Germans and the consequent mass sacrifice of Soviet people to save the native land. The victims are counted in many millions, though numbers are unfeeling abstractions, and feeling is essential to the understanding of a collective mentality. In Soviet memories Stalin and his Party are soaked with sacrificial blood, as butchers or saviors or both together. Stalinists after Stalin may be perceived as self-serving manipulators of an increasingly stultified system, but Stalin and his Party carry about their brutish heads the red aura of imposed revolution, mass terror, and patriotic war to victory over 'advanced' foreigners bent on enslavement.

Intense feelings, of admiration and of hatred, attach to that aura, for insiders. Outsiders take distant note, and puzzle over the pragmatism of berserkers. Berserk pragmatism seems an impossible combination when one does not share it, when one can see the warriors in frenzy and hear their bellowing insistence on practicality, but cannot join the contrary elements within one's own mind — which is an unavoidable confession of failure. Seeing how the mentality of Stalinists worked without understanding how it made sense, one too quickly falls into talk of abnormal minds, delusions, madness. Yet it is also insane for the outsider to imagine himself master of a global madhouse, handing out straitjackets to patients who will not accept his authoritative diagnoses. That is the way of the anti-Communist crusader. Better to cultivate the calm pragmatism that simply confesses an ultimate inability to get inside the Stalinist mentality, to grasp its inward subjectivity.

12

The Criterion of Practice

Psychologists' claims of practical expertise provoke odd mixtures of trustful hope, alarm, and mocking disbelief. If they really do know how to bring madmen to sanity, workers to willing labor, children to model adulthood, as masterfully as other engineers make sewage systems or weapons of mass destruction, they obviously deserve very great hope or even greater alarm, depending on the goals of such human engineering, and on the underlying decision whether we want ourselves to be engineered for any purpose. If they cannot, they deserve mockery for claims that they can, perhaps prosecution for playing confidence games in a world so full of people yearning for technological escape from difficult problems.

Stalin and his Party had the usual twentieth-century mixture of inconsistent attitudes on applied psychology, but they were unique in their violent fluctuations from one to another. In the 1920s and early 1930s they believed in psychohygiene, psychotechnics, and pedology — and suddenly they turned so completely hostile that they seemed to be dismissing any notion of expertise in mental health, industrial psychology, or child studies. Of course they were still determined to modernize Soviet Russia, which meant that experts were still needed to treat disturbed people, to manage workers, and to school children. In those fields as in all others the Stalinists were intent not only on catching up with the advanced Western states but on forging ahead of them. They were so dreadfully impatient to be through with backwardness and out in front that they soon fell into the habit of picturing their makeshifts as models for the world, or worse, picturing their mistakes as models. Indeed even in the mid-1950s, when they backed away from the extremes of high Stalinism, they went on adoring its models in applied psychology. Aleksei Stakhanov is still praised for his contribution to the rational organization of labor. Anton Makarenko is more than a bygone hero, he is still the supreme model for educational psychology, and Andrei Snezhnevskii stayed in charge of psychiatry until 1987, still insisting that his clinician's sense of practicality must shape the science of madness, which is otherwise a chaos of patternless symptoms and ineffectual treatments.

PSYCHOHYGIENE

Magnates were not the only originators of Stalinism. At every level of the Party there was a scattering of people who were impatient with the compromises of the 1920s and the attendant recognition that progress to socialism would be slow and tortuous. In 1927, for example, while Stalin still seemed a moderate, a small group of Communist psychiatrists opened a campaign against the Moscow Society of Neuropathologists and Psychiatrists.[1] Exclusivity angered those Communists. Membership in the Society was limited to specialists who had published works of merit, as judged by the existing membership. About eighty of the 400 neurologists and psychiatrists in Moscow had been co-opted.[2] They met in private, not only to elect new members but to select the editorial board of the country's leading professional journal, to decide on psychoneurological articles for the *Great Medical Encyclopedia*, and to organize the conventions that were open to the profession at large. That at any rate was the secretive authoritarian picture drawn by the malcontents.

The first attacks on the traditional pattern failed to budge it. At a large conference in 1928 the Stalinists were outraged to hear counter-arguments, demands that professional associations should strengthen their autonomous functions by intensified advocacy of professional interests. No one needed explicit reminders that pre-revolutionary medical associations had used such talk of professional interests to make demands for constitutional representative government. The Civil War was still in everyone's memory, the time when mass terror had chastened such boldness, leaving professional associations quite subdued in politics, though still non-Communist inwardly. The pattern lasted till 1929–30, when a new wave of terror crushed resistance to the rule of Communists within the professional associations and mobilized them into cheering for Communist rule everywhere. In November 1929, while the press was reporting the purge of 'wreckers' from the Academy of Sciences,[3] the Moscow Society of Neuropathologists and Psychiatrists gave in. It dropped the requirement of publication for membership, and elected more than 300 new members *en masse*, along with a new slate of officers. Half were Communists, the other half members of the All-Union Association of Workers of Science and Technology for Aid to the Construction of Socialism (VARNITSO).[4]

Similar upheavals occurred in every other scientific society during 1929–31.[5] All succumbed to Bolshevization, as the process was called — with little change of intellectual substance, at the outset. The old leadership's fear of a decline in standards seemed groundless, for the time being.

The new leadership made grand declarations about a sharp turn to dialectical materialism and to practical service of socialist construction, but intensification of past trends was the only immediate result. The turn to dialectical materialism meant publication of articles on the Behavioral Congress of 1930, which draped new slogans of unity over pre-existing schools. The new devotion to practical service expressed itself in calls for an expanded mental health movement, which had been the pet project of Communist psychiatrists in the 1920s.[6] The base from which they launched their take-over of the professional society was the Moscow Institute of Neuropsychiatric *Prophylaxis*. Nor was that emphasis peculiar to the Communist group of neurologists and psychiatrists; preventive medicine and public health were the main concern of leftist physicians in general, before the 1917 Revolution and after.

'Psychohygiene' was then the Soviet term for the mental health movement. The name was taken from German, but the most admired model had come to be American. The object was to substitute prevention and outpatient care for institutional cure of mental illness, or rather, for the institutional confinement that notoriously fails to cure. In part the Soviet advocates of psychohygiene were forerunners of deinstitutionalization, as it would be called when it took hold in the West at mid-century. In part they were responding to a peculiarly Soviet problem. Pre-revolutionary Russia had too few psychiatrists and mental hospitals to begin with. Then eight years of disaster — world war and civil war, social upheaval, economic collapse, and famine, 1914–22 — had caused a great increase in the need for mental healing. Psychiatrists used various terms to describe what they saw in their clinics and heard from their colleagues. Some spoke of mass neurasthenia, others of mass schizoidization, or the widespread appearance of autistic symptoms, or simply of 'Soviet *iznoshennost"* (exhaustion, or premature aging).[7] Dr P. B. Gannushkin, one of the leaders of the Moscow Society until the Bolsheviks dislodged him, coined a new term: 'early acquired invalidism' (as opposed to congenital invalidism and to the disability that comes with age).[8] Whatever terms were used, there was general agreement on a great increase in the number of psychically wounded and worn out people, tending to shrink into themselves, to become extremely apathetic, or to lose the capacity for work at an early age.

Party activists were a class of special concern, as the upper stratum of any population is to psychiatrists. Repeated studies showed that they suffered from an especially high incidence of neuroses, hypertension, and other cardiovascular disorders. As Dr L. L. Rokhlin put it: 'That by which the Party *aktiv* lives, the brain and the heart, that is what ails them most of all' ('*To, chem zhivet partaktiv — mozgom i serdtsem — tem on bol'she vsego boleet*').[9] In the 1920s Party leaders reacted with sympathetic concern, annually referring nervous comrades to psychiatrists during the lull after the spring campaigns, commissioning special investigations of such sample populations as the activists sent to study at Party schools, and most of all fostering open talk, advising the *aktiv* how to take proper care of themselves. Dr Zalkind, the chief Party expert in the psychoneurological sciences until the revolution from above, set the tone in lectures, *Pravda* articles, pamphlets and books.[10] Commonsense realism was the characteristic viewpoint. The *aktiv* were warned against the widespread habit of crowding too many hours into a working day, skipping a regular day off, grabbing irregular and poorly balanced meals. Concerning other threats to mental health the experts could do little but point warning fingers. Crowded apartments, to take the most serious threat, allowed the *aktiv* no place to do their paper work or studying, or simply to relax in quiet, or to have a proper sexual life.[11] The psychiatrists also noted special problems among those activists – the overwhelming majority – who were shifting from manual work with no formal education beyond primary school. Troubled by repressed fears of inadequacy, unaware of the sedentary worker's need for periodic breaks and physical exercise, a large percentage of such activists developed neurotic symptoms, while some suffered breakdowns.[12]

The initial impact of the revolution from above was to intensify the drive both for preventive and for remedial measures. The newly Bolshevized journals published shocking figures on the insufficiency of hospital beds for the mentally ill, and on the massive need for *vytrezviteli* ('sobering stations', where alcoholics could be dried out, releasing hospital beds and psychiatric personnel for more serious cases). They even called for a campaign to stop rural people from chaining and beating the mentally ill.[13] In general they intensified appeals for an end to 'penitentiary psychiatry', with its 'factories producing chronic inmates'.[14] To a large extent they issued the kinds of appeal that one expects to hear from public-spirited psychiatrists all over the twentieth-century world, acknowledging the faults of their nineteenth-century predecessors. But there were also distinctively Soviet elements of revolutionary utopianism during the revolution from above: socialist society would now accomplish what could only be dreamed of by 'bourgeois' psychiatrists. Early in 1931, for example, Dr L. M. Rozenshtein, who was then joining the Party, forecast 'the creation of working, semi-therapeutic "phalansteries" [for the mentally ill], somewhat like *kolkhozy*, in the vicinity of agro-towns [*agrogoroda*], and especially the creation of forms of light work in socialist town-communes, in *sovkhozy* of an industrial sort, and so on.'[15]

Most of all the stress was on prevention. The mental health movement so much admired in the United States for its extensiveness would become a genuinely mass movement under socialism. Its aim would be not only the elementary 'struggle for culture, against drunkenness, for a real liquidation of illiteracy, for labor consciousness and labor discipline among the working masses and the peasantry'.[16] Dr Rokhlin quoted that characteristic formula from Party resolutions, and spelled out further dreams of his own. During times like the Civil War, he explained, one could hardly speak of 'carefully measured labor, of the culture and rationalization of work and everyday life, of the culture of the personality'. When the Soviet republic had been in danger 'the maddest expenditure of oneself was justified.' But now, with the construction of socialism, the cultivation of the personality through careful organization of work and everyday life was becoming a practical matter.[17]

It takes no great perspicacity for the outsider to see Dr Rokhlin's gross misreading of the new age and the psychiatrist's role in it. The all-out construction of socialism brought a return of the maddest expenditure of individual selves, not the final leap to utopia. Even before the revolution from above some specialists had been apprehensive of Communist backlash against a mental health movement that emphasized moderation in the expenditure of self and warned of serious costs in revolutionary upheaval. Dr Gannushkin, for example, confessed that he deliberately selected an obscure journal for his first articles on 'early acquired invalidism', because he did not want to provoke undue alarm.[18] His students, speaking on the subject at the Behavioral Congress of January 1930, were anxious to explain that Gannushkin intended no criticism of the Revolution by his frank examination of its psychic costs.[19] In February a publication of the Central Committee gave Gannushkin and another psychiatrist space to offer more explanations and reassurances. They insisted that the mental health movement did not call in question the power of intensive work to invigorate, if it is performed under socialism rather than capitalism.[20] The same theme echoed in apologetic notes that the newly Bolshevized journals appended to articles on mental health: these reports of mental illness are one-sided, for they ignore the mental health achieved through socialist labor, but they deserve publication, for they raise issues that need discussion.[21]

Apologies and excuses proved unavailing. In 1931 new bosses put an end to the mental health movement. Dr Semashko was pushed out of the Commissariat of Health, which he had organized in 1917, and a new type of official was installed as Commissar. M. F. Vladimirskii came to medicine from the secretariat of the Central Committee and the Commissariat of Internal Affairs, that is, from the Party's central chancellery and the state's administration of police.[22] When he told a medical conference that it was wrong to publish disruptive stuff like Gannushkin's or Rokhlin's, with or without editorial disclaimers, the physicians did not protest.[23] Professional autonomy had not only been denied in principle. It was now limited in fact by Party discipline, since Party members had been installed as editors of the professional journals and as officers of the professional societies. When publicly rebuked, they hastened to make amends in the abject spirit that prevailed after Stalin's condemnation of 'Menshevizing idealism', the separation of intellectual work from direct service of the Party line. No matter that Party leaders had commended, as recently as 1930, what they condemned in 1931.[24] Abandoned policies were henceforth to be charged as mistakes or crimes against the individuals who had carried them out, not against the Party leaders who had ordered or tolerated them — so long as they remained in the leadership.

Under the headline, 'For a Bolshevik Offensive on the Theoretical Front of Psychoneurology', a former leader of the mental health movement apologized for his sins, such as the assertion that socialist inspiration reduces the worker's *feeling* of fatigue. It reduces the *reality* of fatigue, he now perceived.[25] As usual his self-criticism was mild by comparison with his criticism of others. 'Only a conscious or subconscious enemy of socialist construction' could write, as another specialist had, that activists transferred from manual to mental labor experienced special problems.[26] There were even harsher words for Dr V. A. Giliarovskii, an eminent psychiatrist, who had lectured the Behavioral Congress on the problems created by rapid urbanization, such as 'early arteriosclerosis, premature invalidism, Soviet exhaustion [*iznoshennost'*]':

> So-called 'Soviet exhaustion [*iznoshennost'*]' does not exist in reality. What exists is merely a reactionary delusion [*bred*], by which they are trying to pit the proletariat against its revolutionary tempos, and by sowing fear of non-existent difficulties to hold back our movement forward. This whole theory of Professor Giliarovskii is a theory of bourgeois restoration.[27]

N. I. Grashchenkov, who was emerging as one of the top three new Party leaders on the psychoneurological front,[28] revoked the previous admiration that Soviet writers had expressed for the mental health movement in the United States. He found it hopelessly 'bourgeois' in character. 'In our country', by contrast, the movement 'must be an instrument for mobilizing the masses for the execution of the tasks of construction, an instrument for creating a personality that fully meets the requirements of socialist society [*polnotsennaia lichnost' sotsialisticheskogo obshchestva*]'.[29]

That formulation was a bit vague. M. B. Krol', another of the new top three Party leaders on the psychoneurological front, was more specific. In his celebration of the Revolution's fifteenth anniversary, he argued that the mental health of workers and collectivized peasants was assured by their dedication to labor as a matter of honor, glory, and heroism; by their participation in the sociopolitical life of the native land. Those were the chief means for achieving the *ozdorovlenie*, the health improvement, of the nervous system. What then could specialists contribute? Krol' offered a concrete example. An 'express brigade' (*skvoznaia brigada*) from the Belorussian Institute of Health Care had gone to a factory and persuaded a group of workers to use five minutes of their lunch break for calisthenics. The result was an increase in their productivity as well as an improvement in their mental health.[30] Another authority tells of a nationwide movement for calisthenics during rest periods in 1931–2.[31] 'We have no figures at hand,' Krol' confessed in November 1932. 'But every neurologist and every physician will confirm that nervous disorders, functional ones in particular – hysteria, neurasthenia – show a clear tendency to decline.'[32] Indeed. Psychoneurological specialists would have had to be crazy themselves to withhold confirmation.

That was how the revolution from above transformed the mental health movement and solved the practical problem of mental illnesses less serious than schizophrenia, such as 'Soviet exhaustion'.[33] By shouts of agreement such lesser illnesses were cured. Eminent specialists who had been studying psychological disorders shifted to organic illnesses, the consequences of brain damage, during the revolution from above.[34] They were moving away from the characteristic preoccupations of comfortable classes in advanced countries, back to the more elemental problems of Stalinist Russia. The dominant emphasis of Russian psychiatrists all along had been on neuropathology and organic illnesses, with schizophrenia as a possible exception to the rule, for it is a major disorder which may nor may not be an organic disease, or indeed a single disease. The revolution from above intensified the psychiatrists' traditional preoccupation with the most severe problems, their disregard for mere neurotics, as forced industrialization piled up mental patients faster than the country's hospitals could accommodate them. From the 1930s schizophrenia, the diagnosis that sent most of them in, became an acute problem for Soviet psychiatrists and for the public health officials who did not want to spend large sums on merely mental disorders. Within that context a distinctively Stalinist psychiatry began to take shape, as we shall see below.[35]

Whether it is a sensible strategy for a backward country to concentrate its psychoneurological expertise on the most serious organic disorders is less difficult to decide than how. How does one know whether the absentee worker lying abed in fearful isolation is suffering from a serious organic disorder or a mental illness that will yield to positive thinking? And how do public health officials and medical personnel find rational solutions to such problems when caught up in a warlike mood of assault on age-old miseries endured too long? Outsiders may calmly discuss such questions; the Stalinist way was to dismiss them with angry contempt. Concern for lesser psychological disorders – such things as neurasthenia or 'Soviet exhaustion', as contrasted with brain tumors or aneurysms or schizophrenia – was not consciously postponed to a future time of greater ease. It was denounced as a subversion of shock-brigade tempos, a counter-revolutionary denial that mind and body are invigorated by 'built-in-battles socialism'.[36] Violent mystifications of that sort accumulated in great number during the revolution from above, leaving to future generations the task of demystification, the internal struggle to overcome self-deception. The most insidious effect of Stalinism on psychological science would prove to be the Stalinist sense of practicality that grew within the clinical mentality of psychiatrists, and emerged in force after Stalin died.[37]

The clash between professional expertise and practical bossing was sharp and short in psychotechnics, as the application of experimental psychology to the management of labor was then called (another German loan-word). In that area the scientific expert is readily typed as either an intruder or a toady, since he is entering the inner realm of bossing, arranging people in hierarchies and telling them what to do. Soviet experts in psychotechnics were careful to emphasize that their science 'does not in any way try to replace the political leadership of social life'.[38] Trying only to help the leadership, they moved to a peak of striving during the early 1930s, with the stifling of their discipline as the swift result.

In the 1920s they promoted the new profession by denying a distinction between 'bourgeois' and Marxist approaches; psychotechnics was offered to the bosses as an applied science, part of technology, which is much the same whether used for the capitalist's profit or the worker's benefit. It was like the rifle that can serve either the whites or the reds, in the favored metaphor of I. N. Shpil'rein, certified leader of the discipline.[39] Of course, he and his colleagues recognized the presence of ideological issues, most notably in Taylorism or Fordism, which had a considerable vogue in Soviet Russia. Lenin had expressed an interest in that American way to super-efficiency, and A. K. Gastev had won support for a Central Institute of Labor, where researchers sought the 'scientific organization of labor' through analysis of the industrial process as an interaction of machines, with human beings included in the concept of machine.[40]

The psychotechnicians criticized that approach as the mechanization of man that grows with capitalism. They preferred to seek the scientific organization of labor through analysis of the human subjects in the work process. One of their central concerns was to devise standardized placement tests and types of vocational counselling that would match individual capabilities to appropriate jobs. Another major concern was to find precise measures of fatigue in various types of labor, so as to achieve an optimum arrangement of exertion and rest in each workplace. As they pursued such tasks they were uneasily aware of potential conflicts with Soviet bosses and their policies. Standardized tests might not 'push up' enough individuals from the lower classes and the lesser nationalities that the Party favored for special encouragement. (Until the late 1930s revolutionary campaigns for national equality, against 'Great-Russian chauvinism', were still in evidence.) Nor was analysis of fatigue a neutral technology. The expert in that area might come dangerously close to playing the judge over the boss in the arrangement of the work process, setting of tempos, or even fixing of piece-rates.

When the revolution from above required specialists to flagellate themselves for separation from practice and lack of partyness, psychotechnicians knew where to apply the lash. Shpil'rein confessed that his discipline was *not* like the rifle that can serve either whites or reds; he had concrete examples to show how 'bourgeois' psychotechnics, uncritically absorbed, had caused violations of Party policies: 'The chief right danger ... is ... in fetishism of bourgeois technology, which manifests itself in the uncritical use of tests borrowed from bourgeois authors. That leads to perversion of the class line in the placement of personnel ... and to great-power perversion of national policy. ....'[41] Psychotechnicians shared that danger with educational psychologists. Whether in job placement or in educational assignment, their pledge of great efficiency won the support of Stalinist officials for a few years of intense effort, only to pile up results that clashed with 'the class line' and with 'national policy'. In psychotechnics the process seems to have been less extensive and briefer than in education. Boasts of 'approximately a million' placement tests in 1931 were a peak, it seems, for later figures are not given.[42] That same year a self-critical congress of psychotechnicians resolved to shift their emphasis from tests for job placement to 'training the masses for their political and economic tasks'.[43] In education IQ testing went on till 1936, as we will see.

Studies of fatigue brought analogous trouble with practical authorities. Some experts had the courage − or the stupidity − to argue for optimum work norms rather than maximum records of output, which were the targets of intense competition among shock brigade workers and ambitious managers in the early 1930s. One of the leading experts, S. I. Kaplun, even warned against 'exploitation of labor', while arguing that too great an increase in tempos of production might be self-defeating, since chronic fatigue would lower productivity in the long run.[44] In 1931 he was sharply rebuked in *Pravda*, and retreated thereafter to a field called 'labor hygiene', restricted to the less sensitive aspects of health and safety in the workplace, indeed to campaigns among workers for self-conscious observance of rules worked out by their superiors.[45]

In 1935 the coalminer Stakhanov won enormous publicity for showing how to involve the workers in the scientific organization of labor. He changed the division of labor within his team and achieved a spectacular increase in the amount of coal produced on a single shift. Other miners were then reorganized on Stakhanov's model, with appropriate increases in quotas, and the Party led a campaign for a mass movement of Stakhanovites in all industries. In effect, the Party mobilized eager beavers to show how the workers themselves could raise tempos and quotas by rationalizing their own work processes. Proper rhythms of labor and rest would be arranged without the aid of outside experts, democratically. Which meant that practical leaders drawing on intuitive psychology were to have undis-puted sway over a field where Bolsheviks had looked for scientific counsel before they took the great leap forward. In 1934 the journal of psychotech-nics ceased publication; by 1936 their research centers and laboratories were closed, and Shpil'rein's disappearance in the late 1930s was widely attributed to his leadership of a field that the Party had outlawed.

An outside observer of the terror is free to note that other leaders of the field were not arrested. The most surprising case is that of O. A. Ermanskii, a well-known ex-Menshevik, who came under severe attack — by Shpil'rein, among others[46] — for his stubborn advocacy of optimal rather than maximal workloads. In 1940 he even published a critical study of the Stakhanov movement.[47] I am not suggesting that the administrators of terror were tolerant; they were capricious — to a terrifying degree. Shpil'rein may have suffered arrest because of his heavy involvement with foreigners. In 1930 he had been publicly attacked for accepting election — along with Chelpanov — to the honorary presidium of an international congress of psychology,[48] and in 1931 he had been the principal host to another international congress in Moscow.[49] The non-arrest of some stalwart independents — such as Ermanskii or Chelpanov — I would call the Priannishnikov effect, in honor of the leading agricultural chemist who openly disapproved the Party line in his field. In 1936 he even disobeyed an order to preside over a meeting on 'wrecking' in his field. He took the chair, but ruled out of order anyone who tried to talk about 'wrecking'.[50] *Pravda* called him terrible names for that defiance, but the NKVD refrained from arresting him. Perhaps they were curious to see how many would follow his example. Perhaps they felt less suspicious of such audacious types than they did of those who concealed autonomous principles beneath compliance.

In principle, Stalinist ideology was committed to scientific rationality, and therefore Stalinists at their highest rage never denounced the abstract idea of scientific expertise in the efficient organization of labor. On a sufficiently abstract level, above such discouraging problems as fatigue, faith in managerial expertise as a science survived the Stalin era to inspire once again a flourishing academic industry. It was called by the acronym NOT, the Scientific Organization of Labor, in the 1920s and 1930s, and would be called by the same name when strongly revived in the post-Stalin era. Indeed, there might well have been no interruption but for the caprice of the administrators of terror. They seized the colorful leader of the field, A. K. Gastev, a poet of the man-machine, whose institute preached a Soviet version of the gospel named for Taylor or Ford in bourgeois America. The central vision was not efficient adaptation of machine pro-duction to the physiological and psychological requirements of humans, but vice versa: exploitation of the machine-like qualities of humans to achieve a maximum continuous flow of assembly-line production. When the terror snatched Gastev in 1938, his institute was closed, which suggests that high Party leaders lacked a very strong commitment to his field of inquiry. But I have found no evidence that they were angered by it, that his notion of practicality in the management of labor was offensive to theirs. He did not presume to set limits.

The military field of applied psychology presents another revelation of the conflicting attitudes that prompted fellow-travelling specialists to speak of limits, and Stalinist bosses to condemn such talk. During the 1920s the Red Army referred 335 cases of suspected malingering to a psychiatrist, who summarized his findings in a 1931 article that provoked instant condemnation.[51] He was trying to tell Soviet military physicians and other officers how to deal with a worldwide problem. Conscious faking to evade service he had found to be extremely rare. He discovered that soldiers who complain of invisible illnesses are usually unbalanced. Accusations of malingering and rough orders to shape up accomplish nothing, he warned, except perhaps to precipitate a physical attack on the accuser. This 'narrow-minded specialist' received the familiar Stalinist rebuke: he did not see the problem as a whole. He failed to appreciate the therapeutic value of the Red Army's training and indoctrination, and thus he had come to recommend psychiatric coddling of malingerers.[52]

Analogous irritation was directed against Iu. P. Frolov, who was emerging as one of Pavlov's most prolific disciples. He had been doing conditioned-reflex studies of soldiers to understand endurance of military stress.[53] These studies were tolerated, perhaps considered useful when first published in 1928, but they were sharply attacked in 1930−1, from two sides. Marxist psychologists who had no faith in Pavlov's reduction of mind to neural process were joined by Party militants who charged Frolov with degrading Red Army men to the level of Pavlovian dogs, failing to see that indoctrination and morale, not reflexes, determine the soldier's ability to withstand stress.[54] Frolov himself was hardy enough to keep on offering professional help to the military, but he had the sense to switch from the investigation of psychological stress to toxicology.[55] And Marxist psychologists, Rubinshtein in particular, perceived in such episodes the mentalist psychology implicit in Stalinism, and thus the appeal that a doctrine of consciousness as reality would have to Stalinists.

PEDOLOGY

The most significant conflict over the practical uses of psychological science focused on *testy*, an Anglo-American word that the Russians borrowed to describe an ideal of human technology: objective measurements of individual capabilities and personality traits. To Anglo-American psychologists 'test' was a native word, the product of a society that had made the shift long ago from the traditional emphasis on ascribed status − the value of persons dependent on their race, sex, caste or class — to notions of achieved status, the modern dream of a society that never assigns persons to pre-ordained functions and places but rewards or punishes individuals for their carefully measured degrees of success or failure. The dream world of the athlete and the entrepreneur, of the artist as celebrity, of the elected ruler acclaimed by willing subjects, becomes the dream of society at large. In its most intense forms this is a vision less of society than of individuals *en masse* striving with each other to define everyone's worth by invidious comparison. In this dream each person's dignity or disgrace is earned by rising above or falling below others. The scorecard is the essence of the person; there are winners and losers and there is no soul that might claim respect in any social station, in any activity or inactivity. The reigning deity is the bitch-goddess success, as William James put it, and mass testing of children's individual differences seems essential to start them off in her service.[56]

But the problem here is less our advanced selves, world pioneers of intelligence testing, than it is people in a backward country, striving to overtake and surpass us. In Russia the reality of ascribed status was still acutely sensed, as a great injustice and obstacle to progress. The peasants were an enormous presence, born to their lowly station and held there by *nekul'turnost'*, lack of modern culture, even when legally emancipated, even after their revolutionary triumph over their former owners. The controlling assumption among educational psychologists, before the Revolution and especially after, was the need to set free the great abilities of the lower classes and the despised ethnic groups, not to prove that they were lower and despised because they lacked such abilities.

I have been unable to find Russian analogues[57] of Lewis Terman or Cyril Burt, the American and English pioneers of IQ testing, who sought to justify those at the top by proving the innate inferiority of those at the bottom.[58] The controversy over 'nature and nurture', which seems to Americans the essential issue in IQ testing, seems that way only to a society that is living within the dream of purely achieved status and is therefore anxious to improve the techniques of justifying inequality. In Russia the pioneers of IQ testing were drawn to the ideal of achieved status as to a dream, not to be confused with reality. They shared the populist ideology that prevailed in the educational profession of their country, the conviction that poor people at the bottom did not put themselves there, that great talents were imprisoned within the uncivilized (*nekul'turnye*) masses, to be set free by revolutionary abolition of social constraints and by educators bearing modern culture to the liberated masses.

Within that very different context of social structure and ideology, the technical issues of objective testing seemed for a while to be the same as in the West. Russian psychologists adopted the Anglo-American term, *testy*, along with the claim — by some, disputed by others — that their science could provide objective measurements of individual capabilities and personality traits. Thus the psychologist would help discover lower-class individuals with frustrated talents. Some made the claim in job placement of adults, but it was pressed most strongly in pedology, as the interdisciplinary study of children was called in the 1920s and 1930s. Skeptical psychologists doubted the ability of their immature science to fulfill such promises as the efficient matching of individual children to the types of education best suited for each. The reader may recall that Chelpanov, the founding father of experimental psychology in Russia, was the chief skeptic concerning *testy*, but his influence declined sharply in the Soviet period, because of his resistance to the campaign for Marxism in psychology.

The detailed history of arguments over *testy* has remained shut up in the archives of the Commissariat of Education, for argument was replaced by simple execration in 1936. But the large pattern is quite clear in the professional literature and the public press. In the Soviet Union as in the West intelligence testing marked the emergence of psychology as authentic science, a high-point of shared faith in technology, and Stalinist leaders were at first among the faithful children of the age. In 1931, after Lunacharsky had been dismissed and ardent Stalinists had taken over the Commissariat of Education, it decreed support for pedology, including the development of *testy* for placement and the establishment of special schools for children who would be found by testing and by teachers' observation to be in need of special programs.[59] Thus psychologists seemed to be passing their own test, of technological power, which is the sacred mark of authentic science for twentieth-century minds, more sacred to more people, I would guess, than the dream of purely acquired status. But fashions change in the public reputation of particular sciences, rather easily when the indisputable power of 'hard' science is lacking. Since the 1930s belief in technological power and purely acquired status has not faded, but faith in the intelligence test has declined in all countries, and with it the scientific reputation of psychologists. In Stalin's Russia the decline came as an abrupt fall, by resolution of the Party's Central Committee on July Fourth 1936 — a declaration of independence from the pseudo-science of pedology or a political suppression of a flourishing academic discipline, or both.

The major practical reasons for the abrupt turnabout were laid out in the resolution. The pedologists' *testy* were more effective in discovering defects than merits, of lower-class groups more than individuals. Special schools for allegedly defective children had grown at an alarming rate, as more and more children were certified to be too stupid or undisciplined to stay within the regular schools. And it was largely the children of workers and peasants who were put out and down, in spite of the Party's efforts to 'push up' meritorious individuals of lower-class origin. The Party's Central Committee therefore rebuked the Commissariat of Education for its 1931 endorsement of pedology and of special schools. Most of the children labeled backward and unruly were immediately to be put back in regular classes. Only a few special schools were to be retained for the clearly defective and ungovernable. All textbooks and monographs of pedology were to be withdrawn, and a campaign of criticism was to be mounted against its pseudo-scientific notion that human capabilities are biologically and socially determined. That notion had been uncritically borrowed from the West, where it served to maintain the lower classes in supposedly deserved subjection to the supposedly superior capabilities of the exploiting minority. Henceforth, in place of pedology, traditional 'pedagogy' was to be re-established as the guiding discipline in teacher training and in educational research.[60]

The rude violence of the Stalinist mentality was evident in that resolution but so was a knot of difficulties that was exposed later on in the more genteel Western attack on the IQ test and its cousins. In standardized versions for mass use they do not validly and reliably measure individual differences as distinct from group differences. That is, they tend to show that children of the lower classes and the despised ethnic groups share the mental characteristics of their classes and groups, while children of the superior classes and favored ethnic groups share the traits of theirs. But that demonstration of obvious differences between groups is disguised as an objective test of individual capabilities and personality traits.[61] Such criticisms were made by Soviet pedologists in the 1920s and early 1930s, for they were wholeheartedly devoted to the encouragement of lower-class children. They set themselves the task of reducing the group bias of supposedly individual tests,[62] and then had the bitter experience of hearing their criticisms of testing thrown at themselves in coarsened form, as accusations.

The accusations of willful bias, which fell on pedologists in 1936, were a scapegoating escape from shared responsibility. Whether in the 1920s, when Lunacharsky flattered the educational profession to win their co-operation, or in the early 1930s, when ardent Stalinists took over the Commissariat and started hectoring, the dream of educational democracy was not a point of conscious division between educators and political leaders. The dream was generally shared, and *testy* were supposed to serve it. Evidence for that generalization was most vigorously provided by the Stalinists who took control in 1931, attacking the former leadership of psychology for pseudo-Marxism and bourgeois bias, yet promoting testing as a way to discover the talents of lower-class children. Some of the leading Marxist psychologists of the 1920s had sympathized with Chelpanov's warning, which was neither Marxist nor un-Marxist in inspiration, merely cautious: mass testing represented a misleading claim of technical power by an immature science.[63]

Such caution was quite alien to Stalinists of the early 1930s. The IQ test seemed as American as the assembly line and the fastfood cafeteria, and

Stalin himself taught that Leninist style combined Russian revolutionary sweep with American efficiency (*delovitost'*). Special schools for problem children seemed the efficient way to give them a chance to learn, while freeing normal children and their teachers from the retarding influence of slow and disruptive pupils. But all of a sudden that was all wrong. The resolution of 1936 abruptly denounced such segregation as inherently prejudicial to lower-class children, and arbitrarily laid the blame on the pedologists and their theories. In equally arbitrary fashion it ordered a return to 'mainstreaming', to use the current American jargon for keeping problem children in regular classes. We outsiders are free to say that Stalinist officials had changed their minds in their characteristic slam-bang manner. They had no genuinely tested policy before or after. To test a policy is to approach examination of self and of system, and their mentality repressed serious thought about both. They could not confront the most obvious question, whether four years of testing and attendant increases in special schools changed appearance or reality in the educational system. I would guess appearance more than reality; testing and segregation of un-successful children probably threw into prominence rates of educational failure that had been masked by traditional schooling, and would be masked once more after the decreed return to tradition. American experience suggests that pattern.

Nevertheless, within the red-faced accusations of bias hurled at the pedologists I sense something more than scapegoating evasion of shared responsibility. There was some genuine difference in educational ideology between pedologists and Stalinist bosses. I am *not* suggesting that the Stalinists were denouncing any system of individual distinctions within the mass. They had briefly lunged toward that kind of equalitarianism in 1930, when individual grading was replaced by collective grading, but all-together-or-none-at-all pointed too dangerously toward generalized failure to learn. Besides, Stalin himself denounced analogous equalitarianism in wages, insisting on individualized reward and punishment until full communism would be reached. Individualized advancement out of the mass was still to be a sacred value, though it had somehow to be combined with the equally sacred faith that the whole mass must rise as one. How the Stalinists thought to square that circle is not revealed in the accusations that started falling on the pedologists in 1936.[64] Those one-sided, self-serving polemics simply assumed that the whole mass would rise along with the chosen few, if educators used other methods than *testy* for choosing the few, and if they repressed the notion that capabilities are determined by interaction of the brains we are born with and the social conditions of our growth. Educators must stop thinking of any determining cause except their own work as educators; theirs was the full responsibility for the success or failure of their charges. With that familiar shout for teacher responsibility came something more than the usual unloading on to teachers of everyone's disappointment with mass education. The resolution of 1936 was explicit on the way for teachers to bear their responsibility: it called for traditional 'pedagogy' to replace pedology in teacher training and educational research. That order signalled the triumph of Anton Makarenko, a traditional pedagogue who had a long-standing quarrel with pedologists over deeper issues than tests.

Before the Revolution he had been a conventional teacher at the primary level, already showing the itch to write but otherwise without a sign of crusading spirit.[65] The crusader and writer came to life when the Civil War and economic collapse swelled the numbers of *besprizornye*, 'unsupervised' children – vagrants, as we would say, who lived by begging and stealing. In 1920, aged thirty-two, Makarenko was recruited by the Cheka to leave the conventional classroom and take on the challenge of a wretched 'colony' for delinquents, nominally in the jurisdiction of the Cheka, but actually in the control of the toughest 'colonists'. The professional staff hardly pretended to be in charge, much less to reform and educate. The new director began to change the world by asserting his authority. At a critical moment he slapped the face of a disobedient tough, to show that the director's concern for his charges knew no bounds, not even fear of death at their undisciplined hands. From that beginning he went on to mobilize intense *esprit de corps*, or sense of the collective, as he preferred to say. His ultimate sanction was not physical punishment but threat of expulsion; to avoid *that* the children began to observe civilized rules first as a small sacrifice and then as a point of pride, reinforced by semi-military manners, including parades to martial music.

Makarenko was scornfully indifferent to psychological science. Intuitive psychology was his sufficient guide, passionately expressed in an autobiographical account of his achievement, a forceful picture of chaos brought to order by stern rectitude. He called the book *A Pedagogical Poem*, with a challenge to pedological science that was implicit throughout and explicit in intermittent tales of clashes with visitors from the Commissariat of Education. The Cheka and its successor, the OGPU, had shielded him from administrative interference by those officious prophets of individualized 'child-centered' education. But he could not contain his outrage at their audacity to criticize his molding of disorderly children into a disciplined collective. *A Pedagogical Poem* was his counter-attack, encouraged by Maxim Gorky, who edited and published the book serially from 1933 to 1935.[66]

Pedologists offered no defense if only because they had lost their professional journal; it stopped without explanation in 1932.[67] Anyhow, the highest authorities soon raised Makarenko above criticism from any source. His book became the bible of Soviet education, psychologists included.[68] An outsider is struck by the simple appeal to commonsense practicality, the lack of any effort to test his methods, beyond *the* test described in *the* book. He proved his theories by telling of their application in two colonies, without noting, much less pondering, the large questions implicit in the tale. Concerning expulsion, for example. Could expulsion from well-functioning collectives serve as a *universal* sanction against bad behavior, without some parallel system of malfunctioning sink-holes to collect the expelled? Concerning academic achievement, for another example. *A Pedagogical Poem* dwelt with special pride on individual colonists who qualified for admission to college preparatory schools (*rabfaki*) – with such special pride that the outside reader begins to note how few those individuals were, how rare the achievement must have been in the mass, how large must have been the common acquiescence in most children's inferiority to the outstanding few. Measured inequality, driven away with the pedologists and their tests, returned unmeasured with Makarenko and traditional pedagogy.

Both issues have remained unexamined. I have not found detailed comparisons between Makarenko's two colonies and other reformatories, with the personalities and methods of the directors related to rates of honorable discharge *v.* punitive expulsion, of recidivism *v.* productive lives. Nor have I found studies of results in regular schools for normal children, with Makarenko's methods measured against his rivals'. Such studies are not merely unavailable to outsiders; they almost certainly do not exist.[69] His two colonies were the equivalent for Soviet educators of the 'beacon light' collective farms that the Stalinists raised above the peasantry, demonstrations of exemplary success for those in outer darkness. The notion that the leaders' policies should depend on statistical measurement of results was not simply ignored by Stalinist leaders; they angrily denounced the notion as an ideology of 'wreckers', especially on the economic front but also in other fields of battle.[70] In education they briefly supported tests and measurements as applied to schoolchildren, hardly to government programs.

Makarenko delighted such leaders not only by his success in two colonies for delinquent children, but even more by the evangelical vision that he shared with the leaders and spread to delinquents, educators and the reading public. He adapted to Soviet ideology the central values of stern *Kulturträger* struggling to transform 'uncivilized' (*nekul'turnye*) masses – the culturally deprived, in our own jargon:

> I ventured to question the correctness of the generally accepted theory of those days [the 1920s and early 1930s], that punishment of any sort is degrading, that it is essential to give the fullest possible scope to the sacred creative impulses of the child, and that the great thing is to rely solely upon self-organization and self-discipline. I also ventured to advance the theory, to me incontrovertible, that, so long as the collective, and the organs of the collective, had not been created, so long as no traditions existed, and no elementary habits of labor and mores had been formed, the teacher was entitled – nay, was bound! – to use compulsion. I also maintained that it was impossible to base the whole of education on the child's interests, that the cultivation of the sense of duty frequently runs counter to them,

especially as these present themselves to the child itself. I called for the education of a strong, toughened individual, capable of performing work that may be both unpleasant and tedious, should the interests of the collective require it.

Summing up, I insisted upon the necessity of a strong, enthusiastic, if necessary a stern collective, and of placing all hopes on the collective alone. My opponents could only fling their pedological axioms in my face, starting over and over again from the words 'the child'.[71]

Makarenko and his opponents were far beyond a debate over the technical issues of objective tests. They were involved in a clash of fundamental judgments about modern culture as it impinges upon the lower classes in a backward country ruled by the supposed vanguard of the lower classes. A retrospective outside observer is at liberty to make forthright statements of their most sensitive assumptions, which they could not state directly, much less question and debate straightforwardly. The attentive reader will have noted Makarenko's assertion that 'the collective ... had not been created, ... no traditions existed, and no elementary habits of labor and mores had been formed'. He was referring to his groups of delinquent youths, but he can also be read as referring to many other Soviet children,[72] perhaps even to very broad sections of the adult population. The passages in *A Pedagogical Poem* which deal with peasants reveal the unspeakable mistrust that guided the collectivizers of agriculture.[73]

The difference between Makarenko and the pedologists was a difference within the mentality of *Kulturträger*. He was sternly demanding where they were mildly patronizing. They devised tests to discover which individuals within the 'uncultured' mass were ready to rise, assuming that the rest would somehow be taught something of value for a modernizing society. He insisted on disciplining the entire mass to reach a minimal level of modern culture, assuming that outstanding individuals would somehow rise to higher levels in the process. From either point of view the characteristic mentality of the lower classes was an obstacle to be overcome, and Makarenko was the grimmer of the two in his version, the closer to regarding lower-class children as little savages in need of conversion. The basic assumption could be hinted at, with supporting appeal to Lenin's authority: 'Makarenko's pedagogical system is a response to Lenin's appeal to "... figure out how we may (and must) build communism with a mass of human material that is spoiled by ages and millennia of slavery, serfdom, capitalism. ..."'[74] But to this day the implicit assumptions cannot be spelled out and frankly analyzed in any version, mild or grim, for the masses are sacred as well as uncivilized.

Kulturträger appears in the Soviet Russian vocabulary as an ironical loanword; Soviet dictionaries pin it to 'imperialists', who pretend to be educating the colonial peoples whom they rule and exploit.[75] In the official Soviet view there are a few equivalents of American Indians, who may frankly be called primitive and openly relegated to tutelary status. But the official outlook has required a strangely self-contradictory approach to the 'toiling masses' of most Soviet nationalities. On the one hand, their education was supposed to be a development of their own culture, guided by their own vanguard. Psychologists who sought to disclose the primitive quality of peasant thinking were severely chastised for their insulting arrogance.[76] On the other hand, Communist leaders habitually called the masses 'uncultured', which is tantamount to saying uncivilized. That side of the official outlook was an unacknowledged approach to the forbidden view of the lower-class mentality as primitive. The numerical results of the pedologists' tests made it difficult to resist acknowledgment. Makarenko's evangelism submerged the self-contradiction in a torrent of self-righteousness.

The unexamined inconsistency does not prove that the official outlook was blatant hypocrisy. After all, the Communists had come to power in 1917 with considerable mass support. The toleration that they showed in the 1920s for old *zemstvo* specialists in peasant studies, and even more the active support for 'pedologists' in educational psychology and for 'psychotechnicians' in industrial psychology, were based upon a benign assumption still lingering from the heady experience of 1917. The grand vision of Marxist-Leninist social science was supposed to accord with the nitty-gritty social realities discoverable by learned experts. With Stalin's revolution from above came a violent revulsion against that benign assumption. Scholars who went on reporting nitty-gritty realities were charged at best with narrow-minded failure to see the big picture. At worst they were literally charged, in the policeman's sense, with the capital crime of 'wrecking' (*vreditel'stvo*, literally pestiferousness, from the word for pests or vermin). Their petty reading of 'practice' subverted the grand vision of 'practice' that guided official policies.[77]

That was the transformation that turned pedologists from technical experts of socialist construction into 'bourgeois' obstructionists, and changed Makarenko from a reformer of delinquent youth into a model for all educators. Educational psychology was not destroyed as an academic field; it was subordinated to his kind of pedagogy. It became one of the two fields of applied psychology — the other was psychiatry — that survived Stalin's revolution from above. But educational psychology was transformed in the process from an autonomous discipline, proud to resemble its Western kin, into a peculiarly Stalinist, nativist enterprise. A Soviet philosopher would complain that it came to be 'characterized by fear of experiment. Developing almost entirely as a part of pedagogy, psychology became a purely descriptive science.'[78] He neglected to specify what it was descriptive of, but we outsiders are free to speak plainly: it hung upon the intuitive judgment of school administrators and their political bosses, who made every educator read Makarenko to understand the mind institute at Lehigh University were graciously helpful in showing me how psychologists approach the history of their problematic science. Similar assistance came from James Wertsch and Michael Cole. Fellow historians Mitchell Ash and Martin Miller were also helpful. I thank George Kline, Norman Birnbaum, Maurice Mandelbaum, Edward Geremek, and Philip as spirit and every psychiatrist read Pavlov to explain the mind as brain. Beyond such crude, separate approaches — the one to humanist under-standing, the other to scientific explanation — there seemed no place for psychological science in the mentality of Stalinists. But they did not live by practice alone; they were also passionately devoted to the dream of a grand theory that would bring together all the human sciences within 'practice', explained and guided by Marxism-Leninism.

13

Theoretical Impasse

A liberal without a sense of history would say that Kornilov and his colleagues earned the anathema that fell on them in 1930–1. They pushed for a monopoly of Marxism in psychology and of one true school within Marxist psychology. In 1927 a devotee of Kornilov's school cast a censorious eye over the first years of

> the so-called Marxist group: the Freudian deviation flourished luxuriantly; mechanists appeared (behaviorists and reflexologists), empiricists (old and new), and a small weak group appeared, to this day still not fully formed (Kornilov with two or three adherents), trying to find and formulate a rigorously sustained Marxist, dialectical materialist view of the psyche.[1]

Implicit in such talk was the acceptance of leadership in the Soviet style, including the power to anathematize false claims of Marxism and quiet submission when the power shifted to new leadership. Such minds made the tyranny that abruptly chastized them.

A liberal with a sense of history would note that limits on tolerance do not automatically bring tyranny; universities can be places of free inquiry while denying positions to astrologers and alchemists. Bukharin leaned heavily on such analogies in explaining why his Party of social scientists had no reason to tolerate its critics, any more than Pavlov had to let spiritualists impede his experiments.[2] Kornilov and his colleagues extended Bukharin's arrogance into psychology, yet somehow they managed to combine the intolerance inherent in claims of true Marxism and scientific truth with the tolerance that is generated by persistent rivalry of claims, if not by wonder whether any of them have merit. (Such wonder comes with an extreme sense of history.)

At the Pedological Congress of January 1928, the organized predominance of Kornilov's school was sufficiently obvious to incite Pavlovian
protest, a pattern of thrust and counter-thrust repeated at the All-Union
Conference of Marxist-Leninist Research Institutions in April 1929.[3] In
theory such meetings were bringing to scientists the Party habit of deciding
truth by prefabricating resolutions for rubber-stamp conferences. In gritty
practice scientists were still committed most of all to the notions of truth
that prevailed at their separate research centers or in their individual heads.
Kornilov's school might be presented at showy congresses as the officially
approved leadership for psychological science, but Pavlov's institutes —
and those of other schools scattered about the country — were sure to
ignore the message.

Bekhterev's disciples, entrenched in their large Leningrad establishment,
attempted a counter-attack in 1929. They held two small conferences,
adopting resolutions that asserted their right, if not to the imperial sway
which Bekhterev had projected, at least to an important place in the human
sciences.[4] With some such end in view they tried to arrange an all-Union
congress of the psychoneurological or behavioral sciences. *Glavnauka*, the
department within Lunacharsky's Commissariat of Education which
administered science, shunted organization of the congress to Kornilov's
Institute.[5] Toward the end of 1929 inspirational 'seminars' were held
throughout the country, to spread the message that institutions which
failed to send delegates would be revealing 'poverty in ideas and in social
involvement' (*ideino-obshchestvennaia bednost'*)[6] — at a time when the Party
was going into its all-out offensive for socialism along the entire front.

Bekhterev's disciples might complain about 'the illegitimate monopoly
of Marxism' that Kornilov's school was claiming for itself,[7] but the pressure
to show the proper social involvement was irresistible. In January 1930
about 1,400 specialists gathered in Leningrad with enough 'guests' to provide an audience of 3,000 for the keynote speeches by Zalkind, Kornilov,
and two allies speaking for applied psychology — psychotechnics and
pedology. Zalkind gloried in the large turnout, evidence of 'an organic
urge [*tiaga*]. Even skeptics can see now that the Congress was not "ordered",
was not artificially "made", but grew organically out of the whole history
of Soviet psychoneurological science.'[8] Evidently there were some who
wondered about that.

Yet the result was not a 'discussion' of the Stalinist sort, a rectification of
thought, as Mao would say. Soviet scholars came to picture the Congress
that way, as the climax of 'the discussion of reflexology', by which they
mean the condemnation of reflexology. But that Stalinist stereotype hardly
fits the actual record of the Congress, which shows unrectified diversity
even in its uncertain title. It was a Congress on 'the psychoneurological
sciences' or 'the study of human behavior', the first phrase pointing toward
the mind-body duality, the second toward behaviorist and reflexological

claims to overcome it. Bekhterev's disciples were well represented, Pavlov's less so, presumably because the master's disapproval of the Soviet regime was especially acute in 1929–30.[9] (The Congress corrected the imbalance by a special session to hear L. N. Fedorov, the unique Pavlovian who had enlisted in the Red Army and joined the Party during the Civil War.)[10] Chelpanov and Nechaev were scandalously excluded – they had been labeled anti-Marxist if not treasonous – but otherwise the famous individualists were there. Vagner, Ukhtomskii, Uznadze, and Beritashvili presented their distinctive approaches to psychological science.[11]

The keynote speeches that opened the Congress and the resolutions that closed it declared an urgent need for theoretical unification within the Marxist-Leninist framework, but the bulk of papers in between demonstrated continuing diversity. Indeed, Kornilov's school, the supposed organizer of the new unity, was itself a loose alliance of his own reactology with the cognitive psychology of Vygotsky and Luria, the comparative psychology of Borovskii (a disciple of Vagner's), and the neuropsychology of Sapir. In short, Kornilov was still an administrative eclectic as he moved beyond the Institute of Experimental Psychology to a triumphant moment as All-Union chief of the drive for Marxist unity. I say that in wistful admiration of his eclectic bent, wondering why Stalinists said it in execration, as they cast him down before the year was out.

An ominous chill descended even while the Congress was in session at the end of January 1930. Just three weeks earlier Stalin had electrified theorists with his complaint that they were separated from practice, and presumably psychologists were included. Lunacharsky had just been pushed out of the Commissariat of Education, which had arranged for the Congress. He came to speak, but not as the chief spokesman of Party and state, nor even on the central issues. As an individual theorist addressing his special topic, he discussed the psychology of art.[12] Two representatives of the philosophical leadership, who did address the central theme of ways to unify the psychoneurological sciences, were already ceasing to be officially recognized leaders of philosophy; they were on their way to condemnation as 'Menshevizing idealists'.[13] That context enables one to read the nonappearance of the new Commissar of Education and the strange silence of the media. Neither *Pravda* nor *Izvestiia* nor *Bol'shevik* (the Central Committee's chief journal of theory) carried a line of news or comment.[14] Evidently the ideological establishment was not sure that the Congress was what it pretended to be, a triumphant rallying of forces under Kornilov's leadership to end discord and guild-like seclusion (*raznoboi* and *tsekhovshchina*) in the psychoneurological sciences or the study of behavior, and so to mobilize all-out practical aid for the construction of socialism.

In the months that followed the Congress the Party cell within Kornilov's Institute accused the leadership of 'separation from practice', which brought investigators from the government inspector's office (RKKI), and a purge or cleansing (*chistka*), reported by *Izvestiia* in November 1930.[15] In June 1931 the Party cell adopted a resolution summing up the results of the 'discussion', and Kornilov was removed from the director's post.[16] That brief brutal process is still called 'the discussion of reactology' (that is, Kornilov's school) by psychologists and historians who must like sick jokes. Or maybe they lack the wit to see black humor in stamping 'discussion' on the conclusion of a brief inquisition.

The 'discussion of reflexology' had shown some elements of a genuine discussion; the 'discussion of reactology' was thoroughly Stalinist. It began abruptly with obscurely motivated attacks on foredoomed individuals, provoked little or no defense from them, nor even any clear or believable arguments against them, and was quickly brought to a close. Busy bossy people were getting obstructionists out of their way — to what? That question was not clearly answered; the inquisitors expressed themselves in vague slogans. The inspector's office that purged the Institute of Experimental Psychology condemned its 'absolutely insignificant results in adapting its work to the needs of socialist construction and in particular in the field of developing applied forms of psychology'.[17] Specifications were not provided, if only because psychotechnics and pedology, the forms of applied psychology which the Institute had favored, were still in favor with the Party and state. Stalin's ardent disciples knew that theorists were separated from practice — Stalin had said so — but they were groping to discover what exactly that meant in psychological science. One thing they and the inspector's office were sure of: 'The Institute is not in any degree the methodological center in the field of Marxist psychology'[18] — which is to say that the Institute had not suppressed the nationwide diversity of viewpoints.

In the course of the 'discussion' the handful of young Communists who initiated it convinced themselves of one major new principle: to be truly Soviet and Marxist, psychology had to become radically different from schools that were Western and 'bourgeois'. They were all bankrupt in science, evil in ideology, and useless or harmful in practical applications. That charge was hurled not only at the open forms of 'bourgeois' psychology exhibited in the West, but also at the analogous forms that had been called Marxist in the Soviet Union. The resolution of the Institute's Party cell, which summed up the 'discussion' as of June 1931, rebuked 'crudely biologizing Bekhterevian reflexology', and the 'militant eclecticism' and the 'pseudo-Marxism of Kornilov's reactology', and 'the "apolitical culturist" [*kul'turnicheskaia*] psychology of Vygotsky and Luria', and 'the efforts to explain the whole complex and varied behavior of man with the conditioned reflex methods of Pavlov's school.'[19] The resolution failed to mention the theorizing of Ukhtomskii, Uznadze, or Beritashvili, but that may have been an oversight.

One might have thought every effort at psychological science was about to be liquidated. Certainly there were signs pointing in that direction. The major journal of the discipline, *Psychology*, which Kornilov's Institute had started so hopefully in 1928, lapsed into irregularity in 1931, devoting most of its space to reports of the 'discussion', and then, in 1932, stopped forever. Lesser journals of psychology, which had multiplied in the late 1920s, also disappeared in 1932−4, leaving a single journal of psychiatry and neuropathology to serve all the psychoneurological sciences till the mid-1950s − two, if one counts *Soviet Pedagogy*, the conduit of official views to educational personnel.[20] The Institute of Experimental Psychology was reorganized, briefly, into an Institute of Psychology, Psychotechnics, and Pedology − note the stress on supposedly practical applications − and then, when faith in those applications collapsed, into an Institute of Psychology within the Academy of Pedagogical Sciences. In short, psychologists were put to work on educational problems. In 1936, when the Party's Central Committee condemned the standardized tests that were their main claim to usefulness, the discipline seemed indeed on the verge of annihilation.

But that did not happen. The handful of young Stalinists who initiated the attack on all existing schools of psychology did not persist. They sank into routine work as educational psychologists, with some attrition owing perhaps to the terror.[21] The one with the most persistent urge to attack exhausted it by 1936, after he had done hatchet jobs on Borovskii, Vygotsky, Luria, and Zalkind. Then he joined the others in routine production of educationist pap on training tomorrow's citizens.[22] That was the springtime of the *vydvizhentsy*, the young lower-class people 'pushed up' by Stalin's revolution from above, yet psychological science had only one major success story of that sort. V. N. Kolbanovskii was made Director of the central Institute of Psychology in 1931, when he was twenty-nine.

His biography is silent on the touchy issue of class, which means that he was not of worker or peasant origin, but during the Civil War, when he was only sixteen or seventeen, he joined the Red Army and the Communist Party.[23] We must credit him with a flammable imagination. When peace came, he took training in medicine, with a specialty in psychiatry and a penchant for discussions of Marxism and science, perhaps as a result of association with Bogdanov at the Institute of Blood Transfusion.[24] Of course he spoke as an orthodox Leninist opponent of Bogdanov's philosophy; the point is that his mind was involved. He was not part of the Party cell that started the 'discussion of reactology'; he seems to have been assigned to the Institute of Psychology after the inspector's office had purged it, as the Party man who would set the place in order. Once there, under the spell of Vygotsky's theorizing, he became a defender of psychological science. That was not an uncommon adaptation, the Party's agent absorbing the culture of the autonomous community he was supposed to control. It happened in collective farms as well as scientific institutes, provoking recurrent complaints in the central press.[25]

Kolbanovskii's first publications on psychology stressed its application in

industry and especially in education.[26] His mandate after all was to close
the gap between theory and practice. Educational psychology remained the
focus of his professional writing for the rest of his life, and Vygotsky's
emphasis on studies of child development seemed obviously relevant. But
Kolbanovskii was no narrow practitioner; he was entranced by Vygotsky's
broad theorizing on psychology's problems as the would-be science of
mind. When consumption finally carried Vygotsky off in 1934 — he was
only six years older than the new Director of the Institute — Kolbanovskii
wrote a long laudatory obituary, which emphasized 'The Historical Meaning of the Psychological Crisis' as Vygotsky's major work, gave a précis of
it, and hoped that it would be published soon.[27] The ideological authorities
would not allow that until 1982, when Kolbanovskii would himself be
twelve years dead. But he did succeed, in 1934, in bringing out a little
collection of Vygotsky's essays on *Thinking and Speech*, which would be
the public's chief access to Vygotsky's thought — virtually the only one —
until the post-Stalin thaw.[28] Indeed, translated into English in 1962, it
retains that function for the Western public to the present time; which is a
pity, for the selection and the editing give a partial view of Vygotsky —
even in the expanded edition of 1986. The broad irenic theorist of 'the
psychological crisis' is concealed; one sees a specialist in cognitive psychology trying to be militant, to meet the demands of Stalinism.

I do not know how much of the selection and editing were the editor's,
how much the author's, aware of death approaching while his major books
were blocked from publication. I am inclined to believe Kolbanovskii's
insistence that he made only 'the most necessary corrections', mostly in the
last part, which was dictated during the author's final weeks.[29] But that
hardly matters; the new pattern is more important than the hand that
fashioned it. The 1934 collection omitted Vygotsky's basic concept of 'the
psychological crisis', which, as recently as 1929, had introduced his central
essay on 'The Genetic Roots of Thought and Speech'.[30] Deprived of those
opening pages, the reader does not learn Vygotsky's characteristic argument
that the clash between natural scientific explanation and humanist understanding generates a constant war of schools in the would-be science of the
mind, which entangles all psychologists, Marxists no less than non-Marxists.
In place of that ecumenical vision the 1934 collection featured the harsh
critique of Piaget that Vygotsky had published in 1932,[31] when the 'discussion of reactology' had shown the need to put a great distance between
Western 'bourgeois' learning and Soviet Marxism.

VYGOTSKY'S VERSION

Before 1932 Vygotsky resisted the notorious dichotomy between Marxist
us and 'bourgeois' them. His basic distinction was between explanation and

understanding, and he was generously appreciative of solid work on both sides, in all the schools.[32] That generosity reinforced his central theme of crisis in psychology: each school had hold of some truth, yet all together were incoherent. He had praised Piaget's work on the development of cognitive functions in children as the foundation for anyone entering the field, himself included.[33] In that spirit he had offered a correction of Piaget's concept of egocentric speech — what is ordinarily called talking to oneself, very common in early childhood. Vygotsky questioned the analogy that Piaget drew with autism, the notion that egocentric speech expresses inner desires and fantasies, defense of the self against hurtful socialization. Vygotsky argued that egocentric speech is less withdrawal than expansion, a child's way of organizing its active participation in learning, a stage in the internalization of patterns of thought and speech that the child is actively deriving from social intercourse. When Piaget learned of that correction, in the 1960s, he gratefully accepted it, as an enrichment of his doctrine.[35]

That is the spirit in which Vygotsky had offered his amendment before 1932, without any suggestion of a Marxist revolt against Piaget's approach to cognitive psychology. Indeed, he had explicitly disapproved of efforts to reconstruct psychology according to the precepts of dialectical materialism. 'Our science', he had declared, 'will become Marxist to the degree that it will become true, scientific; and we will work precisely on that, its trans-formation into a true science, not on its agreement with Marx's theory.'[36] He had delighted in Gestalt psychology for showing '*that the objective immanent driving forces of the development of psychological science are acting in the same direction as the Marxist reform of psychology.*'[37] He had steadfastly pictured Marxism as a very general methodology or philosophy of science, a guide to theorizing on the most general level, not a source of scientific theories or a test of their merit. In 1929, for example, writing in the journal *Natural Science and Marxism* on Köhler's experimental demonstrations of apes' reasoning powers, Vygotsky had quoted Marx, Engels, and Plekhanov to make the modest point that 'the latest discoveries in zoopsychology are not, in theory, absolutely new for Marxism.' The classic authors had all along assumed continuities as well as discontinuities between human and subhuman minds.[38]

In 1932–4 Vygotsky still held back from Stalinist talk of psychology remade according to Marxism-Leninism, and he still refrained from pinning the label 'bourgeois' on Piaget, whose doctrine he still pictured as funda-mental to the field. But there was now a harsh ideological edge in his evaluation. He likened Piaget to Mach and Bogdanov: all were prisoners of philosophical agnosticism and psychological mechanism, which begins with attempted reduction of mind to biological functions and ends un-avoidably in idealism. The reduction cannot succeed, so mind becomes a mysterious substance, an hypostasis, separated from the bodily functions and from the historico-cultural process by which the human mind has shaped itself. Vygotsky now charged that 'the central point of Piaget's entire construction' was the 'attempt to deduce the child's logical thought and its development from some pure exchange of conscious minds [*soznanii*], in complete separation from reality, without any consideration of the child's social practice directed toward the mastery of reality.'[39] He backed up that accusation with a quote from Lenin on the perversity of such metaphysical idealism. He could hardly quote Piaget to sustain the indictment, for Piaget emphatically declared the opposite:

> The idea that dominates ... this work is that the thought of the child cannot be deduced only from innate psychobiological factors and from influences of the physical environment, but must be understood also and predominantly from the relationships that are established between the child and the social environment that surrounds him. I do not mean simply that the child reflects the opinions and ideas of those about him; that would be banal. The very structure of the individual's thought depends on the social environment.[40]

An outsider without access to private papers or freely speaking survivors can only guess at the balance of faith and calculation that brought Vygotsky to that Stalinist mannerism: twisting foreign scholars into gorgons to scare off evil spirits — creating apotropaic symbols, as the anthropologists say. This one was originally fashioned as the introduction to the 1932 translation of Piaget's *Speech and Thought of the Child*. Previously, right through 1930, Vygotsky had introduced Russian translations of Western psychologists — Koffka, Thorndike, Bühler, Köhler — in his typical fair-minded way, insisting indeed that they were 'acting in the same direction as the Marxist reform of psychology'.[41] When the Bolshevizers of science attacked such 'apolitical eclecticism', he may have calculated that getting them to read Piaget was a great enough good to justify some apotropaic caricature in the introduction.

Or maybe that was less a calculated act than a defensive reflex, like the warning that Kolbanovskii placed in *his* introduction to Vygotsky's posthumous collection: this is not yet Marxist-Leninist psychology, it defers too much to Piaget and other 'bourgeois' scientists.[42] Nor did the chained reflex stop there; a reviewer censured Kolbanovskii for insufficient criticism of Vygotsky and his foreign sources.[43] The alien book with a cautionary caricature in the introduction, and reviews harrumphing about the harmful spirits that get past such amulets, remained a recurrent feature of the Soviet intellectual scene until Gorbachev's call for 'new thinking' in 1987. In the late 1930s a Stalinist neologism appeared to deride the suspect motive of such artistry: *perestrakhovka*, literally 'reinsurance', defined by a Soviet dictionary as 'protecting oneself from possible responsibility for something'.[44] But that sneer is superficial. At some level the mannerism merges with substantive thought.

In Vygotsky's case the substantive element was only briefly visible — he died so soon after 1932 — but it was plain to see. His sudden effort to mark off the alien element in Western science, to separate Soviet thought from the clutter of schools whose collective 'crisis' he had so recently lumped with Soviet psychology, drove his critical theorizing to increasing abstraction. He was moving deeper into the characteristic Soviet obsession with metapsychology, the philosophical justification of the possible science of mind rather than work at the science itself. At the same time, striving to close the gap between theory and practice, Vygotsky intensified his work on child development and on the disruption of normal thought in schizophrenics, as a contribution to education and to psychiatry. In both respects he moved with the whole profession, away from the intermediate level of theory, where it interacts with experimental practice, to an awkward layering of metapsychology over an authoritarian pragmatism, a blanket of incongruously abstract ideology cast over a science that appeals to the intuitions of practical officials — in short, an ideology and a science for men in charge of training children and treating the insane.

Vygotsky was still an extraordinarily creative and basically honest thinker, who could illuminate a subject even when he was trying to treat it in the Stalinist manner. In 1932, to take a notable example of his metapsychology, he gave a lecture at the Academy of Communist Education on 'Contemporary Currents in Psychology', which condensed his 'Historical Meaning of the Psychological Crisis' into a grim demonstration of hopeless impasse.[45] He said nothing of a Soviet Marxist school with a will to get out of the impasse, as he had in the 1920s. He spoke only of schools in the West, which he did not call 'bourgeois', but he did not show great sympathy, as he had in the 1920s, for the particular truth that each school built itself upon. He pictured an irremediable conflict of equally unacceptable philosophies, mechanism and vitalism, the one nourishing various schools of explanatory or natural-scientific psychology, the other nourishing a clutter of descriptive or phenomenalistic psychologies. Once again he saw the scientific explanation of mind as opposed to the humanistic understanding of it, with shifting hybrids coming and going, and each school obliged to be inconsistently eclectic as it tried 'to sew a methodological coat on the factual button it had found'.[46]

But now he discerned a recent trend overall, a weary retreat of each school into sullen isolation from the others, a growing abandonment of the struggle for a unified psychological science. His peroration described a vicious circle

> emerging from the very nature of the methodological basis on which psychology has been developing in the West; therefore within itself it has no solution. Even those efforts that start with the idea of resolving the crisis and emerging from the impasses to which it has led, in fact

do not overcome the difficulties to which mechanism and vitalism have brought psychology. And if it were possible for them to do reasonable research for say ten years, then ten years hence such research would lead again into an impasse with a greater factual foundation, under another name, an impasse that would be experienced as immeasurably more tragic and more acute, inasmuch as it would take place on a higher level of the science, where all the clashes and contradictions would appear more acute and more insoluble.

... If we wanted to characterize the very newest of psychological trends, ... it is a methodological mood rather than a full-formed idea.

... It is the notion that overcoming mechanism, overcoming the crisis of explanatory and descriptive psychology and constructing a unified psychology on the basis of the old psychological assumptions, is impossible. The very foundation of psychology must be reconstructed.[47]

With that he stopped. Eloquent silence replaced his previous assurance that Marxism-Leninism inspired Soviet psychologists with the will to get out of the crisis.

Of course he could not repeat his previous invocations of Trotsky's and Kautsky's predictions that a new psychology would emerge as 'new men' would create themselves along with socialism;[48] triumphant Stalinism would tolerate those names only for execration. But Vygotsky no longer offered futuristic reassurance under the aegis of Marx's name, or any of those he had cited as recently as 1930, the last time he declared his faith that the 'psychological crisis' would be transcended along with the 'socialist remaking of man'.[49] He had calmed impatience with the wry simile drawn from Spinoza: present man and his psychology resemble their future perfection no more than the dog, a barking animal, resembles the constellation Canis.[50] By 1932 both revolutionary willfulness and stoical humor were conspicuously absent from Vygotsky's review of the 'psychological crisis'. He pictured the would-be science of the mind as a muddle, a tragic impasse, and stopped.

Also absent from that 1932 review was Vygotsky's dream of psychological science enriched, if not unified, by an 'historico-cultural' approach. He and Luria were just then suffering heavy abuse for their two valiant efforts to turn the vague slogan into concrete knowledge. In 1930 they published a little outline of stages in the mind's historico-cultural development. *Studies in the History of Behavior* they called it, with a subtitle that declared the basic pattern: *Ape, Primitive, Child*.[51] Those three creatures exhibited the phylogenetic and ontogenetic steps toward the fully developed mind of civilized men — or woman; the authors were not sexist. Nor were they Stalinist. In the liberal spirit of the 1920s they drew elements of their theorizing from such thinkers as Levy-Bruhl, Piaget, and Freud — and found themselves denounced in the vituperative spirit of the 1930s. They were called prisoners of 'bourgeois' ideology, trying to reduce the human mind to the animal level, defaming Soviet toiling people by attributing childish and primitive elements to their thinking.[52] 'Vygotsky and Luria ... "find" identical forms of thought in an adult Uzbek woman and a five-year-old child; under the flag of science they smuggle in ideas that are harmful to the cause of national-cultural construction in Uzbekistan.'[53]

That particular accusation was hurled at their second valiant effort on behalf of 'historico-cultural' psychology, a field study that Vygotsky helped to design, which Luria supervised and began to write up in 1931–2. A team of investigators tested the mentality of Uzbek peasants, with the aid of bilingual natives, I assume, for it is a rare Russian who speaks Uzbek, and the principal investigators were Russians or Russian Jews. They showed no concern for the attitudes that historico-cultural experience had built into such a three-cornered encounter between *intelligent* and illiterate peasant of a subject nationality, with a Russified member of the native intelligentsia as intermediary. The psychologists from Moscow were not testing the scientific purity of their own minds. They were testing the intellectual abilities of their subjects, whom they knew in advance to be intermediate between the primitive mentality and the civilized.

So they achieved exchanges such as this, in the test of power to reason syllogistically:

Investigator   Cotton can grow only where it is warm and dry. In England it is cold and damp. Can cotton grow there?
Subject (37-year-old male, illiterate, from a remote village of Kashgariia)   I don't know.
Investigator   Think.
Subject   I have only been in Kashgariia, I don't know any more.
Investigator   But based on what I told you, can cotton grow there?
Subject   If the land is good, cotton will grow there, but if it is damp and poor, then it won't grow. If it's like we have in Kashgariia, it will grow. ...[54]

And the subject went on listing conditions that allowed cotton to grow, insistently apologetic for the limited nature of his experience, to which the investigator insistently responded: 'But what follows from my words?' Finally the subject told him what follows: 'Look, we are Moslems, of Kashgariia, a dark people [*temnyi narod*]; we've not been anywhere; we don't know if it's cold there or warm.'[55]

Luria did not notice the historico-cultural discovery that his investigator had made: Dobroliubov's characterization of Russia as 'a dark realm' (*tëmnoe tsarstvo*) had penetrated the sense of self of an illiterate peasant in one of the empire's remotest spots. Or maybe that is a simplistic and unjust endorsement of the peasant's self-abasement. Maybe all the superior people who had been describing the lower classes as uncivilized or dark were creatures of the historical process no less than the lower classes, two ends of an imperial polarity in the sense of self, a dialectic unity that simultaneously defines the superior minority and the subordinated mass by their reciprocating sense of superiority and subordination. At one point the peasant subject who placed himself among the 'dark people' offered a tantalizing bit of historico-cultural theorizing that suggested such a dialectic.

The investigator had been rigidly ignoring the peasant's insistence that he could not speak about things he did not know at first hand. The investigator simply moved on with his schoolbook syllogisms from the logical impossibility of cotton-growing in England to the logical inevitability of white bears in Novaia Zemlia, given the rule that all bears are white in snowy regions and Novaia Zemlia is a snowy region. The peasant came back with recollections of bears he had seen, none of them white, which the investigator stubbornly ignored, insistently asking: 'But what follows from my words?' 'Look', said the Uzbek peasant, 'the point is this: our tsar is not like your tsar, and your tsar is not like ours. The only one who can reply to your words is one who has seen, and one who has not seen can tell nothing from your words.'[56] Luria subsumed that mentality in the category 'graphical-actional' (*nagliadno-deistvennoe*) or 'situational' thinking, which he contrasted with conceptual or rational thinking, the former a characteristic of young children and primitives, the latter of fully civilized adults. The field study discovered, he was happy to report, that Uzbek peasants who had some schooling and some experience of modern economic and governmental affairs quickly picked up the civilized mentality. They told the investigator what followed from his words.

Forty years after the field study, when Luria finally got the chance to publish the results, he acknowledged the imperfection of its 'methodological design and ... system of concepts'.[57] But he made no effort to spell out such criticism, whether in the graphical-actional manner that I have affected or in the abstractions that social scientists prefer. The Soviet capacity for authentic self-criticism was crippled by Stalinist 'criticism and self-criticism', which should be called accusation and confession, as in Catholic inquisitions or Protestant revival meetings. The main function of those notorious practices is to strengthen the collective sense of rectitude and solidarity, not to question hierarchical divisions along lines of status and power. Such divisions were unwittingly revealed in the testing of Uzbek peasant subjects by Russian scientific investigators, and the Stalinists were instantly incensed. They did not permit publication and they did not request clarification by more sophisticated studies; their 'criticism' was vituperative denunciation of any who would ask how the peasant mind differs from the leaders' plans:

> Dozens of interview records, where the experimenters literally extorted
> the situational thinking that they presupposed. ... cannot hide or veil

their reactionary theory, hostile to Marxism. This pseudo-scientific, anti-Marxist and class hostile theory in practice leads to the anti-Soviet conclusion that the policy of the Soviet Union is being accomplished by people and classes who think primitively, who are incapable of any abstract thinking, which, it goes without saying, is utterly at odds with reality.[58]

Stalinist 'reality' had no room for peasant studies, which had flourished in Russia since the 1860s, while everyone acknowledged that Russian psychology divided along class lines. The will to have done with that division, to bind leaders and led in a single mentality, precluded inquiry into the separate qualities of the led.[59] The same refusal of rational inquiry applied to temporarily 'backward' or 'uncivilized' peoples throughout the world. Their minds were adequately understood by the vanguard elements who would lead them to socialism, and scholars were no longer to debate the intellectual difficulties of combining the vanguard's belief in progressive stages of human improvement with its democratic respect for people at the lower stages. To raise such problems was to obstruct the universal movement to democratic equality. In short, the rulers' will to have done with the wretched past paralyzed anything like a serious historico-cultural approach to psychology.

The minds of children and of disturbed adults were a residual area of legitimate inquiry, since they were acknowledged to be different types that must be realistically studied if they are to be improved. Vygotsky's last major articles concerned special problems in child development and the mentality of schizophrenics.[60] For almost thirty years Western psychologists knew him for that residual fragment of his restless striving for an all-inclusive theory of the mind — indeed, for a bit of the fragment: a technique for grading the mental capacities of children and mental 'defectives'. It became known in the West as the Vygotsky test, though it had actually been devised by one of his colleagues who had been studying 'backward children'.[61] The subject is presented with a jumble of differently colored and shaped blocks, and asked to sort them into four types or categories, explaining as he tries and errs and tries again what he thinks the principle of classification may be which will divide all the blocks into four sets of equal numbers. The key features, he must discover, are neither color nor shape but size and height. The correct classification is small-short, big-short, small-tall, big-tall. The clues that seize the eye — red, blue, green; triangle, circle, polygon — are irrelevant since they will not divide the blocks into four equal sets.

That Vygotsky-Sakharov test of concept formation in children and 'defective' adults is obviously much less authoritarian than the Vygotsky-Luria test of syllogistic capacity in peasants. The subject is asked to think out loud as he tries his hand at an intriguing little puzzle, and the investigator quietly infers what follows from the subject's words. But the whole procedure rests on the assumption that the investigator is the agent of an unquestionably correct intellectual and social hierarchy which is putting the subject to a test, challenging him to show where he should be placed on a scale of inferiority and superiority in mental power. A psychological science that would avoid such invidious comparison and its implicit authoritarianism is hard to imagine. Wordsworth praised the peasant woman who loves her idiot child no less than the others,[62] but his poem celebrating such freedom from invidious comparison is meaningful only to non-idiot and non-peasant minds, in particular to romantic rebels against the endless testing and grading of modern authoritarian systems. The comprehensive psychology that Vygotsky sought would have included understanding of such rebellion; the culture that generates psychological science mocks that understanding or even rules it out.

Luria retreated from historico-cultural psychology to intense study of mental disorder in brain-damaged patients. He earned a medical degree in the 1930s so that he could be fully professional on both sides of the mind-brain distinction. On the psychological side he developed fine distinctions among particular forms of mental disruption, aphasia most notably, on which he wrote a world-renowned monograph.[63] On the neurological side he correlated precisely established areas of brain damage with nicely distinguished forms of mental disruption, using each type of expertise to help the other. An over-simplified example may show how tricky such work is, in its scientific significance for brain localization and cognitive psychology, in its bearing on medical practice, and in its potential link to 'historico-cultural' analysis. A patient with damage to the visual cortex in the back of the head may suffer 'acalculia', impairment of ability to do arithmetic. Careful psychological tests may show the impairment to appear when calculation goes beyond 9, where 10 is confused with 01, 12 with 21, and so on. Such a conjunction of psychological and neurological tests shows that damage to a visual function, the discrimination between left and right, which can be assigned to a particular brain area, has affected an abstract function of discursive reasoning, which involves many different areas.[64]

As Luria did such painstaking back-and-forth between psychology and neurology he enriched the conviction that brain-mind analysis is not point-to-point correlation between localized brain centers and atomized psychic functions. He pushed both brain studies and cognitive psychology toward dynamic theories of enormously intricate interaction among many different structures and functions. He also drew rehabilitation of brain-damaged patients into ingenious modes of compensation, that is, training undamaged parts of the brain to take on the tasks of damaged parts. If that physical sort of compensation fails, as it often does, a purely mental compensation may be sought, by getting the patient to believe that his trouble is neural rather than mental. He has not become stupid; some wires are broken; he should feel reassured.[65] In Soviet culture as in ours physical disability is usually less damaging to social status and self-esteem than mental defect.

Those final observations are mine, not Luria's. I am trying to suggest ways in which his work in 'defectology', as the field is called in the Soviet Union, might have taken him back to historico-cultural issues. Luria stayed away from such questions. In like manner Vygotsky's other disciples, such as A. N. Leont'ev, who devoted their energies to studies of child development, avoided other possibilities of historico-cultural inquiry.[66] They did not ask, for example, how the development of speech in bilingual situations is shaped by the perceptions of status that attach to the two languages in question. That sort of question begs to be asked in the Soviet Union, with its multitude of languages and its tendency to exalt Russian above all others. An outside observer should be gentle in noting the blind eye that Vygotsky's school has turned to such opportunities for historico-cultural studies; they would be rebels rather than specialists if they so directly challenged the Stalinist rule that the national question needs no examination since it has been solved.

It is harder to be understanding of the Stalinist twist that Luria repeatedly put into his writings after 1931, beginning with reviews of 'bourgeois' and Soviet psychologies in which he crudely denounced viewpoints that he had previously endorsed.[67] Even at the age of seventy-two, when Stalin was long gone and Luria got the chance to publish the field study of peasant thinking that he had supervised at thirty, he retained the crippled swagger of the Stalinist style. He stolidly ignored the forty-year delay, and set his review of the theoretical issues within the simplistic framework of reactionary *v*. progressive, those who deny the democratic equality of peoples *v*. those who affirm it.[68] He ticked off the 'biogenetic law', for example, as a reactionary creed,[69] with never a hint that he and Vygotsky had explicitly and repeatedly endorsed the 'law', looking within the mental development of the child for a recapitulation of the species's mental evolution from subhuman to primitive to civilized[70] – until Stalinists shut down the whole field of inquiry.

The anti-cosmopolitan campaign of the early 1950s generated more humiliating instances of Luria bowing to the rod that chastised him, even ritually flagellating himself, as we will see,[71] but the pattern was plain already in the 1930s. He went on with his autonomous work in neuropsychology to the extent that he could do so in submissive cooperation with Stalinist authorities. He was closer than he imagined to the mentality of a peasant – not the illiterate type who sharply distinguished between his own tsar and the tsar of superior people; the type with enough understanding of superior people to tell what follows from their words.

RUBINSHTEIN'S VERSION

S. L. Rubinshtein was a much more puzzling hybrid of the autonomous academic and the submissive Stalinist. Or perhaps he was a mutant.

Suddenly in the mid-1930s he came out of academic obscurity to be the leading theorist of psychology, whose first stroke was to demonstrate the plastic scholasticism that proves the changing truth by quotations from the 'classics of Marxism-Leninism'. Psychologists of Vygotsky's school were annoyed, and have never lost their irritated sense of Rubinshtein as an opportunist, who used 'citationism' (*tsitatnichestvo*) and backstairs intrigue to take over the leadership that should have been theirs.[72] There may be something to that perception, but the record shows something more significant. Scholastic philosophizing about a science can be a serious enterprise, even — or especially — when it mediates between the academic discipline and Stalinist authorities.

Rubinshtein was already twenty-eight and a Ph.D. at the time of the Bolshevik Revolution. In his German dissertation, at Marburg in 1914, he had described himself as a lawyer's son from Odessa, who 'belongs to the Jewish religion and is a Russian subject'.[73] With profound thanks to his mentors, Hermann Cohen and Paul Natorp, he offered a study of Hegel's 'absolute rationalism', that is, a philosophy which attempts to transcend such dualities as mind and body by noting that rationality is the fundamental condition of any scientific inquiry. Thinking and being must be a unity, since the same principles of reason apply in the explanation of both. Rubinshtein argued that Hegel had not succeeded in his grand project, and seemed quite unaware of Karl Marx's claim to have done the job right, to have 'set Hegel on his feet'. Not Marxism but the Kantian tradition was Rubinshtein's next project; he promised a sequel on 'dualistic rationalism'.[74]

Right after he received the Ph.D. he went home to Odessa and started teaching in a secondary school, which seems to have checked his scholarly development only a little, for he wrote another philosophical treatise, though Revolution and Civil War obstructed its publication.[75] His hardworking mind was, in short, a product of the German metaphysical tradition, in particular of its romantic urge to prove that thinking and being, existence and essence can be fused in 'creative self-activation'. Husserl and Heidegger came of that tradition, which also fertilized the unique genius of Sartre, who had *his* first teaching job in a provincial secondary school. Some will make invidious comparison of unequal talents; I prefer to emphasize the shaping influence of the Russian Revolution in the one case, the German and French versions of the intellectual's isolation in the other cases. Rubinshtein could hardly concentrate on the transcendental ego in its *Lebenswelt* (Husserl), or on the anguished forlorn and despairing person condemned to be free (Sartre), while the Nazis took over both Germany and France and Heidegger cheered from his professorial chair. The Russian Revolution thrust Rubinshtein out of philosophy into the profession of psychology, to educate future teachers to serve the construction of socialism. He took upon himself the task of justifying the profession to the Bolshevik authorities.

In the public record there is no direct evidence of Rubinshtein's first reaction to the Bolshevik Revolution. A peculiar silence in Soviet accounts of his life, put together with bits of information vouchsafed to foreigners, suggests that he became a professor of philosophy at Odessa University in 1919, while the city was held by anti-Bolshevik forces, and lost the post in 1922, when the triumphant Soviet state drove non-Marxist philosophers out of higher education, if not altogether out of Russia.[76] At that point Rubinshtein became an instructor in psychology at a teacher-training institute, and simultaneously director of a regional research library. A few small publications in 1921–2 were drawn from his large manuscript on 'the principle of creative self-activation' (*samodeiatel'nost'*), with a footnote wondering when he 'would be given the possibility of publishing this work'.[77] The small pieces that he got into print showed that he was carrying on with the main line of thought of his dissertation.[78] He saw positivism as the chief error of the age, in its basic assumption that the human subject is presented with objective reality as an independent given, which the mind must somehow reproduce within itself and adapt itself to. Rubinshtein argued that the subject actually forms a dynamic unity with the object, a dialectic process in which the active mind simultaneously creates both itself and its world. And still he showed no slightest sense of affinity with Marxism. It would be nice to think that he was unwittingly retracing Marx's way from Hegelian reason to socialist revolution, less pleasant to think that he was preparing himself for surrender to the Stalinist arbiters of what Marx really meant.

During the decade of comparatively free debate over ways to bring Marxism and psychology together Rubinshtein's few publications quite ignored both Marxism and psychology; they were dry-as-dust reports on librarianship and bibliography.[79] But he was teaching psychology, and somehow in 1930 he won a striking promotion, up from Odessa and away from librarianship, to the prestigious Herzen Pedagogical Institute in Leningrad, where he became Director of the Psychology Department in 1932. The accounts of his life offer those bare facts, with studied silence on the obvious question: By what display of talent, by what attractiveness to Stalinist officials, who were striving just then to 'push up' young lower-class *vydvizhentsy*, did this forty-three-year-old with the wrong class background and alien philosophical record achieve such a signal advancement? Without access to the archives or to freely reminiscing survivors even a speculative response is pointless.

But an outsider can see one obvious element in his success that insiders have deliberately ignored, though it was the central feature of his intellectual development. From the German metaphysical tradition Rubinshtein took the principle that neatly served to justify psychological science in the Stalinist context: *activity* is the two-in-one concept of human thinking and being that transcends the traditional dualities — mind and brain, individual and society, theory and practice. Of course he could not openly declare the genealogy of his thought, and to this day no Soviet scholar has seen fit to consider it. But it is immediately obvious to an outsider who compares what Rubinshtein wrote before and after his decade of silent conversion. The 1934 article that announced his arrival on the Marxist scene, 'Problems of Psychology in the Works of Karl Marx', relied most of all on the 1844 manuscripts — they had been published just two years earlier — in which young Marx worked his way from Hegel to the essence of man:

> The point of departure for the reconstruction [of psychology] is the Marxist concept of human activity. ... Marx, using Hegelian terminology, defines [activity] as the objectification of the subject, which is at the same time the deobjectification of the object. 'The greatness of Hegel's *Phenomenology* — the dialectic of negativity as the moving and creating principle —' Marx writes, 'consists in this, that Hegel considers the generation of man as a process, considers objectification [*Vergegenständlichung*] as deobjectification [*Entgegenständlichung*],★ as alienation and transcendence of this alienation, and in this, that he therefore grasps the nature of labor and understands objective man, true, actual man, as the result of his own labor.'[80]

Rubinshtein's 1934 article did not develop that theme either as philosophy or as psychology. He was writing Marxolatry, as we may call extended quotation and paraphrase designed to elicit reverence for ultimate wisdom. Against that awesome standard he measured the pitiful struggles of Western psychologists to make a science of their one-sided schools, which presented man either as pure object (for example, in behaviorism) or as introspective subject (for example, in Wundtian psychology), or took flight into abstractions (for example, in Husserl's or Rickert's phenomenology). Concerning Soviet psychologists he was courteously diplomatic, silent about their past, vaguely reassuring about their future. They would succeed in creating an authentic science of the mind if they based their work on the wisdom of Marx — and Lenin and Stalin, who also appeared among the reverent citations in Rubinshtein's landmark article.[82] It was a landmark because it brought into psychology the plastic scholasticism that can enclose any doctrine in a film of reverence, provided only that it suits the current mood of the current chiefs of human activity.

★ A recent Soviet definition may help the puzzled reader. 'Objectification [*opredmechivanie*] is the conversion into an object of the process accomplished by a subject, the transformation of the ability that is acting into the form of the object. De-objectification [*raspredmechivanie*] is the opposite conversion of objectivity [*predmetnost'*] into a living process, into the ability that is acting: it is the creative principle of the assimilation by the subject of the objective forms of culture, and by means of them also of nature.'[81]

Within a year Rubinshtein showed how easy it was to accommodate psychological science within such an ideology. He published the lecture course that he had been giving at the Herzen Pedagogical Institute, which adapted to the Soviet context the worldwide style of the introductory class in psychology. He retailed to students the conventional factual matter (or supposed factual matter) that seemed most important to the judicious instructor, with intermittent comments on the way the matter connects (or fails to connect) with some favored methodology. He felt no crushing obligation to work out a grand methodology, much less a coherent synthesis of the whole discipline. After all, by common recognition Soviet Marxist psychology was only just entering its proper path of development after years of fruitless theoretical clashes over deceptive imitations of 'bourgeois' schools. And methodology, he emphasized on the first page, should not be a prescription for science but a cluster of principles and methods disclosed within concrete material.[83] The result was a typical twentieth-century textbook in the human sciences: one thing after another, loosely linked by the individual professor's predilections.

In this case the professor was mainly intent on sharing an abundance of traditional and contemporary knowledge (or supposed knowledge), while intermittently reminding students that Marx and Lenin had exposed the crisis of such knowledge and shown the way to rise above it. American behaviorists, for example, make interesting factual discoveries which reflect 'the mechanization of man' that is characteristic of capitalism. Pavlov attempts the same on the physiological level, and Lashley provides a profound self-criticism of that trend. Gestalt is 'that school of psychology, if you please, that more than any other is striving for a rigorously scientific construction of psychology', by its emphasis on the wholeness and dynamism of psychic activity.[84] But in the last analysis Gestalt too is mechanistic, based on 'a philosophy not of human freedom but of human slavery', 'a peculiarly interpreted Spinozism'.[85] On the ideological level he even suggests a link between Gestalt and German fascism, finding no contradiction there with his admiration of the school as science. His brief review of Soviet schools shows every one to be critically flawed[86] — on the ideological level, which he treats calmly, without the tragic sense of Vygotsky's final review of a discipline that resists coherence everywhere and earns Stalinist condemnations in the Soviet Union. Rubinshtein's tone is basically relaxed and cheerful, since the coherence and ideological orthodoxy that are lacking in psychological science are readily found in the 'classics of Marxism-Leninism'. The essence of man is conscious activity; we know that on Marx's authority, and willy-nilly the science of psychology is bound to confirm such ultimate wisdom. Meantime students must learn what psychologists have established about sensations, perception, memory, will, and the other mental functions.[87]

If Soviet ideologists and rival psychologists had been in one of their

bloody-minded periods, they would have berated this textbook for eclecticism and insufficient 'partyness'. Such criticisms were made, but in a
comparatively restrained manner. At a little conference on psychology,
which was arranged in 1936 by the editors of *Under the Banner of Marxism*,
the keynote speaker made those points — eclecticism, insufficient partyness
— not only against Rubinshtein but all other notable Soviet psychologists
as well.[88] Kolbanovskii was the main speaker, who was himself criticized
for insufficient partyness by the others. Mitin, the chief philosopher of the
Stalinist ideological establishment, revealed the ultimate reason for withholding the usual vehemence in such criticisms. He was ambiguous concerning the right of psychology to be a separate science, saved somehow
from dissolving into neurophysiology at one level and historical materialism
at another.[89] That uncertainty entailed indifference to the particular schools
claiming to be Marxist psychology — a threatening indifference if psychology deserved to be liquidated, a patient indifference if not.

In short, during the 1930s and 1940s no one knew any better than
Rubinshtein what the 'correct' line in psychology was or would prove to
be. On a very limited scale research and teaching went on — such as Luria's
in defectology, Leont'ev's in child development, Rubinshtein's in philosophical psychology and teaching future teachers — but theorists were
treading water. Rubinshtein claimed to be the boldest among them. 'In
contrast to the very widespread tendencies of recent times,' he boasted in
the preface to a 1940 revision of his textbook, 'I have not tried in this book
to avoid a single one of the sharp issues.'[90] In an important sense that was
true. He did not avoid sharp issues, he dulled them to suit the mood of the
ideological establishment. That is, he did philosophical translations of
metapsychology into the principle of activity, he repeatedly confessed that
psychology is a very imperfect science, and he was ever ready to oblige
when the ideological establishment condemned this or that idea or demanded
some other.

As he worked on the new edition of the textbook, the ideological
establishment began the campaign for Russian patriotism that would mount
to xenophobia and anti-Semitic heights in the post-war period. In 1938–9
Soviet Pedagogy assailed the received idea that pre-revolutionary Russian
psychology had been a subordinate provincial offshoot of advanced Western
science, which was a metaphysical pseudo-science in any case. Sechenov
had shown the world the way to a genuine science of the mind, a momentous turning point that had been scandalously ignored:

Up to now we still have had almost no correct evaluation of I. M.
Sechenov as a psychologist. Sechenov is linked with the Russian
liberal bourgeoisie, Sechenov is represented as a vulgar materialist, his
philosophical views are undervalued, even though all his life Sechenov
propagandized philosophical materialism.[91]

The newly perceived truth was that Sechenov had brought into psychology the progressive materialist philosophy of the Russian revolutionary democrats. Pavlov had developed Sechenov's idea into the scientific study of higher nervous activity, which was the basis for an authentic science of the mind.

Rubinshtein dutifully revised the historical sections of his textbook to accord with this indisputable discovery.[92] Yet he managed to avoid the reduction of psychology to physiology by emphasizing Sechenov's insertion of a middle element in the brain's reflexes; between stimulus and response came the delay for consciousness.[93] Rubinshtein also showed great care in his ultimate formulation of Pavlov's achievement: not psychological science but 'serious physiological preconditions for the construction of a scientific, neurologically based psychology'.[94] To be sure, there were other passages on the history of psychology that were less careful, or even dishonest, but they hardly affected the non-historical bulk of the textbook, which was still devoted to functional analysis of the conscious mind (*soznanie*), broken down into traditional functions or faculties: perception, memory, speech, thought, imagination, inclinations, needs, interests, emotions, attention, and will.

He apologized for 'the contemplative intellectualism . . ., the traditional abstract functionalism,' which had been justly criticized in the first edition.[95] He claimed that he had drastically altered the book in the light of that criticism — indeed, he called it a new book rather than a new edition — but the same basic divisions were still in evidence: consciousness, broken down into perception, memory, etcetera. He had added, however, a section on 'action and activity', which became in effect a portmanteau faculty that gathered all the others into Marxist ideology.[96] Thus he was able to claim that he had met the fundamental demand of his critics, to end the separation between Marxist philosophy of psychology and psychological science itself. And thus, the outside observer notes, he had managed to preserve the traditional content of the lecture course while adjusting its ideological décor to suit official critics.

One such adjustment was the switch from derogation of the Russian past to the obligatory new pride — in the pre-revolutionary past, one must specify, for Rubinshtein felt obliged to be quite harsh on Soviet Marxist psychologists. Their first twenty years of striving had not been authentically Marxist and had not benefited psychological science. What other conclusion could one draw from the 'discussions' of reflexology and reactology in 1930−2 and the Central Committee's condemnation of pedology in 1936? 'The mechanism of reflexology, the eclecticism of reactology (K. N. Kornilov), the uncritical pursuit of fashionable foreign theories (L. S. Vygotsky), which were presented as Marxist psychology, and the distortions of pedology led [Soviet] psychology into an impasse.'[97] The way out, to 'a broad and fruitful development' of authentically Marxist psychology, was opened by 'the period of discussions' in 1930–2 and especially by the Central Committee's decree on educational psychology in 1936.

The outside observer may think that a paradox – discovery of impasse opening the way to fruitful development – but the establishment was pleased. In 1942 Rubinshtein was promoted from the Herzen Pedagogical Institute in Leningrad to the country's chief university, in Moscow, where he was empowered to found a Department of Psychology. Indeed, he was simultaneously elevated to the directorship of the central Institute of Psychology at the Academy of Pedagogical Sciences. But that approach to total rule over the discipline lasted only to 1945, when a separation of powers was arranged, leaving Rubinshtein at one of two summits. He gave up the Institute of Psychology to a specialist in child psychology and founded a 'Psychological Sector' within the central Institute of Philosophy at the Academy of Sciences.[98] That was not a demotion; he had a Stalin Prize for his book and membership in the Academy of Sciences. He was to be not the chief psychologist but the chief philosopher of psychology – briefly. The ideological establishment that had given so much suddenly took it all away. In 1949 all psychology but Pavlov's doctrine of 'higher nervous activity' was condemned. Rubinshtein and his textbook, so recently exalted, were execrated. He was not of Pavlov's school, and he belonged to 'the tribe of rootless cosmopolitans',[99] which is to say the inadequately Russian Jews.

Must we then conclude that Rubinshtein's triumph was a brief accident, a momentary pause in the decline and fall of psychology as the establishment succumbed to Pavlovian psychology and Russian nativism? Hardly. In the very act of condemning all psychology but Pavlov's reduction of it to nerve action, the ideological establishment insisted that Pavlov intended no such reduction.[100] By the mid-1950s we shall see non-Pavlovian psychology come out of the shadows, Rubinshtein among the leaders, writing textbooks no more but treatises of metapsychology, demonstrating the discipline's place within Marxism-Leninism. Evidently the ideological establishment was of divided mind. It shared with Rubinshtein the conviction that consciousness is a reality – I am tempted to say a substance – which requires study by an autonomous science of psychology. And it also shared with Pavlov the opposite conviction, that reduction of mind to neural matter is the only way for science to deal with mind.

The reader may wonder exactly who was, or were, 'the ideological establishment'. Individuals cannot be cited in response. Bukharin was gone, reviled as a deviationist in 1929, executed as a traitor in 1938. Lunacharsky and Pokrovsky probably escaped a similar fate by natural deaths in the early 1930s. Trotsky was not simply exiled and execrated, but was clubbed to death as he sat writing in Mexico. Thousands of lesser Party intellectuals with individualized records of ideological endeavor were expelled, imprisoned, or executed. Stalin was the only one of the chief ideologists with the right to speak in his own voice, and he was notoriously close-mouthed. Andrei Zhdanov, viceroy of the ideological establishment from the mid-1930s to his death in 1948, imitated Stalin's rarity, brevity, and crudity in public pronouncements.[101] Neither master nor man ever spoke in public to the issues of psychology or neurophysiology, unless one reads such significance into the tiny reports of Stalin's 1932 meetings with writers and physiologists in Gorky's apartment. Zhdanov elucidated Stalin's job classification of writers — 'engineers of human souls' — and said nothing of the chief's comments on physiology.[102]

So we outsiders, like the Soviet intelligentsia of the time, are reduced to guesswork, reading the minds of the ultimate chiefs from the changing policies pursued under their largely silent gaze: rebukes to all would-be Marxist psychologists in the 1930s, honors lavished on Rubinshtein in the 1940s, rebukes to would-be Marxist psychologists once again in 1949–53 along with deification of Pavlov, and renewed respect for mentalistic psychologists in the mid-1950s. To find the changing messages from on high we must pore over the official organs of the ideological establishment — such journals as *Bol'shevik, Under the Banner of Marxism, Soviet Pedagogy* — which fell largely silent on psychology in the 1930s. We cannot know which magnates might have privately expressed what thoughts in unreported council chambers. By the mid-1930s that vast impersonality, serving the cult of a single personality, was the characteristic style of the bureaucracy in charge of Soviet culture. Writers and scholars were supposed to step out on the public stage and speak in their own voices, while Party chiefs sat in the shadows and judged, emerging only at rare moments to shatter the dull murmur of scholarly voices with a godlike declaration, such as the Central Committee decree on pedology in 1936.

As one grows accustomed to that style, it becomes possible to read the collective mentality of an ideological establishment that wore one man's mask. Its central commitment, stressed in all its handouts, was to 'the priority of practice'. Whatever else that might mean, in the early 1930s it meant hope of benefit from applied psychology, which quickly turned to angry conviction of its uselessness or actual harm. A residual sense of practical need for psychiatry and pedagogy of some kind saved psychology from total condemnation, and the intellectual orientation to 'practice' persistently revealed a powerful yearning for metaphysical reassurance.

Like Christian princes of an earlier age, Stalinist magnates felt the need to be, or to have about them, learned defenders of the faith. Their flip-flop pattern — the intermittent approach to anathema on all psychology but physiological, and the backing off from anathema — all that start-stop-go evinced disdain rather than concern for the professional issues that divided psychologists, an irritated refusal to believe that coherent scientific explanation cannot encompass mind as well as matter. Like many other modern people, Bolshevik ideologists felt a need to know that there is a comprehensive scientific truth of the mind; not a need to know the science of mind, just to know that there is one, in the care of trustworthy experts. When various schools of experts offered partial satisfactions of that need for universal truth, they mocked the hunger for a single faith by their resemblance to the clutter of congregations claiming to have it in religion.

During the Second World War, while Soviet Russia had Western allies, the ideological establishment liked Rubinshtein's metaphysical reassurance that diversity in appearance is unity in essence, as Marx had shown long ago. When Soviet Russia found itself isolated once again from the Western world that it must overtake and surpass, the establishment turned to a cruder, bellicose type of reassurance, suitable for the most intense moment of the desperation to believe that twentieth-century thought is a 'bourgeois' deception, from which Soviet Russians must extricate themselves.

14

The Pavlov Solution

Pavlov's quarrel with the Bolsheviks flared up for a third time just before their embrace. It was intense during the Civil War, when political dictatorship and economic ruin prompted him to talk of emigration, and the Bolsheviks responded with extra rations, a nice apartment, and generous research support. It flared again in 1923, when he publicly ridiculed the Bolshevik claim of scientific knowledge in political affairs and they responded with respectful polemics, offering a separation of intellectual powers: physiology was his realm, social science theirs.[1] Calm ensued until 1929, when the Bolsheviks forced the Academy of Sciences to elect Communist members, and then sent in a purge commission to get rid of subversives. Pavlov seems to have agitated for resistance to that assault on academic autonomy, or at least to have expressed strong disapproval. The evidence in the public record gives no details, but its import is clear, most notably in a speech that Kornilov gave at a public meeting in March 1930. He said that 'Pavlov's recent political speeches are clearly counter-revolutionary and demand intervention by the appropriate organs.'[2] He meant of course the OGPU; in the context of the time he was calling for Pavlov's arrest.

Zalkind, who was still the chief Communist on the psychoneurological front, warned the meeting that Kornilov was 'tactically to the "left" of the Central Committee'. Its tactics still prescribed 'political struggle with Pavlov while supporting his enormously important scientific work'.[3] Such a sensible balance could hardly endure in the rage for monolithic unity of politics and culture, which was just then beginning, but it was Kornilov and Zalkind who would be squashed. Within two years of Kornilov's effort to sic the political police on Pavlov he and Zalkind would be stripped of their leadership on the psychoneurological front, and the central press would be hailing Pavlov's main institute as 'the Dneprostroi for the all-round study of man', following the meeting in Gorky's apartment between Stalin and 'a group of scientists'. By 1935 the press would be celebrating

Pavlov as a great Soviet patriot and a virtual Marxist, while Kornilov would be struggling to hold on as an educational psychologist, and Zalkind would be approaching the choice between arrest and suicide.[4]

The caprice of tyrannical power obviously played a part in that absurd twist, but persistent patterns of thought were also at work. The simple-minded admiration of Pavlov's doctrine that had been expressed in the 1920s by Bukharin, Trotsky and Zinoviev was not affected by their personal disgrace. The particular phrase, 'a weapon from the iron arsenal of materialism', was recognizably Bukharin's tribute to Pavlov's doctrine, but the idea it conveyed was too commonplace to carry anyone's copyright: radicals favor the reduction of mind to brain because it undercuts belief in the soul, which serves the cause of priests and reactionaries. That still seemed an obvious truth to Bolshevik ideologists, but so did Marx and Engels' ridicule of physiological reduction, their insistence that minds are determined by the historical experience of class and society. How to re-concile those different forms of materialism, physiological and historical? And how to reconcile either or both with Bolshevik insistence on the supreme power of the conscious will? Such questions were not explicitly confronted; Marx–Engels–Lenin had settled them. Any residual issues were brushed aside as technicalities, to be handled by Marxist specialists in physiology, psychology, and philosophy — who suddenly lost the trust of Party ideologists during Stalin's revolution from above. Rubinshtein offered a way out of that impasse, through complex philosophy to universal truth, but then Pavlov, though dead, showed a simpler way out, through science to native pride.

IDEOLOGY AND SCIENCE

In the 1920s, while *Red Virgin Soil, Under the Banner of Marxism*, and the *Herald of the Communist Academy* provided a fairly autonomous forum for Soviet Marxist intellectuals, they could read sophisticated arguments con-cerning the unresolved tensions among various interpretations of Marxism and various schools of psychological science. As late as 1930 Borovskii was able to tell the Marxist public that 'the reflex as "the unit of behavior" is a myth, an invention.'[5] He drew his evidence from such technical studies as the way newborn fish learn to swim, but he also noted such ideological silliness as Pavlov's 'reflexes of freedom and of purpose', which failed to overcome the inadequacy of his teaching: 'The doctrine of reflexes does not fit the dynamic and labile qualities of behavior as it is factually observed.'[6] He wound up crediting Pavlov with far less than he claimed for himself: he had not discovered the unit of all individually acquired behavior, he had found a method for distinguishing one particular type. And the neural mechanism of it, which Pavlov claimed to know, was actually unknown.

Borovskii's article proved to be the end of genuine discussion, the last time that the general public could read an informed and uninhibited critique of Pavlov's doctrine. Abruptly, in 1930–1, the journals that carried such autonomous discussion were transformed into zealously obsequious mouth-pieces for the ideological establishment, and articles on psychology and neurophysiology simply stopped. The Bolsheviks did not abruptly lose confidence in their long-standing claim of a universal scientific philosophy. They had reached a new level in their equally long-standing reluctance to think about disputatious objections, in their preference for a vague dog-matism that brushes off major problems as perverse inventions of enemy scholars or technicalities for specialists, or both fiendishly entangled. Now they insisted that the specialists must prove themselves to be no enemies but Party thinkers within their technical disciplines, an impossible task while Party thought was both dogmatic and willfully vague. The specialists were damned if they brought their conflicting 'bourgeois' schools within the temple of Marxism-Leninism, where the congregation sings in har-mony with the choirmaster, and they were damned if they didn't, if they tried to avoid sacrilege by isolating their scientific knowledge from the all-inclusive wisdom of the Party.

Pavlov of course was haughtily indifferent to such Bolshevik concerns. But some of his disciples were trying to fit their minds within a Marxist framework, even the new kind of Marxism that sought exclusiveness, separation from such 'bourgeois' schools of science as the Pavlovian. Those earliest Pavlovian Marxists gave papers at the Behavioral Congress in January 1930, which was supposed to rally psychoneurological specialists within a single ideology, and Zalkind, who was still the Party chief on that front, approved their demonstrative defiance of the master's politics – he was as usual absent from a Soviet meeting, though it took place in his own city. But Zalkind also criticized the disciples who gave papers at the Congress, or rather, he pinned ideological labels on them as representatives of 'trends within the Pavlov school'. He put Ivanov-Smolenskii together with Anokhin as 'militant mechanists', for he perceived in their papers an effort to reduce mind to a physiological process. He saw other Pavlovians as 'pseudo-neutralists', who claimed to avoid philosophical issues. K. M. Bykov exemplified an 'elemental dialectician', for he unwittingly approached the union of opposites in his efforts to explain the neural mechanisms of liver and kidney functions.[7]

All these were Zalkind's arbitrary attributions of ideological significance to scientific papers that made no explicit claims of it. He may have had a point. I think he certainly did for the category 'pseudo-neutralist', which I leave without an individual's name, since it included the silent majority of Pavlovian physiologists.[8] They wanted no part of philosophizing with Stalinists. The three individuals to whom Zalkind attributed some ideo-logical stance beyond neutralism – Ivanov-Smolenskii, Anokhin, Bykov –

were subsequently key figures in the imbroglio that reached its Stalinist climax in 1950. Perhaps they were already trying to address Bolshevik sensibilities in 1930, without an explicit avowal of a philosophical position, by the demonstrative act of reading scientific papers under the banner of a Marxist-Leninist unity conference. By finding 'mechanism' or 'elementalism' (*stikhiinost'*) in their papers, Zalkind let them know that was not enough. He preferred Pavlovians who made explicit avowals of a Marxist-Leninist approach; he labeled them 'the group approaching conscious Marxism' − I count three individuals − and singled out one for unalloyed praise. That one had shown how a Pavlovian should bring his doctrine together with the Party's.

He was L. N. Fedorov, virtually unique among Pavlov's disciples for having joined the Red Army and the Party during the Civil War, when he was almost thirty.[9] A special evening session of the Behavioral Congress was arranged so that all might hear this indisputably Communist Pavlovian appraise the master's doctrine. For the most part he presented it quite as the master did, mingling well-established patterns of stimulus and response with hypothetical neural explanations, which he offered without a hint of criticism, as proven inferences from the patterns of stimulus and response. At the end of his lecture Fedorov turned to explicit issues of ideology and openly criticized Pavlov, a startling departure for one of the disciples.[10] That is how the other two in the 'group approaching conscious Marxism' showed such consciousness: they deplored Pavlov's notorious equation of revolution with calamities such as war, caused by 'dark forces' that could be explained and overcome only by physiological science.[11] Fedorov tried to go deeper in his criticism. He objected to Pavlov's identification of 'the human' with 'the subhuman', his reduction of 'the social' to 'the biological'. He held Pavlov responsible for the exaggerated versions of those sins in certain disciples, calling special attention to 'Ivanov-Smolenskii, who ... identifies psychic phenomena with higher nervous processes, and thus denies the psychic, the subjective, as a special quality of highly organized matter'. Against such one-sided mechanism Fedorov upheld 'the monistic viewpoint ... [which] is not the identity ... but the unity of the objective and the subjective, as two sides of one and the same process'.[12]

The most significant feature of Fedorov's pioneering mixture of Marxism with Pavlov's doctrine − one can see this with hindsight − was the separation that appeared in the ostensible mix. Pure science was separated from ideology not only in the body-and-tail structure of the paper − pages of ostensibly pure science wagging a bit of explicit ideology at the end − but also within the two parts. Ideological criticism was kept apart from serious issues in science, and even from the serious kind of ideology that merges into philosophical inquiry. The brief generalities that he offered in criticism of Pavlov's doctrine were left that way, as inane opposition of 'the human' and 'the subhuman', 'the social' and 'the biological', 'the subjective' and 'the objective', which Fedorov no less than Pavlov failed to unite within the discipline of physiology.

Who has? Who can? an outsider will ask. Marx–Engels–Lenin, an insider was obliged to answer, but − or therefore − Fedorov would not apply his own mind at that superhuman level. Indeed, within neurophysiology narrowly construed his exposition of Pavlov's doctrine revealed uncritical reverence. Scientists who stood outside the circle of Pavlov's disciples were making telling criticisms of Pavlovian neurology, and some individuals within the school were beginning to chafe at the master's refusal to pay attention. But while he lived they refrained from public declaration of such dissidence. It was I. D. Sapir, a leading Communist neurologist and Soviet pioneer of neuropsychology, who tried to alert the Behavioral Congress to some of the faults in Pavlov's scheme of brain function. He dwelt on Pavlov's model of conditioning as 'temporary associations' among a 'mosaic' of points in the cerebral cortex, in contrast to a model of 'systemic' interaction.[13] But Sapir's was a lonely effort to bring talk of mechanism-*v.*-dialectics down to concrete issues in experimental science; it had no appeal to the Pavlovians who were trying to be Marxists. Neither did it appeal to Zalkind, nor to the man who soon replaced him as the Party chief on the psychoneurological front. In the Stalinist intellectual culture meaningful intercourse between science and ideology was stubbornly evaded, while the air was split with ceaseless calls for their union. This may be a special version of the pattern we see in our culture: scientists are revolted by explicit ideology, love it when it is insinuated unnamed, while doing pure science.

Zalkind's replacement was a prime case in point. He was the neurologist N. I. Grashchenkov, also known as Propper, just turning thirty in 1931 and still a postgraduate at the Institute of Red Professorship when Zalkind was denounced and leadership on the psychoneurological front passed to him. His path to eminence had begun, like Kolbanovskii's, with Party enrollment during the Civil War, when he was still an adolescent. Afterwards he trained in medicine at Moscow University, stayed on in its faculty, and was almost certainly a leader in the Communist campaign to take over the Moscow Society of Neuropathologists and Psychiatrists. When control was achieved at the end of 1929, Grashchenkov was added to the editorial board of the chief journal in neurology and psychiatry, and introduced its first Bolshevized issue with a review of Pavlov's school at the Behavioral Congress.[14] He was more detailed than Zalkind, yet equally evasive of serious issues in neurophysiology.

In the next few years he continued that pattern in repeated articles on reflexology, a term still applied to Pavlov's school as well as Bekhterev's.[15] Grashchenkov was certainly aware that neurological criticisms of Pavlov's doctrine were accumulating. He even paid tribute to Beritashvili − for his efforts to be a Marxist, ignoring his critique of Pavlov's hypothetical brain processes. When Grashchenkov became a major administrator of medical research in the late 1930s, he showed in action his awareness of Pavlovian tendencies to claim far more than their doctrine could deliver.[16] But he eschewed such matters when he wrote his Marxist-Leninist evaluations of Pavlov's doctrine. In explicit talk of ideology and science he held to the line that Pavlov was 'an idealist and reactionary ... in his explanation of social relations,' but 'in the science of human behavior he emerges as a materialist, and in some places even as an elemental dialectician.'[17] Technical objections are hardly appropriate to such an exalted scientist.

That was the Party line in the early 1930s, and it was reinforced but not substantially changed by Stalin's personal involvement in October 1932. Fedorov, and maybe Grashchenkov too, were present at the meeting with Stalin in Gorky's apartment, as a result of which Pavlov's Institute of Experimental Medicine won a major increase in support and official boosting.[18] In 1933 *Under the Banner of Marxism* broke a three-year silence on the psychoneurological sciences with an article by another of the rare Pavlovian disciples who was a Party member. He opened with a proud contrast between the West, where brain scientists have no theory to unify the information that piles on them like snow, and the Soviet Union, where they meet with Comrade Stalin and reach a decision to turn Pavlov's Institute into 'the all-union center for the all-round study of man.'[19] The rest of the article was the same sort of abstract praise for Pavlov's doctrine as Grashchenkov was then publishing, with the same kind of abstract criticism for its mechanistic elements, which give rise to idealism.[20] Lacking specifics, ignoring the points where Pavlov's doctrine conflicted with other theories of brain action, not to mention other theories of the mind, such ideological evaluation was little more than a vague cheer ending with a sigh: what a pity that the great creator of brain science is opposed to the Soviet cause and to Marxism!

And then the creator changed, toward the Soviet cause if not toward Marxism. In October 1934 Pavlov sent an open letter to the Sechenov Society of physiologists, thanking them for a meeting held in his honor. He had previously stayed away, in body and spirit, from any Soviet gathering, demonstrating an attitude of internal exile. In 1930, at the insistence of Bolshevik delegates, a physiologists' congress had finally responded in kind: they deliberately omitted the usual telegram informing Pavlov of his election *in absentia* to the honorary presidium, and sent the telegram instead to the entire Politburo.[21] Against that background Pavlov's open letter of October 1934 was a political event, declaring his pride in 'our indisputable Russian achievement in world science.'[22] The great scientist was joining the Soviet community. And he went on with other public messages in the two years of life still left to him. (After protracted digestive and respiratory disorders, he died of pneumonia in February 1936.) From expressions of gratitude to a Soviet physiologists' meeting he moved to praise of the Soviet state and its grand strengthening of the native land: 'Whatever I am doing, I constantly think of the cause that I am serving as much as my energies permit, above all my fatherland. In my native land just now a grand social reconstruction is proceeding. The savage gulf between the rich and the poor has been abolished. I want to live until such time as I can see the final results of this social reconstruction.'[23]

The grand climax of the conversion came in August 1935, when an international congress of physiologists met in Leningrad and Moscow. Pavlov opened it with a speech expanding the themes of his recent messages: excitement over the great social experiment under way in his native land, joy to see improvements in the people's condition, gratitude to the Soviet government for its generous funding of his work, and finally the determination that he shared with the entire people and its state to shout 'Not one inch of foreign land' as their slogan of struggle against the threat of another war. That was a quote from Stalin, which set off 'stormy applause'.[24]

Later, in a toast at a Kremlin reception – a toast without alcohol, for Pavlov was a teetotaler – he wondered whether he could justify all the funds that the government was pouring into his research. Molotov called out, 'We are sure that you will unconditionally', and Pavlov returned the compliment: 'As you know, I am an experimenter from head to foot. All my life has consisted of experiments. Our government is also an experimenter, only of an incomparably higher category. I want passionately to live, so that I might see the successful completion of this historic social experiment.'[25] *Pravda* published that exchange, and *Izvestiia* carried a front-page photograph of Pavlov standing next to Molotov and two other Party leaders among the honored foreign guests.[26] In subsequent reprints the two other leaders, victims of the terror, were brushed out, and so were the foreign guests, leaving a Stalinist icon of Molotov and Pavlov in purified unity, which still decorates Pavlov's *Works*.[27]

The Nazi German threat was an obvious reason for this change of heart. Equally obvious was Pavlov's willingness to approve what he had ridiculed in 1923. Marxism might not be authentic science – he never retracted that part of the lecture that had provoked the highest Party leaders to argue with him – but now he conceded one of Bukharin's main points: Soviet leaders were involved in a great experiment comparable to scientists' tests of their masterful knowledge. Pavlov may have been strengthened in that standard Soviet vision by hearing it from the leftist minority of American and British scientists, whom he saw repeatedly whether at home or abroad.[28] In particular I would guess that he heard admiration of Soviet accomplishments from W. B. Cannon and A. V. Hill, who are standing there with Pavlov and Molotov and the short-term leaders in the unaltered photo.[29] But most Western scientists were not admirers of Soviet achievements, and most were not as respectful of Pavlov's achievement as he thought they should be. They might praise him for taking neurophysiology into the borderland between brain and mind, but very few followed his lead, and the few who did were likely to dismay him, as Beritashvili and Lashley had, by setting aside his neurological explanations of learned behavior, the essence of his doctrine as he conceived it.

Like most Russian scientists Pavlov was quite sensitive to the opinions of eminent Western colleagues, eager for their praise, quick to be incensed by lack of proper recognition, ready to be defiantly isolated if the metropolitan leaders were not properly receptive. That potent mixture of scientific conviction, provincial sensitivity, and wounded pride found expression in a lecture of May, 1934, as Pavlov was entering his period of conversion to the Soviet cause. He recalled that Sherrington, twelve years previously, 'frightened me' with the remark, '"Your conditioned reflexes will hardly have much success in England, for they smell of materialism."'[30] Yet his doctrine, Pavlov boasted, was currently taught throughout England and America — by psychologists far more than physiologists, he neglected to specify.

He did note that his doctrine lacked much success as yet in Germany. There physiologists were likely to dismiss studies of conditioned reflexes with the remark, 'Keine Physiologie'.[31] Indeed physiologists everywhere did not properly appreciate what he had given them:

> It must be added that physiologists in general to the present time do not know where to place conditioned reflexes in a textbook of physiology. It seems to me that these reflexes deserve by right to have first place in the exposition of the physiology of the cerebral hemispheres, as the normal, objectively verified work of the hemispheres. The analytical data that have so far been gathered by [brain] stimulations, extirpations and other means of studying the cortex should naturally take their place after the description of the [brain's] normal work.[32]

That was his longstanding boastful complaint: the fragmenting methods favored by most brain scientists revealed only fragmented truths, which required unifying organization by the doctrine of conditioned reflexes. The physiology of the brain was in confusion, and would continue to be so until its adepts learned to order their chaotic material according to Pavlov's doctrine.

That theme resounded again in Pavlov's messages of Soviet patriotism. On his eighty-fifth birthday in October 1934, he sent public thanks to the Leningrad physiological society named for Sechenov, which had informed him of a special meeting in his honor. After a line of conventional gratitude, he added a paragraph of defiant boasting:

> Yes, I am glad that together with Ivan Mikhailovich [Sechenov] and a regiment of good colleagues, we have brought within the mighty power of physiological research the whole indivisible animal organism

in place of the fragmented one [*polovinchatogo*]. And this is entirely our indisputable Russian achievement in world science, in general human thought.[33]

I call that defiant boasting since Pavlov was telling 'world science' and 'general human thought' where they were bound to go, not where they perceived themselves to be. Only five months earlier he had been recalling the 'Keine Physiologie' of a German colleague and the failure of physiological textbooks in every country to place conditioned reflexes where they belonged, as the opening theme in the chapter on brain function. Those who strain toward a future that they know for sure have the impatient habit of seeing its signs before others do, and of dismissing contrary knowledge in annoyance or anger. Stalinists had an extreme case of that common infirmity; Pavlov's was far less severe, but still pronounced. He and the Stalinists discovered ideological comradeship in their conviction that Russia, despite superficial appearances of provincial backwardness and isolation, was leading the rest of a largely hostile or indifferent world, he in brain science, they in social reconstruction.

Once Pavlov recognized that comradeship and death removed the possibility of further change, all qualifications dropped away from Bolshevik praise for him — on the popular level, where twentieth-century political leaders keep their minds. On that level no one knew or cared about the widening gulf between Pavlov's doctrine of brain function and the technical material presented in physiological textbooks. In high culture, when writing for learned journals, Party ideologists might recall that Pavlov had traveled a long and difficult path to proper appreciation of the Soviet cause, but that would be a brief prelude to extended celebration of his ultimate patriotism. Similarly with their former caution concerning Pavlov's mechanistic version of materialism; it shrank into a brief gloss on talk of his unwitting dialectics or was altogether explained away.[34] If some feature of his doctrine was blatantly offensive to Marxism — for example, the expectation that physiology would explain social phenomena — it was attributed to 'immoderately zealous "followers"', not to Pavlov himself.[35] When Anokhin, writing for *Under the Banner of Marxism*, told of Pavlov's *mashinnost'*, his machine theory of the animal organism, his habit of holding up his watch as the model of a man, the editors demurred. Pavlov, they protested, was speaking figuratively, merely calling attention to 'the materiality of the processes in the nervous system'.[36]

Of course Pavlov's express disavowals of materialism were brushed aside if not altogether suppressed. Orbeli, the disciple chosen by Pavlov to inherit supreme leadership of the large research enterprise, tried to forget that his own doctoral dissertation had endorsed an agnostic philosophical interpretation of Pavlov's doctrine. A Communist disciple who was working up a history of the doctrine ignored Pavlov's published disclaimer of materialism, but recalled a remark in conversation: 'I am not a materialist or an idealist, I am a monist or, if one must choose, a methodological materialist.'[37] For an outsider the obvious way to make sense of that declaration is to emphasize *methodological*, which points back to Pavlov's neglected declarations of utter absorption in the way that science works, his avowed indifference to philosophical questions about the ultimate reality that science is trying to get at.[38] That was the sentiment that Orbeli had provided with philosophical sanction in his pre-revolutionary dissertation, but of course he did not try to revive it in the 1930s, for it was obviously what Leninist ideologists denounced as Machism.[39] They tolerantly ignored Orbeli's past, for the time being, while he endorsed their line on Pavlov's doctrine: the scientific complement to Lenin's philosophical theory of reflection, which quite demolished Machism.

That became the standard line, and still is. The laws of higher nervous activity founded on the conditioned reflex (Pavlov's doctrine) show how the human brain generates the knowledge that reflects external reality (Lenin's doctrine). In Russian Pavlov's reflexes (*refleksy*) and Lenin's reflection (*otrazhenie*) are not cognates, as they are in English, but the metaphorical resonance is very strong anyhow. Of course, the admiring believer may not reflect — another cognate lacking in Russian — on the difference between the passive animal that is the model object of Pavlov's experiments and the extremely willful, active creature whose knowledge reflects objective reality in Lenin's philosophy. Serious Leninist thinkers might worry about incongruities of that sort — they had as recently as 1935[40] — but no longer out loud, unless they wished to seem apostates from official doctrine. Lenin's philosophy of the mind had its scientific complement in Pavlov's doctrine, and that was that.

To subdue the unavoidable sense of an enormous difference between dogs salivating to bells and people making a revolution, ideologists gestured toward Pavlov's occasional suggestion of a 'second signal system'.[41] That is the hypothetical part of the human nervous system lacking in lower animals. Or maybe it is not a distinguishable anatomical part but a distinguishable physiological function of the whole; no one has ever made a serious effort to pin it down in either sense.[42] An outside observer feels free to note the obvious: the second signal system was a vaguely neurological fantasy to accommodate speech and thought within the doctrine of conditioned reflexes. Leninists seized upon it as the phrase that would accommodate Pavlov's biological theory of a passive mind within their social theory of a willful mind. More than a phrase was not wanted, for both doctrines were objects of worship rather than thought.

For thirteen years after Pavlov's conversion that rough-and-ready comradeship of science and ideology sufficed. The ideological establishment did not pry into the work of Pavlov's disciples, to see if they were true to the grand old doctrine, and they did not attempt sophisticated correction of the popular notion that Pavlov's doctrine was the final word in brain science. Ivanov-Smolenskii seems to have been the only one who was hurt by that arrangement, perhaps because he was the only one who seriously persisted in the effort to explain human mentality by conditioning. He was therefore viewed as an 'overzealous "follower"', who 'vulgarized the doctrine of the psyche' by claiming reduction of it to physiology.[43]

For a time in the late 1930s he seemed in danger of losing a research center. Moves were made to close the psychiatric research clinic that he directed within the Institute of Experimental Medicine. Evidently Orbeli, Grashchenkov, and other administrators of medical science were skeptical of his claims, which were to translate Pavlov's doctrine into meaningful psychiatric insights and clinical practice. The quarrel over that clinic was confined to bureaucratic politics, with rare muffled reports in the press.[44] With support from someone on high Ivanov-Smolenskii was given a laboratory in Moscow in place of the clinic he lost in Leningrad, and he and his critics refrained — or were restrained — from expanding their quarrel into a major polemical conflict, for the time being. Open debate could hardly be confined to problems of experimental science narrowly construed. Pavlov and his doctrine had become names like Marx-Engels-Lenin and their doctrine, that is, focal points of organized veneration, not of discussion or argument. For thirteen years the organizers of veneration showed little concern with the research and teaching that were ostensibly being done in his name. Then, quite suddenly, they flew into a rage over the incongruities.

PAVLOV'S SCHOOL

Students and observers of Pavlov agreed that he was a severe master with a loud voice and a terrible temper, but disagreed on the effect. Some said that his habit of shouting and cursing, sometimes even striking subordinates, frightened and stifled them; others said that it was a mannerism one got used to, that he himself disapproved of it. According to one anecdote, he stopped cursing his assistants in vivisection after one of them cursed back.[45] Anokhin recalled him flying out of temper at a lecture assistant and shouting 'Get out!' before a crowded amphitheater, to which the assistant shouted, pre-revolutionary style, 'I obey, your excellency!'[46] With such anecdotes fond disciples rebutted the charge that their master's 'intense and unceasing supervision [*rukovoditel'stvo*] oppresses, inhibits self-activation [*samodeiatel'nost'*].'[47] His character 'was formed on the bumps and ruts of primordial Russian nature', which was why he railed at subordinates for the slightest failing, but the net result was the opposite of inhibiting; he built independent characters like himself.[48] Or so they said, in obvious self-justification. Anokhin, who proved to be the most independent and creative, suggested something darker in his judgment that Pavlov 'united in necessary doses

gentle sensitivity of feeling and frequently depressing severity'.[49] From the
new world the émigré disciple Babkin brushed the whole issue aside as a
peculiarity of national styles: pre-revolutionary Russian officials 'considered
it necessary to instill fear in their subordinates by raising their voices. . . .
The Germans were worse in this respect. . . . In England one was amazed
to find that much better results were achieved without raising the voice at
all.'[50]

The important question is whether or to what degree Pavlov turned his
assistants into factory hands,[51] made them do science in the regimented
way that stifles creativity regardless of voice level or other peculiarities of
command and execution. He was a pioneer of the twentieth century's 'big
science', which raises that troubling question everywhere. In his case the
organizational issue was entangled with messy substantive problems in
brain science, a disorderly hybrid of neurophysiology and psychology in
which he clung to an untenable position. He was a physiologist who had
come into psychology with a claim of conquest, yet he had lost connection
with his home discipline. He combined rigorous experimental objectivity
in the psychological part of his research − correlations of stimulus and
response − with loose speculative subjectivity in the neurological part −
the disclosure of neural mechanisms. He called that mixture pure physiology,
and had a powerful motive for shutting his mind to criticism. He was
distressed by the chaos that he had left behind in neurophysiology, as it
descended to the cellular level; he thought to maintain systemic neurophysiology by studying a pattern of 'higher nervous activity'. Yet he was
aware of his isolation in the world community of neurophysiologists, and
also among American psychologists, who absorbed his experimental method
and set aside his neurology. That was the scientific situation − the fortress
mentality − within which Pavlov clung to an autocratic style of doing big
science with teams of researchers carrying out assigned tasks.

No doubt the man and his method stifled creativity in many submissive
souls, who cranked out routine data and went their quiet way to dull
obscurity, their passage marked by a few entries in dusty bibliographies. I
have not attempted a precise count of their numbers; a few hundred I
would guess.[52] But there is also no doubt that the Pavlovian mill cranked
out results which were willy-nilly at odds with the master's neurological
explanations, if one had a mind to think carefully about them. Experimental
scientists can win such triumphant defeats. When two Americans compiled
a thorough review of conditioning in 1940, they used work done by
Pavlov's school to make a judgment on his doctrine: 'What passes for
physiology in Pavlov's theory is nothing more than the translation of
behavioral facts into neurophysiological language' − largely imaginary,
one should add.[53] There is also no doubt that Pavlov's style did build
character and stimulate creativity in a minority of disciples. The obvious
evidence is their explicit disagreement with his opinions, if not in print

while he lived, then in private discussion. Jerzy Konorski, the Polish disciple who published the most extensive critique of Pavlov's doctrine — in English, twelve years after the master's death — gratefully recalled 'vital and sometimes stormy exchanges of opinion and ideas in his laboratories'.[54] Samoilov gave convincing testimony while Pavlov was still alive: he thanked Pavlov in print for driving him away to work with Sechenov.

The reader may recall Samoilov as the pioneer of electrophysiology who left Pavlov's laboratory in the 1890s, because Pavlov was passionately indifferent to research at the cellular and molecular levels while Sechenov encouraged it. Samoilov told of his experience while honoring the master's seventy-fifth birthday in 1924: Pavlov's 'imperious temperament' and single-minded vision had challenged a young scientist to make an independent thinker of himself.[55] And Pavlov was pleased by such a tribute. Within his laboratories his doctrine was law, but in science at large he firmly believed in 'absolute freedom, as much diversity as possible in viewpoints and modes of action'.[56] In 1931, when Samoilov died prematurely, Pavlov wrote a handsome obituary, trying to show respect for the deserter who had achieved fame in a rival school. He could not remember 'whether we had a talk or what kind it was concerning his motives for moving away' — a onesided outburst by Pavlov, in the other man's vivid memoir — but he could understand the difference in 'mental set' (*sklad golovy*) that caused the separation.

> I was and remain a pure physiologist, that is a researcher investigating the functions of separate organs, the conditions of those organs' activity and the synthesis of the separate organs' work in the general mechanics of one or another division of the organism or of the entire organism — and I have little interest in the final, deep foundations of the organ's functioning, of its tissue, for which chemical or physical analysis is primarily required. Hence the division of physiologists into pure physiologists, physiological chemists, and physiological physicists. In my place for certain periods, even exclusively at times, vivisection and surgical operations prevailed, while Ivan Mikhailovich Sechenov worked almost always only with chemical methods and with physical instruments.[57]

That is true, but it is also inadequate and evasive. Pavlov could not meaningfully describe the research of Samoilov and Sechenov's other students, for it was an unanswerable challenge to his doctrine.[58] They were painstakingly working out precise neural circuitry, which comes down to extremely complex summations of bioelectric processes at the cellular level. In the records of Pavlov's 'Wednesdays', his regular discussions with disciples, I find no evidence that he ever seriously confronted the challenge that such work was presenting to his hypotheses of brain function. Indeed, I find no evidence of 'stormy exchanges of ideas and opinions' on any topic. But the bland effect may be a product of the record-keeping, which began only in 1929 as brief minutes, mostly summarizing what Pavlov said. A stenographer appeared to make a verbatim record for the ages beginning in 1933, after the momentous meeting with Stalin in Gorky's apartment. Maybe the resulting exaltation of Pavlov's enterprise is one reason why the disciples — even Konorski — appear in the stenographic record as deferential reporters of their assigned tasks or largely silent listeners.[59]

Pavlov, speaking extemporaneously and at length, occasionally touched upon outside critics of his doctrine, invariably caricatured them beyond recognition, and met with little or no corrective protest. He systematically moved such disagreements quite out of neurophysiology, to a clash of world views or worse. In his American critics he found 'veiled animism, dualism, mysticism, and "verbalism"'; in Sherrington he found dualism so extreme as to indicate 'a sick mind'.[60] At that point P. S. Kupalov, a somewhat independent disciple who had once trained to be a priest, objected. Sherrington was using concepts in a different sense, to get at 'subjective experiences as such', to express the notion 'that if we understood each other quite thoroughly, through and through, it would be absurd, stupid, impossible to live'. That was close to a theme that Pavlov had sounded thirty years earlier, when he first announced his work on conditioned reflexes, and he softened a bit: 'In your words I see the torments of thought trying to solve that problem, but there is no clarity.'[61] With other disciples coming in on Pavlov's side, Kupalov fell silent.

The striking feature of the little argument was not only its rarity but its confinement to ideology; even Kupalov did not press the issue of subjectivity into physiology itself — in that discussion; in his research he tried to measure the emotional influence in conditioning. Nor did he allude to the discrepancies between Sherrington's account of brain processes and Pavlov's. When Anokhin wrote in suggesting that Sherrington's *The Brain and Its Mechanisms* be translated, Pavlov wrote back: 'Why translate [it]? There is almost nothing in it but a ridiculous pretense that our mind, perhaps, has no relationship to our brain.'[62] In fact, there was an argument that reduction of mind to brain is absurd, an argument that Pavlov could not confront, whether philosophically or scientifically.

The disciples may have offered Pavlov something closer to scientific argument than the stenographer recorded, but I doubt it. About 1934 one of the older generation wrote privately to Babkin in Canada that the old man was mostly talking while the others listened. 'In this his old age is most apparent. In our day he would have given up a piece of bread for the sake of an argument or a fight!'[63] But was it merely old age that generated monologues before a subdued audience, or was it also the disciples' inability, through courtesy or mindlessness, to tell the old man of his growing isolation? We may leave aside speculative psychologizing, and address the social facts that are obvious in the public record. Pavlov's laboratories were cranking out mounds of data, largely ignoring problems of discordance with mainstream neurology and emergent neuropsychology. That pattern suggests teams of scientists working as mill-hands, but some of their data were implicitly subversive, and there are bits of evidence that suggest some self-critical capacity even in Pavlov himself.

I do not include in such evidence his tinkering with the dogma of cortical localization. He still insisted that the 'temporary connections' which establish conditioned reflexes are formed in the cortex, even though extirpation experiments obliged him to stop imagining obligatory sites for the connections. If a dog could be conditioned to a light signal after removal of the visual cortex, and it could, Pavlov imagined that scattered throughout the cortex were cells with the capacity to 'analyze' light signals and to connect them with the equally scattered cells for feeding signals.[64] Such dodges evinced resistance rather than capacity for self-criticism. To back off from his cortical dogmatism, to start looking for the mechanisms of conditioned reflexes in subcortical structures — indeed, in the brainless nerve systems of insects or worms, which can also be conditioned — was to join the descent from a grand vision of systemic physiology into an endless mess of micro-processes, to acknowledge that the grand vision had been a fantasy.

Pavlov's appointments are my bits of evidence that his mind was not closed to all change. He delegated vital parts of his expanding enterprise to individuals with minds of their own, with the capacity to diverge from his obsessive schemes. In the physiological division of the Institute of Experimental Medicine, the place where Pavlov did most of his own research, his second in command and successor was Kupalov, who spent 1928–30 studying in England with A. V. Hill.[65] Kupalov's commitment to a cortical scheme for conditioning was almost as strong as Pavlov's, but he was also willing to try and work in evidence that subcortical structures were somehow involved, and we have seen that he was willing to disagree with the master in private discussion. Yet — or maybe therefore — Pavlov favored Kupalov, and two other disciples who were capable of moving the school away from orthodoxy. They were certainly not rebels, but they were creative scientists, of different types.

Orbeli was a pre-revolutionary type (b. 1882), a Russified Georgian who got all his training before 1917, including the classic journey to the West to study with famous scientists.[66] He was not a demonstrative individualist in his relations with Pavlov. Even on the political level he followed the master's example as late as 1930, and stayed away from the Behavioral Congress, though he was sufficiently eminent for the absence to be noted and publicly condemned as 'reactionary' behavior.[67] But Orbeli soon managed to win the trust of the Bolshevik establishment — perhaps as Pavlov changed his political outlook — and so became the indisputable crown prince, certified by multiple directorships and by the ultimate accolade in 1935: full membership in the Academy of Sciences. Following Pavlov's death in 1936 he became the scientific director of three Pavlovian institutes with twenty-eight laboratories in the Leningrad area, while others, Grashchenkov most notably, were the administrative chiefs presiding from Moscow, where new large centers had just sprung up.[68] By 1940 the All-Union Institute of Experimental Medicine boasted a staff of 2,750, a count that may have included Orbeli's Institute of the Evolution of Higher Nervous Activity, but probably did not include the Physiological Institute of the Academy of Sciences, which was also under his direction.[69] To be sure, not all the people in that astonishing count were scientists in the usual sense of the term, but the result is plain enough. Orbeli emerged in the 1930s as a major administrator of big science.

Typed as an orthodox Pavlovian by outsiders, he was sufficiently thoughtful, and sensitive enough to other trends of scientific thought, to edge away from the rigidities of Pavlov's doctrine. In his own research on the physiology of the sense organs he felt obliged to make the Helmholtzian − or Sechenovian, or Sherringtonian, or simply built-in − distinction between the merely physical and the also subjective process. Bioelectric impulses in the optic nerve must be distinguished from visions of color and shape in the brain-mind, the kind of distinction that entangles the physiologist in psychological concepts, if only in the steps he takes to exclude them from his work.[70] Pavlov himself, in the last year or so of his life, started talking to Orbeli and other lieutenants about establishing a psychological laboratory among their enterprises. But he made no written statement of the intention, and Orbeli held back. He merely added a laboratory on the physiology of the sense organs.[71] That was closer to his own research interests anyhow, and was not the shock that a psychological lab would have been to the orthodox conviction that Pavlov's doctrine was the antithesis of psychology. Besides, the Central Committee decree against pedology came soon after Pavlov's death, and many perceived it as Bolshevik anathema on psychological science.

When the occasion suited, Orbeli invoked Pavlov's concept of a second signal system to justify study of distinctively human processes, but he fostered no research on the topic. It was Ivanov-Smolenskii who invoked the concept to legitimize his research in conditioning human subjects with verbal stimuli. He claimed to be showing that speech is also a function of conditioned reflexes, and to be developing techniques of use in psychiatric treatment. Orbeli co-operated with Grashchenkov to close the clinic where some of that research was being done, but smiled benignly when Ivanov-Smolenskii managed to continue it at a new laboratory in Moscow.[72] Toward non-Pavlovian cognitive psychologists, such as the beleaguered disciples of Vygotsky, Orbeli was authentically neutral or even benevolent, for they were studying the subjective experience that was inaccessible to physiology. Toward the comparative or animal psychologists such as

Borovskii, who was driven away from Moscow to a provincial teacher-training institute in the late 1930s, he was hostile. Pavlov had denied the legitimacy of their discipline, and Orbeli did too.[73]

In Orbeli's Institute of the Evolution of Higher Nervous Activity no effort was made to consider the comparative study of animal behavior at various evolutionary levels, the sort of work that Borovskii and his mentor Vagner had used to challenge Pavlov's doctrine. The Institute was established in 1932 ostensibly to meet the comparativists' challenge, that is, to show how the conditioned reflex can be the universal building block of all individually acquired behavior. But Orbeli tacitly evaded that doctrinal obligation, as his researchers investigated physiological mechanisms, for they did not try to show that the increasing complexity at higher evolutionary levels is reducible to conditioned reflexes.[74] In short, he was a statesman of science, with a good mind of his own and a sense of the practical. When he was asked in private to account for the endorsement of philosophical agnosticism in his 1911 doctoral dissertation, 'he explained that that was the dominant philosophy at that time, but now it is the philosophy of dialectical materialism'.[75]

Anokhin was a post-revolutionary type (b. 1898), who also knew how to combine scientific thoughtfulness and diplomacy, with more individuality, less emphasis on corporative enterprise, and a heartfelt engagement with Marxism-Leninism. He received his higher education almost entirely in the Soviet period — at Bekhterev's Institute of the Brain for a short time before he moved to Pavlov in 1922.[76] He was probably the first Pavlovian to start thinking about 'dialectical materialism and the problem of the "psychic",' certainly the first to publish on the subject, in 1926.[77] He showed the manuscript beforehand to Pavlov, who grew angry, and obliged Anokhin to delete his argument that the work in their laboratory showed the dialectical materialist solution to the problem of the psyche.[78] With the purity of his doctrine preserved by that excision, the scientistic liberal shrugged off his disciple's ideological philandering. A humanistic liberal looks eagerly in the article for some fruitful result of Anokhin's first involvement with Marxism, but none is there. He had merely picked up some current formulas on Marxism and psychology, and applied them confusedly. He criticized Kornilov for subjectivity, praised Vygotsky for objectivity, and without any sense of inconsistency also praised the *enfant terrible* of Pavlovian reductionism, A. K. Lents, who equated canine salivation to bells with human shopping for food. Proof again, if proof were needed, that the science of the nervous system, unlike the science of the mind, resists explicit involvement in ideological affairs.

In 1930 Anokhin once again demonstrated his independence of Pavlov in explicit ideology, still with uncritical reverence for his science. He went to the Behavioral Congress, where he gave a paper defending the simple-minded scheme of a cortical mosaic and heard Sapir criticize it.[79] Perhaps that was when Anokhin began to have doubts, influenced by Soviet Marxist critics such as Sapir or Borovskii. The most comprehensive was Mogendovich, who pictured Pavlov in 'a tragic collision' between physiology and psychology, and mocked his attempt to escape by denying 'the distinction between such different actions as the beating of the heart, the pupillary reflex to light, the phenomenon of nystagmus, the sucking motions of an infant, and playing the piano or speaking'.[80] My guess is that Anokhin was initially influenced less by such general arguments than by the experimental results of Pavlov's American admirers, who took his concepts seriously enough to test them.

Remember the animal that breathes with muscles in the pharynx when the nerves to rib muscles and diaphragm are cut, or the rat that learns to run through a maze and then, when the nerves that work its legs are cut, somersaults its learned way to the food at the exit. The *Gestalt* persists, though the reflex arcs are drastically altered. Such experiments made it impossible to go on thinking of all behavior as chains of reflexes in the three-part scheme of the pupil's contraction to light or the eyeblink to approaching object: afferent signal, central switchboard, efferent signal. Evidently an extremely complex back-and-forth links brain with muscles and glands – a feedback system, as we say now, centrally orchestrated by controlling purposes, whether as elemental as getting air into the lungs or as refined as drawing music from a piano. Three-piece reflex arcs accidentally associated with each other in a cortical switchboard simply cannot explain the overwhelming abundance of the creature's finely integrated nerve actions, the *Gestalten* that persist in a welter of changing parts.

In 1930, when he moved from Pavlov's laboratory to a medical institute in Gorky, Anokhin started experiments that led to his preoccupation with 'return afference', as he would call the stream of signals informing the central nervous system of the results of its outgoing commands to the apparatuses that are getting the air or the food at the end of the maze or the music from the piano. His first step was the simplest possible move toward 'operant' conditioning, as the Americans called experiments that require the animal to take some action in order to get food, and to modify its action as circumstances change. Beritashvili called his version 'natural experiments', in contrast with the artificiality of Pavlov's dog trained to stand passively in harness till a bell triggers automatic salivation. Anokhin required the dog to move left or right when the bell rang, by presenting the food sometimes to one side, sometimes to the other. Of course he did not declare himself a partisan of the Americans who had so upset Pavlov, or of Beritashvili, who had been making analogous criticisms before them and was doing much more of it in the 1930s. Anokhin simply presented his work as a further development of Pavlov's doctrine, engaging it with a type of problem that could not be avoided.[81]

Pavlov's response was to call him back from the provinces in 1932, to give a presentation at one of the Wednesdays, and then, in 1934, to organize a section at the newly established Moscow center of the Institute of Experimental Medicine.[82] I take it for granted that such an appointment was Pavlov's doing, though I can only guess whether or how much he sensed Anokhin's growing divergence from orthodoxy. The crucial fact is the divergence. As soon as Pavlov died Anokhin published his conviction that 'the most vulnerable point in the doctrine of conditioned reflexes is its separation from world thought in general neurology.'[83]

He put that manifesto in a major journal of biology and in *Under the Banner of Marxism*.[84] To be sure he softened the impact on simple-minded worshippers by withholding a crushing bill of particulars. With a reassuring historical explanation he worked gently up to the plain statement of 'separation from world thought in neurology'. It had been necessary for Pavlov to concentrate on 'analysis' of conditioned reflexes, to isolate the new problem from the search for its neural mechanisms, which would have been premature. Now the time had come to work on 'synthesis', by which Anokhin meant joining the behavioristic laws of conditioning with the mechanisms of nerve action discovered by 'world thought in neurology'. He added that Pavlov himself had approved, in conversations of his last years, efforts to save the doctrine from becoming dead dogma. I find the quoted conversations too imprecise to support Anokhin's interpretation, but that hardly matters. However he won Pavlov's confidence, however carefully he spoke while the master lived and freely interpreted after he was gone, he was eager to start studies of conditioning on a new track, the one that Beritashvili and Lashley and a growing number of others were traveling — to neuropsychology, the plainly acknowledged hybridization of physiology and psychology. That was another meaning that he packed into his call for 'synthesis'.

He recalled how startled people had been to hear rumors that Pavlov, in the last years of his life, was reversing his views on psychology, even to the extent of talking about a psychological laboratory within one of his institutes. Everyone knew that Pavlov's school was founded on scorn for the would-be science of the mind. He was changing, Anokhin declared, in part because he had been reading Gestalt psychologists. I am skeptical on that score, for the references to Gestalt in Pavlov's 'Wednesdays' are uniformly antagonistic. If any progression can be found, it is from brief contradiction to extended rebuttal, as Pavlov sensed that many people considered Gestalt a subversion of his doctrine. In 1931 he thought it enough to declare that an ape's selection of a long stick to knock down a banana suspended above its reach was 'simply the working out of a conditioned reflex to the long stick. ...'[85] By 1934 he was giving demonstrations with a chimpanzee to prove that Köhler's concept of *Gestalt* was unnecessary, a reversion to animism.

The 'associative process' adequately explained the supposed 'intelligence' in the chimp's behavior.[86] 'Is Zelenyi here?' he asked, when none of those present could explain what possible sense there was in Köhler's views.

> Pity he's not, I'd give him hell [*baniu zadal*]. ... This G. P. Zelenyi started out very well. His dissertation was good, he thought energetically. He was the first to get a reflex to an interval, first to get a second-order reflex, and so on. But when he got a professor's rank, an authoritative label, he gave up energetic work. ... Recently in the organ of the Academy of Sciences he published an article where he takes his stand precisely on Köhler's viewpoint. Instead of trying not to use an ax after he has learned to work with a plane, he left our exact experiments and got involved with phraseology, wordplay, and now like Köhler disputes these experiments.[87]

With that outburst the Wednesday ended; no one could or would defend the absent apostate, or respond to Pavlov's intermittent pleas for explanation of a viewpoint he found simply incredible.

So Anokhin, I would guess, was describing himself when he told of Pavlov privately changing his mind under the influence of Gestalt psychology, coming to the conclusion that conditioned reflexes cannot be the explanatory unit of all individually acquired behavior, that there are various types of such behavior, which must be 'analyzed' by psychological science and 'synthesized' with the neural processes disclosed by physiological research. Perhaps Anokhin was discussing such things with the Soviet psychologists who had been heavily influenced by Gestalt.[88] Luria and Anokhin came in time to be outspoken admirers of each other's work. Perhaps he was reading N. A. Bernshtein, a non-Pavlovian physiologist who published a landmark book on 'the biodynamics of locomotion' in 1935, arguing that walking is a finely integrated pattern of too many sensory inputs and motor commands to be possibly explained by chance concatenations of stimuli and responses.[89] Certainly Anokhin was aware of Beritashvili's major book, *The Individually Acquired Activity of the Central Nervous System* (1932), a massive compilation of evidence and theorizing that required the abandonment of Pavlov's simplistic doctrine.[90] In 1936 the twenty-fifth anniversary of Beritashvili's labors was celebrated with a handsome Festschrift that included articles by Luria and by a disciple of Pavlov's, but not by Anokhin.[91] He was not a renegade from the master's doctrine, or a revisionist, he was merely trying to develop it further. I borrow those invidious distinctions from the Stalinist vocabulary for change in Marx's doctrine, when the change cannot be ignored.

So we can understand Anokhin's gentle manner when the master's death allowed him to speak his mind in public. Uninhibited criticism of the revered doctrine would have invited conflict both with the ideological establishment and with disciples content to go on with routine Pavlovian research. Anokhin declared his respect for those who wanted to go on 'gathering experimental data within the limits of the classical scheme of the conditioned reflex', even though he also called such work dogmatic, threatening the immortality that Pavlov's doctrine deserved.[92] Such inconsistent mixtures of courteous praise and critical depreciation are the academic manner everywhere, and so is responsive silence from those who like established routine and do not like public quarrels. Nevertheless there was a strange, Stalinist intensity in the complete silence that followed Anokhin's manifesto of 1936. The editors of *Under the Banner of Marxism* tagged it 'For discussion', but no discussion ensued — until 1949, when a Stalinist 'discussion' was organized, that is, a vituperative campaign against renegades like Anokhin.

In the intervening years research and teaching drifted away from the master's eccentric neurology, without acknowledgment of the drift by such leaders as Orbeli, Kupalov, or even Anokhin. He contributed as much as the others to Stalinist reverence for Pavlov's 'monolithic' doctrine, as he called it in 1938.[93] Only muffled sounds of disagreement occasionally found public expression. At a 1940 conference on the localization of brain functions, for example, nearly everyone praised Pavlov but ignored his ideas, to the dismay of Ivanov-Smolenskii.[94] 'Brain morphology' was his characterization of what was replacing Pavlov's concept of temporary associations in the cortex. There was no extended argument to make the disagreement more precise, if only because he and the others were unwilling or unable to get deeply involved in each other's ideas. Ivanov-Smolenskii still labored under ideological disapproval for his crude version of Pavlov's doctrine, but he was able to get a little murmur of sympathetic concern from *Pravda* on the closing of his research clinic.[95]

For a while in the mid-1930s one of Pavlov's disciples won official support for an end to such silence, but it was on behalf of his own doctrine, not Pavlov's. A. D. Speranskii claimed that a revolution in medicine would follow recognition of his simple principle: 'In every pathological process the neural component is the governing factor.'[96] He based that vision, not on Pavlov's concept of 'nervism', but on the obsolete notion of a 'trophic' or nourishing function of the nervous system. He had discovered that the contrary also obtained: nerves not only nourished healthy tissues, they also spread diseased processes from their points of origin to the rest of the body. Along with the radical theory he offered a simple panacea: novocaine blockage of nerves in the diseased part would help stop the spread of an infection or a cancer to the rest of the body.[97] When Speranskii started offering that vision in the 1920s, no one paid attention, except for a popular science writer excited by the utopian possibilities.[98] Pavlov was silently unimpressed, and so were the other disciples and medical scientists at large. In the mid-1930s Speranskii's fortunes improved after he got a boost from another popular science writer — or ideologist — this time in *Under the Banner of Marxism*.[99] The Central Committee, while reviewing the work of the All-Union Institute of Experimental Medicine in 1936, worried over its insufficient interest in practically useful research, as pursued, for example, by the pathology laboratory that Speranskii headed. Molotov, the press reported, showed special interest during a visit to the Institute, and K. Ia. Bauman, chief of the Central Committee's division of science, complained about the specialists' indifference to Speranskii.[100]

That was the period when people in high places were eager to support revolutionaries in science, especially those who combined know-it-all theories with cure-all applications. It was the time of Stalin's toast to the science that does not fear to smash what is old and moribund. The most smashing favorite was the young agronomist Lysenko, but the usual type was an older scholar like Speranskii (b. 1888), whose revolutionary claims had been ignored or brushed aside by fellow specialists. There was V. R. Vil'iams (or Williams, born in 1863 to an American railroad engineer), the soil scientist who urged grass as nature's way to restore fertility, and there was N. Ia. Marr (b. 1864), the Georgian linguist who pointed the way to a grand union of nationalities outside of Russian domination. Two elderly physicists who opposed relativity and quantum mechanics were less success-ful; the ideological establishment blew alternately hot and cold on their arguments, which did not in any case include claims of practical achieve-ments.[101] Speranskii's was a much cooler case, with marginal success, for a while. The ideological establishment obliged medical scientists to have a 'discussion' of his theory in 1936−7, but afterward seemed to lose interest.[102] Medical scientists did not feel free to call his doctrine nonsense, but neither were they obliged to pay much attention to it. And when the ideological establishment moved in forcefully in the late 1940s, to establish proper reverence for Russian masters, Speranskii hardly benefited. He was one of the many who were rebuked in 1950, for he had made no effort to attach Pavlov's doctrine to his own.[103] In short, his 'new theory of medicine' lacked both a sacred aura in theory and testimonials of success in medical practice, so the ideological establishment lacked any strong or persistent motive to intervene on his behalf. Which is another way of saying that Soviet leaders were typically modern; they respected the autonomous knowledge claimed by the medical profession − with respect to the nervous system and physical disease. When it came to the mind and its disturbances they were less respectful, and the professionals − the psychiatrists − were more divided in their claims of knowledge, with a stronger contingent of impatient know-it-alls. But even in psychiatry that Stalinist type did not win control until the 1950s, as a result of the final convulsion in Stalin's revolution from above.

THE MONOLITH

The German invasion killed Soviet people in uncounted millions − twenty is the usual estimate − and drove survivors into a new ideological bond.

We customarily speak of an intense revival of Russian patriotism or nationalism, which the government seized upon and magnified, at the expense of the international or universal or cosmopolitan creed that inspired the 1917 Revolution. The choice of synonyms matters less than the bitter truth that is concealed in that conventional wisdom. To speak of nationalism and internationalism as opposites, each excluding the other, is to mask the inflamed interdependence of the two. Each requires the other while making it impossible. Our nation deserves limitless devotion because its way of life shows the way for all nations, including 'them', the adversary, those countries that would perversely obtrude their way on us. The USA and the USSR share that creed, and therefore quarrel violently over the specifications. For present purposes it is immaterial to ask which side did more, whether in universalist preaching or in imperial practice, to turn their wartime alliance into endless enmity. The problem here is not the enmity but the ideological justification that attended it, the way of pumping up belief that our nation state deserves limitless sacrifices because it is defending the ultimate good of all against the ultimate evil that threatens all. I need not rehearse the American version of the creed; it springs to place reflexively at any signal of the Soviet adversary. The problem here is to see if we can decondition ourselves for awhile, if we can suspend reflexive hostility long enough to grasp the Soviet version of the creed as it appears to them.

In some respects the post-war ideological imperative came quite naturally to Soviet citizens. Everyone knew from the most painful experience that the native land had paid terribly for victory over murderous invaders, and for the right to secure itself against any possible recurrence. 'They' out there who would deny that obvious truth must indeed be wicked monsters. Moreover, the universality of Soviet values was attested by comradely parties in all lands and by victorious revolutions in some – China most notably, the largest country in the world though one of the most backward. And that was the intolerable rub, the flaw in the world scene as it naturally presented itself to Stalinist minds. Comrades and admirers were most evident in backward places; enemies were concentrated in the most advanced centers of the culture shared by the Soviet Union. Against that intolerable reality Stalin's Party whipped up the final campaign of its revolution from above, to overturn Russia's provincial relation to the West, to make Russia, not the Western nations, the leader of world civilization. Note well *Russia*, the historic nation state, not some abstract concept of a federal union.

From the start it was an incoherent campaign. There were the notorious claims of Russian priorities in 'contributions to the world treasure-house' of culture, and there were the notorious denunciations of any cosmopolitan notions. The claims of priority assumed a universal community of culture developed jointly by Russians and larcenous partners in the West. The denunciations of cosmopolitanism set Russia apart, in a world of truth that aliens could not enter. In technology the distinction was tolerably clear:

Russians had invented things that everyone valued — the steam engine, the electric light, the potato — and Westerners had somehow stolen the credit. In science there were tormenting confusions; alien scorn for Russian beliefs was evidence of their superior truth, which would someday win over the world, provided that native reverence for them was strictly protected against the seductive power of Western beliefs.

The most tormenting of such confusions was Marxism-Leninism itself, the official faith of Russia that was supposed to be a universal social science. It did win significant conversions in various parts of the world, but the more effectively it took hold here and there the less it resembled the Russian original, the more it changed reverence for Russia into reverence for places like Yugoslavia or China. The most startling of such confusions between nativist truth-for-us and universal truth-for-all was 'Michurinism', a new biology revealed by an unschooled plant breeder in old Russia and developed further by the Soviet agronomist Lysenko. It was much in evidence before the Second World War, when the crisis of collectivized farming made officials hungry for cheap cure-alls, but definitive Party support, with a ban on the decadent pseudo-biology of the West, came in 1948, as part of the campaign for Russian pride, against cosmopolitanism.

In all fields the great urge was to have knowledge distinctive to Russia, and by extension to 'the toiling masses' or 'progressive humanity' all over, who were expected to look to the Soviet homeland as Christians to Rome. Within such internationalism an outsider cannot fail to see national exclusiveness, an implicit rejection of the internationalist concepts that Stalinists uttered with pious reverence, defending Russian priority in 'the world treasure-house of culture'. Even the universal standards of rational discourse were implicitly rejected, most notoriously in the insistence that 'our' doctrines are scientific truth and therefore may not be questioned. In short, an irrational nativism asserted itself in post-war Russian culture more strongly than ever before, unless we go back to the pre-Petrine era, when Russians created their sense of nationhood in conflict with domineering neighbors.

The incongruities were especially inflamed because they involved internal as well as external relations of nationality. In the campaign against cosmopolitanism 'Soviet' and 'Russian' were casually conflated, though their proper meanings overlap no more than Christian and Roman. The last vestiges of Leninist resistance to Russian chauvinism disappeared in the late 1940s. Official ideology used the metaphor of fraternity to prettify the change: in the Soviet family of nationalities Russians were the elder brother, the others were junior. And there were levels of status among the junior brothers, unacknowledged in explicit ideology but quite obviously present in behavior and symbolism. Just below the Russians were fellow Slavs, Ukrainians and Belorussians, with other nationalities descending toward the frankly tutelary status of the primitive peoples of Siberia. Somewhere in an unacknowledged limbo were pariah nationalities, such as the Volga

Germans and Crimean Tartars, who had been driven into the wilderness during the war. And then there were the Jews, in an especially anomalous vicious circle. The pre-war toleration of autonomous Yiddish culture abruptly ceased — with some attendant murders — which seemed to reinforce the long-standing push toward assimilation of Jews to Russianness, but startling new moves pushed Jews in an opposite direction, toward exclusion from the Soviet family altogether, as an irremediably alien element. Even if they seemed quite Russian and opposed to Zionism, a form of 'bourgeois' nationalism that linked believers with Western powers, they could be charged with cosmopolitanism, the insidious assimilation of Russian culture to Western models. That had long been a powerful tendency among educated Russians; now it was made to seem the mark of Jews, passportless wanderers in humanity.

No ideology of explicit anti-Semitism was ever worked out; indeed, anti-Semitism as such was still officially condemned as an instrument of reactionaries and Nazi invaders. 'Anti-cosmopolitanism' was the approved new term, with typecast names to convey the meaning — as in T. S. Eliot's poem on 'Bleistein with a Cigar' in the decaying temples of the culture that Eliot guarded against aliens. The drawings in Soviet publications were as explicit as Eliot's verbal cartoon:

> But this or such was Bleistein's way:
>   A saggy bending of the knees
> And elbows, with the palms turned out,
>   Chicago Semite Viennese.

The words were not explicit. No one put 'Semite' on such cartoons, or openly declared:

> The rats are underneath the piles.
> The jew is underneath the lot.[104]

It was an extraordinary scandal when a Soviet magazine carried a cartoon like Eliot's Bleistein with the word *Zhid* on the hook-nosed cosmopolitan's suitcase, and a follow-up explanation to alarmed observers: André Gide was intended, not the Russian analogue to Yid.[105] Communist ideology is pliable, but it does constrain anti-Semitic utterance, more severely than Eliot's Christianity did.

Deeds were less constrained than words. Jews were systematically removed from positions of authority, to which they had risen in considerable numbers during the first two decades of the revolutionary regime. If they were famous, a public explanation might be offered, as in this 1949 attack on S. L. Rubinshtein: He 'belongs to the tribe of rootless cosmopolitans. . . . The sooner we purge Soviet psychology of rootless cosmopolitans, the sooner we will open its way to fruitful development.'[106] Something worse than demotion colored the announcement that Lina Solomonovna Shtern and the people in her research group, 'Kassil, Shatenshtein, Khvoles, Rosin, Tseitlin', had lost their power to 'dirty Soviet science' with 'full-blown', 'naked cosmopolitanism, kowtowing to foreign pseudo-authorities'.[107] She had been the most celebrated Communist among physiologists — an exile who returned, she had joined the Party in 1938, aged sixty — the only woman scientist to enjoy celebrity status. In 1939 she was elected to the Academy of Sciences, in 1943 awarded a Stalin prize — and in 1948 she disappeared.[108] Secretly arrested and 'tried' for conspiring to detach the Crimea and make it a Jewish state in collaboration with foreign powers, she was lucky to get life imprisonment; twenty-three co-conspirators were shot.[109] Terror was intensified by the whispered way the news went round, while the press revealed only the abrupt change from celebrated Communist scientist to rootless cosmopolitan, who had 'insolently' dismissed Pavlov's doctrine and had slavishly imitated Western physiologists in her neurological research.

Even at the front in time of battle soldiers continue the ordinary business of life, leaping for cover only when necessary. So too in Stalin's Russia. The anti-cosmopolitan campaign, though punctuated by bursts of fire, did not keep scientists constantly in foxholes. They went on with their usual work, while prudently arranging defenses here and there. The typical defenses were new editions of textbooks, removing the names of famous Western discoverers and greatly emphasizing the contributions of Russians. But the subject matter was essentially unchanged. In 1948 the 'August Session' of the All-Union Agricultural Academy was supposed to put an end to such pretense, and it did in biology for geneticists. Lysenko announced that he had the official support of the Central Committee and of Comrade Stalin personally for his Michurinist doctrine. That detonation demolished the laboratories and classrooms of geneticists, who took shelter in odd spots like pharmaceutical institutes or forestry stations until such time as they might emerge and start up their science again. Almost none converted to Lysenkoism in their actual work, though a few mouthed pledges of intent.[110]

The ideological establishment insisted that the August Session was a model and a warning for all the sciences: they must all become authentically Marxist-Leninist and distinctively Russian. In physiology, psychiatry, and psychology that meant a determined campaign for Pavlov's doctrine, against slavish continuation of Western science. To that end meetings were organized, speeches delivered, articles printed, culminating in two intensely publicized 'Pavlov Sessions' of the All-Union Academy of Sciences and the Academy of Medical Sciences — for physiology in the summer of 1950, for psychiatry in the fall of 1951, with psychology dragged in at both and finally subjected to a less publicized Pavlov Session of its own in the summer of 1952.[111] Each time the playbill announced a repeat performance of the August Session to which genetics had been subjected in 1948.

Decorative words of reverence for the native doctrine would no longer suffice; the substance of science was to be changed from cosmopolitan to Pavlovian.

But it was not, and the Sessions themselves revealed that it would not be. The irresistible authority of the Central Committee was invoked against all rivals to Pavlov's doctrine, but no analogue to Lysenko mounted the tribune to put destructive force in such authority. Stalin's personal intervention was repeatedly invoked — on behalf of free thought. That was the most astonishing incongruity in the Stalinist drive for monolithic unity in exclusively Russian culture: at the climactic moment Stalin insisted on the need for a clash of opinions. In June 1950, just before the first Pavlov Session, *Pravda* carried a long interview with the coryphaeus of the arts and sciences, which contained the following exchange:

> *Question* Has *Pravda* acted properly in opening a free discussion on questions of linguistics?
> *Answer* [Stalin] It has. . . . The discussion has revealed . . . a regime that is alien to science and scientists. The least criticism, the most timid attempts at criticism, of the so-called 'new doctrine' in linguistics have been persecuted and suppressed by the leading circles of linguistics. . . . [But] It is generally known that no science can develop and flourish without a struggle of opinions, without freedom of criticism.[112]

Most of Stalin's intervention was especially concerned with the change of Party line in linguistics. The ideological establishment was removing its support from Marr's crackpot school, which was not sufficiently respectful of the Russian language. Stalin deplored the 'Arakcheev regime' (stupid despotism) in linguistics, and used the occasion to ponder the nature of science in general. He implied that it is not an ideology which must be transformed when the proletariat replaces the capitalists as the ruling class. Like language, science may be an instrument used by all classes. Thus Stalin could be read as opening the door to non-ideological debates over scientific truth, urging scientists to go on through and do their duty as free thinkers.[113]

The theme was caught up by the press, as an abstract generality, with particulars to be worked out by bold specialists in their various disciplines, at their own risk. *Bol'shevik*, the theoretical magazine of the Central Committee, derided professors who lacked the courage to defend their views when criticized in the press.[114] Of course *Bol'shevik* did not call on them to defy the Arakcheev regimes that flourished in genetics and all the social sciences, or to challenge the campaign for monolithic unity of a distinctively Russian culture, focused on Pavlov's doctrine in the sciences of brain and mind. That campaign was still overwhelmingly on, yet Stalin and his Party were suggesting that science is not an exclusive ideology of particular classes or countries, that it is universal and requires the free clash of opinions for its argumentative mode of development.

The outsider sees the obvious self-contradiction, but Stalin did not acknowledge it and bless it in the name of dialectics, as he had done in the 1930s for his most notorious innovation in Marxist theory. The power of the state and its violence against 'the class enemy' were increasing enormously, while the Party in charge still preached the disappearance of class conflict and the withering away of the state. That, Stalin had declared, was a dialectical contradiction, the pattern of progress.[115] In 1950 he made no such grand principle of his insistence on freedom of thought at a peak of thought control. He simply ordered scientific specialists to be boldly disputatious, or science would not develop. I do not think he was merely indulging in cynical politics, prodding potential dissidents to get them out in the open. (Nor, do I think, was Mao at the analogous moment in his Party's history, when he invited a hundred flowers to bloom.) The need to overtake and surpass the West coexisted with the need to stop kotowing to the West, each inflaming the other. However inconsistently, the Stalinist mentality laid both demands on scientists, to be true to their own Russian knowledge and to surpass Westerners in universal knowledge; to take a rock-solid stand in the native monolith and to be as disputatiously creative as scientists in the West.

Within that context the bizarre mixture of elements at the Pavlov Session of 1950 becomes understandable. Two officials of higher learning opened it with the demand for a genuine transformation of neurophysiology. They reprimanded Orbeli and the other leading disciples of Pavlov, who had strayed from the master's way, and gave measured praise to K. M. Bykov, the one, they said, who had remained true and was therefore to replace Orbeli as director of the major centers of Pavlovian research. Yet they also thanked Stalin for revealing the need of a free contest of opinions, and called for 'creative, comradely criticism [which] has nothing in common with slap-in-the-face criticism of enemies. That was condemned and is condemned by the Party.'[116] When the major officials sat down, Bykov laid out his criticism of the demoted disciples and his program of genuine Pavlovian neurophysiology — with restraint, both in substance and in tone. Even Ivanov-Smolenskii, who gave a companion main speech, reaffirming his long-standing Pavlovian fundamentalism, was comparatively mild. He did not thunder for the annihilation of all views contrary to his, which were not the same as Bykov's anyhow. And when the floor was opened for Stalinist 'discussion', elements of genuine discussion appeared. Orbeli, most notably, not only defended his views on physiology; he startled the audience by deriding the rules of 'discussion' that required those attacked to assist in their own condemnation.

The choice of Bykov as successor to Orbeli was itself a sign of moderation. He had long been known for his investigation of 'cortico-visceral relations,' as he chose to call conditioning of internal organs with attendant speculation on the role of the cerebral cortex. Since glandular secretions and blood pressure can be altered by conditioning, he saw possible medical applications of his research, in the control of such maladies as stomach ulcers and hypertension.[117] No doubt that claim of presumptive utility endeared him to the Stalinist establishment; they had grumbled about the Pavlovian absorption in pure science, the neglect of practical applications. Pavlov's latter-day dabbling in psychiatry was almost the only exception, which was played up at the Session, with repeated calls to use the 'sleep therapy' that he had recommended for the mentally ill. Bykov's work on interoceptive conditioning suggested remedies for more widespread maladies than insanity, but he was sensibly restrained in suggesting such prospects. The humiliation of Speranskii was a warning to potential Lysenkos in medical science.

Chances are that Bykov had no inclination to make rash claims anyhow. He had been cautious in speculative theorizing on issues of pure science, indulging a bold venture only twice. He had suggested a 'third signal system', and he had shown some interest in Western talk of psychosomatic medicine. The first signal system, as the reader may recall, was supposed to mediate classical conditioning to stimuli such as ringing bells with food to follow. A second signal system was Pavlov's occasional suggestion of a separate neural mechanism or function that mediates verbal stimuli and responses among human beings. In 1946 Bykov had hypothesized a third signal system to mediate interoceptive stimuli and responses flowing back and forth between the brain and the body's internal organs.[118] A burst of orthodox indignation had turned him quickly to apology;[119] mere disciples may not presume to speculate as boldly as the master. He was also quick to back off from his brief interest in the psychosomatic trend then popular in Western medicine.[120] In response to the anti-cosmopolitan campaign he came to insist on a radical opposition between such Western pseudo-science and his own 'cortico-visceral' studies. In short, he was a careful disciple of Pavlov's, who could be counted on to avoid unnecessary disturbance whether to Party ideologists or to the routine fulfillment of inoffensive research programs.

Ivanov-Smolenskii was a different sort. He had been odd man out for twenty years, scorned by Soviet Marxists for insisting that the conditioned reflex is literally the constituent element of which all behavior is compounded, including speech and thought. He crowed at the Pavlov Session, attacking those who had enjoyed superior reputations for drawing distinctions between the conditioned reflex and more complex modes of reaction, and for pursuing the mechanism of the conditioned reflex to subcortical regions of the nervous system.[121] Orbeli and Kupalov, not to mention Beritashvili and Anokhin, who had openly criticized Pavlov's doctrine, were now in disgrace. Many speakers at the Session attacked them and repeated the theme: no more lip service to Pavlov while research leads away from his doctrine. Yet there were notably few speakers who repeated Ivanov-Smolenskii's explicit identification of the cosmopolitan science that must now be rooted out of Soviet neurophysiology. He called it 'the psychomorphological trend', meaning the correlation of precisely distinguished psychic patterns with rigorously demonstrated neural structures and processes. When referring to psychiatry the foe he named was 'brain pathology', which involves the same approach to abnormal psychic patterns: making careful psychological distinctions among them and seeking rigorous proof of the neural pathology that is assumed as their particular causes. Ivanov-Smolenskii had been objecting to those dominant trends for a long time, in isolation, and now he seemed to have vaulted to the forefront of the profession. He was a main speaker at the Pavlov Session. But his was the second of two main speeches, and the first, Bykov's, did not urge suppression of 'brain pathology' or 'the psychomorphological trend'. Nor did most of the speakers who followed. A persistent silence left Ivanov-Smolenskii still in isolation at the moment of triumph.

Some speakers took Stalin seriously on the need for the free clash of opinions. Kupalov vigorously defended his innovation in Pavlovian theorizing. He had devised the term 'reflex without a beginning' to indicate self-activation, the capacity of the cerebral cortex to initiate actions without immediate external stimuli. That was *not*, he insisted, heretical alteration of Pavlov's doctrine; he could find sanction in the master's words. But he also addressed the rules of scientific discourse, and approached a much more serious kind of heresy — from Stalinism:

> I want to ask this exalted scientific audience, before which I am now speaking: Is it possible that our scientific Russian Soviet mind, is it possible that we — the heirs of Pavlov, of Sechenov — have lost our right to create new scientific terms and concepts and to systematize the new facts that we have gathered? I think that we have not lost that right.[122]

He provoked 'noise' and 'laughter' in the hall, and won applause as he ended.

Anokhin was much closer to the model of Stalinist behavior. He apologized at great length for his grievous ideological and political errors. He should not have written *From Descartes to Pavlov*; Zhdanov's pronouncements had revealed to him how wrong it was to put Pavlov in a context that detracted from his priority.[123] Nor was it permissible to criticize Pavlov as he had done in the 1930s. He lacked time, he said, to deal with scientific issues, but he could not forbear on cortical localization, for

Pavlov had encouraged his first steps away from that. Moreover, his exploration of subcortical mechanisms had not revised Pavlov's doctrine but developed it further, a Stalinist distinction that led smoothly into a finale for unity, for the cause of Michurin and Lysenko, for following in the footsteps of Comrade Stalin.[124] Of course he was applauded; he had chanted Stalinist shibboleths without conceding anything of substance in neurophysiology.

Orbeli used a similar peroration to win applause at the end of the most daring speech that the Session heard. He mocked those who had criticized him, even the new chief who was taking his place. He bowed low, he said, in admiration of Bykov's enormously important research in cortico-visceral activity, but hadn't Konstantin Mikhailovich exaggerated its importance? 'Permit me to ask [him] if all his scientific activity is determined by impulses from his bladder and rectum?'[125] A leader like Grashchenkov was safer game, but Orbeli was more daring in going after him, for he entered the sacred preserve of Marxism-Leninism. Grashchenkov had pinned the label of idealism on Orbeli's distinction between physical phenomena and the symbols we use in speaking or writing of them. Surely, Orbeli retorted, when we say 'la' or put the appropriate mark on the staff, our spoken sound or written mark are not the same thing as the musical sound we are signifying.

> But if I say that between the signification of a physical phenomenon and the phenomenon itself there is nothing in common except the connection of signifying, the conclusion is drawn that I am an idealist. I found it very strange to hear that from N. I. Grashchenkov, who went through the Institute of Red Professorship and ought to be philosophically literate. (*Laughter, applause.*)[126]

He must have known that he was offending orthodox Leninists, who took their stand for the 'reflection' theory of knowledge, against the notion that human thought manipulates 'hieroglyphic' symbols of external reality. Plekhanov's endorsement of the hieroglyphic metaphor counted against it, for the Stalinists had written him off as a Menshevik. Helmholtz's endorsement was even stronger reason to stay clear of the notion; he was a 'bourgeois' and a German. Sechenov's endorsement was taboo, not to be recalled; the Stalinist ideological establishment had elevated him to sacredness, certainly above derivative connections to such as Helmholtz.

Orbeli's most daring thrust opened his speech, and closed the discussion part of the Session, for he felt obliged to take the floor again and apologize. The first time up he mocked the Stalinist mode of 'discussion'. He was bothered, he said, by all the references to 'self-criticism', since actual criticism 'has been directed at several predetermined individuals', of which he was one.

And I, unfortunately, must reproach the very organization of this session. If predetermined individuals are selected for rather severe criticism, then, if it is to be a free scientific discussion, it would be extremely important to let them know beforehand what they are to be accused of and criticized for. Even when criminals are involved, they are given an indictment to read, so that they can defend themselves or say something in their defense. In the present case that wasn't done, and we, the accused, find ourselves in a difficult situation. ....[127]

Hearing the accusations for the first time, he could not tell when his ideas were being quoted out of context or otherwise suffering distortion. 'But this is a trifle', he suddenly declared, 'not worth dwelling upon', and coolly turned to Pavlov's doctrine.

He must have known what disciplined pride and repressed shame he was challenging. Many thousands of dead and silent ex-comrades, executed or jailed in far more arbitrary ways, were silent witnesses to the supreme law of submission when criticized. Speakers following Orbeli found his 'scorn' intolerable, were 'indignant' at his 'demagogy'.[128] Kolbanovskii ominously observed: 'though there are not and cannot be accused people at our Session, there are guilty ones' − and piously offered himself and other psychologists as examples.[129] A former student of Orbeli's recalled failed efforts to get from him a proper self-criticism of the Machist or neo-Kantian introduction to his doctoral dissertation, instead of this dismissive explanation: 'that was the dominant philosophy at that time, and now the philosophy of dialectical materialism is dominant.'[130] Finally Orbeli took the floor to apologize for the 'utter tactlessness and political illiteracy' of his comments on the organization of the meeting, his 'impermissible comparison with "defendants" and "criminals".'[131] As for the erroneous philosophy in his doctoral dissertation, he spelled out, with Schweikish precision, the explanation that had seemed an insulting shrug at changing trends in philosophy. He had written the dissertation, and Pavlov had approved it, before Lenin published the book that put an end to the philosophical confusion which was dominant before Lenin published. Undoubtedly, he concluded, he needed to deepen his study of the Marxist classics, especially the newest 'guideline' in the linguistic articles of 'our dear chief and teacher, the genius, the coryphaeus of science, Joseph Vissarionovich Stalin'.[132] And of course he was applauded once again, as he had been for a similar ending to his original speech.

The Pavlov Session of 1950 was very crowded, with would-be speakers as well as listeners. Over 200 asked for the floor; 81 got it, and 51 others were given space in the published proceedings for their 'undelivered presentations'. All that was in markedly civilized contrast to the berserk style and the abridged record of the August Session of 1948, which raised

Lysenko to dictatorial power over genetics and breeding. A thoroughly civilized Pavlov Session, if that can be conceived, would have given Beritashvili a place alongside the main speakers or put him first in the discussion period, for he was the first neurophysiologist outside Pavlov's school to take conditioned reflexes seriously, to include them in his teaching and research even before the 1920s, and to try meaningful ways of replacing Pavlov's imaginary neural mechanisms with the experimental discovery of real ones. He was not allowed to speak at all, but it was no small concession to civilized debate that his long review of arguments over Pavlov's doctrine was included in the 'undelivered presentations'.

His first aim was to correct the vulgar distortions of his views by many polemicists, but much more than self-defense was at stake. He wanted to clarify the basic issues. The method of conditioned reflexes, he insisted, studies a particular component of individually acquired behavior, not all of it. He took that issue into philosophy by noting that dialectical materialism recognizes qualitatively different levels of emergent behavior, each one 'aufgehoben' or 'sniat' (sublated and preserved) in the higher ones. It is not dialectical to seek reduction of all types of behavior to a single constituent unit. He could spell out that philosophical issue in a cluster of scientific problems, and most of his presentation did so. With respect to psychological science he asked orthodox Pavlovians to open their eyes to non-automatic behavioral processes, especially those that precede automatized patterns of individually acquired behavior.

With respect to neurophysiology he stressed the issue that had separated his research from theirs since his first publications in the 1920s: cortical localization and the precise meaning of inhibition. 'There can be no genuinely scientific understanding of [conditioned reflex] activity, if we don't put an end to the cursed vagueness in this problem.' He reminded them that fourteen years had passed since Pavlov's death, 'hundreds of scientists' had been working on the problem, and 'hypothetical constructs of cortical inhibition still prevail, which absolutely did not satisfy Pavlov himself'.[133] That effort to picture Pavlov on his side, to deny the basic differences between them was Beritashvili's one concession to the Stalinist ethos. Some may say that his talk of dialectical materialism was also Stalinist, but I think it expressed genuine thought as well as reverence.

Stalinist 'discussion' was not only organized campaigning for certain solutions but also organized disregard of uncertainty. Psychological science was the major uncertainty at the Pavlov Session of 1950, dealt with in large silences punctuated by stereotyped phrases of solution ready at hand. The second signal system was the key phrase, which had never been developed before the Session, and would not be developed after it. Everyone who approached the problem of encompassing speech and thought in Pavlov's doctrine uttered the phrase 'second signal system', and stopped. Everyone

lamented everyone else's persistent failure to develop that further, pledged
to start right away, and neglected to say how. Ivanov-Smolenskii's conditioning experiments with verbal stimuli were largely ignored, because —
as one orthodox Pavlovian explained — they oversimplified the comparison
between dogs salivating to bells and humans speaking and thinking about
dogs and experiments and all manner of things.[134]

Pavlov's notorious hostility to psychological science, several speakers
agreed, was to be explained away, by picking at the words he had used or
by emphasis on his change of mind in the last few years of his life. But
such appeals to *magister dixit* were too vague to decide what kind of
psychological science he might have approved. No one dared to recall his
communications of best wishes to Chelpanov at the founding of the
Psychological Institute, with their liberal endorsement of free competition
among rival schools.[135] Monolithic unity was the framing assumption of
the Session; it required a choice — psychology or no psychology, and if
psychology, which school? — a definitive choice that no one dared to
propose. The Pavlovian who criticized Ivanov-Smolenskii's experiments
was isolated in her proposal that courses in psychology should be replaced
by courses in 'higher nervous activity'. If that proposal had been endorsed
by the leaders and placed in the resolutions of the Session, psychological
science would have been on its way toward decreed oblivion along with
genetics or the economics of marginal utility. 'Higher nervous activity' was
the name for an ostensibly new field or discipline, which would extend
Pavlov's doctrine beyond classical conditioning, even to the analysis of the
conscious mind. Thus existing schools of psychological science would be
superseded by Pavlovian studies, but no one could specify how, and no one
pressed for the immediate suppression of existing schools.

Nevertheless — or therefore — psychologists were very subdued. It was
not until the third day of the discussion that one of them ventured to speak,
or rather to do a profuse display of Stalinist breast-beating. He and his
colleagues had been wrong to pay so little attention to Pavlov, wrong to
say in their textbooks that human brains have higher levels than those
which mediate conditioned reflexes, wrong to imply dualism by insisting
that psychic and physiological processes are not identical, wrong to repeat
the Gestalt notion that complex wholes cannot be reduced to the action of
their parts. Pavlov's associationism must be the basis of psychology; with
that in mind psychologists must henceforth seek 'the fusion, the marriage
of physiology and psychology'.[136] That was the point of the servile effusion,
the plea to be acknowledged as a spouse, not simply cast aside.

On the ninth day Kolbanovskii took the rostrum for a dignified defense
of his discipline. He noted 'the abnormal and unpropitious relations between
physiologists and psychologists', which he attributed to their separate
historical development. He acknowledged that Sechenov and Pavlov could
be quoted for the suppression of psychology, but Sechenov had in mind

the idealist psychology of the pre-revolutionary period, and Pavlov had softened in his later years. Of course the physiology of higher nervous activity must be extended into the study of psychic processes. 'But can those processes be fully explained by physiological methods of research? Can all the wealth and variety of man's subjective world be reduced to basic physiological laws? To these questions Marxism answers in the negative.'[137]

No one chose to disagree explicitly, yet no one was bold enough to confront the implicit judgment on Pavlov's doctrine: even if it were a comprehensive physiology of higher nervous activity, it could not pretend to be a comprehensive science of psychology. Rubinshtein, still around though in cosmopolitan disgrace, took the floor to bury the problem in doubletalk.[138] Luria offered an undelivered presentation, which argued for the correlation of psychological and neural processes as the Pavlovian way – and inconsistently apologized for his work on aphasia, which correlated disturbed psychological processes with damaged structures of the brain.[139] Silence was the overwhelming response. Of nearly 150 presentations less than ten addressed the fate of psychological science in any detail, and the lengthy resolutions adopted at the end of the Session touched on it only with a passing phrase: Pavlov's doctrine was to be 'the foundation in natural science for the reconstruction of medicine and psychology on scientific principles'.[140] No effort was made to specify what that entailed, beyond the invocation of the 'second signal system' and insistence on sleep therapy.

Unified sloganeering out front and squabbling behind the scenes followed that portentously indecisive Session of 1950. A Scientific Council on Problems of Pavlov's Doctrine was unable to get a satisfactory self-criticism from Orbeli and Beritashvili, or to press other physiologists beyond Pavlovian slogans, into the reconstruction of their discipline that had been resolved upon at the Session. Phrases of compliance prefaced and concluded research and teaching of the routine sort. Psychologists were especially eager to please – with slogans, which changed little of substance in their discipline, and at least one person was so undisciplined as to challenge the slogans in a letter to *The Teacher's Gazette*. Brain processes, the writer argued, cannot explain why different persons have different world views. (The editorial rebuttal was to call the letter-writer a dualist.)[141]

In psychiatry there was far more stubborn diversity, including some public squabbling over the leadership: which eminent individuals did or did not have the right to call themselves Pavlovian? Implicit in such personal issues were substantive disagreements within psychiatry, to which Pavlov's doctrine was largely irrelevant, though no one dared say so. But the urge for monolithic unity was still powerful. In July 1951 *Pravda* marked the first anniversary of the Pavlov Session by starting preparation for another. Bykov published a detailed complaint of continuing resistance and evasion among physiologists. The most scandalous case was in Georgia, where an

'Arakcheev regime', as Bykov chose to call Beritashvili's school, clung to their founder's views even though he had been dismissed from his post. Such disorder would presumably be suppressed through further administrative measures, but psychiatry would need a 'discussion'. The Pavlov Session of 1950, Bykov declared, 'is still being ignored by psychiatrists, and the Academy of Medical Sciences does not expose the anti-Pavlovian positions that prevail in several psychiatric "schools".'[142] In spite of the derisive quotation marks the schools that divided psychiatrists were real, and significant conflict would be precipitated by a campaign to amalgamate them in anti-cosmopolitan Pavlovian unity. At the next Pavlov Session, in October 1951, psychological science would once again be a fitfully present apparition, which no one had strong reason to confront unambiguously, or push to the choice between spectral existence and Pavlovian non-existence. But psychiatry was a field of applied science, where the Stalinist criterion of practice could be applied, with consequences that would long outlast Comrade Stalin.

15

Treating the Insane

Psychohygiene was a transient episode, an effort of fellow-traveling psychiatrists to bring a mental health movement to the population at large, to start the 'dispensaries' that might in the long run reduce the need for insane asylums. Soviet authorities approved the movement in the 1920s when it was mostly futuristic talk — funds and staff were lacking, whether for dispensaries or for asylums — and condemned it in the 1930s, for talk of mental health encouraged a take-it-easy attitude, a concern to protect the mind against excessive strain. In either period, with or without official approval, psychohygiene was a minor concern of Soviet psychiatrists, who were so few in such a large population that seriously demented patients had to be their overwhelming concern. And that concern entangled physicians of the mind with agents of state power, for seriously demented people are typically confined.

Psychiatrists tried to deny the entanglement, especially before the Revolution, when they could express autonomous dreams of themselves as pure healers. There were times, they complained, when the police dumped derelicts, alcoholics, and political offenders in mental hospitals without even asking for the doctors' approval.[1] But police requests for professional judgment were more common and more troublesome, for then psychiatrists could hardly avoid complicity with power. Shackles hung on the criminal suspects or convicts brought in for mental testing, to decide whether they were to be confined by doctors or by jailers. The shackles must be removed, a congress of psychiatrists heatedly and unanimously demanded in 1909.[2] With such a gross symbol of state power removed, the criminal would be a genuine patient, long enough for the physician to decide whether to recommend the jail or the madhouse.

That eagerness to distance the psychiatrist's role from the policeman's, if only by symbolic rituals, precipitated the first intervention of the Communist regime in the psychiatric profession. At the newly founded Serbskii Institute for Forensic Medicine in the early 1920s, specialists routinely judged criminals to be *nevmeniaemye*, 'unchargeable', in need of treatment rather than punishment. On a theoretical level such findings were consciously linked with the naturalistic belief that criminal responsibility is a dubious concept, since human behavior is determined by our particular heredities and environmental histories. On a political level the forensic psychiatrists were showing liberal disapproval of the Soviet regime that would try and punish 'chargeable' criminals.[3]

Very soon the political authorities grew angry. In their view liberal psychiatrists were coddling criminals under the pretense of treating sick people. In the mid-1920s and early 1930s, virtually the entire staff of the Serbskii Institute was dismissed. The new staff was politically sympathetic to the Soviet regime, and therefore willing to put very sharp limits on findings of *nevmeniaemost'*, unchargeability. Only the most extreme cases of insanity were to be given such exculpation; the rest were to be turned over to the judicial system for punishment. By the early 1930s Cecilia Feinberg, the new director of the Serbskii Institute, was boasting that the percentage of psychopaths found to be unchargeable had dropped from 46.5 per cent in 1922 to 6.4 per cent in 1930.[4] It has remained low ever since, for the authorities' vindictive view of criminals and their indignation at psychiatric exculpation have persisted.[5]

That first political intervention in psychiatry was a fairly minor infraction of professional autonomy, for most psychiatrists are not forensic specialists, and most mental patients are not involved in criminal charges. The overwhelming majority of psychiatrists and of patients relate to each other with very little external regulation by courts or bureaucracy, and with very little feeling among psychiatrists that there is any need to worry about the lack of regulation. One must search to find a Soviet psychiatrist noticing the possibility of a problem in the profession's exercise of autonomous power over patients, and then only to brush the problem aside – unless a criminal is involved. This is how a leading psychiatrist explained the difference to a 1935 conference:

Properly speaking, in a narrowly medical sense compulsory treatment goes on in our psychiatric practice every day, without legal proceedings. For example, every day we see cases of forceful isolation of the mentally ill, when that is required by their mental illness, of such degree and form that they cannot remain with other people. And we have no reason to reconsider this kind of practice, which has been established in the course of decades or maybe even centuries. Nor does this provoke theoretical disagreements. ... [But] the system of compulsory treatment of the mentally ill who have been placed by force in psychiatric hospitals after breaking the law — that is rather more complicated. ... Both practice and theoretical considerations indicate that here there is an essential difference. If, for the placing of ordinary citizens in psychiatric hospitals, the criterion is merely the condition of the patient, for patients who have committed a crime the criterion is far more complex. Here we must take into account the reaction of society. That is, the pathological behavior of the mentally ill person has acquired a special social resonance.[6]

In the Soviet context the 'special social resonance' of criminal cases has entailed complex transactions within bureaucracies, not adversary proceedings in courtrooms, but the result has been analogous: checks and balances on the exercise of power by forensic psychiatrists. At repeated conferences one finds them discussing their complex role in mediating between criminals and the judicial authorities, with constant awareness of two other interested parties.[7] Prison authorities do not want insane prisoners even if the judicial authorities are determined to be severe, and administrators of mental hospitals do not want intractable criminals as patients. Beginning in 1939, the establishment of special prison hospitals for 'compulsory treatment of especially dangerous mentally ill people' eased that problem of conflicting interests, but did not stop forensic psychiatrists from insisting upon their strictly limited powers. They merely advise the judicial authorities, who alone have the responsibility to decide between jail and madhouse — or the hybrid 'special hospital' for a criminal.[8]

Of course, in the daily intercourse of psychiatric advisers and judicial deciders there is probably more co-operation than conflict — as, indeed, there is in much forensic practice in the West, where constitutional protections of the accused are only as significant as the independent expertise that money can buy. The Soviet Union is not the only place where expert psychiatric opinions are written and rewritten to suit police opinions on the treatment of particular troublemakers. Until the archives are opened we cannot know how much professional autonomy Soviet forensic psychiatrists are in the habit of demanding in such transactions. We know only that the judicial authorities have persistently disapproved the coddling of criminals through psychiatric findings of 'unchargeable', and that forensic psychiatrists have strong, persistent motives not to challenge the judicial authorities. By lending their skills to findings of 'chargeable', fit for prison rather than hospital, they are more likely to avoid trouble and to keep their self-image as doctors of the mind, not punishers of criminals.

Political offenders have not been an exception to this rule, by and large. Only a small minority of them have been subjected to psychiatric examination, and most of that minority have been pronounced 'chargeable', tagged for explicit punishment rather than medical treatment. That pattern emerges in the exposés of flagrantly political misuse of psychiatry, which flared up in the 1930s, caused a major court case in the 1950s, and became a persistent scandal in the 1960s and 1970s, when the state was trying to suppress a vigorous dissident movement. Since then many people have taken it for granted that political bosses and venal psychiatrists have co-operated to make confinement in the madhouse a favorite method of punishing dissidents. But careful scrutiny of the record does not bear out that impression. Through the scandals of the 1960s and the 1970s the overall pattern was still the one that had been established in the late 1920s. Malefactors were to be punished, not coddled by doctors of the mind. The most thorough review of punitive psychiatry, by Bloch and Reddaway, estimated 'about 365' cases between 1962 and 1976, or 'three hundred or so', as Reddaway put it in 1980.[9] The scandalous fact is that those political offenders were examined by psychiatrists in intimidating circumstances; the significant fact, confirming the long-term trend, is that most were pronounced 'chargeable', fit for prison or banishment rather than the insane asylum.

Preoccupation with blatantly political misuse of psychiatry overlooks the far more insidious and persistent problem of the psychiatrist's routine authority. Against those 300 or so politicals, who were examined and mostly pronounced sane during a period of fourteen years, one must set the 313,000 people who were in Soviet mental institutions in 1975, when the annual reports of their rapidly increasing numbers stopped.[10] They are the 'mentally ill', routinely treated by autonomous psychiatrists with scant concern for problems of explicitly political authority or the due process of law that is supposed to govern exercise of power even in the Soviet system.[11] I am calling attention to the chimeric nature of the psychiatrist's authority: he is part doctor, part psychologist, part jailer. And I am suggesting that unconscious abuse of that chimeric authority has been far more common than the exceptional, deliberate misuse of it in blatantly political cases. The authoritarian Nurse Ratchit was a pervasive type in mental hospitals long before *One Flew Over the Cuckoo's Nest* alarmed Americans with a fearsome portrait of her, and her type — male no less than female — has probably dominated Soviet hospitals as well. In 1970, when the dissident Medvedev spent ten days under observation in a psychiatric ward, he got to know a young patient who annoyed the staff by asking once too often why Medvedev was denied the visiting rights that the other patients had. A doctor ordered him to the hospital wing with bars on the windows. She acted on impulse, without formal procedures, and the young patient did not demand them; attended by a powerful orderly, he went.[12]

In published records of forensic specialists I note casual reports of 'querulants', as they would be called in the American branch of the profession: confined people who evince their derangement by complaining and demanding their rights.[13] In such reports the psychiatrist's mind routinely notes 'recalcitrance' (*nepokornost'*) as a symptom of derangement in the patient's.[14] An American psychiatrist who had great sympathy for her Soviet colleagues was nevertheless troubled, during an extended visit, by their comparative freedom in locking up unruly adolescents.[15] She was observing, I would suggest, the freedom that American psychiatrists also enjoyed before the movement for patients' rights restrained the doctors' right to treat patients as they saw fit.[16] That was the long period when popular culture ridiculed the loonies hunted down by white-coated men with huge butterfly nets. In high culture Blanche Dubois's tragic reliance on the kindness of the white-coated men focused blame on her relatives rather than the psychiatrist who helped them put Blanche away. Until 1987, when the new 'openness' exposed latent discontent, Soviet culture seemed quite willing to rely on the kindness of psychiatrists.

Until that year the psychiatrist's routine power to impose medical treatment on non-criminal patients was never thoroughly examined in any Soviet publication that I could find. I have already quoted the perfunctory dismissal of the problem by an eminent psychiatrist, as he turned to the criminal cases which did impose checks and balances on the Soviet psychiatrist's professional authority. Textbooks of psychiatry offered brief reports of rules governing enforced treatment of ordinary patients, but detailed explanations were not public.[17] The rules were information for use within the bureaucracy, and psychiatrists showed hardly any sign of worrying about their adequacy. Only political dissidents raised the issue in their clandestine (*samizdat*) writings.[18]

We are approaching paradoxical contrasts. In countries with strong constitutional traditions psychiatrists have been notoriously self-assertive and fractious, and significant legal restrictions have been placed upon their power to treat patients without consent.[19] In the Soviet Union until very recently the profession has enjoyed almost unrestricted autonomy in its power to treat patients, and psychiatrists have displayed very little self-assertive or fractious spirit. They have been almost as submissive to the authoritarian leaders of their profession as their patients have been to them.

There were five waves of political assault on the psychiatric profession, which destroyed its capacity to resist a despotism that finally emerged from within. In the late 1920s, while forensic psychiatrists bowed to the judicial authorities' vindictive view of criminal behavior, the rest of the profession surrendered Freud, on the insistence of the ideological bureaucracy.[20] The surrender was eased by a distinction between Freud's doctrine as a general ideology, which was utterly condemned, and his doctrine as therapy, which was tolerated until the late 1940s.[21] Of course, the distinction between ideology and therapy was hard to maintain, and Freudians of any kind were increasingly subdued in the 1930s and early 1940s. But that throttling of psychoanalysts seemed to be of little consequence to the profession as a whole, since Freud had relatively few disciples among Russian psychiatrists. In that respect, as in many others, they resembled the German center of the profession, which was cool to psychoanalysis, rather than the new center developing in America with a heavy Freudian influence.[22]

A far more serious assault on professional autonomy was mounted during Stalin's revolution from above of 1929–32, when the very principle of professional autonomy was rejected in favor of *partiinost'*, the party principle. For psychiatrists, as for all other specialists, there were violent changes of the 'leading cadres', as professional organizations and publications were subjected to loudly proclaimed control by the Party's Central Committee. But only a few substantive issues were explicitly involved in those upheavals, most notably the Soviet version of the mental health movement which was suppressed.[23] The 'pushed-up' builders of socialism (*vydvizhentsy*) wanted no experts fussing over their mental health. For them, as for many hard-driving 'positive thinkers' in America, minds are healthy if we work hard and don't worry about them.

Once again, as in the ban on forensic liberals and on Freudians, only marginal concerns of Soviet psychiatrists were at stake. Their overriding concern had all along been psychoses and neuropathology, not neuroses and psychotherapy – as one would reasonably expect of a very small profession in a very large and backward country. (In 1916 there were 350 psychiatrists in the Russian Empire; in 1932 the Soviet Commissar of Health reported 538, plus 743 neuropathologists.)[24] In spite of all the Communist denunciation of 'bourgeois' psychiatrists in 1929–32, their competence to deal with severe derangement and neuropathology was never challenged in those years. The intellectual autonomy of the profession was largely preserved in fact, though vehemently denied in principle, during Stalin's revolution from above. But the profession was laid open to further political intervention, which soon touched substantive issues of major concern, especially the diagnosis of schizophrenia, the major cause of long-term confinement in mental asylums.

That further history requires understanding of the intertwined problems that schizophrenia presented to psychiatrists, to public health officials, and to the political bosses who were intent on building heavy industry rather than mental hospitals. Schizophrenia is the most common of the most extreme mental disorders. It is *not* a 'split personality' on the model of Jekyll and Hyde, as many people imagine. Schizophrenia is a label for severe disruptions of mental functions, with such alarming symptoms as fearful delusions, hallucinations, and senseless speech, and a consequent inability to be a normally functioning member of society. Such disorders may begin insidiously, in the absence of unusual external stress. From within a person may feel a mounting sense of worthlessness, an irresistible urge toward increasing isolation, and may begin to offer delusions by way of explanation, such as an unbearable stench driving others away from oneself, or terrible voices that others cannot hear. The experienced clinician may sense, without being able to prove, that a cumulative disintegration of mental functions is beginning. Thus the psychiatrist may feel impelled to intervene with some vigorous, not to say violent, empiric remedy – such as sulfur injections or insulin coma in the 1930s, prolonged drugged sleep or electric shock in the 1940s and 1950s, or heavy doses of major tranquilizers since the 1960s.[25]

Such forceful interventions are justified by the clinicians' interlocking circle of intuitions, actions, inferences, convictions. If an empiric remedy fails to halt the disintegration of the mind, the diagnosis is confirmed: schizophrenia is an irreversible endogenous disease of unknown etiology. Some other empiric remedy needs to be tried in place of the one that failed. If the disintegration of the mind is halted, the diagnosis of an irreversible process still stands: the empiric remedy has put the disease 'in remission'. In short, severe mental disorder puts the psychiatrist under pressure not only to act with insufficient knowledge but also to repress awareness of his ignorance, to become a 'clinical dogmatist'.

In this respect the clinical psychiatrist resembles other practical authorities who feel duty bound, like the ideal psychiatrist in a Soviet textbook, to 'reconstruct the patient's entire way of life, his entire system of values. ... The goal is the arrangement of his destiny [*ustroistvo ego sud'by*].'[26] The author of that grand pronouncement was Dr A. V. Snezhnevskii, who was the uncontested boss of Soviet psychiatry from 1951 to 1987, when he died. Like policemen and military officers, or teachers and parents, psychiatrists are constantly drawn toward the intuitive self-assurance that is essential to action, and thus toward repression of the question whether they can reasonably justify what they feel compelled to do. The Stalinist mentality is an extreme example of the type, a species of violent insistence that *praktiki*, men of practice, must be right if they are to act on other people, and conversely, that such action proves them to be right.

The natural affinity between Soviet political *praktiki* and 'clinical dogmatists' in psychiatry appeared only fleetingly in the 1930s. In 1933, when Dr Snezhnevskii was twenty-nine, he reported that chaos had been overcome in a terribly overcrowded provincial mental hospital, using the characteristic political language of the time. The work had been stormy, the struggle intense. On orders from local Party organs, the old staff had been driven out, replaced by Snezhnevskii's team, which had raised 'bed turnover' from one to three per year and depressed the death rate 'from 10 per cent to 2 per cent'. The characteristic bluster of the time was in those percentages, unsupported by tables of absolute numbers. But – or maybe therefore: Stalinist bluster may have been essential to Stalinist achievement – Dr Snezhnevskii probably did improve the hospital, if only by moving some patients out to the empty houses of transported 'kulaks', and by imposing orderly procedures of hygiene and organized activities.[27]

Concerning psychiatric theories Snezhnevskii had little to say in 1933, but that little was revealing. His practical success proved that 'psychiatry was transformed into a science, capable of curing, and of curing far from poorly'. He stressed organized 'work therapy and cultural therapy', rather than the physiological remedies that would later become an obsession with him, but the obsessive frame of mind was already apparent. Indeed, young Snezhnevskii rediscovered a basic conviction that Pinel and Tuke, the founding fathers of modern psychiatry, had bequeathed to the profession. Science and morality are fused in the personal authority of the psychiatrist.

> Work therapy and cultural therapy do not in the slightest exclude, but on the contrary they presuppose the personal individual influence of the doctor's personality on the patient and on his manifestations of illness. The authority of the personality [*avtoritet lichnosti*] of the doctor giving the treatment, and his educative influence both in work-therapy and in culture-therapy, are decisive.[28]

Foucault and Szasz would no doubt seize upon that declaration as an admission of the authoritarianism that they angrily charge against modern psychiatry.[29] They might even make much of the uncanny similarity between Snezhnevskii's stress on 'the authority of the personality' and the 'cult of the personality' that Stalin built about himself. But Foucault and Szasz are not quite fair in their criticism of psychiatric authoritarianism. They ignore the self-corrective liberalism of the profession as a whole, its collective self-questioning, embodied in the toleration of competing schools and doctrines. Liberalism of that type still prevailed in the Soviet profession of the early 1930s, in spite of such portents as the *Gleichschaltung* of forensic psychiatrists, the suppression of Freudianism, and the imposition of *partiinost'*, the party principle, within professional organizations.

We need the advantage of hindsight to perceive the ominous affinity between the authoritarian pragmatism of a clinical boss like Snezhnevskii and the authoritarian pragmatism of the political bosses who would ultimately raise him to power over the whole profession. In the 1930s the crisis of over-crowding in mental hospitals, which gave Snezhnevskii a little fame as an administrator, generated far more fame and authority for Dr V. P. Osipov, who exposed the political misuse of sloppy diagnoses of schizophrenia, and campaigned for strict science and professional self-restraint. Under that banner Osipov led the fourth wave of political intervention in psychiatry, which came at a peak of Stalinist authoritarianism in society at large — on behalf of rigorous self-questioning and truly objective standards in psychiatric practice.

Previously, in the 1920s, there had been much talk of 'dispensarization' — or 'deinstitutionalization', as an analogous campaign would be called in the West — without much impact on theory or practice. While the profession dreamed of a great increase in out-patient clinics, as we would call dispensaries, talk of pinning the schizophrenic label to mildly disturbed people was not perceived as a threat to overburden the system. Dr L. M.

Rozenshtein, the chief advocate of 'dispensarization', argued that the population was full of incipient or 'mild' schizophrenics, who needed out-patient care, not confinement. His concept of the disease was broad − perhaps sloppy is the better term − reaching out for millions of new patients.[30] But his scheme of out-patient treatment seemed socially manageable, while political leaders and economists were still indulging in dreams of socialist planning that would produce a great leap forward on all fronts at once, in the health and welfare of the present generation no less than the industrial base for the future. Rozenshtein's opponents criticized 'mild schizophrenia' as a contradiction in terms, but the controversy was relatively sedate, for it was apolitical or 'purely scientific'[31] − until the mid-1930s, when Rozenshtein's concept of schizophrenia was retrospectively, and unfairly, blamed for the acute crisis that overwhelmed psychiatric care during Stalin's 're-volution from above'.

In June 1932 Soviet psychiatrists held a major conference on schizophrenia, the last one, as things turned out, that indulged in a free contest of 'teachings' on the subject, that had no official line established in advance. Rozenshtein presented a paper defending his broad concept of the disease. O. V. Kerbikov argued for a different but equally broad concept. Other participants countered with arguments for narrower concepts, more rigorous methods of diagnosis. The participants criticized each other keenly but politely, ignoring the social crisis that had put their courteous debate in jeopardy.[32] Forced collectivization and rapid urbanization, with every possible ruble being squeezed into heavy industry, were blasting the dream of 'dispensarization', while creating havoc in the old-fashioned practice of confining schizophrenics for long periods. Mental hospitals were being overwhelmed by a flood of new patients, and psychiatrists were responding in the usual style of learned specialists. They were holding a conference, politely debating their divergent concepts of diagnosis and treatment.

Experts argue whether hereditary vulnerability to schizophrenia pulls individuals down into the urban lower classes or whether the shattering experiences of the urban lower classes precipitate schizophrenia. Both causal factors may be at work. In any case the correlation is beyond dispute. 'Schizophrenia is common in all races and cultures ... and is commonest in the lower socio-economic groups in dilapidated areas of large cities.'[33] Stalin's 'revolution from above' caused a huge increase in such groups down below, while the number of psychiatrists and of hospital beds for mental cases probably declined. Reliable statistics are lacking, but official comments make it certain that, even if beds and personnel increased slightly, they were grossly inadequate to a huge increase in need.[34]

The characteristic response of Stalinist officials was to rebuff pleas for increased funding of psychiatric facilities and staff.[35] Instead they stressed the need for administrators like young Dr Snezhnevskii, who imposed order on overcrowded hospitals without requiring large amounts of extra funds. At the same time public health officials gave eager support to psychiatrists who deplored broad, sloppy concepts of schizophrenia, the most common cause of long-term confinement. The rigorists were mostly associated with 'the Leningrad school' of psychiatry, as opposed to 'the Moscow school', which produced both Kerbikov and Snezhnevskii. Those stereotypes may be unfair, but one can understand their appeal. It was the elderly dean of the Leningrad school, Dr V. P. Osipov, who precipitated the campaign for 'narrowing' the concept of schizophrenia by exposing the political misuse of psychiatry that the 'broad' concept can facilitate. As chief of psychiatry at the Military Medical Academy in Leningrad he reviewed cases of army personnel treated for mental illness, and thus he discovered, and published in 1935, a scandalous history of bold young officers who had been certified as schizophrenic when they dared to criticize their superiors.[36]

At a major psychiatric conference in 1936 the Stalinist mode of discourse was clearly in evidence. No speaker questioned the demand for 'narrowing' the concept of schizophrenia, or challenged Osipov's keynote speech in any way. In place of collective self-criticism, as we may call the liberal habit of open debate among conflicting views, the conference witnessed scapegoat 'self-criticism', the lurid Stalinist ritual of public confession by errant individuals, including *ex post facto* sinners, who had strayed from the official line before it was laid down. Most notably, O. V. Kerbikov contritely apologized in 1936 for the paper he had presented to the 1932 conference. He had argued that psychiatrists must be intuitively bold in thought and action, that they must learn to recognize 'schizophrenia without schizophrenic symptoms', if they want to stop the disintegration of the mind before the insidious process becomes irreversible. At the 1936 conference he repudiated that argument, and promised to support a narrow view.[37] By such humiliating rituals the Stalinist system pushed psychiatrists toward greater scientific rigor, toward more scrupulous self-doubt when placing the dread label of schizophrenia on disordered minds. Or so it seemed in the mid-1930s.

Seemed — that must be stressed, for dissembling is the natural result of enforced belief. Kerbikov did not really change his mind. Like many other participants in Soviet rituals of the Stalinist type, he put on a mask. In the 1950s, when another political intervention reversed the field of force in psychiatry, Kerbikov took off his mask, and demanded self-criticism from skeptical critics of broad concepts. In short, he resumed his argument of 1932: timid hesitation to diagnose schizophrenia until mental disintegration is far advanced misses the critical period of insidious onset, when vigorous intervention with shock therapy or drugged sleep might still arrest the disease process.[38]

THE TRIUMPH OF CLINICAL DOGMATISM

That sudden reversal in the field of political force, like so many others in Soviet intellectual history, was absurdly irrelevant in origin, quite unconnected with the scientific issues of schizophrenia, or with such relevant social circumstances as overcrowding in mental hospitals. It was the 'anticosmopolitan' drive of the late 1940s and the resulting 'Pavlov Sessions' that raised Snezhnevskii and Kerbikov to power over psychiatry. Neither one had any connection with Pavlov's school or his doctrine. Russian chauvinism gave them power, which they proceeded to use autonomously, on behalf of their 'clinical dogmatism'. But the irrelevance of cause and consequence is mainly in the eye of the academic observer, who seeks coherence in articulate thought. In the world of authoritarian pragmatists, inhabited by Snezhnevskii and the political bosses, comrades recognize one another by other signs. He did not join the Party until fairly late — in 1945 at the age of 41 — but he had proved his Stalinist administrative skills in the heroic 1930s, he was a no-nonsense clinician who lectured with authority and hardly bothered to publish, and he was 'pure Russian'. That invidious distinction was and still is common in the Soviet Union despite the official repudiation of racism and the urge toward Russification. No matter how well they spoke the language and shared the folkways, Jews could not be 'pure Russian', as Snezhnevskii was by birth, an especially important qualification in a profession that had a considerable number of Jews among its leaders.

So Snezhnevskii was ripe for a political boost to the top of the profession, though it was hardly aware of his existence. At a major psychiatric conference in May 1948 his name was mentioned only twice (and misspelled),[39] while the recognized leaders of the profession tried to reconcile the demand for a unified, uniquely Soviet Russian science of the mind with their ongoing toleration of diverse views on major unsolved problems, such as schizophrenia. But only a few months later the August Session of the Agricultural Academy raised Lysenko to absolute power over biology and intensified the drive for distinctively Soviet Russian science in all fields. Then recognition came to Snezhnevskii, from the ideological establishment, which appointed him to the commission preparing a new classification of mental illnesses. (That is the Soviet equivalent of the American Psychiatric Association's *Diagnostic Manual*, which is periodically revised as professional opinion rearranges the categories of mental disturbance.) He was added to a roster of distinguished scholars for the express purpose of rooting out 'enemy ideology'.[40] From there he moved quickly into major administrative posts. In 1950 he replaced Cecilia Feinberg as Director of the Serbskii Institute of Forensic Psychiatry, while the press attacked her for insufficient patriotism. Early in 1951 he took charge of the country's one journal of psychiatry and neuropathology, and moved from the Serbskii Institute to the

Central Institute for Postgraduate Medical Training, where he took over as chief of psychiatry.

Thus he was prepared to step into the limelight as the chief speaker at the Pavlov Session for psychiatrists, in October 1951. He appeared as head of a new team – with Kerbikov as chief theorist – which would remake the psychiatric profession in a distinctively Soviet Russian style. Their roots were in Soviet clinical practice, as opposed to academic research and theorizing, and the distinctive new quality that they would bring to academic psychiatry was the rough-and-ready decisiveness of men who command in adverse circumstances. Hindsight reveals that. At the time of sudden promotion, in 1950–1, they seemed distinguishable only by their 'anti-cosmopolitan' abuse of the leaders they were replacing, with emphasis on the Jewish names among them: 'As a result of the activity of some psychiatrists with cosmopolitan moods (Professors Shmar'ian, Gurevich, Sereiskii, Edel'shtein), the materialist ideas, the independent originality of our fatherland's psychiatry, have been willfully suppressed.'[41] Limitless devotion to Russia's native traditions, Snezhnevskii insisted, must be proved by disdain for Western authorities and by oaths of allegiance to 'Pavlov's teaching'.

We may give Snezhnevskii credit for hypocrisy in mouthing such rhetoric. Before 1948 he had shown no signs of Russian chauvinism. In two modest articles, which were his complete scholarly *oeuvre* before his sudden rise to power, he had shown the usual reverence for German authorities, and had paid special tribute to some of the Jewish teachers and supervisors whom he began to denounce after 1948.[42] Even in the most fervid years of the nativist crusades he was comparatively restrained. He gave only a little lip service to Lysenko, the most exalted god of nativist science at the moment. Belief in diathesis, an hereditary predisposition to mental illness, was and remained basic to Snezhnevskii's clinical assumptions.[43] Of course he joined the crusade for Pavlov's doctrine, which he had previously ignored – and freely turned it to his own uses. In his speech to the Pavlov Session he attacked one of the very few psychiatrists who *had* previously shown a serious interest in Pavlov's views on schizophrenia. A. S. Chistovich was that nearly unique person; he had presented patients during Pavlov's visits to a mental hospital, and had analyzed Pavlov's speculations in a 1949 article.[44] Snezhnevskii attacked the article for 'nosological agnosticism', foreshadowing the campaign he would mount after 1951, as he pressed his 'clinical dogmatism' on the profession – in the guise of Pavlov's doctrine.[45] Chistovich made a little show of 'self-criticism' at the 1951 session, but afterward became one of the few hardy souls who offered open resistance to Snezhnevskii, until he too was ground down into silent acceptance of Snezhnevskii's leadership.[46]

We may credit Snezhnevskii with hypocrisy in the nativist campaign not only because he joined it late but because he left it early. Within a few years after 1951, as the post-Stalin political leadership reopened Russia's respectful window to the West, Snezhnevskii's school hastened to stop embarrassing displays of chauvinism. They even dropped Pavlov, except for ceremonial occasions. Pavlov's celebrated 'teaching' had served as a ladder, quickly climbed, soon pushed away. The teacher they most imitated in actual clinical thought — and soon restored to reverence on ceremonial occasions — was Emil Kraepelin, the German founder of the nosological school.[47]

To understand the Stalinist version of that school one must appreciate the tensions within psychiatric nosology, which do constantly threaten agnosticism, 'anarchy', and 'nihilism', as Snezhnevskii has repeatedly warned. Nosology is the classification of diseases. Kraepelin's school, whether in Germany or Russia or the United States — it is indeed cosmopolitan — centers its faith on the power of clinicians to impose taxonomic order on the enormously variable symptoms that mental patients present, to perceive patterns of development, disease 'courses', which may be classified as disease entities. Dementia praecox was Kraepelin's original name for schizophrenia, and a more revealing one too. It is the endogenous dementia that appears precociously, that is, the mental disorder that emerges within young people who have no apparent lesions in their nervous systems, as opposed to senile dementia, which emerges within aging nervous systems.

Kraepelin admitted that the concept of dementia praecox or schizophrenia is a taxonomic *Riesentopf* or giant pot; 'wastebasket' is the harsher metaphor of a recent American psychiatrist.[48] Into this concept the nosologist throws diverse symptoms that perhaps should be classified separately, and perhaps should not be linked to one particular disease entity any more than fever or fainting or nausea. In other words, the concept of schizophrenia bundles together phenomenal symptoms that should perhaps be considered separately, and ties the bundle to a noumenal reality that is still unproved and may be unprovable. Those viciously circular weaknesses — lumping varied symptoms of mental disorder on the unproved assumption that they jointly evince an underlying process of one particular disease entity — have been the focus of skeptical attack for nearly a century.

In a normally functioning community of psychiatrists the tension between skeptics and believers defines the community. (Of course, many versions of this tension are constantly in evidence, and participants are frequently too annoyed with each other to feel much sense of professional community. I am here offering a schematic outline.) Skeptics note the incongruities that result from the patchwork-quilt of success and failure in reducing mental disorders to physical causes. A patient's delusions and hallucinations may be caused by infections such as malaria or syphilis, or by poisoning as in alcoholism, or by vitamin deficiency as in pellagra. When physical causes are unknown, delusions and hallucinations are ascribed to a mysterious disease process called schizophrenia. Symptoms are hypostatized, transformed from evidence into the thing evinced, the substance or essence of a disease entity. Thus the skeptics. Believers oppose such subversion by appeal to analogies of another kind: somatic processes such as cancer or 'essential hypertension', which are recognized as disease entities though the etiologies are unknown. Note especially that quaint use of 'essential', which equates the evidence with the thing evinced. The symptom, high blood pressure, is declared the essence of the disease — until it may be reduced to some other physical phenomena. Mental causes are generally assumed to be of secondary importance.

The implicit metaphysics of the profession — medical materialism in William James's plain speech — is rarely confronted as a problematic issue that requires discussion. The explicit faith of nosological believers is in 'clinical experience', as epitomized in 'case histories'. They are the physician's equivalent of the exemplary stories that politicians, novelists, and historians draw from *their* experience. Such examples are intended to embody universal truths, which may be disgraced if separated from concrete evidence and presented as abstract formulas. Kerbikov crossed the line when he talked of recognizing 'schizophrenia without schizophrenic symptoms'.[49] So too do psychiatrists who support a diagnosis with the remark: 'This case has the smell of schizophrenia.'[50] Clinicians are expected to use such intuitive flair (from the French for smell; compare Russian *chut'ë* and German *Spürsinn*), but they may not simply point to the nose in proof. They must tell stories that evoke the persuasive odor in the collective olfactory apparatus of their experienced audience.

In the 1920s the German psychiatrist Kurt Schneider started a movement toward systematic restraint of subjectivity and imprecision in the diagnosis of schizophrenia.[51] This rigorously self-questioning movement significantly limited the incidence of schizophrenic diagnoses in Europe, as contrasted with the United States, where the heavy influence of Freudian or 'psychodynamic' thought expanded the role of subjectivity in psychiatric practice. At first the Soviet branch of the profession followed the European rigorists, especially when the acute shortage of hospital beds and resulting political pressure reinforced the self-questioning approach in diagnosis. In 1935 the official *Soviet Medical Encyclopedia* declared schizophrenia:

> a problem, one of the most difficult in psychiatry. ...˙ Every new work on schizophrenia raises more problems than it solves. The situation is best characterized by the [German] authors of the large monograph [recently translated into Russian] ..., who declare: Concerning the essence of schizophrenia 'we do not know anything.'[52]

By such self-doubt the Soviet profession moved toward cautious self-restraint, until Snezhnevskii took command in the 1950s. He drove — or led — his colleagues to bold self-confidence. By 1973, when the World Health Organization published a comparative study, Soviet psychiatrists had overtaken and surpassed America in diagnoses of schizophrenia.[53]

Snezhnevskii began to challenge the diagnostic self-restraint preached by the leaders of his profession only when he felt the mantle of authoritative leadership on his shoulders. He opened his campaign against 'nosological agnosticism' in 1951, when he was promoted to the editorship of the country's single journal of psychiatry and neuropathology.[54] From that commanding height, which he held until his death in 1987, along with directorships of key institutes, he issued continual pronouncements on the nature of schizophrenia and nosology in general, with occasional conferences organized to demonstrate virtually unanimous support for his views.

The transformation of Snezhnevskii from an unpretentious clinician to an unanswerable boss fits a very widespread Soviet pattern. He was dutifully quiet until the higher powers chose him to mount the appropriate tribune and 'lay down' or 'formulate' − *oformit'*, a favorite term of the Soviet bureaucracy − the theoretical implications of his promotion, which was proof of his practical success. Stalin's career once exemplified that pattern, and hundreds of others, including Khrushchev's and Brezhnev's, have since been held up as ideal types in the Soviet press. The circular logic of the faith that informs those tales of success is one of the crucial meanings of the Stalinist rule that, while theory guides practice, practice has primacy over theory. One might consider analogies with our own cult of success, the pragmatic ideology of those who 'make it' in Western countries. 'Winners' take it for granted that they know something which 'losers' do not, and 'losers' often agree. Thus hierarchy is sanctified and confidence in knowledge is strengthened.

For a few years in the early 1950s Snezhnevskii organized a 'discussion' of schizophrenia in his journal. It was a classic Stalinist caricature of a genuine discussion. With disapproving editorial footnotes he published a few brief defenses of views labeled 'incorrect' from the start, and many long expositions of the 'correct' view. At a conference in 1954 he announced the end of the 'discussion'. (To be precise, he said he was not ending discussion; he was suspending it until decisive data might be collected.) He brushed aside the charge that he was denying freedom of research and publication to psychiatrists with legitimate differences of opinion. He was merely resisting 'agnostics' and 'nihilists', who would subvert the whole progress of science:

> Science can develop only on condition of historical continuity [*preem-stvennost'*], and denying the achievements of preceding generations of psychiatrists, denying efforts to define this disease [schizophrenia] − that signifies interruption of the continuity of science, that means opposing scientific development, opposing the progress of science.[55]

In pitiful fact the critics of Snezhnevskii's 'clinical dogmatism' were very far from such audacious opposition. They were few in number and subdued in tone. Suffice to note that 'clinical dogmatism', the accurate name for

Snezhnevskii's outlook, was offered almost apologetically by a distinguished forensic psychiatrist, who took instant pains to cushion the blow by declaration of his respect for Snezhnevskii's school.[56] By 1963, when Snezhnevskii assembled the next conference to endorse his views, he could note with satisfaction that even fewer critics spoke out. His triumph was supreme: 'The rivulets flowing in a single direction have fused in a mighty torrent. . . . [Our data] will permit us to specify the precise boundaries of schizophrenia, to erect, so to speak, the boundary marks whose absence has tormented some psychiatrists.'[57]

Western psychiatrists have focused on that claim of 'boundary marks', Snezhnevskii's nosological scheme of schizophrenia, as the distinguishing feature of his school.[58] However important, that focus misses a deeper and more constant theme, which persisted even through the 1970s, when Snezhnevskii felt obliged to shift the 'boundary marks' of schizophrenia, though still insisting on his larger nosology. His abiding obsession was 'nosological agnosticism', 'nihilism', or 'anarchism', as he variously called the threat to his most basic value: *preemstvennost'*, continuity, or more precisely, the principle of proper succession, from the Russian root for the successor to a throne or office. He found that essential continuity in the ongoing tradition of 'the clinic', another favorite term of his, which resonated as powerfully in Snezhnevskii's mind as in Foucault's (with opposite feeling, to be sure). He blamed researchers for the 'nihilism' that threatens the continuity of clinical wisdom. In his universe 'the laboratory' was granted a place, explicitly subordinate to 'the clinic'. The practicing psychiatrist could not allow his self-confidence to be shaken by the academic researcher, who might be of great technical assistance — for example, in the development of new drugs — but must not be allowed to subvert the lessons of the clinic.[59]

In typically Stalinist fashion Snezhnevskii erected a crude, scholastic theory to dignify his vital faith in practice. It may be dealt with summarily here. His scheme of schizophrenia has been well reported and critically analyzed in the West, especially by Dr Walter Reich.[60] The crushing response of virtually all psychiatrists outside the Soviet Union — including those of East Germany — has been cold indifference, relieved occasionally by little courteous flatteries.[61] Imitation, the sincerest form of flattery, has, as usual, been paid to the West by the backward East, first in the adoption of psychotropic drugs, finally in the attendant theoretical upheavals. In the mid-1970s Snezhnevskii felt obliged to acknowledge 'a crisis in the development of clinical psychiatry', and began to publish extensive reports of Western research in his journal.[62]

He kept his school intact by restating his nosological scheme, emphasizing the inanity that protects scholastic theories from refutation by any possible evidence. Schizophrenia can be recognized early and confidently, as an hereditary disease process that must follow one of three courses: continuous, intermittent, or transitory. I have used less obscure terms than Snezhnevskii, in order to bring out more clearly the irrefutable nature of his scheme. The clinician may apply the schizophrenic label with complete confidence, for the patient's symptoms will get worse (continuous course), or they will come and go (intermittent course), or they will disappear (transitory course). In the last case the diagnosis still stands, for the patient without schizophrenic symptoms is still a schizophrenic. 'Even as a result of complete recovery the organism does not return entirely to the condition that preceded the disease.'[63]

The absence of boundary marks does not torment the Snezhnevskian psychiatrist, whose clinical nose can still discern the insidious presence of schizophrenia. All mental illnesses are still enclosed within the schemes that Snezhnevskii's intuition has drawn from clinical experience. He has literally *drawn* the schemes of classification as nested circles, oddly resembling medieval drawings of the earth nested in concentric cosmic spheres (see plate 18). Snezhnevskii thinks he has charted the taxonomic relationship of every mental disturbance with every other one, from neuroses to manic depression and schizophrenia, including even epilepsy and feeble-mindedness.

Even when he began to concede some significance to contemporary disturbances in nosology, Snezhnevskii clung to faith in historical continuity or succession, in part by recalling that Wilhelm Griesinger, one of the founding fathers of modern psychiatry, conceived the diversity of symptoms as manifestations of disorder in the brain, and therefore in some sense a single disease.[64] Snezhnevskii reconciles that stratospheric vision with the grubbing nosology of the Kraepelin tradition by one breathtaking stroke: '*Any* form of mental disorder may emerge in the course of development of many, or of *all* mental diseases.'[65] If a patient treated the logic of classification in such a wild manner, a Snezhnevskian psychiatrist might well write 'cognitive slippage' in his notebook, and leap to a diagnosis of incipient schizophrenia. Imagine someone saying that any form of animal may emerge in the course of development of all animals, that a crab, let us say, may emerge in a woman's womb or in the belly of a man.

Dr Walter Reich takes exception to my argument here, and very likely many other psychiatrists would too. We agree that Dr Snezhnevskii deserves to be mocked for disgracing present standards of rigor in psychiatric nosology. My language may suggest mockery of the whole nosological tradition. I do not intend that, but I am a layman. I have no license to draw a precise line between sensible and ridiculous nosological reasoning in psychiatry. But the licensed authorities are notoriously discordant; they have not drawn a precise line to which a layman can reverentially point. So I can only confess my intuitions, which laugh at Snezhnevskii's mode of reasoning, and respect Kurt Schneider's.

Snezhnevskii's belated retreat to almost explicit inanity was forced by foreign, not by Soviet, research and debate. In the 1950s and 1960s, just when he was imperiously suppressing 'the anarchy in this whole problem' of schizophrenia,[66] psychiatrists in other countries were letting loose a new wave of anarchy by the use of psychotropic drugs and by intense efforts to achieve objectivity in research. Used as empiric palliatives, major tranquillizers brought sufficient abatement of symptoms to permit a great increase in the release of patients from mental hospitals, but efforts at scientific explanation have been persistently frustrated. Probabilistic correlation of particular drugs with the abatement of particular symptoms has exacerbated rather than relieved the problems of nosology, that is, of clustering symptoms and processes in disease entities. Neurochemical research on the cellular level has painstakingly pursued an obvious hypothesis — that subtle disorders in neurotransmitters give rise to mental disorders — but without much success. Masses of data have been accumulated, holding out tantalizing possibilities of comprehension, but leaving schizophrenia still an essentially unsolved problem.[67]

MODERN WAYS

For more than twenty years, from the 1950s to the 1970s, Snezhnevskii's 'clinical dogmatism' kept the Soviet profession from significant participation in those new trends of research, including the rising insistence on rigorous skepticism in diagnostics. During the same period the sloppy diagnostic habits that he fostered helped to fill mental hospitals as fast as new ones could be built and staffed. The critically significant social fact is that they were built. The political triumph of Snezhnevskii's 'clinical dogmatists' in 1951 was crowned by a decree of the Minister of Health ordering a great increase in spending on mental care. At long last the Soviet Union was to get a truly modern number of psychiatrists, mental hospitals, and patients to occupy them, and Snezhnevskii's school was to be in charge of the modernizing process.[68]

The dramatic results can be seen in table 1. In twenty years the number of hospital beds for the mentally ill almost tripled (from 106,500 in 1955 to 312,600 in 1975), while the number of psychiatrists almost quadrupled (from almost 4,800 to 18,700). And then, after 1975, those indicators of nerve-racking modernity became a state secret — until *glasnost*. No doubt one of the reasons for the new secrecy was the embarrassing contrast with Western trends. The 1950s to 1970s were the years of 'deinstitutionalization'. In the United States, for example, the number of mental patients in governmental hospitals declined from a peak of 558,900 in 1955 to 307,900 in 1971.[69] One might compare the ironic process to the Soviet catch-up in steel production just as it peaked and began to decline in the USA Whether either process

– deinstitutionalization or deindustrialization – should be regarded as
progress is too serious a problem to be sloughed off with cynical laughter.

It is impossible to get precise figures on the role of schizophrenia diagnoses
in the Soviet Union's rising tide of hospitalization for mental illness. Even
in the earlier years, while Soviet health officials had boasted of their low
rate of mental illness compared with the decadent West, they had never
offered comprehensive data on the incidence of particular illnesses. They
may have lacked good data even in their private discussions; in 1948 an
Assistant Minister of Health made such a complaint to a conference of
psychiatrists.[70] Solid epidemiological studies of mental disorders have begun
to appear in Soviet publications only very recently, and they are still very
limited. But they suggest that the incidence of schizophrenia has been
going up more swiftly than the total increase in all types of mental illness.[71]
Snezhnevskii's school can claim only some of the credit for that dispropor-
tion. They are notoriously quick to pin the label of schizophrenia on
disturbed people, but continuing urbanization has been piling up the 'lower
socio-economic groups in dilapidated areas of large cities', and such groups
have the highest rates of schizophrenia even with the most rigorous diagnostic standards.

Snezhnevskii's belated retreat from extreme self-confidence, his admission of 'a crisis in clinical psychiatry',[72] may have been prompted by
dissatisfied health officials, envious of the dramatic 'deinstitutionalization'
of mental patients in the West during the 1960s and 1970s. We may
imagine the Minister of Health chiding Snezhnevskii on the need to reduce
hospital confinement – but only in private. After 1964, when they over-
threw Khrushchev, Soviet political leaders were extremely fearful of 'dis-
organizing the cadres'. They allowed nothing like the public campaign of
the 1930s for 'narrowing' the concept of schizophrenia. Nor did they allow
anything like a return to the open, autonomous debate of the 1920s, which
culminated in the 1932 conference on schizophrenia. Snezhnevskii shared
his superiors' immunity to public criticism, whether of the politically
organized type, as in the 1930s, or of the autonomous academic type, as in
the 1920s. Like so many other little Stalins commanding a host of Soviet
fiefdoms, he maintained his unquestioned authority while changing his
line, offering an insultingly vague explanation and no trace of apology. He
and his lieutenants simply began to publish reports of foreign trends in
schizophrenia research, eliminating or toning down the most glaring sub-
versions of the original Snezhnevskii scheme, and raising the scheme to a
splendid level of irrefutable generality.

The latterday tactics of Snezhnevskii's school resembled those of
Lysenko's in the 1950s and early 1960s, when Lysenko conceded the legitimacy of DNA research, and offered sophistries to justify his continuing
rejection of genetics.[73] But there has been a striking difference between the
passivity of the psychiatrists and the assertiveness of the geneticists, who

TABLE 1 Doctors and beds for the mentally ill: (a) 1890–1940

Years for which figures, sometimes inconsistent, are available in the public record

	1890	1895	1902	1909	1912	1916	1922	1924	1925	1928	1932	1935	1940
(Numbers in thousands)													
All hospital beds					208					250			790.9
Hospital beds:													
for 'mentally ill'				35	42.2[a] 48[a]		12.9[a]	14	16.6[a]	26.4[b]	31.3[b]	48	82.9
for 'neurally ill'													
for forensic psychiatric cases													10
Approximate ratio of beds for mentally ill to all hospital beds													1 to 9.5
All physicians	14	16	20	25[c]	23					65			142
Psychiatrists	0.18	0.26	0.41			0.35					0.538[b]		1.55
											1.39		2.36
													2.4
Neuropathologists											0.743[b]		2.66
													3.21

(The following numbers are not in thousands)

Approximate ratio of psychiatrists to all physicians	1 to 80	1 to 60	1 to 50	1 to 60
Number of all hospital beds per 10,000 of population		13		40
Number of all physicians per 10,000 of population		1.5		7

TABLE 1   Doctors and beds for the mentally ill: (b) 1950–80

Years for which figures, sometimes inconsistent, are available in the public record

(Numbers in thousands)

	1950	1951	1955	1958	1959	1960	1963	1970	1974	1975	1980
All hospital beds			1288.9	1532.5	1618	1739.2		2663.3	2933	3009	3324
Hospital beds:											
for 'mentally ill'	71.8		106.5	138.2	149.6	162.2		267.9	300.6	312.6	d
for 'neurally ill'	15.1		18.9	23.8	26.1	29.9		71.5	89.4	94	d
						30.5					
for forensic psychiatric cases							1.65				
Approximate ratio of beds for mentally ill to all hospital beds			1 to 12	1 to 11	1 to 11	1 to 11		1 to 10	1 to 9.5	1 to 9.5	
All physicians	265		310	362	380	431.7		668.4	799	835.2	995.6
						402					
Psychiatrists	3.1	2.82	4.78	5.76	6.15	6.39		14.3	17.7	18.7	d
								14.5			
Forensic psychiatrists							0.67				
Neuropathologists	5.1	4.21	7.57	9.24	9.85	10.5		18.1	20.5	21.4	d
								17.9			

(The following numbers are not in thousands)

Approximate ratio of psychiatrists to all physicians	1 to 90	1 to 65	1 to 65	1 to 65	1 to 65	1 to 65	1 to 45	1 to 45	1 to 45
Number of all hospital beds per 10,000 of population	65	73	76	80			109.2	117.2	124.9
Number of all physicians per 10,000 of population	16	17	18	19			27.4	32.7	37.4

Ratios of psychiatrists to all physicians are only roughly comparable before and after 1940, when the published data begin to give numbers of psychiatrists and neuropathologists as separate categories. The distinction between the 'mentally ill' and the 'neurally ill' raises analogous problems.

[a] Patients, rather than beds.

[b] RSFSR only; in 1932 add 11,000 beds outside hospitals (in sanitoria, 'colonies', homes). Cf. n. 34.

[c] Estimate for 1910 by Nancy Frieden, *Russian Physicians in an Era of Reform and Revolution, 1856–1905* (Princeton, 1981), p.323. Cf. Gordon Hyde, *The Soviet Health Service; A Historical and Comparative Study* (London, 1974), and Michael Kaser, *Health Care in the Soviet Union and Eastern Europe* (Boulder, Colo., 1976).

[d] No further data in the public record until 1987: 335 for 'mentally ill', 142.3 for 'neurally ill', and 125.5 for 'narcological' cases. For the years since the Second World War, see especially the statistical series, *Narodnoe khoziaistvo SSSR v 1960 godu* (Moscow, 1961), *et seq.* For earlier years, see especially the psychiatric journals, monographs, and proceedings of congresses, as cited in notes.

Diverse publications have provided the figures in this table.

attacked Lysenkoism as it retreated, until they finally achieved the withdrawal of political support from that pseudo-science. By contrast, non-
Snezhnevskian psychiatrists continued to show the restraint that they learned
so quickly in the 1950s. The so-called Leningrad school, to take the most
notable center of silent disagreement, was not totally deprived of print by
Snezhnevskii's control of the country's one psychiatric journal. Leningrad
research institutions published occasional volumes, in which they systematically avoided offense to Snezhnevskii. They published very little on
schizophrenia; they never made explicit criticism of Snezhnevskii's views;
they inserted little tokens of explicit obeisance to him, if only in vague
terms.[74] One can only assume that these timid psychiatrists were censoring
themselves to avoid reprimand by officials in the medical and ideological
bureaucracies, who would presumably object to conflicts that might 'dis-
organize the cadres'.

Let us seek appropriate standards of criticism, both of the cosmopolitan
profession and of the national milieux within which particular branches are
submerged. The intellectual fragmentation of the psychiatric profession can
approach chaos, as we in the scandal-mongering West are reminded every
time a mass murderer brings a carnival of discordant psychiatrists into the
courts and the newspapers. In the West we still feel free to indulge our taste
for such scandal, as an exciting flirtation with social chaos. Soviet authorities
are still obsessively fearful of such flirtations — even as they venture into
'openness' and 'new thinking' — and most of their subjects give dutiful
signs of sharing the fears. There may be much genuine feeling, along with
cynical pretense, in those submissive signs of shared fearfulness. The living
memory of Soviet rulers and subjects retains terrible experiences of murderous chaos on such a massive scale, of such a wild intensity, as we in the
West retain only in the ghostly memory of historians.

We must keep in mind not only major differences in social contexts, but
also differences in the internal standards of knowledge, the implicit
epistemologies, of the various learned professions. Soviet geneticists were
pushed into militant defense of their profession not simply by the political
pressure of Lysenkoism but also by the highly formal character of their
discipline. They simply could not do their work without the concepts and
methods that Lysenko denounced. In other branches of biology specialists
could avoid that clash, and they tended to do so. Plant physiologists, for
example, resembled the 'Leningrad school' of psychiatrists in avoiding
controversial topics, such as plant hormones and stages of growth, which
were areas of conflict with Lysenko's pseudo-scientific beliefs. Plant physiology is such a sprawling discipline that its devotees could find tasks to
keep them busy without challenging Lysenko's beliefs.[75] They did so, and
so did the non-Snezhnevskian psychiatrists, whose discipline is even further
than plant physiology from the formal character, the monistic epistemology
of genetics. Epistemological pluralism has permitted the Soviet devotees of

many disciplines to be conscientious professionals while evading conflict with their little Stalins. They can have the sweet cake of a successful career without spending the penny of professional self-respect. Geneticists were an exception to that rule — as mathematicians and physicists would have been if the Party-state had attacked their mode of inquiry.

The natural sciences have not been major breeding grounds of the Stalinist mentality, or of resistance to it. When Soviet political authorities have intruded upon the intellectual autonomy of the natural sciences, specialists have usually been able to find some respectable way to evade conflict. The most widespread and persistent types of political intrusion have been in the explicitly philosophical or ideological interpretations of the sciences, in the political views of the scientists, and in their organizational ethos. That last has been the least noticed but probably the most significant in its effects. A tendency toward extreme centralization of authority within a discipline tends to inhibit creativity, even when the lines of authority converge upon a genuine scientist. Most natural scientists have found it possible to be professionally respectable, though not very creative, while kowtowing to all three types of political intrusion, or finding modes of evasion. The strictly professional commitment of their disciplines has only rarely got in the way of such kowtowing and evading, though creativity has suffered. Thus, there is little in the natural sciences that might push either scientists or political leaders toward liberalization, except the yearning for creativity, the shame of boasting the world's greatest number of scientists and the smallest number of Nobel laureates, not to speak of the persistent Soviet lag in applied science.

One might expect the human sciences to generate a lot of conflict with the Stalinist mentality, since they overlap so much with the knowledge claimed by political leaders and have been so grossly subjected to political interference. Yet the human sciences have generated relatively little resistance to the Stalinist mentality. Indeed, they have engendered many autonomous models of Stalinist thinking, as in the case of Snezhnevskii's school of psychiatry. Little Stalins with advanced degrees have dominated such disciplines as history and economics longer, and more ruinously, than Snezhnevskii ruled over psychiatry. I would offer a general rule: the broader the commitment to a scientific understanding of human beings, the greater the vulnerability to the Stalinist mentality.

Many people will prefer the familiar contrast of 'soft' science and 'hard', as the crucial difference that makes for vulnerability or invulnerability to the Stalinist mentality. Authoritarian pretense of scientific knowledge is much easier when a discipline is 'mushy' than when it is 'firm'. But such terms are themselves a fuzzy way of distinguishing between the sciences that explain people and those that explain utterly impersonal objects. Psychiatry is an exceptionally revealing case, for it combines the two types of knowledge. To the extent that human beings can be studied as bodies, the pattern of the natural sciences emerges. To the extent that human beings are persons, forms of mental stuff, a strikingly different pattern emerges, both within the learned professions and among outsiders such as Soviet political authorities. Where minds are to be explained, learned specialists divide into warring schools, and their professional disputes are connected in obvious ways with ideological and political issues, if only with the issue of liberal open-mindedness *v.* illiberal certainty. Of course warring schools and plainly political intrusion occasionally appear in the natural sciences, as in the Lysenko affair or the current American dispute over creationism. But such divisions and conflicts are so much more frequent and intense in the human sciences as to suggest a difference not just in degree but in kind. There is something in the study of human beings as minds or persons which obstructs the unforced consensus that is so prominent a feature of the natural sciences.

To get a clear view of that obstructive something one must look past the human sciences to the frankly humanistic disciplines, and beyond them to the frankly ideological and artistic modes of explaining and comprehending ourselves as human beings. There the possibility of somatic reduction becomes wholly metaphysical, or achieves concrete expression in obviously metaphorical forms, as in Freud's doctrine. Knowledge of ourselves as minds or persons is irremediably ideological or artistic and therefore pluralist, teetering on the edge of chaotic disorder. Political authorities intent on *Gleichschaltung* find themselves in constant conflict with artists, whose profession it is — in modern societies — to be not merely pluralist but even individualist in the knowledge they offer of ourselves as persons. That type of knowledge necessarily fuses fact and feeling, and therefore generates tensions that help define a community, by holding opposed visionaries in fearful respect of each other — or they help explode a community into civil war, as in Russia in our century. Different countries, with different experiences of the precarious balance between cohesion and disintegration, have developed different ways of maintaining a balanced tension, or striving to beat back incipient chaos.

The practical art of treating disturbed people reveals the different ways in starker fashion than the fine art of treating characters in fiction or drama. The most striking difference appears between 'backward' and 'advanced', or 'underdeveloped' and 'developed', countries. Incidence of hospital confinement for mental illness is low in 'backward' or 'underdeveloped' countries, high in 'advanced' or 'developed' ones. Let us call that Esquirol's law, to honor the first discussion of the pattern in 1824, by one of the founding fathers of modern psychiatry.[76] He noted that the number of psychiatric patients rises to meet or exceed the supply of hospital beds and mental doctors provided for them. He attributed the trend to progress in diagnostic science and in social benevolence, and beat back the gloomier possibility, that the stress of advancing civilization causes more and more minds to break down. He did not even consider the possibility that confinement for mental illness is an artifact of those who would dominate modern society by scientific reason, a way of maintaining confidence in the healthiness and rationality of the existing system, by shutting away the sick, irrational people who do not spontaneously fit themselves into it.

When we say that the sloppy diagnostic habits of Snezhnevskii's school helped to fill Soviet mental hospitals as fast as they could be built and staffed, we are noting a special instance of Esquirol's law, and we are doing so in hostile fashion. We are showing our eagerness to blame those who dominate the Soviet version of modern development. We are judging them too eager to confine, excessively anxious in their forceful claims of a rational and humane system. In 1980 a Soviet author still had an inclination to read the increase in psychiatric patients and confining doctors in Esquirol's manner, as evidence of progress in social benevolence and 'improvement in diagnostics', and she was glad to note that 'this viewpoint remains dominant among psychiatrists to the present time.'[77] She did not ponder the recent decrease in hospitalized patients in Western countries, or wonder whether her own country should start trying to catch up with *this* trend. It may indicate a decline of arrogant self-confidence among doctors of the mind and political authorities, or a new departure in social benevolence, perhaps toward greater respect for the autonomy of disturbed people, perhaps toward greater stinginess in caring for them, a growing indifference that comes disguised as self-restraint among the people at the top and freedom for wretches at the bottom. In 1988 the Soviet press disclosed that a new chief of psychiatry has indeed started his country in that direction.[78]

Scientific explanation of people is still alienated from human understanding of them, more so than it was when Vygotsky tried to overcome the alienation. His grand theorizing is published now, and largely ignored. Foucault caught some attention with his denunciation of the scientific belief that the insane cannot be understood as persons, that they must be explained as malfunctioning objects in need of repair. Foucault had no practicable alternative, just inane enthusiasm for Freudian efforts to commune with 'the madman'.[79] He ignored the record of Freudian or psychodynamic theories of schizophrenia, which were as sloppy as Snezhnevskii's in putting terrible labels on disturbed people, and sometimes crueler in speculative constructs that were supposed to join human understanding with scientific explanation. The 'schizophrenogenic mother' was a special shocker of the psychodynamic school: she induces schizophrenia by putting her children in a 'double bind', getting them to believe that nothing is more important than pleasing mother and nothing they might do could possibly please her.[80] Offering such explanation-cum-understanding to disturbed people and their parents seems to me as savagely pseudo-scientific as the physical treatments that the dominant medical materialists have used upon severely disturbed people: surgical excision of organs supposed to be infected, shock to the errant brain by insulin or electricity or induced fever, protracted drugged sleep, and ugliest of all the lobotomy: an icepick through the eye socket into the forebrain. (In the West a Nobel Prize was given in 1949 to one of the inventors of the lobotomy, which was discouraged and then banned in Soviet Russia, in part because Pavlov recommended drugged sleep.[81])

Szasz denounces his fellow psychiatrists as quasi-Stalinist authoritarians, who lord it over disturbed people by pretending to have scientific explanations of their disturbances and thus the know-how of treatment. But Szasz is as far as Foucault from a practicable alternative, perhaps farther, for he mocks the whole notion of schizophrenia while accepting the medical materialism that engenders it. He promises to accept the reality of schizophrenia if and when it is rigorously defined and demonstrably reduced to specific neural disorders. Until such time he is free to feel holier than the average practitioner confronting severely disturbed persons, knowing the inadequacy of his knowledge yet compelled to do something, especially when suicide is a strong possibility. Snezhnevskii turned that situation to self-pitying justification of authority, mouthing a cliché about 'the tragic position of psychiatry', obliged to act with insufficient knowledge.[82] Kurt Schneider turned such self-awareness toward self-restraint, by exposing the paradox within the concept of *Wahn* (delusion, mania, madness): 'Where there is genuine *Wahn*, there understanding of psychic character ceases; and where understanding is possible, there is no *Wahn*.'[83]

That is a psychiatrist's confession, that his profession cannot understand the seriously disturbed person as a person. We — the profession of mental doctors and the society that sustains it — cannot help treating the insane mind as the symptom of some physical disorder, even when we know that we lack knowledge of the disorder. The insane are persons whom we must reduce to physical objects and 'treat', whether or not we have the necessary knowledge, sometimes winning their submission to the culturally imposed project, sometimes forcing it. We are not as different as we suppose from Snezhnevskii's school and the Stalinist society that engendered it. Indeed, the medieval French doctor who drove evil spirits from a woman by incising a cross in her scalp and rubbing salt in it seems uncomfortably similar to the mental doctors of our century.[84] The main difference is in the figurative symbols that the doctor's confident mind-brain-hand projects upon the patient's disjointed mind and body.

Part V
After Stalin

16

Psychologies and Ideologies

'Psychology' points either to mental process or to the study of it, and within that ambiguity of the word are at least four more of the concept, expressing different notions of what mind is. *Scientific*: Mind is a function of nervous systems, to be explained by neurophysiology, behavioral analysis, and neuropsychology. *Aesthetic*: Mind is the creator of human meaning, expressed in human intercourse, above all in language and art forms. Studying such works of the mind yields psychology as understanding. *Ideological*: Mind is a collective function of social relations, organized in historically changing ways, above all in ideologies that mobilize individual minds to serve group purposes. Studying those ideological aspects of social relations yields psychology, whether as scientific explanation or as expressive understanding. Many tidy minds have tried to bring order to this plurality of psychologies either by monistic edict, or by eclectic diplomacy, or by retreating to some *philosophical* dreamworld of essential or authentic mind — a fourth type of psychology that deserves especially gentle solicitude in its present ruin.

The types are frequently mixed up, though usually without acknowledgment, for their underlying premises are too obviously in conflict. In our time the most common defense against such disorder has been isolation, shrinking within some community of fellow believers in one particular type of psychology, trained to ignore the others, which are supposed to wither away as the chosen type grows irresistibly perfect — like antagonistic classes and the state vis-à-vis authentic community in the dream of communism. The withering away visibly fails to occur, the dreamers grow dispirited, but they go on with their varied labors. Scientific, aesthetic, and ideological psychologies develop inertially, each with its own kind of cacophonous multiplicity, and all together making such a chaos of the mind that heaven would surely call a halt, if heaven were still there to put meaning in human affairs. A realistic appraisal of modern psychology must take note of all that.

Russia has provided an extreme test of these incongruities. The Tsarist regime was determined to keep heaven and hell and the immortal soul working for the old order, and therefore tried for some years to block the rise of scientific psychologies. But in the 1860s, striving also to achieve modern power, Tsarist authorities backed off from that hopeless quarrel with modern high culture. Within the country's academies and universities soulless physiology and secular philosophy were permitted to engender increasingly soulless psychologies, while outside, among the population at large, official ideologists went on pointing to heaven and hell and the immortal soul as the ultimate justification of the old order. Meantime imaginative literature and unofficial ideologies were undermining the official faith among the educated, and also, in cruder and angrier ways, among the lower classes. Fifty years of such cultural disintegration, exacerbated by industrialization, chronic agrarian distress, and defeat in war, culminated in the popular overthrow of the old order, which the intelligentsia applauded, only to wring their hands as the emancipated lower classes used the new freedom to dissolve the armed forces, take over the factories, seize the land − maybe put an end to Russia as a multi-national state. The Bolsheviks took power; theirs was the only party that combined a will to state power with endorsement of the lower-class revolution.

Among the main sources of the Bolshevik will to power was the conviction that their understanding of human beings was scientific; so they were doubly angry, for intellectual as well as political reasons, when they met hostile disapproval among nearly all the intelligentsia, including professionals in the human sciences. The initial Bolshevik response was a mixture of political repression and ideological courtship, which permitted a brief continuation of genteel cultural disintegration. A new official ideology developed its claim to human understanding, while varied parts of high culture developed theirs, and little bands of Marxist intellectuals strove for harmony or unity through various mediations and compromises − until 1929, when Stalin's revolution from above started a frenzied crusade for a total unification of culture, a twenty-four-year period of all-out assault and pause, and renewed intensified assault and pause, and once again assault till all evidence of cultural disunity was destroyed or covered up. Three Pavlov Sessions punctuated that process in neurophysiology (1950), in psychiatry (1951), in psychology (1952). Each community of scholars was marshalled in a floodlit arena to criticize their non-Pavlovian past and make pledges of devotion to Pavlov's doctrine, which was supposed to unify the science of the mind-brain as the doctrine of Marx-Engels-Lenin-Stalin unified social science. Imaginative writers were supposed to work as 'engineers of human souls' within that frame of scientific reference.

The vehemence of the Stalinist assaults on high culture confessed their intellectual failure. Party discipline and state power were forcing outward confession of an ever cruder credo, ever further from the actual beliefs of the confessing scholars and writers. Even before Stalin's death (in 1953) the ideological establishment was already beginning its tacit retreat, the painfully protracted withdrawal of political compulsion from high culture, which still claims to be no retreat but a consolidation of victory. The established ideology still divides psychology into conflicting universes, the 'bourgeois' – foreign, decadent, divided against itself – and the Soviet, which is native, progressive, unified by Marxism-Leninism and Pavlov's doctrine. Yet the dichotomy has become largely ceremonial; the establishment has mostly conceded in practice what it still denies in principle, the striving of Soviet psychologists to do as their Western colleagues do, to seek kudos in the cosmopolitan contest of scientific disciplines and schools.

This wavering between two worlds, a Russian-Orthodox or Russian-Communist dreamworld of meaningful unity *v.* the real world of modern cultural disorder, can be observed throughout the past 150 years, often within the minds of individual thinkers. But the wavering has also taken the startling form of an extreme historical zigzag by people in power: a drift toward cosmopolitan acceptance of cultural pluralism in the last half-century of the Tsarist regime, a plunge toward nativist unification in the first thirty-five years of the Soviet regime, and once again, since the mid-1950s, a drift toward cultural pluralism. An analogous wavering of minds and a similar zigzag in cultural policies have been apparent in China and the other countries that have had indigenous Communist revolutions, which suggests a broad simple explanation to many observers: Marxist ideology. *It* has been the cause of the violent plunge for cultural unity, and it has been defeated by the necessity of cultural pluralism that inheres in economic development. Thus, in this common view of Communist history, Marxist ideology must give way to 'pragmatism', a colloquial term that no longer refers to the earnest moral philosophy of William James but simply to the rule: theory be damned, whatever wins is right.

That familiar scheme is less an explanation of Communist revolutions and their aftermath than a sermon against Marxism – a superficial, unhistorical sermon. It ignores the large fact that Marxist ideology has been drastically different things in different contexts, and the fact that 'pragmatism' is found in many of them. Stalinists and Maoists earnestly invoked 'the criterion of practice' in their drives for cultural unity, and so did German Social Democrats in their acceptance of cultural pluralism. Historians cannot explain such diversity by imitating shallow preachers, gesturing toward some abstract bookish ideology, whether of Marxism or of pragmatism, as the source of wisdom or wickedness. We have hindsight, we can see what people back then could not, how particular clusters of belief interacted with other parts of the historical process to produce results at odds with expectations.

We can seek such retrospective foresight with an emphasis either on political or on intellectual culture in their interaction. We may ask, for example, whether the Tsarist state helped to bring on its own collapse by piecemeal surrender to cultural pluralism — the obvious answer is yes, but what else could it do? — or whether the state that the Bolsheviks rebuilt was strengthened more than weakened by their extreme ideological mobilization of culture. The obvious answer once again is yes, but — in this case still unresolved, for the Bolshevik state is still in place. Its rulers and subjects are still struggling to find some endurable balance of unity and diversity. However that works out, even if the state should collapse tomorrow, its seventy years of power will still demand explanation, which requires illumination of the regime's changing hold on the beliefs of various groups, and vice versa: the changing influence of those groups on the evolving ideology of state.

Thus political inquiry must be interwoven with intellectual, asking for example to what extent various intellectual enterprises have supported or subverted this or that cluster of official beliefs, or have labored away indifferently in neutral space. The quickest way to sense the bite of such inquiry is to wonder why imaginative writers are often said to be an alternative government, both in the Tsarist and the Bolshevik context, but scientific psychologists are not. Chernyshevsky dreamed that the scientists would play the rebel, but Sechenov and all the others have steadfastly refused to accept the part. The refusal is an integral part of their scientific project. Whether working at the neural basis of mental functions or seeking their objective laws some other way, scientific psychologists try hard to eliminate 'subjectivity' from psychology. They cannot agree on how to accomplish such an amputation, but they share the underlying assumption that it must be done, since mind is not a self-expressing entity but a function of something other than itself. It is adaptive and so are they. Imaginative writers are often quite different, for they are obsessed with subjectivity, the conscious 'I' at the center of experience that may or may not approve what it experiences. Such troublesome writers seemed to disappear during the twenty-four years of Stalinist assaults on deviant minds, but some were there all along, and emerged to view at the first sign of Stalinist retreat.

SCIENTISTS AND IDEOLOGIES

In 1955 Piaget and two eminent French psychologists visited the Institute of Psychology in Moscow, fearing to see their discipline ruined by the official drive for Pavlov's doctrine. They were delighted to find almost a hundred well-equipped researchers working at projects very like those they knew at home. Each prefaced explanation of their work with 'a simplistic reference to Pavlov. Then came an account of the concrete research, full of riches, based on adequate methodologies, in which there was no longer any question of conditioned reflexes or higher nervous activity, except when those explanations were pertinent.'[1] In the evening the three Westerners found themselves with

> the five big men of the time: Leont'ev, Luria, Smirnov, Rubinshtein, and Teplov, munching dried fruit and eating oranges. One of them – in an aside – picked up two halves of an orange that had been emptied of their content, put them together, and said to me: 'You see, Pavlovianism is like this orange; it is very beautiful,' and separating the two peels, he added: 'But you see, inside it is empty.' An excessive quip, to be sure, but it illuminated a climate.[2]

It did indeed illuminate a climate – Soviet, post-Stalin thaw – though not as simply as scientists would like to believe, laughing off ideology and returning to talk of pure science. After all, students of the mind-brain extracted some scientific nourishment from the Pavlovian orange, which needs to be distinguished from the discarded peel that the ideological establishment imposed upon psychologists and physiologists. Ideologies are never as distinct from other types of knowledge as when an external authority makes them mandatory. That is one reason for the fascination of Soviet intellectual history, with its scandalous clashes between ideas imposed by an ideological establishment and ideas maintained by thinkers under pressure. As we discover what psychologists and physiologists stubbornly or slyly insisted upon, and what they obliged the ideological establishment to concede, we go beyond gross palpable differences between scientific inquiry and ideological conviction. We illuminate the internal differences between inquiry and conviction within the two types of community, scientific researchers and political bureaucrats. Neither type has a purely open or an utterly closed mind; learning is possible within both.

We also gain insight into the evolution of the Soviet system, its new twists in the Russian tension between *vlast'* and *obshchestvennost'*, state power and educated opinion. The scholar's quip that laughed off officially imposed belief was told in private; none of the psychologists ever hinted at such heresy in public. Even at the headiest moment of the post-Stalin thaw they regularly deferred to established orthodoxy, which continued to require lip service to Pavlov's doctrine, and still does. But it is also true that psychologists refused to give more than lip service even while Stalin lived, and the ideological establishment did not seriously press them for more, not even in the fearful last months of Stalin's reign when another peak of mass terror seemed in the works.

In 1952–3 the anti-cosmopolitan campaign mounted to a climactic announcement, portending show trials, that nine physicians – six of them Jewish – had been arrested for killing high officials.[3] But only a few scientists collapsed in fearful self-criticism and strenuous disavowals of suspect ideas. Luria felt sufficiently endangered – by his Jewishness, I would imagine, by his medical connection, by his renown in the West — to repudiate the work that had won the renown: precise correlations of particular types of aphasia with particular areas of brain damage. He had been un-Pavlovian, he confessed, 'in superimposing the non-spatial concepts of contemporary psychology on the spatial construction of the brain'.[4] In the newspaper of the medical profession he published a denunciation of the Western world that fostered such neuropsychology, singling out Sherrington's 'reactionary' school of neurophysiology and all of American psychology; serving imperialism, it had 'ceased to be a branch of scientific knowledge'.[5] But such groveling was not typical of the profession. When the psychologists had their Pavlov Session, in the summer of 1952, the keynote speakers did not endorse, they attacked 'the nihilist attitude toward the psychological legacy', 'the troglodyte moods we encounter in some comrades, who believe that the reconstruction of psychology on the basis of Pavlovian physiology means the obliteration of Soviet psychology and all its achievements'.[6]

Stalin was still in charge in 1952, but the post-Stalin thaw was beginning. The Pavlov Session for psychologists was an exercise in swearing hollow oaths to an established cause that no one wished to serve but no one knew how to disestablish. That had not been the dominant pattern at the first Pavlov Session, in 1950 for neurophysiologists; the ideological establishment had seriously disturbed their discipline by thrusting a literal version of Pavlov's doctrine upon it. At the second Session, in 1951 for psychiatrists, Pavlov's banner was fluttered over issues to which it had no relevance, while Stalinist clinicians rose to command a practical profession, as they would for the next thirty-six years. At the third Pavlov Session, in 1952 for psychologists, the sacred doctrine was potentially quite relevant — it beckoned toward behaviorism and the reduction of mental to neural processes — but almost no one wanted to go that way.

Not the ideological establishment, which condemned behaviorism as a dehumanizing ideology in the service of capitalism and still remembered Karl Marx's scorn for physiological materialism; not Pavlov's creative disciples, who had moved away from the master's simplistic scheme of reduction, toward the correlation of mental and neural processes; and least of all the psychologists. Since the emergence of their profession in the pre-revolutionary period — from the school of Wundt through Chelpanov, with a strong subsequent influence of Gestalt — Russian psychologists had been overwhelmingly mentalist and therefore indifferent to Pavlov's doctrine. The battering they had suffered in the 1930s, when the Central Committee denounced intelligence tests, had driven them still further from behaviorism or physiological reduction. They had been pressed to justify themselves in applied psychology by following Makarenko's educational doctrine, which is as far from any kind of physiology as the doctrines of self-improvement preached by popular psychologists in America. In research the most respected psychologists did cognitive studies of child development or of brain-damaged people, and those kinds of research simply cannot be reconciled with the notion that the conditioned reflex is the elemental unit of all learned behavior.

To be sure, in 1952 there were some ideologists who were virtually demanding the liquidation of psychological science, its replacement by a single science of nerves, with Pavlovian studies of 'higher nervous activity' as the highest level. Such abolitionists were prominent in philosophical publications, but they were hardly in evidence at the Pavlov Session for psychologists.[7] The keynote speakers there were A. A. Smirnov and B. M. Teplov, old-timers of the eclectic school that derived from Chelpanov. Though the tub-thumping theme of the Session was the Pavlovian reconstruction of psychology, the more telling counterpoint was the confession that no one knew how to realize that dream. Vague gestures toward a future reconstruction were all that anyone could manage. Meantime Pavlovian quotations and paraphrases were beaded into a metapsychology that justified the continued coexistence of two sciences, psychology as well as neurophysiology. Pavlovian study of 'higher nervous activity' was supposed someday to unify the two, but no one could say how or when.

Everyone leaned especially on the master's brief references to a 'second signal system', which he imagined to mediate speech and thought. The phrase pointed toward an undiscovered system of nerves or perhaps a mysterious function of the known system — in either case, a realm unknown to neurophysiology, and thus by default the domain of psychological science. That continuing duality of scientific disciplines suggested philosophical dualism to the guardians of ideology, but the leading psychologists stood up for their autonomous discipline anyhow. Teplov, author of the most widely used textbook of psychology, defended it against the charge of dualism that had appeared in the central press. Indeed, he defiantly repeated the basic observation that had provoked the charge: 'In a system of physiological concepts there is no place for such concepts as sensation, thinking, feeling, etc.; they are the subject matter of psychology.'[8]

The metapsychology that linked the two disciplines reached above Pavlov to Lenin for its justification: the brain 'reflects' reality in a single process studied by two scientific disciplines and sanctified by a third, dialectical materialist philosophy. With that trinitarian reassurance to the ideological establishment the psychologists at the 1952 Session went beyond apology to demands. They resolved that the recently created Scientific Council on Pavlov's Doctrine must be balanced by an equally dignified Council on Psychology, and they demanded the revival of a professional journal, which had been denied to their discipline since the mid-1930s.[9] Their 1952 resolution even chose the title, *Problems of Psychology*, which the journal had when it materialized in 1955.

Stalin was dead by that time, the thaw was on, and the editors boldly displayed, with the iconic magic of photocopy, the handwritten letter that Pavlov had sent to Chelpanov in 1914, warmly congratulating him on the founding of the Institute of Psychology.[10] It was the same Institute that Piaget came to visit in 1955, for it was still the center of the profession though it had been transferred from Moscow University to the Academy of Pedagogical Sciences and ostensibly transformed from a 'bourgeois' to a Marxist world view. The job of explaining the brain, Pavlov wrote,

> is so inexpressibly large and complex that all the resources of thought are demanded: absolute freedom, complete renunciation of stereotypes, as great a diversity as possible in points of view and modes of activity, and so on, in order to guarantee success. All mental workers, from whatever angle they may approach the subject, all will discover something in their field, and the fields of all sooner or later will combine to solve the greatest problem of human thought.
>
> That is why I, who exclude in my laboratory work on the brain the slightest reference to subjective states, with all my heart hail your Psychological Institute and warmly wish you complete success.[11]

However closed Pavlov's mind was within his own scientific discipline, it was determinedly open in external relations with other disciplines and creeds. Illiberal monism was his scientific ideology; his political creed was liberal pluralism.

That is a characteristic incongruity of scientific minds in the modern world, and it was still strong among Soviet scientists in the 1950s, though they did not feel free to confess the liberal part openly. With token oaths of unified allegiance to Pavlov's doctrine they hushed up the continuing rivalry of disciplines and schools in efforts to explain the mind–brain, and of course they suppressed any cry of shame on the ideological establishment for trying to impose a single doctrine on all. Stalin's death and the cessation of mass terror emboldened psychologists to reproduce Pavlov's letter on the need for political pluralism, but they could not bring themselves to express that creed in their own voice. As for *philosophical* pluralism, the thought that mind and nerves may *not* be explainable by a single science, that the universe may be 'all spots and jumps, without unity, without continuity, without coherence or orderliness or any of the other properties that governesses love' — those are Bertrand Russell's words[12] — Soviet psychologists most likely never gave a thought to such a shocking proposal, whether in after-dinner conversations or even in the privacy of their individual minds. It would have been doubly subversive, not only of the ideological establishment that required oaths of allegiance to a present doctrine but also of their own labors toward a unified science of the future, which would command universal acceptance without political force.

Reverence for the monistic ideal, the dream of a single science of the mind-brain, is constantly shown by psychologists and physiologists, without any coercion, in any political context, whether pre- or post-revolutionary, Russian or Western. It is the conventional faith of their worldwide fellowship. They look askance when dissidents like Sherrington or Eccles find dualism in the physiologist's exclusion of mind from the analysis of nervous systems, and they simply ignore suggestions of a pluralist universe, which come occasionally from such mavericks as William James or Bertrand Russell. The conventional faith in monism and its attendant blindsight are even shared by most neuropsychologists, such as Luria, who labor to correlate mental and neural processes but avoid any suggestion that they may both be substantial realities. The neuropsychologist is proud to show, for example, that damage to this or that part of the brain may disrupt this or that arithmetical calculation, but he does not ask whether he has thereby identified the calculation with the machinery that carries it out. The answer, I think, would point too obviously toward some kind of philosophical pluralism.

In the nineteenth century the founders of experimental psychology thought a great deal about such problems, and into the twentieth century exceptionally thoughtful members of the new profession continued to combine some experimental approach with philosophical examination of its premises. But such broadly cultured individuals have grown quite rare; the dominant type is the one that labors at a particular experimental strategy on the unexamined assumption that sometime, somehow, the results will justify the premises, even among the multitudes of unbelievers. The narrowing trend is especially striking in the case of Vygotsky's disciples, who took advantage of the post-Stalin thaw to promote the conviction that theirs was *the* Soviet school of psychology. They quickly republished Vygotsky's 1934 collection of articles, *Thinking and Speech*, in which he had tried to placate the Stalinist shrieking for a distinctively Marxist-Leninist psychology, sharply opposed to 'bourgeois' science.[13] Then with great delays, measured in decades, the disciples brought out Vygotsky's earlier works, which had taken for granted the facts of life that had provoked the Stalinist outburst: the absence of a distinctively Soviet school of psychology, the cosmopolitan competition of various schools, none of which was authentically Marxist.

Entangled with the flammable matter of Soviet pride was the serious question whether a Marxist psychology is already at hand or only a dream, a philosophical possibility of some future solution for the foundational problems that confront all those who aspire to an objective science of the mind. In his major treatises of the 1920s, which Vygotsky could only pass among friends in manuscript form, he had argued that Marxist psychology was the latter, a possibility that would become a fact if Marxist psychologists showed their colleagues how to surmount the crisis of their discipline. His doctoral dissertation spelled out the fundamental antinomy −

scientific explanation *v.* aesthetic understanding – within the psychology of art. Then he examined the antinomy in the discipline at large, in 'The Historical Meaning of the Psychological Crisis'. Reading the manuscript in the late 1920s and early 1930s, the disciples identified it as Vygotsky's major work, but they could not or would not publish it until 1982, when it was discreetly enclosed within the first volume of his *Collected Works*, and was largely ignored by working psychologists.[14]

By the 1980s the book's central heresies had lost their frightful attractiveness. The ideological establishment had come to tolerate the similarity of Soviet and Western psychology, provided that Soviet scholars made ceremonial declarations of differences. And psychologists at large, whether in the Soviet Union or in the West, had stopped brooding over the antinomy that preoccupied Vygotsky. The project for an 'explanatory' science of the mind is still at odds with age-old aesthetic methods of 'understanding' it, and each project is still fragmented among inconsistent, if not incommensurable, disciplines and schools, but most psychologists have learned to keep their eyes down, focused on their own little isolated parts of the grand discord. Vygotsky's school is no exception to the rule. It mostly studies cognitive development in children, very much as Piaget's admirers do in the West.

To be sure, Vygotskians drape the banner of Marxism over their limited investigations. An 'historico-cultural' approach to the mind – that is their slogan, though they make no effort to revive Vygotsky's field studies of peasant mentalities, or his friendly interest in Freudian analysis of the unconscious, or his ruminations on an evolutionary sequence of mentalities rising from subhuman animals through various levels of human cultural development, pointing on toward the authentic humanity that Marx dreamed of. The Stalinist assaults of the 1930s destroyed such freewheeling mixtures of science, philosophy, and prophecy, while keeping some of their phrases as reverential decoration for specialized research.

Without the application of state power analogous shrinkage has been under way in the West, where specialists in child development use Piaget's methods and concepts with little more than token references to his large project on philosophy of mind. So Vygotskians have been doubly unjustified in declaring themselves different and broader. They have long been quite similar on child psychology and equally unconcerned with larger problems. Piaget lived long enough to discover, in the post-Stalin period, that Soviet psychologists were distorting his views to make themselves seem different; he made gentle protests, and gave published as well as verbal assurance that he agreed with Vygotsky on most issues of child psychology.[15] Even so, more than two decades of slow retreat from Soviet sectarianism preceded public acknowledgment that there is 'an analogy if not identity' between the two schools. To be sure, the speaker who conceded that point, at a 1981 conference on Vygotsky's achievement, did not surrender Soviet pride or Marxist hauteur. He made it seem that Piaget had somehow found his way, after Vygotsky though without his help, to a special part of the same grand Marxist vision: 'Although Vygotsky's views were practically unknown to Piaget [until the late 1950s], in its primary principles his genetic psychology can be regarded, in essence, as one of the possible concrete realizations of the historico-cultural understanding of the psyche which was proposed by Vygotsky.'[16]

In time, one would hope, Soviet scholars will feel free to note what is abundantly evident in the public record: that Vygotsky worked out his views on child development after Piaget, expressing generous appreciation to him as he did so — until the 1930s, when Stalinist yahoos shrieked for a uniquely Soviet Marxist mentality. One may even hope for a renewal of peasant studies or of interest in the unconscious. Modest signs of such revivals are already in view — as separate projects, unconnected with the Vygotsky school of cognitive psychology. Anthropologists and sociologists have attempted a revival of village studies, and Uznadze's disciples, the distinctive Georgian school of psychologists, have provided the chief center for renewed interest in the Freudian unconscious.[17] The psychology of art may even hope for some slight development, but it is quite unlikely that cognitive psychologists will try to draw such specialties together by pondering, as Vygotsky did, the underlying concepts and methods that separate them. Thoroughly modern specialists are content, when such issues obtrude, to make gestures of reverent dismissal toward great thinkers of the past, or toward the universal triumph of their favored school in the future.

As Stalinist force ebbs away from various fields in high culture, their self-created walls come in view, separating not only disciplines and schools but even different parts of individual minds. Among Vygotskians Luria provides the most revealing case, for he was so much more creative than the other disciples and he enjoyed twenty-four years of productive life after Stalin. He resumed his active intercourse with congenial Western psychologists and his habit of prolific publication abroad as well as at home, including popularizations and even an autobiography. In spite of his timid reticence and occasional dishonesty on politically sensitive topics, a powerful and original mind comes through to the reader, until one sees at last the deepest reason for the political complaisance of scientific psychology, its built-in protection against the insubordination that afflicts imaginative writers, their readers, and other ordinary devotees of aesthetic psychologies.

The scientific project shares with political bosses, the Soviet version included, an overwhelmingly conformist premise. Conscious striving to perform socially approved tasks is the essence of being human. With that prophylactic conviction the mind is protected against the deviant impulse that repeatedly afflicts imaginative writers, and many ordinary people in everyday life, who want to know what is really there within, at the center of conscious striving, and what is really there without, at the center of social approval. In certain contexts that impulse may move political types to radical action, but scientific types are inwardly protected against such waywardness.

Consider the record in more than a century of Russian history: during the period of Tsarist disintegration, while the intelligentsia at large was breeding radical activists by the thousand, I have found a single case of a psychologist who may possibly be counted in those ranks (Blonskii). During the post-Stalin decades of agitation for basic reforms I have found no case of a psychologist writing or speaking as a dissident. In between, during the revolutionary transformations named for Lenin and Stalin, numerous psychologists professed revolutionary Marxism, but that hardly alters the pattern of political complaisance, for the revolutionary regime strongly urged, then absolutely required, such demonstrations of conformity. The same pattern holds for neurophysiologists, with the possible exception of a few young men who joined the Party during the Civil War and became neuroscientists afterward.[18] If the long-term record of psychiatrists and medical neurologists has been marginally different — lots of radical speeches before 1917, and a few bold dissidents after Stalin — clinical practice is to blame, drawing them away from a purely scientific vision of their work, toward recognition of complicity in power.[19] They disliked such complicity before 1917, when the state was quite stingy to them; they have been overwhelmingly complaisant since the state became generous.

All that is evidence *en gros*, sociological. Consider the inward psychological evidence provided by Luria. His broadest summation, *The Working Brain: An Introduction to Neuropsychology*,[20] presents human beings as self-activating servo-mechanisms, programmed by their social context. There are distinctively Soviet elements in his version, but it is fundamentally similar to a major premise of the American behaviorists, who built into their science the worship of social winners, the contempt for losers, that form the operative faith of bosses and would-be bosses and submissive subjects in the USA no less than the USSR. At the same time, as Luria reveals in *The Man with a Shattered World*, he had a sensitive clinician's understanding of losers, such as his patient Zasetsky, whose dream of becoming a successful engineer was ruined by war damage to the problem-solving parts of his brain. The parts that maintained self-awareness and imagination were left intact. He could perceive and understand the revulsion that his incoherent speech and abnormal movements provoked in other people. His struggle to be human was confined to an effort, alone in a room, writing his experiences in notebooks, to transcend his '"know-nothing" world of emptiness and amnesia.'[21]

That is very close to the defiant reason that modern authors have given for writing, whether they speak of creating a momentary stay against confusion, or of carving on the wall of time some variant of the tourist's 'I was here', or of accepting the despot's rule that creative writing is an actionable deed.[22] Luria did not perceive that affinity between imaginative writers and his patient Zasetsky; he was reporting the case of a damaged mind, not an engineer of human souls. The implicit premises of scientific psychology exclude the notion that lonely defiance may be the essence of a physically normal brain-mind seeking to express itself. In the scientific as in the political vision the poet building a monument to himself (or to some city of God) is understandable only if humanity bows down, as it does to political idols.

Philosophical psychology has been conspicuously avoided in the writings of experimental psychologists, even such extraordinary ones as Luria, but it did not vanish in Soviet Russia. Indeed, it was heavily emphasized in the first two decades after Stalin died, as the apparent unity and uniqueness of Soviet culture began to crumble, and ideologists scrambled to explain and justify, still clinging to the official insistence on unity and uniqueness. So S. L. Rubinshtein enjoyed a great comeback, tacitly cleansed of the anti-cosmopolitan taint that had ruined his career during Stalin's final years. In 1956 he simply reappeared as Director of the Psychological Sector in the central Institute of Philosophy, with a renewed stream of publications to show that he was once again, in intellectual accomplishment as well as rank, the chief Marxist–Leninist interpreter of psychological science.

No effort was made to account for the six-year interval of ostracism and public abuse. Official ideologists retreated into silence on the Jewish question, unable to explain in public the whys and wherefores of governmental policies toward Jews, such as their systematic exclusion from governmental office – a policy that was continued and intensified after Stalin died – or the highly restrictive quotas on their admission to higher education – a policy enacted by unpublished decree in the late 1960s. The resemblance to policies of the late nineteenth century is evident not only in such particulars but also in the officials' inability to speak of them, in the strangulated silence that expresses inward conflict between nationalist conviction and the formal requirements of internationalist ideology. The silence is more intense now than it was back then, for Marxism–Leninism is much more insistently internationalist than the Tsarist claim to represent the divine order for all nations.

There is not a breath of such forbidden issues in Rubinshtein's publications. He had no inclination toward dissidence, though – or because – he was a grand ideologist of the vanishing breed that sought to connect everything with the one-in-all. In his seven years of life after Stalin he showed that mentality most notably in *Consciousness and Being* and in *Psychology's Principles and Paths of Development*, philosophico-historical treatises that expressed his distinctive thought more directly than the textbook of psychology which had been his chief work in the 1930s and

1940s.[23] In one obvious respect the works of the late 1950s were less
forthright: in reverence for Pavlov they went beyond a few perfunctory
gestures, and effusively kowtowed to him as the god of psychological science
— in the midst of arguments that are obviously non- or even anti-Pavlovian.
At some points an outsider begins to wonder if Rubinshtein was deliberately
mocking the cult of this god by draping absurdly ill-fitting clothes on him.
He even implied that Pavlov was sympathetic to Gestalt psychology,
giving references to passages that attacked that school, where Pavlov declared that the chimp solves puzzles as the dog is conditioned to salivate, by
a process of chance association, not by holistic insight.[24] It seems strange
that Rubinshtein made such a show of Pavlov-worship during the post-
Stalin thaw, when it became legitimate to say that the Pavlov Session of
1950 had been a bit excessive, and many psychologists — Luria among
them — were shrinking the ritual of Pavlov references toward the vanishing
point. One may suppose that Rubinshtein was offering extravagant reassurance to the officials who had staged the Session, and that he had no
fear of offending them by excess since Stalinist officials require excess.
Between adulation and rejection they perceive nothing but treacherous
concealment or timid indecision.

In any event Rubinshtein's voice was quite audible through the Pavlovian
static. 'The brain is only the *organ* of psychic activity, the man [*chelovek*] is
its *subject*. The feelings, and also the thoughts, of a man emerge in the
activity of the brain, but it is not the brain that loves and hates, knows and
changes the world, it is the man.'[25] Declarations of that sort hark back to
Rubinshtein's 1914 dissertation at Marburg and to his writings of the early
1920s, when he was still weighing the pros and cons of philosophical
idealism, absolute *v.* relative. In the 1930s he seized upon young Marx's
concept of revolutionary practice as the ontological basis of the human
world, and entered the Stalinist 'discussions' of rival psychologies brandishing that talisman. The scientific rivals dissolved into minor technicalities
within his grand vision:

> The interaction of the individual [*individ*] with the world, his *life*,
> whose demands are what led to the emergence of the brain as the
> organ of man's psychic activity, *practice* — that is the real material
> basis, in the frame of which the cognitive relationship to the world
> discloses itself; that is the 'ontological' basis on which is formed the
> subject's cognitive relationship to objective reality.[26]

On that ground, as a metaphysical philosopher might say, Rubinshtein
constructed not so much a system as a sequence of ruminations on mind as
'activity', which has been the central concept in Soviet philosophical psychology, lending itself then to metaphysical discourse, now mostly to
cybernetic modeling.[27]

Rubinshtein's purpose was less to judge the various trends and schools of psychology on their merits as science than to fit them within a Marxist-Leninist frame of judgment. A few — Freudianism most notably — he summarily condemned, and he found none worthy of unqualified blessing. But the judge's overall mood was balanced and cheerful. On the one hand he faulted psychologists who pictured the brain-mind as nothing more than a problem-solving machine within the natural order — of course he did not cite Pavlov in this connection — and on the other hand he deplored those — Sartre most notably — who dwelt painfully on the subjective mind as an alien presence in mindless nature. Rubinshtein sought the in-between. His ponderous prose labored to bring back confidence in the mind's harmonious participation both in objective nature and in the authentic subjectivity that creates itself in the historical process. Within the grand old dream of the official ideology he positioned himself as arbiter of rival psychologies, inviting specialists to enter the structure as he laid it out, to debate their scientific articulation of his metaphysical premises.

Only a few did so, in an elusive way, on issues of marginal import. Rubinshtein himself set the evasive pattern. He turned Pavlov's doctrine into holy water, and evinced his dislike for Vygotsky's school by an insulting disregard of their work. When his writings came to matters on which Vygotskians were eminent authorities, Rubinshtein conspicuously ignored them, citing Western authors instead, and the comparatively obscure Soviet psychologists who had some link to him.[28] The Vygotskians returned the snub, which suggests some petty hostility over appropriations and appointments, and also the sullen indifference between philosophical and experimental psychologists that has prevailed everywhere for a long time, not only in a country with an ideological establishment that paralyzed debate on fundamentals by insisting that everyone shares the same fundamental beliefs.

Rubinshtein was the master demonstrator of the Stalinist and neo-Stalinist commonality, with all its awkward silences and self-deceptions obscuring his authentic reflections on consciousness and being. So his similarities with Western blenders of Marxism, phenomenology, and existentialism went unnoticed. Further West than East Germany his works have been untranslated and unread, except by a handful of specialists in Soviet studies.[29] Even within the Soviet Union the continuing decay of the Stalinist context has been draining his texts of their significance for philosophers of mind. 'The "ontological" basis ... [of] the subject's cognitive relationship to objective reality' — with or without Rubinshtein's apologetic quotation marks — has scant significance for scholars who are less and less preoccupied with the ideologists' one-in-all and more and more with cybernetic modeling of cognitive systems.

Given that trend one might expect the Pavlovian legacy to be enjoying a fresh flowering, and it is — of a kind that cannot be celebrated in his own country. There 'Pavlov's doctrine' has remained a sacred term for everything of value in all the diverse fields of psychology and neuroscience, so it can hardly be a subject of meaningful discussion or testing. Outside the Soviet Union scientists speak plainly of 'Pavlovian' or 'classical conditioning' as a certain type of individually acquired behavior, distinct from other types, its mechanism to be discovered, its place in the taxonomy of behavior to be defined. Pavlov's insistence that he had accomplished both tasks — discovered the mechanism, defined the taxonomic place — was set aside long ago, but a large number of scientists have continued to share his conviction that conditioning is the most promising area of inquiry for the explanation of mind as neural function. Fresh experimentation and theorizing keep branching out of that conviction in the prolific manner that indicates a powerful source of scientific creativity. The persistent hope is to achieve at last the reduction of cognitive psychology to neuroscience. The persistent result, as the historian of ideas sees it, is the regeneration of separateness, of division between the two fields.

There is no space here to support that conclusion by a thorough review of studies of conditioning since the 1920s, when American behaviorists distressed Pavlov by taking his ideas seriously enough to test and change them.[30] Suffice to say that some — Lashley most notably — pointed the inquiry toward the neural mechanisms of conditioning, and ended by imagining a hypothetical engram distributed who-knows-where in the nervous system, some alteration of nerve tissue that keeps results of past experience available for future use. For a long time most behaviorists preferred the black-box approach, correlating stimuli and responses to achieve fine distinctions among behavioral patterns, postponing the effort to discover the neural mechanisms even of the simplest pattern. Since the 1960s neuroscientists have come into the field in increasing number, confident, as they like to say, that the time has come to open up the black box. But they have been opening so many — that is, establishing so many correlations between alterations of behavior and alterations of neural action — that generalization seems impossible; catalogs seem the only way to store their data. But Edward Manier, a philosophical outsider, carefully studying the output of two leading research groups, has discerned a bifurcation that seems quite familiar to this historian. I therefore feel free to simplify his analysis, and adapt it to my perspective.[31]

Down below linkages in the cerebral cortex, where Pavlov thought he had located the mechanisms of conditioning, below the subcortical circuits of mammalian brains, where Beritashvili and Anokhin hunted — and many scientists are still searching — down among the tiniest parts of the most elementary nervous systems in animals without brains — roaches, locusts, jellyfish, snails — the hardest of the mind's hard scientists have been seeking its most elementary mechanism. In their most notable work of the recent past — with sea-slugs — aversive behavior induced by tactile stimuli has been correlated with biolectric processes at synaptic membranes. The neuroscientists who have accomplished that feat of microscopic engineering think they have discovered the ultimate molecule of mind, the unit of which all learning, or individually acquired behavior, is compounded. That claim is implicitly contested by psychologists who have used pigeons and rats and hypothetical neurologizing to develop systemic explanations of individually acquired behavior. They insist upon distinctions between emergent levels, and place the sea-slug experiments below authentic Pavlovian conditioning. It requires a 'second-order' stimulus, such as the buzzer that precedes feeding, and is therefore a higher level than mere sensitization or habituation, the intensification or dulling of an innate reaction as it is repeatedly provoked directly, by a 'first-order' stimulus.

The distinction can be illustrated with familiar examples: the dental patient who flinches at the merest touch of the drill is sensitized rather than conditioned; the person near an air hammer who ceases to flinch at its noise is habituated rather than conditioned. Authentic conditioning emerges when an additional stimulus elicits the reaction — coming to flinch, or ceasing to flinch, at the sight of the hand taking hold of the air hammer or the dentist's drill. At that level a visual image signals the forthcoming assault on the ears or teeth, and the psychologists bring in mentalist concepts such as representation and knowing, and hypothesize neural explanations by reference to circuits of a higher order than local changes in action potentials at particular membranes.

The historian notes that these psychologists are keeping faith in Pavlov's insistence on the whole-animal approach — what he called 'organ physiology', as distinct from cellular or molecular physiology — but they are deserting his faith in 'pure physiology', by which he meant strict exclusion of mentalist concepts, adherence to the rule that the physiologist must point to the neural processes that accomplish determinate actions of muscles or glands. It was that twin faith that took Pavlov into studies of conditioning, when neurophysiology started its descent to the neuronal level, and kept him stubbornly attached to his scheme of linkages in the cerebral cortex, insisting that he had not deserted physiology for psychological hypothesizing. Rigorous neuroscience was a slippery slope with a chaos of neurons and ions at the bottom, while frankly hypothetical neurologizing about conditioning was a slippery slope with 'subjective' psychology and its mentalist concepts at the bottom. In angry hope Pavlov clung to his doctrine, a dream of firm ground above the choice.

Studies of conditioning since his time have persistently refashioned the dream, and just as persistently sent it down one or the other of these slopes. Insistence on rigorous demonstration of actual neural processes drives researchers away from the whole-animal study of individually acquired behavior, down below the 'higher nervous activity' that the analysis of conditioning was supposed to bring within physiological science. And vice versa: insistence on the whole-animal approach drives researchers

to mentalist concepts, away from rigorous demonstration of neural processes. The researchers I am referring to have not been scientific dreamers
like Wundt or Brentano, James or Freud, Bekhterev or Vygotsky, who
hoped by grand theorizing to achieve some comprehensive explanation and
understanding of the mind in all its aspects. I am referring here to the
narrower or harder type of scientist, such as Pavlov or Lashley, who strives
for experimentally proven explanation, if only of the mind's most elementary function, and shrugs off larger issues as problems for the future or
pseudoproblems — 'the poetry of the problem', in Pavlov's sneering dismissal. Among such blinkered scientists mind-body dualism is still regenerated as persistently as it was in the nineteenth century, when physiologists achieved great consistency and explanatory power by excluding
mentalist concepts from the analysis of neural processes, and psychologists
began their endless struggles to achieve analogous power in the study of
mental processes by experimental methods. Optimists may speak of a
dialectical relationship or mutual enrichment then and since, and call in
evidence the combination of physical and mental concepts that has flourished
in medical neurology, such as the correlation of damage to particular areas
of the brain with deficits in particular mental functions. Pessimists speak of
frustration in the would-be science of mind-brain that keeps breaking into
separate sciences of mind and brain, and splintering further within each
realm, reminding all parties of their separate inadequacies and joint incongruities.

The paradoxical development of Pavlovian conditioning, its continual
defeat in victory, has not been confronted by Soviet scientists. The post-
Stalin thaw released them from the obligation to support his 'cortical
dogmatism' and other obviously wrong parts of the sacred doctrine, but
correction had to be tacit and partial, without open criticism.[32] Pavlov's
creative disciples, such as Anokhin, and his critical sympathizers, such as
Beritashvili, simply resumed publication of their increasingly neuropsycho-
logical research: investigations of conditioning which required subcortical
neurology, some frankly hypothetical neurologizing, and the use of some
mentalist concepts. Neither they nor the younger Soviet scientists who
have been pursuing research of that kind more recently have been willing
or able to confront the persistent division within the Pavlovian legacy.
That is probably one reason why Soviet research in conditioning has
persistently lagged behind the pacesetters,[33] who are still clustered in Western
countries, as the foremost neurophysiologists and psychologists were eighty
years ago, when Pavlov and Bekhterev seemed at one leap to bring their
country into the front rank — and ended by contributing to the primacy of
the West.

But that depressing pattern of lost opportunities has been so common in
so many fields of Russian and Soviet science that one cannot single out the
sacralization of Pavlov's doctrine as the decisive cause. It was as much a

symptom as a cause, a symptom of the Soviet tendency to accompany huge increases in scientific education and research with a powerfully organized effort to maintain faith in old dreams of unified scientific vision. The result has been a depressingly familiar pattern. At the research bench of the working scientist specialized labor generates fragmented truths, while high up and far away the ideological establishment makes hollow claims of faith justified in one grand truth. In between, at those intermediate levels of interactive theorizing and experimentation where the most creative scientific thinking is done,[34] few venture, and they feebly. Add to that intellectual polarization the stifling of initiative that is built into a very large, highly centralized research system with a strong tradition of personal authoritarianism, and one begins to see how it is that the Soviet government can claim the world's largest number of scientists yet have the least to boast in numbers of Nobel laureates or young scientists coming in from abroad to study with the luminaries. Laurelled masters surrounded by multi-national apprentices are an obvious indication of a metropolis, and the Soviet Union, like its Tsarist predecessor, is still comparatively poor in such glitter.

The Soviet situation is not dark night to Western sunlight. Everywhere the mass production of data in the life sciences rises on an accelerating curve, and creative thought is rare. The bulk of scientists in all countries tend to avoid the risky places where creative thought occurs. The Soviet Union differs in number more than in kind; the bulk of timid souls is greater, the minority of daring innovators smaller, than in countries where ideologists have long since learned to ignore the intellectual content of the sciences while manipulating the symbols that hold the world in awe. Soviet ideologists have been very slow in mastering that lowbrow skill, hampered as they are by Stalinist pretenses and fears. They still pretend that their political leaders have scientific vision, partly because they still fear that the intelligentsia may have political pretensions as well as claims of knowledge. The fear seems quite absurd, if we consider only the scientific psychologists, who have never approached political pretensions and are eager to please established authority in their offers of practical insight. But there are other, much more potent analysts of human psychology whom Soviet leaders have good reason to view with apprehension.

WRITERS AND IDEOLOGIES

Imaginative writers, the reader will have noticed, dropped out of this history when it moved from the 1920s into the period of high Stalinism. Of course industrious typewriters continued to manufacture novels, plays and poems, but they no longer revealed authors in search of the authentic self and true community, as the works of Olesha and Babel had, not to speak of the pre-revolutionary masters. From 1930 to 1953 Stalin's engineers of human souls typed out their works to formula. Their product has its fascinations, like mass-market fiction and popular drama in the West, but hardly for understanding the psychologies of high culture. They help one understand mass psychology in its relation with the authorities.

Writers who are eager to please the authorities must not only write for the editor and the censor, they must win a large audience. Their words can be read as reciprocating transmission belts — to adapt Stalin's metaphor — between the establishment and the mass of readers, with influences going both ways even under Stalinist tyranny. The popular taste for heroic fantasy expanded beyond the likes of Horatio Alger or Tarzan to the likes of Gladkov's engineers, who raised giant factories out of Russian *stikhiia* (elemental chaos), or Sholokhov's rural organizers, who didn't need a gun to get peasants into collective farms, or Bek's front-line officer who did use a gun to turn panicky conscripts into disciplined victors over German supermen.[35] When I speak of socialist realism as heroic fantasy I do not call in question the reality of new factories, collective farms, or defeated invaders. I am noting the dreams that attended their achievement, that raised the consciousness of the mass reader above a multitude of unheroic realities.

That was the original type of socialist realism; in time Stalinist editors and censors conceded the legitimacy of a mindset focused on mundane satisfactions, which had been decried as philistine or petty bourgeois in the heroic periods of the Revolution — finding love and a livable apartment, for example. One way or another, the flow of routine literary works illuminates the interacting mentalities of officials and ordinary people in Stalin's time, and before and afterward.[36] But the student of high culture, on first looking into Stalin's time, finds mere destruction. He sees an iron flood that just wiped his subject off the Soviet sixth of the earth. Serious artists striving for authenticity were forced into formulaic phoniness, or utterly silenced, or physically destroyed — or first one then the other. Yet a closer look discovers another reality within that devastation. The pre-revolutionary tradition of the writer as spokesman for *obshchestvennost'* in combat with *vlast'*, educated opinion *v.* state power, was given a terrible new vitality by the violent campaign to crush it. Stalinist officials ploughed the earth with writers' blood, and writer warriors grew as weeds among the intended crops of writer engineers. Space permits only an exemplary case, to epitomize the development of a psychology that is simply lacking among those who seek a science of the mind.

Osip Mandelstam is an exceptionally illuminating case, for he connects the generations of the intelligentsia from the pre-revolutionary time, when his mind took shape, through the 1920s and 1930s, when he wrote his greatest poetry and prose, to the post-Stalin thaw, when his work became a vital part of the dissident movement. We need not guess whether Mandelstam's decision to stay in Russia after 1917 signified 'acceptance' of the Revolution, in the stock phrase of the time, for he was not content with stock phrases. He worked out his response to the Revolution in a series of poems and essays that began in the first year of the new regime and did not stop until it arrested and destroyed him twenty years later. Some were published at home during the 1920s; many others were preserved by his widow and published abroad in the post-Stalin thaw. The *Complete Works* are still prohibited in the poet's own country even though he has been posthumously 'rehabilitated', and is universally acknowledged to be one of the great modernist poets. His response to the Revolution has too much of tragedy and rebellion in it to be confronted by the Soviet ideological establishment, up to now at any rate.

Mandelstam 'accepted' the Revolution in a painfully literal sense. He took it within his conscious mind; he took it upon himself to be in his writing a conscious participant in the historical process. He would not permit himself the idle luxury of the bystander or even the industrious virtue of 'the citizen', who performs certain functions in the historical process, with this party or against that, to the extent that such politics is feasible. Within 'the citizen' Mandelstam sought 'the man', the conscious self as agent of its purposeful history, the hero who is not content with feasible functions.[37] In a poem of 1918, which made a considerable stir, Mandelstam celebrated 'the twilight of freedom' − or dawn, the word can mean either − as a test of manliness, the courage to make oneself a conscious part of a process that is unconscious, elemental, *stikhiia*.[38] It was as great a burden as ever Calvin laid upon those of tender conscience, to make oneself responsible for a process that is infinitely greater than an individual's power to comprehend or to influence it.

Mandelstam wrote reverently of 'the word', or poetic culture, but did not claim that it shapes the historical process. Indeed, he acknowledged that the modern secular state assigns to 'the word' a decorative function, lending appearance of holiness to institutions that have been separated from religious faith. Yet he took upon himself a desperate form of the vatic tradition, telling men of power what they should be thinking and feeling as they struggled to control a beastly age − telling that to revolutionary men who were passionately convinced that *they* spoke for history, and needed literary artists merely to give their words extra force. In 'The Twilight of Freedom' Mandelstam called them to celebrate 'the fateful burden that the people's leader takes up in tears, the somber burden of power', on a ship of state that is simultaneously floating on elemental chaos and sinking to the bottom, in a modernist conflation of metaphors that jars the reader loose from a reassuring sense of position or direction.[39] Yet − or therefore − Bukharin himself, chief of ideology in the 1920s, acted as Mandelstam's personal adviser, and even close-mouthed Stalin, when he took over the ideological post in the 1930s, made a famous telephone call to Pasternak to ask if Mandelstam was really such a good poet. Pasternak might have replied: he is the only modernist master who provoked such a question from Comrade Stalin, who acknowledges thus both Mandelstam's genius and the Revolution's need of poetic justification.[40]

Mandelstam was not at all a political type in the usual sense. He felt no obligation to comment on current events or even on momentous events as journalists and politicians measure the momentous. His poetic vision worked upon intensely personal experience of the historical process, which provoked him in 1930–1, while Stalin's revolution from above was reaching its wild climax, to write an angry declaration of independence. He had been accused of plagiarism for using one Gornfel'd's translation of a German poet without requesting permission or paying a fee. A publisher's oversight was turned into a petty scandal by manipulators of literary politics, who wrote attacks on Mandelstam and summoned him to an 'arbitration court'. While he was preparing his reply, the police came at night to arrest a small businessman on the other side of the Mandelstams' thin apartment wall, with floorboards ripped up in search of valuables, the wife shrieking, and a boy sobbing for his father, at the time and for weeks after. About the same time an officious critic visited Mandelstam at the Communist newspaper that employed him, to give advice on writing poetry, which Mandelstam had been scanting in favor of prose. He swore at the critic in his office – Would the authorities advise him on frequency and choice of position in coupling with his wife? – and expanded the polemic against Gornfel'd and his partisans beyond their accusation of plagiarism into the whole business of 'obtaining permission'.[41]

> All the works of world literature I divide into those permitted and those written without permission. The first are trash, the second are stolen air. As for the writers who write previously permitted things, I want to spit in their face, I want to beat them about the head with a stick, and sit them all down behind a table in Herzen House [headquarters of the writers' organizations], placing before each a glass of police tea and giving each the job of analyzing Gornfel'd's urine.[42]

To distinguish that breed of writer from his own Mandelstam offered a contrast of ethnic stereotypes: people of a wandering, dirty, thieving, servile tribe, whose elders had tried to perform upon him a disgusting ritual of 'cutting off and dishonoring' – he called them interchangeably 'the race of professional writers' or 'gypsies' – and a race of 'sheepbreeders, patriarchs, and kings', with 'the honorable name of Jew, which I take pride in'. (Of course he was taunting anti-Semitic gentiles by inversion of their stereotypes.) The thieving servile tribe

> camps and sleeps in its own vomit, is expelled from cities and persecuted in villages, yet it is forever close to authority [*vlast'*], which finds a place for it in red light districts, as prostitutes. For literature always and everywhere fulfills a single assignment: it helps the bosses

[*nachal'nikam*] keep soldiers in obedience and helps judges execute punishment on the condemned.[43]

As for himself, or his kind of writer, Mandelstam swore that he would henceforth run away from the pieces of silver, the fur coat, the special apartments and shops that he had been accepting in return for literary pieces done on contract. In a final thrust at sacred concepts he swore that he would never be a 'toiler' (*trudiashchiisia*), no matter how hard he worked. 'My toil, however it expresses itself, is perceived as mischief, as lawlessness, as fortuity. But that is my choice, and I agree to that, I put my signature to that with both hands.'[44]

This 'Fourth Prose', as he called it — he counted three preceding works in prose — seems to reject any more fellow-traveling, yet he was still determined to be a conscious participant in his country's development, and he had no wish to play the martyr. So he wrote 'Fourth Prose' for the drawer, as the Russians say, or more precisely for his wife's handbag, lest it be found too readily. The poem that was found in the drawer, when the police came for him in 1934, was a rueful boast of his quixotic valor.[45] 'For the thundering prowess of ages to come' he had deprived himself of joy and honor. His own age was a wolfhound that 'leaps upon my shoulders, though I am not a wolf by blood'. The poet yearns for Siberian exile, where he won't see cowards or bloody bones, but night and pines and blue foxes: 'For a wolf I am not by blood, and the man [*chelovek*] will not die in me.' Mandelstam left three variants of that last line, which all converge, with rueful or defiant pride, on the human self, 'me', indestructible even by a beastly age.[46]

In the usual accounts Mandelstam's valorous poetry — the irrepressible man against the implacable state — reached its climax in the satirical poem on Stalin and his lieutenants, which Mandelstam read out loud to a group of friends in 1933, knowing that he was inviting arrest, for there was bound to be a Judas in the audience. There is truth in that usual tale, but it is a one-sided truth, which misses the ultimate torment of the poet determined to make his voice an expression of the historical process. Without the semi-public reading he might well have been arrested anyhow, as many fellow-travelers, time-servers or mere bystanders were; the terror intensified its effect by wanton caprice in its random blows. More importantly, if our concern is not the terror itself but Mandelstam's expressions of consciousness within it, we must note that his satirical poem on Stalin was not a classical rapier thrust, such as Pushkin fashioned against the despots of his time. It was a grotesque montage of modernist images, which magnify Stalin more than belittle him, making him fearsome more than contemptible.[47]

The painful facts must be confronted. Mandelstam wrote other poems in *praise* of Stalin. The poet's admirers usually note only one, and explain it away as a desperate effort by a persecuted man *in extremis*, trying to purchase his life by flattering the despot who was torturing him to death rather than having him shot at once. No doubt there is truth in that version, but once again it is a one-sided truth that evades the bitterest part of Mandelstam's determination to be a conscious part of the time that worshiped Stalin. He tried to join in. The most tragic instance is the most ambiguous, 'If it were me our enemies arrested', written in 1937 as the terror reached a peak of accusations against 'enemies of the people', summarily exposed and imprisoned or shot. Mandelstam pictured himself as the kind of prisoner who still proclaimed his faith in the justice of the people's cause, personified by Lenin and Stalin.[48]

The poem is ambiguously disturbing from the first line to the last. Does 'our enemies' refer to the subversives being unmasked in the few show trials and the multitude of secret tribunals, or to those who were running the trials and the tribunals, arresting hundreds of thousands of innocent people? Is the final line a declaration of faith that Stalin will wake up (*budit'*) reason and life, or that he will destroy (*gubit'*) them? There are two versions, and the whole poem can make sense with either verb at the end: the people's cause will triumph over mass injustice either with Stalin or in spite of him. But it is a tortured sense in either case, a pathological extreme of the poet who would not simply curse the collective experience called history, who knew that he was part of it and tried to find a voice that would be authentically both his and its. Critics may look for precedents to Tiutchev's celebration of contagious disease[49] or to Baudelaire's litany to the satanic majesty of science and war,[50] but such flaunting of perversity is clarity itself compared to Mandelstam's 'If it were me ...' The perverse romantics maintain a distinction between the poet's voice and the horror that he declares himself to love or revere. Mandelstam's poem tries to dissolve that distinction by imagining himself as innocent victim of official torture shrieking his faith in the official doctrine that even this kind of history makes sense; not by an end in oblivion (Tiutchev's notion) or by the final triumph of Satan (Baudelaire's), but by moving through horror to the realization of good.

'If it were me ...' is a small part of Mandelstam's *oeuvre*, but tormenting ambiguity of some form attends all his efforts to situate the conscious self in history. The best of them achieve an aching beauty by failing in their effort, that is by aesthetic transcendence of history's rebuke to the conscious self. One of the loveliest of such paradoxical triumphs appeals beyond history to the cosmic order, or rather, to an ambiguous possibility of order: a flickering light at a fearsome height that may be a star, brother of Petrograd, which is dying.[51] Perfect harmony of images, thought, and verbal music proved again what has often been noted, that the modernist sensibility is at odds with the traditional religions and with the secular ideologies that fit the mind within an historic plan and a cosmic order.

Some modernist masters at the beginning of our century responded to that fact of life by laboring at nostalgic revivals — such as Eliot's rightist Christianity or Yeats's national spirituality — which make the reader more conscious than ever of the naturalist metaphysic that prompts such labors and subverts them. Mandelstam's was a far more serious effort to engage his poetic mind with a great revolution while it was in process. The result was a keener form of modernist reflection on the place of the conscious self in history and the cosmos, a more vivid reminder that aestheticism is the other side of modern naturalism: the sense of the conscious self as a trivial episode in a noisy infinity of episodes, signifying nothing until the episode utters words that signify. Scientists of the mind and Communist bosses share the naturalist metaphysic, but insist on reading other meanings out of it: either that we must explain our conscious selves away, or that we must dissolve them within the cause that makes us all conscious agents of a great historical purpose. In the latter, the Communist project, there was enough of poetry to attract a mind like Mandelstam's, enough indeed to provoke angry objection or anguish at its self-destructive inconsistency.

By 1956, with Stalin dead and Khrushchev exposing his crimes, a Soviet critic imagined walls dissolving and 'the Boss' (*Khoziain*) speaking directly to 'the writer', who has just put on paper his conviction that 'the word' is the primal human deed or action (*delo*).

> 'Court action', the Boss corrects me. 'Do you hear me, storyteller? If there is a word, it is a word of accusation. If there is an action, it is a court action. Word and action!'
>
> I hear him.
>
> The court is in session, it is in session throughout the world. And ... all of us, however many we may be, are being daily, nightly taken to court for interrogation. And that is called history.
>
> The doorbell rings. Surname? First name? Date of birth?
>
> That's when you begin to write.[52]

That startling clarification of the Soviet writer's involvement in history appeared in a philosophical tale, which winds up with the writer digging ditches in a labor camp, alongside a foolish young Marxist-Leninist who dared to dream out loud about a truly communist society and a Jewish doctor who was somehow overlooked in the post-Stalin pardons. The actual writer of the fiction, Andrei Siniavsky, was accurately forecasting the bosses' response to his work, which he published in the West under the pen-name Abram Tertz. (He deliberately affected a Jewish identity for his *alter ego*.) When the police tracked Tertz to Siniavsky's apartment in 1965, after the highest bosses had dismissed Khrushchev and stopped reform, they took the writer into a closed court, where his books served as evidence of his crime against the Soviet system, and did in fact pack him off to a labor camp.[53] He spent almost six years there, still writing for publication in the West, to which the bosses sent him, stripped of Soviet citizenship, in 1973.

Of course they did not rid themselves of defiant writers by banishing Siniavsky, and many others like him, who have continually accepted the bosses' insulting challenge to their valor by writing against or around official prescriptions. Siniavsky's work is especially illuminating of the vicious circle, for he gives a searching analysis of the mindsets that egg each other on. The official justifies sacrifice of individuality, his own as well as the writer's, for the sake of disciplined movement toward a great goal, which the writer ridicules as a phantasm, if not a hypocritical fraud. Siniavsky's ridicule is charged with pained sympathy, for he does not reject the underlying assumption that some shared belief in an ideal goal is essential to authentic human beings. Completely self-centered individuals are contemptible or pitiful objects in his stories, condemned to self-defeat in their mean projects. In his contest with the bosses Siniavsky moved from Marxism-Leninism as the vision of the ideal goal to a sort of Orthodox Christianity infused with the existentialist sensibility, the conviction that faith is the mind's defiant refusal to be merely a social artifact, an object in nature.[54] His writing suggests faith in a communion of souls, emerging within the tragicomic suffering of people who are pursuing phantasms of other faiths. Literary artists are still essential to the process, as they were in the days of Gogol and Dostoevsky, for they bring out the phantasms that people discover when they open their minds to self-scrutiny.

Philosophical psychology of that or any sort is not to be found in Solzhenitsyn, the most famous of the dissident writers, who shares with the bosses a tough inner protection against profound self-questioning. A simple typology seals his mind against tormenting depths: some people are righteous, some loathsome, and many are mixed types, with the capacity to go good or bad at decisive moments. The challenge of writing, and of life at large, is to assert the righteous self and its true community in defiance of their loathsome opposites. That urgent business tends to suppress the question, But what are the authentic self and its true community? They are to be found in struggle against their opposites − a psychology surprisingly similar to Lenin's and to the radical tradition that fostered Lenin. In the psychology of such writers as Siniavsky and Mandelstam rebellious self-assertion is also essential, but they examine it, asking what is being asserted and how and why, and thus bring in the characteristic anguish of modern thinkers, who have no ready-made scheme of reassuring self-righteousness.

Official editors and censors have been slowly retreating from the Stalinist ban on the soul-searching type of writer, which is a tacit admission of self-doubt emerging within the official mentality. The most revealing case in point is the work of Iurii Trifonov, or was until an embolism cut him off in 1981, aged 56, a soul-searching writer who was not jailed or banished or confined to *samizdat* and *tamizdat* (self-publication and 'there-publication', in hand-copied manuscripts and Western print). He managed somehow to get the official imprimatur for novels that probe the official psychology in decay. They mark off older people, who went violently through revolutionary storms, and younger people, himself included, who no longer believe that human authenticity is defined by disciplined participation in 'the cause'. There is a search for the true character of both generations, back then when the fathers did terrible things with passionate conviction of rectitude, and here now, when the sons are shallow self-seekers or, at best, troubled searchers for an authentic self in a deadened present. The novels end in failure; neither fathers nor sons are justified, except perhaps by the tragedy of the unavailing quest, the sense gained of irremediable inadequacy, which reveals a distinctively human mind within the social artifact, the natural object.[55]

Young Marx might have related those expressions of the Soviet sensibility to the *Gattungswesen*, the generative essence of humanity, which has so far realized itself only in grotesquely alienated forms, each one transforming itself through time into yet another alienated form. If we ask what is the authentic form, the standard by which we know this or that particular case to be inadequate or estranged, we find no direct answer in Trifonov. He provides no model human beings, no 'positive heroes'. Nor does Siniavsky, who finds authentic forms of humanity in dreams of religious perfection. Solzhenitsyn does offer 'positive heroes': simple people heroically suffering, and intellectuals in revolt against the scoundrel system that makes the people suffer.[56] It might seem that his version of socialist realism portends the collapse of the Soviet system, maybe even another outburst of revolution, as radical literature did in the last decades of the Tsarist era. But there are other possibilities, as we have seen in other countries, Western countries included. Expressions of outrage can provoke leaders to reform — can even reinforce stasis, if the constituency of the outraged is hopelessly overpowered by those of complacent or divided mind. The imprimatur for novels such as Trifonov's indicated the growth within officialdom of the divided or the reforming mentality, of people ill at ease with the existing condition of 'Soviet man', anxious to find or make some improved versions. Waiting in reserve to reinforce such tendencies are the visions of Siniavsky and Mandelstam and other presently banished writers, ostensibly excluded from the Soviet experience but actually working their way underground back into the consciousness of the country that generated them.

Many believe that the psychology which the Bolsheviks brought to power is moribund if not altogether dead, and only brute power sustains the appearance of belief in it. This history, it may seem, has borne out that view: Chernyshevsky's dream of the confident scientific revolutionary, encouraged by a naturalist metaphysic to construct new men and women, was already moribund in high culture by the end of the nineteenth century.

The dream survived within the Bolshevik minority of the intelligentsia as part of their willful refusal to accept contemporary 'bourgeois' culture, while trying to share in the science and art of their time. That incongruity was in evidence before 1917, within the Bolshevik mentality and in their relations with the intelligentsia at large. Bolshevik intellectuals like Bogdanov and Lunacharsky inclined more toward sharing in the high culture of the age, at the risk of waking from Chernyshevsky's dream, while Lenin and his disciples inclined more toward purging high culture of its 'bourgeois' elements, at the risk of hostile relations with the intelligentsia. The Bolshevik mentality has never been all of one piece or the other, not even in the years of high Stalinism, when the ideological establishment was squeezing socialist realism out of writers and forcing from psychological scientists confessions of faith in the scientific revolutionary, the mythic comradeship of Chernyshevsky-Sechenov-Lenin-Pavlov. Wild campaigns of enforced confession were driven in part by Bolshevik awareness of their growing isolation from modern high culture, their last-ditch will to believe that high culture would become Communist if only they forced it. Thus the slow retreat since the early 1950s seems to many a confession of intellectual bankruptcy.

Seeing Soviet history that way is seeing only part of a complex drift, while ignoring another side of the Bolshevik mentality, which was still operative even at the height of Stalinist willfulness. Even when 'psycho-technics' and 'pedology' were being abolished as intolerable intrusions of supposedly objective expertise in the management of human beings, the bosses still insisted upon the need for such expertise in the treatment of the insane. Indeed, they demanded that the psychiatrists be scientifically rigorous and therefore frugal in selecting patients for institutional treatment. In general the Stalinist bosses continued to support the *idea* of a scientific psychology, both pure and applied, and thus confessed their affinity to non-revolutionary people all around the modern world who regard the brain-mind as something like the circulatory or genito-urinary systems, objects in nature to be managed most effectively by scientific experts. The person or self is perceived as an adaptive function of the individual brain-mind interacting with the social group. That reductive vision has had enormous appeal for almost two centuries now, in 'advanced' countries and in those aspiring to escape 'backwardness'. It has found expression not only in the creation of psychological science but in such other phenomena as the triumph of the industrial assembly line, the disciplined citizen soldiery, the mental health industry, and the huge boom in pornography.

Let us call this the functionalist faith, and note its purest expression in the public's eagerness to believe exaggerated claims of psychological science, the endless capacity to accept new schools and trends as often as old favorites die of inanition. The disputable claims of successive favorites are less significant than the persistent common sense that we must have knowledge of the kind they claim. A society that maintains scientific psychology is implicitly doubting its own ideological and aesthetic psychologies, trying to persuade itself that they are elaborate signalling devices in the human species, like ratsqueak or birdsong or the shrieks of chimpanzees. Such a society wrangles for a while over the incompatibility of scientific psychology with traditional modes of self-knowledge, but ultimately learns to ignore or evade the issue. In cultural function, adepts of the scientific discipline become modern replacements of the religious scholars who once fostered faith in a dominant vision of human nature that could not be abandoned though it could not be proved. The obvious difference between the old style and the new — replacement of the soul by some systemic function of the brain-mind-group — may be less significant than the rarely noticed similarity: masters of esoteric knowledge about persons serve as reminders, even to the bosses who command workforce and armed force, of mysteries within that correspond to cosmic mysteries without. They hold out promise of regularized control over the mysteries, and so reduce the fearful wonder and the wayward excitement that literary artists and rebel ideologists bring to awareness.

This current of modern sensibility has been at work in the Bolshevik mentality all along, in spite of the implicit conflict with Marx's vision of human nature realizing itself through a series of alienations generating successive revolts against alienation. Suffice to recall the Bolshevik leaders' response when they discovered, on taking power, that they had among their subjects a scientist who had discovered the molecule of which all mental activity is compounded: the conditioned reflex. (Do not sneer at their credulity; even so knowledgeable a thinker as Bertrand Russell took Pavlov's claim for granted.) In spite of Pavlov's express hostility to their government and their ideology, the Bolsheviks lavished support on his project; when he turned friendly, they raised him to their pantheon just beneath Marx-Engels-Lenin. And they have kept him there, while ideologists and historians have labored to keep some semblance of logic in the bizarre combination, the vision of revolutionary transformation joined to the vision of functional adaptation. While Russia was going through its revolutionary transformation the combination had great appeal: a new version of humanity was supposed to be emerging along with a new kind of industrial society in a new Russia rescued at last from 'backwardness'. But revolutionary transformation has become a dying dream and functional adaptation the overwhelming reality, in their society as in ours.

The Russian Revolution may still generate something more than that. After all, it continued into the twentieth century the persistent revolt against subordination that began with the German Reformation and the French Revolution. Whether it is individual conscience against established church, or ordinary citizen against aristocracy and king, or worker against boss, or 'backward' people against 'advanced', the persistent faith is in some authentic person within some true community, each freely generating the other. The very fact that reality mocks that faith keeps it alive, as knowledge that we are not what we know true human beings would be — free, insubordinate.

Notes

References are abbreviated; see bibliography for full citations.

CHAPTER 1 PSYCHOLOGICAL SCIENCE AND IDEOLOGIES

1 For an exceptional brain scientist who confronts the concept of mind, see Pribram. Note his observation that 'neurology has little to contribute to the study of consciousness even today.' IV, p. 501. For the characteristic attitude of brain scientists, see Blakemore. For an effort 'to dispel the myth that philosophical speculation regarding the concept of the body is only sporadic', see Spicker. Physiology is conspicuous by its absence from the essays in that anthology. For a recent effort to bridge the gap, see Churchland.
2 The phrase is Robert Frost's, in 'Lucretius and the Lake Poets'.
3 For the most generous to the church, see Langford. See Koestler for accusation of Galileo, and de Santillana or Geymonat for balanced interpretations.
4 For neat examples of Descartes divided, see the contrasting articles on him in *Encyclopedia of Philosophy* and in *Dictionary of Scientific Biography*. Cf. Guéroult, II, entitled *L'âme et le corps*, which manages to ignore physiology. On the other hand, see Caton, for an exceptional effort to achieve a whole view of Descartes and his place in the development of modern thought. See also Rosenfield, for a history that brings together physiology, philosophy, theology, and poetry. Vartanian, *Diderot and Descartes*, pays little attention to physiology.
5 See, e.g., Canguilhem, *La formation*, p. 85; C. C. Gillispie, 'Diderot', in *Dictionary of Scientific Biography*; and Arthur M. Wilson, especially p. 570 and p. 834 n. 63. For a modernization of Diderot's views on neurophysiology, see *Kindlers Literatur Lexikon*, IV (1970), p. 3139; and Jean Mayer. See also Mayer's very informative 'introduction', in Diderot, *Éléments*.
6 For Lamettrie's alternating moods, see Vartanian, *Lamettrie's*, pp. 9 ff. There is a striking similarity of materialist outlook and alternating mood in *Danton's Death*, by George Büchner. Many people have seen materialism as a threat to belief in some 'eternal relation', without which 'life is trivial.' The quoted phrases are Brunetière's. See Chadwick, p. 243.
7 See Keats, 'Lamia'. Cf. Bate, p. 270.
8 Schiller, 'Die Götter Griechenlandes'.
9 Rousseau may be an exception. See the reproaches cast at mechanistic physiology in the famous credo of a Savoyard priest, in *Émile*.

10 Cf. the _succus nerveus_ of Borelli and the _vis nervosa_ of Unzer, in Boring, p. 17. For a history of such concepts, see Hall.

11 See Schiller, _Aesthetic Letters_. For special studies of Schiller's physiological views, which attempt to modernize them, see Tarkhanov, 'Psikhofiziologicheskie ...', pp. 472–5; Benesch; and Metts. Cf. Kerry, ch. 2, for an analysis of the physiological treatises that almost entirely ignore physiology.

12 Quoted in _Philosophy, Politics, and Society_, 3rd series, p. 148.

13 Oldfield, 'Hartley', _International Encyclopedia of Social Sciences_, VI, with bibliography.

14 Beach, pp. 128 ff.

15 For the posthumous recognition, see Du Bois-Reymond's 1875 lecture, in his _Reden_, pp. 178–210. 'Gray philosophy' refers to Goethe's comment on Lamettrie. See Sherrington, _Man_, p. 198.

16 Clarke and O'Malley, pp. 336–7. Cf. French.

17 Fearing, pp. 74–82.

18 _Ibid._, ch. XI, 'The Pflüger-Lotze controversy.'

19 _Ibid._, p. 133.

20 Fearing, p. 152. Bischoff was not unique. Unzer did experiments on beheaded criminals, and so did Aldini. See _Dictionary of Scientific Biography_, I, p. 198, and XIV, p. 321. Cf. Nathan, p. 232, for a physiologist of our time who jokes about Aldini's experiments.

21 Cf. William James's lively description, in his _Principles_, I, pp. 9–10.

22 Quoted in Marx, _Capital_, I, pp. 418–20. For the rise of feedback mechanisms and the extension of the metaphor to social phenomena, see Mayr.

23 See Fearing, pp. 128–45.

24 See Boring, pp. 41 ff.

25 Widely quoted in the scholarly literature, e.g., in Boring, p. 708. The quoted words are Du Bois-Reymond's telling what he and Brücke swore. The point of view was shared by Ludwig and Helmholtz. For the mechanistic triumph see Lenoir, especially chapter 5.

26 Laycock, 'On the reflex function ...'; Griesinger, 'Über psychische. ...' Griesinger proudly called attention to this article in his landmark textbook, _Mental Pathology_ ..., p. 42. (The original German version appeared in 1845, with a major new edition in 1861 and numerous reprints and translations throughout the nineteenth century.) The article was also reprinted in his _Gesammelte_ ..., I (1872). Laycock repeated his idea in his _Mind and Brain_ ... (1860, and 2nd ed., 1869). These bibliographic data are important in view of the claim that Sechenov's 1863 essay initiated the reflex approach to mental function.

27 Cabanis seems to have been the first to use the secretion metaphor, or at least to make it popular, in an 1802 publication. Dessoir, p. 164.

28 See below, p. 17.

29 Laycock, 'On the reflex function ...', p. 311.

30 Griesinger, _Mental Pathology_ ..., p. 6 _et passim_.

31 Marshall Hall, who did the experiment with the turtle, insisted that reflexes 'are in reality _physical_, not _psychical_', and also insisted that '_volition_ may _modify_ the acts of the reflex function.' Quoted in Fearing, pp. 138–9. Cf. Sechenov on consciousness (_soznatel'noe chuvstvovanie_) as 'an indispensable factor' in 'the

evacuation of the bladder and of the rectum'. Sechenov, *Biographical*, p. 344; or Sechenov, *Izbrannye*, I, p. 184.

32 Jefferson, pp. 303–20. Cf. Riese, *History*, pp. 68–9 *et passim*, for another eminent neurologist disturbed by Marshall Hall's mingling of two 'principles of interpretation, the mechanical and teleological'.

33 The phrase is Ryle's, in his *Concept of Mind*.

34 Note especially the succession of great British neurologists, from Hughlings Jackson to Sherrington and Eccles, who have followed this pattern. See, e.g., C. U. M. Smith; Riese, 'Hughlings Jackson's doctrine ...'; Young, *Mind, Brain* ..., pp. 232–3 *et passim*; Swazey, *Reflexes* ..., pp. 28, 80, 204–6 *et passim*; Ekehorn, and Eccles.

35 Coleman, pp. 145–6.

36 Fleming, p. xli.

37 See the remarks of Helmholtz in 1877, disowning extreme mechanism yet looking back to the 1840s with nostalgia: 'It was a period of fermentation, of the fight between learned tradition and the new spirit of natural science. ...' Helmholtz, p. 199. Cf. the quotation, on 'his youth, when we strove in the combat together', which adorns the dedication to Brücke in Du Bois-Reymond's *Reden*, I.

38 See *OED Supplement*.

39 Cf. William James on 'the scandalous vagueness with which this sort of "chromo-philosophy" is carried on'. *Principles*, I, pp. 149 *et passim*. Boring, p. 243, quotes a crushing epigram from a letter of James to Peirce.

40 I am not aware of a general history of positivism in the broad sense. Simon, *European* ..., is an essay on Comte's philosophy and its influence. Merz, *History* ..., includes much information, but treats it from a viewpoint that can hardly be taken seriously any more: 'the unification of thought' on the basis of Herman Lotze's philosophy. Kolakowski, *Alienation*, is an insightful essay.

41 For learned exceptions that prove the rule, see the abortive effort of Neurath, et al., *International Encyclopedia of Unified Science*, and the continuing project of Bunge, ed., *Methodological Unity* ..., and Bunge, *Furniture*. ...

42 Huysmans, *Against Nature*, p. 158. The original, *À rebours*, appeared in 1884. See below, p. 245.

43 There is no general history of the process—aside from Crum's brief *Scientific Thought in Poetry* — and there are too many special studies to cite here. Suffice to note Beach, a thorough history of the process in English poetry. Gode-von Aesch deals with the first wave, and is not nearly as clear and penetrating as Beach. See the following notes for other references to special studies.

44 See Stevenson for a sentimental account. Beach is better.

45 See Heller.

46 *In Memoriam*, stanza CXIX.

47 Quoted and analyzed in Leakey, pp. 103–4. Previously Baudelaire had admired 'le culte de la nature, cette grande religion de Diderot et d'Holbach, cet unique ornement de l'athéisme', which he distinguished from 'the drab cult of Science'. *Ibid.*, p. 24.

48 Waggoner, p. 75. Another example that comes to hand: 'The nothingness [Wallace] Stevens looks at ... is that of mathematical abstraction, the universe of 20th-century science, emptier and even more discouraging than Hardy's

19th-century universe ..., emptier than the darkness and deprivation of ... Eliot. ...' Litz, p. 23. One could add such quotations endlessly.

49 Hemmings, p. 20.

50 See Fusil.

51 See, e.g., Hemmings, pp. 59, 155–6, *et passim*; and Angus Wilson, p. 34.

52 See, e.g., Lemaitre's essay on Zola in his *Literary Impressions*.

53 Quoted in Hemmings, p. 41.

54 Zola, *L'Assommoir*, trans. Tancock (1970), pp. 413–21. I have altered this translation, to get closer to my sense of the original, in Zola, *L'Assommoir* (Paris, 1969), pp. 436–43.

55 Zola, *Le Docteur Pascal.*

56 'The puppet animal' is Sherrington's phrase, to describe the 'decerebrate preparations' with which he traced neural pathways. Sherrington, *The Integrative Action*, p. xii. He sought refuge from study of the puppet animal in humanistic studies of history and literature, a separate realm of his dualistic universe. Zola allowed himself no such refuge; he tried to see the world monistically.

57 Tiutchev, *Stikhotvoreniia*, p. 177.

58 The classic of this genre is I. A. Richards, *Poetries and Sciences*, originally published in 1926 as *Science and Poetry*. In later editions he protests unconvincingly that he has been misunderstood. Cf. Wheelwright for a sharply different view.

59 See, e.g., George A. Miller. There are many other, more tendentious histories of psychology. Boring is exceptional in his breadth and philosophical sensitivity. So too are recent works from some specialists in the history of psychology. See, e.g., Woodward and Ash and Ash and Woodward; also *Wundt Studies*.

60 Boring tries so hard to be comprehensive and fair to all schools that he comes close to being an analyst of confusion. James, *Principles*, originally published in 1890, is still an extraordinarily lively book precisely because James approached his subject as an analyst of confusion, not as a preacher of a sectarian faith. Recent specialists in the history of psychology have gentler ways of dealing with the fact that 'the psychologies of the founding fathers passed from the scene without laying permanent conceptual foundations on which later generations of psychologists could build.' Kurt Danziger, in *Wundt Studies*, p. 371.

61 Boring, ch. 14.

62 *Ibid.*, p. 286.

63 Fechner, *Elements.* ...

64 See the witty dismissal of Fechner by William James, *Principles*, I, p. 549.

65 Quoted *ibid.*, I, p. 131. 'Shamefaced materialism' is the term that Engels applied to Huxley.

66 Büchner, p. 146.

67 See, e.g., Engels, *Anti-Dühring*, p. 394.

68 Du Bois-Reymond, *Über die Grenzen* ..., p. 35. A somewhat different English version can be found in *Popular Science Monthly*, 5 (1874), p. 28. Tyndall made the same point in a famous speech of 1874, and William James in 1890 reported that it was very widely taken for granted. *Principles*, I, p. 147.

69 Hughlings Jackson, p. 417.

70 Young, *Mind*, pp. 232—6.
71 Riese, *History*, pp. 94—5. Cf. Rothschuh, pp. 216 ff. Hans Berger, the discoverer of the EEG, was also a maverick in his belief that he was measuring psychic energy. See *ibid.*, pp. 226 ff.
72 Stevens, 'Connoisseur of Chaos'.
73 See Hagstrom for a sober statement of this theme. Blissett, *Politics in Science*, takes it to an absurd extreme, where objective standards disappear.
74 John B. Watson set the pattern. See his *Behaviorism*, pp. 3—4. This famous tract was originally published in 1924.
75 William James, *Psychology*, p. 468.
76 Brentano, *Psychologie* (1874), p. vi. The (Leipzig, 1924) reprint contains a crucial misprint: 'psychic realm' is turned into 'physical realm'.
77 See Boring, chs. 17 and 19. For another recent historian of psychology who is unusually broadminded in acknowledging the significance of Brentano, see O'Neil.
78 Pribram, IV, pp. 9—10, and 395—432; and Merlan.
79 The principal connection was through Gestalt. See below, pp. 361 ff.
80 For an incisive introduction, with bibliography, see Richard Schmitt, 'Husserl', in *Encyclopedia of Philosophy*, IV.
81 James, *Principles*, I, p. 145.
82 Boring, ch. 12. For an analysis that stresses the contribution of the British and deplores Boring's emphasis on the Germans, see Young, 'Scholarship ...'.
83 See Tjoa on Lewes. On Carpenter, see Fearing, pp. 154—7, 161.
84 Boring, pp. 505 ff; Roback; and Heidbreder.
85 See especially Darwin's *Descent of Man*. Cf. Robert Richards.
86 See Pavlov, *Lectures*, p. 59. Cf. Loeb, 'Znachenie ...', p. 108.
87 See, e.g., Bohn, *passim*; and Vagner, 'Fiziologiia ...'.
88 Loeb, 'Zur Theorie ...', pp. 456—7; and cf. Loeb, *Comparative ...*, pp. 181—2, 232—3, *et passim*.
89 See, e.g., Vagner, *Vozniknovenie ...*, *vypusk 3*.
90 Quoted in Colp, p. 333. Note the recent discovery that Marx did *not* offer to dedicate *Capital* to Darwin: see Fay.
91 See Marvyn Harris; and Stocking.

CHAPTER 2   SOCIAL SCIENCE AND IDEOLOGIES

1 Papmehl, p. 23. For more detail on that and similar absurdities — e.g., a 1756 ban on a book for using only secular sources in analyzing human beings — see *Russkii vestnik*, 1902, No. 1, pp. 259—64.
2 Arthur M. Wilson, chs. 37 and 44 for the involvement with Catherine; ch. 9 for the previous imprisonment in France.
3 Vartanian, *Lamettrie's*, *passim*. Frederick's eulogy is included in Lamettrie, *Oeuvres philosophiques* (Berlin, 1796), and in the (Paris, 1865) edition of his *L'Homme-Machine*.
4 Olmsted and Olmsted, pp. 126—7.

5 For a neat illustration of Bernard's essentially mechanistic approach in experimental biology, see the incident reported by F. B. Churchill, in Giere and Westfall, pp. 192–3. The literature on Bernard's elusive philosophy is very large. For a sympathetic introduction, with leads to further reading, see Coleman, pp. 154–9, 182. For an illustration of Bernard's ability to seem many things to many people, see his famous lecture on the heart, as reported by Olmsted and Olmsted, pp. 126–8, and as reported by a dualistic contemporary, below, pp. 123–5. For divergent appraisals of Bernard's political stance, compare Tsion, *Nauchnye besedy*, p. 189, and Tarkhanov, 'Klod Bernar', pp. 106, 108.

6 For biographies, see the *Dictionary of Scientific Biography*. For an analytical history, see Chadwick.

7 Degen, pp. 271–7. Degen's remarks on 'the Göttingen seven', who had been dismissed from the University in 1838 for their protest at the suppression of the constitution, imply a very repressive atmosphere on the issue of mechanism in science. Compare the relaxed, joking mood of Helmholtz's letter to Ludwig concerning the incident, in Schröer, *Carl Ludwig*, p. 61.

8 *Ibid.*, p. 210.

9 *Ibid.* To be precise, Ludwig noted that Volkmann found such a message in a speech by Helmholtz.

10 *Ibid.*, *passim*.

11 Virchow. At an earlier scientific congress, in 1863, Virchow had called for an understanding between science and religion. See Degen, p. 277.

12 Du Bois-Reymond, *Über die Grenzen* ....

13 Helmholtz, 'On thought in medicine', in his *Popular Lectures*.

14 For bibliographical information, text, and some commentaries, see Marx, *Early Writings*, pp. xvii-xix, 61–219; McLellan, *passim*; and Marx, *Ökonomisch-philosophische Manuskripte* (Leipzig, 1968), with introduction and notes by Joachim Höppner.

15 I refer of course to the *Grundrisse*, especially to those parts that Hobsbawm has selected as Marx, *Precapitalist Economic Formations*, pp. 67–120. For more bibliographical information, text, and some more leads to the commentaries, see Hobsbawm's 'Introduction', David McLellan's selective translation, *Marx's Grundrisse*, and Martin Nicolaus's complete translation, Marx, *Grundrisse*. Pp. 471–514 of Nicolaus's translation correspond to Hobsbawm's selections.

16 For Marx's abandoned first drafts, see Marx-Engels, *Werke*, XIX, pp. 384–406. Cf. Shanin.

17 Perhaps the most famous evidence is the letter that Proudhon wrote to Marx, warning him that he might be another Luther, establishing a new intellectual tyranny in place of the one he was trying to overthrow. Quoted in Edmund Wilson, pp. 154–5. Perhaps the most convincing evidence are the efforts of Marx's admirers to rescue him from his reputation. See, e.g., McLellan, *Karl Marx*, pp. 455–6.

18 For the crisis of confidence at the turn of the century, see Hughes. Perhaps the most poignant evidence is Herbert Spencer's sense, in old age, that his dream was mocked by intensified imperialism and drift toward total war. See Peel (ed.), *Herbert Spencer*, pp. xxxvii-xxxviii; and at greater length, Peel, *Herbert Spencer*.

19 For Marx's link with romanticism, as part of Hegel's influence, see Cottier. The influence of Schiller and other romantic poets has not been thoroughly studied, as far as I know. Nor have biographers paid sufficient attention to the sentimentality of everyday life, a strong romantic residue in Marx as in so many of us, with intellectual consequences that we are only dimly aware of. In this connection see the remarkable letter that Marx wrote to his wife in 1856, confessing in ironical self-mockery that his stress on 'the relations of production and exchange' may be the obverse of his 'role of lover in a second-class theater'. McLellan, *Karl Marx*, pp. 273–4.

20 *Ibid.*, pp. 121–2.

21 Marx, *Ökonomisch-philosophische Manuskripte*, pp. 191–2 (my translation). Bottomore's translation, in Marx, *Early Writings*, p. 162, tried to make sense of Marx's play on the word 'sense' (*Sinn*) by elegant variation, which spoils the word play.

22 Note that the 1st ed. of the *International Encyclopedia of the Social Sciences* (1930), had an article on human nature by John Dewey. The 2nd ed. (1968) has no such article by anyone. Similarly, the recent *Encyclopedia of Philosophy* has many historical references to human nature (see the Index) but no contemporary article on the subject.

23 Quoted in McLellan, *Karl Marx*, pp. 147–8. Cf. pp. 149–50 for an analogous passage from *The German Ideology*, predicting the end of 'the subordination of the artist to some definite art. . . . In a communist society there are no painters but, at most, people who engage in painting among other activities.'

24 Karl Marx, *Der 18te Brumaire*, p. 9. The English translations of this famous exclamation wobble on 'ein Alp', which is a mountain when feminine, an incubus or nightmare when masculine.

25 Marx-Engels, *Werke*, II, p. 132.

26 The knowledgeable reader will recognize the influence of Lichtheim, *Marxism*. I differ from Lichtheim in giving Marx credit for a basic incoherence, a painful sense of antinomies obstructing the grand goal he set himself in his youth.

27 See Schumpeter.

28 For a review of Marxist debates on pre-capitalist modes of production see Baron. See also references in Hindess and Hirst, p. 335 n. 1.

29 For a handy collection of Marx's rare comments on the future communistic society, see McLellan, *The Thought* . . ., pp. 212–24. For Marx's famous refusal – in the 'Afterword' to the 2nd ed. of *Capital* – to satisfy critics by 'writing recipes (Comtist ones?) for the cookshops [*Garküche*] of the future', see *Capital*, I, p. 17.

30 See again Schumpeter; also Robinson.

31 Marx, *Critique of the Gotha Program*, written in 1875, first published in 1891 (posthumously), and since republished many times.

32 Quoted in R. Medvedev, *Let History Judge*, p. 550. For the Russian post-revolutionary conflict over economic calculation, see A. Erlich; and Spulber.

33 Marx, *Capital*, I, p. 760, for a somewhat different translation.

34 Marx, *Der 18te Brumaire*, p. 9.

35 *Ibid.*, p. 138.

36 Black, p. 242.

37 I am offering here a highly compressed, personal reaction to the turn-of-century argument over the special qualities of history as a mode of inquiry. See Mandelbaum.

38 Quoted in Duncan, I, pp. 80−1.

39 Marx, *Ökonomisch-philosophische Manuskripte*, pp. 192−3.

40 *Ibid.*, pp. 193−4. Cf. the nervous footnote appended by the Communist editor, Joachim Höppner, who denies that Marx was here rejecting the separation of the natural and human sciences or predicting that they would all be dissolved into a single science of history. Höppner confines Marx to a philosophic repair of the gap that 'idealism' had opened between man and nature.

41 See, e.g., Aliotta, a reprint of a 1914 book. Cf. also Merz, *passim*.

42 Convincing evidence of the drift is the admission, by Lichtheim and McLellan, that it occurred, for each of them is strongly committed to a non-positivist interpretation of Marx's thought. See Lichtheim, p. 243; McLellan, *Karl Marx*, p. 423.

43 See his biography, with bibliographies, in *Encyclopedia of Social Sciences*, 1st ed., V, and *Encyclopedia of Philosophy*, II. Cf. Adamiak.

44 Engels, *Anti-Dühring*, pp. 13−4.

45 See, e.g., Levine. For a very careful assessment of the relationship between Marx and Engels, which goes far beyond the limited theme of its title, see Krader.

46 See Marx and Engels, *Briefwechsel*, IV, pp. 521−3, 539−40, *et passim*.

47 It is noteworthy that the reference to Hegel which opens *The 18th Brumaire* was suggested to Marx by Engels: *Briefwechsel*, I, p. 354. For Engels's intellectual development, see Henderson; and Gustav Mayer.

48 Engels, *Anti-Dühring*, p. 36.

49 *Ibid.*, pp. 168−9.

50 See ch. 1 of Joravsky, *Lysenko*, for my analysis of ideology, with references to other authors on the subject.

51 Georges Sorel is the best-known spokesman for that transformation. Among Marxists, Bogdanov, Lukács and Gramsci have provoked controversy by leanings in that direction.

52 James, *Principles*, I, p. 194.

53 Penfield, p. 144.

54 See Gay.

55 See Kolakowski, *Main Currents*, II, *passim*. Bogdanov was exceptionally bold and energetic in arguing this view.

56 See, e.g., Kautsky, *Materialistische Geschichtsauffassung*, and Lenin, *Filosofskie tetradi*, various editions.

CHAPTER 3   NEUROPHYSIOLOGY AND OBVIOUS IDEOLOGIES

1 See O. W. Müller. Note that German and French once used *Intelligenz* and *intelligence* as designations for the educated class, but that usage has faded into

obsolescence. For recent Soviet scholarship, see Leikina-Svirskaia, 'Formirovanie ...', and Leikina-Svirskaia, *Intelligentsiia*.

2 See Shils, 'Intellectuals', with bibliography. Also Heyck.

3 Quoted in OED, *Supplement*, p. 505.

4 The first phrase is Lavrov's, the second Dobroliubov's. See Masaryk's classic *Spirit of Russia*, and more recent works as cited in note 1.

5 See, e.g., *Otechestvennye zapiski*, 1874, No. 8, pp. 130–4, for a classification of scientists in *four* categories. I am simplifying a complex argument. Cf. Omelianskii, 'Razvitie ...', for a defense of scientists against the accusation of *zamknutost'*.

6 To be precise, they have felt obliged to tell the story that way since the 1940s. For the turning point, see below, pp. 374–5. For the abundant Soviet literature on Sechenov and Chernyshevsky, see *Istoriia estestvoznaniia ...*, *passim*. For the most scholarly effort to preserve the main lines of the story while respecting historical facts, see Iaroshevskii, *Sechenov*, especially ch. III.

7 See, e.g., Zenkovsky, II, pp. 733–6 for Sechenov, *et passim* for the emphasis on pluralism.

8 For a convenient introduction, with bibliography, see *FE*, IV, 66–7, and Novikov, ch. II.

9 For introductory bibliographies of the three authors in Russian translations, see appropriate entries in *FE* and *BS*.

10 See Lavrov, *Historical Letters*, with introduction by Scanlan; Utkina; Vucinich, *Social Thought*; and bibliographical references in all of them.

11 Quoted by Scanlan in Lavrov, p. 36.

12 Mechnikov, 'Vospominaniia ...'. Cf. the unconvincing effort of Gaisinovich, a Soviet scholar, to explain away the obvious significance of the contrasting funerals, in Mechnikov, *Stranitsy*, pp. 202–3.

13 The obit in *VE* is quoted in Bogdanovich, p. 62. See also *Russkoe bogatstvo*, 1905, No. 10, pp. 193–6; and the condolence sent by a group of writers to Moscow University, in *Nauchnoe nasledstvo*, III, p. 159.

14 N. E. Vvedenskii, *PSS*, VII, pp. 46–9.

15 See the detailed account of the invitation – from Nekrasov through Dr Bokov – and of Sechenov's response, in Iaroshevskii, *Sechenov*, pp. 89–90.

16 The essays are conveniently collected in Sechenov, *Izbrannye*, I.

17 *Nauchnoe nasledstvo*, III, p. 238. The moderate liberalism of Sechenov was routinely acknowledged by Soviet scholars until the 1930s. See, e.g., Semashko's introduction to *Bor'ba za nauku ...*, ed. Shtraikh.

18 Sechenov, *Izbrannye*, I, pp. 9–10 (his italics).

19 Quoted in Iaroshevskii, *Sechenov*, p. 115.

20 *Ibid.*, p. 93. For the complete text of the censor's ruling, see *Nauchnoe nasledstvo*, III, pp. 58–9.

21 *Ibid.*

22 See Balmuth, *passim*, and the very large literature that he refers to. Cf. Todes, ch. II.

23 *Ibid.*, pp. 116 *et passim*. The texts of the various censors' opinions are published in *Nauchnoe nasledstvo*, III.

24 See especially Sechenov, *Izbrannye*, I, pp. 142–3. Iaroshevskii, *Sechenov*,

pp. 195—6, acknowledges the implicit dualism in some of Sechenov's writing, but attempts to prove it a temporary departure from the alleged materialism of 'Reflexes of the Brain'. Shaternikov, the disciple chosen by Sechenov to be executor of his will, was free to state the plain truth in 1905: 'While he was neither an extreme sensationalist nor even less a narrow materialist, Ivan Mikhailovich saw the task of psychophysiology to be the searching out of the material substrate of psychic phenomena.' That passage in Shaternikov's obituary of Sechenov, *Nauchnoe slovo*, 1905, No. 10, p. 47, was deleted from the reprint in *Bor'ba za nauku* ... Nor does any comment of that sort appear in the biographical essay that Shaternikov wrote for Sechenov's, *Selected Works* in 1935.

25 The lawyer was V. D. Spasovich (or Wlodzimierz Spasowicz). See *Nauchnoe nasledstvo*, III, pp. 67—73.

26 *Ibid.*, pp. 70—1. Todes, pp. 117—19, tells a somewhat different story.

27 V. A. Obruchev, 1836—1912. See his reminiscences, *VE*, 1907 and 1908. Son of a highly placed officer, he became a general himself after his radical interlude and punishment. See *Bor'ba za nauku* ..., p. 77, and Bogdanovich, pp. 426ff. Maria Obrucheva is usually referred to as Bokova, after her first husband.

28 P. P. Tsitovich, *Otvet* ..., pp. 26—7.

29 P. P. Tsitovich, *Chto delali* ..., p. 44 for the hint of homosexuality, p. 46 for the women posing nude and being kissed all over.

30 Mechnikova; Mechnikov, 'Vospominaniia ...'; Pypina, 'Iz vospominanii o Sechenovykh', in Bogdanovich; Vitmer, 'Sviatoi chelovek', *Istoricheskii vestnik*, 1915, pp. 819—29.

31 I am essentially agreeing with Reiser, 'Legenda ...'. For reminiscences of Olga, see references in preceding note. Cf. also Pypina, *Liubov'* ..., and Nabokov's satirical portrait of Chernyshevsky in *The Gift*.

32 Chernyshevsky, *What Is To Be Done?*, *passim*. Cf. Shelgunov for a similar experience.

33 Quoted by Mechnikov, in *VE*, 1915, No. 5, pp. 80—1.

34 *Nauchnoe nasledstvo*, III, pp. 105—6.

35 *Ibid.*, pp. 116—19.

36 See *ibid.*, pp. 230—3 for a few of his letters to N. V. Stasova, leader in the struggle for women's right to higher education. Cf. p. 235 for a letter of 1863 to his future wife, urging her not to weaken in her effort to enter the Medical Academy, 'for you are defending the general cause of women'. For his support of the shortened working day, see Iaroshevskii, *Sechenov*, pp. 339—41. For his liberalism on the nationality question, see below, pp. 68—70. Note too his contribution of an article to a publication in aid of starving Jews. Sechenov, *Izbrannye*, I, p. 756.

37 See Dobrovol'skii, for a catalog of forbidden books with dates and references. See also the catalog in Brockhaus and Efron, *ES*, LXXV (1903), pp. 1—8. Cf. Todes, ch. II.

38 For evidence see the fading of those subjects from *ZhMNP* in the last two decades of the nineteenth century. Cf. the tolerant eclecticism in Verzhbolovich, one of the rare reviews of psychology by a defender of the traditional ideology.

39 Popel'skii, p. 77.
40 Bekhterev, *Avtobiografiia*.
41 Granat, *ES*, XVIII, p. 198.
42 Sechenov, *Avtobiograficheskie*.
43 *Ibid.*, pp. 40–2.
44 *Nauchnoe nasledstvo*, III, pp. 155–8.
45 Sechenov, *Izbrannye*, I (1952), p. 748.
46 Iaroshevskii, *Sechenov*, p. 373, citing a reminiscence of Tarkhanov.
47 For almost identical words by the psychiatrist Korsakov to his students – 'Earn the bread the *muzhik* is providing you' – see the reminiscence in *Sovremennaia psikhiatriia*, 1911, No. 1–2.
48 Sechenov, *Avtobiograficheskie*, p. 76.
49 *Ibid.*
50 *Ibid.*, p. 95.
51 See his letters in *Nauchnoe nasledstvo*, III, pp. 208–12.
52 Sechenov, 'Nauchnaia deiatel'nost' ...'.
53 Sechenov, *Avtobiograficheskie*, pp. 87 ff.
54 See, e.g., Todes, and Vucinich, *Science, passim*.
55 Mechnikova. See Mechnikov, *Stranitsy*, p. 145, for his single autobiographical reference to his mother's 'Jewish origin'. The maternal grandfather was L. N. Nevakhovich, 1776–1831. See *Evreiskaia entsiklopediia*, XI, pp. 622–4. Another of his grandsons also became a well-known scientist: L. I. Mechnikov, 1838–1888, geographer and sociologist. A third, Ivan Il'ich, was the jurist whose premature death inspired Tolstoy's great story.
56 Sechenov, *Avtobiograficheskie*, p. 132. Mechnikov, 'Vospominaniia ...', pp. 73–4, disagrees with his friend's account, but also does not confront the issue of Jewishness, which crops up persistently in other accounts – by innuendo rather than explicit confrontation. See, e.g., V. M. Kaganov's use of the opposites, '*nashi*' (our kind) *v.* '*chuzhie*' (strangers, aliens), in his introduction to Sechenov, *Izbrannye* (1947). Kekcheev and Shustin, p. 5, and Iaroshevskii, *Sechenov*, p. 218, are explicit but cryptically brief on the Jewish issue in the Medical Academy's rejection of Mechnikov.
57 Quoted in Mechnikov, *Stranitsy*, pp. 206–8; cf. *Nauchnoe nasledstvo*, III, pp. 46 ff, for some more of the documents, including Sechenov's letter of resignation.
58 Quoted in *FZ*, 1936, No. 1, pp. 5–6, and in Mechnikov, *Stranitsy*, p. 207.
59 See *Nauchnoe nasledstvo*, III, pp. 213–14; cf. Mechnikova, and Omelianskii, *Mechnikov*, p. 6.
60 Mechnikov, *Stranitsy*, pp. 165–6.
61 See *Protokoly zasedanii ... Voenno-meditsinskoi Akademii*, 1872, for the major collection of source materials, including the Director's report of the affair, pp. 436–47, and the official reports of the opposed sides. Cf. the summary in Popel'skii, pp. 71–80. Todes, pp. 389 ff, repeats allegations concerning Tsion's father which I have chosen not to accept, since they first appear, without documentation, in an American account of 1938. Todes also repeats the story that I. F. Tsion wrote, or helped to write, the *Protocols of the Elders of Zion*. I find the story not only unproved but unlikely.

62 Most of these details come from Tsion, 'Nigilisty ...', *Russkii vestnik*, 1886, Nos. 5–6 and 7–8, and separate publication. To be sure, I have been obliged to use my judgment in selection and emphasis. See, e.g., in his *Études sociales*, pp. 29–30, his denial that his failing of students influenced the protests against him.

63 Strakhov, writing to Leo Tolstoy. *Tolstovskii muzei*, II, pp. 53–4.

64 *Evreiskaia entsiklopediia*, XV, p. 118. The article, dated 1912, lists at least two people who were no longer on any faculty (N. Bakst and M. E. Mandel'shtam), but seems to have omitted Jews who had converted (such as the two Khvol'sons, father and son) and people of partly Jewish origin (such as Mechnikov).

65 Jewish writers who confronted the issue openly were likely to become spokesmen of Jewish opinion, and thereby isolated from Russian *obshchestvennost'*. That is how I read the rich evidence assembled by Frankel, *Prophecy*. Note especially the career of M. E. Mandel'shtam.

66 *Otechestvennye zapiski*, 1874, No. 7, p. 25.

67 *Ibid.*

68 See especially the second installment of Mikhailovskii's polemic, *ibid.*, No. 8.

69 See, e.g., Tsion (or Cyon), *La guerre à Dieu* ..., pp. 20–1, for angry thrusts at Sechenov and at Miliutin.

70 Tsion, *Raboty* ..., pp. 187–8.

71 *Russkii vestnik*, May 1886, pp. 764–5.

72 For Tsion's campaign against Witte, see Kennan. For a little sample of Tsion linking Witte with Jewish financiers and liberalism and the ruin of Russia, see his letter in *Pobedonostsev* ..., II, p. 971.

73 Tsion, *Études politiques*, p. 314.

74 Tsion, *Études politiques*, pp. 313–15.

75 Tsion, *La guerre à Dieu* ..., p. 10.

76 *Russkii vestnik*, May 1886, pp. 770–1.

77 See again 'La question des Juifs', in Tsion, *Études politiques*. Cf. Rollin, p. 332, for a quote from a letter of Tsion to Drumont, without citation of source.

78 *Russkii vestnik*, 1886, No. 7–8, p. 826. But cf. Tsion, *École médicale pour les femmes* ..., for a surprising streak of liberalism on higher education for women.

79 See *Pobedonostsev* ..., II, pp. 675, 716, 719–20, 804, in particular. Cf. Tsion's public appeal to Alexander III to play the statesman, and moderate the hostility to Jews that is understandable in a private individual. *Études politiques*, pp. 328–32.

80 The most notorious was the biologist N. Ia. Danilevskii, who crusaded against Darwinism and for Russian nationalism. Cf. A. I. Sikorskii, eminent professor of psychiatry who served as an expert for the prosecution at the Beiliss trial, testifying that the mentality of the accused was compatible with ritual sacrifice of a Christian boy. Bekhterev, chief expert for the defense, was far more representative of psychiatrists.

81 V. S. Solov'ev was the most celebrated spokesman of the religious revival, and he was dismayed by Pobedonostsev's efforts to enforce religious belief.

82 The searching was done by Soviet scholars after Stalinist ideologists revived

old-fashioned Russian nationalism. But they have been inhibited from praising such figures as N. Ia. Danilevskii, or from acknowledging the truculent chauvinism of, say, N. N. Zinin, a distinguished chemist who provoked angry despair in Sechenov. See *Nauchnoe nasledstvo*, III, pp. 110 *et passim*. Zinin took a leading role in the opposition both to Mechnikov and to Tsion.

83 *VFiPs*, 1894, kn. 25(5), p. 730.

84 See editorial comment, *ibid.*, pp. 729–30.

85 Mechnikova.

86 See above, pp. 68–70, for Du Bois-Reymond to that effect, and p. 75, for Tsion. For the history of such reasoning, see S. J. Gould.

87 *Trudy Obshch. russk. vr.*, 1907, p. 248. Cf. Pavlov, *PSS*, VI, p. 266, where the quoted words are surreptitiously omitted, without ellipsis points.

88 See above, p. 75. Note also Tsion's admiration of Houston Stuart Chamberlain, in Tsion, *Dieu et science*, p. 384.

89 Pavlov, *PSS*, III, pt. 1, p. 345. Available in Pavlov, *Lectures*, p. 286.

90 Sherrington, *The Integrative Action*, pp. 116 *et passim*. Cf. Lents, 'Ob osnovakh ...', for a Pavlovian using that audacious notion to justify limitless metaphorical use of the reflex concept.

91 Cf. Joravsky, 'The scientist ...', *NYR*, 12 October 1978; 'Scientists ...', *ibid.*, 28 June 1979; and 'Sin ...', *ibid.*, 17 July 1980.

92 See *Letopis'* ... *Pavlova*, pp. 9–12, with references. Note also Babkin; Savich; and Frolov, *Ivan* ..., 1949 and 1953 eds., for rather different reports of Pavlov and religion and the conversion to faith in science, by three disciples with long personal acquaintance. For his own brief autobiographical report, see Pavlov, *PSS*, VI, p. 441. For his revealing *obiter dicta* on religion, including his conversion to faith in science, see references under 'Religiia' in *Pavlovskie klinicheskie sredy*, III, p. 483.

93 See her letter to Babkin after Pavlov's death, quoted in Babkin, p. 28.

94 The incident occurred in Babkin's presence in 1929. He told of it in the unabridged typescript of his biography, which is in McGill University Library.

95 I quote from a picture postcard of the cross, copyright 1929, purchased in Montreal in 1974.

96 See Pavlova, p. 101.

97 Cf. the contrasting accounts by Pavlov's disciples – e.g., Anokhin, *Pavlov*, pp. 72 ff, and Babkin, pp. 14–16 – and by Tarkhanov's disciples, Eristavi and Semenskaia, pp. 9–11 *et passim*.

98 *Perepiska* ... *Pavlova*, pp. 61–2.

99 *Tovarishcheskaia pamiatka* ..., p. 115 and Pavlova, p. 135.

100 Pavlov, *PST*, V, p. 372, and *PSS*, VI, p. 442.

101 See 'Botkin', *BSE*, 1st ed. Since the 1940s Stalinist veneration has erased such comments on Botkin and Pavlov.

102 See *BS*, I, p. 101, with bibliography.

103 Pavlov, *PSS*, VI, pp. 108, 443.

104 Pavlov to Babkin, 28 September 1929. Babkin papers at McGill University Library.

105 See above, p. 57.

106 See Babkin, pp. 27–54, for a detailed picture based on much testimony of

Mrs Pavlov, including quotes from her letters to Babkin. Cf. also her memoir in *Novyi mir*, 1946, No. 3, and the correspondence in *Moskva*, 1959, No. 10.

107 Minkowski, 'Iwan ...', in Kolle, I, p. 211.

108 *Protokoly zasedanii ... Voenno-meditsinskoi Akademii*, 1906–7.

109 *Iz istorii studencheskikh volnenii*.

110 Minkowski, 'Iwan ...', in Kolle, I, p. 213.

111 Pavlov, 'Nauchnyi institut ...', in *Rechi i privetstviia....* Omitted from his *PST* and *PSS*, though Soviet scholars were aware of its existence: see *Bibliografiia trudov Pavlova ...*, p. 115. The speech was finally republished in *Neopublikovannye ...*, pp. 74–6, with alteration and omission at the point of his most fulsome tribute to German primacy in science and therefore in national power.

112 Zinoviev said so, in *Pravda*, 25 November 1923. See Orbeli, *Vospominaniia*, pp. 53–4, for a different version: other professors withdrew their signatures, and the petition was aborted.

113 Cf. the depreciatory acknowledgment of his 'bourgeois-liberal ... "oppositionism"' by the editors of Repin, p. 8.

114 Tarkhanov, 'Klod Bernar'.

115 See Eristavi and Semenskaia for bibliography.

116 *Ibid.*, p. 42.

117 Tarkhanov, 'Svobodnaia nauka'.

118 For Ol'denburgskii and the founding of the Institute, see *Letopis' ... Pavlova*, pp. 39, 191–2; Chebysheva; Savich; Brockhaus and Efron, *ES*, XXIA, 1901, p. 916; Orbeli, *Vospominaniia*, pp. 49–50; and Pavlov's tribute to Ol'denburgskii in the speech cited above, note 111. For Tarkhanov's part in Pavlov's appointment to the Medical Academy, see *Letopis' ... Pavlova*, p. 34.

119 Averbukh and Miasishchev omit the donations and the allocation of crown lands, which Bekhterev, *Avtobiografiia*, pp. 32ff, was proud to report.

120 *Ibid.* V. A. Vagner became the titular director.

121 *Ibid*, p. 39.

122 *Protokoly zasedanii ... Voenno-meditsinskoi Akademii*, 1906–7.

123 Reported by Batalov, *Filosofskie*.

124 Reported by Bekhterev, *Avtobiografiia*, p. 49.

125 *Trudy vtorogo s'ezda ...*, p. 2.

126 *Ibid.*, pp. 33, 46.

127 *Ibid.*, p. 424. The theme was repeated in the closing remarks by Serbskii, pp. 503–4, and popularized by Khoroshko.

128 Dobroliubov, V, pp. 7–140 and 560–2.

129 See Frieden. Cf. also Julie Brown, for a somewhat different appraisal of the psychiatric part of the medical profession.

130 See below, p. 434.

131 See Tager, ch. 12. Cf. Bekhterev, 'Ubiistvo Iushchinskogo ...'.

132 *Russkii vrach*, 1912, Nos. 20 ff., pp. 700–2, 738–41, 951–8, 967–8, 980–1, 1015–16, 1050–1, 1449–56. Pavlov's contributions to this extended polemical exchange have been omitted from both editions of his 'complete' works, *PST* and *PSS*. For a list of Bekhterev's extensive publications on the problem of alcoholism, see his *Izbrannye*, p. 519.

133 See the unabridged typescript of Babkin, *Pavlov*, in McGill University Library. The abridged version is still harsh in its portrait of Bekhterev.
134 Batalov.
135 *Trudy tret'iago s'ezda* ..., p. 62.
136 *Ibid.*, p. 46.
137 *Ibid.*, pp. 264–5.
138 See Julie Brown, 'Professionalization ...'.
139 Chekhov, *PSS*, pt. 1, XIII, pp. 63–4.
140 *Ibid.*
141 *Ibid.*, pp. 401–2, and pt. 2, X, pp. 404–5, 438.
142 Cf. Grossman, p. 50, for the memory of the 1902 performance turning into a talisman for a Russian Jewish physician shunned by her non-Jewish compatriots as the Nazi Germans close in.
143 *Trudy tret'iago s'ezda* ..., pp. 868–9.

CHAPTER 4 PSYCHOLOGIES AND LESS OBVIOUS IDEOLOGIES

1 Cited by Ivanovskii, in *VFiPs*, 1900, kn. 51, pp. 12–13.
2 *Ibid.*
3 See biography by Radlov, in Brockhaus and Efron, *ES*, LXXXI, p. 420. See philosophical report by Solov'ev, a pupil of Iurkevich, in *ZhMNP*, Dec. 1874, pp. 294–318.
4 Iurkevich, 'Iazyk ...', and 'Iz nauki ...', reprinted (abridged) in *Russkii vestnik*, 1861, No. 4–5.
5 See Wundt, *Dusha*, II, pp. 1–53, for the censors' case against the book, and the trial record.
6 *Ibid.*, pp. 7 ff.
7 *Ibid.* Spasovich republished his courtroom speech in his *Za mnogo let*, pp. 333–42. Cf. Todes, pp. 104–10, for a detailed account of the censors' reasoning.
8 See below, *passim*.
9 Troitskii, *Nemetskaia*. Still remembered in the Soviet period as a landmark; see Vygotsky, 'Psikhologicheskaia nauka', p. 28.
10 *ZhMNP*, July and August 1867, pp. 174–208, 499–539.
11 Some learned believers kept on trying. See, e.g., Ostroumov, and Metropolitan Antonii. The 'problematic science' is Mitchell Ash's and W. R. Woodward's neat phrase. See their book of that title.
12 See Shenrok's biography in *Nikolai Iakovlevich Grot*, pp. 18–19, and Ivanovskii, pp. 63 ff.
13 *VFiPs*, 1889, kn. 1. The Society was founded in 1885.
14 See biography in *FE*, I, 230. Cf. A.I. Vvedenskii, 'Nauchnaia ...'.
15 A. I. Vvedenskii, *Psikhologiia*. See pp. 80–1 for his account of his original article on the theme, in 1892, with ensuing polemical exchange.
16 *Ibid.* For the reaction of Pavlov and his disciples, see below, pp. 158 *et passim*.
17 See especially Orbeli, *Uslovnye ...*, pp. 13 *et passim*, and Zelenyi, 'Sovremennaia ...'.

18 That is abundantly evident in A. I. Vvedenskii, *Psikhologiia*. See also his *Dekart*, and the items cited in *FE*, I, p. 230.

19 G.E. Struve, *Samostoiatel'noe*, previously published in *Russkii vestnik*, February, March 1870. Cf. Usov; Aksakov; and Iaroshevskii, 'Iz istorii'. For a biography of Struve, see Brockhaus and Efron, *ES*, XXXIa, 1901, p. 832.

20 Samarin, VI, pp. 374–5 *et passim*. That account is much closer to the event than Sechenov, *Avtobiograficheskie*, p. 129, which implies that the discussion with Kavelin followed the printed exchange.

21 Kavelin, 'Zadachi psikhologii', *VE*, January and April 1872; conveniently republished in his *Sobranie*, III, together with rejoinders to Sechenov's replies.

22 Sechenov, *Izbrannye*, I (1952), p. 140.

23 See above, pp. 7–8.

24 See especially Sechenov, *Sobranie*, I, p. vi.

25 Sechenov, 'Komu i kak razrabotyvat' psikhologiiu ...', *Izbrannye*, I (1952), pp. 173 ff. Originally published in *VE*, April 1873.

26 Kavelin, *Sobranie*, III.

27 Sechenov, *Izbrannye*, I (1952), pp. 138–9.

28 *Ibid.*, pp. 144–5.

29 *Ibid.*, p. 139.

30 *Ibid.*, pp. 148 ff. Note the Soviet editor's discomfiture at that point, bound by Marxism-Leninism to take Kavelin's side against Sechenov. See pp. 709–10.

31 *Ibid.*, p. 178.

32 See especially, *ibid.*, pp. 153 ff.

33 *Ibid.*, p. 173.

34 *Ibid.*, p. 713 n. 162.

35 *Ibid.*, pp. 427 ff, and Sechenov, *Avtobiograficheskie*, pp. 115–16. It was not only conservatives who objected to Sechenov's argument against free will. See especially Antonovich, 'Professor Sechenov ...', and particularly p. 204, for a radical who sounded like Dostoevsky on the issue of freely given love.

36 See, e.g., Rosenberg, *passim*.

37 Mechnikov, 'Vospominaniia ...', p. 79.

38 Note especially Kavelin, *Zadachi etiki*, and the extended critique by Spasovich, in *VE*, 1885, No. 5, conveniently republished in Spasovich, *Sochineniia*, IV, pp. 155–210, which includes interesting commentary on Sechenov as well as Kavelin.

39 Cf. Canguilhem, 'Le concept ...', for the broad provenance of the distinction commonly attributed to Helmholtz.

40 Sechenov, *Izbrannye*, I (1952), pp. 449, 474, *et passim*. Cf. Iaroshevskii's article on the subject in *FE*, II, 239–40.

41 Plekhanov, I, pp. 480–1, 500–1, and III, pp. 240–3.

42 Lenin, *Sochineniia*, XIV, pp. 219 ff. Lenin seems unaware that 'physiological idealism' was Feuerbach's criticism of Johannes Müller.

43 In 1904 Lenin wrote for a copy of Sechenov's *Elementy mysli*. That is the only reference to Sechenov in all of Lenin's writing.

44 See below, pp. 374–5.

45 The neatest summary of the evidence is provided by Drapkina, in her protest against continuation of the tradition: 'Up to now we have had almost no

correct evaluation of I. M. Sechenov as a psychologist ... Sechenov is pictured as a vulgar materialist, his philosophical views are undervalued ...'. *Sovetskaia pedagogika*, 1939, No. 6, p. 105. Rubinshtein tried to correct the subsequent exaggeration of Sechenov's role as a psychologist: 'if one is speaking of the history of science, considered organizationally, above all as official university science, Sechenov in reality played almost no role in it.' Rubinshtein, *Printsipy*, p. 246.

46 See many references to Spencer in index of Sechenov, *Izbrannye*, I (1952), p. 762.

47 For his point of departure, see Grot, *Psikhologiia chuvstvovanii*; for his ultimate view, see his article, 'Psikhologiia', in Brockhaus and Efron, *ES*, L, pp. 677–83. See Rubinshtein, *Printsipy*, pp. 242–4, for Grot's 'Copernican revolution'.

48 *Ibid.*

49 For his own account of early interest and rapid disillusion, see Sechenov, *Avtobiograficheskie*, and cf. *Nauchnoe nasledstvo*, III, pp. 235 ff.

50 Sechenov, *Études*, with introduction by Vyrubov.

51 See Tutundzhian for an embarrassing effort to make much of that isolated review.

52 See below, pp. 135 ff. For Bekhterev's first notice of Sechenov's possible influence on his 'objective psychology', see Iaroshevskii, *Sechenov*, pp. 388–9.

53 Brentano in 1895, as quoted by Kraus in Brentano, *Psychologie* ... (1924), p. xviii.

54 James, *Psychology*, p. 468. For the young man's hopes in 1867, see Hearst, p. 1.

55 James, *Principles*.

56 Grot, 'Psikhologiia', in Brockhaus and Efron, *ES*, L, 1898, p. 680.

57 N. N. Lange, *Psikhologicheskie*, pp. xxi ff.

58 *VFiPs*, 1894, kn. 24(4), p. 588.

59 N. N. Lange, *Psikhologiia*, p. 42.

60 *Ibid.*, pp. 63–4. The individual in question was Munsterberg.

61 *Ibid.*, p. 251.

62 See the entire report of Lange's doctoral defense, *VFiPs*, 1894, kn. 24(4), pp. 564–616.

63 Iudin, p. 153.

64 N. N. Lange, *Psikhologiia*, facing p. 128, has a portrait of Sechenov, but the text pays very little attention to him.

65 Lenin, *Sochineniia*, XIV, p. 286.

66 See references in Chekhov, *PSS*, pt. I, vol. VII, pp. 694–5.

67 *Ibid.*, p. 454.

68 For a different, or additional, set of contemporaneous references in 'The Duel', see Tulloch, who finds Max Nordau in Chekhov's young biologist.

69 The educational psychologist was Lazurskii; the sociologist M. M. Kovalevskii, the historian of culture Kareev, the religious philosopher Losskii. For additional names, see Averbukh and Miasishchev, pp. 4 ff. Note their omission of Losskii. See *Vestnik psikhologii, kriminal'noi antropologii i gipnotizma*, 1904, No. 5, pp. 273 ff, and 1910, No. 3, pp. 259 ff, for accounts of the Institute.

70 See Chelpanov's account in *Psikhologicheskii institut imeni* . . . .
71 Ebbinghaus, *Abriss*. For an absurd interpretation of the apothegm − 'Much of psychology's history has been written in retrospect' − see Eysenck, ed., *Encyclopedia of Psychology*, II, p. 62.
72 See especially Chelpanov, 'Ob eksperimental'nom metode . . .', and 'Ob otnoshenii . . .'.
73 Rubinshtein, *Printsipy*, p. 244.
74 Psikhologicheskii institut, *Rechi i privetstviia* . . ., p. 47. See also work cited in note 70.
75 Psikhologicheskii institut, *Rechi i privetstviia* . . ., p. 16.
76 *Ibid.*, p. 36.
77 See *VPs*, 1955, No. 3, pp. 99−100, for a belated publication of one of his two messages. See below, pp. 451−2.
78 Timiriazev, IX, p. 232. That pre-revolutionary article was reprinted in Timiriazev's *Nauka i demokratiia* (1920), and was used in the campaign to discredit Chelpanov. See Frankfurt, 'Ob odnom . . .', pp. 185−6.
79 A. I. Vvedenskii, *Psikhologiia*, 1917 ed., pp. 348−9.
80 *Ibid.*, p. 334. Wundt and Vvedenskii used the term 'artisans'; I have added the specific workplaces.
81 See, most notably, Nechaev, *Sovremennaia* . . . (1901), and his 'Pervyi kongress . . .', pp. 428−42. For a major argument between him and Chelpanov, see *Trudy vtorogo vserossiiskogo s'ezda po pedagogicheskoi psikhologii*, pp. 56−68, *et passim*.
82 See Lazurskii, *Ocherk nauki o kharakterakh* and *Klassifikatsiia lichnostei*; and Rossolimo, *Psikhologicheskie profili*.
83 Charlotte Bronte, *Jane Eyre*, Penguin ed., pp. 385, 415, for 'the British peasantry', and *passim* for her inconsistent fantasies of self-sacrifice to educate the worthy ones.
84 See Sokolov, 'Kritika . . .'.
85 See Eklof.
86 *VPs*, 1957, No. 4, p. 4.
87 See Kornilov, *Uchenie*, for the summation of that work.
88 Kornilov, *Shkola* . . ., pp. 7−8 quoting Paulsen.
89 *Ibid.* On that basis he argued for the separation of religious education from the public schools.
90 Blonskii, *Moi vospominaniia*.
91 Blonskii, 'Fridrikh Paul'sen . . .', p. v.
92 *Nikolai Iakovlevich Grot* . . ., p. 207.
93 Tolstoy, *PSS*, L, pp. 172−3.
94 *Ibid.*, pp. 20−1.
95 *Ibid.*, XXXVIII, p. 589.
96 *Ibid.*, LXVI, p. 62.
97 The major statement of this argument is Tolstoy's *Confession*. For the Russian, with rich explanatory notes, see Tolstoy, *PSS*, XXIII.
98 *Ibid.*, XXXI, p. 93. I use the Maude translation, from Tolstoy, *Essays and Letters* (1903), p. 227.
99 See note 92.

100 Tolstoy, *PSS*, LVII, pp. 158–9. He took Wundt more seriously, though he was convinced that Wundt was trying 'to do the impossible, by laws of matter to explain the life of the spirit'. *Ibid.*, LII, pp. 14–15.

101 Chekhov, *PSS*, series II, vol. 3, p. 207. I have translated *fiktsiia* as fabrication rather than fiction, to avoid confusion with literary fiction, which Chekhov took quite seriously.

102 For example, *Russkaia mysl'* at the turn of the century had a category of book reviews called 'Philosophy and Psychology', which gave occasional heed to issues of *VFiPs* – most intensely when Tolstoy published in it.

103 For a rare example of the genre, see Rakhmanov.

104 Ovsianiko-Kulikovskii, p. 146.

105 Verzhbolovich, pp. 133–4.

106 *Ibid.*, p. 123. The quoted words are from Kireevskii.

CHAPTER 5 NEUROPHYSIOLOGY AND THE POETRY OF THE PROBLEM

1 See below, p. 134.
2 See below, p. 386.
3 Pavlov, *PSS*, VI, p. 248.
4 Bernard, 'Étude …'.
5 *Ibid.*, p. 237.
6 *Ibid.*, p. 250.
7 Tsion, 'Serdtse i mozg', p. xviii.
8 *Ibid.*, p. xxiii. There is a separate publication, *Serdtse i mozg* (St Petersburg, 1873).
9 For Tsion's views on religion, science, and politics, see above, pp. 70–7. For his major accomplishment in neurophysiology, see Schröer, 'Carl Ludwig …', pp. 176–7. Tsion's scientific works are conveniently gathered in his *Gesammelte* ….
10 See above, pp. 96ff.
11 Quoted in N. E. Vvedenskii, *Ivan* …, p. 11.
12 Quoted in N. E. Vvedenskii, *Pamiati* …, p. 4.
13 *Nauchnoe nasledstvo*, III, p. 240. For his public tribute to Weber, see Sechenov, *Izbrannye*, I (1952), p. 20.
14 For Griesinger's pioneering role in the reflex concept of the brain-mind, see above, pp. 7–8. In Sechenov's published works I have been unable to find any reference to Griesinger, but I note the repeated observation of Griesinger's influence. See, e.g., Kannabikh, *Istoriia*, p. 275; Grashchenkov, 'Shkola … Pavlova', p. 5; and Snezhnevskii, *Obshchaia psikhopatologiia*, pp. 7–8. The persuasive facts are that Griesinger published the major textbook of psychopathology in 1845 (2nd ed., 1861), and that Sechenov in the 1860s was trying to set 'medical psychology' upon an experimentally proven foundation. I would not be surprised if the Stalinist editors of Sechenov's letters—in *Nauchnoe nasledstvo*, III—have omitted laudatory references to Griesinger, in keeping with the dogma that Sechenov originated the reflex concept of the mind. See

especially *ibid.*, p. 245, where he is responding to his wife's recommendation that he study Griesinger.

15 See Schröer, *Carl Ludwig*, pp. 190 *et passim*, and Sechenov, *Avtobiograficheskie*, pp. 112, *et passim*.

16 Conveniently republished in Sechenov, *Izbrannye*, II, pp. 361–87, with bibliographical information on pp. 918–19.

17 See the cool characterization of Bernard in Sechenov, *Avtobiograficheskie*, pp. 110–11.

18 See the review of the controversy in Pankratov. For a less partisan review, see Fearing, pp. 191 *et passim*.

19 *Nauchnoe nasledstvo*, III, p. 237.

20 *Ibid.*, pp. 237 ff.

21 *Ibid.*

22 T. Lauder Brunton was the author. See Fearing, pp. 194–5.

23 *Nauchnoe nasledstvo*, III, pp. 248–9.

24 See especially his comments, in 1901, on a critical article by S. J. Meltzer, which had appeared in the *New York Medical Journal*, 1899. Sechenov, *Izbrannye*, II, pp. 548–53. Cf. the note that Sechenov in 1904, preparing his *Collected Works*, appended to his 1863 article on inhibition: Sechenov, *Sobranie* ..., I, p. 27. Cf. *Izbrannye*, II, pp. 919–20. Pankratov, p. 228, acknowledges that 'Sechenov, in his later comments, left the question of inhibition open', but declares that 'he did not renounce his views.'

25 N. E. Vvedenskii, *Ivan* ... (1906), originally published in *Trudy Sankt-Peterburgskogo obshchestva estestvoispytatelei*, 1906, No. 2, and reprinted in Vvedenskii, *PSS*, VII. He published another memoir of Sechenov in *Russkii vrach*, 1905, No. 4, and reviewed his achievements in a paper to educational psychologists. Note Vvedenskii's persistent effort to make the studies in gas absorption seem Sechenov's major accomplishment.

26 See *BME*, 1st ed., XXX (1934), pp. 374–9, a biography by his student Shaternikov, who attributes the resignation to Sechenov's 'miserable mood as a result of the fate of his research in gas absorption'. Shaternikov's expanded version, in Sechenov, *Biographical*, p. xxxi, is unconvincing in its effort to disprove Sechenov's gloomy assessment of his research. Cf. Iaroshevskii, *Sechenov*, pp. 295 and 333.

27 Sechenov, *Fiziologiia* ....

28 Sherrington, 'Spinal reflexes', II, p. 838.

29 See Vvedenskii's notes in the Russian translation of Fredericq and Nuel, *Osnovy*, II.

30 Sherrington, 'Spinal reflexes', pp. 840–1.

31 See especially Swazey, *Reflexes* ....

32 *Nauchnoe nasledstvo*, III, p. 257.

33 Karl Ewald Hering presents a crucial test of this generalization, for he worked at the boundary between physiology and psychology, trying to keep them joined. See discussions, with further references, in Boring, pp. 351 ff, and in *Dictionary of Scientific Biography*, VI.

34 J. B. Watson took this ideology to an extreme. Note his tormenting experiment on a human infant, and his advocacy of 'etherization' for the 'hopelessly

insane' and of forced labor for other defectives. See Watson, *Behaviorism*, pp. 147–64 and 185–86. Cf. Ben Harris, pp. 151–60, for a critique of Watson's notorious experiment on 'Little Albert'. Except for a fleeting reference to Watson's possibly 'callous' failure to 'recondition' Albert–the child had been made to cry at the sight of stuffed toys, since metal objects were banged whenever the toys were presented–Watson's critic is concerned only with the experimental data. For Watson and behaviorism placed in historical context – 'the consummate psychology for the manipulative, outer-directed man' – see O'Donnell, p. 242 *et passim*.

35 See, e.g., Umov, 'Predislovie', in Sechenov, *Avtobiograficheskie*, and the previously cited commemorations by N. E. Vvedenskii.

36 *Trudy pervogo* . . ., p. 148.

37 Iaroshevskii, *Sechenov, passim*.

38 *Ibid.*, pp. 151 ff, 394 ff. It is worth noting that two Soviet historians of neurophysiology credit Charles Bell with anticipating the concept of the feedback loop, and picture Sherrington as the experimenter who proved that nervous systems operate on that model. See Airapet'iants and Batuev, introduction and afterword, in Sherrington, *Integrativnaia* . . . .

39 Pavlov, *PSS*, VI, p. 255 *et passim*. The two disciples of Sechenov were M. P. Kravkov and Tarkhanov.

40 *Ibid.*, pp. 253, 255.

41 *Ibid.*, p. 258.

42 Pavlov, *PSS*, III, pt. 1, p. 14.

43 For examples of authors who should have known better, see Frankfurt, *Refleksologiia*, II, pp. 94 *et passim*; V. P. Osipov, 'Fiziologiia . . .', p. 59; Grashchenkov, 'Shkola . . . Pavlova', pp. 5–6; Koshtoiants, 'I.M. Sechenov', p. 11. Boring, p. 636, noted that Pavlov was not Sechenov's student, and that there was a time lag of more than thirty years between the older man's essay on reflexes of the brain and the younger man's venture into conditioning, but Boring felt obliged to repeat the formula about the one inspiring the other. For less cautious repetitions of the formula, see Brazier, 'Historical', in *Handbook*, p. 55; Clarke and O'Malley, *Human Brain*, pp. 365, 377; Graham, *Science*, pp. 355 ff; Kussmann, p. 31; Frank, *Dostoevsky, The Seeds*, p. 93. The list could be extended indefinitely. For a refreshing contrast, see Roger Smith, p. 85.

44 Pavlov, *PSS*, I, p. 190.

45 *Letopis'* . . . *Pavlova*, p. 31.

46 See Dionesov's notes to Orbeli, *Vospominaniia*, p. 113. Sechenov recommended V. Ia. Danilevskii; Pavlov was recommended by the chemist N. A. Menshutkin, according to *Letopis'* . . . *Pavlova*, p. 33. (Dionesov refers to a different Menshutkin.) Vvedenskii was recommended by F. V. Ovsiannikov, who had been Pavlov's first teacher of physiology.

47 *Nauchnoe nasledstvo*, III, p. 225. In his *Avtobiograficheskie*, p. 111, written after Pavlov had received the Nobel Prize, Sechenov repeated that brief bit of praise: 'the most artful vivisectionist in Europe'.

48 Pavlov, *PSS*, VI, p. 26.

49 The note of congratulation is quoted in Kostiuk, pp. 46–7, as evidence of Sechenov's pride in Russia, which was indeed the theme of the note. The

Festschrift was a special appendix of *Arkhiv biologicheskikh nauk*, 11 (1904), which had been planned to celebrate Pavlov's twenty-fifth anniversary of scientific work, and happily coincided with the Nobel award.

50 Pavlov, *PSS*, III, pt. 1, p. 23, for the opening of the 1903 article. Gantt translated *obrashchenie* as 'the physiologist's *shifting his attention* from purely physiological to so-called psychical questions'. Pavlov, *Lectures*, p. 47. [Italics added.] For Pavlov's previous use of the concept 'psychic secretion', see references under that heading in his *PSS, ukazateli*, p. 42.

51 Pavlov, *PSS*, III, pt. 1, pp. 23—39.

52 *Ibid*.

53 Rozhanskii, p. 158. That was a common theme of Pavlov and his disciples. See, e.g., Zelenyi, 'Sovremennaia ...'.

54 Pavlov, *PSS*, II, pt. 2, pp. 99 ff.

55 *Ibid*., VI, p. 151.

56 See Minkovskii (or Minkowski), 'Uchenie Pavlova', p. 261.

57 I. F. Tolochinov was the assistant. See biography, with bibliographical references, in *Fiziologicheskaia shkola*, pp. 246—7. Cf. *Letopis' ... Pavlova*, pp. 96—7, for the conference in Helsingfors, July 1902, at which Tolochinov and three other Pavlovian assistants gave papers that involved either 'the psychic influence' or 'the conditional reflex'.

58 Orbeli, 'Pamiati', pp. 27 ff. Note his emphasis on the crucial role of V. N. Boldyrev in persuading a stubbornly resistant Pavlov that 'artificial (psychic) conditional reflexes' deserve to be studied. The quote is from the title of Boldyrev's first article on the subject. See his bibliography in *Fiziologicheskaia shkola*, pp. 50—2.

59 Orbeli, *Uslovnye ...* (1908), pp. 1—17. See also the work of G. P. Zelenyi, as cited in *Fiziologicheskaia shkola*, pp. 112—13; and Leporskii.

60 Pavlov, *PSS*, VI, p. 441. For a belated tribute to Chernyshevsky's influence, see *Pavlovskie klinicheskie sredy*, I, p. 533.

61 Babkin, pp. 214—15; *I. P. Pavlov v vospominaniiakh*, p. 364; Pavlov, *Lectures* ..., p. 170.

62 Lewes, II, pp. 7 ff.

63 F. V. Ovsiannikov, *Izbrannye*.

64 See especially Pavlov, *PSS*, VI, p. 27, for his defense of the vivisectionist against the charge of cruelty. Note, p. 26, the incidental report of what made Carl Ludwig weep: relentless checking of his results by a rival laboratory.

65 Samoilov, 'Obshchaia ...', p. 8.

66 *Ibid*., p. 17.

67 Conveniently republished in Pavlov, *PSS*, II, pt. 2, and in English, *Work ...* (1902).

68 K. A. Lange, p. 14; and Chebysheva.

69 See below, p. 211, for Pavlov's non-response to Trotsky's comparison. Cf. *Pavlovskie klinicheskie sredy*, I, p. 42, and II, 296—97, for *obiter dicta* on Freud. For a rare moment of tacit approval of an effort to fuse his doctrine with Freud's see Pavlov's endorsement of Lents, *Vysshaia ...*, p. 1. For Freud on himself as 'not really a man of science ... but a conquistador', see Jones, I, p. 348.

70 Lashley, *Neuropsychology*, pp. 217, 248. He cites in particular an 1881 paper that Heidenhain wrote with Bubnov.

71 Pavlov, *PSS*, VI, p. 248.

72 *Ibid.*, p. 107.

73 *Ibid.*, I, p. 197.

74 *Ibid*, II, pt. 1, p. 263.

75 Eristavi and Semenskaia, pp. 11, 173 ff.

76 Pavlov, *PSS*, I, p. 197.

77 Savich, in *Sbornik ... Pavlova*, pp. 16, 413.

78 Pavlov, *PSS*, II, pt. 2, p. 173.

79 I am disregarding other possibilities, which were read into Pavlov's work by some Stalinist ideologists, who contrasted his 'nervism' with emphasis on 'humors' or glandular secretions. I am also ignoring complex weighing of 'psychogenic' *v.* 'neurogenic' factors. As I read Pavlov, he turned decisively against any weighing of 'psychogenic' factors in animal behaviour.

80 Samoilov, 'Obshchaia ...', p. 7.

81 *Ibid.*

82 *Ibid.*

83 *Ibid.*, pp. 10−13.

84 *Ibid.*, pp. 18−19.

85 Pavlov, *PSS*, III, pt. 1, p. 38.

86 *Ibid.* On Loeb see Fleming; and Pauly. On Pavlov's debt to Loeb, see Pavlov, *PSS*, III, pt. 1, p. 14, and IV, pp. 19−20. Before the rise of Stalinist xenophobia Pavlov's disciples regularly placed Loeb at the origin of Pavlov's doctrine. See, e.g., Orbeli, *Uslovnye ...*, p. 16; Zelenyi, 'Sovremennaia ...'; and Lents, *Vysshaia ...*, pp. 12 *et passim.*

87 Pavlov, *PSS*, IV, p. 20. Reference was to Bethe, Beer, and Uexküll, 'Vorschläge ...', 1899. Of the three, Bethe continued to interest Pavlovians. See, e.g., Anokhin, *Problema tsentra ....*

88 Pavlov, *PSS*, IV, p. 20, and III, pt. 1, pp. 15, 17.

89 See most notably G. B. Shaw, *Everybody's*, ch. 23.

90 See Gantt's response to Brazier, in Brazier, ed., *Central*, pp. 170−1.

91 *Ibid.*

92 Yerkes and Morgulis. See Hilgard and Marquis, pp. 22 ff. For Yerkes's ideology see Sokal, *Psychological, passim.*

93 Watson, 'The place ...'.

94 See note 34. Watson's admirers like to dwell on his lower-class Southern origin, ignoring his fierce determination to rise, which expressed itself when young in '"nigger-fighting"', when mature in advertizing. See O'Donnell, pp. 186, 237.

95 For an extensive bibliography, see Bekhterev, *Izbrannye* (1954), pp. 471−523. See biography by Miasishchev, *ibid.*, pp. 3−20; and Miasishchev, ed., *V. M. Bekhterev.* Other biographical articles are listed in *Istoriia estestvoznaniia, passim.* That bibliography omits *Sbornik ... Bekhterevu*, which contains much biographical material.

96 See Bekhterev, 'Eksperimental'nye ...', *Vrach*, 1884, No. 1, for his earliest work along these lines. Cf. his *Avtobiografiia*, for his basic ideas occurring to

him in 1884—6 while studying with Flechsig. See also Blumenau, 'O lokali-zatsii ...'.

97 Bekhterev, *Psikhika* .... There are French and German translations.
98 Bekhterev, *Kollektivnaia*, pp. 122—5.
99 Quoted by Averbukh and Miasishchev, pp. 3—4.
100 Bekhterev, 'Ob'ektivnaia ...', and Bekhterev, *Ob'ektivnaia* .... For later transmutations, see references in note 95.
101 See Bekhterev, *Obshchie, passim*.
102 *Ibid.*, ch. 12 *et passim*.
103 Gerver, 'O vliianii ...', pp. 191—8, 275—83. See comments of Pavlov and Bekhterev in Pavlov, *PSS*, VI, pp. 150—1.
104 *Ibid.*, p. 204.
105 See Pavlov, *PSS*, VI, pp. 289 ff, for a convenient republication of the stenographic record.
106 *Ibid.*, p. 294.
107 Pavlov, *Neopublikovannye*, pp. 110—11.
108 See above, p. 134.
109 Bekhterev, 'Znachenie ...', pp. 1107 *et passim*.
110 Pavlov, *PSS*, III, pt. 1, p. 317; IV, pp. 23—8.
111 See Lents, 'Ob osnovakh ...', and *Vysshaia* .... Note Pavlov's endorsement of the book.
112 Zelenyi, 'Espèce ...', pp. 458 ff. Zelenyi actually used chilling of the skin to signal a metronome that signaled acid in the mouth, and by ingenious manipulation achieved linkage. But the usual pattern, he makes clear, is no such linkage.
113 From the preface to the first edition of Bekhterev, *General Principles*, p. 17, dated 'Petrograd, July, 1917'.

CHAPTER 6   THE POETRY OF THE THING, AND THE POLITICS

1 Pavlov, *PSS*, III, pt. 1, pp. 323—39.
2 *Psikhiatricheskaia gazeta*, 1917, No. 8, p. 202.
3 *Ibid.*, p. 201.
4 *Ibid.*, p. 202.
5 *Ibid.*, p. 202—3.
6 *Ibid.*, p. 202.
7 For Pavlov's disciples taking pride in neo-Kantianism, see Orbeli, *Uslovnye* ...; Zelenyi, 'Sovremennaia ...'; Leporskii, 'Uchenie ...'. For those who turned to Marxism after 1917, see below, pp. 381 ff.
8 For leads into the large literature by and about Solov'ev, see articles in *Encyclopedia of Philosophy*, VII, and in *FE*, V.
9 Bekhterev, 'Razvitie ...', pp. 169—75, 193—9.
10 See above, pp. 136 *et passim*.
11 See Maiorov, *Istoriia*, 2nd ed., p. 21.
12 Pavlov, *PSS*, III, pt. 1, p. 27.
13 *Ibid.*, p. 39.

14 Pavlov, 'Pis'ma ...', pp. 155–81.
15 *Pavlovskie klinicheskie sredy*, III, p. 189.
16 *Ibid.*, p. 190.
17 *Ibid.*, p. 191. The helpful doctor was S. N. Davidenkov.
18 See below, pp. 210 *et passim*.
19 Vagner, 'Renan ...'; 'Staryi ...'.
20 The Library of Congress has an extensive bibliography of Vagner's works, evidently compiled by himself, bound with his work of summation, *Psikhologicheskie* ... (1929). For a sample of his evolutionary criticism of Pavlov, see Vagner, *Vozniknovenie* ..., *vypusk 3*.
21 See Timiriazev, *Sochineniia*, IX, p. 232, for his scorn of Chelpanov's psychology. For his admiration of Pavlov's doctrine, see IX, pp. 114 ff. For Timiriazev wrestling with the problem of subjectivity and consciousness as possibly useful products of evolution, see V, pp. 353–4. For Pavlov's gratitude to Timiriazev in the struggle against subjective psychology, see Pavlov, *PSS*, III, pt. 1, pp. 321–2.
22 Timiriazev, *Sochineniia*, VIII, p. 177.
23 Omelianskii, 'Razvitie ...', p. 144.
24 Reprinted, e.g., in Briusov, *Rasskazy* ..., and in English: Brussof, *Republic* ....
25 Ashukin, ed., *Briusov v avtobiograficheskikh* ..., pp. 16–17 *et passim*, and Mochul'skii, *Briusov*, p. 17.
26 Briusov, *Sobranie*, VI, pp. 167–8; originally published in 1909. He was ostensibly paraphrasing Ghil, and obviously extending and agreeing with his view.
27 One who did was Ia. P. Polonskii. Note how Mirsky, *History*, pp. 220–1, treats his effort to be romantic and scientific: Mirsky simply brushes aside the claim of science.
28 Briusov, *Sobranie*, I (1973), p. 497. I thank Henry Cooper for sharing with me his sensitive interpretation of Briusov.
29 Briusov, *ibid.*, p. 593.
30 Quoted in *New Yorker*, 21 April 1973, p. 27.
31 Briusov, *Sobranie*, VI, p. 61.
32 Mochul'skii, *Briusov*, p. 118.
33 For a lead into the abundant Soviet literature on Briusov, see the editorial notes and articles in his *Sobranie*.
34 See Dobroliubov, V, p. 28.
35 See Gregg, pp. 219–20.
36 See Solov'ev, *Sobranie*, VI, pp. 470–1 *et passim*.
37 See Nabokov, *Pushkin* ..., p. 54, *et passim*.
38 Tiutchev, *PSS* (1933); *idem, Izbrannye* ... (1952); *BSE*, 1st ed., XXXXV (1947), p. 455.
39 Quoted in Gregg, p. 76.
40 *Ibid.*, p. 133.
41 Tiutchev, *PSS*, p. 204. Cf. comment by Briusov, p. 25.
42 Briusov, *Sobranie*, VI, p. 167.
43 *Ibid.*, p. 195.

44 Nabokov, *Pushkin* ..., p. 54. For the original, see Tiutchev, any edition.
45 See Tiutchev, 'Silentium', any edition. Cf. commentary by Briusov, *Sobranie*, VI, p. 204, and by V. Ivanov, as reported by Rice, pp. 95–6.
46 Stevens, 'The Snowman'.
47 As cited in note 45.
48 *Ibid.*
49 Solov'ev, *Stikhotvoreniia*, p. 16. Cf. p. 46, for streams of tears flowing toward the irretrievable past. For the 'dark root of being', see Solov'ev, *Sobranie*, VI, pp. 463–80.
50 Briusov, *Sobranie*, VI, p. 197.
51 Turgenev, p. 352.
52 See Mochulskii, *Dostoevsky*, p. 256; Frank, *Dostoevsky: The Stir*, p. 328; and R. L. Jackson, pp. 27–8.
53 Frost, 'Lucretius and the Lake Poets'.
54 See again works cited in note 52.
55 The most famous is *The Possessed* or *The Devils*, as *Besy* has been called in translation.
56 Tolstoy, *PSS*, XXVI, p. 112.
57 Tolstoy, *Great* ..., p. 301.
58 See Ariès, pp. 563 ff.
59 Tolstoy, 'Tri smerti', in *PSS*, V, pp. 53–65; and see p. 301 for his moral explication of the story. Cf. Ariès, pp. 561–2.
60 Tolstoy, *Great* ..., p. 294.
61 Tolstoy, *PSS*, LX, pp. 357–8. I have adapted the translation of R. F. Christian, in *Tolstoy's Letters*, I, pp. 141–2. This famous letter has been repeatedly published beginning in 1890.
62 See especially Tolstoy, *PSS*, XXXI, pp. 87–95, and 'Modern science', in his *Recollections* ... (translated by Maude), originally written in 1898.
63 *Ibid.*, pp. 185–7. See Tolstoy, *PSS*, XXXI, pp. 93–5 for original.
64 That is the argument of Russell, *Scientific* ..., and of Mumford, and of many others.
65 See, e.g., Chekhov, *Letters*, pp. 61–3, 243–4, 261.
66 Chekhov, *PSS*, pt. 1, vol. 7, p. 671.
67 *Ibid.* Cf. pt. 2, vol. 3, pp. 234, 447.
68 Chekhov, *PSS*, pt. 2, vol. 3, p. 252.
69 Chekhov, *ibid.*, pt. 1, vol. 7, p. 291.
70 See, e.g., Kuznetsov, *Nigilisty?* and Novikov, *Nigilizm.*
71 Reported in the memoirs of Gregory Gurevich (Gershon Badaner), YIVO, *Studies in History*, 3 (Vilno, 1939), in Yiddish. I am grateful to Irwin Weil for providing me with a translation.
72 See Ascher.
73 See, e.g., Plekhanov, IV, p. 351, and V, p. 338.
74 The first phrase is Marx's, the second Lenin's.
75 Lenin, *PSS*, I, p. 140.
76 *Ibid.*, p. 438.
77 *Ibid.*, pp. 141–2.
78 See Joravsky, *Soviet*, p. 27.

79 *Ibid.*, pp. 28 ff.
80 See Cohen, pp. 14–15.
81 See Joravsky, *Soviet*, pp. 41–2, 135, 347 n. 14.
82 *Ibid.*, especially p. 347 n. 16.
83 Bogdanov, *Iz psikhologii* ..., p. 41. Cf. Grille, pp. 141 ff, for Bogdanov's attraction to Sechenov's definition of thought as an interrupted reflex.
84 Bogdanov, *Empiriomonizm*.
85 See especially Plekhanov, 'Materialismus militans', in his *Izbrannye*, III. Cf. Plekhanov's earlier incidental attacks on Bogdanov's philosophy, as indexed, *ibid.*, p. 764.
86 See Joravsky, *Soviet*, p. 42.
87 See Lenin, *Sochineniia*, XIV, *passim*.
88 *Ibid.*, XXXVIII, p. 204. Lenin is here summing up his reading of Hegel, but he records no disagreement.
89 See Joravsky, *Soviet*, pp. 39–40, for Lunacharsky in 1909 mocking his comrades' churchy attitude toward orthodoxy and heresy, without drawing any response from Lenin.
90 Bogdanov, *Iz psikhologii*, pp. 184 ff.
91 *Ibid.*, p. 213.
92 *Ibid.*
93 *Ibid.*, pp. 213–14.
94 His brief comment on relativity, in 1922, is not an exception to this rule. See Joravsky, *Soviet*, p. 280.
95 *Ibid.*, ch. 2.
96 Quoted *ibid.*, pp. 15–16.
97 See her letter of 10 August 1909, in *Protokoly soveshchaniia ... 1909*, pp. 250–1.
98 Iushkevich, pp. 6 ff.
99 See especially Deutscher's discussion of 'substitutism', in his *Prophet Armed*, pp. 90 *et passim*.
100 Trotsky, *Sochineniia*, XX, p. 78.
101 *Ibid.*, p. 79.
102 See especially the introduction to the post-revolutionary edition of Conrad, *Under Western Eyes*.
103 Conrad, *Heart of Darkness*.
104 Conrad, *Nostromo*, and *Under Western Eyes*. Cf. Fleishman.

CHAPTER 7   A GREAT UNIFYING IDEA

1 See, e.g., Lenin, *Sochineniia*, XXXIII, p. 54; XXXII, pp. 118–19; XXXI, p. 263.
2 I have run together elements of two famous exhortations. See Stalin, *Sochineniia*, XIV, p. 59, and XII, p. 38.
3 Quoted by Fitzpatrick, *Commissariat*, p. 12, from *Novaia zhizn'*, 1917, No. 176, p. 3. I have altered her translation.
4 Lenin, *Sochineniia*, XLIV, p. 227. Gorky's protest at the arrest of intellectuals

was the occasion for this outburst, which is used by Solzhenitsyn, *Gulag*, p. 329, to epitomize the Bolshevik attitude toward the intelligentsia.

5 Trotsky, *Sochineniia*, XXI, pp. 110–12.

6 *Ibid.*

7 Trotsky, *Literature*, p. 109.

8 *Ibid.*, p. 107.

9 *Ibid.*, p. 214. Demian Bednyi was the model poet.

10 *Ibid.*, p. 14.

11 *Ibid.*, p. 15.

12 Kalinin, 'Nauka . . .', *Novaia Petrovka*, 1923, No. 3–4, pp. 5–7. Cf. *ibid.*, 1922, No. 2, pp. 26–7, for Kalinin preaching the 'need for fiery faith that our Republic, which is agriculturally backward, will not only overtake but will surpass the agriculture of Western Europe'.

13 *Pravda*, 8 September 1925.

14 Lenin, *Sochineniia*, XLIV, pp. 325–6.

15 *Ibid.*, XXXII, p. 48. For a photograph of the celebrated document, see K. A. Lange, p. 15. For a complete translation, see Babkin, p. 165.

16 See, e.g., Kornilov, 'Sovremennaia . . .'.

17 Pavlov, *PSS*, III, pt. 1, pp. 340–5. Originally published in *Russkii vrach*, 1918, No. 1–4.

18 Bukharin, *Historical Materialism*, *passim*.

19 Lenin, *Sochineniia*, XXXIII, pp. 209–10. For the news of banishment, see *Pravda*, 31 August 1922. Cf. Chagin and Klushin, pp. 73–4.

20 Zh. Medvedev, *Soviet Science*, pp. 8 *et passim.*, for the difficult task of specifying what is meant by 'scientist'.

21 Pavlov, *PSS*, III, pt. 1, p. 17.

22 Quoted by Zinoviev, 'Intelligentsiia . . .'.

23 Trotsky, *Sochineniia*, XXI, p. 260.

24 *Ibid.*

25 Frolov, *Ivan* . . ., pp. 154–5. The metaphor has become tunneling in a mountain. Cf. an American reminiscence of Pavlov expecting a fusion of psychoanalysis with his theory of neurosis. Reported in Corson and Corson, pp. 150–1.

26 Trotsky, *Sochineniia*, XXI, pp. 275–7, 430–1, 488–91.

27 Bukharin, 'O mirovoi . . .', *Krasnaia nov'*, 1924, Nos. 1, 2; republished as *O mirovoi* . . . (1924); and in *Ataka*.

28 Bukharin, 'Enchmeniada', *Krasnaia nov'*, 1923, No. 6; and in his *Ataka*.

29 See Joravsky, *Soviet*, p. 339 n. 39.

30 Bukharin, *O mirovoi* . . ., p. 3.

31 *Ibid.*, p. 11.

32 *Ibid.*, p. 4.

33 The most notable case is Vygotsky. See below, pp. 265 *et passim*.

34 A. K. Lents, *Vysshaia* . . . . Pavlov's endorsement is on p. 4.

35 Bukharin, *Historical Materialism*, pp. 53–8, implies that view.

36 *Ibid.*, p. 98.

37 Bukharin, *O mirovoi* . . ., p. 11.

38 Bukharin, *Historical Materialism*, p. 98.
39 Sapir, 'Freidizm ...', p. 76; and Sapir, *Vysshaia*, p. 156.
40 Vygotsky, most notably. See below, p. 260.
41 *Pravda*, 29 June 1924. Cf. Joravsky, *Soviet*, pp. 40 *et passim*.
42 *Pravda*, 29 June 1924.
43 *VKA*, 1926, *kn.* 16, pp. 285–7.
44 *Ibid*. See also 1928, *kn.* 26/2, pp. 249 ff. D. B. Riazanov was the historian.
45 See Joravsky, *Soviet*, pp. 56, 100 *et passim*.
46 See above, pp. 93 ff. Some Russian translations of Western psychologists may have been 'arrested', if only for a time, by the pre-revolutionary censor – e.g., Krafft-Ebing, and, more surprisingly, Ribot's *Philosophy of Schopenhauer*.
47 See especially I. D. Ermakov, ed., *Psikhologicheskaia* ..., 22 issues, 1922–5. And see studies by Martin Miller, and by James Rice.
48 The last Russian translation seems to be Freud, *Budushchnost' odnoi illiuzii* (1930). Cf. Shirvindt, 'Psikhoanaliz', in *Osnovnye techenie* ... (1930), for the last effort at a balanced appraisal of Freud's psychology.
49 Koffka, *Osnovy psikhicheskoi razvitiia* (1934), with introductory matter by Kolbanovskii and by Vygotsky, is the last I am aware of, until the post-Stalin period.
50 Bukharin, *O mirovoi* ..., p. 36.
51 Bukharin, *Ataka*, p. 133.
52 *Ibid*.

CHAPTER 8   PSYCHOLOGY AND PHILOSOPHY

1 Blonskii, *Moi vospominaniia*.
2 *Ibid*., pp. 143 ff.
3 *Golos rabotnika prosveshcheniia*, 1922, No. 6, p. 43.
4 Blonskii, *Reforma*; and Blonskii, *Ocherki nauchnoi*.
5 Blonskii, *Reforma*, p. 37.
6 *Ibid*., p. 31.
7 Musil, I, p. 103.
8 Blonskii, as cited in note 4.
9 See editor's report in Blonskii, *Moi*, pp. 5–6.
10 Efrussi, p. 20, attributes his absence to illness.
11 See Zaluzhnyi for Zalkind's end in the 1930s.
12 See above, p. 113.
13 Petrovskii, p. 59. Cf. A. N. Leont'ev's introduction to Vygotsky, *Sobranie*, I, p. 11, and A. A. Smirnov p. 139. The very heavy emphasis on the clash of ideas – inaccurately reported – and hasty by-pass of the administrative action are evidence, I hope, of persistent bad conscience among Soviet psychologists. Cf. Efrussi for a more accurate account of the clash of ideas, without any administrative history.
14 R. Medvedev, *Let History Judge*, p. 339.
15 Kornilov, *Shkola* ....

16 Kornilov, *Uchenie* (1922).
17 *Ibid.*, p. 8.
18 *Ibid.*, p. 24.
19 *Ibid.*, pp. 8, 141–2. Cf. Efrussi, pp. 31–2, for keen, polemical analysis of Kornilov's treatise.
20 Kornilov, 'Sovremennoe …', p. 19.
21 See Petrovskii and Smirnov, as cited in note 13.
22 Kornilov, *Uchenie* 2nd and 3rd eds. Note also excision of any credit to Chelpanov. Cf. Teplov.
23 Kornilov, 'Sovremennaia …'.
24 See *ZhPNP*, 2 (1923), pp. 290–1, and 3 (1923), pp. 246–319. This extensive record simply does not support the account of the meeting in Petrovskii, *Istoriia*, pp. 53 ff. Neither do his references to *Izvestiia* and *Pravda*.
25 *Pravda*, 11 January 1923.
26 *ZhPNP*, 3 (1923), pp. 259–60; and Efrussi, pp. 20 ff.
27 Bukharin, 'Kul'turnyi front …'.
28 Efrussi is an exception to this rule. She seems to have published this pamphlet before the dismissal of Chelpanov.
29 See note 13.
30 A. B. Zalkind, 'Psikhonevrologiia i revoliutsiia'.
31 Daian.
32 Chelpanov, *Psikhologiia i marksizm* and *Psikhologiia ili refleksologiia*.
33 Chelpanov, *Psikhologiia ili refleksologiia*, p. 27.
34 See, e.g., Kornilov, 'Sovremennoe …', *passim*.
35 See virtually all the references in the preceding notes, except for Efrussi and Chelpanov himself.
36 See above, p. 213.
37 Portugalov, ed., *Detskaia*, p. v.
38 *Ibid.*, p. 18. Kornilov's opposition to energeticism was part of his Marxist metamorphosis.
39 Kornilov, as cited in n. 34, pp. 18–19.
40 Samoilov, 'Dialektika …'.
41 See Joravsky, *Soviet*, pp. 152 *et passim*.
42 Kornilov, 'Sovremennoe …', pp. 11–13.
43 *Ibid.*
44 'I think that the place of psychology is in the series of natural scientific disciplines, both with respect to the method of its work and the object of its study …'. Kornilov, *Uchenie*, p. 8.
45 Kornilov, 'Psikhologiia …', p. 9. Italics in original.
46 See below, p. 262 ff.
47 Vygotsky, 'Psikhologicheskaia nauka', p. 39.
48 See Petrovskii, Leont'ev, and Smirnov, as cited in note 13.
49 See Joravsky, *Soviet*.
50 This correlation emerged in the 1920s, e.g., in Frankfurt, 'K bor'be …', and in Chuchmarev. It is central to the pioneering Western study by Bauer, and has been constantly repeated in various forms by more recent authors, both Soviet and Western.

51 See index for both in Joravsky, *Soviet*.
52 See Institut Krasnoi Professury, *Trudy*, I (1923); and Rakhman, with introduction by L. I. Aksel'rod.
53 L. I. Aksel'rod, 'Nadoelo!', pp. 179–80.
54 See Joravsky, *Soviet*, pp. 162–3. Z. A. Tseitlin is my source.
55 See her introduction to Rakhman.
56 See, e.g., Vygotsky, as cited in note 47, p. 32. Cf. Sapir, *Vysshaia*, pp. 194–5, for a stress on consciousness at the end of a heavily reductionist book.
57 Vygotsky and Luria, *Etiudy*.
58 *Deiateli* ..., pp. 52–6.
59 See 'Freud' in index of Vygotsky, *Sobranie*; Luria, 'Psikhoanaliz, kak sistema ...'; Luria, *Psikhoanaliz* ...; Luria, 'Die moderne ...'; Zalkind, 'Freidizm ...'; and Malis. For reviews of these efforts, see Voloshinov, pp. 138 ff; Martin Miller; and James Rice. Note the emphasis on Luria's role in Ellenberger, p. 847.
60 See, e.g., Vnukov, 'Psikhoanaliz', *BME*, 1st ed., XXVII (1933); and Luria, 'Psikhoanaliz', *BSE*, 1st ed., XLVII (1940).
61 See *Sovetskaia meditsina v bor'be* ..., p. 176, for the mere citation, without texts, of the papers on treatment of neuroses, which three Freudians (Kannabikh, Assatiani, and Zalkind) delivered at a psychiatric congress in late 1925.
62 Wilhelm Reich, 'Psikhoanaliz ...'.
63 Zalkind, 'Zabolevaniia ...'; and *Umstvennyi* ....
64 *EIM*, 1929, No. 4, pp. 115–20; and Reich's response, pp. 124–5.
65 Kannabikh, *Istoriia*.
66 *Pedologiia*, 1929, No. 3, p. 436.
67 See Zaluzhnyi.

CHAPTER 9   LITERATURE AND PSYCHOLOGY

1 Voloshinov, p. 137. (Bakhtin published some of his work under that name.)
2 *Ibid.*
3 Prangishvili.
4 *Pravda*, 14 June 1925, p. 7. Cf. Petrovskii, pp. 88–9, for a presentation of that tiny reference in *Pravda* as the beginning of the 'all-out assault on psychoanalysis'.
5 Zetkin, *Reminiscences*, pp. 11–12.
6 *Ibid.*
7 Franklin, p. 103.
8 Zetkin, *Reminiscences*, pp. 12–13.
9 Zetkin, *Vospominaniia*, editions of 1959, 1968, 1971. The edition of 1955 contains the sexual discussion.
10 See Mathewson for analysis of the positive hero.
11 Note especially the public protest of General Budennyi, reported in *Babel*, pp. 384–9. Cf. Maguire, pp. 312ff.

12 Babel, *Collected*, p. 72. I have slightly altered Walter Morison's translation. See Babel, *Izbrannoe*, p. 44.

13 Babel, *Konarmiia*, p. 169. Morison translates 'kak stado platianykh vshei' 'like a multitude of bugs swarming in clothes'. Babel, *Collected*, p. 192.

14 *Ibid.*, p. 193. Cf. Babel, *Konarmiia*, p. 170.

15 'Argamak', in Babel, *Collected*, pp. 194–200. See Babel, *Detstvo* ..., pp. 390–1, for bibliographical information.

16 Carden, p. 151.

17 Babel, *Izbrannoe* (1966), p. 10. Repeated and endorsed by Levin, p. 118.

18 See below, p. 279.

19 See Beaujour; Olesha, *No Day*; and Olesha, *Izbrannoe*.

20 For analysis of the novel and the controversy it provoked, see Beaujour.

21 Olesha, *Izbrannoe*, p. 229. The original appeared in *Izvestiia*, 1929.

22 Huysmans, *À rebours*, p. 321. In the English translation, *Against the Grain*, that becomes 'a trained engineer of the soul', which Havelock Ellis catches up and repeats in the introduction, in tribute to Huysmans. See pp. 259 and 29.

23 Quoted in Willett, p. 152.

24 See Tumarkin, pp. 165–206.

25 Olesha, *Izbrannoe*, p. 427, or *No Day* ..., p. 142.

26 See below, pp. 463 ff.

27 See especially Rossolimo, *Psikhologicheskie profili*; and Lazurskii, *Ocherk*. Rossolimo's orientation was to psychiatry, Lazurskii's to education. Both continued their work into the Soviet period. See the Festschrift for Rossolimo, *Neurologie* ..., and the third edition of Lazurskii, *Klassifikatsiia* ... (1924).

28 Luria, *The Making* ..., p. 18. See p. 197 for Cole's explanation of the book's origin. Note, pp. 198–200, Cole's effort to repair Luria's omission of personal information, beginning with Jewishness. Cole writes that Luria's father was denied a teaching post before the Revolution, which I find hard to square with Luria's text.

29 For a lead into these tangled issues, see Gitelman.

30 Luria, *The Making* ..., p. 19.

31 *Ibid.*, pp. 19–20.

32 *Ibid.*, p. 27.

33 Luria, 'Psikhoanaliz, kak sistema ...', p. 79. Italics in original.

34 *Ibid.*, pp. 54–5, 60, 66–7.

35 See Luria, *The Nature* .... Cf. Petrovskii, pp. 278–9, for a hostile report of a psychologist who dared to do such experiments of a political nature.

36 Kornilov, 'Sovremennoe ...', p. 24.

37 *Ibid.* Such self-criticism and preaching were common. At the 1930 Congress on the Study of Man's Behavior Artemov opened his report on social psychology by declaring 'the absence of any well-developed social psychology' to be 'one of the greatest contradictions in the development of our school of psychology'. *Psikhonevrologicheskie*, pp. 105–6. At the outset of the campaign for a Marxist psychology in the early 1920s, social psychology had seemed the obvious field of choice. See Omel'chenko; and Struminskii. Mention should be made of M. A. Reisner (or Reusner), 1868–1928, whose writings on social psychology were largely ignored by Soviet professionals in psychological science. See his bibliography below, and in *FE*, IV, pp. 485–6.

38 *EIM*, 1929, No. 3, p. 216.

39 *Ibid.*

40 Luria, *The Nature....* Introduction by Adolph Meyer. See Luria, *The Making* ..., p. 36, for his fond gratitude to Meyer.

41 See below, p. 365

42 Luria, *The Making* ..., p. 56. See pp. 130–31 for the precise years of his medical training, which began part-time in the late 1920s and became full-time in 1936.

43 Quoted in *VIEiT*, 1983, No. 4, p. 83.

44 See Joravsky, *Soviet.*

45 See Vygotsky, *Sobranie*, I, pp. 439–40, for rare admissions of that fact by Soviet psychologists of the present day.

46 Rainov, *VKA*, No. 14, p. 95.

47 See Martin Jay. See Poster for the period since the Second World War.

48 See Rainov, *VKA*, No. 14, p. 82, for Bukharin presented as an opponent of Pavlov's doctrine. For another Marxist criticism of Pavlov and Bekhterev, see Malis.

49 Vygotsky, *Sobranie*, I, p. 374. Cf. Vygotsky, 'Psikhologicheskaia nauka', pp. 25 and 44.

50 See below, pp. 255, 262.

51 Levitin, pp. 24 ff. I thank Alex Kozulin for telling me of this book.

52 See, e.g., the vague passage in Kolbanovskii, 'Lev ...', p. 388. Luria was even less informative in 'Professor ...'. Cf. Leont'ev, 'O tvorcheskom ...', and the joint article by Leont'ev and Luria in Vygotsky, *Izbrannye*, pp. 4–36. For further references see Petrovskii; and A. A. Smirnov.

53 *Novyi put'* and *Letopis'*. Thanks to Alex Kozulin for information on the former.

54 Vygotsky, *Psikhologiia iskusstva* (1965), (1968), (1986), and (1987). The English translation, *The Psychology of Art*, seems to be from the first edition.

55 *Ibid.*, pp. ix-x.

56 See studies of Vygotsky cited in preceding notes. Cf. the conference devoted to his thought: *Nauchnoe tvorchestvo* ... (1981). Three of the fifty-seven papers dealt with his views on art.

57 Vygotsky, *Psychology of Art*, passim.

58 See references to Marx in the Index, *ibid*.

59 See Victor Erlich.

60 See above, pp. 245 ff.

61 See, most notably, Michael Cole et al., 'Introduction' and 'Afterword' in Vygotsky, *Mind in Society*; and Bruner's introduction to the Vygotsky memorial issue of *Soviet Psychology*, 1967, No. 3. An illuminating cross-cultural review of Vygotsky is provided by Alex Kozulin, who moved from the USSR to the USA: see his *Psychology in Utopia*.

62 Vygotsky, *Psychology of Art*, p. 246.

63 *Ibid.*, pp. 246–8. It must be noted that Sherrington did *not* have a reductive view of art; he was explicitly dualistic.

64 The most detailed account is by Daian.

65 From various accounts I gather that he spoke extemporaneously, at two sessions. Two of his articles appear to be subsequent written versions of what he said. See Vygotsky, 'Soznanie', and 'Metodika'.

66 Daian, No. 2, pp. 164–6.
67 See the writings of Leont'ev and Luria, as cited above. See especially the chapter on Vygotsky in Luria's autobiography, *The Making* ....
68 See the original *Uchenye zapiski* of the Institute. For an index of the Institute's publications, see APN Institut psikhologii, *Ukazatel'* ... (1967).
69 See above, pp. 210–12.
70 Bukharin, 'Enchmeniada'. Cf. Rainov's use of the article, as cited in note 48.
71 Zinoviev; and Trotsky, 'K pervomu ...'.
72 Bukharin, 'O mirovoi ...'.
73 Bukharin, *Historical Materialism*, p. 98. See above, pp. 213 ff, for the mixture of irony and literal mechanism in Bukharin's repeated use of such tropes.
74 Vygotsky, 'Soznanie'.
75 *Ibid.*, pp. 179 *et passim*.
76 *Ibid.*, p. 190.
77 *Ibid.*, p. 179.
78 *Ibid.* For Vygotsky at length on Gestalt psychology see his 'Strukturnaia ...'.
79 See, e.g., historical surveys cited in note 52. The pioneering study by Bauer, *The New Man*, offered a variant of that theme. See Thielen, p. 87, for his agreeing with that theme, and disagreeing with McLeish, *Soviet Psychology*. McLeish notes the obvious contest of schools in Soviet psychology of the 1920s, but misses the peculiar twist given to that contest by the Party ideologists who unthinkingly equated psychology with Pavlov's and Bekhterev's outlook.
80 Since Kornilov was the Director, I assume that he invited Vygotsky, as Leont'ev implies, in Vygotsky, *Sobranie*, I, p. 13. Luria implies that Kornilov opposed Vygotsky's outlook, and that he, Luria, was responsible for bringing Vygotsky to Moscow (*The Making* ..., pp. 38–9). Luria is too vague to be convincing – and inaccurate in his picture of Kornilov.
81 See above, p. 216. Kornilov chose to interpret Bukharin that way. See *Problemy sovremennoi psikhologii*, III (1928), pp. 15–17.
82 See, e.g., Vygotsky, 'Psikhologicheskaia nauka', pp. 32, 45.
83 Vygotsky, *Sobranie*, I, pp. 330–9. Luria read this work, 'The Historical Meaning of the Psychological Crisis', in manuscript, and cited it in admiration, both in the 1920s and in a 1935 commemoration of Vygotsky.
84 Vygotsky, *ibid.*, pp. 361–3, 422–3, 432. To be sure, the criticism is imbedded in praise – extravagant praise, in my reading – but Vygotsky does lump Kornilov with 'eclectics', and explicitly disapproves of Kornilov calling his psychology Marxist or dialectical materialism.
85 See references to Marx and Spinoza in Vygotsky, *ibid.*, conveniently indexed.
86 The editors declare, *ibid.*, p. 7, that they are 'publishing the text of the original without alterations'. It seems to me highly probable that they have omitted Vygotsky's quotations from proscribed authors, such as Trotsky, Bukharin, and Kautsky. (See below, note 90.) But they did publish his heretical arguments – against the notion of a Marxist psychology, most notably – with critical notes warning the reader against heresy. See especially p. 472.
87 Vygotsky frequently repeated this fundamental distinction in works published in his lifetime. See, most notably, the opening passage of 'Geneticheskie',

pp. 106–8, where he adds other synonyms to each side of the contrast; e.g., 'phenomenological' alongside 'understanding'. The posthumous republications of that article in his best-known book, *Myshlenie i rech'* – and in his *Izbrannye* – silently omitted the crucial opening pages, and the omission is carried into the English translation, *Thought and Language*, ch. 4, and into his *Sobranie*, II. See *ibid.*, pp. 480–1, for the editors implying that Vygotsky himself altered the text.

88 Spinoza, *Ethics*, Part III, Proposition 2, Scholion, translated by R. H. M. Elwes, as quoted in Vygotsky.

89 *Ibid.*

90 Compare Vygotsky, *Sobranie*, I, p. 436 – taking care to note the ellipsis points just before the final paragraph – with the close of Vygotsky, 'Psikhologicheskaia nauka', p. 45, where the quotes from Kautsky and Trotsky are highlighted. For the original of the quote from Trotsky see above, p. 205. For Kautsky's forecast of a superman, see Joravsky, *Lysenko*, p. 256.

91 Vygotsky, *Sobranie*, I, p. 436. His reference is to theorem 17 of Spinoza's *Ethics*. Cf. again the closing paragraph of Vygotsky, 'Psikhologicheskaia nauka'.

92 For evidence that Vygotsky was sensitive to modernist absurdity, see again his analysis of *Hamlet*. Cf. his review of Belyi's *Petersburg*, in *Letopis'*, 1916, No. 12, pp. 327–8.

93 The main texts are Lenin's *Materialism and Empiriocriticism* (1908) and his 1922 essay, 'On the Significance of Militant Materialism'. See Lenin, *Sochineniia*, XIV and XXIII.

94 Kornilov, *Uchebnik*. There were also 2nd and 3rd eds., 1928.

95 Vygotsky, *Sobranie*, I, pp. 434–5.

96 See Joravsky, *Soviet, passim*.

97 Vygotsky, *Sobranie*, I, p. 436.

98 For a plain statement of that policy, see Stalin, *Sochineniia*, V, pp. 223–5.

99 Vygotsky, 'Psikhologicheskaia nauka', p. 40.

100 See especially Vygotsky, as cited in n. 65. Those articles are conveniently republished in his *Sobranie*, I. For Vygotsky at greater length on Pavlov's achievement, see references to Pavlov in the index, *ibid.*

101 See, e.g., *ibid.*, pp. 388 *et passim*.

102 Vygotsky, 'Psikhologicheskaia nauka', pp. 44–5.

103 Vygotsky and Luria, *Etiudy*.

104 See *Psikhologiia*, 1931, No. 1, p. 3, and Razmyslov, 'O kul'turno-istoricheskoi teorii . . .'.

105 See below, pp. 360 ff.

106 Vygotsky, 'Biogeneticheskii . . .'. And see the work cited in note 103.

107 See below, p. 367. For his earliest Western renown, see Hanfmann and Kasanin.

108 See especially the works of V. M. Borovskii, beginning with his 'K voprosu . . .'. A partial list of his works is in the index cited in note 68.

109 Vygotsky and Luria, *Etiudy*, pp. 140–1.

110 For an intermediate stage, see Vygotsky, *Voobrazhenie* (1930), republished in 1967.

510   *Notes to pages 272 to 279*

CHAPTER 10   THE TRUTH IN NEUROPHYSIOLOGY

1 That interpretation of the Revolution is scattered through Bekhterev, *Kollektivnaia*, pp. 81, 97–9, 116–18, 142–3, 176 ff, 249–51, 271–2, 291, 399 ff, especially 406–7.
2 Bal'dysh, pp. 225–8.
3 *Ibid.*, pp. 242–3. I was unable to find the statement in the place that Bal'dysh cites, but I assume that it was published somewhere.
4 See, e.g., 'Smenovekhovstvo', *Sovetskaia istoricheskaia entsiklopedia*, XIII (1971), pp. 73–75.
5 Bekhterev, *Obshchie*; translated as *General Principles*.
6 For Lenin's polemic see *Materialism*, pp. 276–81, *et passim*.
7 Nevskii, 'Politicheskii ...', and 'Khoroshie ...'.
8 See Bekhterev, *Kollektivnaia*, pp. 122–3, with citation of original report. Note that Ivanov-Smolenskii was a participant in these ESP experiments.
9 See, e.g., Bekhterev, *General Principles*, pp. 87, 118–19, 150–1.
10 Bal'dysh, p. 226 *et passim*. Cf. the cryptic accounts of Bekhterev's institutional expansion, and subsequent contraction, in Averbukh and Miasishchev, pp. 3–6; and in Miasishchev and Khvalitskii, eds., *V. M. Bekhterev*. Cf. Miasishchev's very broad conception of reflexology in his 'Refleksologiia ...', pp. 42–5. He became Director of the shrunken Institute in 1939.
11 Mozhaiskii, pp. xii–xiii. Cf. the somewhat different list of component institutes in *Nauka i nauchnye rabotniki* ..., II (1926), pp. 190–3.
12 *Izvestiia*, 28 December 1927.
13 Bekhterev, *General Principles*, p. 20.
14 Compare the ending of ch. XV in the 2nd and 3rd eds.
15 Bekhterev, *Psikhologiia* ..., especially pp. 30 ff, where he replies to Frankfurt, *Refleksologiia*, with introductory matter by Kornilov and Zalkind.
16 Bekhterev, *General Principles*, p. 17.
17 Bekhterev and Dubrovskii, 'Dialekticheskii ...'.
18 *Ibid.*, p. 69.
19 Bekhterev, *General Principles*, pp. 19–20.
20 See works cited in note 17, pp. 87–9, and in note 15, pp. 59–64.
21 Ivanov-Smolenskii, pp. 91 ff. On pedology see Fitzpatrick, *Commissariat*.
22 Bekhterev, *General Principles*, p. 87.
23 Cited in A. A. Smirnov, p. 144.
24 Bekhterev, *General Principles*, p. 151.
25 *Ibid.*, pp. 149–50.
26 See below, pp. 287 ff.
27 See Joravsky, *Soviet*, p. 189. The interpretation offered there is not accurate, I now realize.
28 See Shmidt et al., pp. 54–8.
29 See *NR* (1930) for basic biographical data. For his major works on psychology, see Zalmanzon, 'V zashchite ...', 'Protiv eklekticheskogo ...', and the single publication of KA, Institut vysshei nervnoi deiatel'nosti, *Vysshaia* ....

30 See Zaluzhnyi, for the public cursing. Zalkind's bibliography is too extensive to give here.

31 Sapir was still a major figure at the Behavioral Congress of 1930. See his speech 'On the Problem of Marxist Methodology in the Science of Behavior', Vsesoiuznyi povedencheskii s'ezd, *Stenograficheskii*. Within the year he was sharply attacked. See *ZMLE*, 1931, No. 1, p. 151, for his self-criticism. His bibliography is too extensive to give here. For his resurfacing after a long silence, see Vsesoiuznyi s'ezd nevropatologov i psikhiatrov, III. *Trudy*, p. 422.

32 Among Bekhterev's disciples S. I. Fedorov still talked that way, and so did V. P. Protopopov. On the former, see Shnirman, p. 90. On Protopopov, see his *Vvedenie*, p. 2, and criticism by Chuchmarev, p. 65. Among Pavlov's disciples Lents still talked that way, in a book that Pavlov endorsed. See below, p. 214. For the major Russian source of such philosophizing, A. I. Vvedenskii, see above, pp. 95–6.

33 *Refleksologiia ili psikhologiia*.

34 *Refleksologiia i smezhnye napravleniia*.

35 Work cited in note 33, pp. 78–9.

36 Work cited in note 34, p. 108.

37 Quoted in Merkulov, *Ukhtomskii*, p. 39.

38 *Ibid., passim*. See also Merkulov, 'O vliianii ...'.

39 Ukhtomskii, *Sobranie*, VI, pp. 13–40.

40 See especially Sherrington, *Man*; and Swazey, *Reflexes*.

41 Merkulov, *Ukhtomskii*, p. 95.

42 Ukhtomskii, *Izbrannye*, p. 9; and Lenin, *Materialism, passim*.

43 See, e.g., Ukhtomskii, 'Dominanta', *BSE*, 1st ed., XXIII (1931), 135–40.

44 See, e.g., Ukhtomskii, *Izbrannye*, pp. 74–5, and the 1926 article cited there. Cf. *Pavlovskie klinicheskie sredy*, I, p. 211, for Pavlov's awareness of the criticism, which he did not reply to in print.

45 Ukhtomskii, 'Dominanta ...', *VKA*, 1927, No. 22. Republished in his *Sobranie*, I, and in his *Izbrannye*, pp. 63–90.

46 Sherrington, *The Integrative Action*, p. 116.

47 Ukhtomskii, *Izbrannye*, p. 75.

48 See above, p. 260.

49 Schrödinger, *What Is Life?*

50 Ukhtomskii, *Izbrannye*, p. 79.

51 *Ibid.*, p. 87.

52 *Ibid.*, pp. 87–9.

53 See, e.g., *KN*, 1924, No. 3, p. 225.

54 Ukhtomskii, *Izbrannye*, p. 90.

55 *Sbornik ... Pavlova*.

56 Frequently recalled, e.g., in *Pavlovskie sredy*, I, p. 208, and III, p. 66.

57 Cited by Gantt in Pavlov, *Lectures*, p. 24. The physiologist was Robert Tigerstedt.

58 Pavlov, *Conditioned*, p. 7, says 'over a hundred'. See Pavlov, *PSS*, IV, p. 21, for 'a hundred'.

59 See above, pp. 153–4, for that pre-revolutionary pattern. In the 1920s they mostly ignored each other.

60 Karl Pribram taught me that useful verb, signifying the construction of hypothetical neural explanations of psychological processes. See his commentary in Pribram, ed., *Brain and Behavior*.

61 Jennings.

62 See Boring, p. 690. For Pavlov's difficulties with Munk's data and language, see Pavlov, *Conditioned*, p. 336. Also *PSS*, III, pt. 1, pp. 214−16, and VI, pp. 280−2.

63 I. S. Tsitovich, 'O proiskhozhdenii . . .'. He was awarded the Pavlov Prize for that report. *Trudy Obshchestva russkikh vrachei v SPb*, LXXIX (1912), pp. 81−2.

64 Pavlov, *PSS*, IV, p. 36. See also III, pt. 1, pp. 330−1, and pt. 2, p. 386. For an admirer of Pavlov's confronting the difficulty that Pavlov avoided, see Sapir, *Vysshaia*, pp. 52−3.

65 Pavlov, *Conditioned*, pp. 33−5.

66 See above, p. 165.

67 See Borovskii, 'Uslovnye . . .', and 'Novoe . . .'.

68 See above, p. 260.

69 E.g., M. A. Minkovskii (or Minkowski), 'Zum gegenwartigen Stand . . .'. Pavlov is not explicitly criticized but his concepts are undermined. Cf. Minkowski's contribution to *Sbornik . . . Pavlova*, which starts with apparent acceptance of Pavlov's scheme of cortical localization and ends by doubting it. For plain talk, see Russkikh and Krylova, 'O lokalizatsii . . .'.

70 R. Magnus was the Dutch scientist. See Beritashvili, *Biobibliografiia*, p. 27.

71 Beritov, 'Über . . .'.

72 Beritov, 'On the fundamental . . .', p. 110.

73 I think Beritov was not conscious of Sechenov's thoughts on this matter until the 1930s, when the Stalinist legend of Sechenov was created. See Beritashvili, *Izbrannye*, p. 659, for references to Sechenov. Before the 1930s Beritov drew from Sechenov strictly neurophysiological ideas, unconnected with problems of the psyche.

74 *Ibid.*, p. 646.

75 See Hilgard and Marquis, pp. 336 and 359; and Konorski, pp. 56−60.

76 P. K. Anokhin, quoted in Beritashvili, *Izbrannye*, p. 514.

77 Beritashvili, *Biobiblicgrafiia*, p. 27.

78 Pavlov, *PSS*, IV, p. 123.

79 See, e.g., Pavlov, *Conditioned*, pp. 219 ff.

80 See, e.g., Pavlov, *PSS*, III, pt. 1, pp. 156−7 *et passim*. For implicit comparison of his work with that of Galileo and of Darwin, see *ibid.*, pp. 113 ff and 236 ff.

81 Beritov, 'On the fundamental . . .', p. 359.

82 See references in Pavlov, *PSS, ukazateli*, p. 43, under 'rastormazhivanie'.

83 Beritov, 'On the fundamental . . .', p. 115.

84 Richard Semon, *Die Mneme* . . . .

85 See references in Pavlov, *PSS, ukazateli*, p. 61, under 'Uslovnye refleksy − sledovyi [*sic*]'.

86 The experimenter was N. P. Studentsov. See biography with citations in *Fiziologicheskaia shkola*, p. 242. See Pavlov, *PSS*, III, pt. 1, p. 273, for the transformation of conditioned reflexes into unconditioned, i.e., the inheritance of acquired characters.

87 *Pravda*, 13 May 1927. The letter has not been republished in either edition of Pavlov's 'complete' works. Cf. *I. P. Pavlov v vospominaniiakh*, pp. 112–16, for N. K. Kol'tsov, the famous geneticist, recalling conversations with Pavlov on this issue. Better yet, see the original, Kol'tsov, 'Trud ...'; the republished version has been cut.

88 The Division of Evolutionary Physiology was created in 1932 within the Institute of Experimental Medicine in Moscow, under the direction of Pavlov's major disciple, L. A. Orbeli. See below, p. 394. The bust of Mendel – along with Descartes and Sechenov – was erected outside the laboratory at Koltushi. See *I. P. Pavlov v vospominaniiakh*, pp. 360–1.

89 See Beritashvili, *Izbrannye*, pp. 367 ff.

90 Watson and Rayner. Also in Watson, *Behaviorism*, pp. 159 ff. Cf. Ben Harris, especially p. 154, where Harris notes Watson's failure to 'recondition' the child – i.e., to restore its pleasure in stuffed toys – and wonders whether that might be considered 'callous'.

91 See, e.g., Kimble et al., pp. 233–4, for a summary of C. L. Hull's efforts.

92 See *FE*, V, p. 271, for brief biography with bibliography.

93 See articles by Prangishvili and Natadze in *Psikhologicheskaia nauka*, II. Cf. Clauss et al., pp. 122 ff, for a German perspective.

94 Borovskii, 'Uslovnye ...', p. 26. That seems to be a paraphrase of Pavlov, *PSS*, III, pt. 1, pp. 336–9.

95 *Ibid.*, III, pt. 2, pp. 21–2. Cf. III, pt. 1, pp. 288–9 for a less harsh dismissal.

96 Pavlov to Babkin, 23 October 1924, in Babkin papers in McGill University Library.

97 Anokhin, 'Dialekticheskii ...'. For Pavlov's annoyance, see *I. P. Pavlov v vospominaniiakh*, pp. 39–40.

98 See Graham, *Soviet Academy*, pp. 116–18.

99 Lents, *Vysshaia* ..., p. 5, ascribes the publication delay to the size of his book.

100 Lents, 'Ob osnovakh ...'.

101 See denunciation by Krol', '"Nauka" ...', pp. 25–34; and note abrupt cessation of his busy pen in the mid-1930s.

102 *Pavlovskie sredy*, III, p. 318. Quoted deadpan by Beritashvili, *Izbrannye*, p. 435.

103 Pavlov, *PSS*, VI, pp. 257–8. For the many efforts to condition the pupillary reflex, some successful, see Kimble et al., p. 51.

104 *Ibid.*

105 See below, p. 400.

106 See, most notably, his speech to the International Physiological Congress in Rome, 1932: Pavlov, *PSS*, III, pt. 2, pp. 219 ff. Note that Gantt omitted 'several paragraphs dealing with old material', in the English translation: Pavlov, *Lectures*, II, p. 87.

107 Pavlov, *Conditioned*, chs. 19–21.

108 Cited by Gantt, in Pavlov, *Lectures*, II, p. 30.

109 Pavlov, *Conditioned*, p. 407, and *PSS*, IV, pp. 428–9.

110 *Ibid.*, p. 415.

111 *Ibid.*, III, pt. 1, pp. 15–17; pt. 2, p. 322; IV, p. 20.

112 Watson, 'The place ...'. Cf. his snide comments on imagined physiological explanations, in his *Behaviorism*, pp. 206 *et passim*.

113 Sokal pp. 1248–49; and Borovskii, 'Otchet ...'.
114 Lashley, 'Basic ...', p. 1. Conveniently republished in Lashley, *Neuropsychology*, pp. 191 ff. Also published in Russian, in *Psikhologiia*, 1930, No. 3.
115 Lashley, 'Basic ...', p. 12.
116 *Ibid.*, pp. 17–23.
117 *Ibid.*, p. 3.
118 *Ibid.*, p. 8.
119 *Ibid.*, p. 9.
120 See Iaroshevskii, *Sechenov*, p. 393, for the legend. Cf. *Filosofskie voprosy v. n. d.*, p. 151, for Kupalov's eyewitness reference to 'a conversation ... of Pavlov with ... Lashley'. I wish to thank George Windholz for alerting me to the legendary nature of Pavlov's 'speech' in New Haven.
121 Guthrie, 'Conditioning ...'.
122 Pavlov, 'The reply ...'; and *PSS*, III, pt. 2, pp. 153–88; and *Lectures*, II, pp. 117–45.

CHAPTER 11   COMRADE STALIN AND HIS PARTY

1 Stalin, *Sochineniia*, XII, pp. 141–72.
2 *Ibid.*, taken from *Pravda*, 29 December 1929, indicates no ovation, but *Nauchnyi rabotnik*, 1930, No. 1, p. 100, reports one.
3 See Joravsky, *Soviet*, ch. 17.
4 *Ibid.*
5 *Ibid.*, ch. 2.
6 Kol'man, 'Politika ...', p. 27. This is a speech to the Society of Materialist-Dialectical Mathematicians in November 1930. It is republished in Kol'man, *Na bor'bu* ....
7 R. Medvedev, *Let History Judge*, p. 301. Djilas, *Conversations*, pictures a talkative Stalin in private, playing cat-and-mouse games with his subordinates.
8 Trotsky, *Stalin*, p. 244; Deutscher, *Stalin*, p. 119; Marie, *Staline*, pp. 48–9.
9 For a bit more pre-revolutionary evidence of disdain for émigré revolutionaries, and possibly of anti-intellectualism, see Tucker, p. 149.
10 Antonov-Ovseyenko, p. 254.
11 Trotsky, *Stalin*, p. 414.
12 Sukhanov, as cited in Tucker, pp. 178–9. Cf. Sukhanov, II, pp. 265–6, and note that he mentioned Stalin several other times – e.g., VII, p. 242, as the obvious choice for Commissar of Nationalities.
13 Lenin, *PSS*, XLV, pp. 345–6.
14 *Ibid.*, XLVIII, p. 162.
15 Maiakovskii seems to be the author of this line, inscribed everywhere in the Soviet Union. See Tumarkin, pp. 163 *et passim*.
16 Stalin, *Sochineniia*, VI, pp. 69 ff. Cf. Tucker, *Stalin*, pp. 315 ff.
17 See Joravsky, *Soviet*, pp. 59–60.
18 Barbusse, *Stalin*.
19 See above, p. 205.
20 Radek in August 1930. See Joravsky, *Soviet*, p. 236.

21 See Fitzpatrick, *Education*, *passim*; and Bailes, pt. 3.
22 Cited from the archives, in Kim, p. 140.
23 Stalin, *Sochineniia*, XIV, p. 60.
24 *Ibid.*, p. 94.
25 *Ibid.*, VI, pp. 186−8. Tucker, *Stalin*, p. 318, finds that Stalin borrowed this concept from Bukharin.
26 See especially the interventions of Stetskii, as reported in Joravsky, *Soviet*, pp. 246, 269, *et passim*.
27 Ushakov, *Tolkovyi*. See Stalin, *Sochineniia*, XIII, pp. 72−3, and note the inconsistency with much of his preceding talk of 'wrecking'.
28 *Ibid.*, XIV, pp. 395−9.
29 *KPSS v rezoliutsiiakh*, II, p. 865.
30 Stalin, *Sochineniia*, XIII, p. 39.
31 *Ibid.*, X, p. 175. See Tucker, pp. 366 *et passim*. On Trotsky's vacillation, see Deutscher, *Prophet Unarmed*, pp. 137 *et passim*. This was not the first, or the only, time that Stalin boasted of his *grubost'*. See Stalin, *Sochineniia*, IV, p. 261, for a 1921 telegram, which was published in December 1929, just before his speech to the agrarian theorists, and subsequently cited by such admirers as Kol'man, 'Stalin . . .', p. 178.
32 As quoted in R. Medvedev, 'K sudu istorii', manuscript of 2nd ed., p. 459.
33 Trotsky, as cited in Tucker, pp. 422−3.
34 Deutscher, *Prophet Unarmed*, pp. 366−7.
35 Stalin, *Sochineniia*, XIII, pp. 84 ff.
36 For Stalin's acknowledgment that 'this was one of the most dangerous periods in the life of our Party', see *ibid.*, XIV, p. 235.
37 *Ibid.*, XIII, p. 38, 41, *et passim*.
38 Quoted in Joravsky, *Soviet*, p. 204. Many other examples could be given, e.g., Adoratskii; and Krivtsov.
39 Stalin, *Sochineniia*, IV, p. 261, and Kol'man, as cited in note 31.
40 Stalin, *Sochineniia*, XIV, pp. 275−8.
41 *Ibid.*, XVI, p. 144.
42 See Joravsky, *Lysenko*, ch. 1, especially notes 8 and 9.
43 Stalin, *Sochineniia*, XVI, pp. 114 ff, and 188 ff.
44 *Ibid.*, p. 144.
45 E.g., A. A. Maksimov, the ideological foe of modern physics. See index of Joravsky, *Soviet*, and note his exclusion from the philosophical discussion of physics in the 1950s. Another example is I. I. Prezent, Lysenko's chief ideologist.
46 See Weil, *Gorky*.
47 See *PZM*, 1933, No. 6, p. 217; Stalin, *Sochineniia*, XIII, p. 410; *Gor'kii i nauka*, pp. 243−4, 251−2. Cf. *Rabochaia Moskva*, 18 June 1938, and VIEM, *Materialy*, pp. 10−11, for the reports of two participants, which are censored in *Gor'kii i nauka*. See also Speranskii, et al., 'Detishche . . .'. (Thanks to Michelle Marrese for providing me with a copy of that article.) See Speranskii's biography in *Fiziologicheskaia shkola*, pp. 254−6.
48 *Izvestiia*, 16 and 18 October 1932.
49 See below, p. 385.
50 See above, p. 213.

51 Stalin, *Sochineniia*, XIII, p. 410.
52 *Pervyi s'ezd sovetskikh pisatelei*, p. 9.
53 See above, p. 245.
54 *Pervyi s'ezd sovetskikh pisatelei*, pp. 278–80.
55 See especially Skvorecky.
56 Lenin, *Sochineniia*, X, pp. 26–31.
57 Nabokov, *The Gift*, p. 9.
58 See above, p. 206.
59 See Stalin, *Sochineniia*, XIV, pp. 279–326, for the chapter, which appeared over Stalin's signature in *Pravda*, 12 September 1938, and also in numberless editions of the *History of the CPSU (Short Course)*, all languages.
60 Mao Tse-tung, 'On Practice', and 'On Contradictions', in his *Selected*, I, II. For the evidence of plagiary (from Soviet works) see Wittfogel.
61 See, most notably, Popper, *The Open Society*; Arendt, *Totalitarianism*; and Camus, *The Rebel*. For a latter-day continuation of the theme, see Kolakowski, *Main Currents*.

CHAPTER 12   THE CRITERION OF PRACTICE

1 See the account in *ZhNiPs*, 1930, No. 3, pp. 98–107.
2 *Ibid*. Cf. Zalkind's somewhat different figures in *Pedologiia*, 1930, No. 2, pp. 161–2.
3 'Vrediteli v akademii nauk', *Izvestiia*, 16 November 1929. Cf. *Nauchnyi rabotnik*, 1930, No. 1, pp. 96–7. For the full account, see Graham, *Soviet Academy*, ch. IV.
4 See items cited in notes 1 and 2. Cf. *Vrachebnaia gazeta*, 1930, No. 1, p. 52.
5 See Joravsky, *Soviet*, pp. 241 *et passim*.
6 See *ZhNiPs*, 1930, Nos. 3ff, for the Society's journal under the new leadership.
7 See, e.g., Rozentsveig; Giliarovskii, 'Urbanizatsiia'; and Dekhterev.
8 Gannushkin, 'Ob okhrane . . .'.
9 Rokhlin, 'Psikhogigienicheskaia . . .', p. 25. Rokhlin repeated this apothegm in a number of publications.
10 See, e.g., Zalkind, 'Zabolevaniia . . .'. For a collection of his articles on the subject, see Zalkind, *Rabota i byt*. And see Zalkind, *Umstvennyi* . . . .
11 Rokhlin, *Trud*, especially chs. 5 and 6. Note his references to previous publications by other authors.
12 *Ibid*., p. 131, for a summary of five studies of the *aktiv* in scattered places. Those suffering from nervous illnesses ranged from a low of 41.5% to a high of 88.7%. Cardiovascular disorders ranged from a low of 12.0% to a high of 75.0%. In earlier editions of this book Rokhlin was more forthright in discussion of these problems.
13 Strel'chuk and Rumshevich. For grim figures on the availability of psychiatric care, see Prozorov, No. 3, pp. 109–10; No. 4, pp. 120–3, 127–8.
14 Rozenshtein, 'Sotsial'no-profilakticheskoe . . .', p. 5; and Rozenshtein, 'Psikhogigienicheskoe . . .', p. 123.
15 *Ibid*.

16 Rokhlin, as cited in note 11, p. 9.

17 *Ibid.*, pp. 7−8.

18 Gannushkin, as cited in note 8, pp. 43−4. The original articles appeared in *Trudy Psikhiatricheskoi Kliniki MGU* (1926), which was unavailable to me.

19 *Psikhonevrologicheskie nauki v SSSR*, pp. 301−4. Note on pp. 301−2 the repudiation of the notion that transfer of manual workers to mental labor can cause mental illness.

20 Gannushkin, as cited in note 8; and Vnukov, 'Reshaiushchie . . .'.

21 See, e.g., *ZhNiPs*, 1930, No. 3, pp. 22−3.

22 See his autobiography in *Deiateli SSSR*, I, pp. 84−5. Note his occasional enrollment in medical school during his pre-revolutionary years of Party work.

23 *ZhNiPs*, 1931, No. 1, p. 3. Cf. No. 2, p. 83, for report of a long delay in publication following the Commissar's speech, which led people to believe that he had suspended the journal.

24 The editors of *ZhNiPs* were slightly heretical in pointing that out, as they apologized for the offensive articles, which had originally been papers at the Behavioral Congress of 1930, and which had been sent to press before the *razvoroshenie* (turning upside down) of the Commissariat of Health in the spring of 1930 and the *razvoroshenie* of 'theoretical positions' in February−March 1931. *ZhNiPs*, 1931, No. 1, p. 3.

25 Subbotnik. Note that Commissar Vladimirskii had singled out Subbotnik for criticism, *ZhNiPs*, 1931, No. 1, p. 3.

26 *Ibid.*, 1931, No. 2, p. 14. The 'conscious or subconscious enemy' was Dekhterev. See note 7.

27 *Ibid.*, p. 14.

28 He then signed himself 'Propper'. See his biography in *Biograficheskii slovar'*, I, pp. 260−1. The other two leaders were Kolbanovskii (see below, p. 359) and M. B. Krol'. Note that all three had a medical background.

29 Grashchenkov (Propper), 'Itogi . . .', No. 5, p. 13.

30 Krol', 'Uspekhi . . .', p. 1.

31 Kaplun, pp. 91−2.

32 Krol', as cited in note 30.

33 See Giliarovskii, 'Dostizheniia', for a review that seems to show real progress, until one reads very carefully, with special attention to the omissions.

34 See especially the case of Luria, below, p. 368. A similar shift is observable in the publications of I.D. Sapir, who probably fell to the terror in the late 1930s. One of his last articles was 'O rasstroistve . . .'.

35 See below, ch. 15.

36 The phrase is Maiakovskii's. See his *The Bedbug* . . ., p. 220.

37 See below, ch. 15.

38 Artemov, p. 208.

39 Quoted in Petrovskii, *Istoriia*, p. 274.

40 There is a fairly large literature by and about Gastev and NOT, the standard acronym for Scientific Organization of Labor. See, e.g., Bailes, *Technology*, and his article cited on p. 50. Cf. Shpil'rein, in *Obshchestvennye nauki SSSR*; 'Organizatsiia', in *FE*, IV, pp. 160−1.

41 Quoted in Petrovskii, *Istoriia*, pp. 280−1, from *Sovetskaia psikhotekhnika*, 1931, No. 2−3, p. 105.

42 Petrovskii, *Istoriia*, p. 277.

43 *Ibid.*

44 See *Vrachebnaia gazeta*, 1931, No. 13, pp. 1013−18, for his speech to the All-Union Congress of Psychotechnics, in May 1931, apologizing and explaining.

45 See *Pravda*, 16 June 1931, for the attack on Kaplun: 'Za partiinost' v gigiene i fiziologii truda'. Cf. Kaplun, p. 11, for confession of errors before 1931, and pp. 75−6 for brief dismissal of the problem of fatigue. Cf. Siegelbaum, 'Okhrana truda'.

46 Shpil'rein, 'Psikhotekhnika', p. 166. Note announcement of Ermanskii's expulsion from the Communist Academy. (Thanks to Sheila Fitzpatrick for this reference.)

47 Ermanskii, *Stakhanovskoe*. Siegelbaum, 'Okhrana truda', p. 26, describes it as still the most interesting work on Stakhanovism. For the best study of the subject, see Siegelbaum, *Stakhanovism*.

48 See *Trud*, 24 May 1930, and Lunacharskii's defense of Shpil'rein in *Psikhotekhnika*, 1930, No. 5, p. 460.

49 See *Izvestiia*, 9, 10, 11, 15 September 1931, for reports of the Seventh International Psychotechnical Congress. Shpil'rein led the Soviet attacks on 'bourgeois' psychotechnics, to the astonishment of the foreign visitors, who knew their Soviet colleagues from past meetings as amiable fellow specialists.

50 See Joravsky, *Lysenko*, p. 124.

51 See Galant.

52 *Ibid.*, p. 20, for the editors' criticism of the article. The article was published in the fleeting period when the new Bolshevik editors were balancing between publishing professional advice to officials and delivering official preconceptions to professionals. For another example, see *ZhNiPs*, 1931, No. 1, p. 41, where Rozenshtein offers 'psychohygiene' as 'an ally of the command, educational and political service of the Army'.

53 Frolov, 'Chto takoe ...'. The work seems to me an inane translation of conventional wisdom about army morale into Pavlovian terminology.

54 See *Sovetskaia psikhotekhnika*, 1930, No. 2−3, p. 232; Aleksandrovskii, p. 43; and *ZhNiPs*, 1931, *prilozhenie*, p. 20.

55 See Frolov, *Vysshaia*.

56 See Myers, p. 415, for the quotation from James. For the American context of mass testing, see Sokal, *Psychological*.

57 Stalinists did the search for me, when they turned against pedology in 1936. They searched the works of pedologists, looking for depreciation of lower-class capabilities. Evidently they found none, for their polemics offer in evidence only the pedologists' assumption that there are individual differences in capacities.

58 See S. J. Gould.

59 See *Pedologiia*, 1931, No. 3 (15), pp. 80−3. Note the heavy emphasis on sensitivity to the special problems of 'national minorities' and workers' and peasants' children. Cf. *ibid.*, 1931, No. 7/8, pp. 134−5, for bibliography of articles on such problems.

60 The Decree is conveniently translated in Wortis, pp. 242–5.

61 See Kamin; and see again S. J. Gould.

62 For a convenient review of their work as of 1930, see Molozhavyi, pp. 18–21, and pp. 210–44, for summaries of the papers on tests at the Behavioural Congress. See also the critical report of the First All-Union Psychotechnical Congress, May 1931, in *Vrachebnaia gazeta*, 1931, No. 13, pp. 1014–18. And see references in note 59, and *Pedologiia*, 1931–2 *passim*, for harsh, Stalinist attacks on testers accused of bias.

63 See above, p. 110.

64 See, for example, 'Pedologiia', *BSE*, 1st ed., XLIV (1939), pp. 461–2.

65 See Bowen. There is a very large literature about him in Russian. For a bibliography, see Khrustalev. And see Balabanovich.

66 See Makarenko, *Sochineniia*, I, for a convenient reprint, with a detailed history of its writing and publication, pp. 749–57.

67 In 1931 *Pedologiia* reached its peak output of eight issues. In 1932 it stopped with an extremely delayed No. 4, sent to press in December. *Sovetskaia pedagogika* began publication in mid-1937, with declarations of holy war on pedology.

68 See Hillig for responses to the book in 1934–7.

69 The works on Makarenko that appeared in the post-Stalin period make no reference to such studies. See, e.g., Kostelianets; Lukin; Balabanovich.

70 See, e.g., Malyshev. Cf. Joravsky, *Lysenko*, pp. 73 *et passim*.

71 Makarenko, *Sochineniia*, I, p. 128. I have used, with slight alterations, the translation by Ivy and Tatiana Litvinov: Makarenko, *Road*, I, pp. 217–18.

72 Makarenko occasionally cautioned that normal children required different methods than those suitable for delinquents, but his major emphasis, repeated by his admirers, was on the common elements in the education of both.

73 See Makarenko, *Road*, I, pp. 70–1, 87, 103, 140 ff.

74 *FE*, III, p. 278.

75 Akademiia nauk, *Slovar'*, V, p. 183.

76 See below, p. 366.

77 The first notable victims were such agrarian specialists as A. V. Chaianov and A. G. Doiarenko. See Susan Solomon, *Soviet, passim*, and Joravsky, *Lysenko*, p. 37 *et passim*.

78 AMN, *Sessiia* ... (1951), p. 393. The speaker was K. K. Platonov.

CHAPTER 13   THEORETICAL IMPASSE

1 Frankfurt, 'K bor'be ...', p. 170. That Frankfurt spoke for Kornilov's school is evinced by Kornilov's preface to Frankfurt, *Refleksologiia*, a 1924 critique of Bekhterev.

2 Bukharin, *O mirovoi* ...; and Bukharin, 'Kul'turnyi front ...'.

3 See above, pp. 276–7.

4 See above, p. 280.

5 See *Psikhologiia*, 1928, No. 2, p. 175, for news of the start of these complex maneuvers.

6 *Vrachebnaia gazeta*, 1930, No. 1, p. 53.
7 *Refleksologiia ili psikhologiia*.
8 Zalkind, 'Povedencheskii ...', p. 503; and Zalkind, 'Pervyi ...', pp. 161–2.
9 See below, p. 379.
10 See his biography in *Fiziologicheskaia shkola*, pp. 254–6. Fedorov, 'Metod ...', seems to be the speech he gave at the special session of the Congress. For report of that, see Grashchenkov (or Propper), 'Shkola ... Pavlova', especially p. 11.
11 See *Psikhonevrologicheskie*, the proceedings of the Congress.
12 Lunacharsky, 'Iskusstvo ...', *ibid.*, pp. 222–49.
13 The two were Karev and Luppol, *ibid.*, pp. 15–77. For attacks on them by Stalinist zealots, see Joravsky, *Soviet*, pp. 250–3.
14 Propper (or Grashchenkov), 'Izuchenie ...', was a belated, exceptional report in a mass-circulation journal.
15 *Izvestiia*, 20 November 1930.
16 'Itogi diskussii po reaktologicheskoi psikhologii', *Psikhotekhnika i psikhofiziologiia truda*, 1931, No. 4–6, pp. 387–91.
17 *Ibid.*, 1931, No. 1, p. 98.
18 *Ibid.*
19 'Itogi ...', as cited in note 16, *passim*. Note the harsher condemnations of Chelpanov and Nechaev on p. 387: 'remnants of bourgeois idealist theories, which are direct reflections of counter-revolutionary elements' resistance to socialist construction.'
20 See *Periodicheskaia pechat' SSSR, passim*. I count three ongoing journals in the years 1917–28, plus six with very brief lives. Six journals were ambitiously started in 1928–31, and were gone by the mid-1930s.
21 See publication records of A. A. Talankin, A. V. Vedenov, and F. N. Shemiakin, in *Ukazetel' literatury ... psikhologii*.
22 See P. I. Razmyslov's entries, *ibid.*
23 See his obituary in *VPs*, 1970, No. 6, pp. 184–5.
24 See *EIM*, 1929, No. 3, pp. 203–4 *et passim*.
25 See Joravsky, *Lysenko, passim*. Note especially the careers of Zhebrak, Alikhanian, and Lobashev.
26 See, e.g., Kolbanovskii, 'Psikhologiiu ...'.
27 Kolbanovskii, 'Lev ...'.
28 Vygotsky, *Myshlenie*. The English translation is *Thought and Language*.
29 Vygotsky, *Myshlenie*, p. v.
30 Compare Vygotsky, *ibid.*, pp. 76–102, with the original: Vygotsky, 'Geneticheskie'.
31 Vygotsky, 'Problema ...'; republished in Vygotsky, *Myshlenie*, pp. 16–66.
32 See above, pp. 262 ff.
33 See, e.g., Vygotsky and Luria, *Etiudy*, pp. 133–4.
34 *Ibid.*, p. 138, with references to his original publication on the subject.
35 See his 'Comments', a fourteen-page brochure distributed as an insert in Vygotsky, *Thought*. His agreement with Vygotsky's correction is on p. 7. At the very end he gently sets aside the Stalinist caricature of his views on socialization. Note at the outset, p. 3, his explanation of 'cognitive egocentrism

(no doubt a bad choice [of terms])' as a general historico-cultural concept, which is certainly compatible with Vygotsky's outlook.

36 See above, p. 264.

37 Vygotsky, *Sobranie*, I, p. 102. Originally published in 1926. Italics are Vygotsky's.

38 Vygotsky, 'Geneticheskie', p. 129. The 1934 version of that article shifted to ambiguous language, which can imply that Marxism predicted the findings of experimental psychologists. See Vygotsky, *Thought*, pp. 48–49. For Vygotsky at greater length – before the great break – on Marxist expectations and Köhler's experiments, see Vygotsky, *Sobranie*, I, pp. 214 ff.

39 Vygotsky, 'Problema ...', p. 50; and *Myshlenie*, p. 62. The translation, in Vygotsky, *Thought*, omits this section of the original.

40 Piaget, *Rech'*, p. 55.

41 The introductions are conveniently gathered in Vygotsky, *Sobranie*, I. The quoted phrase is on p. 102. Note the criticism of Bühler's hereditarian assumptions, pp. 206–9, for a good example of Vygotsky's capacity to be sharply critical while remaining fair, without distortion of the foreign scholar or appeals to Marxist authorities for ultimate truth.

42 Kolbanovskii in Vygotsky, *Myshlenie*, pp. v ff.

43 See *Kniga i proletarskaia revoliutsiia*, 1935, No. 4, pp. 100–5. The reviewer was F. I. Georgiev.

44 Ozhegov, p. 451. Cf. Ushakov, III, pp. 202–3, for the 1938 decree that established this neologism in the literary language.

45 Vygotsky, 'Sovremennye ...'. The lecture was published in 1960.

46 *Ibid.*, p. 460.

47 *Ibid.*, p. 481.

48 See above, p. 265. Cf. the explicit attack on Trotsky's and Kautsky's remarks concerning psychology: Shemiakin and Gershenovich, 'Kak Trotskii ...'.

49 Vygotsky, 'Sotsialisticheskaia ...'. Note his appeals to Marx, Engels, Krupskaia, even to Nietzsche's concept of the superman (with cautionary amendment, of course). Stalin's name is conspicuously absent.

50 *Ibid.*, p. 44.

51 Vygotsky and Luria, *Etiudy*.

52 See, e.g., Feofanov; also Abel'skaia and Neopikhonova.

53 Razmyslov, 'O 'kul'turno–istoricheskoi teorii', p. 82.

54 Luria, *Ob istoricheskom*, p. 112.

55 *Ibid.*

56 *Ibid.*, p. 113.

57 *Ibid.*, p. 4.

58 Razmyslov, 'O 'kul'turno–istoricheskoi teorii', pp. 83–4.

59 For the end of peasant studies, see Susan Solomon, 'Rural ...'.

60 See Vygotsky, *Myshlenie*, pp. 321–3, for his list of works arranged chronologically. For another, fuller list, arranged topically, see Luria's obituary in *SNPsPs*, 1935, No. 1, especially p. 168, 'Psychopathology and defectology'.

61 The colleague was L. S. Sakharov. See his 'Obrazovanie ...', and his 'O metodakh ...'. Cf. Vygotsky, 'Thought in schizophrenia', and Hanfmann and Kasanin, for the transfer to Western specialists.

62 Wordsworth, 'The Idiot Boy', in his *Lyrical Ballads*. See his note, p. 158, and cf. pp. 143–4.

63 Luria, *Travmaticheskaia*.

64 This oversimplified example is adapted from Luria, *The Working Brain*, pp. 154–5, 335–40.

65 For an especially poignant case, see Luria, *Man*.

66 See, e.g., A. N. Leont'ev, *Ocherk*, an outgrowth of his dissertation, and *Problemy*, 1st to 4th eds.

67 Luria, 'Krizis ...', and Luria, 'Put' ...'.

68 Luria, *Ob istoricheskom*, pp. 3–24.

69 *Ibid.*, p. 8.

70 See, e.g., Vygotsky and Luria, *Etiudy*; and Vygotsky, 'Biogeneticheskii ...'.

71 See below, pp. 413, 449–50.

72 Hints of this resentment appeared in print from time to time. For a fairly open expression, see Kozulin, *Psychology*, p. 23.

73 Rubinshtein, *Eine Studie* ..., p. 68.

74 *Ibid.*, pp. 66–7. I thank Mitchell Ash for getting me a copy of this work. Cf. Payne, pp. 68–70, for a summary of the dissertation.

75 See Rubinshtein, 'Printsip ...', p. 154.

76 See Levitin, pp. 126–7, for detail on Rubinshtein's employment in Odessa from 1915 to 1932. I thank Alex Kozulin for telling me of this book, which contains information not vouchsafed to Soviet readers. For the sequence of rival forces that held Odessa during the Civil War, see *Sovetskaia istoricheskaia entsiklopediia*, X, pp. 470–1. There was a period from April to August 1919, in which Soviet troops held the city, but I assume that Rubinshtein's appointment to the University was not connected with that transient presence.

77 Rubinshtein, 'Printsip ...'.

78 The small pieces are listed in Rubinshtein, *Problemy*, p. 420. Note 'Nikolai ...', his first publication in psychology.

79 See, e.g., Rubinshtein, *Sovremennoe sostoianie* ....

80 Rubinshtein, 'Problemy ...', pp. 6–7. In the quotation from Marx I have used, with alterations, the translation in Bottomore, p. 202.

81 *FE*, IV, p. 154.

82 Rubinshtein, 'Problemy ...', p. 14.

83 Rubinshtein, *Osnovy psikhologii*, p. 6.

84 *Ibid.*, p. 28.

85 *Ibid.*, p. 31.

86 *Ibid.*, pp. 35–7.

87 Three hundred of the book's five hundred pages are devoted to 'Functional Analysis of Consciousness', beginning with sensations and ending in will. The last fifty pages are devoted to personality, while the first sections do the traditional review of the history, subject matter, and methods of the discipline.

88 See *PZM*, 1936, No. 9, pp. 87–90.

89 *Ibid.*, pp. 97–9.

90 Rubinshtein, *Osnovy obshchei psikhologii*, p. 4.

91 Drapkina, 'Filosofsko-psikhologicheskaia ...', p. 105. The call was sounded originally by Anan'ev, 'Zadachi ...'. He was a disciple of Bekhterev who reformed his outlook in the 1930s.

92 See Rubinshtein, as cited in note 90, pp. 70–86, for a greatly expanded section on the history of Russian psychology.

93 *Ibid.*, pp. 74–5.

94 *Ibid.*, p. 82.

95 *Ibid.*, p. 3.

96 *Ibid.*, pp. 535–616.

97 *Ibid.*, pp. 83–4.

98 These facts have been pieced together from brief biographical notices and other fugitive information. There is no thorough institutional history of the institutes and departments in question. Kolbanovskii was director of the central Institute of Psychology 1931–7; Kornilov resumed the directorship 1938–41. Rubinshtein held the post 1942–5, when A. A. Smirnov took over. Whether there was a transient occupant between Kolbanovskii and Kornilov, or between Kornilov and Rubinshtein, I do not know.

99 Plotnikov, p. 16.

100 See below, p. 411.

101 See Zhdanov, *Essays*, which begins with his 1934 explication of Stalin's job classification for writers ('engineers of human souls') and closes with his complaints, in 1946–7, that writers, philosophers, and composers were disappointing their employers. In between there was nothing else in Zhdanov's *oeuvre*.

102 See above, p. 329.

CHAPTER 14   THE PAVLOV SOLUTION

1 See above, pp. 210–11.

2 *Pedologiia*, 1930, No. 3, pp. 422–3.

3 *Ibid.*

4 See above, pp. 279 ff.

5 Borovskii, 'Novoe ...', p. 200.

6 *Ibid.*, p. 206.

7 *Pedologiia*, 1930, No. 3, p. 421.

8 The example he gave was N. A. Podkopaev, whose paper at the Behavioural Congress seems quite mechanistic to me. See the précis by Grashchenkov, 'Shkola ... Pavlova', pp. 9–10.

9 See his biography in *Fiziologicheskaia shkola*, pp. 254–6. Cf. pp. 158–61 for the biography of F. P. Maiorov, who joined the Red Army in 1919 and the Party in 1925; and p. 174 for N. N. Nikitin, who joined the Party in 1920 and came to Pavlov's Institute much later, evidently as a Party activist and supervisor as much as a scientist in training. His sudden death in August 1936, without honorific notice in any scientific journal, suggests that he fell victim to the terror.

10 Fedorov, 'Metod ...'. Cf. Grashchenkov's account, as cited in note 8, p. 11.

11 Maiorov, 'Uchenie ...', p. 66. I assume that Nikitin spoke to similar effect.

12 Fedorov, 'Metod ...'.

13 Sapir, 'K voprosu ...'.

14 See Grashchenkov, 'Shkola ... Pavlova'. For his biography see *Biograficheskii slovar'*, I, pp. 260–1.

15 N. I. Propper (i.e., Grashchenkov), 'Refleksologicheskoe ...'; 'Raboty ...'; 'Refleksologiia'. These articles grew out of a seminar paper written at the Institute of Red Professorship.

16 See below, p. 394.

17 Grashchenkov, 'Shkola ... Pavlova', p. 8.

18 See above, p. 328. In 1931 Fedorov had become the Director of the Institute, and Grashchenkov had become Director of the miniature Pavlovian institute within the Communist Academy.

19 Nikitin, p. 217.

20 *Ibid.*, pp. 227–30.

21 Zavadovskii, 'Itogi ...'.

22 Pavlov, *PSS*, I, p. 13.

23 *Izvestiia*, 6 July 1935. The version in Pavlov, *PSS*, I, p. 15, is abridged. See also the longer interview, *ibid.*, 17 August 1935.

24 Pavlov, *PSS*, I, pp. 16–18.

25 *Ibid.*, p. 19.

26 *Izvestiia*, 18 August 1935. The other leaders were G. M. Kaminskii, Commissar of Health, and I. A. Akulov, Secretary of the Central Executive Committee.

27 Pavlov, *PSS*, I, plate facing p. 18.

28 See Pavlov's express delight at the comments of his foreign friends on Soviet progress, in *Izvestiia*, 17 August 1935.

29 *Ibid.*, 18 August 1935. Cf. the speech of Cannon's, *ibid.*, 12 August, and the commemoration of the Congress in 1985, reported in *VIEiT*, 1986, No. 2, pp. 166–8, with heavy emphasis on Pavlov's friendship with Cannon.

30 Pavlov, *PSS*, III, pt. 2, p. 295. Cf. *Pavlovskie sredy*, II, p. 446, for Pavlov at greater length on Sherrington's remark.

31 Pavlov, *PSS*, III, pt. 2, p. 295.

32 *Ibid.*

33 *Ibid.*, I, p. 13.

34 See, e.g., Maksimov; and Mitin.

35 See, e.g., Krol', 'I. P. Pavlov ...'. The favorite scapegoats were Lents, Savich, and Zelenyi.

36 *PZM*, 1936, No. 9, p. 65.

37 Quoted by Maiorov, 'O mirovozzrenii ...', p. 17. Cf. Maiorov, 'Pavlov' (1932), for a different account of Pavlov's philosophy, and the apology for that in Maiorov, *Istoriia*, 2nd ed. (1954), p. 6.

38 See above, pp. 158–9.

39 Orbeli, *Uslovnye*, pp. 3–17. Cf. Orbeli, 'Tvorcheskaia ...', p. 53, for an assertion as late as 1936 that Pavlov's doctrine is purely empirical, compatible with any epistemology.

40 See especially Megrelidze, 'Ot zhivotnogo ...'.

41 For the earliest reference, see above, p. 303. For later comments on the second signal system, see Pavlov, *PSS*, III, pt. 2, pp. 214–15, 232–3, 260, 335–6, 345, and 424. And note *Pavlovskie sredy*, I, pp. 243, 272; II, 468; III, p. 8.

42 Suffice to note Orbeli's summation on the tenth anniversary of Pavlov's death: 'The role of the second signal system has not yet been taken in hand in the proper way, and we still know very little about it.' Quoted in AN, *Sessiia* (1950), p. 129. Orbeli, ed., *Ob'edinennaia sessiia* ..., pp. 15–17, is more optimistic, but no less unclear. Cf. *FE*, V (1970), p. 5, for acknowledgment that the second signal system is still 'primarily the indication of a problem'.

43 See Vsesoiuznyi s'ezd nevropatologov i psikhiatrov, III, *Trudy*, p. 87, for a fairly late — 1948 — public comment of that sort. They were frequent in the early 1930s.

44 See *Pravda*, 7 June 1941. *VIEM*, the newspaper of the Vsesoiuznyi Institut Eksperimental'noi Meditisiny, carried articles on the subject, but I have not been able to consult them.

45 Babkin, p. 121.

46 Anokhin, 'Tvorcheskii ...'.

47 Zavadskii, p. 167.

48 *Ibid.*

49 Anokhin, 'Tvorcheskii ...'.

50 Babkin, p. 120.

51 I take the metaphor from Kol'tsov, 'Trud ...'.

52 See *Fiziologicheskaia shkola*, for a fairly complete listing with brief biographies.

53 Hilgard and Marquis, p. 42. See pp. 336–8 for their use of work by Pavlov's disciples.

54 Konorski, p. 53.

55 Samoilov, 'Obshchaia ...'.

56 Pavlov to Chelpanov, 24 March 1914 (Old Style), in *VPs*, 1955, No. 3, p. 100.

57 Pavlov, 'Pamiati ...', p. 331.

58 Cf. Ukhtomskii, 'Fiziologiia ...', for an explicit contrast between the school of Pavlov and the school of Sechenov as the two most important trends in Soviet neurophysiology. Of course, Ukhtomskii presents them as complementary rather than contradictory.

59 For Konorski's participation, see his name in the index, *Pavlovskie sredy*, III, p. 416.

60 The comments on the Americans were made in a 1934 interview with Razran. The comments on Sherrington are in *Pavlovskie sredy*, III, pp. 444ff.

61 *Ibid.*, pp. 447–8. For Kupalov's biography see *Fiziologicheskaia shkola*, pp. 150–2.

62 Letter to Anokhin of 1933, quoted in Anokhin, 'Uzlovye ...', p. 14. The work in question was a lecture by Sherrington, *The Brain* ....

63 V. V. Savich to Babkin, in Babkin papers, McGill University Library.

64 See, e.g., Pavlov, *PSS*, III, pt. 2, pp. 178–9.

65 See biographical information on Kupalov, as cited in note 61, and in *ZhVND*, 1958, No. 5, pp. 781–5, and 1965, No. 2, pp. 195–201. Cf. Ukhtomskii, 'Fiziologiia ...', p. 1176, for plain talk about his study with Hill.

66 See Orbeli, *Vospominaniia*; and Popovskii; and Shilinis; and other references in *Fiziologicheskaia shkola*, pp. 177–80.

67 *EIM*, 1930, No. 2–3, p. 154.

68 K. A. Lange, pp. 61–2 *et passim.*

69 VIEM, *Materialy* ..., pp. 16 *et passim.*

70 See, e.g., Orbeli, *Lektsii* ..., lectures 7 and 8.

71 See his account in AN, *Sessiia* ... (1950), pp. 170–1.

72 For the quarrel over the clinic, see above, note 44. For Orbeli's benign smile at Ivanov-Smolenskii's work, see Orbeli, ed., *Ob'edinennaia sessiia* ..., pp. 15–17.

73 See AN, *Sessiia* ... (1950), p. 169.

74 See Orbeli, 'O perspektivakh ...', for an admission that there had been no search for an evolutionary sequence of neural mechanisms.

75 Quoted in AN, *Sessiia* ... (1950), p. 462.

76 See *Fiziologicheskaia shkola*, pp. 28–30.

77 Anokhin, 'Dialekticheskii ...'.

78 *I. P. Pavlov v vospominaniiakh*, pp. 39–40.

79 See reports in *Sovetskaia psikhotekhnika*, 1930, No. 2–3, p. 226, and in *Pedologiia*, 1930, No. 3, p. 421, where Anokhin is lumped with Ivanov-Smolenskii as extreme mechanists, who received a deserved rebuff. For an account of his paper, see Grashchenkov, 'Shkola ... Pavlova', pp. 10–11.

80 Mogendovich, 'Problema ...', No. 4, p. 10, and No. 5, p. 111. A third installment was promised, but I did not have access to the volume in which it was to appear. Mogendovich was part of Bekhterev's school, whose prolonged silence from the mid-1930s to the 1950s indicates time spent in the camps.

81 Anokhin, 'Aktivnyi ...', was the first of a series. Cf. Anokhin, ed., *Problema tsentra* ....

82 See *Pavlovskie sredy*, I, pp. 184–6 for the 1932 presentation.

83 Anokhin, 'Analiz ...', p. 78.

84 *Ibid.* Also in *Uspekhi sovremennoi biologii*, 1936, No. 4.

85 *Pavlovskie sredy*, I, p. 131.

86 *Ibid.*, II, pp. 386 ff.

87 *Ibid.*, III, pp. 47–9.

88 See Scheerer.

89 Bernshtein, *Issledovaniia* ....

90 Beritov (or Beritashvili), *Individual'no-priobretennaia* ....

91 Beritashvili Festschrift: *Problemy nervnoi* .... The Pavlovian contribution is by N. A. Rozhanskii.

92 Anokhin, 'Analiz ...', pp. 77–8.

93 Anokhin, 'Tvorcheskii ...'.

94 See *NiPs*, 1940, No. 6.

95 See references in note 44.

96 Quoted in *BME*, 1st ed., XXXXI (1935), pp. 251–2.

97 See Speranskii, *Elementy* ... for his major statement. There is an English translation: *A Basis* ....

98 See *Zhizn' i tekhnika budushchego* ..., pp. 385–8.

99 Karlik, 'Nekotorye ...'.

100 See work cited in note 69, p. 12; and Bauman.

101 See Joravsky, 'The Stalinist mentality ...', with bibliographic references. The two elderly physicists were A. K. Timiriazev and V. F. Mitkevich.

102 *Arkhiv biologicheskikh nauk*, 1937, XLVI, No. 2, pp. 116–58, and No. 3, pp. 92–118, for the discussion, which was held at the Institute of Experimental Medicine in December 1936.

103 See, e.g., AN, *Sessiia* ... (1950), pp. 11, 26–9, 639–44, *et passim*. See pp. 116–25 for Speranskii's defense.

104 T. S. Eliot, *The Complete Poems and Plays 1909–1950*, p. 24.

105 See Pinkus, pp. 112–13.

106 Plotnikov, pp. 16, 19. See also Zankov, p. 67.

107 AN, *Sessiia* ... (1950), p. 101. D. A. Biriukov was the speaker, an especially virulent 'anti-cosmopolitan', who got no applause at the end. Cf. pp. 405–8, for the speech by D. I. Shatenshtein, one of Shtern's group, who writhed in abject apology, and got no applause.

108 For biographical information, see *Front nauki i tekhniki*, 1936. No. 3, p. 65; *Biograficheskii slovar'*, II, p. 390; and her *biobibliografiia* (1960), esp. pp. 16–17 for a list of articles celebrating her.

109 Pinkus, pp. 196–7. Cf. 106–7 *et passim*, for other reports on 'the Crimean Affair'.

110 See Joravsky, *Lysenko, passim*.

111 See AN, *Sessiia* ... (1950); AMN, *Sessiia* ... (1951); APN, *Izvestiia*, No. 45.

112 Stalin, *Sochineniia*, XVI, p. 144.

113 See *ibid.*, especially pp. 148–57.

114 *Bol'shevik*, 1950, No. 11, pp. 7–14. Cf. Petrushevskii, *ibid.*, No. 15, for a furious attack on Orbeli, in the usual style of the Stalinist press.

115 Stalin, *Sochineniia*, XII, pp. 369–70.

116 AN, *Sessiia* ... (1950), p. 11. The speaker was I. P. Razenkov, Vice President of the Academy of Medical Sciences. The other official who opened the Session was S. I. Vavilov, President of the Academy of Sciences.

117 See especially Bykov, *Kora* ... (1942 and later editions, including an English translation of 1957); and Bykov, 'Novye puti ...'. Cf. Beritashvili, *Ob osnovnykh* ..., pp. 56, 71–2, 79, and 98, for an argument that Bykov was implicitly acknowledging the differences among various types of individually acquired behavior.

118 See Bykov and Chernigovskii; and Bykov, 'O signal'nykh ...'.

119 Recalled by Airapet'iants in AN, *Sessiia* ... (1950), pp. 138–9.

120 See Bykov, ed., *Nauchnaia konferentsiia* ..., for his sympathetic interest. See AN, *Sessiia* ... (1950), p. 212, for M. G. Durmish'ian ridiculing Bykov's volte-face.

121 *Ibid.*, pp. 44–81.

122 *Ibid.*, p. 162.

123 *Ibid.*, p. 362. The book he apologized for was Anokhin, *Ot Dekarta* ....

124 AN, *Sessiia* ... (1950), pp. 367–9.

125 *Ibid.*, pp. 171–2.

126 *Ibid.*

127 *Ibid.*, p. 165.

128 *Ibid.*, pp. 182, 187.

129 *Ibid.*, p. 425.

130 *Ibid.*, p. 462.

131 *Ibid.*, p. 501.
132 *Ibid.*, pp. 503–4.
133 *Ibid.*, p. 547.
134 *Ibid.*, pp. 340–41. The speaker was M. M. Kol'tsova.
135 See above, note 56, and see below, p. 452.
136 AN, *Sessiia* ... (1950), pp. 153–9. The speaker was B. M. Teplov.
137 *Ibid.*, p. 427.
138 *Ibid.*, pp. 310–15.
139 *Ibid.*, p. 633.
140 *Ibid.*, pp. 524–5.
141 *Uchitel'skaia gazeta*, 20 August 1951.
142 *Pravda*, 24 July 1951.

CHAPTER 15   TREATING THE INSANE

1 See Julie Brown, 'Professionalization ...', pp. 282–3, *et passim*, and Julie Brown, 'Psychiatrists ...'.
2 *Trudy tret'iago s'ezda otechestvennykh psikhiatrov* (St Petersburg, 1911), pp. 532–49.
3 See the account by Feinberg.
4 *Ibid.*, p. 15. Cf. the figures she gave at Vsesoiuznoe soveshchanie po sudebnoi psikhiatrii, I-oe, *Trudy* (1937), p. 12.
5 See Morozov, et al., p. 169 *et passim*. I thank Walter Reich for giving me this book.
6 Ukrainskii s'ezd ..., *Trudy*, p. 885. The speaker was the leading forensic psychiatrist (and psychoanalyst) V. A. Vnukov.
7 See, e.g., conferences cited in notes 4 and 6, and cf. *Voprosy sudebnoi psikhiatrii*.
8 That is the major theme of the speech by D. R. Lunts, *ibid.*
9 Bloch and Reddaway, Appendix I; and Reddaway in *NYR*, 20 March 1980.
10 See below, p. 436.
11 See Medvedev and Medvedev, *Question*, for a change of law in 1961, which moved challenges to psychiatric confinement from the courts to administrative procedures.
12 *Ibid.*, pp. 110–11.
13 *Voprosy sudebnoi psikhiatrii*, pp. 141–6.
14 *Ibid.*, p. 144.
15 Holland, pp. 138–40.
16 See A. D. Brooks.
17 See, e.g., Giliarovskii, *Psikhiatriia*, pp. 495–6, a one-page 'chapter' on the legal position of mentally ill people; and *Sudebnaia psikhiatriia*, pp. 409–22.
18 See, e.g., Medvedev and Medvedev, *Question*, pp. 66, 72–4, *et passim*, and other *samzidat* writings cited by Bloch and Reddaway. See also Segal in Corson and Corson.
19 See again A. D. Brooks.
20 See above, pp. 236–7. The surrender of the psychiatric profession is evident in the disappearance of Freudian articles from psychiatric publications. For

some of the last to hold out, see Vnukov, 'Psikhoanaliz' (1933), with biblio-graphy of Russian Freudians. Cf. the closing sentence of Giliarovskii's article on Freudianism in *ES Granat*, XIV (1927), p. 616: 'The efforts of some Russian psychoanalysts to present Freudianism as a strictly materialist system of psychology have been rebutted by competent spokesmen of dialectical materialism.'

21 See Luria, 'Psikhoanaliz', in *BSE*, 1st ed., XLVII (1940). At a conference in May 1948, A. S. Chistovich made a little plea for a renewal of interest in Freud and the unconscious. See *Vsesoiuznyi s'ezd* ..., III—ii, *Trudy*, p. 80. The reaction was so scandalized that he felt obliged to apologize.

22 For the cool reaction of the German profession, see Decker. For a very detailed Stalinist history of the profession, with a little highly distorted account of Russian Freudianism, see Iudin, pp. 381 ff.

23 See above, pp. 336 ff.

24 See table 1, pp. 434—7.

25 There is an enormous literature on schizophrenia. The clearest, most sensible introduction that I have seen is O'Brien. On a more advanced level, see Shershow, which is honestly historical and pluralist in its assortment of views on an unresolved problem. Note especially the contribution by Klerman, *ibid*. For the changing official views of the American Psychiatric Association, see its *Diagnostic* ..., three editions. For a history of extreme treatments, see Valenstein.

26 Snezhnevskii, *Obshchaia psikhopatalogia*, p. 189, as paraphrased by S. Ia. Rubinshtein, in *ZhNiPs*, 1980, No. 4, p. 619. As editor of the journal, Snezhnevskii must have approved the paraphrase.

27 Snezhnevskii, 'Oblastnaia', pp. 149—54.

28 *Ibid.*, p. 153.

29 See Foucault, *Madness*, an abridged translation of his *Histoire*; and Szasz. Foucault charges such authoritarianism against modern medicine in general — see his *Birth of the Clinic* — while Szasz does not.

30 See the memorial issue of *SNPsPs*, 1934, No. 5, devoted to 'Rozenshtein and the clinical-prophylactic-psychohygienic trend in psychiatry'.

31 See the fine review article by Kannabikh, 'K istorii', *ibid.*, pp. 6—13.

32 The papers were published as *Sovremennye problemy shizofrenii*.

33 *Encyclopedia of Psychology*, III, p. 177, with references on p. 179. The problem of hereditary vulnerability is most carefully studied by Gottesman and Shields. Comparative studies of socio-cultural factors are summarized in Petrakov. The extreme paucity of Soviet data is scandalously evident in Petrakov's review of the epidemiological literature. Cf. Hyde, pp. 262—4.

34 In 1930 there was plain talk of a crisis of overcrowding in mental hospitals, with exemplary figures of up to 1,300 patients in a Moscow hospital that had 450 planned (*stroitel'nykh*) beds; or 1,080 hospital beds available for mental patients in the Ural district (*oblast'*), where the 'strictest norms' indicated 4,200 patients in need of hospitalization. See *ZhNiPs*, 1930, No. 3, pp. 109—10; No. 4, pp. 127—8. For the virtual disappearance of reliable global statistics during the first Five Year Plan, see the report in *SNPsPs*, 1934, No. 5, pp. 133—8. Restricting himself to the RSFSR, the author claims an

increase in hospital beds for mental patients from 26,377 in 1928 to more than 31,000 in 1932, plus about 11,000 beds in 'colonies', sanitoria, and private homes. The statistical compilations that began to appear in the post-Stalin era invariably leap over the 1920s and 1930s in their data on hospital beds and specialists for the mentally ill.

35 See the repeated complaints by psychiatrists, with occasional agreement of officials. E.g., *ibid.*, 1933, No. 1, p. 124, and 1936, No. 6, pp. 1078–9. At a major conference in December 1936, A. L. Shnirman complained that psychiatry was the stepchild of health care, and the Commissar of Health, G. N. Kaminskii (soon to be snatched by the administrators of terror), exclaimed '*Pravil'no!*' ('True!'). *Vtoroi vesesoiuznyi s'ezd psikhiatrov* ..., *Trudy*, I, p. 78.

36 See Osipov, 'O raspoznavanii ...', and 'Granitsy ...'. Osipov was also the Director of the Bekhterev Institute of the Brain. The clash between the Moscow and Leningrad schools has pre-revolutionary origins. See Julie Brown.

37 See Kerbikov, 'O gruppe ...', for the 1932 paper, and *Vsesoiuznyi s'ezd psikhiatrov ... II–oi*, *Trudy*, II, pp. 516–18, for the self-criticism.

38 See Kerbikov's speeches at AMN, *Sessiia ...* (1951), pp. 10–41, 85–92. See especially his articles in *ZhNiPs*, 1952, No. 5, pp. 8–15, No. 11, pp. 8–13ff.

39 See *Vsesoiuznyi s'ezd nevropatologov ... III-ii*, *Trudy*, pp. 257, 351.

40 *NiPs*, 1950, No. 1, pp. 63–5. Cf. *ibid.*, 1947, No. 2, p. 15, for the original commission.

41 *NiPs*, 1951, No. 4, p. 34. All four of the names cited were recognizably Jewish.

42 See Snezhnevskii, 'O pozdnikh', p. 269, for his 'profound thanks, for the direction of the present work', primarily to M. A. Sereiskii, whom he would denounce as a cosmopolitan in 1951. For his other modest article before the late 1940s, see the bibliography after 'Snezhnevskii, A. V.', in *BME*, 2nd ed., XXX (1963), pp. 756–7. Note the omission of his 1933 article, 'Oblastnaia'.

43 See especially Kerbikov's amusing use of Lysenko to support an argument *for* diathesis. *ZhNiPs*, 1952, No. 5, pp. 21–5. Cf. *ibid.*, No. 11, pp. 63–5.

44 Chistovich, 'O vzgliadakh ...'. For Chistovich presenting mental patients to Pavlov, see *Pavlovskie klinicheskie sredy*, III, pp. 373–4, and 430ff.

45 See AMN, *Sessiia ...* (1951), p. 33.

46 For Chistovich's self-criticism at the 1951 Session, see *ibid.*, pp. 266–7. For his subsequent resistance, see his speech at the 1954 *Vsesoiuznaia nauchno-prakticheskaia konferentsiia ...*, *Trudy*, pp. 204–5. See also the articles he was permitted to publish in *ZhNiPs*, during the brief 'discussion' of schizophrenia: 1953, No. 4; 1955, No. 11; and a letter of protest, 1960, No. 9, p. 1241. Cf. his remarks at the 1963 *Vsesoiuznyi s'ezd nevropatologov ... IV-yi*, *Trudy*, III, pp. 132–6.

47 See Kerbikov, 'Emil' Kraepelin'. For the virtual dismissal of Pavlov except as a totem, see Kerbikov, 'O nekotorykh ...'.

48 Kraepelin is quoted in *Allgemeine Zeitschrift* ..., 65 (1908), pp. 472–3. The wastebasket metaphor can be found in O'Brien, pp. 27, 40. It has been used by critics of other diagnostic labels than schizophrenia. See Goldstein, p. 211.

49 Kerbikov, 'O gruppe ...', pp. 99–100.
50 *Ibid.*, p. 154. The speaker was deriding that style of diagnosis. He was V. I. Akkerman, a leading forensic psychiatrist and a persistent advocate of rigor in the diagnosis of schizophrenia.
51 See Schneider.
52 Giliarovskii, 'Skhizofreniia', p. 129. He was quoting from Bumke, ed., translated into Russian in 1933.
53 World Health Organization, *Report*, and *idem, Schizophrenia*, especially pp. 142–3. For a pointed summary, see Walter Reich, 'The spectrum concept', pp. 493 ff.
54 To be precise: *NiPs*, 1951, No. 1, announced the appearance of Snezhnevskii as 'deputy editor', replacing the 'cosmopolitan' A. S. Shmar'ian. O. V. Kerbikov was added to the board of editors in the next issue, and other transformations led to Snezhnevskii's formal designation as 'editor' in 1952, No. 1. (He took the place of N. I. Grashchenkov, also known as Propper.) The journal's patriotic title, which had been dropped in the radical 1930s, was restored: *Zhurnal nevropatologii i psikhiatrii im. S. S. Korsakova.*
55 Vsesoiuznaia nauchno-prakticheskaia konferentsiia ..., *Trudy*, pp. 205 *et passim*. For the accusations of repression, and other criticisms of Snezhnevskii's school, see the speeches of P. E. Vishnevskii, A. L. Epshtein, A. S. Chistovich, and A. I. Zelenchuk. The overwhelming majority of speakers were either pro-Snezhnevskii or evasive.
56 *Ibid.*, p. 210. The speaker was A. N. Buneev. Snezhnevskii preferred 'traditional clinical psychiatry' as the name for his school. See his *Obshchaia psikhopatologiia*, p. 163. Cf. p. 187 for his effort to rebut the charge of 'nosological dogmatism'. A Snezhnevskian has characterized his master's school as 'clinical-syndromal'. See *ZhNiPs*, 1980, No. 4, p. 628. That marked a retreat toward the 'phenomenological' outlook which Snezhnevskii derided in 1970, before his recognition of a 'crisis in clinical psychiatry'.
57 Vsesoiuznyi s'ezd nevropatologov ..., IV-yi, *Trudy*, p. 521.
58 See especially Walter Reich, 'The spectrum concept ...', with many bibliographic notes. See also Reich, 'Kazanetz', and 'The world ...'.
59 For characteristic statements of these themes, see Snezhnevskii's editorial note in *ZhNiPs*, 1953, No. 11, p. 909, and his major articles: 'O nozologicheskoi', pp. 201 *et passim*; 'Ob osobennostiakh ...'; 'Mesto kliniki ...', pp. 1341 *et passim*. And see his course of lectures: *Obshchaia psikhopatologiia*.
60 See items cited in notes 53 and 58.
61 Note the persistent Snezhnevskian complaints concerning the indifference of foreigners. They occurred especially in the reports of foreign psychiatric literature by E. Ia. Shternberg, e.g., in *ZhNiPs*, 1980, No. 4, pp. 624–30. For foreign indifference underscored by occasional courteous flattery, see the papers by East Germans and by an Englishman (John Wing) at an international conference in the Soviet Union: *ibid.*, 1975, No. 9, pp. 1359–61 and 1390–3. For a convenient summary of East German views, see relevant articles and references (e.g., 'Schizophrenie') in Clauss et al., eds., *Wörterbuch*.
62 For Snezhnevskii's acknowledgment of 'a crisis' see his article, 'O nozologii ...', p. 138, with footnote reference to the 'discussion' that he began in his

journal in 1973, No. 9. Note his acknowledgment of the connection between the crisis in nosology and the growing use of psychotropic drugs. 'One may say that [the concept of] a single psychosis, driven out the door by nosologists, has come back through the window in the form of psychotropic remedies'. (p. 139). In other words, the disease entities postulated by nosologists cannot be correlated with the effects of psychotropic drugs, and therefore psychiatrists have allegedly been turning back toward belief in a single mental disease with multiple symptoms.

63 Snezhnevskii, 'Mesto kliniki ...', p. 1344.

64 See Snezhnevskii, as quoted in note 62. For another of his appeals to the authority of Griesinger, see 'Prognoz ...', pp. 84–5.

65 *ZhNiPs*, 1975, No. 1, p. 140. Italics added.

66 The quoted words were actually uttered by Kerbikov, at the 1954 conference cited in note 55, p. 201.

67 See Swazey, *Chloropromazine* .... For the impact on diagnosis – descent from confident nosology to skeptical empiricism – contrast the 1st, 2nd, and 3rd editions of American Psychiatric Association, *Diagnostic* .... For the origins of that statistical effort to overcome diagnostic confusion, see Plunkett and Gordon, pp. 21–4. See also Altschule, 'Whichophrenia', and Altschule, ed., *Development*. The best history I have come across is Klerman.

68 See *ZhNiPs*, 1952, No. 2, pp. 3–8. Note the stress on the Snezhnevskii-Kerbikov theme, that schizophrenia 'begins with neurotic symptoms' and can be cured if caught early. Note also the complaint that previous calls for increases in psychiatric beds and specialists had been ineffectual.

69 See the chart in Swazey, *Chloropromazine*, p. 241.

70 Vsesoiuznyi s'ezd nevropatologov ..., III–ii, *Trudy*, p. 439. Nevertheless he boasted, in the spirit of the time, that the healthy superiority of Soviet society to the decadent West was attested by its lower rate of mental illness.

71 The most detailed and revealing study, in Tomsk, for the period from 1948 to 1971, is reported by Krasik and Semin, 'Epidemiologicheskie aspekty'. Cf. Snezhnevskii, 'Prognoz ...', for a few global figures, including the remark that 'up to 70%' of chronic mental patients are schizophrenics. And, see again the study by the World Health Organization cited in note 53.

72 See above, note 62.

73 See Joravsky, *Lysenko*, pp. 212–16.

74 See especially publications of the Bekhterev Institute: Nauchno-issledovatel'skii psikhonevrologicheskii institut im. V. M. Bekhtereva, *Trudy*. Note, e.g., Zenevich. See also Lebedinskii and Miasishchev, with special attention to the evasive discussions of schizophrenia, *passim*. Cf. V. M. Smirnov for a report of a very subdued 'discussion' in Leningrad.

75 Joravsky, *Lysenko*, pp. 187–201.

76 See Esquirol, II, ch. XIX. Cf. the 1832 paper, pp. 312 ff, which calls for reform of the law to protect the insane against arbitrary confinement.

77 L. M. Shmaonova, reviewing Häfner, in *ZhNiPs*, 1980, No. 5, p. 784.

78 See, e.g., *Izvestiia*, 27 April 1988.

79 See Foucault, *Madness*, and *Histoire, passim*.

80 See Arieti, especially 2nd ed., pp. 81–2.

81 See Valenstein.

82 Snezhnevskii, 'Mesto kliniki ...', p. 1340.
83 Quoted in Huber and Gross, p. 32. For continuing disapproval of the 'narrow' view that Schneider preached, see E. Ia. Shternberg, in *ZhNiPs*, 1980, No. 4, p. 628.
84 See Haskins, pp. 326—7.

CHAPTER 16   PSYCHOLOGIES AND IDEOLOGIES

1 Fraisse, in Massucco Costa, p. 5.
2 *Ibid.*
3 For a convenient review, with citation of sources, see Pinkus, pp. 198—201.
4 AMN, *Sessiia* ... (1951), p. 205. Cf. Luria, 'Voprosy ...'.
5 *Meditsinskii rabotnik*, 26 June 1952.
6 *Sovetskaia pedagogika*, 1952, No. 8, p. 91. The stenographic record of the session is in APN *Izvestiia*, vyp. 45 (1953).
7 See, e.g., Petrushevskii et al. for the virtual abolitionists. Cf. Kussmann, pp. 65 *et passim*.
8 *Sovetskaia pedagogika*, 1952, No. 8, p. 95.
9 *Ibid.*, pp. 102—3.
10 *VPs*, 1955, No. 3, pp. 99—100.
11 *Ibid.*
12 Russell, p. 95. Originally published in 1931.
13 Vygotsky, *Izbrannye*. For the original, see above, pp. 453 ff.
14 See above, pp. 262 ff. For the lack of significant impact on working psychologists of the present, see *VPs, passim*; Wertsch, *Culture*; and Wertsch, *Vygotsky*.
15 See especially Piaget, 'Comments'. Cf. J. A. Martin for the similarity between Piaget's and Vygotsky's account of child development.
16 *Nauchnoe tvorchestvo* ..., p. 143. Cf. p. 159 for a bit of the old grumbling about the Westerners' failure to understand Vygotsky's Marxist approach.
17 See especially *Bessoznatel'noe* .... For an analysis of the peasant studies, see Dunn and Dunn.
18 See above, pp. 382, 523 n. 9, for L. N. Fedorov, F. P. Maiorov, and N. N. Nikitin. They became physiologists after the Civil War, as did N. I. Grashchenkov (Propper), who joined the Party in 1918, at the age of seventeen.
19 See especially Koriagin; and E. F. Kazanets.
20 Luria, *Working Brain*.
21 Luria, *Man* ..., p. 86.
22 The acceptance of the despot's rule is Siniavsky's metaphor. See below, p. 469. The 'momentary stay' is Frost's metaphor; the tourist's inscription is Faulkner's.
23 Rubinshtein, *Bytie*, and *Printsipy*.
24 Rubinshtein, *Bytie*, pp. 137, 157.
25 *Ibid.*, p. 7.
26 *Ibid.*
27 For a major sign of the shift to cybernetic modeling, see the 1962 conference, *Filosofskie voprosy* ....
28 See, e.g., Rubinshtein, *Bytie*, pp. 75, 91, 165 ff. Cf. pp. 288—9 for a rare

reference to A. N. Leont'ev – approving, with correction, his scholastic reconciliation of Pavlov's doctrine and psychology. Rubinshtein's hostility to Vygotsky's school may have been fueled by the major role of Kolbanovskii, an admirer of Vygotsky, in the anti-cosmopolitan campaign against Rubinshtein. See Kolbanovskii, 'Za marksistskoe ...'.

29 See Payne; and Graham, *Science*, pp. 377–92.

30 See above, pp. 306–7, for Pavlov's distress. For thorough reviews of work on both sides of the divide between psychologists and neuroscientists, see Kimble, et al. (with special attention to the seminal ideas of Tolman); Farley and Alkon; Woody; and Gould.

31 Manier, 'Cognitive ...', and 'Problems ...'. I am very grateful to Edward Manier for giving me these illuminating articles.

32 For examples of muted criticisms of Pavlov's doctrine, see Serzhantov; and Slonim. For an exceptionally plainspoken criticism of Pavlov's doctrine, see Megrelidze, *Osnovnye* ... (2nd ed., 1973), pp. 26 *et passim*. The book was written in 1935, before the author's destruction as an 'enemy of the people'.

33 For an admission that work on conditioning 'has been more intensive abroad than among us in recent years', see introduction to Sherrington, *Integrativnaia* .... For overwhelming evidence, see the relative paucity of Soviet items in the bibliographies of the review articles cited in note 30.

34 See Merton, *passim*.

35 See Bek, *And* ...; Sholokhov, *Virgin* ...; Gladkov, *Cement* .... For popular heroic fantasy before socialist realism, see J. P. Brooks.

36 See Dunham; Clark; Mathewson.

37 See N. Struve, pp. 35 *et passim*; Broyde, pp. 2–3; and Mandelstam, 'On the Nature of the Word', in his *Complete Critical Prose*, pp. 117 ff, and *Sobranie*, II, pp. 283 ff.

38 Mandelstam, *Sobranie*, I, No. 108.

39 *Ibid.* For a translation and commentary see Broyde, p. 47, *et passim*. Ehrenburg, in his memoirs, attested to the stir that the poem made. See quotation in Mandelstam, *Sobranie*, I, pp. 443–4.

40 See N. Mandelstam, *Hope Against Hope*, pp. 145–9. Maiakovskii was of course another modernist master who provoked questions among Soviet leaders.

41 For the circumstances of the writing, see *ibid.*, pp. 177–8 *et passim*, and N. Mandelstam, *Hope Abandoned*, pp. 526 *et passim*; and Mandelstam, *Complete Critical Prose*, pp. 660 ff.

42 *Ibid.*, p. 316. I have altered the translation in this edition to fit my sense of the original. See Mandelstam, *Sobranie*, II, p. 220.

43 *Ibid.*, pp. 225–6, and *Complete Critical Prose*, p. 321.

44 *Ibid.*, p. 324, and *Sobranie*, II, p. 229.

45 Ehrenburg reports that find. See his *Liudi* ..., as quoted in Mandelstam, *Sobranie*, I, p. 491. Cf. p. 512 for Akhmatova's vivid memory.

46 *Ibid.*, No. 227. Cf. p. 490 for an alternate ending, and also Baines, p. 21.

47 Mandelstam, *Sobranie*, I, No. 286. Cf. Baines, pp. 84–5; N. Struve, pp. 73–4.

48 Mandelstam, *Sobranie*, I, No. 372. Cf. p. 513 for reference to other poems praising Stalin. See also N. Struve, pp. 90–1; and Clarence Brown, 'Heart'; Baines, pp. 201 *et passim*; and Struve, pp. 88–91.

49 Tiutchev, 'Mal'aria', in any edition.
50 Baudelaire, 'Les Litanies de Satan', in any edition.
51 Mandelstam, *Sobranie*, I, No. 101. For an English version see Mandelstam, *Selected Poems*, pp. 21−2. Cf. Broyde, pp. 62−70; N. Struve, pp. 34−5; and Clarence Brown, *Mandelstam*.
52 Tertz, *The Trial* . . . , p. 59; and *idem, Fantasticheskii* . . . , p. 233.
53 See A. Ginzburg, comp., *Belaia kniga*, for the trial record, which was surreptitiously made and smuggled out of the courtroom.
54 See, e.g., Siniavskii, *Unguarded*, p. 79. Cf. Dalton; and Fanger, 'Conflicting . . .', in Morson, ed., *Literature* . . . .
55 See especially Trifonov, *Another Life and The House* . . . ; and *The Old Man*. Cf. Ivanova, *Proza* . . . .
56 See especially Solzhenitsyn, *One Day* . . . ; 'Matrenin dvor', in Solzhenitsyn *Sochineniia*; and *The First Circle*, with special attention to the hero Nerzhin, a descendent of Chernyshevsky's Rakhmetov and Gorky's Pavel Vlasov. Cf. Mathewson.

Bibliography

This list is limited to items cited in the notes in abridged or abbreviated form. Periodicals have not been given separate entries here; for full bibliographic information on them, see such reference works as the *Union List of Serials*.

ABBREVIATIONS

AHR	*American Historical Review*
AMN	Akademiia meditsinskikh nauk
AN	Akademiia nauk SSSR
APN	Akademiia pedagogicheskikh nauk RSFSR
BME	*Bol'shaia meditsinskaia entsiklopediia*. 1st ed., 35 vols. M., 1928–36; 2nd ed., 36 vols. M., 1956–64.
BS	*Biograficheskii slovar' deiatelei estestvoznaniia i tekhniki*. 2 vols. M., 1958–9.
BSE	*Bol'shaia sovetskaia entsiklopediia*. 1st ed. 65 vols. M., 1926–47; 2nd ed. 51 vols. 1950–8; 3rd ed. 30 vols. 1970–81.
EIM	*Estestvoznanie i marksizm*
ES	*Entsiklopedicheskii slovar'*, either Brockhaus and Efron, 41 vols. in 82, St Petersburg, 1890–1904, or Granat, 52 vols., M., 1910–34, as indicated in each citation.
FE	*Filosofskaia entsiklopediia*. 5 vols. M., 1960–70.
FZ	*Fiziologicheskii zhurnal*
IEM	Institut Eksperimental'noi Meditsiny
KA	Kommunisticheskaia Akademiia
KN	*Krasnaia nov'*
L.	Leningrad
M.	Moscow
NiPs	*Nevropatologiia i psikhiatriia*
NPsPs	*Nevropatologiia, psikhiatriia i psikhogigiena*
NR	*Nauka i nauchnye rabotniki SSSR*. 4 vols. M., 1924–34.
N.Y.	New York
NYR	*New York Review of Books*

OED   *Oxford English Dictionary*
PSS   *Polnoe sobranie sochinenii*
PST   *Polnoe sobranie trudov*
PZM   *Pod znamenem marksizma*
SNPsPs   *Sovetskaia nevropatologiia, psikhiatriia, i psikhogigiena*
SPb   St Petersburg
VAN   *Vestnik akademii nauk SSSR*
VE   *Vestnik Evropy*
VF   *Voprosy filosofii*
VFiPs   *Voprosy filosofii i psikhologii*
VIEiT   *Voprosy istorii estestvoznaniia i tekniki*
VIEM   Vsesoiuznyi Institut Eksperimental'noi Meditsiny
VKA   *Vestnik kommunisticheskoi akademii*
VPs   *Voprosy psikhologii*
VPsKAG   *Vestnik psikhologii, kriminal'noi antropologii i gipnotizma*
ZhMNP   *Zhurnal Ministerstva narodnogo prosveshcheniia*
ZhNiPs   *Zhurnal nevropatologii i psikhiatrii*
ZhPNP   *Zhurnal psikhologii, nevrologii, i psikhiatrii*
ZhVND   *Zhurnal vysshei nervnoi deiatel'nosti*
ZMLE   *Za marksistsko-leninskoe estestvoznanie*

Abel'skaia, R. and Neopikhonova, Ia. S. 'Problema razvitiia v nemetskoi psikhologii i ee vliianie na sovetskuiu pedologiiu i psikhologiiu', *Pedologiia*, 1932, No. 4.

Adamiak, R. 'Marx, Engels, and Dühring', *Journal of the History of Ideas*, No. 1, 1974.

Adoratskii, V. V. 'I. V. Stalin, kak teoretik leninizma', *Izvestiia*, 21 December 1929.

Akademiia meditsinskikh nauk. *Fiziologicheskoe uchenie akademii I. P. Pavlova v psikhiatrii i nevropatologii: materialy stenograficheskogo otcheta obedinennogo zasedaniia rasshirennogo Prezidiuma AMN SSSR i plenuma Pravleniia Vsesoiuznogo obshchestva nevropatologov i psikhiatrov. 11–15 okt., 1951 g.* M., 1951.

——. *Problemy vysshei nervnoi deiatel'nosti.* M., 1949.

Akademiia nauk. *Nauchnaia sessiia, posviashchennaia problemam fiziologicheskogo ucheniia Akademika I. P. Pavlova, 28 iiunia-4 iiulia 1950 g.: stenograficheskii otchet.* M., 1950.

Akademiia pedagogicheskikh nauk SSSR, Institut psikhologii. *Ukazatel' literatury vypushchennoi institutom psikhologii za 50 let.* M., 1967.

Aksakov, N. *Podspudnyi materializm: po povody dissertatsii-broshiury Gospodina Struve.* M., 1870.

Aksel'rod, L. I. 'Nadoelo!' *KN*, 1927, No. 3.

Aleksandrovskii, A. B. 'Protiv burzhuaznykh techenii v psikhotekhnike i fiziologii truda', *ZMLE*, 1931, No. 2.

Aliotta, Antonio. *The Idealistic Reaction against Science.* N.Y., 1975.

Altschule, M. D., ed. *The Development of Traditional Psychopathology.* N.Y., 1976.

——. 'Whichophrenia, or the confused past, ambiguous present, and dubious future of the schizophrenia concept', *Journal of Schizophrenia*, 1967, No. 1.

American Psychiatric Association. *Diagnostic and Statistical Manual of Mental Disorders.* Washington, D. C., 1st ed., 1952; 2nd ed., 1968; 3rd ed., 1980.

Anan'ev, B. G. 'Zadachi izucheniia istorii russkoi psikhologii', *Sovetskaia pedagogika*, 1938, No. 4.

Anokhin, P. K. 'Aktivnyi sekretno-dvigatel'nyi metod izucheniia vysshei nervnoi deiatel'nosti', *FZ*, 1933, No. 5.

——. 'Analiz i sintez v tvorchestve akademii I. P. Pavlova', *PZM*, 1936, No. 9. Also in *Uspekhi sovremennoi biologii*, 1936, No. 4.

——. 'Dialekticheskii materializm i voprosy psikhologicheskogo', *Chelovek i priroda*, 1926, No. 1.

——. *Ivan Petrovich Pavlov: zhizn', deiatel'nost' i nauchnaia shkola.* M., 1949.

——. *Ot Dekarta do Pavlova.* M., 1945.

——, ed. *Problema tsentra i periferii v fiziologii nervnoi deiatel'nosti: sb. rabot.* Gorky, 1935.

——. 'Tvorcheskii oblik I. P. Pavlova', *KN*, 1938, No. 3.

——. 'Uzlovye voprosy vysshei nervnoi deiatel'nosti', in AMN, *Problemy vysshei nervnoi deiatel'nosti.* M., 1949.

Antonii, Metropolitan of Kiev and Galich. *Psikhologicheskiia dannyia v pol'zu svobody voli i nravstvennoi otvetstvennosti.* St Petersburg, 1888.

Antonovich, M. A. 'Professor Sechenov o nesvobode voli', *Novoe obozrenie*, 1881, No. 2.

Antonov-Ovseyenko, Anton. *The Time of Stalin: Portrait of a Tyranny.* N.Y., 1981.

Arendt, Hannah. *The Origins of Totalitarianism.* 3 vols. N.Y., 1968.

Ariès, Philippe. *The Hour of Our Death.* N.Y., 1981.

Arieti, Silvano. *Interpretation of Schizophrenia.* N.Y., 1955; 2nd ed., 1974.

Artemov, V. A. 'K voprosu o sotsial'noi psikhotekhnike', *Psikhonevrologicheskie nauki v SSSR* ..., 1930.

Ascher, Abraham. *Pavel Axelrod and the Development of Menshevism.* Cambridge, Mass., 1972.

Ash, Mitchell and Woodward, W. R., eds. *Psychology in Twentieth-Century Thought and Society.* N.Y., 1987.

Ashukin, N. S., ed. *Valeryi Briusov v avtobiograficheskikh zapisiakh, pis'makh, vospominaniakh sovremennikov i otzyvakh kritiki.* M., 1929.

Averbukh, E. S. and Miasishchev, V. N. 'Kratkii ocherk nauchnoi deiatel'nosti Psikho-nevrologicheskogo instituta im. V. M. Bekhtereva', in *Nauchno-issledovatel'skaia deiatel'nost' instituta za 50 let: kratkii ocherk i bibliografii.* L., 1958.

Babel, Isaac. *The Collected Stories*, trans. Walter Morison. N.Y., 1960.

——. *Detstvo i drugie rasskazy.* Tel-Aviv, 1979.

——. *Izbrannoe.* M., 1966.

——. *Konarmiia.* M., 1928; 5th–6th ed., 1931; 7th–8th ed., 1933.

Babel: The Lonely Years, 1925–1939: Unpublished Stories and Private Correspondence, ed. Nathalie Babel. N.Y., 1964.

Babkin, B. P. *Pavlov, a Biography.* Chicago, 1949.

Bailes, K. E. *Technology and Society under Lenin and Stalin: Origins of the Soviet Technical Intelligentsia, 1917–1941.* Princeton, 1978.

Baines, Jennifer. *Mandelstam: The Later Poetry.* Cambridge, 1976.

Balabanovich, E. Z. *A. S. Makarenko: chelovek i pisatel'*. M., 1963.

Bal'dysh, G. *Bekhterev v Peterburge-Leningrade*. L., 1979.

Balmuth, Daniel. *Censorship In Russia, 1865–1905*. Washington, D. C., 1979.

Barbusse, Henri. *Stalin: A New World Seen Through One Man*. N.Y., 1935.

Baron, Samuel. 'Marx's *Grundrisse* and the Asiatic mode of production', *Survey*, 1975, No. 94/95.

Batalov, A. A. *Filosofskie vzgliagy V. M. Bekhtereva i mesto v nikh problema lichnosti.* Sverdlosk, 1969.

Bate, W. J. *John Keats*. Cambridge, Mass., 1963.

Bauer, Raymond. *The New Man in Soviet Psychology*. Cambridge, Mass., 1952.

Bauman, K. Ia. 'Polozhenie i zadachi sovetskoi nauki', *Pravda*, 6 September 1936, and *PZM*, 1936, No. 9.

Beach, J. W. *The Concept of Nature in 19th-Century English Poetry*. N.Y., 1956.

Beaujour, Elizabeth K. *The Invisible Land: A Study of the Artistic Imagination of Iurii Olesha*. N.Y., 1970.

Bek, Alexander. *And Not to Die*. N.Y., 1949. Also translated as *Volokolamsk Highway*, M., 1961; 2nd rev. ed., 1969.

Bekhterev, V. M. *Avtobiografiia*. M., 1928.

———. 'Eksperimental'nye issledovaniia nad vyrazheniem dushevnykn dvizhenii u zhivotnykh', *Vrach*, 1884, No. 1.

———. *General Principles of Human Reflexology*. N.Y., 1932.

———. *Izbrannye proizvedeniia*. M., 1954.

———. *Kollektivnaia refleksologiia*. Petrograd, 1921.

———. *Ob'ektivnaia psikhologiia*. 3 vols. St Petersburg, 1907–10.

———. 'Ob'ektivnaia psikologiia i ee predmet', *VPsKAG*, 1904, Nos. 9, 10.

———. *Obshchie osnovy refleksologii cheloveka: rukovodstvo ob'ektivnomy izucheniiu lichnosti.* 1st ed., Petrograd, 1918; 2nd ed., Petrograd-M., 1923; 3rd ed., L., 1926; 4th ed., M., 1928.

———. *Psikhika i zhizn'*. St Petersburg, 1902.

———. *Psikhologiia, refleksologiia i marksizm*. L., 1925.

———. 'Razvitie polovogo vlecheniia c tochki zreniia refleksologii', *Russkii vrach*, 1918, Nos. 29–32, 33–6.

———. 'Ubiistvo Iushchinskogo i psikhiatro-psikhologicheskaia ekspertiza', *Vrachebnaia gazeta*, 1913, No. 50.

———. 'Znachenie issledovaniia dvigatel'noi sfery dlia ob'ektivnogo izucheniia nervno-psikhicheskoi sfery cheloveka', *Russkii vrach*, 1909, Nos. 33–5.

Bekhterev, V.M. and Dubrovskii, A.V. 'Dialekticheskii materializm i refleksologiia', *PZM*, 1926, No. 7–8.

Bekhterev Institute (Gosudarstvennyi nauchno-issledovatel'skii psikhonevrologicheskii institut im. V. M. Bekhtereva.) *Nauchno-issledovatel'skaia deiatel'nosti instituta za 50 let: kratkii ocherk i bibliografiia*. L., 1958.

Benesch, Hellmuth. 'Friedrich Schillers Dissertation zum psycho-physischen Grundproblem', *Wissenschaftliche Zeitschrift der Friedrich-Schiller Universität Jena. Matematischnaturwissenschaftliche Reihe*, 1954–5, No. 1.

Beritashvili, I. S. *Biobibliografiia*. Tbilisi, 1977.

———. *Izbrannye trudy: neirofiziologiia i neiropsikhologiia*. M., 1975.

———. *Ob osnovnykh formakh nervnoi i psikho-nervnoi deiatel'nosti*. M., 1947.

Beritashvili Festschrift. *Problemy nervnoi fiziologii i povedeniia: sbornik posviashchennyi 25-letiiu nauchnoi, pedagogicheskoi i obshchestvennoi deiatel'nosti I. S. Beritashvili.* Tiflis, 1936.

Beritov, I. S. *Individual'no-priobretennaia deiatel'nost' tsentral'noi nervnoi sistemy.* Tiflis, 1932.

_____. 'On the fundamental nervous processes in the cortex of the cerebral hemisphere', *Brain*, 47 (1924), pp. 109–48 and 358–76.

_____. 'Über die neuro-psychische Tätigkeit der Grosshirnrinde', *Journal für Psychologie und Neurologie*, 30 (1924), pp. 217–56.

Bernard, Claude. 'Étude sur la physiologie du coeur', *Revue des deux mondes*, 56 (1865), pp. 236–52.

Bernshtein, N. A. *Issledovaniia po biodinamike lokomotsii.* M., 1935.

Bessoznatel'noe (ego priroda, funktsii i metody issledovaniia). 2 vols., ed. A. S. Prangishvili, et al. Tbilisi, 1978.

Bethe, A., Beer, T. and Uexküll, J. 'Vorschläge zu einer objektivierenden Nomenklatura in der Physiologie des Nervensystems', *Biologisches Zentralblatt*, 19 (1899), pp. 517–21.

Bibliografiia trudov I. P. Pavlova i literatury o nem, ed. E. Sh. Airapet'iants. M., 1954.

Biograficheskii slovar' deiatelei estestvoznaniia i tekhniki. 2 vols. M., 1958–9.

Black, Max. *Models and Metaphors.* Ithaca, 1962.

Blakemore, Colin. *Mechanisms of the Mind.* London, 1977.

Blissett, M. *Politics in Science.* Boston, 1972.

Bloch, Sidney and Reddaway, Peter. *Russia's Political Hospitals: The Abuse of Psychiatry in the Soviet Union.* London, 1977.

Blonskii, P. P. 'Fridrikh Paul'sen kak filosof i pedagog', *VFiPs*, 1908, No. 4.

_____. *Moi vospominaniia.* M., 1971.

_____. *Ocherki nauchnoi psikhologii.* M., 1921.

_____. *Reforma nauki.* M., 1920.

Blumenau, L. V. 'O lokalizatsii i strukture sochetatel'nykh mekhanizmov kory', *Sovremennaia psikhonevrologiia*, 1930, No. 4–5.

Bogdanov, A. A. *Empiriomonizm: stat'i po filosofii.* 3 vols. M., 1905–7.

_____. *Iz psikhologii obshchestva (stat'i 1901–1904).* 2nd ed. St Petersburg, 1906.

Bogdanovich, T. A. *Liubov' liudei shestidesiatykh godov.* L., 1929.

Bohn, Georges. *La nouvelle psychologie animale.* Paris, 1911.

Bor'ba za nauku v tsarskoi Rossii, ed. S. Ia. Shtraikh. M., 1931.

Boring, E. G. *A History of Experimental Psychology.* N.Y., 1950.

Borovskii, V. M. 'K voprosu ob instinkte v nauke o povedenii', *Psikhologiia i marksizm.* M., 1925.

_____. 'Novoe v uchenii o refleksakh', *PZM*, 1930, No. 2–3.

_____. 'Otchet o IX internatsional'nom psikhologicheskom kongesse v Amerike', *Psikhologiia*, 1930, No. 1.

_____. 'Uslovnye refleksy s tochki zreniia sravnitel'noi psikhologii', *Problemy sovremennoi psikhologii*, 3 (1928), pp. 26–36.

Bottomore, T. B., ed. *Karl Marx: Early Writings.* N.Y., 1963.

Bowen, James. *Soviet Education: Anton Makarenko and the Years of Experiment.* Madison, Wisc., 1962.

Brazier, Mary A. B., ed. *The Central Nervous System and Behavior: Transactions of the First Conference.* N.Y., 1959.

——. 'The historical development of neurophysiology', *Handbook of Physiology.* Section I: *Neurophysiology.* Vol. I. Washington, 1959.

Brentano, Franz. *Psychologie vom empirischen Standpunkt.* Leipzig, 1874. Reprint, 1924.

Briusov, V. Ia. *Rasskazy i povesti.* Munich, 1970.

——. *Sobranie sochinenii.* 7 vols. M., 1973–5.

Bronte, Charlotte. *Jane Eyre.* Penguin ed. 1966.

Brooks, Alexander D. *Law, Psychiatry, and the Mental Health System.* Boston, 1974.

Brooks, Jeffrey P. *When Russia Learned to Read: Literacy and Popular Literature, 1861–1917.* Princeton, 1985.

Brown, Clarence. 'Into the Heart of Darkness: Mandel'stam's ode to Stalin', *Slavic Review,* 1967, No. 4.

——. *Mandelstam.* Cambridge, 1973.

Brown, Julie. 'The Professionalization of Russian Psychiatry: 1857–1911', Dissertation, University of Pennsylvania, 1981.

——. 'Psychiatrists and the State in Tsarist Russia', in A. Scull and S. Cohen, eds., *Social Control and the State.* N.Y., 1983.

Broyde, Steven. *Osip Mandel'stam and His Age: A Commentary on the Themes of War and Revolution in his Poetry, 1913–1923.* Cambridge, Mass., 1975.

Brussof, Valéry. *The Republic of the Southern Cross and Other Stories.* N.Y., 1919.

Büchner, Ludwig. *Force and Matter.* London, 1872.

Bukharin, N. I. *Ataka.* M., 1924.

——. 'Enchmeniada', *KN,* 1923, No. 6.

——. *Historical Materialism.* Ann Arbor, Mich., 1969.

——. 'Kul'turnyi front i intelligentskii pessimizm', *Pravda,* 24 June 1923.

——. 'O mirovoi revoliutsii, nashei strane, kul'ture i prochem (otvet prof. I. Pavlovu)', *KN,* 1924, Nos. 1, 2. And separately, M., 1924.

Bumke, Oswald, ed. *Handbuch der Geisteskrankheiten.* 11 vols. Berlin, 1928–32.

Bunge, Mario. *The Furniture of the World.* Dordrecht, 1977.

——, ed. *The Methodological Unity of Science.* Dordrecht, 1973.

Bykov, K. M. *Kora golovnogo mozga i vnutrennie organy.* Kirov, 1942; 2nd ed., 1944; 3rd ed. 1947; 4th ed., 1954. Translated as *The Cerebral Cortex and the Internal Organs.* N.Y., 1957.

——, ed. *Nauchnaia konferentsiia po problemam psikhosomatiki.* L., 1948.

——. 'Novye puti v izuchenii deiatel'nosti vnutrennikh organov', *FZ,* 32 (1946).

——. 'O signal'nykh sistemakh organizma', *Sovetskii vrachebnyi sbornik,* 1 (1946).

Bykov, K. M. and Chernigovskii, V. N. 'O printsipe vremennoi sviazi i ego znachenii v fiziologii', *FZ,* 33 (1947), No. 6.

Camus, Albert. *The Rebel: An Essay on Man in Revolt.* N.Y., 1956.

Canguilhem, Georges. *La formation du concept de réflexe aux XVIIe et XVIIIe siècles.* Paris, 1955.

——. 'Le concept de réflexe au XIXe siècle', in *Von Boerhaave bis Berger,* ed. K. E. Rothschuh. Stuttgart, 1964.

Carden, Patricia. *The Art of Isaac Babel.* Ithaca, 1972.

Caton, Hiram. *The Origin of Subjectivity: An Essay on Descartes.* New Haven, 1973.

Chadwick, Owen. *The Secularization of the European Mind in the 19th Century.* Cambridge, 1975.

Chagin, B. A. and Klushin, V. I. *Bor'ba za istoricheskii materializm v 20-e gody.* L., 1975.

Chebysheva, N. A. 'Nauchno-organizatsionnaia rol' I. P. Pavlova v Institute eksperimental'noi meditsiny v 1891–1916 gg', *Ezhegodnik IEM*, 1957.

Chekhov, A. P. *Letters of Anton Chekhov*, ed. Simon Karlinsky. N.Y., 1973.

——. *Polnoe sobranie sochinenii i pisem.* 30 vols. in two parts. M., 1974–83.

Chelpanov, G. I. 'Ob eksperimental'nom metode v psikhologii', *Novye ideiv filosofii*, sb. 9 (St Petersburg, 1913).

——. 'Ob otnoshenii psikhologii k filosofii', *VFiPs*, 1907, No. 4.

——. *Psikhologiia ili refleksologiia.* M., 1926.

——. *Psikhologiia i marksizm.* M., 1924.

Chernyshevsky, N. G. *What Is To Be Done? Tales About New People.* N.Y., 1961.

Chistovich, A. S. 'O vzgliadakh Pavlova na shizofreniiu', *NiPs*, 1949, No. 5.

Chuchmarev, Z. I. *Marksizm, psikhofiziologiia, uslovnye refleksy.* Kharkhov, 1928.

Churchland, Patricia Smith. *Neurophilosophy: Toward a Unified Science of the Mind-Brain.* Cambridge, Mass., 1986.

Clark, Katerina, *The Soviet Novel: History as Ritual.* Chicago, 1981.

Clarke, Edwin and O'Malley, C. D. *The Human Brain and Spinal Cord. A Historical Study.* Berkeley, 1968.

Clauss, Gunter, et al., eds. *Wörterbuch der Psychologie.* Leipzig, 1978.

Cohen, Stephen. *Bukharin and the Bolshevik Revolution: A Political Biography, 1888–1938.* N.Y., 1973.

Coleman, William R. *Biology in the 19th Century.* N.Y., 1971.

Colp, Ralph. 'The contacts between Karl Marx and Charles Darwin', *Journal of the History of Ideas*, April–June, 1974.

Conrad, Joseph. *Heart of Darkness.* N.Y., 1972.

——. *Nostromo: A Tale of the Seaboard.* N.Y., 1961.

——. *Under Western Eyes.* N.Y., 1951.

Corson, Samuel A. and Corson, Elizabeth O'Leary, eds. *Psychiatry and Psychology in the USSR.* N.Y., 1976.

Cottier, Georges M.-M. *Du romantisme au marxisme.* Paris, 1961.

Crum, R. B. *Scientific Thought in Poetry.* N.Y., 1931.

Daian, G. 'Vtoroi psikhonevrologicheskii s'ezd', *KN*, 1924, Nos. 2, 3.

Dalton, Margaret. *Andrei Siniavskii and Julii Daniel': Two Soviet 'Heretical' Writers.* Würzburg, 1973.

Darwin, Charles. *The Origin of Species and The Descent of Man.* N.Y., 1936.

Decker, Hannah. *Freud in Germany: Revolution and Reaction in Science, 1893–1907.* N.Y., 1977.

Degen, Heinz. 'Vor hundert Jahren: Die Naturforscherversammlung zu Göttingen und der Materialismusstreit', *Naturwissenschaftliche Rundschau*, 1954, No. 7.

Deiateli SSSR i Oktiabr'skoi Revoliutsii (Avtobiografii i biografii), prilozhenie k tsiklu statei 'SSSR'. Granat *ES*, XLI. And photo-reprint.

Dekhterev, V. V. 'Dispanserizatsiia kak osnova bor'by s istoshcheniem', *Klinicheskaia meditsina*, 1930, No. 19–20.

de Santillana, G. *The Crime of Galileo.* Chicago, 1955.

Dessoir, Max. *Ocherk istorii psikhologii.* St Petersburg, 1912.

Deutscher, Isaac. *The Prophet Armed: Trotsky: 1879–1921.* N.Y., 1954.

——. *The Prophet Unarmed: Trotsky: 1921–1929*. N.Y., 1959.

——. *Stalin: A Political Biography*. N.Y., 1949.

Dictionary of Scientific Biography. 16 vols., ed. C. C. Gillespie. N.Y., 1970–80.

Diderot, Denis. *Éléments de physiologie*. Paris, 1964.

Djilas, Milovan. *Conversations with Stalin*. N.Y., 1962.

Dobroliubov, N. A. *Sobranie sochinenii*. 9 vols. M., 1961–4.

Dobrovol'skii, L. M. *Zapreshchennaia kniga v Rossii, 1825–1904*. M., 1962.

Drapkina, S. E. 'N. T. Chernyshevskii i I. M. Sechenov', *FZ*, 28 (1940), No. 2–3.

——. 'Filosofsko-psikhologicheskaia polemika 1860–62 gg. i I. M. Sechenov', *Sovetskaia pedagogika*, 1939, No.6.

Du Bois-Reymond, E. H. *Reden und Schriften*. Leipzig, 1886.

——. *Über die Grenzen des Naturerkennens: Die sieben Welträthsel*. Leipzig, 1884.

Duncan, David. *Life and Letters of Herbert Spencer*. N.Y., 1908.

Dunham, Vera. *In Stalin's Time: Middleclass Values in Soviet Fiction*. N.Y., 1976.

Dunn, Ethel and Dunn, Stephen P. *The Peasants of Central Russia*. N.Y., 1967.

Ebbinghaus, Hermann. *Abriss der Psychologie*. Leipzig, 1908.

Eccles, J. C. *Facing Reality: Philosophical Adventures by a Brain Scientist*. N.Y., 1970.

Efrussi, P. O. *Uspekhi psikhologii v Rossii*. Petrograd, 1923.

Ehrenburg, Ilia. *Liudi, gody, zhizn'*. M., 1961.

Ekehorn, Gosta. *Sherrington's 'Endeavor of Jean Fervel' and 'Man on His Nature'*. Stockholm, 1949.

Eklof, Ben. *Russian Peasant Schools: Officialdom, Village Culture, and Popular Pedagogy, 1861–1914*. Berkeley, 1986.

Eliot, T. S. *The Complete Poems and Plays, 1909–1950*. N.Y., 1958.

Ellenberger, Henri F. *The Discovery of the Unconscious*. N.Y., 1970.

Encyclopedia of Philosophy. 8 vols., ed. Paul Edwards. N.Y., 1967.

Encyclopedia of Psychology. 3 vols., ed. Hans Eysenck. N.Y., 1972.

Encyclopedia of Social Sciences. 1st ed. 15 vols. N.Y., 1930–5.

Engels, F. *Herr Eugen Dühring's Revolution in Science (Anti-Dühring)*. N.Y., 1939.

Eristavi, K. D. and Semenskaia, E. M., eds. *I. R. Tarkhanishvili: zhizn', nauchnaia i obshchestvennaia deiatel'nost'*. Tbilisi, 1953.

Erlich, A. *The Soviet Industrialization Debate, 1924–1928*. Cambridge, Mass., 1960.

Erlich, Victor. *Russian Formalism*. The Hague, 1980.

Ermakov, I. D., ed. *Psikhologicheskaia i psikhoanaliticheskaia biblioteka*. 23 issues. Moscow-Petrograd, 1922–5.

Ermanskii, O. A. *Stakhanovskoe dvizhenie i stakhanovskie metody*. M., 1940.

Esquirol, E. *Des maladies mentales considerées sous les rapports médical, hygiénique et médico-légal*. Bruxelles, 1838.

Evreiskaia entsiklopediia. 16 vols. St Petersburg, 1906–13.

Fanger, Donald. 'Conflicting imperatives in the model of the Russian writer: the case of Tertz/Sinyavsky', in *Literature and History: Theoretical Problems and Russian Case Studies*, ed. G. S. Morson. Stanford, 1986.

Farley, Joseph and Alkon, Daniel L. 'Cellular mechanisms of learning, memory, and information storage', *Annual Review of Psychology*, 36 (1985), pp. 419–94.

Fay, Margaret A. 'Did Marx offer to dedicate *Capital* to Darwin?', *Journal of the History of Ideas*, January-March, 1978.

Fearing, Franklin. *Reflex Action: A Study in the History of Physiological Psychology*. N.Y., 1964.

Fechner, Gustav. *Elements of Psychophysics*. N.Y., 1966.

Fedorov, L. N. 'Metod uslovnykh refleksov v izuchenii vysshei nervnoi deiatel'-nosti', *Chelovek i priroda*, 1930, No. 4.

Feinberg, Ts. M. *Sudebno-psikhiatricheskaia ekspertiza i opyt raboty Instituta im. Serbskogo*. M., 1935.

Feofanov, M. P. 'Teoriia kul'turnogo razvitiia v pedologii kak eklekticheskaia kontseptsiia imeiushchaia v osnovnom idealisticheskie korni', *Pedologiia*, 1932, No. 1–2.

Filosofskie voprosy fiziologii vysshei nervnoi deiatel'nosti i psikhologii. M., 1963.

Fitzpatrick, Sheila. *The Commissariat of Enlightenment: Soviet Organization of Education and the Arts under Lunacharsky. October, 1917–1921*. Cambridge, 1970.

——, ed. *Cultural Revolution in Russia, 1928–1931*. Bloomington, 1984.

——. *Education and Social Mobility in the Soviet Union, 1921–1934*. Cambridge, 1979.

Fiziologicheskaia shkola I. P. Pavlova: portrety i kharakteristiki sotrudnikov i uchenikov, ed. D. G. Kvasov. Leningrad, 1967.

Fleishman, Avrom. *Conrad's Politics: Community and Anarchy in the Fiction of Joseph Conrad*. Baltimore, 1967.

Fleming, Donald. 'Introduction', in Jacques Loeb, *Mechanistic Conception of Life*. Cambridge, Mass., 1964.

Foucault, Michel. *The Birth of the Clinic: An Archaeology of Medical Perception*. N.Y., 1973.

——. *Histoire de la folie*. Paris, 1961.

——. *Madness and Civilization: A History of Insanity in the Age of Reason*. N.Y., 1965.

Frank, Joseph. *Dostoevsky: The Seeds of Revolt, 1821–1849*. Princeton, 1976.

——. *Dostoevsky: The Stir of Liberation, 1860–1865*. Princeton, 1986.

Frankel, Jonathan. *Prophecy and Politics: Socialism, Nationalism, and the Russian Jews, 1862–1917*. Cambridge, 1981.

Frankfurt, Iu. V, 'K bor'be za marksistskuiu psikhologiiu', *KN*, 1927, No. 10.

——. 'Ob odnom izobrazhenii marksizma v oblasti psikhologii', *KN*, 1925, No. 4.

——. *Refleksologiia i marksizm: uchenie Bekhtereva i marksizm*. L., 1924.

Franklin, Benjamin. *Autobiography*. N.Y., 1954.

Frédericq, Léon and Nuel, J. P. *Osnovy fiziologii cheloveka*. St Petersburg, 1897–9.

French, R. K. *Robert Whytt, the Soul and Medicine*. London, 1969.

Freud, Sigmund. *Budushchnost'odnoi illiuzii*. M., 1930.

Frieden, Nancy. *Russian Physicians in an Era of Reform and Revolution, 1856–1905*. Princeton, 1981.

Frolov, Iu. P. 'Chto takoe fiziologiia voennogo truda?', in *Voprosy fiziologii voennogo truda i voenno-professional'nogo otbora*, ed. N. A. Zelenev. M., 1928.

——. *Ivan Petrovich Pavlov: vospominaniia*. M., 1949; 2nd ed., 1953.

——. *Vysshaia nervnaia deiatel'nost' pri toksikozakh (po materialam BOV). Dlia voennikh vrachei i toksikologov*. M., 1944.

Fusil, C. A. *La poésie scientifique de 1750 à nos jours*. Paris, 1917.

Galant, I. B. 'Rezul'taty psikhoekspertizy 335 krasnoarmeitsev', *ZhNiPs*, 1931, No. 2.

Gannushkin, P. B. 'Ob okhrane zdorov'ia partaktiva', *Revoliutsiia i kul'tura*, 1930, No. 4.

Gay, Peter. *The Dilemma of Democratic Socialism: Eduard Bernstein's Challenge to Marx.* N.Y., 1952.

Gerver, A. V. 'O vliianii golovnogo mozga na otdelenie zheludochnogo soka', *Obozrenie psikhiatrii, nevropatologii, i eksperimental'noi psikhologii*, 5 (1900), pp. 191–8, 275–83.

Geymonat, L. *Galileo Galilei: A Biography and Inquiry into His Philosophy of Science.* N.Y., 1965.

Giere, R. N. and Westfall, R. S., eds. *Foundations of Scientific Method: The Nineteenth Century.* Bloomington, 1973.

Giliarovskii, V. A. 'Dostizheniia v sovetskoi psikhiatrii za poslednie 15 let i ee blizhaishie perspektivy', *SNPsPs*, 1933, No. 1.

——. 'Freidizm', Granat, *ES.* XLV, 1927, pt. 1.

——. *Psikhiatriia: rukovodstvo dlia vrachei i studentov.* 4th ed., M., 1954.

——. 'Skhizofreniia', *BME*, 1st ed., XXXII (1935).

——. 'Urbanizatsiia i zabolevaniia nervno-psikhicheskoi sredy', *Psikhonevrologicheskie nauki v SSSR.* M., 1930.

Ginzburg, Aleksandr, compiler. *Belaia kniga po delu A. Siniavskogo i Iu. Danielia.* Munich, 1967.

Gitelman, Z. Y. *Jewish Nationality and Soviet Politics: The Jewish Sections of the CPSU, 1917–1930.* Princeton, 1972.

Gladkov, F. V. *Cement: A Novel.* N.Y., 1929.

Gode-von Aesch, A. *Natural Science in German Romanticism.* N.Y., 1941.

Goldstein, Jan. 'The hysteria diagnosis and the politics of anticlericalism in late 19th-century France', *Journal of Modern History*, June 1982.

Gor'kii i nauka: stat'i, rechi, pis'ma, vospominaniia. M., 1964.

Gottesman, I. L. and Shields, J. *Schizophrenia and Genetics: A Twin Study Vantage Point.* N.Y., 1972.

Gould, James L. 'The biology of learning', *Annual Review of Psychology*, 37 (1986), pp. 163–92.

Gould, S. J. *The Mismeasure of Man.* N.Y., 1981.

Graham, L. R. *Science and Philosophy in the Soviet Union.* N.Y., 1971.

——. *The Soviet Academy of Sciences and the Communist Party, 1927–1932.* Princeton, 1967.

Grashchenkov, N. I. (or Propper) 'Itogi diskussii na estestvenno-nauchnom fronte i bor'ba na dva fronte v meditsine', *ZhNiPs*, 1931, Nos. 1, 2, 5.

——. 'Izuchenie povedeniia cheloveka', *Molodaia gvardiia*, April 1930.

——. 'Raboty fiziologicheskoi laboratorii Pavlova', *ZMLE*, 1932, No. 3–4.

——. 'Refleksologicheskoe napravlenie v fiziologii', *ZMLE*, 1932, No. 3–4.

——. 'Refleksologiia', *BME*, 1st ed., XXVIII (1934), pp. 737–55.

——. 'Shkola akademika Pavlova na povedencheskom s'ezde', *ZhNiPs*, 1930, No. 3.

Gregg, R. A. *Fedor Tiutchev: The Evolution of a Poet.* N.Y., 1965.

Griesinger, W. *Gesammelte Abhandlungen.* 2 vols. Berlin, 1872.

——. *Mental Pathology and Therapeutics.* N.Y., 1965.

——. 'Über psychische Reflex-Aktionen', *Archiv für physiologische Heilkunde*, 2 (1843).

Grille, Dietrich. *Lenins Rivale; Bogdanov und seine Philosophie.* Köln, 1966.

Grossman, Vasilii. *Zhizn'i sud'ba: roman.* Lausanne, 1980.

Grot, N. Ia. 'Psikhologiia', in Brockhaus and Efron, *ES*, L (1898).

———. *Psikhologiia chuvstvovanii v eia istorii i glavnykh osnovakh*. St Petersburg, 1879–80.

Guéroult, M. *Descartes selon l'ordre des raisons*. 2 vols. Paris, 1953.

Guthrie, E. R. 'Conditioning as a principle of learning', *Psychological Review*, 37 (1930), pp. 412–28.

Häfner, H., ed. *Psychiatrische Epidemiologie: Geschichte, Einführung, und ausgewählte Forschungsergebnisse*. Berlin, 1978.

Hagstrom, W. O. *The Scientific Community*. N.Y., 1965.

Hall, Thomas S. *Ideas of Life and Matter: Studies in the History of General Physiology, 600 B.C.–1900 A.D.* Chicago, 1969.

Hanfmann, E. and Kasanin, J. 'A method for the study of concept formation', *Journal of Psychology*, 1937, No. 3.

Harris, Ben. 'Whatever happened to Little Albert?', *American Psychologist*, February 1979.

Harris, Marvyn. *The Rise of Anthropological Theory: A History of Theories of Culture*. N.Y., 1968.

Haskins, C. H. *The Renaissance of the Twelfth Century*. Cambridge, Mass., 1928.

Hearst, Eliot, ed. *The First Century of Experimental Psychology*. Hillsdale, N.J., 1979.

Heidbreder, Edna. *Seven Psychologies*. N.Y., 1933.

Heller, Erich. *The Artist's Journey Into the Interior*. N.Y., 1965.

Helmholtz, H. L. F. von. *Popular Lectures on Scientific Subjects*. London, 1881.

Hemmings, F. W. J. *Émile Zola*. London, 1952.

Henderson, W. O. *Life of Friedrich Engels*. 2 vols. London, 1976.

Heyck, T. W. *The Transformation of Intellectual Life in Victorian England*. N.Y., 1982.

Hilgard, E. R. and Marquis, D. G. *Conditioning and Learning*. N.Y., 1940. Cf. Kimble, et al.

Hillig, Götz. 'Makarenkos 'Pädagogiches Poem' in der zeitgenössischen Kritik (1934–1937)', *Pädagogik und Schule in Ost und West*, 1980, No. 4, and 1981, No. 1.

Hindess, Barry and Hirst, Paul Q. *Precapitalist Modes of Production*. London, 1975.

History of the CPSU (Short Course), edited by a Commission of the Central Committee of the CPSU. N.Y., 1939.

Holland, Jimmie. 'A comparative look at Soviet psychiatry', in *Psychiatry and Psychology in the USSR*, ed. S. A. and E. O. Corson. N.Y., 1976.

Huber, G. and Gross, G. *Wahn: eine deskriptiv-phänomenologische Untersuchung schizophrenen Wahns*. Stuttgart, 1977.

Hughes, H. Stuart. *Consciousness and Society: The Reorientation of European Social Thought, 1890–1930*. N.Y., 1958.

Huysmans, J. K. *À rebours*. Paris, 1981. Translated as *Against the Grain*, N.Y., 1931, and as *Against Nature*, Baltimore, 1971.

Hyde, Gordon. *The Soviet Health Service: A Historical and Comparative Study*. London, 1974.

Iaroshevskii, M. G. 'Iz istorii bor'by materializma s idealizmom v russkom estestvoznanii XIX veka', *VF*, 1956, No. 1.

_____. *Ivan Mikhailovich Sechenov, 1829—1905*. L., 1968.

Ignat'ev, E. I., ed. *Voprosy psikhologii lichnosti*. M., 1960.

International Encyclopedia of the Social Sciences. 2nd ed. 16 vols. N.Y., 1968.

I. P. Pavlov v vospominaniiakh sovremennikov. L., 1967.

Istoriia estestvoznaniia: literatura opublikovannaia v SSSR (1917—1980). 9 vols. M., 1949—85.

Istoriia Rossii v XIX veke. 9 vols. St Petersburg, 1907—11. Reprint: Ann Arbor, 1960.

Iudin, T. I. *Ocherki istorii otechestvennoi psikhiatrii*. M., 1951.

Iurkevich, P. D. 'Iazyk fiziologov i psikhologov', *Russkii vestnik*, 1862, Nos. 4—6, 8.

_____. 'Iz nauki o chelovecheskom dukhe', *Trudy Kievskoi dukhovnoi akademii*, 1860, No. 4. Also in *Russkii vestnik*, 1861, No. 4—5.

Iushkevich, P. S. *Stolpy filosofskoi ortodoksii*. St Petersburg, 1910.

Ivanova, Natal'ia. *Proza Iuriia Trifonova*. M., 1984.

Ivanovskii, V. N. 'N. Ia. Grot', *VFiPs*, 1900, kn. 51.

Ivanov-Smolenskii, A. G. *Estestvoznanie i nauka o povedenii cheloveka*. M., 1929.

Iz istorii studencheskikh volnenii (Konovalovskii konflikt). St Petersburg, 1906.

Jackson, J. Hughlings. *Selected Writings*. 2 vols. London, 1931.

Jackson, R. L. *Dostoevsky's Underground Man in Russian Literature*. The Hague, 1958.

James, William. *Principles of Psychology*. 2 vols. N.Y., 1950.

_____. *Psychology*. N.Y., 1892.

_____. *The Varieties of Religious Experience: A Study in Human Nature*. N.Y., 1902.

Jay, Martin. *The Dialectical Imagination: A History of the Frankfurt School and the Institute of Social Research*. Boston, 1973.

Jefferson, Geoffrey. 'Marshall Hall, the grasp reflex and the diastaltic spinal cord', in *Science, Medicine, and History: Essays on the Evolution of Scientific Thought and Medical Practice, Written in Honour of Charles Singer*, II, London, 1953.

Jennings, Herbert Spencer. *Behavior of the Lower Organisms*. Bloomington, 1962.

Jones, Ernest. *The Life and Work of Sigmund Freud*. 3 vols. N.Y. 1953—7.

Joravsky, David. *The Lysenko Affair*. Cambridge, Mass., 1970.

_____. 'The scientist as conformist', *NYR*, 12 October 1978.

_____. 'Scientists as servants', *NYR*, 28 June 1979.

_____. 'Sin and the scientist', *NYR*, 17 July 1980.

_____. *Soviet Marxism and Natural Science, 1917—1932*. N.Y., 1961.

_____. 'The Stalinist mentality and the higher learning', *Slavic Review*, Winter 1983.

Kalinin, M. I. 'Nauka i liudi truda', *Novaia Petrovka*, 1923, No. 3—4.

Kamin, L. J., *The Science and Politics of IQ*. Potomac, Md. 1974.

Kannabikh, Iu. V. *Istoriia psikhiatrii*. L., 1928.

_____. 'K istorii voprosa o miagkikh formakh shizofrenii', *SNPsPs*, 1934, No. 5.

Kaplun, S. I. *Obshchaia gigiena truda*. M., 1940.

Karlik, L. N. 'Nekotorye itogi rabot shkoly professora Speranskogo (o nervnoi trofike v teorii i praktike meditsiny)', *PZM*, 1934, No. 3.

Kautsky, Karl. *Materialistische Geschichtsauffassung*. Berlin, 1927.

Kavelin, K. D. *Sobranie sochinenii*. 4 vols. St Petersburg, 1897—1900.

_____. *Zadachi etiki: uchenie o nravstvennosti pri sovremennykh usloviiakh znaniia.* St Petersburg, 1885.

_____. 'Zadachi psikhologii', *VE*, January, April 1872.

Kazanets, E. F. 'Differentiating exogenous psychiatric illness from schizophrenia', *Archives of General Psychiatry*, 36 (1979).

Kekcheev, K. Kh. and Shustin, N. A. 'K ukhodu I. M. Sechenova iz Mediko-khirurgicheskoi akademii v 1870 g. (Arkhivnie mateialy)', *FZ*, 21 (1936), No. 1.

Kennan, George F. *The Fateful Alliance: France, Russia, and the Coming of the First World War.* N.Y., 1984.

_____. 'The curious Monsieur Cyon', *American Scholar*, Autumn 1986, pp. 449–75.

Kerbikov, O. V. 'Emil' Kraepelin i problemy nozologii v psikhiatrii', *ZhNiPs*, 1956, No. 12.

_____. 'O gruppe shizofrenii tekushchikh bez ismeniia kharaktera', *Sovremennye problemy shizofrenii.* M., 1933.

_____. 'O nekotorykh spornykh voprosakh psikhiatrii', *ZNiPs*, 1952, No. 5.

Kerry, S. S. *Schiller's Writings on Aesthetics.* Manchester, 1961.

Khoroshko, V. K. 'Gigiena dushi i biurokratiia', *Russkaia mysl'*, 1905, No. 12.

Khrustalev, V. A., compiler *A. S. Makarenko: bibliograficheskii ukazatel'.* M., 1959.

Kim, M. P., ed. *Sovetskaia intelligentsiia (Istoriia formirovaniia i rosta 1917–1965 gg).* M., 1968.

Kimble, G. A., et al. *Hilgard and Marquis' Conditioning and Learning.* N.Y., 1961.

Kindlers Literatur Lexikon. 8 vols. Zürich, 1965–74.

Klerman, G. L. 'The evolution of a scientific nosology', *Schizophrenia: Science and Practice*, ed. J. C. Shershow. Cambridge, Mass., 1978.

Koestler, Arthur. *The Sleepwalkers.* N.Y., 1959.

Koffka, Kurt. *Osnovy psikhicheskoi razvitiia.* M., 1934.

Kolakowski, Leszek. *The Alienation of Reason: A History of Positivist Thought.* N.Y., 1961.

_____. *Main Currents of Marxism.* 3 vols. Oxford, 1978.

Kolbanovskii, V. N. 'Lev Semenovich Vygotskii', *Sovetskaia psikhotekhnika*, 1934, No. 4.

_____. 'Psikhologiiu na sluzhbu promyshlennosti', *Psikhologiia*, 1932, No. 3.

_____. 'Za marksistskoe osveshchenie voprosov psikhologii', *Bol'shevik*, 1947, No. 17.

Kol'man, E. G. *Na bor'bu za materialisticheskuiu dialektiku v matematike.* M., 1931.

_____. 'Politika, ekonomika i matematika', *ZMLE*, 1931, No. 1.

_____. 'Stalin i nauka', *PZM*, 1939, No. 12.

Kol'tsov, N. K. 'Trud zhizni velikogo biologa', *Biologicheskii zhurnal*, 5 (1936), No. 3.

Kommunisticheskaia Akademiia, Institut vysshei nervnoi deiatel'nosti. *Vysshaia nervnaia deiatel'nost'.* 1929.

Konorski, Jerzy. *Conditioned Reflexes and Neuron Organization.* London, 1948.

Koriagin, Anatolii. 'Unwilling patients', *The Lancet*, 11 April 1981.

Kornilov, K. N., ed. *Psikhologiia i marksizm.* L., 1925.

_____. 'Psikhologiia i marksism', in *ibid.*

_____. *Shkola i zakon Bozhii.* M., 1919.

_____. 'Sovremennaia psikhologiia i marksizm', *PZM*, 1923, No. 1.

_____. 'Sovremennoe sostoianie psikhologii v SSSR', *Problemy sovremennoi psikhologii*, 3, 1928.

_____. *Uchebnik psikhologii, izlozhennoi s tochki zreniia dialekticheskogo materializma.* L., 1926; 2nd ed., 1928.

_____. *Uchenie o reaktsiakh cheloveka.* M., 1922; 2nd ed., 1925; 3rd ed., 1927.

Koshtoiants, Kh. S. 'I. M. Sechenov', in I. M. Sechenov, *Selected Physiological and Psychological Works.* M., 1952[?].

_____. *Sechenov.* M., 1945.

Kostelianets, B. *A. S. Makarenko: kritiko-biograficheskii ocherk.* M., 1954.

Kostiuk, P. G., et al. *Ivan Mikhailovich Sechenov: k 150-letiiu so dnia rozhdeniia.* M., 1980.

Kozulin, Alex. *Psychology in Utopia.* Cambridge, Mass., 1984.

_____. 'Vygotsky and crisis', *Studies in Soviet Thought*, 1983, No. 26.

_____. 'Georgy Chelpanov and the establishment of the Moscow Institute of Psychology', *Journal of the History of the Behavioral Sciences*, Jan., 1985.

KPSS v rezoliutsiiakh i resheniiakh s'ezdov, konferentsii i plenumov TsK. 7th ed. 4 vols. M., 1953–60.

Krader, L. 'The works of Marx and Engels in ethnology compared', *International Review of Social History*, 1973, pt. 2.

Krasik, E. D. and Semin, I. R. 'Epidemiologicheskie aspekty pervichnoi gospitalizatsii bol'nykh shizofrenii', *ZhNiPs*, 1980, No. 9.

Krivtsov, S. S. 'I. V. Stalin (k 50–letiiu so dnia rozhdeniia)', *PZM*, 1930, No. 2–3.

Krol', M. B. 'I. P. Pavlov i ego znachenie dlia nevropatologii', *NPsPs*, 1936, No. 6.

_____. 'Nauka' o povedenii na sluzhbe u natsional-demokratov', *ZhNiPs*, 1931, No. 1.

_____. 'Uspekhi sovetskoi nevropatologii za 15 let', *SNPsPs*, 1933, No. 1.

Kussmann, Thomas. *Sowjetische Psychologie auf der Suche nach der Methode: Pavlovs Lehren und das Menschenbild der marxistischen Psychologie.* Bern-Stuttgart-Wien, 1974.

Kuznetsov, F. F. *Nigilisty? D. I. Pisarev i zhurnal 'Russkoe slovo'.* M., 1983.

Lamettrie, J. O. de. *L'Homme-Machine.* Paris, 1865.

_____. *Oeuvres philosophiques.* Berlin, 1796.

Lange, K. A. *Institut fiziologii imeni I. P. Pavlova: ocherk istorii organizatsii i razvitii.* L., 1975.

Lange, N. N. *Psikhologicheskie issledovaniia.* Odessa, 1893.

_____. *Psikhologiia.* M., 1914.

Langford, Jerome J. *Galileo, Science, and the Church.* N.Y., 1966.

Lashley, K. S. 'Basic neural mechanisms in behavior', *Psychological Review*, January 1930. Also in Russian, *Psikhologiia*, 1930, No. 3.

_____. *The Neuropsychology of Lashley: Selected Papers*, ed. F. A. Beach, et al. N.Y., 1960.

Lavrov, P. L. *Historical Letters.* Trans. and intro. James P. Scanlon. Berkeley, 1967.

Laycock, T. *Mind and Brain, or the Correlations of Consciousness and Organization.* Edinburgh, 1860.

_____. 'On the reflex function of the brain', *British and Foreign Medical Review*, January 1845.

Lazurskii, A. F. *Klassifikatsiia lichnostei.* 3rd ed. L., 1924.

——. *Ocherk nauki o kharakterakh.* St Petersburg, 1906.

Leakey, F. W. *Baudelaire and Nature.* Manchester, 1969.

Lebedinskii, M. S. and Miasishchev, V. N. *Vvedenie v meditsinskuiu psikhologiiu.* L., 1966.

Leikina-Svirskaia, V. R. 'Formirovanie raznochinskoi intelligentsii v Rossii v 40-x godakh XIX veka', *Istoriia SSSR,* 1958, No. 1.

——. *Intelligentsiia v Rossii vo vtoroi polovine XIX veka.* M., 1971.

Lemaître, Jules. *Literary Impressions.* London, 1921.

Lenin, V. I. *Filosofskie tetradi.* M., 1933.

——. *Materialism and Empiriocriticism; Critical Comments on a Reactionary Philosophy.* M., 1947.

——. *Polnoe sobranie sochinenii.* 5th ed. 55 vols. M., 1958–65.

——. *Sochineniia.* 4th ed. 45 vols. M., 1941–67.

Lenoir, Timothy. *The Strategy of Life: Teleology and Mechanics in Nineteenth-Century German Biology.* Dovdrecht, 1982.

Lents, A. K. 'Ob osnovakh fiziologicheskoi teorii chelovecheskogo povedeniia', *Priroda,* 1922, No. 6–7.

——. *Vysshaia reflektornaia deiatel'nost' pri progressivnom paraliche: eksperimental'no-klinicheskoe issledovanie po metody uslovnykh refleksov.* Minsk, 1928.

Leont'ev, A. N. *Ocherk razvitiia psikhiki.* M., 1947.

——. 'O tvorcheskom puti L. S. Vygotskogo', in Vygotsky, *Sobranie,* I.

——. *Problemy razvitiia psikhiki.* 1st to 4th eds. M. 1959–81.

Leporskii, N. I. 'Uchenie ob uslovnykh refleksakh', *Uchenye zapiski imp. Iur'evskogo universiteta,* 1913, No. 2.

Letopis' zhizni i deiatel'nosti Akademika I. P. Pavlova, vol. I, *1849–1917.* L., 1969.

Levin, F. *Isaak Babel.* M., 1972.

Levine, Norman. *The Tragic Deception: Marx Contra Engels.* Oxford, 1975.

Levitin, K. *One is Not Born a Personality: Profiles of Soviet Education Psychologists.* M., 1982.

Lewes, George Henry. *The Physiology of Common Life.* 2 vols. Edinburgh, 1959–60.

Lichtheim, George. *Marxism: An Historical and Critical Study.* N.Y., 1961.

Litz, A. Walton. *Introspective Voyager.* N.Y., 1972.

Loeb, Jacques. *Comparative Physiology of the Brain and Comparative Psychology.* London, 1900.

——. *The Mechanistic Conception of Life.* Cambridge, Mass., 1964.

——. 'Znachenie tropizmov dlia psikhologii', *Novye idei v filosofii,* sb. 8 (St Petersburg, 1913).

——. 'Zur Theorie der physiologischen Licht- und Schwerkraftswirkungen', *Pflüger's Archiv,* 66 (1897), pp. 439–66.

Lukin, Iu. B. *A. S. Makarenko: kritiko-biograficheskii ocherk.* M., 1954.

Lunacharsky, A. V. 'Iskusstvo i psikhologiia', in *Psikhonevrologicheskie nauki v SSSR.*

Luria, A. R. 'Die moderne russische Psychologie und die Psychoanalise', *Internationale Zeitschrift für Psychoanalyse,* 12 (1926), pp. 40–53.

——. 'Krizis burzhuaznoi psikhologii', *Psikhologiia,* 1932, No. 1–2.

——. *The Making of Mind.* Cambridge, Mass., 1979.

——. *The Man with a Shattered World: The History of a Brain Wound.* N.Y., 1976.

——. *The Nature of Human Conflicts.* N.Y., 1932.

——. *Ob istoricheskom razvitii poznavatel'nykh protsessov: eksperimental'no-psikhologi- cheskoe issledovanie.* M., 1974.

——. 'Professor L.S. Vygotskii, 1896–1934', *SNPsPs*, 1935, No. 1, pp. 165–9.

——. 'Psikhoanaliz', *BSE*, 1st ed., XLVII (1940).

——. 'Psikhoanaliz, kak sistema monisticheskoi psikhologii', in *Psikhologiia i mark- sizm*, ed. K. Kornilov. L., 1925.

——. *Psikhoanaliz v svete osnovnykh tendentsii sovremennoi psikhologii*, Kazan', 1923.

——. 'Put' sovetskoi psikhologii za 15 let', *Sovetskaia psikhonevrologiia*, 1933, No. 1.

——. *Travmaticheskaia afaziia.* English translation: The Hague, 1970.

——. 'Voprosy slukha i rechi v svete ucheniia I. P. Pavlova o dvukh signal'nykh sistemakh', *Vestnik oto-rino-laringolii*, 1951, No. 4.

——. *The Working Brain: An Introduction to Neuropsychology.* N.Y., 1973.

Maguire, R.A. *Red Virgin Soil: Soviet Literature in the 1920's.* Princeton, 1968.

Maiakovskii, Vladimir. *The Bedbug and Selected Poetry*, ed. and intro. Patricia Blake. N.Y., 1960.

Maiorov, F. P. *Istoriia ucheniia ob uslovnykh refleksakh. Opyt raboty Pavlovskoi shkoly po izucheniiu vysshego otdela golovnogo mozga.* 1st ed. M., 1948; 2nd ed. M., 1954.

——. 'O mirovozzrenii I. P. Pavlova', *VAN*, 1936, No.3.

——. 'Pavlov, I. P.', *BME*, 1st ed., XXIII (1932).

——. 'Uchenie akademika I. P. Pavlova ob uslovnykh refleksakh', *Vrachebnaia gazeta*, 1930, No. 1.

Makarenko, A.S. *The Road to Life.* 3 vols. M., 1951. Translation of his *Pedagogical Poem* (1933–5) by Ivy and Tatiana Litvinov.

——. *Sochineniia.* 7 vols. M., 1957–8.

Maksimov, A. 'Ivan Petrovich Pavlov', *PZM*, 1936, No. 2–3.

Malis, G. Iu. *Puti Psikhologii.* L., 1929.

Malyshev, A. 'Za marksistsko-leninskuiu teoriiu i praktiku sovetskoi statistiki', *Problemy ekonomiki*, 1938, No. 1.

Mandelbaum, Maurice. *The Problem of Historical Knowledge.* N.Y., 1938.

Mandelstam, Nadezhda. *Hope Abandoned.* N.Y., 1974.

——. *Hope Against Hope: A Memoir.* N.Y., 1980.

Mandelstam, Osip. *The Complete Critical Prose and Letters*, ed. Jane Gray Harris, trans. Harris and Constance Link. Ann Arbor, 1979.

——. *Selected Poems*, trans. Clarence Brown and W. S. Merwin. London, 1973.

——. *Sobranie sochinenii.* 1st ed. 3 vols. Washington, D. C., 1964–9; 2nd ed. 4 vols. Washington, D. C., 1967–84.

Manier, Edward. 'Cognitive and cellular accounts of associative learning', unpub- lished paper at October 1986 meeting of History of Science Society and Philoso- phy of Science Association.

——. 'Problems in the development of cognitive neuroscience', in *PSA 1986* (published by the Philosophy of Science Association), pp. 183–97.

Mao Tse-tung. *Selected Works.* 5 vols. London and N.Y., 1954–n.d.

Marie, Jean-Jacques. *Staline.* Paris, 1967.

Martin, Janis Allan. 'A Comparison of the Developmental Stages Proposed by L. S. Vygotsky and J. Piaget', Ph.D. dissertation, University of Alberta, 1973.

Marx, Karl. *Capital*, vol.I. N.Y., 1967.
——. *Der 18te Brumaire des Louis Napoleon*. Allgau, 1965.
——. *Early Writings*, trans. and ed. by T. B. Bottomore. N.Y., 1963.
——. *Grundrisse*, trans. Martin Nicolaus. N.Y., 1973.
——. *Ökonomisch-philosophische Manuskripte*. Leipzig, 1968.
——. *Precapitalist Economic Formations*, ed. E. Hobsbawm. London, 1964.
Marx, Karl, and Engels, Friedrich. *Briefwechsel*. Berlin, 1950.
——. *Werke*. 39 vols. Berlin, 1960—8.
Masaryk, Thomas. *The Spirit of Russia*. 3 vols. London, 1961—7.
Massucco Costa, Angiola. *Psychologie soviétique*. Paris, 1977.
Mathewson, Rufus W. *The Positive Hero in Russian Literature*. N.Y., 1958.
Mayer, Gustav. *Friedrich Engels*. N.Y., 1936.
Mayer, Jean. *Diderot, homme de science*. Paris, 1959.
Mayr, Otto. *The Origins of Feedback Control*. Cambridge, Mass., 1970.
McLeish, J. *Soviet Psychology: History, Theory, Content*. London, 1975.
McLellan, David. *Karl Marx: His Life and Thought*. N.Y., 1973.
——. *Marx's Grundrisse*. London, 1971.
——. *The Thought of Karl Marx*. London, 1971.
Mechnikov, I. I. *Stranitsy vospominanii: sbornik avtobiografícheskikh statei*. M., 1946.
——. 'Vospominaniia o Sechenove', *VE*, 1915, No. 5.
Mechnikova, Ol'ga. *Zhizn' Il'i Il'icha Mechnikova*. M., 1926.
Medvedev, Roy A. *Let History Judge: The Origins and Consequences of Stalinism*. N.Y., 1971. And Russian original: *K sudu istorii: genezis i posledstviia stalinizma*. N.Y., 1974; 2nd ed. forthcoming.
Medvedev, Zhores. *The Medvedev Papers*. L., 1971.
——. *Soviet Science*. N.Y., 1978.
Medvedev, Z. A. and Medvedev, R. A. *A Question of Madness*. N.Y., 1971.
Megrelidze, K.R. *Osnovnye problemy sotsiologii myshleniia*. 2nd ed., Tbilisi, 1973.
——. 'Ot zhivotnogo soznaniia k chelovecheskomu', *Iazyk i myshlenie*, 5 (1935), pp. 5—62.
Merkulov, V. L. 'O vliianii F. M. Dostoevskogo na tvorcheskie iskaniia A. A. Ukhtomskogo', *VF*, 1971, No. 11.
——. *Aleksei Alekseevich Ukhtomskii. Ocherk zhizni i nauchnoi deiatel'nosti, 1875—1942*. M., 1960.
Merlan, P. 'Brentano and Freud', *Journal of the History of Ideas*, 1945, No. 6, and 1949, No. 10.
Merton, Robert K. *Social Theory and Social Structure*. N.Y., 1957.
Merz, John T. *History of European Thought in the 19th Century*. 4 vols. London, 1903—14.
Metts, Alexander. 'Schillers physiologische Schriften in ihrer Beziehung zur heutigen Hirnphysiologie', *Aufbau*, October 1955.
Miasishchev, V. N. 'Refleksologiia i smezhnye distsipliny', *Refleksiologiia ili psikhologiia*. L., 1929.
——. and Khvalitskii, T. Ia., eds. *V. M. Bekhterev i sovremennye problemy stroeniia i funktsii mozga v norme i patologii*. L., 1959.
Miller, George A. *Psychology: The Science of Mental Life*. Harmondsworth, 1962.
Miller, Martin. 'Freudian theory under Bolshevik rule: the theoretical controversy during the 1920s', *Slavic Review*, Winter 1985.

Minkovskii, M. A. 'Uchenie I. P. Pavlova ob uslovnykh refleksov v sviazi s istoriei razvitiia i lokalizatsiei funktsii v tsentral'noi nervnoi sisteme', *Sbornik* . . . *75-letiiu Pavlova*, ed. V. L. Omelianskii and L. A. Orbeli. L., 1924.

———. 'Zum gegenwartigen Stand der Lehre im den Reflexen', *Schweizer Archiv für Neurologie und Psychiatrie*, 15 (1924), 16 (1925).

Minkowski, M. A. 'Iwan Petrowitsch Pawlow', in K. Kolle, ed., *Grosse Nervenärzte*, I. Stuttgart, 1956.

Mirsky, D. S. *A History of Russian Literature*. N.Y., 1949.

Mitin, M. B. 'Pamiati velikogo fiziologa-materialista', *PZM*, 1936, No. 2–3.

Mochul'skii, Konstantin. *Dostoevsky: His Life and Work*. Princeton, 1967.

———. *Valerii Briusov*. Paris, 1962.

Mogendovich, M. R. 'Problema refleksa v psikhologii', *Sovetskaia psikhonevrologiia*, 1933, Nos. 4, 5.

Molozhavyi, S. S. 'Printsipal'nye voprosy pedologii', *Psikhonevrologicheskie nauki v SSSR* . . . . M., 1930.

Morozov, G. V., Lunts, D. R., and Felinskaia, N. I. *Osnovnye etapy razvitiia otechestvennoi sudebnoi psikhiatrii*. M., 1976.

Morson, Gary Saul, ed. *Literature and History: Theoretical Problems and Russian Case Studies*. Stanford, 1986.

Mozhaiskii, V. M. 'Vladimir Mikhailovich Bekhterev (ocherk zhizni i deiatel'nosti)', *Sbornik* . . . *V. M. Bekhterevu*. L., 1926.

Müller, O. W. *Intelligenciia: Untersuchungen zur Geschichte eines politischen Schlagwortes*. Frankfurt, 1971.

Mumford, Lewis. 'An appraisal of Lewis Mumford's "Technics and Civilization" (1934)', *Daedalus*, Summer 1959.

Musil, Robert. *The Man Without Qualities*. 3 vols. London, 1954.

Myers, Gerald E. *William James: His Life and Thought*. New Haven, 1986.

Nabokov, Vladimir. *The Gift*. N.Y., 1963.

———, trans. and ed. *Pushkin, Lermontov, Tyutchev, Poems*, London, 1947.

Natadze, R. G. 'Eksperimental'nye osnovy teorii ustanovki D. N. Uznadze', in *Psikhologicheskaia nauka v SSSR*, II. M., 1960.

Nathan, Peter. *The Nervous System*. Philadelphia, 1969.

Nauchnoe nasledstvo. 3 vols. M., 1948–56. Publication of Institut istorii estestvoznaniia i tekhniki.

Nauchnoe tvorchestvo L.S. Vygotskogo i sovremennaia psikhologiia. M., 1981.

Nauchno-issledovatel'skaia deiatel'nost' Instituta [Bekhtereva] *za 50 let: kratkii ocherk i bibliografiia*. L., 1958.

Nauka i nauchnye rabotniki SSSR. 5 vols. M., 1925 and 1930 (for M.); 1926 (for institutions of Leningrad); 1928 (for all parts of USSR but M. and L.); 1930 (for M.); 1934 (for L.).

Nechaev, A. P. 'Pervyi kongress eksperimental'noi psikhologii', *VPsKAG*, 1904, No. 6.

———. *Sovremennaia eksperimental'naia psikhologiia v ee otnoshenii k voprosam shkol'nogo obucheniia*. St Petersburg, 1901.

Neurath, Otto, ed.-in-chief. *International Encyclopedia of Unified Science*. Chicago, 1955.

Nevskii, V. I. 'Khoroshie raboty estestvennikov i nekhoroshie vyvody iz nikh', *Voinstvuiushchii materialist*, 3 (1925).

_____. 'Politicheskii goroskop uchenogo akademika', *PZM*, 1922, No. 3.

Nikitin, N. N. 'Estestvennaia nauka o cheloveke i sotsializm', *PZM*, 1933, No. 6.

Nikolai Iakovlevich Grot v ocherkakh, vospominaniiakh i pis'makh tovarishchei i uchenikov, druzei i pochitatelei. St Petersburg, 1911.

Novikov, A. I. *Nigilizm i nigilisty: opyt kriticheskoi kharakteristiki.* L., 1972.

Novye idei v biologii, ed. V. A. Vagner. 7 *sborniki.* St Petersburg, 1913–14.

Novye idei v filosofii, ed. N. O. Losskii and E. P. Radlov. 17 *sborniki.* St Petersburg, 1912–14.

O'Brien, Patrick. *The Disordered Mind: What We Know About Schizophrenia.* Englewood Cliffs, N.J., 1978.

Obruchev, V. A. 'Iz perezhitogo', *VE*, May and June, 1907.

_____. 'Posle ssylki', *VE*, Oct., 1908, pp. 504–43.

Obshchestvennye nauki SSSR, 1917–1927. M., 1928.

O'Donnell, John. *The Origins of Behaviorism: American Psychology, 1870–1920.* N.Y., 1985.

Olesha, Iu. K. *Envy.* Garden City, 1967.

_____. *Izbrannoe.* M., 1974.

_____. *Ni dnia bez strochki.* M., 1965.

_____. *No Day Without a Line.* Intro. and trans. Judson Rosengrant, Ann Arbor, 1979.

Olmsted, J. M. D. and E. H. *Claude Bernard.* N.Y., 1952.

Omel'chenko, A. 'Eksperimental'naia sotsiologiia', *Zapiski nauchnogo obshchestva marksistov*, 1923, No.5(1).

Omelianskii, V. L. *I. I. Mechnikov.* Petrograd, 1917.

_____. 'Razvitie estestvoznaniia v Rossii v posledniuiu chetvert' XIX veka', *Istoriia Rossii v XIX veke,* 9 (1911).

O'Neil, W. M. *The Beginnings of Modern Psychology.* Harmondsworth, 1968.

Orbeli, L. A. *Lektsii po fiziologii nervnoi sistemy.* L., 1934.

_____. 'O perspektivakh razvitiia nauchnogo nasledstviia I. P. Pavlova', in *idem*, ed., *Sbornik trudov* . . . (1938).

_____, ed. *Ob'edinennaia sessiia posviashchennaia 10-tiletiiu so dnia smerti I. P. Pavlova. Trudy sessii.* M., 1948.

_____. 'Pamiati I. P. Pavlova', *VAN.* 1936, No. 3.

_____, ed. *Sbornik trudov pamiati Akademika I. P. Pavlova.* L., 1938.

_____. 'Tvorcheskaia deiatel'nost' I. P. Pavlova', *Priroda*, 1936, No. 1.

_____. *Uslovnye refleksy s glaza u sobaki.* St Petersburg, 1908.

_____. *Vospominaniia.* L., 1966.

Osipov, V. P. 'Fizologiia i refleksologiia', in *Refleksologiia ili psikhologiia.* L., 1929.

_____. 'Granitsy shizofrenii i ikh legkomyslennoe raspoznavanie', *NPsPs*, 1935, No.7.

_____. 'O raspoznavanii skhizofrenii', in Vtoroi vsesoiuznyi s'ezd psikhiatrov i nevropatologov, 25–29 dek. 1936 g., *Trudy*, I. M., 1937.

Osnovnye techeniia sovremennoi psikhologii, ed. B. A. Fingert and M. L. Shirvindt. M., 1930.

Ostroumov, M. A. 'O fiziologicheskom metode v psikhologii', in *Vera i razum*, II, pt. 2. 1888.

Ovsianiko-Kulikovskii, D.N. 'Vozrozhdenie pozitivizma', *VE*, March 1914.

Ovsiannikov, F. V. *Izbrannye proizvedeniia.* M., 1955.

Ozhegov, S. I. *Slovar' russkogo iazyka*. M., 1968.

Pankratov, M. A. 'Uchenie I. M. Sechenova o tormozhenii', *Izvestiia nauchnogo instituta im. P. F. Lesgafta*, 22 (1940).

Papmehl, K. A. *Freedom of Expression in Eighteenth Century Russia*. The Hague, 1971.

Pauly, Philip. *Controlling Life: Jacques Loeb and the Engineering Ideal in Biology*. N.Y., 1987.

Pavlov, I. P. *Conditioned Reflexes: An Investigation of the Physiological Activity of the Cerebral Cortex*, trans. and ed. G. V. Anrep. London, 1927.

——. *Lectures on Conditioned Reflexes*. 2 vols., trans. and ed. W. H. Gantt. N.Y., 1928—41.

——. 'Nauchnyi institut v pamiat' 27-go fevralia 1917 g.', in *Rechi i privetstviia* . . . . Petrograd, 1917.

——. *Neopublikovannye i maloizvestnye materialy I. P. Pavlova*. L., 1975.

——. 'Pamiati Aleksandra Filippovicha Samoilova', *Kazanskii meditsinskii zhurnal*, 1931, No. 4—5.

——. 'Pis'ma Pavlova k neveste', *Moskva*, 1959, No. 10.

——. *Polnoe sobranie sochinenii*. 2nd ed. 6 vols. in 8 parts. M., 1951.

——. *Polnoe sobranie trudov*. 5 vols., ed. L. A. Orbeli. M., 1940—9.

——. 'The reply of a physiologist to psychologists', *Psychological Review*, March 1932.

——. *The Work of the Digestive Glands*. London, 1902.

Pavlova, S. V. 'Iz vospominanii', *Novyi mir*, 1946, No. 3.

Pavlovskie klinicheskie sredy: stenogrammy zasedanii v Nervnoi i Psikhiatricheskoi klinikakh. 3 vols. M., 1954—7.

Pavlovskie sredy: protokoly i stenogrammy fiziologicheskikh besed. 3 vols. M., 1949.

Payne, T. R. *S. L. Rubinstein and the Philosophical Foundations of Soviet Psychology*. Dordrecht, 1968.

Peel, J. D. Y., ed. *Herbert Spencer on Social Evolution*. Chicago, 1972.

——. *Herbert Spencer: The Evolution of a Sociologist*. N.Y., 1971.

Penfield, Wilder. *The Second Career*. Boston, 1963.

Perepiska I. P. Pavlova, ed. E. M. Kreps. L., 1970.

Periodicheskaia pechat' SSSR, 1917—1949: Bibliograficheskii ukazatel'. 10 vols. M., 1955—63.

Pervyi vsesoiuznyi s'ezd sovetskikh pisatelei. Stenograficheskii otchet. M., 1934.

Petrakov, B. D. *Psikhicheskaia zabolevaemost' v nekotorykh stranakh v XX veke*. M., 1972.

Petrovskii, A. V. *Istoriia sovetskoi psikhologii*. M., 1967.

Petrushevskii, S. A., et al. *Uchenie I. P. Pavlova i filosofskie voprosy psikhologii*. M., 1952.

Petrushevskii, S. A. 'Vointsvuiushchii materializm I. P. Pavlova', *Bol'shevik*, 1950, No. 15.

Philosophy, Politics, and Society. 3rd series. Oxford, 1967.

Piaget, Jean. 'Comments', insert in Vygotsky, *Thought and Language*. Cambridge, Mass., 1962.

——. *Rech' i myshlenie rebenka*. M., 1932.

Pinkus, Benjamin. *The Soviet Government and the Jews. 1948—1967: A Documented Study*. Cambridge, 1984.

Plekhanov, G. V. *Izbrannye filosofskie proizvedeniia*. 5 vols. M., 1956—8.

Plotnikov, P. I. 'Ochistit' sovetskuiu psikhologiiu ot bezrodnogo kosmopolitaniz- ma', *Sovetskaia pedagogika*, 1949, No. 4.

Plunkett, R. J., and Gordon, J. E. *Epidemiology and Mental Illness*. N.Y., 1960.

Pobedonostsev [K. P.] *i ego korrespondenty: pis'ma i zapiski s predisloviem M. N. Pokrovskogo*. 2 vols. M., 1923.

Popel'skii, L. B. *Istoricheskii ocherk kafedry fiziologii v Voenno-meditsinskoi akademii za 100 let*. St Petersburg, 1899.

Popovskii, A. D. *L. A. Orbeli*. M., 1961.

Popper, Karl. *The Open Society and Its Enemies*. London, 1945.

Portugalov, Iu. V, ed. *Detskaia psikhologiia i antropologiia*. Samara, 1925.

Poster, Mark. *Existential Marxism in Postwar France*. Princeton, 1975.

Prangishvili, A. S., et al. *Bessoznatel'noe: priroda, funktsii, metody, issledovaniia*. 2 vols. Tbilisi, 1978.

Prangishvili, A. S. 'Obshchepsikhologicheskaia teoriia ustanovki', in *Psikholo- gicheskaia nauka v SSSR*, II. M., 1960.

Pribram, K.H., ed. *Brain and Behaviour*. 4 vols. Harmondsworth, 1969.

Problemy sovremennoi psikhologii. M., 1926 and 1928. Vols. II and III of *Uchenye zapiski Instituta Psikhologii*.

Propper, N. I. See Grashchenokov.

Protokoly soveshchaniia rasshirennoi redaktsii Proletariia iiun' 1909 g. M., 1934.

Protokoly zasedanii konferentsii Imperatorskoi Voenno-meditsinskoi Akademii. St Peters- burg, 1872 and 1906—7.

Protopopov, V. P. *Psikhologiia, refleksologiia, uchenie o povedenii*. Khar'kov, 1929.

———. *Vvedenie v izuchenie refleksologii*. Khar'kov, 1924.

Prozorov, L. A. 'Obzor polozheniia dela psikhiatricheskoi pomoshchi v RSFSR', *ZhNiPs*, 1930, Nos. 3, 4.

Psikhologicheskaia nauka v SSSR. 2 vols. M., 1959—60. Published by APN, Institut Psikhologii.

Psikhologicheskii institut imeni L. T. Shchukinoi pri Imperatorskom Moskovskom Univer- sitete (Istoriia, opisanie ustroistva i organizatsiia zaniatii). M., 1914.

Psikhologicheskii institut. *Rechi i privetstviia na otkritii Psikhologicheskogo instituta*. M., 1914.

Psikhologiia i marksizm, ed. K. N. Kornilov. L., 1925.

Psikhonevrologicheskie nauki v SSSR (Materialy I Vsesoiuznogo s'ezda po izucheniiu povedeniia cheloveka). M., 1930.

Pypina, V. A. 'Iz vospominanii o Sechenovykh', in Bogdanovich, *Liubov'* . . . . L., 1929.

———. *Liubov' v zhizni Chernyshevskogo*. Petrograd, 1923.

Rainov, T. I. 'Otchuzhenie deistviia', *VKA*, 1925—6, Nos. 13, 14, 15.

Rakhman, D. *Dzhon Lokk: ego uchenie o poznanii, prave i vospominanii: sub'ektivnaia i ob'ektivnaia psikhologiia*. M., 1924.

Rakhmanov, V. V. *Dushevnoe zdorov'e: obshchedostupnye besedy o dushevnoi zhizni cheloveka, o dushevnykh zabolevaniiakh, o tom, kak predupredit' eto neschast'e i kak ukhazhivat' za bol'nymi*. M., 1908.

Razmyslov, P. I. 'O "kul'turno-istoricheskoi teorii psikhologii" Vygotskogo i Luriia', *Kniga i proletarskaia revoliutsiia*, 1934, No. 4.

——. 'Ob eklekticheskikh i psevdonauchnykh vzgliadakh prof. Zalkinda', *Nachal'-naia shkola*, 1936, No. 10.

——. 'Ob oshibkakh t. Borovskogo', *Kniga i proletarskaia revoliutsiia*, 1934, No. 3.

——. 'Protiv mekhanitsizma v psikhologii', *Kniga i proletarskaia revoliutsiia*. 1933, No. 10.

Razran, G. *Mind in Evolution: An East-West Synthesis of Learned Behavior and Cognition*. Boston, 1971.

Rechi i privetstviia, proiznessennye na trekh publichnykh sobraniiakh, sostoiavshikhsia v 1917 g. 9 i 16 aprelia v Petrograde i 11 maia v Moskve. Petrograd, 1917.

Refleksologiia ili psikhologiia. L., 1929.

Refleksologiia i smezhnye napravleniia. L., 1930.

Reich, Walter. 'Kazanetz, schizophrenia, and soviet psychiatry', *Archives of General Psychiatry*, 36 (1979).

——. 'The spectrum concept of schizophrenia: problems for diagnostic practice', *Archives of General Psychiatry*, 32 (1975).

——. 'The world of Soviet psychiatry', *N. Y. Times Magazine*, 30 January 1983.

Reich, Wilhelm. 'Psikhoanaliz kak estestvenno-nauchnaia distsiplinna', *EIM*, 1929, No. 4. Also in *VKA*, 1929, No. 35–6, with discussion.

Reiser, S. A. 'Legenda o prototipakh "Chto delat" Chernyshevskogo', *Trudy Leningradskogo gosudartsvennogo bibliotechnogo instituta imeni Krupskoi*, 2 (1957).

Reisner (or Reusner), M. A. 'Sotsial'naia psikhologiia', in Granat, *ES*, XLI.

——. 'Sotsial'naia psikhologiia i marksizm', in *Psikhologiia i marksizm*, ed. K. Kornilov. M., 1925.

Repin, I. E. *Pis'ma k E. P. Tarkhanovoi-Antokol'skoi i I. R. Tarkhanovu*. M., 1937.

Rice, James. 'Russian stereotypes in the Freud-Jung correspondence', *Slavic Review*, Spring 1982.

Rice, Martin. *Valery Briusov and the Rise of Russian Symbolism*. Ann Arbor, 1975.

Richards, I. A. *Poetries and Sciences*. N.Y., 1970.

——. *Science and Poetry*. N.Y., 1926.

Richards, Robert. *Darwin and the Emergence of Evolutionary Theories of Mind and Behavior*. Chicago, 1987.

Riese, Walter. *A History of Neurology*. N.Y., 1959.

——. 'Hughlings Jackson's doctrine of consciousness', *Journal of Nervous and Mental Disease*, 120 (1954).

Roback, A. A. *A History of American Psychology*. N.Y., 1964.

Robinson, Joan. *An Essay on Marxian Economics*. London, 1966.

Rokhlin, L. L. 'Psikhogigienicheskaia rabota sredi partaktiva', *ZhNiPs*, 1930, No. 3.

——. *Trud, byt i zdorov'e partiinogo aktiva*. Dvou, 1931.

Rollin, Henry. *L'Apocalypse de notre temps*. Paris, 1939.

Rosenberg, Charles E. *The Trial of the Assassin Guiteau: Psychiatry and Law in the Gilded Age*. Chicago, 1968.

Rosenfield, L. D. *From Beast-Machine to Man-Machine*. N.Y., 1968.

Rossolimo, G. I. *Neurologie, neuropathologie, psychologie, psychiatrie. Mémoires publiées à l'occasion du jubilé du Prof. G. Rossolimo, 1884–1924*. M., 1925.

_____. *Psikhologicheskie profili. Kolichestvennoe issledovanie psikhicheskikh protsessov v normal'nom i patologicheskom sostoianiiakh*. M., 1910.

Rothschuh, K. E., ed. *Von Boerhaave bis Berger*. Stuttgart, 1964.

Rozenshtein, L. M. 'Psikhogigienicheskoe dvizhenie v SSSR i ego zadachi v sviazi s rekonstruktsiei', *Vrachebnaia gazeta*, 1931, No. 2. Also in *ZhNiPs*, 1931, No. 1.

_____. 'Sotsial'no-profilakticheskoe napravlenie v psikhiatrii', *ZhNiPs*, 1930, No. 4.

Rozentsveig, B. M. 'Osnovy psikhnevrologicheskoi dispanserizatsii v edinom dispansere', *Moskovskii meditsinskii zhurnal*, 1929, No. 11–12.

Rozhanskii, N. A. 'Rabota I. P. Pavlova nad tsentral'noi nervnoi sistemoi', *Izvestiia Severno-Kavkazskogo Gosudarstvennogo Universiteta*, 8 (1926).

Rubinshtein, S. L. *Bytie i soznania*. M., 1957.

_____. *Eine Studie zum Problem der Methode Absoluter Rationalismus*. Marburg, 1914.

_____. 'Nikolai Nikolaevich Lange', *Narodnoe prosveshchenie*, 1922, Nos. 6–10.

_____. *Osnovy obshchei psikhologii*. M., 1940; 2nd ed., 1946.

_____. *Osnovy psikhologii*. M., 1935.

_____. 'Printsip tvorcheskoi samodeiatel'nosti; k filosofskim osnovam sovremennoi pedagogiki', *Uchenye zapiski vysshei shkoly g. Odessy*, II (1922), pp. 148–54.

_____. *Printsipy i puti razvitiia psikhologii*. M., 1959.

_____. *Problemy obshchei psikhologii*. M., 1973.

_____. 'Problemy psikhologii v trudakh Karla Marksa', *Sovetskaia psikhotekhnika*, 1934, No. 1.

_____. *Sovremennoe sostoianie i ocherednye zadachi nauchnoi bibliografii v SSSR*. M., 1930.

Russell, Bertrand. *The Scientific Outlook*. N.Y., 1931. Reprint, 1962.

Russkikh, V. N. and Krylova, E. S. 'O lokalizatsii assotsiatsii', *ZhNiPs*, 1931, No. 2.

Ryle, Gilbert. *The Concept of Mind*. N.Y., 1949.

Sakharov, L. S. 'Obrazovanie poniatii u umstvenno otstalykh detei', *Voprosy defektologii*, 1928, No. 2.

_____. 'O metodakh issledovaniia poniatii', *Psikhologiia*, 1930, No. 1.

Samarin, Iu. F. *Sochineniia*. 12 vols. M., 1877–1911.

Samoilov, A. F. 'Dialektika prirody i estestvoznaniia', *PZM*, 1929, No. 4–5.

_____. 'Obshchaia kharakteristika issledovatel'skogo oblika I. P. Pavlova', *Zhurnal eksperimental'noi biologii*, series B, 1925, No. 1–2.

Sapir, I. D. 'Freidizm i marksizm', *PZM*, 1926, No. 11.

_____. 'K voprosu o marksistskoi metodologii v nauke o povedenii', *Psikhonevrologicheskie nauki v SSSR*. M., 1930.

_____. 'O rasstroistve intellekta pri porazhenii lobnoi doli. K teorii voprosa', *NPsPs*, 1936, No. 9.

_____. *Vysshaia nervnaia deiatel'nost' cheloveka*. M., 1925.

Savich, V. V. 'Ivan Petrovich Pavlov: biograficheskii ocherk', *Sbornik posviashchennyi 75-letiiu Pavlova* . . . . L., 1924.

Sbornik posviashchennyi 75-letiiu Pavlova akademika Ivana Petrovicha, ed. V. L. Omelianskii and L. A. Orbeli. L., 1924.

Sbornik posviashchennyi Vladimiru Mikhailovichu Bekhterevu. K 40-letiiu professorskoi deiatel'nosti (1885–1925). L., 1926.

Schäfer, E. A. S., ed. *Textbook of Physiology*. 2 vols. Edinburgh, 1898–1900.

Scheerer, Eckart. 'Gestalt psychology in the Soviet Union', *Psychological Research*, 41 (1980).

Schiller, Friedrich. *Aesthetic Letters*. New Haven, 1954.

——. *Sämtliche Werke*. Munich, n.d.

Schneider, Kurt. 'Wesen und Erfassung des Schizophrenen', *Zeitschrift für die gesamte Neurologie und Psychiatrie*, 99 (1925), pp. 542–7.

Schrödinger, Erwin. *What is Life? and Mind and Matter*. Cambridge, 1944. Reprint, 1977.

Schröer, Heinz. *Carl Ludwig: Begrunder der messenden Experimentalphysiologie*. Stuttgart, 1967.

——. 'Carl Ludwig', in *Von Boerhaave bis Berger*, ed. K. E. Rothschuh. Stuttgart, 1964.

Schumpeter, Joesph. *Capitalism, Socialism, and Democracy*. N.Y., 1942.

Sechenov, I. M. *Avtobiograficheskie zapiski*. M., 1907. Republished 1945.

——. *Biographical Sketch and Essays*. N.Y., 1973. Photo-reprint, in part, of his *Selected Works*. M., 1935.

——. *Elementy mysli: sbornik izbrannykh statei*. M., 1943.

——. *Études psychologiques*. Paris, 1884.

——. *Fiziologiia nervnykh tsentrov*. St Petersburg, 1891.

——. *Izbrannye filosofskie i psikhologicheskie proizvedeniia*. M., 1947.

——. *Izbrannye proizvedeniia*. 2 vols. M., 1952–6.

——. 'Nauchnaia deiatel'nost' russkikh universitetov po estestvoznaniiu za poslednee 25-letie', *VE*, 1883, No. 11.

——. *Selected Works*. M., 1935.

——. *Sobranie sochinenii*. 2 vols. M., 1907–8.

Segal, B. M. 'Involuntary hospitalization in the USSR', in *Psychiatry and Psychology in the USSR*, ed. S. A. and E. O. Corson. N.Y., 1976.

Semon, Richard. *Die Mneme als erhaltandes Prinzip im Wechsel des organischen Geschehens*. Leipzig, 1920.

Serzhantov, V. F. *Filosofskie problemy biologii cheloveka*. L., 1974.

Shanin, Teodor, ed. *Late Marx and the Russian Road: Marx and 'the Peripheries of Capitalism'*. N.Y., 1983.

Shaw, G. B. *Everybody's Political What's What*. London, 1944.

Shelgunov, N. V. *Vospominaniia*. M., 1923.

Shemiakin, F. N. and Gershenovich, L. 'Kak Trotskii i Kautskii revizuiut marksizm v voprosakh psikhologii', *Psikhologiia*, 1932, No. 1.

——. 'Protiv trotskistskikh i kautskianskikh pozitsii v voprosakh psikhologii', *ZMLE*, 1932, No. 3–4.

Sherrington, Charles S. *The Brain and Its Mechanisms*. Cambridge, 1933.

——. *The Integrative Action of the Nervous System*. New Haven, 1906. Republished 1961.

——. *Integrativnaia deiatel'nost' nervnoi sistemy*. L., 1969.

——. *Man on His Nature*. N.Y., 1941.

——. 'Spinal reflexes', in *Textbook of Physiology*, ed. E. A. S. Schäfer, II. Edinburgh, 1900.

Shershow, John C., ed. *Schizophrenia: Science and Practice*. Cambridge, Mass., 1978.

Shilinis, Iu. A. *L. A. Orbeli.* M., 1967.

Shils, Edward. 'Intellectuals', *International Encyclopedia of the Social Sciences*, VII, 1968, pp. 398–415.

Shirvindt, M. L. 'Psikhoanaliz', *Osnovnye techeniia sovremennoi psikhologii.* M., 1930.

Shmidt, O. Iu., et al. *Zadachi marksistov v oblasti estestvoznaniia.* M., 1929.

Shnirman, A. L. 'Refleksologiia i uchenie ob uslovnykh refleksakh', in *Refleksologiia i smezhnye napravleniia.* L., 1929.

Sholokhov, Mikhail. *Virgin Soil Upturned.* N.Y., 1959.

Shpil'rein, I. N. 'Nauchnaia organizatsiia truda', *Obshchestvennye nauki SSSR, 1917–1927.* 1928.

_____. 'Psikhotekhnika v rekonstruktivnyi period', *VKA*, 1930, No. 39.

Shtern, Lina Solomonovna. M., 1960. Materialy k biobibliografii uchenykh SSSR.

Siegelbaum, Lewis. 'Okhrana truda: Industrial hygiene, psychotechnics, and industrialization in the USSR', unpublished paper, University of Toronto conference on the history of Russian and Soviet public health, 7–10 May 1986.

_____. *Stakhanovism and the Politics of Productivity in the USSR, 1935–1941.* Cambridge, 1988.

Simon, W. M. *European Positivism in the 19th Century.* Ithaca, 1963.

Siniavsky, Andrei. *Unguarded Thoughts.* L., 1972.

Skvorecky, Josef. *The Engineer of Human Souls.* N.Y., 1985.

Slonim, A. D. *Sreda i povedenie. Formirovanie adaptivnogo povedeniia.* L., 1976.

Smirnov, A. A. *Razvitie i sovremennoe sostoianie psikhologicheskoi nauki v SSSR.* M., 1975.

Smirnov, V. M. 'Zasedanie psikhiatricheskoi sektsii Leningradskogo nauchnogo obshchestva nevropatologov i psikhiatrov, posviashchennoe kontseptsii edinogo psikhoza (14/V 1974g.)', *ZhNiPs*, 1975, No. 8.

Smith, C. U. M. 'Evolution and mind', *Journal of the History of Biology*, 1982, pp. 55–88, 241–62.

Smith, Roger. 'The background of physiological psychology in natural philosophy', *History of Science*, vol. II (1973), pp. 75–123.

Snezhnevskii, A. V. 'Mesto kliniki v issledovanii prirody shizofrenii', *ZhNiPs*, 1975, No. 9.

_____. 'Oblastnaia psikhiatricheskaia bol'nitsa v g. Kostrome', *SNPsPs*, 1933, No. 10.

_____. 'Ob osobennostiakh techneiia shizofrenii', *ZhNiPs*, 1960, No. 9.

_____. *Obshchaia psikhopatologiia. Kurs lektsii.* Valdai, 1970.

_____. 'O nozologicheskoi spetsifichnosti psikhopatologicheskikh sindromov', *ZhNiPs*, 1960, No. 1.

'O nozologii psikhicheskikh rasstroistv', *ZhNiPs*, 1975, No. 1.

_____. 'O pozdnikh simptomaticheskikh psikhozakh', *Trudy nauchno-issledovatel'skogo instituta psikhiatrii im. Gannushkina*, V. M., 1940.

_____. 'Prognoz issledovaniia shizofrenii', *Vestnik Akademii Meditsinskikh Nauk*, 1970, No. 6.

Sokal, M.M. 'The Gestalt psychologists in behaviorist America', *AHR*, December 1984.

_____. ed. *Psychological Testing and American Society, 1890–1930.* New Brunswick, 1987.

Sokolov, M. V. 'Kritika metoda testov na russkikh s'ezdakh po eksperimental'noi
    pedagogike, 1910–1916', *VPs*, 1956, No. 6.
Solomon, Susan. 'Rural scholars and the Cultural Revolution', in *Cultural Revolu-
    tion in Russia, 1928–1931*, ed. S. Fitzpatrick Bloomington, 1984.
——. *The Soviet Agrarian Debate: A Controversy in Social Science, 1923–1929*.
    Boulder, 1977.
Solov'ev, V. S. 'O filosofskikh trudakh P. D. Iurkevicha', *ZhMNP*, December
    1874.
——. *Sobranie sochinenii*. 9 vols. St Petersburg, 1901–7.
——. *Stikhotvoreniia i shutochnye p'esy*. Munich, 1968.
Solzhenitsyn, Alexander. *The First Circle*. N.Y., 1968.
——. *The Gulag Archipelego, 1918–1956: An Experiment in Literary Investigation*. 3
    vols. N.Y., 1973–8.
——. *One Day in the Life of Ivan Denisovich*. N.Y., 1963.
——. *Sochineniia*. Frankfurt/Main, 1964.
Sovetskaia istoricheskaia entsiklopediia. 16 vols. M., 1961–76.
Sovetskaia meditsina v bor'be za zdorovye nervy: sbornik statei i materialov [Pervoe
    Vsesoiuznoe soveshchanie po psikhiatrii i nevrologii]. Ul'ianovsk, 1926.
Sovremennye problemy shizofrenii: doklady na konferentsii po shizofrenii v iiune 1932 g.
    M., 1933.
Spasovich, V. D. *Sochineniia*. 10 vols. St Petersburg, 1889–1902.
——. *Za mnogo let. 1859–1871*. St Petersburg, 1872.
Speranskii, A. D. *A Basis for the Theory of Medicine*. N.Y., 1944.
——. *Elementy postroeniia teorii meditsiny*. M., 1935.
——, Lavrent'ev, V. I. and Fedorov, L. N. 'Detishche stalinskoi epokhi', *Meditsin-
    skii rabotnik*, 21 December 1939.
Spicker, S. F., ed. *The Philosophy of the Body: Rejection of Cartesian Dualism*.
    Chicago, 1970.
Spulber, N. *Soviet Strategy for Economic Growth*. Bloomington, 1964.
Stalin, I. V. *Sochineniia*. 13 vols. M., 1946–51; and 3 vols. Stanford, 1967.
Stevenson, Lionel. *Darwin Among the Poets*. Chicago, 1932.
Stocking, George. *Victorian Anthropology*. N.Y., 1987.
Strel'chuk, I. V. and Rumshevich. 'Zhizn' i byt dushevnobol'nykh na sele', *ZhNiPs*,
    1930, No. 5.
Struminskii, V. Ia. *Psikhologiia: opyt sistematicheskogo izlozheniia osnovnykh voprosov
    nauchnoi psikhologii s tochki zreniia dialekticheskogo marksizma*. Orenburg, 1923.
Struve, G. E. *Samostoiatel'noe nachalo dushevnykh iavlenii*. M., 1870.
Struve, Nikita. *Ossip Mandelstam*. Paris, 1982.
Subbotnik, S. I. 'Za bol'shevistskoe nastuplenie na teoreticheskom fronte
    psikhonevrologii', *ZhNiPs*, 1931, No. 2.
Sudebnaia psikhiatriia (Rukovodstvo dlia vrachei). M., 1967.
Sukhanov, N. N. *Zapiski o revoliutsii*. 7 vols. Berlin, 1922–3.
Swazey, Judith P. *Chloropromazine in Psychiatry: A Study of Therapeutic Innovation*.
    Cambridge, Mass., 1974.
——. *Reflexes and Motor Integration: Sherrington's Concept of Integrative Action*. Cam-
    bridge, Mass., 1969.
Szasz, Thomas. *Schizophrenia: The Sacred Symbol of Psychiatry*. N.Y., 1976.

Tager, A. S. *Tsarskaia Rossiia i delo Beilisa*. M., 1933.

Tarkhanov, I. R. 'Klod Bernar', *Slovo*, 1878, No. 5.

_____. 'Psikhofiziologicheskie opyty Shillera', in *Biblioteka velikikh pisatelei. Shiller*, I. St Petersburg, 1902.

_____. 'Svobodnaia nauka', *Znanie i zhizn'*, 1905, No. 7.

Teplov, B. M. 'Bor'ba K. N. Kornilova v 1923−1925 gg. za perestroiku psikhologii na osnove marksizma', in *Voprosy psikhologii lichnosti*. M., 1960.

Tertz, Abram. *Fantasticheskii mir Abrama Tertsa*. N.Y., 1966.

_____. *The Trial Begins and On Socialist Realism*. N.Y., 1960.

Thielen, Manfred. *Sowjetische Psychologie und Marxismus: Geschichte und Kritik*. Frankfurt/Main, 1984.

Timiriazev, K. A. *Sochineniia*. 10 vols. M., 1937−40.

Tiutchev, F. I. *Izbrannye stikhotvoreniia*. N.Y., 1952.

_____. *Polnoe sobranie sochinenii*. 2 vols. M., 1933; 1 vol. L. 1957.

_____. *Stikhotvoreniia*. M., 1970.

Tjoa, Hock Guan. *George Henry Lewes: A Victorian Mind*. Cambridge, Mass., 1977.

Todes, David P. 'From radicalism to scientific convention: biological psychology in Russia from Sechenov to Pavlov', unpublished Ph. D. dissertation, University of Pennsylvania, 1981.

Tolstovskii muzei. 2 vols. S. P., 1911−14.

Tolstoy, L. N. *Essays and Letters*. N.Y., 1903.

_____. *Great Short Works*. N.Y., 1967.

_____. *Polnoe sobranie sochinenii*. 90 vols. M., 1928−58.

_____. *Recollections and Essays*. Oxford, 1937.

_____. *Tolstoy's Letters*, ed. and trans. R. F. Christian. 2 vols. N.Y., 1978.

Tovarishcheskaia pamiatka vrachei vypuska 1879 g. byvshei imperatorskoi Mediko-khirurgicheskoi akademii, izdannaia ko dniu XXV-letiia so dnia okonchaniia kursa. St Petersburg, 1904.

Trifonov, Iurii. *Another Life and The House on the Embankment*. N.Y., 1983.

_____. *The Old Man*. N.Y., 1980.

Troitskii, M. M. *Nemetskaia psikhologiia v tekushchem stoletii*. M., 1867.

Trotsky, L. D. 'K pervomu s'ezdu nauchnykh rabotnikov', *Pravda*, November 24, 1924.

_____. *Literature and Revolution*. N.Y., 1957.

_____. *Sochineniia*. 14 vols. M., 1925−7.

_____. *Stalin: An Appraisal of the Man and His Influence*. N.Y., 1941.

Trudy Obshchestva russkikh vrachei v S. Peterburge, 1879−1914.

Trudy pervogo vserossiisskogo s'ezda po pedagogicheskoi psikhologii. St Petersburg, 1906.

Trudy tret'iago s'ezda otechestvennykh psikhiatrov. St Petersburg, 1911.

Trudy tret'iago vsesoiuznogo s'ezda nevropatologov i psikhiatrov. M., 1950.

Trudy vtorogo s'ezda otechestvennykh psikhiatrov. Kiev, 1907.

Trudy vtorogo vserossiiskogo s'ezda po pedagogicheskoi psikhologii v S. Peterburge v 1909 g. (1−5 iiunia). St Petersburg, 1910.

Tsion, I. F. (Cyon, Élie de). *Dieu et science. Essais de psychologie des sciences*. Paris, 1910.

_____. *École médicale pour les femmes à Saint-Pétersbourg.* Paris, 1879.

_____. *Études politiques: la Russie contemporaine.* Paris, 1892.

_____. *Études sociales: nihilisme et anarchie.* Paris, 1892.

_____. *Gesammelte physiologische Arbeiten.* Berlin, 1888.

_____. *La guerre à Dieu et la morale laïque. Reponse à m. Paul Bert.* Paris, 1881.

_____. *Nauchnye besedy.* St Petersburg, 1880.

_____. 'Nigilisty i nigilizm', *Russkii vestnik*, 1886, Nos. 5—6, 7—8.

_____. *Raboty sdelannyia v fiziologicheskoi laboratorii imp. mediko-khirurgicheskoi Akademii za 1873 god. s prilozheniem kriticheskikh statei.* St Petersburg, 1874.

_____. 'Serdtse i mozg', in Voenno-Meditsinskaia Akademiia, *Protokoly zasedanii konferentsii Imp. Meditsin. Khir. Ak. za 1872 g.* St Petersburg, 1873. And separately, *Serdtse i mozg.* St Petersburg, 1873.

Tsitovich, I. S. 'O proiskhozhdenii natural'nogo uslovnogo refleksa', *Trudy Obshchestva russkikh vrachei v SPb*, 1911.

Tsitovich, P. P. *Chto delali v romane 'Chto delat'?.* Odessa, 1879.

_____. *Otvet na 'Pis'ma k uchenym liudiam'.* Odessa, 1878.

Tucker, Robert C. *Stalin as Revolutionary, 1879—1929.* N.Y., 1973.

Tulloch, John. *Chekhov: A Structuralist Study.* London, 1980.

Tumarkin, Nina. *Lenin Lives! The Lenin Cult in Soviet Russia.* Cambridge, Mass., 1983.

Turgenev, Ivan. *The Borzoi Turgenev.* N.Y., 1950.

Tutundzhian, O. K. 'Uchenie Sechenova vo Frantsii', *VPs*, 1963, No. 5.

Uchenye zapiski Instituta Psikhologii. 3 vols. M., 1925—8. Usually cited under titles of the individual vols. : *Psikhologiia i marksizm* (1925) and *Problemy sovremennoi psikhologii*, II and III (1926 and 1928).

Ukazatel' literatury vypushchennoi institutom psikhologii za 50 let (s 1917 po 1967 gg). M., 1967. APN, Institut Psikhologii. Mimeograph.

Ukhtomskii, A. A. 'Dominanta kak faktor povedeniia', *VKA*, 1927, No. 22.

_____. 'Fiziologiia v Sovetskoi Rossii za 15 let', *Priroda*, 1932, No. 11—12.

_____. *Izbrannye trudy.* L., 1978.

_____. *Sobranie sochinenii.* 6 vols. L., 1945—62.

Ukrainskii s'ezd nevropatologov i psikhiatrov, I-yi. *Trudy.* Kharkov, 1935.

Umov, N. A. 'Predislovie', in Sechenov, *Avtobiograficheskie zapiski.* M., 1907.

Ushakov, D. N. *Tolkovyi slovar' russkogo iazyka.* 4 vols. M., 1935—40.

Usov, S. A. *Po povodu dissertatsii G. Struve.* M., 1870.

Utkina, N. F. *Pozitivizm, antropologicheskii materializm i nauka v Rossii (vtoraia polovina XIX veka).* M., 1975.

Vagner, V. A. 'Fiziologiia i biologiia v reshenii psikhologicheskikh problem', *Novye idei v biologii*, sb. 6 (St Petersburg, 1914).

_____. *Psikhologicheskie tipy i kollektivnaia psikhologiia: po dannym biologicheskikh nauk.* L., 1929.

_____. 'Renan i Nitsshe. O zvere v cheloveke', *VFiPs.* 1901, No. 2.

_____. 'Staryi naturalizm i filosofiia mirovoi skorbi', *Zaprosy zhizni*, 1911.

_____. *Vozniknovenie i razvitie psikhicheskikh sposobnostei. vypusk 3: Ot refleksov do instinktov vysshego tipa u chelokveka i ikh znachenie v zhizni poslednego.* L., 1925.

Valenstein, Eliot S. *Great and Desperate Cures: The Rise and Decline of Psychosurgery and Other Radical Treatments for Mental Illness.* N.Y., 1986.

Vartanian, Aram. *Diderot and Descartes: A Study of Scientific Naturalism in the Enlightenment*. Princeton, 1953.

———. *Lamettrie's L'Homme-Machine*. Princeton, 1960.

Verzhbolovich, M. O. 'Obzor glavneishikh napravlenii russkoi psikhologii', *Vera i razum*, 1895, pp. 117—34.

Virchow, Rudolph. *The Freedom of Science in the Modern State*. London, 1878.

Vitmer, A. N. 'Sviatoi chelovek', *Istoricheskii vestnik*, 12 (1915).

Vnukov, V. A. 'Psikhoanaliz', *BME*, 1st ed., XXVII (1933).

———. 'Reshaiushchie zven'ia v okhrane zdorov'ia kadrov', *Revoliutsiia i kul'tura*, 1930, No. 4.

Voloshinov, V. N. *Friedizm: kriticheskii ocherk*. M., 1927.

Voprosy psikhologii lichnosti. Publication of APN, ed. E. I. Ignat'ev. M., 1960.

Voprosy sudebnoi psikhiatrii. M., 1965. Vol. VIII of IV-yi Vsesoiuznyi s'ezd nevro-patologov i psikhiatrov, *Trudy*.

Vsesoiuznaia nauchno-prakticheskaia konferentsiia posviashchennaia 100-letiiu so dnia rozhdeniia S.S. Korsakova i aktual'nym voprosam psikhiatrii. *Trudy*. M., 1955.

Vsesoiuznoe soveshchanie po sudebnoi psikhiatrii, l-oe. *Trudy*. M., 1937.

Vsesoiuznyi Institut Eksperimental'noi Meditsiny. *Materialy k istoriiu VIEM*. M., 1941.

Vsesoiuznyi povedencheskii s'ezd, I-yi. *Stenograficheskii otchet*. Same as *Psikhonevro-logicheskie nauki v SSSR*.

Vsesoiuznyi s'ezd nevropatologov i psikhiatrov, II-oi (25—29 dek. 1936 g.). *Trudy*. M., 1937.

Vsesoiuznyi s'ezd nevropatologov i psikhiatrov, III—ii. *Trudy*. M., 1950.

Vsesoiuznyi s'ezd nevropatologov i psikhiatrov, IV-yi. *Trudy*. M., 1965.

Vucinich, Alexander. *Science in Russian Culture, 1861—1917*. Stanford, 1970.

———. *Social Thought in Tsarist Russia: The Quest for a General Science of Society, 1861—1917*. Chicago, 1976.

Vvedenskii, A. I. *Dekart i okkazionalizm*. Berlin, 1922.

———. 'Nauchnaia deiatel'nost' M.I. Vladislavleva', *ZhMNP*, June, 1890.

———. *Psikhologiia bez vsiakoi metafiziki*. St Petersburg, 1914; 2nd ed., 1917.

Vvedenskii, N. E. *Ivan Mikhailovich Sechenov. Nekrolog*. St Petersburg, 1906.

———. *Pamiati Ivana Mikhailovicha Sechenova*. n.p., n.d.

———. *Polnoe sobranie sochinenii*. 7 vols. L., 1951—63.

Vygotsky, L. S. 'Biogeniticheskii zakon', *BSE*, 1st ed., VI (1927), pp. 275—9.

———. 'Geneticheskie korni myshleniia i rechi', *EIM*, 1929, No. 1.

———. *Izbrannye psikhologicheskie issledovaniia*. M., 1956.

———. 'Metodika refleksologicheskogo i psikhologicheskogo issledovaniia', in *Prob-lemy sovremennoi psikhologii*. M., 1926.

———. *Mind in Society*. Cambridge, Mass., 1978.

———. *Myshlenie i rech'*. M., 1934.

———. 'Problema rechi i myshleniia rebenka v uchenii Zh. Piazhe', in Piaget, *Rech' i myshlenie rebenka*. M., 1932.

———. 'Psikhologicheskaia nauka', *Obshchestvennye nauki SSSR*. M., 1928.

———. *Psikhologiia iskusstva*. M., 1965 and 1968 and 1986 and 1987.

———. *The Psychology of Art*. Cambridge, Mass., 1971.

——. *Razvitie psikhicheskikh funktsii: iz neopublikovannykh trudov.* M., 1960.

——. *Sobranie sochinenii.* 6 vols. M., 1982.

——. 'Sotsialisticheskaia peredelka cheloveka', *VARNITSO*, 1930, No. 9–10.

——. 'Sovremennye techeniia v psikhologii', in his *Razvitie vysshikh psikhicheskikh funktsii.*

——. 'Soznanie kak problema psikhologii povedeniia', in *Psikhologiia i marksizm.* M., 1925.

——. 'Strukturnaia psikhologiia', in *Osnovnye techeniia sovremennoi psikhologii.* M., 1930.

——. *Thought and Language.* Cambridge, Mass., 1962. 2nd ed., 1986.

——. 'Thought in schizophrenia', *Archives of Neurology and Psychiatry*, 1934.

——. *Voobrazhenie i tvorchestvo v detskom vozraste.* M., 1930.

Vygotsky, L. S. and Luria, A. *Etiudy po istorii povedeniia: obez'ian, primitiv, rebenok.* M., 1930.

Vysshaia nervnaia deiatel'nost'. Publication of the Communist Academy's Institut vysshei nervnoi deiatel'nosti. Sb. 1 (1929).

Waggoner, Hyatt. *The Heel of Elohim.* Norman, Okla., 1950.

Watson, John B. *Behaviorism.* N.Y., 1970.

——. 'The place of the conditioned reflex in psychology', *Psychological Review*, 23 (1916).

Watson, J. B. and Rayner, R. 'Conditioned emotional reactions', *Journal of Experimental Psychology*, 1920, No. 3.

Weil, Irwin. *Gorky: His Literary Development and Influence on Soviet Intellectual Life.* N.Y., 1966.

Wertsch, James, ed. *Culture, Communication, and Cognition: Vygotskian Perspectives.* Cambridge, Mass., 1984.

——. *Vygotsky and the Social Formation of Mind.* Cambridge, Mass., 1985.

Wheelwright, Philip. *The Burning Fountain: A Study in the Language of Symbolism.* Bloomington, 1954.

Willett, John. *Art and Politics in the Weimar Period: The New Sobriety, 1917–1933.* N.Y., 1978.

Wilson, Angus. *Émile Zola.* London, 1952.

Wilson, Arthur M. *Diderot.* N. Y., 1972.

Wilson, Edmund. *To the Finland Station.* N.Y., 1940.

Wittfogel, Karl A. 'Some remarks on Mao's handling of concepts and problems of dialectics', *Studies in Soviet Thought*, December 1963.

Woodward, William R. and Ash, Mitchell G., eds. *The Problematic Science: Psychology in Nineteenth-Century Thought.* N.Y., 1982.

Woody, C. D. 'Understanding the cellular basis of memory and learning', *Annual Review of Psychology*, 37 (1986), pp. 433–93.

Wordsworth, William. *Lyrical Ballads.* London, 1963.

World Health Organization. *Report of the International Pilot Study of Schizophrenia.* Geneva, 1973.

——. *Schizophrenia: A Multi-National Study.* Geneva, 1975.

Wortis, Joseph. *Soviet Psychiatry.* Baltimore, 1950.

Wundt, Wilhelm. *Dusha cheloveka i zhivotnykh.* 2 vols. St Petersburg, 1865–6. Translation of Wundt, *Vorlesugen über die Menschen und Tierseele.* Leipzig, 1863.

Wundt Studies: A Centennial Collection, ed. W.G. Bringmann and R.D. Tweney. Toronto, 1980.

Yerkes, R. M. and Morgulis, S. 'The method of Pavlov in animal psychology', *Psychological Bulletin*, 1909, No. 6.

Young, Robert M. *Mind, Brain and Adaptation in the 19th Century*. Oxford, 1970.

———. 'Scholarship and the history of the behavioral sciences', *History of Science*, 5 (1966).

Zalkind, A. B. 'Freidizm i marksizm', *KN*, 1924, No. 4.

———. 'Pervyi Vsesoiuznyi s'ezd psikhonevrologicheskikh nauk', *Pedologiia*, 1930, No. 2.

———. 'Povedencheskii s'ezd i sovetskaia psikhonevrologiia', *Vrachebnaia gazeta*, 1930, No. 7.

———. 'Psikhonevrologiia i revoliutsiia', *Pravda*, 10 January 1924.

———. *Rabota i byt obshchestvennogo aktiva*. M., 1930.

———. *Umstvennyi trud. Gigiena i ratsionalizatsiia umstvennoi deiatel'nosti*. M., 1930.

———. 'Zabolevaniia partaktiva', *KN*, 1925, No. 4.

Zalmanzon, A. N. 'Protiv eklekticheskogo napravleniia v psikhologii', *VKA*, 1929, No. 34.

———. 'V zashchite ob'ektivnogo napravlenniia v psikhologii', *VKA*, 1926, No. 18.

Zaluzhnyi, A. S. *Lzhenauka pedologiia v 'trudakh' Zalkinda*. M., 1937.

Zankov, L. V. 'Puti psikhologicheskogo issledovaniia i preodolenie burzhuaznykh vliianii', *Sovetskaia pedagogika*, 1949, No. 5.

Zavadovskii, B. M. 'Itogi IV-ogo vsesoiuznogo s'ezda fiziologov', *EIM*, 1930, No. 2–3.

Zavadskii, I. V. 'Vospominaniia: I. P. Pavlov v laboratorii', *Izvestiia Severno-kavkazskogo gosudarstvennogo universiteta*, 8 (1926).

Zelenev, N. A., ed. *Voprosy fiziologii voennogo truda i voenno-professional'nogo otbora*. M., 1928.

Zelenyi, G. P. 'Espèce particulière de réflexes conditionels', *Arkhiv biologicheskikh nauk*, 14 (1909).

———. 'Sovremennaia biologiia i psikhologiia', *Novye idei v filosofii*, sb. 9 (St Petersburg, 1913).

Zenevich, G.V. 'O primenenii kliniko-nozologicheskogo printsipa v psikhiatrii', in Nauchno-issledovatel'skii psikhonevrologicheskii institut im. V. M. Bekhtereva, *Trudy*, XXXIX. L., 1966.

Zenkovsky, V. V. *A History of Russian Philosophy*. 2 vols. N.Y., 1953.

Zetkin, Klara. *Reminiscences of Lenin*. N.Y., 1934.

———. *Vospominaniia o Lenine*. M., 1955, 1959, 1968, 1971.

Zhdanov, A. A. *Essays on Literature, Philosophy, and Music*. N.Y., 1950.

Zhizn' i tekhnika budushchego (sotsial'nye i nauchno-tekhnicheskie utopii). M., 1928.

Zinoviev, G. E. 'Intelligentsia i revoliutsiia', *Pravda*, 25 and 27 November 1923.

Zola, Émile. *L'Assommoir*. Paris, 1969.

———. *L' Assommoir*. Trans. L.W. Tancock. Harmondsworth, 1970.

———. *Le Docteur Pascal*. Paris, 1975.

Index

academic autonomy, 84, 333; *see also* professional autonomy

academic institutions, access to, 65–6, 69–70, 76

Academy of Psychoneurological Sciences, 274

Academy of Sciences, 376, 379, 404

aesthetic psychology, ix, xii, xix

aesthetic reaction to science, 14–15; *see also* imaginative writing

Aksel'rod, Liubov (1868–1946), 231–2

Aksel'rod, P. B., 184

alcoholism, 86

alienation, theories of, 252; *see also under* Marx, Karl

All-Union Association of Workers of Science and Technology for Aid to the Construction of Socialism, 336

American Psychological Association, 304, 425

anaesthesia, development of, 56

analyzers, 293–4, 307

Anokhin, P. K. (1898–1974), 307, 381, 387, 395–9, 460, 462; *From Descartes to Pavlov*, 408; and Pavlov, 301, 389, 392; at Pavlov Session, 408–9

anti-cosmopolitanism, 401–5, 425, 426, 449–50, 534 n. 28

anti-Semitism, 65–6, 69–76, 403

Artemov, V. A. (1900–), 506 n. 37

Asiatic mode of production, 35

associationism, 20, 21, 23; and Pavlov, 294

associative reflex, 150–2, 275, 278

atomism, psychological, 21, 22

Avenarius, Richard (1843–1896), 187, 190, 283

Babel, Isaac (1894–1941), 245, 247, 330, 463; *Red Cavalry*, 240–3

Babkin, B. P. (1877–1950), 390, 392, 487 n. 94

backwardness, Russian, 318–19, 323

Bain, Alexander (1818–1903), 23, 94, 127

Bakhtin, Mikhail (1895–1975), *Freudianism: A Critical Essay*, 238

Bakunin, M. A. (1814–1876), 57, 80

Baudelaire, Charles (1821–1867), 13, 468, 477 n. 47

Bauman, K. Ia. (1892–1937), 400

Bebel, August (1840–1913), 81

Behavioral Congress (1930), 337, 339, 356–7, 381–3, 393, 395–6, 506 n. 37; publication of papers, 517 n. 24

behaviorism, 18, 148, 373; and conditioning, 298; influence of, on Soviet psychologists, 450–1; and mechanists, 231; and Pavlovians, 149, 304–7, 460; and reflexology, 275

Beilis trial, 86, 486 n. 80

Bek, Alexander (1903–1972), 464

Bekhterev, V. M. (1857–1927), xii-xiv, xv, 65, 83–8, 90–1, 107; at the Beilis trial, 486 n. 80; and Bolsheviks, 216, 271–81; *Collective Reflexology*, 84, 273; disciples of, struggle with Kornilov, 356–7; *Foundations of the Science of Brain Functions*, 154; *The General Principles of Human*

447−8, 452; *see also* monism

Pobedonotsev, K. P. (1827−1907), 75, 76, 94, 486 n. 81

poetry: in historical explanation, 38−40; and science, 12−13, 15−16, 168−74, 477 n. 43

Pokrovsky, M. N. (1868−1932), 216, 232, 233, 249, 376

Pol Pot, 323

political offenders, psychiatric evaluation of, 417−18

Polonskii, Ia. P. (1819−1898), 499 n. 27

populism *see* 'people, the'

Portugalov, Iu. V. (1876−?), 226−7

positivism, 11, 94−5, 166, 477 n. 40; and Marxism, 42−4, 185−7, 216, 234; *see also* synthetic positivism

Potebnia, Alexander (1835−1891), 257

practice, criterion of, 238−40, 311−12, 325−6, 377, 429−30

Pravda, statements appearing in, 206, 210, 224, 239, 259, 343, 344, 357, 385, 399, 413

'preparation', idea of, 7, 19, 140, 155, 478 n. 56

Prezent, I. I. (1902−   ), 515 n. 45

Priannishnikov, D. N. (1865−1948), 344

Pribram, Karl (1919−   ), 512 n. 60

Problems of Philosophy and Psychology, 117

Problems of Psychology, 451

professional autonomy, 416−17, 419−21, 424, 425

professionalism, 52, 85−6, 88−91, 113−18

prose writing, 174−81

Protopopov, V. P. (1880−1957), 511 n. 32

Proudhon, P. J. (1809−1865), 480 n. 17

psychiatric nosology, 427−32, 532 n. 62

psychiatrists, routine authority of, 418−19, 422, 442

psychiatry, xix, 88, 236, 246, 341, 413−38, 441−2; and preventive mental health, 337−8; and radicalism, 456; and Red Army, 345

psychic processes: distinguished from physical processes, 101−2, 394; Pavlovian view of, 134, 136−8, 140, 142−56, 376, 382, 390−4, 412−13;

see also mind and brain, duality of; neural processes

psychic secretions, 141−2, 153

psychoanalysis, 236, 419−20

psychohygiene *see* mental health movement

Psychological Review, 306

Psychology, 359

psychology: Bogdanov on, 189−93; Bolsheviks on, 209−19, 473; crisis in, and Vygotsky, 262−6, 360, 364; definition of, 26; diversity of, in nineteenth century, 104−9, 120; and literature, 116−19, 256−7; Marx on, 40−1; Marxist, campaign for, 220−30, 355−89, 404, 453−4; and monism, 452−3; origins of Russian, 54, 92−121; and philosophy, 232, 234; and physiology, 122−59, 258−60, 412−13, 450−1; public attitude towards, 118−21, 472−3; and radicalism, 456; and subjectivity *see* subjectivity; types of, ix, xv, 445; *see also* experimental psychology; history of psychology

Psychoneurological Institute, 83−4, 107, 152, 272, 274

psychophysics, 16, 17

psychotechnics, 342−4

psychotropic drugs, 432, 532 n. 62

purposes, attribution of, 7; *see also* intentional acts

Pushkin, A. S. (1799−1837), 283

race, 68

radicalism, political, and materialist science, 27−31, 53−63, 139, 149, 182−4, 329, 455−6; *see also* Marxism

Rainov, T. I. (1888−1958), 251−3; *A Theory of Creativity*, 251

Razenkov, I. P. (1888−1954), 527 n. 116

reactology, 222−3, 227, 273, 280, 358

reciprocal innervation, 130

Red Army, and psychiatry, 345

Red Virgin Soil, 218, 224, 258, 260, 380

Reddaway, Peter, 418

reflection, doctrine of, 194

reflex of freedom, 78, 209, 278, 380

reflexes and the reflex arc: Bekhterev's concept of, 152−3, 274−5, 277; Pavlov's concept of, 78, 155, 156,

Index by Ken Hirschkopf